KT-197-187

The Green Guide
Provence

Gordes , D. Pazery/MICHELIN

General Manager   Cynthia Clayton Ochterbeck

THEGREENGUIDE **PROVENCE**

Editor   Alison Coupe
Principal Writer   Glenn Harper, Margaret Littman
Production Manager   Natasha G. George
Cartography   Stephane Anton
Photo Editor   Yoshimi Kanazawa
Proofreader   Karolin Thomas
Interior Design   Chris Bell
Layout   Alison Rayner
Cover Design   Chris Bell, Christelle Le Déan
Cover Layout   Michelin Apa Publications Ltd.

Contact Us   The Green Guide
                                       Michelin Maps and Guides
                                       One Parkway South
                                       Greenville, SC 29615
                                       USA
                                       www.michelintravel.com

                                       Michelin Maps and Guides
                                       Hannay House
                                       39 Clarendon Road
                                       Watford, Herts WD17 1JA
                                       UK
                                       ✆01923 205240
                                       www.ViaMichelin.com
                                       travelpubsales@uk.michelin.com

Special Sales   For information regarding bulk sales,
                                       customized editions and premium sales,
                                       please contact our Customer Service
                                       Departments:
                                       USA   1-800-432-6277
                                       UK   01923 205240
                                       Canada 1-800-361-8236

Note to the reader Addresses, phone numbers, opening hours and prices
published in this guide are accurate at the time of press. We welcome
corrections and suggestions that may assist us in preparing the next edition.
While every effort is made to ensure that all information printed in this guide
is correct and up-to-date, Michelin Apa Publications Ltd. accepts no liability
for any direct, indirect or consequential losses howsoever caused so far as
such can be excluded by law.

HOW TO USE THIS GUIDE

PLANNING YOUR TRIP

The blue-tabbed PLANNING YOUR TRIP section at the front of the guide gives you **ideas for your trip** and **practical information** to help you organize it. You'll find tours, practical information, a host of outdoor activities, a calendar of events, information on shopping, sightseeing, kids' activities and more.

INTRODUCTION

The orange-tabbed INTRODUCTION section explores Provence's **Nature** and geology. The **History** section spans from Roman times through empire to the modern day. The **Art and Culture** section covers architecture, art, literature and music, while **Provence Today** delves into modern Provence.

DISCOVERING

The green-tabbed DISCOVERING section features Principal Sights by region, featuring the most interesting local **Sights**, **Walking Tours**, nearby **Excursions**, and detailed **Driving Tours**. Admission prices shown are normally for a single adult.

ADDRESSES

We've selected the best hotels, restaurants, cafes shops, nightlife and entertainment to fit all budgets. See the Legend on the cover flap for an explanation of the price categories. See the back of the guide for an index of hotels and restaurants.

Sidebars

Throughout the guide you will find blue, peach and green-colored text boxes with lively anecdotes, detailed history and background information.

😊 A Bit of Advice 😊

Green advice boxes found in this guide contain practical tips and handy information relevant to the sight in the Discovering section.

STAR RATINGS★★★

Michelin has given star ratings for more than 100 years. If you're pressed for time, we recommend you visit the ★★★, or ★★ sights first:

★★★   **Highly recommended**
★★   **Recommended**
★   **Interesting**

MAPS

- 😊 National Driving Tours map, Places to Stay map and Sights map.
- 😊 Region maps.
- 😊 Maps for major cities and villages.
- 😊 Local tour maps.

All maps in this guide are oriented north, unless otherwise indicated by a directional arrow. The term "Local Map" refers to a map within the chapter or Tourism Region. A complete list of the maps found in the guide appears at the back of this book.

PLANNING YOUR TRIP

Stéphanie Berghaeuser/SXC

INTRODUCTION TO PROVENCE

DISCOVERING PROVENCE

CONTENTS

Welcome to Provence

Along the Mediterranean Coast in the southeast corner of France, nestled next to Italy, lies beautiful Provence. It gets its name from the fact that it was the first Roman province outside Italy. But today the name is synonymous with serene landscapes and rich history. Provence's western border is the Rhône River, one of the country's major commercial routes. Inside these boundaries are mountains comparable with the Alps, plains and reserves that attract natural life, fine, sandy beaches and arable land with bountiful crops.

AIX AND STE-VICTOIRE
(pp104–123)

Sohpisticated and serene, Aix-en-Provence bubbles with religious and art history, just as the natural thermal springs bubble below the town. This town is home to many of Provençal highlights, from Roman ruins to 17C creativity to 20C art, not to mention a little 21C shopping. Highlights include the lovely Cours Mirabeau walkway and Ste-Victoire, which was and remains an inspiration to artists.

THE ALPILLES AND THE MONTAGNETTE *(pp124–153)*

The great outdoors is the appeal of the Alpilles, Provence's majestic limestone hills. This is pristine, preserved and protected land for the most part, so that the flora and fauna are similar to what they were centuries ago when people first began to flock here. At the highest elevations, the vistas are full of stately bare rock formations. Further down, olive, almond and pine trees flourish. Montagnette is a smaller mountain range, but no less bucolic. Once a camping ground for Roman soldiers, the Montagnette is now planted with classic Provençal herbs.

ARDÈCHE/GARD *(pp154–203)*

From bullfighting to caving, seaside resorts to Roman ruins, Ardèche/Gard is a holiday paradise on earth. There are opportunities to lap up the Provençal sun, raft rivers, take in maritime history and otherwise appreciate the sunny climate of Provence. The road between Vallon-Pont-d'Arc to Pont-St-Esprit is particularly picturesque, although underground caving at the Grotte de la Madeleine is also an option. Nature preserves and architectural ruins and wine tasting round off the Provençal experience.

ARLES AND THE CAMARGUE
(pp204–227)

Walking tours are the best way to see this large city and its countryside. Hiking, biking, horse riding and boating open up the world of the Camargue nature and zoological reserve, packed with more than 400 types of birds and wildlife. More native nature is on display close up at the Parc Ornothologique du Pont-de-Gau. In town, there are as many sites to see, from Arles' Roman Theatre and ancient ruins to museums and the many places that were part of Vincent Van Gogh's life.

Flamingos in the Camargue

© Javier Gil/Fotolia.com

Bouillabaisse

©S. Sauvignier/MICHELIN

AVIGNON AND THE COMTAT VENAISSIN *(pp228–261)*

Provence is nothing without its papal history, and Avignon brims with it. The Palais des Papes is world renowned as a home to seven popes in the 14C. Those residents helped transform Avignon from a city of little importance to Provence's centre of art, history and religion. The nearby Comtat Venaissin offers countryside pleasures that balance Avignon's city highlights.

THE LUBERON *(pp262–293)*

Postcard-perfect villages, with quaint homes and narrow streets populate the towns of the Luberon region, which may be why it was the perfect setting for Peter Mayle's *A Year in Provence* books. The limate is classic, sun-filled Mediterranean, which produces remarkable views of the landscapes. *Bories* (dry-stone huts), rock quarries and fields filled with lavender are the backdrop in this region. In the foreground are clusters of quintessential hamlets, with houses, cafés and shops.

MARSEILLES AND SURROUNDS *(pp294–339)*

The large city of Marseille is a bustling port with quaint buildings in the Vieux Port. But, while tourism is important, Marseille is a living inductrial city, where the commercial port still aids in oil pressing, soap-making and flour milling. Marseilles' restaurants rival those in Paris, with their fresh-from-the port seafood, classic *bouillabaisse* and mussels, as well as other creative gastronomic delights.

DENTELLES DE MONTMIRAIL AND MONT VENTOUX *(pp340–355)*

Mountains that look like the edge of a piece of lace are the focal point of this region. They are not particularly tall mountains, although they seem so thanks to a dramatic profile, dotted with rocky ridges, pine and oak trees, and, often snow-covered peaks. Natural springs poke through the rock and, in the springtime, the mountainsides are in bloom with bright yellow foliage.

VAUCLUSE AND THE DRÔME PROVENÇALE *(pp356–371)*

Fertile plains and a good growing season populate the Vaucluse with fruits and vegetables and herbs, not to mention sunflowers and truffless. Equally abundant are the grapes, as this region is also home to the famed wine-growing town of Châteauneuf-du-Pape. Red wines from here are rustic and now in demand across the world. Olive pressing is as important and industry as winemaking; tasting rooms are open to visitors, so they can sample the wonderful produce of this region.

Grignan, Drôme

©A.Cassalgne/MICHELIN

Cassis viewed from Cap Canaille
©Didier Zylberyng/Pictures Colour Library

PLANNING YOUR TRIP

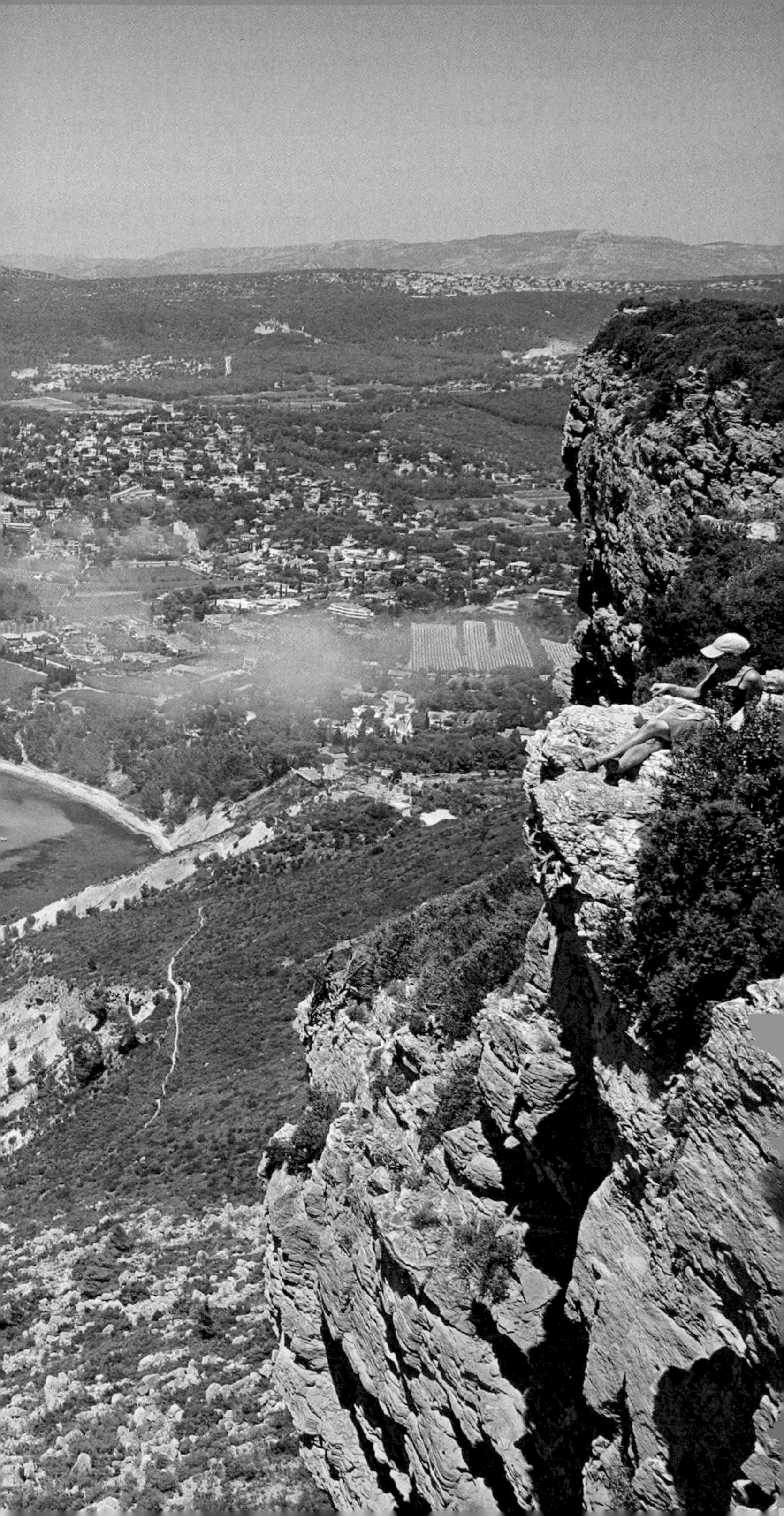

Michelin DrivIng Tours

See the map of Driving Tours on the inside back cover.

1 THE GARD AND THE GORGES DE L'ARDÈCHE

▷ *198km/123mi leaving from Uzès*

The old ducal seat of **Uzès**, with its elegant Tour Fenestrelle, its stately ducal palace, and the charming place aux Herbes, is the starting point for this itinerary. Explore Bagnols-sur-Cèze and its museum of modern figurative art, the old city of Pont-St-Esprit, and have a first look at the Gorges de l'Ardèche: the profusion of caves, cliffs and spectacular viewpoints. The route climbs up the gorges to the astonishing natural arch at Pont d'Arc, near the Orgnac cave and its fantastic rock formations. Explore the Gorges de la Cèze and remember to stop off at Goudargues before admiring the waterfalls at Sautadet in La Roque-sur-Cèze and at Les Concluses. If you're feeling energetic, climb the Guidon de Bouquet, for the view over the typical landscape of the *garrigue* – thyme, rosemary and *arbutus* (also known as strawberry trees) scattered among holm oaks.

2 PROVENCE AND THE ROMAN EMPIRE

▷ *233km/145mi leaving from Orange*

This itinerary starts at **Orange** with a visit to the triumphal arch, the magnificent Roman Theatre and the museum just opposite. From there, continue on to the extraordinary archaeological site at Vaison-la-Romaine. Other sites on the itinerary include a triumphal arch at Carpentras, remains of the Roman wall in Avignon, the Roman monuments of the Plateau des Antiques and the ancient city of Glanum, both situated just outside St-Rémy. Then it's on to Arles: the amphitheatre, the Roman Theatre, the mysterious Cryptoporticus, Constantine's baths, the melancholy necropolis of Les Alyscamps, and the fascinating Musée de l'Arles et de la Provence Antiques. Then to Nîmes: the amphitheatre, the Temple of Diana, the Maison Carrée and the vestiges of the city's fortifications, the most impressive example of which is the Tour Magne. The Castellum, a Roman water distribution tank, is an appropriate introduction to the majestic Pont du Gard, the most spectacular part of the ancient aqueduct that brought water from the Eure fountain near Uzès to Nîmes. This Roman aqueduct crosses 50km/31mi of hinterland.

Driving through lavender fields with a view of Mont Ventoux

©Arco Digital Images/Tips Images

③ NATURAL WONDERS OF THE VAUCLUSE

▷ *258km/160mi leaving from Carpentras, after visiting the old town*

Starting at **Carpentras**, admire the views and landscapes of the Dentelles de Montmirail, with a stop in the picturesque village of Malaucène. Choose a clear day to climb Mont Ventoux and enjoy the spectacular views. From the Nesque gorges, carry on to the remarkable ochre quarries of Colorado de Rustrel, gateway to the Luberon. Climb the Mourre Nègre summit and acquaint yourself with Mount Luberon, and the *villages perchés* (hilltop villages) of Bonnieux, Rousillon (where ochre reigns) and Gordes, with its stepped alleyways and the surprising *village des bories*. Make a stop in Fontaine-de-Vaucluse, where you can see the resurgent spring of the Sorgue river. It comes to the surface here after winding its way below the Vaucluse plateau – while you were winding your way above.

④ BEAUTIFUL VILLAGES IN THE LUBERON

▷ *128km/79.5mi leaving from Cavaillon*

Don't go anywhere without tasting the famous melons of **Cavaillon**. Then set out to visit the town: the synagogue and Jewish museum in the lower town; and the antique shops at L'Îsle-sur-la-Sorgue. If your memory is in high gear, you may wish to recite the poems of Petrarch in Fontaine-de-Vaucluse, his retirement home in the 14C. The curious group of drystone huts known as the *village des bories* may inspire you to write some poetry of your own. In the village of Gordes, go up and down the *calades*, the steep staircases that serve as streets, and admire the view of the Calavon valley. The Abbey of Sénanque is nestled in a lavender field nearby, a heavenly place in more ways than one. Explore Roussillon, with its ochre-coloured buildings and extraordinary quarries

from which ochre is extracted, as well as the workshop where the pigment was processed with time-consuming and complex techniques. Visit Saturnin-lès-Apt, with its mill and cherry orchards, before going to Apt, where you can enjoy the crystallised fruits and the large Saturday market. Climbers will appreciate the rock spur of Buoux, but you can, too, by just resting in the charming hamlet at the base. To round off your tour, take a walk in the cedar forest of Bonnieux before visiting Lacoste and the lovely hillside villages of Ménerbes and Oppède-le-Vieux.

⑤ CAMARGUE

▷ *228km/141.6mi leaving from Arles*

Start in **Arles** with a visit to the Museon Arlaten, founded by the legendary local poet Frédéric Mistral. Next board a boat for a relaxing trip down the Rhône. Off starboard, you can catch a glimpse at the unique and beautiful ecosystem of the Camargue. Discover the intricate network of marshes and streams, and the fabulous flora and fauna of the wetlands. Visit the salt marshes of Salin-de-Giraud and walk the footpaths of the Domaine de la Palissade (the only area of the delta not to have been enclosed by dykes) to Piémanson beach near the mouth of the Rhône. Learn more about the birds and flora on the footpaths around La Capelière or take a seat aboard the small train in Méjanes and visit the shores of the Vaccarès lagoon. The Musée de la Camargue is devoted to the customs of the region's inhabitants; the bird sanctuary at Pont-de-Gau offers a unique opportunity to become better acquainted with the unusual and rare birds that frequent the lagoons. Take a stroll through the streets of Stes-Maries-de-la-Mer, with its white houses nestled around the imposing fortified church, before going to the walled city of Aigues-Mortes, either via the Sylvereal bridge or by boat.

Savour some fish soup and other local specialities in the port of Grau-du-Roi before starting the return journey to Arles. On the way back, explore the profusion of reeds that conceals the Scamandre lagoon and then stop to contemplate the sculptures adorning the façade of the Abbey of St-Gilles, a masterpiece of Provençal Romanesque architecture.

6 PAINTERS AND AUTHORS OF PROVENCE

250km/155mi leaving from Baux-de-Provence

What better place to start this tour devoted to artists than the magnificent town of Baux, which has inspired many painters and writers? It is only fitting to make the pilgrimage to Maillane where the great master of the Félibrige movement, Frédéric Mistral, was born and lived, before going to admire the paintings of Auguste Chabaud in Graveson. A visit to the Château of Tarascon will evoke the pageantry of the court of King René, and be sure to stop off at Tartarin's house before going to explore the landscape and the mill of Fontvieille, which inspired the author Alphonse Daudet. In Arles follow the footsteps of Vincent Van Gogh: visit the foundation that bears his name and the hospice where he was interned, which has been faithfully reconstructed to exactly as it was. The Picasso donation in the Musée Réattu is well worth a visit for the remarkable modern sculpture and fine photographic collection. To learn more about the late 19C Provençal school, go to the Musée Ziem in Martigues, while the Musée des Beaux-Arts in Marseille will deepen your appreciation of the great Baroque master Pierre Puget. Others may prefer to see the installations in the MAC (Musée d'Art Contemporain) or to settle down on Prado beach with one of Jean-Claude Izzo's detective novels.

Classical Aix is the place to go to follow in Cézanne's footsteps (as well as finding out more about Vasarely) and to re-read Zola, who described the city (under the name of Plasson) as the birthplace of the Rougon family in his Rougon-Macquart series of novels. And if you're curious, why not visit Salon to find out what the future holds in Nostradamus' prophecies?

7 THE MOUNTAINOUS SHORE AND THE COUNTRYSIDE BEYOND MARSEILLE

290km/180mi leaving from Marseille

This itinerary is the ideal opportunity to use your walking shoes, or your flippers! Consider that after a pleasant stroll through the Panier and Notre-Dame de la Garde quarters of old Marseille, the Chaîne de l'Estaque provides creeks and *calanques* with some superb seawater for swimmers and divers. Niolon, in particular, is ideal for divers, while the tiny beaches of Ensuès-la-Redonne are good for catching sea urchins and spotting octopuses *(pourpres)*. If you prefer to swim without octopuses, head for Carry-le-Rouet, Sausset-les-Pins or Carro. Aix is a good place for an evening stroll, when the light falls on the façades of the old *hôtels particuliers*. Trace Cézanne's footsteps by exploring Ste-Victoire, where the steep footpaths provide some superb views from the Croix de Provence. A visit to the Royal Monastery at St-Maximin makes an ideal prelude to an excursion on the Ste-Baume massif, which attracts pilgrims, ramblers and climbers who enjoy the challenge of its steep rock faces. The bucolic St-Pons park offers a pleasant rest in the shade before returning to the sea at La Ciotat and travelling up the Corniche des Crètes. Finally, at Cassis get on a boat for a voyage of discovery of the sumptuous *calanques*.

When and Where to Go

WHEN TO GO
SEASONS

The region of Provence is blessed with mild weather throughout the year, especially along the coast. The rhythm of the seasons fluctuates somewhat, especially in the spring; even in winter the temperature can rise or fall dramatically in one day.

Spring

High pressure from Siberia abates from February on, allowing the Atlantic rains to fall. These rains are less violent than those in the autumn and bright and clear days are frequent. The *mistral*, especially in March, can provoke a surprising chill for those who are not used to the whims of a Provençal spring.

Summer

This is *the* season. In those three or four months, the heat and lack of rain attract sun-loving crowds to this popular region. It rains no more than 70mm/2.75in and the temperature rarely drops below 30°C/86°F. The dry heat is not overpowering; its constancy is explained by the presence of a hot air mass from the Sahara, protected from the west's humid depressions by the Massif Central.

Autumn

The reflux of high pressure of tropical origin opens the way to Atlantic depressions. From mid-September to late November, rain appears; sometimes violent rainstorms provoke flash floods. The rainfall can amount to more than 100mm/3.94in in 1hr (annually 600mm/23.6in).

Winter

The cold season – which is often sunny – is relatively mild and dry. The temperature can drop 10°C/50°F in a few hours because of the *mistral* (see Winds, opposite). The Mediterranean's liquid mass reduces the cold front and prevents snowfalls except on the peaks.

WINDS

The wind is an essential part of the Provençal climate. The best known is the *mistral* (*mistrau* means master in Provençal, thus master-wind). This strong, dry, cold north-westerly wind sweeps down when the pressure is high over the mountains. It can rage like a storm, then disappear as suddenly as it arrives. Two other common winds in this region are the southeast *marin*, bringing rain and fog; and the southwest *labech*, bringing rainstorms.

CLIMATE

Writers have acclaimed Provence's temperate climate, low rainfall and exceptional light. Nonetheless, weather conditions are changeable from year to year. Provence's land relief and the sea play an important role. Maritime Provence enjoys a more agreeable climate (less rain and hotter) than the hinterland, where altitude modifies the temperature considerably. But the dominant factor remains the long periods of sunshine (more than 2 500hr per year) in the region.

WHAT TO PACK

As little as possible! Cleaning and laundry services are available everywhere and most personal items can be replaced at reasonable cost. Try to pack everything in one suitcase and a carry-on bag. Take an umbrella – and an extra tote bag for packing new purchases, shopping at the open-air markets, carrying a picnic, etc. Be sure luggage is clearly labelled and old travel tags removed.

IDEAS FOR YOUR VISIT
HISTORICAL ITINERARIES

The historical itineraries, known as *Routes Historiques*, are intended to present France's architectural heritage in its historical context. You can find out more about these many routes by contacting the various tourist offices or *La Demeure Historique* (℘01 55 42 60 00; www.demeure-historique.org). Four important historical itineraries are covered in this region:

♦ **Route Historique du Patrimoine Juif du Midi de la France** Comité Départemental du tourisme de Vaucluse. ℘04 90 80 47 00. www.provenceguide.com.

♦ **Route Historique des Vaudois en Luberon; Routes Historiques en Languedoc-Roussillon** Château de Flaugergues, 1744 av. Albert Einstein, 34000 Montpellier. ℘04 99 52 66 37. www.flaugergues.com.

♦ **Via Domitia** ℘04 91 56 47 00. www.decouverte-paca.fr/us.

You may also be interested in the *Route Historique Musicale* and part of the *Route Historique du Gévaudan au Golfe du Lion*.

Historical itineraries are signposted along country roads. All of them are detailed in handbooks available from local tourist offices.

PAINTERS' PATHS, WRITERS' FOOTSTEPS

The **Route des Peintres de la Lumière en Provence** offers an introduction to the region through the various sites painted by artists who created radiant works suffused with light (*see Introduction to Provence, pp 82–4*). For details, enquire at the *Comité Régional de Tourisme Provence-Alpes-Côte d'Azur* (℘04 91 56 47 00; www.decouverte-paca.fr/us).

The tourist offices in Aix-en-Provence, St-Rémy-de-Provence and Arles (*see AIX-EN-PROVENCE, ST-RÉMY-DE-PROVENCE, ARLES*) have information on thematic itineraries – **"In the steps of Cézanne" (Aix), "The places painted by Vincent van Gogh" (St Rémy)** and **"Arles et Vincent Van Gogh" (Arles)**.

In Aubagne, you can walk or take a bus tour to explore the life of writer/filmmaker **Marcel Pagnol**: enquire at the tourist office in Aubagne (*see AUBAGNE*).

For a tour on **Alphonse Daudet** to visit the sites that inspired his famous, *Lettres de Mon Moulin*: enquire at the tourist office in Fontvieille (*see Les ALPILLES*).

NATURE PARKS

Parc Naturel Régional de Camargue
See La CAMARGUE.
La Maison du Parc, RD 570, Pont-de-Gau, 13460 Les Stes-Maries-de-la-Mer. ℘04 90 97 86 32. www.parc-camargue.fr; Musée de la Camargue, Mas du Pont de Rousty, 13200 Arles. ℘04 90 97 10 82.

Parc Naturel Régional du Luberon
See Le LUBERON.
60 place Jean-Jaurès, BP 122, 84404 APT Cedex. www.parcduluberon.fr.

MARINE PARKS

Marine parks feature preserved areas where fishing and diving activities, as well as boat anchoring, are strictly regulated and where experiments with artificial reefs are being carried out. The aim of these parks is to fulfil a number of well-defined objectives: protecting the natural environment (controlling all activities concerned with the development and survival of plant and animal species); exploiting the available resources (immersion of artificial reefs to encourage the growth of flora and fauna); installing blocks to hinder illicit trawling; and providing information to increase public awareness of ecological issues (www.aires-marines.fr).

Parc Marin de la Côte Bleue

Lying west of Marseille harbour, it laps the Massif de la Nerthe, a rocky mountain range separating the Étang de Berre from the sea.

Information: Parc Marin de la Côte Bleue, Observatoire du Parc Marin, Plage du Rouet, 31 avenue Jean Bart, BP 42, 13620 Carry-le-Rouet. ℘04 42 45 45 07. www.parcmarincotebleue.fr or from local tourist information centres in Carry-le-Rouet, Ensuès-la-Redonne, Martigues, Le Rove and Sausset-les-Pins.

Parc Marin de la Baie de La Ciotat
The park is defined by La Ciotat bay. The underwater topography is remarkably varied: rocks, sand, sloping ledges, underwater slabs, and mossy beds of *posidonia*, home to a great many small molluscs.
Information: Parc Régional Marin de la Baie de La Ciotat, Hôtel de Ville, 13712 La Ciotat, ℘04 42 83 90 09, or from La Ciotat tourist office.

- ⊛ **Never forget** that the marine environment is extremely fragile and needs to be respected by all those who venture near it. Make a point of observing the following rules:
- ⊛ Dispose of plastic bags on shore in closed containers.
- ⊛ Throw any fish you have caught back into the sea.
- ⊛ Do not damage or remove the long, green *posidonia* leaves that cleanse seawater by renewing its oxygen.

OLIVES AND THE OIL INDUSTRY
There are several types of olives in Provence: the *tanche* or *olive de Nyons*, delicious when served pickled in brine; the *angladau*, pressed for its oil; the *grossane*, a big, black fleshy olive; the *salonenque* or *olive des Baux*, a green variety served crushed; the *picholine*, a long, narrow green olive, crushed and then pickled.
To learn more about olives and oils, contact *l'Institut du Monde de l'Olivier* in Nyons (℘04 75 26 90 90; www.monde-olivier.com).
Provence offers thematic circuits that focus on the olive: those in the Bouches-du-Rhône (**Route de l'Olivier des Alpilles et de la Vallée des Baux** and **Route de l'Olivier du Pays d'Aix-en-Provence**); and in the Drôme (**Route de l'Olivier en Baronnies**, around Nyons and Buis-les-Baronnies). These tours include visits to olive groves, mills, presses and museums.
Information: Association Française Interprofessionnelle de l'Olive, Maison des Agriculteurs, avenue Henri-Pontier, 13626 Aix-en-Provence Cedex 1. ℘04 42 23 01 92. www.afidol.org.

LAVENDER FIELDS
Created by the Regional Tourist Committee of the Provence-Alpes-Côte d'Azur area, the **Route de la Lavande** enables you to visit many places associated with the growing and processing of lavender around Mont Ventoux, the Luberon, and the Provençal Drôme. This circuit is complemented by various festivities, such as Fête de la Lavande in Sault between 14 and 15 August, and the **Corso Nocturne de la Lavande** in Valréas at the beginning of August. The *Grande Traversée des Alpes (14 r. de la République, BP 227, 38019 Grenoble Cedex; ℘04 76 42 08 31; www.routes-lavande.com)* publishes a handbook with general information and practical data about each site and can be picked up from local tourist offices.

PAYS DE SAULT ET DU VENTOUX
Ferme St-Agricol in *Savoillans*: tour of the farmhouse and botanical gardens, practical demonstration of distillation techniques: ℘04 75 28 85 78.
Lavender garden in Sault: collection of lavender plants. **Hameau de Verdolier**. ℘04 90 64 14 97.
You can also visit a cooperative at the **Maison des Producteurs de Sault** *(rue de la République; ℘04 90 64 08 98)*.

PAYS D'APT AND LUBERON
The tiny commune of Lagarde d'Apt is known for its lavender distilling and has two distilleries. *www.ot-apt.fr.* Other lavender places to visit in the area can be found at www.casamira.fr/

ot_apt/us/terroir/lavandes/lavandes_
adresse.htm.

PROVENÇAL DRÔME

In Nyons: **Bleu Provence Distillery**
(*04 75 26 10 42*) and **Jardin des
Arômes** (*04 75 26 04 30*): collection
of aromatic plants, promenade along
the pier. .

TRUFFLES

The Vaucluse is the main truffle-
producing region. If you are here
from mid-November to mid-March,
you can enjoy a visit to the regional
truffle markets that take place in the
morning. Be sure to seal the deal with
a good elixir!

- **Carpentras**
  The most important truffle market
  of the Vaucluse, runs from late Nov
  to mid-Mar: Fri 9am.
- **Richerenches**
  A very reputable market: mid-Nov
  to late Mar, every Sat from 10am.
- **Valréas** mid Nov–mid Mar,
  every Wed.

To visit a *truffière*, go to Uzès (*see
UZÈS*) and Grillon (*see VALRÉAS*).

TOURS OF WINE COOPERATIVES

Tours of cooperative wine cellars
(caves) are offered all over the wine-
producing regions: the east and west
banks of the Rhône, areas surrounding
Aigues-Mortes, Aix, Les Baux-de-
Provence, Cassis, etc. Details about
events linked to vineyards and wine
festivals are available at tourist offices.
Also consult Michelin's *The Wine
Regions of France*.

Côtes-du-Rhône Wines
*Maison des Vins d'AOC Côtes-du-Rhône
et Vallée du Rhône* – 6 rue des Trois
Faucons, 84024 Avignon Cedex 1.
04 90 27 24 00. www.vins-rhone.com.
Wine festivals of Vacqueyras, 14 July;
of Véraison to Châteauneuf-du-Pape,
first Sun in Aug; of Rasteau, the

weekend of 15 Aug; in Avignon, third
Thu in Nov.
Ask for the pamphlet **Routes des
Vins**, which details nine itineraries.
*See Dentelles de MONTMIRAIL,
ORANGE, VAISON-LA-ROMAINE.*

Coteaux d'Aix-en-Provence Wines
**Syndicat des Coteaux d'Aix-en-
Provence** – Maison des Agriculteurs,
22 avenue Henri Pontier, 13626 Aix-
en-Provence Cedex 1. *04 42 23 57
14. www.coteauxaixenprovence.com.*

Baux-de-Provence Wines
Syndicat des Vignerons des Baux,
Domaine Saint-Vincent, Route d'Orion,
13810 Eygalières. *04 90 90 61 14.*

Cassis Wines
Syndicat des Vignerons de Cassis –
Château de Fontcreuse, 13260 Cassis.
04 42 01 71 09. A **wine feast** with a
procession and tasting sessions takes
place the first Sun in Sept.

Côtes-du-Luberon Wines
**Syndicat `général des Vins des
Côtes-du-Luberon**, BP 12, La Tour
d'Aigues, 84125 Pertuis Cedex.
04 90 07 34 40.

Côtes-de-Provence Wines
**AOC Côtes de Provence Sainte-
Victoire** – Vinothèque Sainte-Victoire,
1 bd E. Boyer, BP 25, 13530 Trets.
*04 42 61 37 60. www.vins-sainte-
victoire.com.*

Costières de Nîmes Wines
Syndicat des Costières de Nîmes,
19 pl. Aristide Briand, 30900 Nîmes.
04 66 36 96 20.
www.costieres-nimes.com.

Vins de Pays des Sables

du Golfe du Lion
Domaine de la Malgue, 30220 Aigues-
Mortes. *04 66 73 51 13.*

What to See and Do

OUTDOOR FUN
MARINAS

Most of the seaside resorts lying between Le Grau-du-Roi and La Ciotat (*see Where to Stay*) have well-equipped marinas. The main ones, running from west to east, are: Aigues-Mortes, Le Grau-du-Roi, Port-Camargue, Les Stes-Maries/Port Gardian, Port-St-Gervais to Fos-sur-Mer, Martigues, Les Heures Claires at Istres, Carro, Sausset-les-Pins, Carry-le-Rouet, L'Estaque, Le Frioul, Marseille Pointe Rouge and Le Vieux Port, Cassis and La Ciotat.

Le Grau-du-Roi, Marseille, Port-St-Gervais to Fos-sur-Mer, Cassis and Port-Camargue have been awarded the Pavillon Bleu d'Europe (Blue Flag), granted on the basis of the following criteria: clean site and surroundings, special equipment and amenities, reception and information services, educational facilities.

Most seaside resorts have sailing schools where courses are organised. In season, you can hire boats with or without a crew.

For further information, contact the local harbour-master's office or the **Fédération Française de Voile** (*01 40 60 37 00; www.ffvoile.net*).

SCUBA-DIVING

Marseille and its surroundings have always been a privileged setting for diving activities. It was here that Jacques-Yves Cousteau and Émile Gagnan achieved their record-breaking performances that paved the way for modern diving with the invention of the Aqualung.

The most popular spot for deep-sea diving are the *calanques* around Marseille, where the seabed is truly a feast for the eyes. Despite subsequent damage caused by pollutant waste, excessive harpoon fishing and the combing of wrecks for their valuable archaeological significance, the *calanques* still provide exceptional interest for divers with their abundance of multicoloured fish, gorgonia, sponge, purple sea urchins, crayfish and mother-of-pearl.

Six exceptional sites can be explored: *Le Chaouen*, a Moroccan cargo ship, which ran aground on the Île de Planier (off Marseille); *La Drôme*, a shipwreck lying at a depth of 51m/168ft; *Le Liban*, a liner that sank in front of the Île Maïre in 1903; Les Impériaux, a site renowned for its huge gorgonian fish; La Cassidaigne, a seaway teeming with fish at the foot of the lighthouse (4 nautical miles from Cassis) and Île Verte, an islet with luxuriant vegetation peopled with myriads of fish.

This sport requires lengthy and challenging training, which can only be provided by fully qualified instructors holding nationally recognised diplomas. For a list of clubs offering scuba-diving courses, contact the local branch of the **Fédération Française d'Études et de Sports Sous-Marins** (*04 91 33 99 31; www. ffessm.fr*). This organisation publishes the magazine *Subaqua* every two months. The Centre UCPA in Niolon is Europe's biggest training centre for deep-sea diving (*0892 680 599, www.ucpa.com*). Books about diving can be found at the Librairie Maritime bookshop (*26 quai de Rive-Neuve, 13007 Marseille; 04 91 54 79 40; www. librairie-maritime.com*). The Centre Cassidain de Plongée (*04 42 01 89 16; www.centrecassidaindeplongee. com*) in Cassis offers one-to-one first dives in English for 63€. Also check out Plongée Passion Carry (*04 42 45 08 00; www.plongee-passion-carry. com*) on the Côte Bleue, which offers first dives in English from 55€.

SEA FISHING

Although the Mediterranean is not the busiest fishing spot in France, shoals of rock fish abound: red mullet, conger and moray eels as well as numerous octopuses, spider crabs, various squid and even the odd crayfish. In shallow, sandy waters there are skate, sole and dab. Offshore, shoals of sardines, anchovies and tuna fish intermingle with sea bream, bass and grey mullet. No permit is necessary for sea angling, provided that the day's catch is for personal consumption only.

BOAT TRIPS
By Sea
Leaving from Marseille, you can visit the Château d'If, the Îles du Frioul and the *calanques*; leaving from Cassis, you can visit the *calanques* at Port-Miou, Port-Pin and En-Vau. 🕭 See *Massif des CALANQUES*.

Leaving from La Ciotat, you can visit the Île Verte (🕭 *see La CIOTAT*). The excursions leaving from La Ciotat are on board a catamaran-type boat offering views of the sea depths cruising among the *calanques* of La Ciotat, between Cassis and Marseille. For details contact **Les Amis des Calanques** (𝄢06 09 35 25 68; *www.visite-calanques.fr*).

Leaving from the Tour de Constance in Aigues-Mortes, *Le Pescalune* (𝄢04 66 53 79 47; *www.petittrain-aiguesmortes. com*) will take you on a trip along the canals and the Vidourle, a coastal river. *Tiki III* (𝄢04 90 97 81 68; *www.tiki3. fr*), leaving from Les Stes-Maries-de-la-Mer, will take you along the River Rhône between March and November. The trip offers an insight into the Camargue of the *gardian*: herds of bulls and horses grazing on the plains; herons, flamingos and egrets on the banks of the tamarisk-dotted river. In Le Grau-du-Roi, you can hire a boat (🕭*licence required in some cases*) to cruise the canals from Cap 2000 (*ZA Port de Pêche;* 𝄢04 66 51 41 54) or *A2M* at Port-Camargue (𝄢04 66 53 35 18). Sea lovers will enjoy the *Nautiques de Port-Camargue* (𝄢04 66 51 81 65; *www.lesnautiques.com*), a nautical fair devoted to used boats that takes place in March or April.

WALKING/HIKING
Exploring Provence on foot is an enchanting way of discovering the all-encompassing brightness of Provençal light as it sets off the beauty of the landscape to perfection, both in its natural, unspoiled state, and featuring the evidence of humankind's passage through village and countryside.

Leave the car behind and experience a different, more relaxed pace of life in a landscape that rings with the echoes of days gone by.

Many long-distance footpaths (*sentiers de Grande Randonnée* – GR) cover the area described in this guide. The GR 4 crosses the lower Vivarais country as far as Mont Ventoux; to climb up the mountain, you can start in the Bédoin Forest and follow GR 91 and 91B (information in the Bédoin tourist office: 𝄢04 90 65 63 95; *www.bedoin. org*). GR 42 leads along the valley of the Rhône; GR 6 follows the River Gard as far as Beaucaire and then plunges into the Alpilles and Luberon ranges; GR 9 takes the line of the north face of Mont Ventoux, then crosses the Vaucluse plateau, the Luberon range, Montagne Ste-Victoire and the massif of Ste-Baume. Further variations on the above are offered by the GRs 63, 92, 97 and 98. Besides the long-distance footpaths, there are short- to medium-distance paths ranging from walks of a few hours to a couple of days (*Petit Randonnée* – PR).

The **Fédération Française de la Randonnée Pédestre** publishes "topo-guides" available from its information centre (𝄢01 44 89 93 90; *www.ffrandonnee.fr*). Some English-language editions are available. The regional guides describe long-distance trails (GR, for *Grande Randonnée* and GRP for *Grande Randonnée de Pays*) and shorter ones (PR – *Petite Randonnée*) in detail, with distances and approximate times. Another source of maps and guides for excursions on foot is the **Institut Géographique National (IGN)**. Their website (*www.ign.fr*) is available in English. Among their publications,

which you can order online, are France 903, a map showing all of the GRs and PRs in France; the *Série Bleue* and *Top 25* maps, at a scale of 1:25 000 (1cm = 250m), which show all paths as well as refuges, campsites and beaches for a specific area. In Provence itself, you can find many of the publications cited above in bookstores, at sports centres or outdoor equipment shops, and even in local newspaper shops or from the town hall *(mairie)*.
For information on walking the *calanques*, contact **Les Excursionnistes Marseillais** *(16 r. de la Rotonde, 13001 Marseille; ℘04 91 84 75 52; www.excurs.com).*

HORSE RIDING

The **Comité National de Toursime Équestre** *(℘02 54 94 46 80 ; www.ffe. com)* is a useful source of information if you would like to plan a riding holiday. The website lists horse-friendly holiday cottages, riding trails and riding centres. It also publishes "l'Estafette" (12.20€ for a year – four issues + the catalogue), a review of local events and information on maps for riders, children's activities etc, and the catalogue *Cheval Nature* (4.50€ + postage), where you will find further information including the addresses of riding centres *(Centres de Tourisme Équestre)* region by region, and practical tips on holidays for kids, insurance and more. Both can be ordered from the website.
Riding is a favourite pastime in the **Camargue**. Go to Ranch La Brouzetière *(rte d'Arles, 13460 Les Stes-Maries-de-la-Mer; ℘04 90 97 82 40; www.labrouzetiere.camargue. fr)* if you dream of riding one of the famous white horses on the plain, in the marshes or along the beach; they also offer between two- and five-day riding holidays from 590€/1375€.
Another good place on the way into Les Stes-Maries-de-la-Mer is Les Écuries at the Auberge Cavalière hotel *(rte d'Arles, 13460 Les Saintes-Maries de la Mer; ℘06 09 54 24 40; www.ecuries-cavaliere.camargue.fr)*, which has

highly qualified instructors and also offers riding lessons; a 2hr trek will set you back 35€. On the Espiguette road there are several stables: Écurie des Dunes *(℘04 66 53 09 28)*, Mas de l'Espiguette *(℘04 66 51 51 89)*, Ranch du Phare *(℘04 66 53 10 87)*, Ranch Lou Seden *(℘04 66 51 74 75)* and Abrivado Ranch *(℘04 66 53 01 00)*.

CYCLING

For general information concerning France, contact the **Fédération Française de Cyclotourisme** *(℘01 56 20 88 88; www.ffct.org)*. Off-road enthusiasts should contact the **Fédération Française de Cyclisme** *(℘01 49 35 69 00; www.ffc.fr – in French)* and request the *Guide des Centres VTT*. The IGN *(www.ign.fr)* offers Map 906, *Mountain Bike and Cycle Touring in France*. The websites provide addresses of local clubs and a calendar of events. A favourite challenge is to tackle Mont Ventoux by bike. Contact the tourist office in Bédoin for information on trails *(℘04 90 65 63 95; www.bedoin.org)*. Local tourist offices have a list of cycle hire firms (including some SNCF train stations).
Europbike *(1 r. Philippe Lebon, Arles; ℘04 90 49 54 69)* offers bike rental seven days a week for you and yours to discover the Provençal countryside at your leisure. It has offices in Arles, Avignon and Aix-en-Provence. If riding on roads, make sure you have your wits about you.

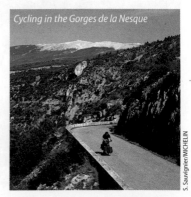

Cycling in the Gorges de la Nesque

S. Sauvignier/MICHELIN

> ### ☺ A Bit of Advice ☺
>
> A French bylaw rules that access to forests and other wooded massifs is strictly forbidden between 1 July and the second Saturday in September, and when winds blow at over 40kph/25mph.

SKIING

You can practice both downhill and cross-country skiing at the Mont-Serein resort (the secondary peak of Mont Ventoux, 1 445m/4 741ft high). For details, contact the town hall (*mairie*) in Beaumont-du-Ventoux on Tuesdays, Thursdays and Fridays (*℘04 90 65 21 13, Reception Chalet/Chalet d'Accueil; ℘04 90 63 42 02; www. stationdumontserein.com*).

ROCK CLIMBING

Rock climbing is possible all year up the Dentelles de Montmirail or the cliffs in the *calanques* near Marseille. ☺*Access to the calanques is forbidden from 1 July to the second Saturday in September, see box above.* The local branch of the **Club Alpin Français de Provence** (*℘04 91 54 25 84; http://cafmarseille.free.fr*) organises accompanied climbing trips.

General information can be obtained from the **Fédération Française de la Montagne et de l'Escalade** (*℘01 40 18 75 50; www.ffme.fr – in French*). For the Dentelles de Montmirail, contact the tourist information centre of Gigondas (*℘04 90 65 85 46; www.gigondas-dm.fr*).

CANOEING

Canoeing is a good way of exploring the less accessible stretches of the Ardèche, Cèze, Gardon, Durance and Sorgue rivers.

As far as the **Gorges de l'Ardèche** are concerned, *see Addresses section in GORGES DE L'ARDÈCHE*. Bear in mind that the stretch between Charmes and Sauze has been designated a natural reserve and special rules are enforced: no windsurfing, no boats with more than three people allowed, compulsory life jackets. Camping is possible only in Gaud and Gournier, for no longer than two nights.

For further practical information, contact the **Maison de la Réserve** at Gournier (*℘04 75 04 36 38; www. gorgesdelardeche.fr*).

The **Association de Protection des Gorges de l'Ardèche** publishes a plastic-coated map showing difficult stretches of river and possible refuelling stops along the river.

Canoeing in the Vallon Pont d'Arc

J. Damase/MICHELIN

It can be found at local tourist information centres.

For a trip in the area around Bagnols-sur-Cèze, contact the association **CAPCANOE** *(route de Barjac, 30500 St-Ambroix; ℘04 66 24 25 16; www.canoe-France.com)*. There is a choice of three routes along the River Cèze (4, 8 and 29km/2.5, 5 and 18mi) and a route of 14km/8.7mi through the Cèze gorges.

Upstream from the Pont du Gard, you can safely practice canoeing on the Gardon (4 trips of 4, 8, 11 and 22km/2.5, 5, 7 and 14mi). Contact Kayak Vert in Collias *(Berges du Gardon, 30210 Collias; ℘04 66 22 80 76; www.canoe-france.com)*.

Between Fontaine-de-Vaucluse and Isle-sur-la-Sorgue, a 8km/5mi trip on the Sorgue will enable you to discover the beauty of the local landscape. Contact **Kayak Vert Aqueduc** in Fontaine-de-Vaucluse *(℘04 90 20 35 44; www.canoe-france.com)*.

In conjunction with the **Fédération Française de Canoë-Kayak** *(℘01 45 11 08 50; www.ffck.org)*, IGN publishes a map called *France, Canoë-Kayak et Sports d'Eau Vive*, which lists all the different excursions, classifying them in terms of difficulty.

BULLFIGHTING EVENTS

The Camargue area, and especially the famous Camargue bull, have always been at the heart of French bullfighting or bull running. *Courses camarguaises* involve men called *raseteurs* chasing a bull around an arena in a bid to remove a rosette *(cocarde)* from between its horns. The bull is not killed and the beasts take part in the games year after year, often becoming famous in their own right: some even have a statue erected in their native village! These events take place in Arles (April to early October) – *Cocarde d'Or* on the first Monday in July, Beaucaire (late July), Les Stes-Maries-de-la-Mer (April to August), St-Martin-de-Crau (May and October), Châteaurenard (May to October) and Le-Grau-du-Roi (April to October). Local newspapers give the dates for these events. You can also find information on the website of the Fédération Française de la Course Camarguaise *(www.ffcc.info)* or at www.camargue.fr.

Originally, bullfighting was a Spanish tradition, but it gradually spread to Provence in the 18C. *Corridas* and *novilladas* are usually held during *férias*, large celebrations that bring huge crowds to the arenas and create a lively atmosphere in the town centre: *abrivados* (bulls are let loose on the streets), *peñas* (brass bands) playing along pavements and in the *bodegas* (bars), dances, etc. The city of Nîmes hosts three *férias* (in February, May and September) every year and Arles stages the famous *Féria de Pâques* at Easter. In Les Stes-Maries-de-la-Mer, the *corridas* are performed on horseback *(Féria du Cheval)*. To attend a *corrida* or a *novillada*, it is best to book in advance by contacting one of the following offices: **Nîmes:** *Bureau de Location des Arènes, 4 rue de la Violette, BP 61480, 30017 Nîmes Cedex 1 (℘08 91 70 14 01; www.arenesdenimes. com)*; **Arles:** *Location Arènes d'Arles, BP 42, 13633 Arles Cedex (℘08 91 70 03 70; www.arenes-arles.com)*; Les **Stes-Maries-de-la-Mer:** *Arènes des Stes-Maries-de-la-Mer (℘04 90 97 85 86)*; **Camargue:** *Arènes de Méjanes (℘04 90 97 10 10; www.mejanes.camargue.fr)*. The best seats are in the front row, on the side of the arena.

There is also an interesting museum dedicated to bullfighting in Nîmes: *Le Musée des Cultures Taurines (6 rue Alexandre Ducros, 30900 Nîmes; ◷open May–Sept Tue–Sun 10am–6pm; ☞4.90€; ℘04 66 36 83 77)*.

ACTIVITIES FOR CHILDREN

In this guide, sights of particular interest to children are indicated with a Kids symbol (♠♠). Some attractions offer discount fees for children. Here are a few things that children will especially enjoy – and it makes a change from a day at the beach!

OK Corral (≈18€, child 15.80€; ℘04 42 73 80 05; www.okcorral.fr), between Aubagne and La Ciotat, is a Wild West theme park with fun rides in a super setting.

Amazonia near Roquemaure in the Gard (≈14€, child 13€; 12.50€/13€ in low season; ℘04 66 82 53 92; www.parcamazonia.fr) is another, with an Aztec-Mayan theme.

The **Bonbon Museum** (℘04 66 22 74 39; www.haribo.com) in Uzès is a sweet treat for children.

At **Parc du Soleil et du Cosmos** (≈11.50€, child 9€; ℘04 90 25 66 82; www.parcducosmos.net) in Les Angles, near Villeneuve-lès-Avignon, the stars and planets are the featured performers.

Fans of birds of prey can watch spectacular displays of falconry in a hilltop castle at **Les Aigles de Beaucaire** (≈10€, child 7€; ℘04 66 59 26 72; www.aigles-de-beaucaire.com). Animal lovers can visit a working version of a 19C farm at **Le Vieux Mas** (℘04 32 61 11 58; www.vieuxmas.com) north of Arles.

More exotic creatures can be found at **La Barben Zoo** (≈13.50€, child 8€; ℘04 90 55 19 12; www.zoo labarben.com) near Salon-de-Provence.

If you are in the area at the end of June, be sure to attend the **Fête de la Tarasque** in Tarascon, an enchantment for all ages!

SHOPPING
VALUE ADDED TAX

There is a **Value Added Tax** (VAT) in France of 19.6% on almost every purchase (books and some foods are subject to a lower rate). However, non-European visitors who spend more than 175€ in any one participating store can apply for a refund of the VAT. Usually, you fill out a form at the store, showing your passport. Upon leaving the country, you submit all forms to customs for approval (they may want to see the goods, so if possible don't pack them in checked luggage).

The refund is usually paid directly into your bank or credit card account, or it can be sent by mail. Big department stores that cater for tourists provide special services to help you; be sure to mention that you plan to seek a refund before you pay for goods (no refund is possible for tax on services). If you are visiting two or more countries within the European Union, submit the forms only on departure from the last EU country. The refund is worthwhile for those visitors who would like to buy fashion, furniture or other fairly expensive items, but remember, the minimum amount must be spent in a single shop (though not necessarily on the same day).

People travelling **to the USA** cannot import plant products or fresh food, including fruit, cheeses and nuts. It is acceptable, however, to carry tinned products or preserves.

Among the souvenirs you might like to bring home are the famous *santons* figurines from Aubagne, Arles or Marseille. Tarascon is famous for its Provençal cloth, although this can be bought throughout the entire region. Provence is famous for its candied fruit (Apt, Aix) or its olive oil (Alpilles region).

SPECIALITIES FROM PROVENCE
Crafts and Workshops

Numerous craft workshops can be found along the coast and inland, representing a wide variety of cottage industries. Most of them welcome visitors during the summer but it is always advisable to book in advance.

Provençal Cloth

♦ Annie Sotinel, Les Pourquiers, route de Goult, 84220 Gordes (hand weaving). ℘04 90 72 05 71.

♦ Souleiado, 39 rue Proudhon, 13150 Tarascon. ℘04 90 91 08 80. www.souleiado.com.

♦ Les Olivades, Avenue Barberin, 13103 St-Étienne-du-Grès. ℘04 90 49 19 19. www.lesolivades.fr.

- Les Indiennes de Nîmes, 2 bd des arènes, 30900 Nîmes. ℰ04 66 21 69 57. www.indiennesdenimes.fr.

Soaps

- Savonnerie du Duché, 7 rue Salin, place du Duché, Uzès. ℰ06 23 61 33 49.
- Savonnerie Marius Fabre, 148 avenue Paul-Bourret, 13300 Salon-de-Provence. ℰ04 90 53 82 75. www.marius-fabre.fr.

Santons and Faïence Pottery

- Atelier Marcel Carbonel (santons), 47 rue Neuve-Sainte-Catherine, 13007 Marseille. ℰ04 91 54 26 58. www.santonsmarcelcarbonel.com.
- Maison Chave (santons), 37 rue Frédéric-Mistral, 13400 Aubagne. ℰ04 42 70 12 86.
- Santons Fouque, 65 cours Gambetta, 13100 Aix-en-Provence. ℰ04 42 26 33 38. www.santons-fouque.com.
- Atelier d'Art-Maison Sicard (santons and faïence), 2 boulevard Émile Combes, 13400 Aubagne. ℰ04 42 70 12 92. www.maison-sicard.com.
- Poterie Ravel (faïence), avenue des Goums, 13400 Aubagne. ℰ04 42 82 42 00. www.poterie-ravel.com.
- Établissement Vernin Carreaux d'Apt (clay tiles), RN 100, 84480 Bonnieux. ℰ04 90 04 63 04

Provençal Furniture

- Meubles Melani, route d'Eyguières, Pont de Crau, 13200 Arles. ℰ04 90 49 72 83. www.meubles-melani. com (tour of workshops for small groups by appointment).
- Meubles Bonjean, 747 route de l'Isle-sur-la-Sorgue, 84250 Le Thor. ℰ04 90 33 82 94 (tour of workshops during the week). http://meubles-bonjean. ifrance.com.

Antiques

Those with a passion for antique furniture will enjoy browsing around

Souleiado in Tarascon

S. Sauvignier/MICHELIN

l'Isle-sur-la-Sorgue, where no fewer than 160 dealers have set up shops in five separate "villages".

- The largest one is the Village des Antiquaires de la Gare, 2 bis avenue de l'Égalité, 84800 L'Isle-sur-la-Sorgue. ℰ04 90 38 04 57.
- Village des Antiquaires du Quartier de Lignane, RN 7, Lignane, 13540 Puyricard. ℰ04 42 92 50 03.

Sweets

- Confiserie Léonard Parli, 35 avenue Victor Hugo, 13100 Aix-en-Provence. ℰ04 42 26 05 71. www.leonard-parli.com.
- Miellerie des Butineuses (honey, nougat, gingerbread), 189 rue de la Source, 84450 St-Saturnin-les-Avignon. ℰ04 90 22 47 52. www.mielleriedesbutineuses.com.
- Confiserie du Mont Ventoux (Berlingot sweets), 1184 ave D Eisenhower, 84200 Carpentras. ℰ04 90 63 05 25. www.berlingots.net.

Alcohol

- Distillerie Liqueur Frigolet (Élixir du Révérend Père Gaucher), 26 rue Voltaire, 13160 Châteaurenard. ℰ04 90 94 11 08. www.frigoletliqueur.com.

Aperitifs and liqueurs from Provence

S. Sauvignier/ MICHELIN

PROVENÇAL MARKETS

The picturesque markets of Provence, which liven up both city streets and village squares, are a must-see for tourists. Marvel at the high-quality local produce and crafts (fruit and vegetables, flowers, spices, herbs, olives, honey, cheese, fabric); chat to the stallholders, if you can understand their broad southern French accents!

Aigues-Mortes – Traditional market Wednesdays and Sundays on avenue F. Mistral.

Aix-en-Provence – Traditional market on place Richelme, daily.
General market on place des Prêcheurs and place de la Madeleine Tuesdays, Thursdays and Saturdays.
Flower market on place d'Hôtel de Ville, Tuesdays, Thursdays and Saturdays.
Flea market on place Verdun, Tuesdays, Thursdays and Saturdays.

Apt – Traditional market, Saturdays. Farmers' market Tuesdays (May–Nov).

Arles – Traditional market Wednesdays (boulevard Émile-Combes) and Saturdays (boulevard des Lices and bd Clemenceau).
Flea market on bd des Lices the first Wednesday of each month.

Aubagne – Traditional market on cours Voltaire, Tuesdays, Thursdays and weekends.
Flea market at La Tourtelle the last Sunday of each month.

Avignon – Traditional market daily except Mondays at les Halles (www.avignon-leshalles.com).
Flower market on place des Carmes, Saturdays.
Flea market on place des Carmes, Sundays.

Beaucaire – Traditional market, Thursdays and Sundays.

Bédoin – Provençal market, Mondays.

Cadenet – Farmers' market, Mondays and Saturdays.

Carpentras – Traditional market around the station, daily.
Truffle market Fridays (November–March).

Cavaillon – Traditional market, Mondays.

La Ciotat – Handicraft market every evening 8pm to midnight at the Vieux Port in July and August.

Fontvieille – Handicraft market, once a week 4pm to 9pm in June, July and August.

Gardanne – Traditional market in the town centre Wednesdays, Fridays and Sundays.

Graveson – Farmers' market on place du Marché, 4pm to 8pm Fridays May–October (www.lemarchepaysan.com).

L'Isle-sur-la-Sorgue – Traditional
market Thursdays and Sundays.
Flea market on avenue des Quatre
Otages, Sundays
Marseille – *See MARSEILLE.*
Nîmes – Indoor food market at
Les Halles every day.
Nyons – Traditional market Thursdays.
Orange – Traditional market
Thursdays.
Pertuis – Traditional market Fridays.
Farmers' market Wednesdays
and Saturdays.
Ruoms – Traditional market Fridays
and Saturdays.
St-Rémy-de-Provence – Traditional
market Wednesdays on place de
la République and place Pélissier.
Les Stes-Maries-de-la-Mer
– Traditional market on place des
Gitans Mondays and Fridays.
Salon-de-Provence – Traditional
market on place Morgan and
along the cours, Wednesdays.
Flea market on place Morgan the
first Sunday of each month.
Tarascon – Traditional market in the
town centre Tuesdays.
Uzès – Traditional market Saturdays.
Vaison-la-Romaine – Traditional
market Tuesdays.
Provençal market in the upper
town Sundays (June–September).
Vallon-Pont-d'Arc – Traditional
market Thursdays.
Valréas – Traditional market
Wednesdays and Saturdays.

FAIRS AND EXHIBITIONS

Arles – Santons Fair *(Salon
International des Santonniers)*
November–January.
Aubagne – Santons and Ceramics
Fair *(Foire aux Santons et à la
Céramique)*, July and August and
early December to early January.
Barjac *(Michelin map no 81 fold 12)* –
Antique Fair *(Foire aux Antiquités)*
Easter weekend and 15 August.
L'Isle-sur-la-Sorgue – Antiques
Fair *(Foire aux Antiquités)* Easter
Sunday and the Sunday around
15 August.

Marseille – International Fair
in September.
Santons Fair *(Foire aux Santons)* at
La Canebière from the last Sunday
in November to 31 December.
St-Quentin-la-Poterie – Biennial
Pottery Fair *(Terralha)* 12–14 July.

SIGHTSEEING
FROM ABOVE

One way of discovering the beautiful
landscapes of Provence from above
is by gliding. The following compnies
organise trips throughout Provence:
Association Vélivole de Carpentras,
BP 8, 84210 Pernes les Fontaines.
℘04 90 60 08 17.
http://pagesperso-orange.
fr/planeurs.carpentras.
Aéro-Club St-Rémy-les-Alpilles,
Aérodrome du Romanin, 13210 St-
Rémy-de-Provence. ℘04 90 92 08
43. www.aeroclub-alpilles.fr.
Centre de Vol à Voile de la Crau,
Aérodrome de Salon-Eyguières,
BP 81, 13300 Salon-de-Provence.
℘04 90 42 00 91.
www.planeur13.com.

General information can be obtained
from the Fédération Française de
Planeur Ultra-léger Motorisé
(*℘01 49 81 74 43; www.ffplum.com*).

ARCHAEOLOGICAL
EXCAVATIONS

Provence is packed with archaeological sites which welcome voluntary dig-
gers during the summer. Every spring,
the journals *Archeologia*, *L'Archéologue*
and *Archéologie* list sites which are
looking for new recruits. Contact
regional archaeology departments
(Services Régionaux de l'Archéologie)
for details.

♦ **Ardèche and Drôme**: DRAC
Rhône-Alpes, 6 quai St-Vincent,
69283 Lyon Cedex 01. ℘04 72 00
44 00. www.culture.gouv.fr/
rhone-alpes.
♦ **Bouches-du-Rhône**, **Var and
Vaucluse**: DRAC Provence-Alpes-
Côte d'Azur, 23 boulevard du Roi
René, 13617 Aix-en-Provence

Cedex. ℘04 42 16 19 00, www.paca.culture.gouv.fr.

◆ **Gard**: 5 rue de la Salle-l'Évêque, CS 49 020, 34967 Montpellier Cedex 2. ℘04 67 02 32 00. www.languedoc-roussillon. culture.gouv.fr.

BOOKS
PERSONAL EXPERIENCE

Village in the Vaucluse by Laurence Wylie *(3rd ed. Harvard University Press, reprinted 2005)*. Written by Wylie, a sociologist, in the years following World War II, this is a sincere, in-depth look at rural France in the years of post-war recovery.

Two Towns in Provence by M F K Fisher *(Vintage, new ed. 2002)*. This is a reissue under one cover of *A Considerable Town* (Marseilles) and *Map of Another Town* (Aix-en-Provence). Well known for her cookbooks and treatises on culinary arts, she has here set down parts of her life story when she was living in southern France in the 1950s.

A Year in Provence, Toujours Provence, Provence Encore by Peter Mayle *(Penguin, all published or reprinted between 1990 and 2000)*. These best-selling books have been credited for stirring up interest in Provence and all things Provençal, including house renovation and the game of *boules*.

The Magic of Provence: Pleasures of Southern France by Yvonne Lenard *(Princetown, 2000)*. Lenard is an American with French origins who, after a teaching stint in Aix, decided to stay on in the Luberon. She tells some entertaining stories about local characters and events, and closes most chapters with a doable recipe.

FOOD AND WINE

The Provence of Alain Ducasse by Alain Ducasse and François Simon *(Assouline, 2001)*. This hardback, coffee-table book is by a Michelin-starred chef whose love for the region of Provence is apparent in every page. In addition to recipes, luscious photographs, information about regional products (flowers, olive oils, herbs, etc.), there are tips on finding the best markets, café terraces, wineries and gardens.

Patricia Wells at Home in Provence: Recipes Inspired by her Farmhouse in France, by Patricia Wells, photographs by Robert Freson *(Fireside paperback, 1999)*. Lovers of French fare, whether prepared at home in the kitchen or savoured in restaurants both grand and humble, are well acquainted with Wells' reviews and recipes.

Markets of Provence: A Culinary Tour of Southern France by Dixon Long, Ruthanne Long, photographs by David Wakely *(HarperCollins, 1995)*. This book offers ways to really blend in to the local life by discovering the daily markets (and asking vendors about their specialities), visiting vintners or finding the freshest goat cheese and bread. It even includes directions to favoured picnic spots.

Flavours of Provence: Recipes from the South of France by Clare Ferguson *(Ryland, Peters & Small, 2007)*. Great cookbook full of regional information and authentic recipes.

FICTION

Hotel Pastis by Peter Mayle *(Penguin, 1994)*. More Mayle, anyone? This one is a tale of fun, love and outlandish schemes in the sunny south.

The Sacred Pool by L. Warren Douglas *(Baen Books, 2001)*. Set in the early Middle Ages and greatly inspired by folklore, this book is full of magic and mysticism but also offers an interesting perspective on history.

Toujours Dead by Susan Kiernan-Lewis *(Abdale Books, 2001)*. A *whodunit* that does it in the setting of a quaint village in

Provence, and involves the handsome heir to an ancient vineyard, who also happens to be a great cook.

Jean De Florette and Manon Des Sources by Marcel Pagnol, translated by W E van Heyningen *(Prion Books, 2004)*. These two books, which follow one another in sequence, are acclaimed works of French literature, and admirable in their faithfulness to the region's character. Visit Pagnol's home in Aubagne to get a real feel for them.

REGIONAL INTEREST AND ART

The Most Beautiful Villages of Provence by Michael Jacobs, photographs by Hugh Palmer *(Thames and Hudson, 1994)*. The villages of Provence are especially photogenic, drenched in colour, bright with flowers, fountains sparkling in the squares.

Colours of Provence by Michel Biehn *(Stewart, Tabori & Chang, 1997)*. This intriguing book is divided into chapters entitled "Red," "Orange," "Yellow," "Green," "Blue" and "White, Black & Gray". The text ventures from Van Gogh and Picasso, to local fabric designs and other crafts, delving into the realm of flower and herb gardens. The photographs of landscapes, villages, interiors and objects illustrate personal reminiscences, historical anecdotes, and descriptions of local culture, poetry, folklore and cuisine.

Crafts of Provence: Projects and Inspiration from the South of France by Amelia Saint George *(Conran Octopus, 2000)*. If you are not quite ready to realise your dream of retiring to southern France, here is a book that will advise you on transforming your home into a bright and sunny place that will make you feel like you're on holiday. Fabrics, ceramics, tiles and gardens are discussed at length and some DIY projects are outlined.

The Women Troubadours by Meg Bogin *(W.W. Norton paperback, 1980)*. This book casts a new light on the famous 12C poetry of Provence: finally we get a peek at courtly love from the feminine perspective.

The Memoirs of Frédéric Mistral by Frédéric Mistral, translated by George Wickes *(W W Norton, 1988)*. This book was first published in Provençal in 1906 under the title *Moun espelido: Memori e raconte*. The region's best-loved bard, Mistral was awarded the Nobel Prize in literature in 1904 and founded the Félibrige association of poets to protect and revitalise the Provençal language. His memoirs are a charming collection of proverbs and stories, hyperbole and myth. Mistral gives us a look at the ordinary people of his time, singing and telling tales, and delights the reader with examples of medieval and modern Provençal poetry.

The Letters of Vincent van Gogh by Vincent van Gogh, translated by Arnold Pomerans *(Penguin Classics, 2003)*. These letters are a precious companion to art book reproductions (⊘ *see below*) and will certainly move any reader interested in Van Gogh's paintings.

Van Gogh in Provence and Auvers by Bogomila Welsh-Ovcharov *(Universe Publishing, 2008)*. This oversize book has 270 excellent reproductions of the artist's paintings, focused on his 15 months in Arles and the last feverish days of his life in Auvers, where he painted 70 pictures in as many days. The text provides insight and analysis of Van Gogh's achievements.

The Yellow House by Martin Gayford *(Penguin, 2008)*. Gaugin and Van Gogh go mad in Arles (literally, for the latter). An account of their ten-week, masterpiece-producing stay in the city in 1888.

Cézanne in Provence by Evmarie Schmitt *(Prestel, 1995)*. This series has become popular for the quality of the text and the reproductions as well as the price range. The artist's work was deeply rooted in his native region, and the 50 paintings reproduced here emphasise the landscapes in particular, but his Bathers and still lifes are also included.

LITERATURE IN FRENCH

Jean de Florette, Manon des Sources, Marius, Fanny, César, Topaze, La Gloire de mon Père, Le Château de ma Mère, Le Temps des Secrets, Le Temps de l'Amour by M. Pagnol *(Éditions de Fallois, collection Fortunio)*. Atmospheric, bittersweet tales set in Marseille or its surrounding countryside.

Lettres de mon Moulin, Tartarin de Tarascon by A. Daudet *(Paris, Presses Pocket)*. The first is a nostalgic look at nineteenth-century village life; the latter is a fictional tale of hunting Tarascon's mythical monster.

GENERAL INTEREST

Caesar's Vast Ghost by Lawrence Durrell *(Faber & Faber, 2002)*. Part history, part colourful memoir, part poetry by British author who lived in the Gard.

French Dirt by Richard Goodman *(Workman, 2005)*. An American's tales of gardening, and living, near Avignon.

New Gardens in Provence: 30 Contemporary Creations by Louisa Jones *(Stewart, Tabori & Chang, 2006)*. Stunning book on Provence's beautiful gardens.

The Roman Remains of Southern France by James Bromwich *(Routledge, 1996)*. All you need to know about the Roman remains in the area.

Wild France: A Traveller's Guide edited by Douglas Botting and Simon Rigge *(Sheldrake, 2000)*. Ideal companion for outdoor types.

Cock and Bull Stories: Folco de Baroncelli and the Invention of the Camargue by Robert Zaretsky *(University of Nebraska, 2004)*. Examines the history of France's Wild West.

Provence: Style of Living by Jerome Coignard *(Hachette Illustrated, 2003)*. A stylish look at some beautiful homes.

FILMS

White Mane (1953) by Albert Lamorisse. A short film about a boy and his Camargue horse (filmed at Hotel Cacharel near Les Stes-Maries-de-la-Mer).

Borsalino (1970) by Jacques Deray. Belmondo and Delon in Marseille-based crime caper.

Caravan to Vaccarès (1974) by Geoffrey Reeve. Charlotte Rampling pouts her way through mediocre action thriller set in the Camargue.

French Connection II (1975) by John Frankenheimer. Action thriller starring Gene Hackman, as Popeye Doyle chases smugglers in Marseille.

Jean de Florette (1986), Manon des Sources (1986) by Claude Berri. Breathtaking interpretations of Pagnol's novels with Depardieu, Béart, Montand and Auteuil.

My Father's Glory (1990), My Mother's Castle (1990) by Yves Robert. More of Pagnol's depiction of eary 20C French provincial life.

Marius and Jeannette (1997) by Robert Guédiguian. Gritty love story set in the suburbs of Marseille.

Taxi (1998) by Gérard Pirès. A lighthearted action comedy set in the streets of Marseille, written by Luc Besson.

La ville est tranquille (2000) by Robert Guédiguian. Social and political drama set in Marseille.

A Good Year (2006) by Ridley Scott. Russell Crowe plays a City boy turned wine-maker in the predictable film of Peter Mayle's book.

Calendar of Events

The list below is a selection of the many events that take place in the region. Contact local tourist offices for further details.

TRADITIONAL CELEBRATIONS

FIRST SUNDAY IN FEBRUARY
Nyons – Festival of New Oil *(Fête de l'Alicoque; www.paysdenyons.com)*.

2 FEBRUARY
Marseille – Candlemas Procession *(Fête de la Chandeleur)* in the Basilique St-Victor *(http://marseille.catholique.fr)*.

SUNDAY BEFORE LENT
Graveson – Carnival Procession of Floats *(Corso carnavalesque; www.graveson.com)*.

LAST WEEKEND IN FEBRUARY
Nîmes – *Féria de Primavera*. Bullfights *(www.ot-nimes.fr)*.

EASTER WEEKEND
Arles – *Féria de Pâques*. Bullfights *(www.feriaarles.com)*.

1 MAY
Arles – Gardians' Festival *(www.tourisme.ville-arles.fr)*.

24 AND 25 MAY
Les Stes-Maries-de-la-Mer – Gypsy Pilgrimage *(Le Pèlerinage)* on 24 May, procession and blessing of

Gypsy Pilgrimage, Les Stes-Maries-de-la-Mer

©Haga Library/JTB/Photoshot

the sea on 25 May *(www.saintesmaries.com)*.

WHITSUN
Nîmes – *Feria de Pentecôte*. Bullfights *(www.ot-nimes.fr)*.
St-Rémy-de-Provence – Transhumance Festival. Sheep procession to the mountains. *(www.saintremy-de-provence.com)*.

23 JUNE
Valréas – Feast of Little St John *(Foire de la St Jean; www.ot-valreas.fr)*.

THIRD WEEK IN JUNE
Martigues – **Le Grau-du-Roi** – **Cassis** Fishermen's Festival on St Peter's Day. Water jousting and sardine scoffing.

LAST WEEKEND IN JUNE
Tarascon – Tarasque Festival. Folklore procession led by the mythical Tarasque monster *(www.tarascon.org)*.

Bullfighting in the amphitheatre, Nîmes

M.-H. Carcanague/MICHELIN

LAST FRIDAY IN JUNE
Arles – *Pegoulado*. Night-time procession in traditional costume *(www.tourisme.ville-arles.fr)*.

EARLY JULY
Marseille – International Folklore Festival at Château-Gombert *(www.roudelet-felibren.com)*.

FIRST SATURDAY IN JULY
Martigues – Venetian Festival. Fireworks display and evening flotilla of decorated boats *(www.martigues-tourisme.com)*.

FIRST SUNDAY IN JULY
Châteaurenard – Festival of St Eligius *(Défilé de St Eloi)*. St Eligius' cart, decorated and drawn by 40 horses in Saracen harness *(http://ot.chateaurenard.com)*.

FIRST MONDAY IN JULY
Arles – *Cocarde d'Or*. Provençal-style bullfights *(www.tourisme.ville-arles.fr)*.

WEEKEND BEFORE 14 JULY
Nyon – International Olive Festival *(Les Olivades; www.paysde nyons.com)*.

ABOUT 14 JULY
Les Stes-Maries-de-la-Mer – *Festival du Cheval*. Competitive events, games in the arena, gypsy flamenco music *(www.festival ducheval.camargue.fr)*.

MID-JULY
Carpentras – *Corso nocturne fleuri*. Evening procession of floats *(www.carpentras-ventoux.com)*.

MID-JULY–MID-AUGUST
Valréas – *Festival des Nuits de l'Enclave*. Concerts, markets and parades *(www.lesnuitsde lenclave.com)*.

LAST WEEK OF JULY
Graveson – Feast of St Eloi. Bull races and *pétanque* competitions *(www.graveson.com)*.

MID-AUGUST
St-Rémy-de-Provence – Feria. Provençal-style bull runs *(abrivados)* and *courses camarguaises (www.saintremy-de-provence.com)*.

AROUND 20 AUGUST
Monteux – Festival of St John's firework display. Concerts and activities on all week *(www.monteux.fr)*.

LATE AUGUST
Aigues-Mortes – Festival of St Louis. Medieval-themed events and costumes *(www.ot-aiguesmortes.fr)*.

FIRST SUNDAY IN SEPTEMBER
Aix-en-Provence – Blessing of the Calissons in the Église St-Jean-de-Malte *(http://moinesdiocesains-aix.cef.fr)*.

WEEKEND AROUND 22 OCTOBER
Les Stes-Maries-de-la-Mer – October Gypsy Pilgrimage *(www.saintesmaries.com)*.

EARLY DECEMBER
Istres – Shepherds' Festival. Shepherds march through the streets with their herds *(www.istres.fr)*.

24 DECEMBER
Allauch – Midnight Mass in Provençal. Shepherds come down from the hill of Notre-Dame du Château.
Les Baux de Provence – Shepherds' Festival. Midnight Mass in Provençal.
Arles – Christmas Eve watch and Midnight Mass in Provençal.
St-Michel-de-Frigolet, **Tarascon**, **St-Rémy-de-Provence** – Midnight Mass in Provençal.

Les Stes-Maries-de-la-Mer –
Midnight Mass with offerings.
Séguret – Enactment of the Li
Bergié de Séguret Mystery.

FESTIVALS
JUNE–SEPTEMBER
Nîmes – *L'Été de Nîmes*. Summer
festival of music, theatre, dance,
art exhibitions *(www.nimes.fr)*.

JULY
Fontaine-de-Vaucluse,
L'Isle-sur-la-Sorgue,
Lagnes, **Le Thor** – *Festival de la
Sorgue*. Music, theatre, dance
(http://festivaldelasorgue.free.fr).
Villeneuve-lès-Avignon –
International Events at the
Charterhouse Theatre *(www.
chartreuse.org)*.
Îles du Frioul – *Festival MIMI*. Jazz,
variety entertainment, folklore
(www.amicentre.biz).
Avignon – Festival of Theatre, Dance
and Music
(www.festival-avignon.com).
Aix-en-Provence – International
Festival of Opera and Music *(www.
festival-aix.com)*.

JULY–AUGUST
Valréas – Evenings of the Papal
Enclave (*Nuits de l'Enclave des
Papes*). Theatre and concerts
(www.ot-valreas.fr).

EARLY JULY–LATE AUGUST
La Tour-d'Aigues – Festival of
South Luberon *(www.
chateaulatourdaigues.com)*.

JULYSEPTEMBER
Luberon region –
International String Quartet
Festival in the Luberon *(http://
pagesperso-orange.fr/festival-
luberon-quatuors)*.
Arles – International Photography
Festival (*Les Rencontres d'Arles;
www.rencontres-arles.com*).
St-Rémy-de-Provence – Organ
Festival. Organ concerts
(http://organa2000.free.fr).

MID-JULY–EARLY AUGUST
Orange – *Chorégies*. Opera,
symphonic concerts
(www.choregies.asso.fr).
Vaison-la-Romaine – *L'Été de Vaison*.
Theatre, dance, music concerts
(www.musiquesdanslesvignes.com).

SECOND FORTNIGHT IN JULY
Carpentras – *Les Estivales*.
International Festival of Theatre,
Opera and Dance
(www.carpentras-ventoux.com).
Marseille – The Marseillaise Pétanque
Competition held in Parc Borély.
Salon-de-Provence – Jazz Festival
(www.salon-de-provence.org).
Uzès – *Nuits Musicales d'Uzès*.
Evening music concerts
(www.nuitsmusicalesuzes.org).

MID-JULY–LATE AUGUST
Bollène – *Polymusicales de Bollène*.
Music Festival
(www.bollenetourisme.com).
Martigues – International Folk
Festival *(www.martigues-
tourisme.com)*.

FIRST THREE WEEKS IN AUGUST
La Roque-d'Anthéron –
International Piano Festival
(www.festival-piano.com).

SECOND FORTNIGHT IN AUGUST
Pont-St-Esprit – *Rencontres Musicales*.
Classical concerts
(www.ot-pont-saint-esprit.fr).

THIRD WEEK IN SEPTEMBER
St-Maximin-la-Ste-Baume –
Autumn Festival. Organ concerts
(www.st-maximin.fr).

OCTOBER
Marseille – *Fiesta des Suds*. Two weeks
of world music with high-profile
performers
(www.dock-des-suds.org).

EARLY NOVEMBER
Vaison-la-Romaine –
Gastronomic Festival
(www.vaison-la-romaine.com).

Know Before You Go

USEFUL WEBSITES

www.ambafrance-us.org,
www.ambafrance-uk.org
The French embassies in the US and UK have a website providing basic information (geography, demographics, history), a news digest, and business-related information. It offers special pages for children and pages devoted to culture, language study and travel.

www.franceguide.com
The French Tourist Office (*Maison de la France*) site is packed with practical information and tips for travelling to France. Choose your country of origin and then click on the French region you're interested in.
You'll find links to individual sites for the Gard, Vaucluse and Bouches-du-Rhône plus contact details for local tourist boards and offices.

www.francekeys.com
This site has plenty of practical information for visiting France. It covers all the regions, with links to tourist offices and related sites. Very useful for planning your trip.

www.provencebeyond.com
Useful site, which as well as providing general information on Provence, has details of local transport.

TOURIST OFFICES

For information, brochures, maps and assistance in planning a trip to France travellers should apply to the official French Tourist Office or Maison de France in their own country.

AUSTRALIA – NEW ZEALAND

Sydney
Level 13, 25 Bligh Street, 2000 NSW, Sydney, Australia.
℘61 (0)2 9231 5244
http://au.franceguide.com.

CANADA

Montreal
1800 avenue McGill College, Suite 1010, Montreal, Quebec H3A 3J6.
℘(514) 288-2026
http://ca-en.franceguide.com.

EIRE

Dublin
℘(1) 560 235 235
http://ie.franceguide.com.

SOUTH AFRICA

Maison de la France South Africa, 3rd floor Village Walk Office Tower, cnr Maude and Rivonia, Sandton.
℘ 00 27 (0) 11 523 82 92
http://za.franceguide.com.

UNITED KINGDOM

London
Lincoln House, 300 High Holborn, London WC1V 7JH.
℘09068 244 123 (60p/min)
http://uk.franceguide.com.

UNITED STATES

Three offices are available, but the quickest way to have a response to any question or request is by phone.
℘514 288 1904
http://us.franceguide.com
East Coast
825 Third Avenue, 29th Floor, New York, NY 10022.

Midwest
205 N Michigan Avenue, Suite 3770, Chicago 60601, IL.

West Coast
9454 Wilshire Boulevard – Suite 210, Beverly Hills 90212 CA.

LOCAL AND REGIONAL TOURIST OFFICES

Visitors may also contact local tourist offices for more precise information, and to receive brochures and maps. The addresses, telephone numbers, and websites of local tourist offices are listed after the symbol ▯ in the Orient Panels of the Principal Sights inthe *Discovering* section of this guide. Below are addresses for the regional tourist offices and the *départements* tourist offices for Provence.

COMITÉ REGIONAUX DE TOURISME

Provence-Alpes-Côte d'Azur
10 place de la Joliette – Les Docks, BP 46214, 13567 Marseille Cedex 02. ✆04 91 56 47 00.
www.decouverte-paca.fr/us.

Languedoc-Roussillon
(For the département of Gard)
954 avenue Jean Mermoz, CS 79507, 34960 Montpellier Cedex 2.
✆04 67 20 02 20.
www.sunfrance.com.

Rhône-Alpes
(For the Gorges de l'Ardèche)
104 route de Paris,
69260 Charbonnières-les-Bains.
✆04 72 59 21 59.
www.rhonealpes-tourisme.com.

COMITÉ DÉPARTEMENTAL DU TOURISME

Ardèche
4 cours du Palais, 07000 Privas.
✆04 75 64 04 66.
www.ardeche-guide.com.

Bouches-du-Rhône
13 rue Roux-de-Brignoles,
13006 Marseille.
✆04 91 13 84 13.
www.visitprovence.com.

Gard
Rue Cité Foulc, BP 122,
30010 Nîmes Cedex 04.
✆04 66 36 96 30.
www.tourismegard.com.

Vaucluse
12 rue Collège-de-la-Croix, BP 147,
84008 Avignon Cedex 1.
✆04 90 80 47 00.
www.provenceguide.com.

INTERNATIONAL VISITORS
EMBASSIES AND CONSULATES IN FRANCE

Australia Embassy
4 rue Jean-Rey, 75015 Paris.
✆01 40 59 33 00
Fax: 01 40 59 33 15
www.france.embassy.gov.au.

Canada Embassy
35 avenue Montaigne,
75008 Paris.
✆01 44 43 29 00
Fax: 01 44 43 29 99
www.international.gc.ca/canada-europa/france.

Eire Embassy
12 avenue Foch, 75116 Paris.
✆01 44 17 67 00
Fax: 01 44 17 67 50
www.embassyofirelandparis.com.

New Zealand Embassy
7 rue Léonard-de-Vinci,
75016 Paris
✆01 45 00 24 11
Fax: 01 45 01 26 39
www.nzembassy.com/france.

South Africa Embassy
59 quai d'Orsay,
75343 Paris Cedex 07.
✆01 53 59 23 23.
Fax: 01 53 59 23 68
www.afriquesud.net.

UK Embassy
35 rue du Faubourg St-Honoré,
75383 Paris.
✆01 44 51 31 00
Fax: 01 44 51 32 34
http://ukinfrance.fco.gov.uk/en.

UK Paris Consulate
18 bis rue d'Anjou, 75008 Paris.
✆01 44 51 31 00
Fax: 01 44 51 31 27.

UK Marseille Consulate
24 ave du Prado, 13006 Marseille.
✆04 91 15 72 10
Fax: 04 91 37 47 06.

USA Embassy
2 avenue Gabriel, 75008 Paris.
℘01 43 12 22 22.
Fax: 01 42 66 97 83.
http://france.usembassy.gov.

USA Paris Consulate
2 rue St-Florentin, 75001 Paris.
℘01 43 12 22 22.

USA Marseille Consulate
Place Varian Fry, 13286 Marseille
Cedex 6.
℘04 91 54 92 00
Fax 04 91 55 56 95.

DUTY-FREE ALLOWANCES	
Spirits (Whisky, gin, vodka, etc.)	10l/2.6gal
Fortified Wines (Vermouth, port, etc.)	20l/5.28gal
Wine (not more than 60 sparkling)	90l/23.7gal
Beer	110l/29gal
Cigarettes	800
Cigarillos	400
Cigars	200
Smoking tobacco	1kg/2.2lb

DOCUMENTS

Passports
Nationals of countries within the European Union entering France need only a national identity card (a passport for UK nationals). Nationals of other countries must be in possession of a valid national **passport**. In case of loss or theft, report to your embassy or consulate and the local police.

Visas
No **entry visa** is required for Canadian, US or Australian citizens travelling as tourists and staying for up to 90 days, except for students planning to study in France. If you think you may need a visa, apply to your local French Consulate.
US citizens are advised to consult www.travel.state.gov for entry requirements, security and other information including contact numbers of US embassies and consulates. In an emergency call the **Overseas Citizens Services** ℘1-888-407-4747 (℘1-202-501-4444 from overseas).

CUSTOMS
In the UK, **HM Revenue & Customs** (www.hmrc.gov.uk) publishes *A Guide for Travellers* on customs regulations and duty-free allowances.
US citizens should view *Tips for Traveling Abroad* online *(travel.state. gov/travel/tips/brochures/brochures_ 1225.html)* for general information

on visa requirements, customs regulations, medical care, etc.
There are no customs formalities for holidaymakers bringing their caravans into France for a stay of less than six months. No customs document is necessary for pleasure boats and outboard motors for a stay of less than six months but the registration certificate should be kept on board. Americans can bring home, tax-free, up to US$ 800 worth of goods (limited quantities of alcohol and tobacco products); Canadians up to CND$ 750; Australians up to AUS$ 900; and New Zealanders up to NZ$ 700.
Persons living in a member state of the European Union are not restricted with regard to purchasing goods for private use, but the recommended maximum allowances for alcoholic beverages and tobacco are listed in the table on p14.

HEALTH
First aid, medical advice and chemists' night service are provided by chemists/drugstores *(pharmacie)* identified by the green cross sign. Since the recipient of medical treatment in French hospitals or clinics must pay the bill, it is advisable to take out comprehensive insurance coverage. Nationals of non-EU countries should check with their insurance companies about policy limitations. Reimbursement can then

be negotiated with the insurance company according to the policy held. All prescription drugs should be clearly labelled; it is recommended that you carry a copy of the prescription.

British and Irish citizens, if they are not already in possession of an **EHIC** (European Health Insurance Card), should apply for one before travelling. The card entitles UK residents to reduced-cost medical treatment. Apply at UK post offices, call *℘0845 606 2030*, or visit *www.ehic.org.uk*. You pay upfront but can reclaim most of the money (see website for details). **Americans** concerned about travel and health can contact the International Association for Medical Assistance to Travelers, which can also provide details of English-speaking doctors in different parts of France: *℘(716) 754-4883. www.iamat.org*.

The American Hospital of Paris is open 24hr for emergencies as well as consultations, with English-speaking staff *(63 boulevard Victor Hugo, 92200 Neuilly sur Seine; ℘01 46 41 25 25; www.american-hospital. org)*. Accredited by major insurance companies.

The British Hospital is just outside Paris: in Levallois-Perret, 3 rue Barbès; *℘01 46 39 22 22; www.british-hospital.org*.

ACCESSIBILITY

The sights described in this guide that are easily accessible to people of reduced mobility are indicated by the symbol ♿. Many of France's historic buildings, including museums and hotels, have limited or no wheelchair access. Older hotels tend to lack lifts. Tourism for All UK *(℘0845 124 9971; www.tourismforall.org.uk)* publishes overseas information guides listing accommodation that they believe to be accessible but haven't inspected in person.

Information about accessibility is available from French disability organisations such as **Association des Paralysés de France** *(17 bd. Auguste Blanqui, 75013 Paris; ℘01 40 78 69 00; www.apf.asso.fr)*.

Useful information on transportation, holidaymaking, and sports associations for the disabled is available from French-language website www.handicap.fr. In the UK, www.radar.org.uk is a good source of info and support and US website www.access-able.com provides information on travel for mature travellers or those with special needs. The **Michelin Green Guide France** and **Michelin Camping and Caravanning in France** indicate hotels and campsites with facilities suitable for people with physical disabilities.

Getting There

BY AIR

You can currently fly direct from the UK to:

Nîmes Airport *(℘04 66 70 49 49; www.nimes.aeroport.fr)* with Ryanair *(www.ryanair.com)*.

Avignon *(℘04 90 81 51 15; www.avignon.aeroport.fr)* with Flybe *(℘0871 700 2000; www.flybe.com)*.

Marseille *(℘04 42 14 14 14; www.marseille.aeroport.fr)* with Ryanair, easyJet *(www.easyjet.com)*, British

Airways *(www.ba.com; ℘0844 493 0777)* and Air France *(℘0871 66 33 777; www.airfrance.com)*.

To compare the cost of flights see *www.skyscanner.net*. No North American airlines currently fly direct to Provence, so you'd need to go to Paris and get a connecting flight or train. American Airlines *(℘1 800 433 7300; www.aa.com)*, Delta *(℘1 800 221 12 12; www.delta.com)* and Continental *(℘1 800 231 0856; www.continental.com)*. All fly from the US to Paris.

BY SEA
FROM THE UK OR IRELAND

There are numerous **cross-Channel services** (passenger and car ferries, hovercraft) from the United Kingdom and Ireland, as well as the **Eurotunnel** rail shuttle through the Channel Tunnel (*℘08705 35 35 35; www. eurotunnel.com*). To choose the most suitable route between your port of arrival and your destination use the *Michelin Tourist and Motoring Atlas France, Michelin map 726* (which gives travel times and mileages) or Michelin maps from the Local series (with the yellow cover). To compare prices, see www.ferrysavers.co.uk or contact:

- **P & O Ferries**
  ℘08705 980 333
  www.poferries.com
- **Brittany Ferries**
  ℘0871 244 0744
  www.brittany-ferries.com
- **Irish Ferries**
  ℘0818 300 400
  www.irishferries.com
- **Seafrance**
  ℘0871 663 2546
  www.seafrance.com
- **Norfolk Line**
  ℘0870 870 10 20
  www.norfolkline-ferries.co.uk

BY RAIL

Eurostar (*℘08705 186 186; www. eurostar.com*) operates a 2hr15min daily service via the Channel Tunnel from **London** (St Pancras) and Ebbsfleet International in Kent to **Paris** (Gare du Nord) or **Lille** (1hr20min). You can then catch a connecting train, the high-speed **TGV**, from **Paris** (Gare de Lyon) to **Marseille** (3hr15min), **Avignon** (2hr40min) and **Nîmes** (2hr55min). You can also catch a train south from **Lille**, which is convenient as you just have to change platforms and not stations. From 11 July to 12 September Eurostar operates a direct service from London to Avignon every Saturday. To book your return tickets from the UK to Provence, contact **Rail Europe** (*℘08448 484 064; www. raileurope.co.uk*).
Eurail (*www.eurail.com*) offers travel passes that may be purchased by residents of countries outside the European Union. In the US, contact your travel agent.
Train tickets in France must be validated *(composté)* by using the orange automatic date-stamping machines at the platform entrance (failure to do so may result in a fine).

BY COACH/BUS

Eurolines has regular overnight services from London and Paris to Marseille, Avignon and Nîmes. For further information go to www.eurolines.com or call ℘08717 818 181.

Getting Around

BY TRAIN/RAIL

France's rail system (SNCF) is an efficient and inexpensive way of getting between cities and larger towns. The TGV *(train à grande vitesse)* network is ever-expanding – see www.tgv.co.uk for a route map. Provence is well served by the TGV: it stops at Nîmes, Arles, Avignon, Aix-en-Provence, Miramas, Montélimar and Marseille. To help you get around during your stay, information on local train schedules and ticket prices can be seen at www.voyages-sncf.com. You'll find many offers and discounts: if you're travelling with children look out for the *Découverte Enfant* ticket, which allows a 25% discount on travel for up to four people accompanying one child under 12.

BY COACH/BUS

Getting around by bus is a cheap way of seeing Provence but services can be infrequent or at odd hours (to coincide with the school run). For

bus timetables in the Gard see www.
stdgard.fr, for the Bouches-du-Rhône
see www.lepilote.com and for the
Vaucluse see www.vaucluse.fr (all
websites in French). You'll find up-to-
date information in local bus stations
and at some tourist offices.

BY CAR
ROUTE PLANNING

The area covered in this guide is
easily reached by main motorways
and national routes. **Michelin map
726** indicates the main itineraries as
well as alternate routes for avoiding
heavy traffic during busy holiday
periods, and gives estimated travel
times. **Michelin map 723** is a detailed
atlas of French motorways, indicating
tolls, rest areas and services along
the route; it includes a table for
calculating distances and times. The
latest Michelin route-planning service
is available at **www.ViaMichelin.
com**. Travellers can calculate a precise
route using such options as shortest
route, a route avoiding toll roads or
the Michelin-recommended route. The
site also provides tourist information
(hotels, restaurants, attractions).
The roads are very busy during the
holiday period (particularly weekends
in July and August) and, to avoid traffic
congestion, it is advisable to follow
the recommended secondary routes
*(signposted as Bison Futé – itinéraires
bis)*. The motorway network includes
rest areas *(aires)* and petrol stations,
usually with restaurant and shopping
complexes attached, about every
40km/25mi, so that long-distance
drivers can stop for a rest regularly.

DOCUMENTS

Travellers from other European Union
countries and North America can
drive in France with a valid national
or home-state **driving licence**. An
international driving licence is
useful because the information on
it appears in nine languages (keep
in mind that traffic officers are
empowered to fine motorists). You'll
also need the vehicle registration

document and a current insurance
certificate as well as an international
sign plate or sticker (e.g. GB).
Certain motoring organisations (AAA,
AA, RAC) offer accident **insurance**
and breakdown service schemes for
members. Check with your current
insurance company in regard to
coverage while abroad. If you plan to
hire a car using your credit card, check
with the company, which may provide
liability insurance automatically (and
thus save you having to pay the cost
for optimum coverage).

RULES OF THE ROAD
Regulations

The minimum driving age in France
is 18. Traffic drives on the right. All
passengers must wear **seat belts**.
Children under the age of 10 must ride
in the back seat. Headlights must be
switched on in poor visibility and at
night; use sidelights only when the
vehicle is stationary.
In the case of a **breakdown**, a red
warning triangle or hazard warning
lights are obligatory; a reflective
jacket must be kept in the car. In the
absence of stop signs at intersections,
cars must **give way** *(cedez le passage)*
to the right. Traffic on main roads
outside built-up areas (priority
indicated by a yellow diamond sign)
and on roundabouts has right of way.
Vehicles must stop when the lights
turn red at road junctions and may
filter to the right only when indicated
by an amber arrow.
The regulations on **drinking and
driving** (limited to 0.50g/l) and
speeding are strictly enforced,
usually by an on-the-spot fine and/or
confiscation of the vehicle. For further
information, the highway code can be
checked at www.legifrance.gouv.fr.

Speed Limits

Although liable to modification, these
are as follows:
- ◆ toll motorways *(autoroutes)*
  130kph/80mph (110kph/68mph
  when raining);

RENTAL CARS – RESERVATIONS IN FRANCE		
Avis France:	☎ 08 20 05 05 05	www.avis.fr
Europcar:	☎ 08 25 35 83 58	www.europcar.com
Budget:	☎ 08 25 00 35 64	www.budget.com
Hertz:	☎ 08 25 861 861	www.hertz.com
SIXT:	☎ 08 20 00 74 98	www.e-sixt.com
CITER:	☎ 08 25 16 12 20	www.citer.fr

- dual carriageways and motorways without tolls 110kph/68mph (100kph/62mph when raining);
- other roads 90kph/56mph (80kph/50mph when raining) and in towns 50kph/31mph;
- outside lane on motorways during daylight, on level ground and with good visibility – minimum speed limit of 80kph/50mph.

Parking

In towns there are zones where parking is either restricted or subject to a fee; tickets should be obtained from the ticket machines (*horoda-teurs* – small change necessary) and displayed inside the windscreen on the driver's side; failure to display may result in a fine, or towing and impoundment. Other parking areas in town may require you to take a ticket when passing through a barrier.
To exit, you must pay the parking fee (usually there is a machine located by the exit – *sortie*) and insert the paid-up card in another machine which will lift the exit gate.

Tolls

In France, most motorway sections are subject to a toll (*péage*). You can pay in cash or with a credit card.

VEHICLES

Car Rental

Car rental agencies are located at airports, at railway stations and in all large towns throughout France. European cars have **manual transmission**; automatic cars are available in larger cities only if an advance reservation is made.
Drivers must be over 21 years of age. Drivers between the ages of 21–25 years are required to pay an extra daily fee. Some companies rent to drivers under 23 years of age only if the reservation has been made through a travel agent.
Rental prices have come down in the last few years but prices still vary. It's often a good idea to check out fly-drive offers or seek advice from a travel agent. There are many online services that will search internationally for the best prices on rental cars.
In the UK, see www.carrentals.co.uk for price comparisons or www.novacarhire.com.
See the Rental Cars coloured box for information and reservations.

Motorhomes
Worldwide Motorhome Rentals

Offers fully equipped camper vans for rent; you can view them on the company's website.
☎ 888 519 8969 *US toll-free*
☎ 1 530 389 8316 *outside the US*
www.mhrww.com.
Also try www.aviscaraway.com and www.motorhome-hire-france.com.

Petrol/Gasoline

French service stations dispense:
- *sans plomb 98* (super unleaded 98)
- *sans plomb 95* (super unleaded 95)
- *diesel/gazole* (diesel)
- *GPL* (LPG).
Petrol (gasoline) is considerably more expensive in France than in the USA.

Prices are listed on signboards on the motorways; it is usually cheaper to fill up after leaving the motorway; check the large hypermarkets on the outskirts of town. You can pay by card at the pump using credit/debit cards, including Maestro.

Where to Stay and Eat

WHERE TO STAY
FINDING A HOTEL

Turn to the **Addresses** within individual sight listings for descriptions and prices of typical places to stay **(Stay)** and eat **(Eat)** with local flair. The key at the back of the guide explains the symbols and abbreviations used in these sections. Use the map of **Places to stay** *(overleaf)* to identify recommended places for overnight stops.

To enhance your stay, hotel selections have been chosen for their location, comfort, value for the money, and in many cases, their charm. Prices indicate the cost of a standard room for two people in peak season. For an even greater selection, use the red-cover **Michelin Guide France**, with its well-known star-rating system and hundreds of establishments throughout France.

The **Michelin Charming Places to Stay** guide contains a selection of 1 000 hotels and guest houses at reasonable prices.

Be sure to book ahead, especially for stays during the high season: Provence is a very popular holiday destination. For further assistance, **Loisirs-Accueil** *(280 bd St-Germain, 75007 Paris; 01 44 11 10 44; www.loisirs-accueil.fr)* is an online booking service. You can also contact the tourist offices for further information on all kinds of accommodation in their respective areas, such as hotel-châteaux, bed-and-breakfasts, etc.

Another resource, which publishes a catalogue listing holiday villas, apartments or chalets in each *département* is the **Fédération Nationale des Locations de France Clévacances** *(54 bd de l'Embouchure, BP 52166, 31022 Toulouse Cedex 2; 05 61 13 55 66, www.clevacances.com).*

For good-value, family-run hotels, **Logis de France**, is one of the best organisations to contact (01 45 84 83 84; www.logis-de-france.fr).

Relais & Châteaux provides information on booking in luxury hotels with character: 0825 32 32 32; within the UK: 00 800 2000 00 02; within the US: 1 800 735 2478; www.relaischateaux.com.

These days, there are many websites which offer discount hotel accommodation.

Try *www.hotels.com*, *www.wotif.com* or *www.lastminute.com*. If you know where you want to stay, do a price comparison at *www.travelsupermarket. com* or *www.comparethemarket.com*.

ECONOMY CHAIN HOTELS

If you need a place to stop en route, these can be useful, as they are inexpensive (around 45€ on average for a double room) and generally located near the main road. While breakfast is available, there may not be a restaurant; rooms are small, with a television and bathroom. Central reservations in France:

- **Akena** 01 69 84 85 17 www.hotels-akena.com
- **B&B** 01 72 36 51 06 www.hotel-bb.com
- **Etap Hotel** 0892 688 900 www.etaphotel.com
- **Hotel Formula 1** 0892 685 685 www.hotelformule1.com
- **Accor Hotels** 0825 88 00 00 www.accorhotels.com/fr
- **Villages Hôtel** 03 80 60 92 70 www.villages-hotel.com

The hotels listed below are slightly more expensive (from 58€), and offer a few more amenities and services. Central reservation numbers:

- **Campanile** ℘01 64 62 59 70 www.campanile.com
- **Ibis** – ℘0892 686 686 www.ibishotel.com

COTTAGES AND BED & BREAKFASTS

The **Maison des Gîtes de France et du Tourisme Vert** is an information service for self-catering accommodation in Provence (and the rest of France). *Gîtes* usually take the form of a cottage or apartment decorated in the local style where visitors can make themselves at home, or bed and breakfast accommodation *(chambres d'hôtes)* that consists of a room and breakfast at a reasonable price. Contact the **Gîtes de France** office in Paris *(56 r. St-Lazare, 75439 Paris Cedex 09; ℘01 49 70 75 75; www. gites-de-france.fr).* You can also order a catalogue to browse in your own time. **Fédération des Stations Vertes de Vacances et des Villages de Neige** *(6 r. Ranfer de Bretenières, BP 71698, 21016 Dijon Cedex; ℘03 80 54 10 50; www.stationsvertes.com)* offers similar options, in the mountains or the countryside, with access to local life and leisure activities.

HOSTELS, CAMPING

To obtain an **International Youth Hostel Federation** card (there is no age requirement, and there is a "senior card" available too), you should contact the IYHF in your own country for information and membership applications *(US ℘1 301 495 1240; UK ℘01629 592 700; Canada ℘1 800 663 5777; Australia ℘61 2 9283 7195).* There is an online booking service *(www.hihostels.com),* which you may use to reserve rooms as far as six months in advance.

There are two main youth hostel *(auberges de jeunesse)* associations in France, the **Ligue Française pour les Auberges de Jeunesse** *(67 r.*

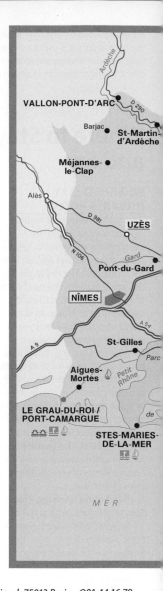

Vergniaud, 75013 Paris; ℘01 44 16 78 78; www.auberges-de-jeunesse.com) and the **Fédération Unie des Auberges de Jeunesse** *(27 r. Pajol, 75018 Paris; ℘01 44 89 87 27; www. fuaj.org).* The Fédération has an informative website providing online booking.

There are numerous officially graded **camping sites** with varying standards of facilities throughout Provence. The **Michelin Camping and**

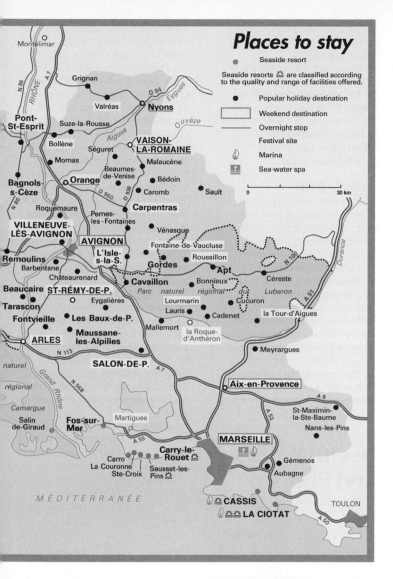

Places to stay

- Seaside resort

Seaside resorts ⚖ are classified according to the quality and range of facilities offered.

- Popular holiday destination
- Weekend destination
- Overnight stop
- Festival site
- ⛵ Marina
- ⚖ Sea-water spa

0   30 km

(Map of the Provence region showing towns including Montélimar, Grignan, Valréas, Nyons, Pont-St-Esprit, Suze-la-Rousse, Bollène, Mornas, Séguret, VAISON-LA-ROMAINE, Malaucène, Bagnols-s-Cèze, Orange, Beaumes-de-Venise, Bédoin, Caromb, Sault, Roquemaure, Pernes-les-Fontaines, CARPENTRAS, VILLENEUVE-LÈS-AVIGNON, AVIGNON, Vénasque, Remoulins, Barbentane, L'Isle-s-la-S., Fontaine-de-Vaucluse, Roussillon, Gordes, Apt, Céreste, Beaucaire, Châteaurenard, Cavaillon, Bonnieux, Tarascon, ST-RÉMY-DE-P., Eygalières, Parc naturel régional du Luberon, Cucuron, Fontvieille, Les Baux-de-P., Lourmarin, Lauris, Cadenet, la Tour-d'Aigues, ARLES, Maussane-les-Alpilles, Mallemort, la Roque-d'Anthéron, Meyrargues, SALON-DE-P., Aix-en-Provence, Camargue, Salin-de-Giraud, Fos-sur-Mer, Martigues, St-Maximin-la-Ste-Baume, Nans-les-Pins, Carro, La Couronne, Ste-Croix, Carry-le-Rouet, Sausset-les-Pins, MARSEILLE, Gémenos, Aubagne, MÉDITERRANÉE, CASSIS, LA CIOTAT, TOULON)

Caravanning in France guide lists a selection of campsites. The area is very popular with campers in the summer months, so it is wise to reserve in advance. Are you going hiking, skiing or kayaking and want a rustic place to stay overnight? Then visit *www.gites-refuges.com*, which provides details of accommodation in France's national parks including the Luberon. You can print out a guide to the Provence region for 5€.

THALASSOTHERAPY

Thalassotherapy uses the virtues of sea water to prevent or cure certain disorders and to improve general fitness and well-being. The healing and relaxing properties of the marine climate (iodine, radiant light, etc.), sea water, sea mud, algae and sand have given rise to a variety of therapeutic cures: fitness programmes, beauty treatments, therapy for relief from backache, stress, and addiction to

41

smoking. The mild Mediterranean climate is a good place to rest and restore your energy.

There are various thalassotherapy centres in the region, at **Le Grau-du-Roi**, **Marseille** and **Les Stes-Maries-de-la-Mer**. Or contact the national association for information: **Le Syndicat National de la Thalassothérapie** ℘02 40 11 72 35, www.thalassofederation.com.

WHERE TO EAT

A selection of places to eat in the different locations covered in this guide can be found in the **Addresses** appearing in the section entitled *Discovering Provence*. The key at the back of the book explains the symbols and abbreviations used in the Addresses. We have highlighted an array of eating places primarily for their atmosphere, location and regional delicacies. Prices indicate the average cost of a starter, main dish and dessert for one person. Use the red-cover **Michelin Guide France**, with its well-known star-rating system and hundreds of establishments throughout France, for an even greater choice. If you would like to experience a meal in a highly rated restaurant from The Michelin Guide, be sure to book ahead. In the countryside, restaurants usually serve lunch between noon and 2pm and dinner between 7.30 and 10pm. It is not always easy to find something in between those two mealtimes, as the "non-stop" restaurant is still a rarity in the provinces. However, a hungry traveller can usually get a sandwich (usually a filled baguette) in a café, and ordinary hot dishes may be available in a brasserie. Throughout France, the culture leans more towards sitting and eating than to grabbing a sandwich on the go, so it's worth planning ahead if you're unsure.

In French restaurants and cafés, a service charge is included. Tipping is not necessary, but French people often leave the small change from their bill on their table, or about 5% for the waiter in a nice restaurant.

For information on local specialities, see the section on Food and Wine in the next chapter, Introduction to Provence.

Useful Words and Phrases

Sights

	Translation
Abbaye	Abbey
Beffroi	Belfry
Chapelle	Chapel
Château	Castle
Cimetière	Cemetery
Cloître	Cloisters
Cour	Courtyard
Couvent	Convent
Écluse	Lock (Canal)
Église	Church
Fontaine	Fountain
Halle	Covered Market
Jardin	Garden

Mairie	Town Hall
Maison	House
Marché	Market
Monastère	Monastery
Moulin	Windmill
Musée	Museum
Parc	Park
Place	Square
Pont	Bridge
Port	Port/harbour
Porte	Gateway
Quai	Quay
Remparts	Ramparts
Rue	Street
Statue	Statue
Tour	Tower

Natural sites

	Translation
Abîme	Chasm
Aven	Swallow-hole
Barrage	Dam
Belvédère	Viewpoint
Cascade	Waterfall
Col	Pass
Corniche	Ledge
Côte	Coast
Forêt	Forest
Grotte	Cave
Lac	Lake
Plage	Beach
Rivière	River
Ruisseau	Stream
Signal	Beacon
Source	Spring
Vallée	Valley

On the Road

	Translation
Car park	Parking
Driving licence	Permis de conduire
East	Est
Garage (for repairs)	Garage
Left	Gauche
Motorway/Highway	Autoroute
North	Nord
Parking meter	Horodateur
Petrol/Gas	Essence
Petrol/Gas station	Station d'essence
Right	Droite
South	Sud
Toll	Péage
Traffic Lights	Feu tricolore
Tyre	Pneu
West	Ouest
Wheel Clamp	Sabot
Zebra Crossing	Passage clouté

Time

	Translation
Today	Aujourd'hui
Tomorrow	Demain
Yesterday	Hier
Winter	Hiver
Spring	Printemps
Summer	Été
Autumn/Fall	Automne
Week	Semaine
Monday	Lundi
Tuesday	Mardi
Wednesday	Mercredi
Thursday	Jeudi
Friday	Vendredi
Saturday	Samedi
Sunday	Dimanche

Numbers

	Translation
0	zéro
1	un
2	deux
3	trois
4	quatre
5	cinq
6	six
7	sept
8	huit
9	neuf
10	dix
11	onze
12	douze
13	treize
14	quatorze
15	quinze
16	seize
17	dix-sept
18	dix-huit
19	dix-neuf
20	vingt
30	trente
40	quarante
50	cinquante
60	soixante
70	soixante-dix
80	quatre-vingt
90	quatre-vingt-dix
100	cent
1000	mille

Shopping

	Translation
Bank	Banque
Baker's	Boulangerie
Big	Grand
Butcher	Boucherie

Chemist	Pharmacie
Closed	Fermé
Cough Mixture	Sirop pour la toux
Cough Sweets	Cachets pour la gorge
Entrance	Entrée
Exit	Sortie
Fishmonger's	Poissonnerie
Grocer's	Épicerie
Newsagent, Bookshop	Librairie
Open	Ouvert
Post office	Poste
Push	Pousser
Pull	Tirer
Shop	Magasin
Small	Petit
Stamps	Timbres

Food and Drink

	Translation
Beef	Bœuf
Beer	Bière
Bread	Pain
Breakfast	Petit-déjeuner
Butter	Beurre
Cheese	Fromage
Chicken	Poulet
Dessert	Dessert
Dinner	Dîner
Fish	Poisson
Fork	Fourchette
Fruit	Fruits
Glass	Verre
Ice Cream	Glace
Ice Cubes	Glaçons
Ham	Jambon
Knife	Couteau
Lamb	Agneau
Lunch	Déjeuner
Lettuce Salad	Salade
Meat	Viande
Mineral Water	Eau minérale
Mixed Salad	Salade composée
Orange Juice	Jus d'orange
Plate	Assiette
Pork	Porc
Restaurant	Restaurant
Red Wine	Vin rouge
Salt	Sel

Spoon	Cuillère
Sugar	Sucre
Vegetables	Légumes
Water	De l'eau
White Wine	Vin blanc
Yoghurt	Yaourt

Personal Documents and Travel

	Translation
Airport	Aéroport
Credit Card	Carte de crédit
Customs	Douane
Passport	Passeport
Platform	Voie
Railway station	Gare
Shuttle	Navette
Suitcase	Valise
Train/plane ticket	Billet de train/ d'avion
Wallet	Portefeuille

Commonly used words

	Translation
Goodbye	Au revoir
Hello/good morning	Bonjour
How	Comment
Excuse Me	Excusez-moi
Thank You	Merci
Yes/no	Oui/non
I am sorry	Pardon
Why	Pourquoi
When	Quand
Please	S'il vous plaît

USEFUL PHRASES

Do you speak English?
   Parlez-vous anglais?
I don't understand
   Je ne comprends pas
Talk slowly
   Parlez lentement
Where's …?
   Où est …?
When does the … leave?
   À quelle heure part …?
When does the … arrive?
   À quelle heure arrive …?
When does the museum open?
   À quelle heure ouvre le musée?

UNESCO World Heritage Sites

Provence boasts four World Heritage Sites, that is, sites deemed to be of outstanding value to humanity. Arles' Roman (amphitheatre, theatre, Alyscamps) and Romanesque (St-Trophime Church) remains have been protected by the organisation since 1981. Orange's well-preserved Roman theatre, probably the best-remaining example of its kind, and Roman triumphal arch are also included. The Pont du Gard aqueduct near Nîmes has been protected since 1985 and is fêted as a magnificent feat of Roman engineering, standing almost 50m/164ft high. Avignon's Papal Palace and bridge stand to remind us of the city's prominent role in the 14C when it was the home of the then popes. These sites will be protected and preserved as shining examples of Provence's contribution to European development for many generations to come.
For further information, see http://whc.unesco.org.

When is the show?
À quelle heure est la représentation?
When is breakfast served?
À quelle heure sert-on le petit-déjeuner?
What does it cost?
Combien cela coûte?
Where can I buy a newspaper in English?
Où puis-je acheter un journal en anglais?

Where is the nearest petrol/gas station?
Où se trouve la station d'essence la plus proche?
Where can I change traveller's cheques?
Où puis-je échanger des traveller's chèques?
Where are the toilets?
Où sont les toilettes?
Do you accept credit cards?
Acceptez-vous les cartes de crédit?

Basic Information

BUSINESS HOURS

Most of the larger shops are open Monday to Saturday from 9am to 6.30 or 7.30pm. Smaller, individual shops often close for 1–2hr at lunch daily and open half-day on Monday. Food shops – grocers, wine merchants and bakeries – are generally open from 7am to 6.30 or 7.30pm; some open on Sunday mornings. Many food shops close between noon and 2pm and on Monday. Hypermarkets usually stay open non-stop until 8pm or later. Many museums are closed on Monday or Tuesday.

DISCOUNTS

Some towns and cities sell passes, available from local tourist offices, which allow entry to several museums and monuments. In **Marseille**, you can get a one- or two-day *City Pass* for 20€ or 27€ respectively, which allows entry to 15 museums, a free trip on the little tourist train, discounts or freebies in some shops and free access to the bus and metro system. In **Arles**, you can get a *Pass Monuments* for 13.50€, which allows entry to six monuments and three museums.

The **International Student Travel Confederation** (*www.istc.org*), global administrator of the International Student and Teacher Identity Cards, is an association of student travel organisations around the world. ISTC members collectively negotiate benefits with airlines, governments, and providers of other goods and services for the student and teacher community, both in their own country and around the world. The non-profit association sells international ID cards for students, youth under age 25 and teachers (who may get discounts on museum entrances, for example). The ISTC is also active in a network of international education and work exchange programmes.

ELECTRICITY

The electric current is 220 volts/50hz. Circular two-pin plugs are the rule. Adapters and converters (for hairdryers, for example) should be bought before you leave home; they are on sale in most airports. If you have a rechargable device (video camera, portable computer, battery recharger), read the instructions carefully or contact the manufacturer or shop. Sometimes these items only require a plug adapter, in other cases you must use a voltage converter as well or risk ruining your device. Also, tourist offices will have details of any special passes or discounts applicable to their town or area.

EMERGENCIES

EMERGENCY NUMBERS	
Police	17
Fire Brigade (Pompiers)	18
Ambulance (SAMU)	15

MAIL/POST

Main post offices usually open Monday to Friday 9am–noon and 2–7pm, Saturday 9am–noon. **Stamps** *(timbres)* are also available from newsagents and *bureaux de tabac*. Stamp collectors should ask for *timbres de collection* in any post office.

France	Letter	(20g) 0.56€
UK	Letter	(20g) 0.70€
North America	Letter	(20g) 0.85€
Australia	Letter	(20g) 0.85€
New Zealand	Letter	(20g) 0.85€

MONEY
CURRENCY

There are no restrictions on the amount of currency visitors can take into France. Visitors carrying a lot of cash are advised to complete a currency declaration form on arrival, because there are restrictions on currency export: if you are leaving the country with more than 7 600€, you must declare the amount to customs.

BANKS

Banks are open 9am–noon and 2–4pm and branches are closed on either Monday or Saturday. Banks close early on the day before a Bank Holiday. A passport is necessary as identification when cashing traveller's cheques in banks. Commission charges vary and hotels usually charge more than banks for cashing cheques. One of the most economical ways to use your money in France is by using an **ATM** to get cash directly from your bank account or to use your credit cards to get cash advances (but be aware that your bank will charge you for this service). Be sure to remember your PIN number; you will need it to use cash dispensers and to pay with your card in most shops, restaurants, etc. Code pads are numeric; use a telephone pad to translate a letter code into numbers. PIN numbers have four digits in France; enquire with the issuing company or bank if the code you usually use is longer. Visa is the most widely accepted credit card, followed by MasterCard; other cards, credit and debit (Maestro, Plus, Cirrus, etc.) are also accepted in some cash machines. American Express is more often accepted in premium establishments. There are now credit cards on the market that don't charge for transactions made abroad (apart from withdrawing money from ATMs). Most places post signs indicating the cards they accept; if you don't see such a sign, and want to pay with a card, ask before ordering or making a selection. Cards are widely accepted in shops, hypermarkets, hotels and restaurants, at tollbooths and in petrol stations. If your card is lost or stolen, call one of the following 24-hour hotlines in France:

American Express: ℘01 47 77 72 00
Visa: ℘08 36 69 08 80
MasterCard: ℘08 00 90 13 87

You must report any loss or theft of credit cards or traveller's cheques to the local police who will issue you with a certificate (useful proof to show the issuing company).

PUBLIC HOLIDAYS

See the box below for a list of major public holidays in France. There are other religious and national festivals days, and a number of local saints' days, etc. On all these days, museums and other monuments may be closed or may vary their hours of admission. In addition to the usual school holidays at Christmas and in the spring and summer, there are long mid-term breaks (ten days to a fortnight) in February and early November.

PUBLIC HOLIDAYS	
1 January	New Year's Day (Jour de l'an)
Mon after Easter Sun	Easter Monday (Pâques)
1 May	Labour Day
8 May	VE Day
Thu 40 days after Easter	Ascension Day (Ascension catholique)
7th Sun after Easter	Whit Monday (Pentecôte)
14 July	**Fête National** France's National Day **(or Bastille Day)**
15 August	Assumption (Assomption)
1 November	All Saints' Day (Toussaint)
11 November	Armistice Day
25 December	Christmas Day (Noël)

SMOKING

In February 2007, France banned smoking in public places such as offices, universities and railway stations. The law became effective for restaurants, cafés, bars, nightclubs and casinos in January 2008.

TELEPHONES
PUBLIC TELEPHONES

Most public phones in France use pre-paid phone cards (télécartes), rather than coins. Some telephone booths accept credit cards (Visa, MasterCard/EuroCard). Télécartes (50 or 120 units) can be bought in post offices, branches of France Télécom, bureaux de tabac (cafés that sell cigarettes) and newsagents and can be used to make calls in France and abroad. Calls can be received at phone boxes where the blue bell sign is shown; the phone will not ring, so keep your eye on the little message screen. Some public telephones have internet access.

NATIONAL CALLS

French telephone numbers have ten digits. Paris and Paris region numbers begin with 01; 02 in northwest France; 03 in northeast France; 04 in southeast France and Corsica; 05 in southwest France.

INTERNATIONAL CALLS

To call France from abroad, dial the country code (+33) + 9-digit number (omit the initial 0). When calling abroad from France, dial 00, then dial the country code followed by the area code and number of your correspondent.

International Dialling Codes
Dial 00 before the country code (℘ see box below) minus the first 0, then the full number.

To use your **personal calling card** dial:
AT&T ℘0800 99 00 11
Sprint ℘0800 99 00 87
MCI/Verizon ℘0800 99 00 19
Canada Direct ℘0800 99 00 16
BT ℘0800 99 02 44
International information, US/Canada: ℘00 33 12 11

Australia	61
New Zealand	64
Canada	1
United Kingdom	44
Eire	353
United States	1

International operator ✆ 00 33
12 + country code
Local directory assistance ✆ 12

MINITEL

France Télécom operates a system offering directory enquiries (free of charge up to 3min), travel and entertainment reservations, and other services (cost per minute varies). These small computer-like terminals can be found in some post offices, hotels and France Télécom agencies and in many French homes. 3614 PAGES E is the code for **directory assistance in English** (turn on the unit, dial 3614, hit the *connexion* button when you get the tone, type in "PAGES E", and follow the instructions on the screen).

MOBILE/CELL PHONES

France has an efficient mobile phone service with several networks to choose from including SFR, Orange and Bouygtel. Check with your network provider that your phone is set up for international roaming before you go – your phone will automatically switch to the local network when you get to France. Bear in mind that calls are more expensive than those made within the UK or US and you also pay to receive a call. If you're going to be making and receiving a lot of calls, it might be worth getting a global sim card (*www.0044.co.uk* or *www.gosim.com*), which will give you a local number and lower calling rates. If you're going to be making a lot of calls in France, you should consider buying a pay-as-you-go (*sans abonnement*) phone from a high-street shop or supermarket.

Alternatively, you could hire a phone (delivery or airport pick-up provided):

- ◆ **World Cellular Rentals**
  www.worldcr.com

TIME

France is 1hr ahead of Greenwich Mean Time (GMT). In France the 24hour clock is widely applied.

WHEN IT IS **NOON IN FRANCE**, IT IS	
3am	in Los Angeles
6am	in New York
11am	in Dublin
11am	in London
7pm	in Perth
9pm	in Sydney
11pm	in Auckland

TIPPING

Since a service charge is automatically included in the price of meals and accommodation in France, any additional tipping is up to the visitor, generally small change, and generally not more than 5%. Taxi drivers and hairdressers are usually tipped 10–15%.

As a rule, prices for hotels and restaurants as well as for other goods and services are less expensive in the French regions than in Paris.

Restaurants usually charge for meals in two ways: a *menu*, that is a fixed price menu with two or three courses, sometimes a small pitcher of wine, all for a stated price or à la carte, the more expensive way, with each course ordered separately.

Cafés have very different prices, depending on where they are located. The price of a drink or a coffee is cheaper if you stand at the counter (*comptoir*) than if you sit down (*salle*) and sometimes it is even more expensive if you sit outdoors (*terrasse*).

CONVERSION TABLES

Weights and Measures

1 kilogram (kg)	**2.2 pounds (lb)**	**2.2 pounds**	*To convert*
6.35 kilograms	14 pounds	1 stone (st)	*kilograms*
0.45 kilograms	16 ounces (oz)	16 ounces	*to pounds,*
1 metric ton (tn)	**1.1 tons**	**1.1 tons**	*multiply by 2.2*
1 litre (l)	**2.11 pints (pt)**	**1.76 pints**	*To convert litres*
3.79 litres	1 gallon (gal)	0.83 gallon	*to gallons, multiply*
4.55 litres	1.20 gallon	1 gallon	*by 0.26 (US)*
			or 0.22 (UK)
1 hectare (ha)	**2.47 acres**	**2.47 acres**	*To convert*
1 sq. kilometre	**0.38 sq. miles**	**0.38 sq. miles**	*hectares to*
(km²)	**(sq.mi.)**		*acres, multiply*
			by 2.4
1 centimetre (cm)	**0.39 inches (in)**	**0.39 inches**	*To convert metres*
1 metre (m)	**3.28 feet (ft) or 39.37 inches**		*to feet, multiply*
	or 1.09 yards (yd)		*by 3.28; for*
			kilometres to miles,
1 kilometre (km)	**0.62 miles (mi)**	**0.62 miles**	*multiply by 0.6*

Clothing

Women	🇪🇺	🇺🇸	🇬🇧		Men	🇪🇺	🇺🇸	🇬🇧
	35	4	2½			40	7½	7
	36	5	3½			41	8½	8
	37	6	4½			42	9½	9
Shoes	38	7	5½		**Shoes**	43	10½	10
	39	8	6½			44	11½	11
	40	9	7½			45	12½	12
	41	10	8½			46	13½	13
	36	6	8			46	36	36
	38	8	10			48	38	38
Dresses	40	10	12		**Suits**	50	40	40
& suits	42	12	14			52	42	42
	44	14	16			54	44	44
	46	16	18			56	46	48
	36	06	30			37	14½	14½
	38	08	32			38	15	15
Blouses &	40	10	34		**Shirts**	39	15½	15½
sweaters	42	12	36			40	15¾	15¾
	44	14	38			41	16	16
	46	16	40			42	16½	16½

Sizes often vary depending on the designer. These equivalents are given for guidance only.

Speed

KPH	10	30	50	70	80	90	100	110	120	130
MPH	6	19	31	43	50	56	62	68	75	81

Temperature

Celsius (°C)	0°	5°	10°	15°	20°	25°	30°	40°	60°	80°	100°
Fahrenheit (°F)	32°	41°	50°	59°	68°	77°	86°	104°	140°	176°	212°

To convert Celsius into Fahrenheit, multiply °C by 9, divide by 5, and add 32.
To convert Fahrenheit into Celsius, subtract 32 from °F, multiply by 5, and divide by 9.
NB: Conversion factors on this page are approximate.

Lavender and Oleander
Stephanie Berghaeuser/SXC

Provence Today

Provence is famous the world over for its colourful landscapes and its relaxed way of life, along with its mouthwatering regional produce and cuisine; it's precisely these desirable attributes that drive a thriving tourist industry. The region still retains a strong cultural identity, most evident in its year-round events calendar, in spite of increased industrialisation and farming.

21ST CENTURY

The beginning of this century has seen Provence posing a familiar question to itself: how to combine modern development and growth, with Marseille being the second-largest city in France, while maintaining their fiercely proud Occitan identity, which has inspired artists and visitors and provided a melting pot for Mediterranean culture throughout its long history.

POPULATION

Provence has a population of around 4.5 million inhabitants, of which 839 000 inhabit the metropolitan area of Marseille; and of which 50% are of working age. The region boasts a growing population with around 55 000 births and around 20 000 marriages per year. Provence also enjoys a higher life expectancy at birth than the rest of the country. Interestingly, it has also become popular with second-home owners, with twice the percentage of second homes than the national average.

LIFESTYLE

The Provençal way of life is synonymous with a tranquil and easygoing charm, epitomised by its Mediterranean climate and alluring scenery. It is fused with bustling markets that can be found on any day of the week in most villages, where the wares of local artisans and fresh farm produce create a forum for communal life, and by the festivals or *férias*, which bring communities together in celebration.

RELIGION

Roman Catholicism is the religion of the majority of France, where there are also significant minorities who practise Islam, Protestantism and Judaism. *Laïcité*, the French concept regarding the separation of Church and State, allows citizens the freedom to practice the religion of their choosing. In this context, religion is seen as a private matter and people generally refrain from discussing their beliefs openly.

SPORT

As well as enjoying France's passion for sports such as football and cycling, Provence also enjoys regional sports such as *pétanque*, a form of bowls played with steel *boules*, which developed from the 17C sport called *jeu provençal*. *Course camarguaise*, a bloodless (at least for the bulls!) form of bullfighting where *raseteurs* snatch rosettes called *cocardes* from the head of a young bull, is regularly contested in villages as well as during festivals in Arles and Nîmes.

MEDIA

As well as Marseille-based newspapers such as *La Provence* and *La Marseillaise*, the region is also served by the *France Bleu Provence* radio station (101.8–103.6 FM) along with local television stations.

ECONOMY

Of all the regions of France, Provence is perhaps the place where the local economy has undergone the greatest

Street sign in Aix-en-Provence

J. Malburet/MICHELIN

changes in the past 50 years. These changes have come about due to the transformation of the agricultural sector, increased industrialisation – especially along the coast – adaptation to large-scale tourism, and runaway urbanisation.

FACETS OF AGRICULTURE

Rural life in the past depended on three crops – wheat, vineyards and olives. These, with sheep raising and a variety of other products gathered locally (herbs, almonds), ensured the existence of small farmers. However, this traditional polyculture has all but disappeared and been replaced by modern speculative agriculture, making the most out of Provence's natural resources, thus turning it into the garden of France.

Early Produce

The alluvial soil of the Rhône plain, the high mean temperature, and irrigation schemes favoured the development of early market gardening and fruit growing, producing several crops a year in the Comtat Venaissin and Petite Crau. The whole region is now divided up into parcels of land protected from the *mistral* winds by screens of cypress trees and reeds.

Strawberries, tomatoes and melons from Carpentras, asparagus, new potatoes and melons from Cavaillon, cabbage from Rognonas, asparagus from Lauris, cherries from Remoulins, and peaches, pears and apricots from the Rhône Valley are all sold in markets throughout France and the world.

Early produce, picked in the morning, is either sold to a private packer or sent to a cooperative where it is sorted, graded, packed and conditioned. Cooperatives have been established in places such as St-Rémy, Châteaurenard, Barbentane, Cabannes and St-Andiol, west of Cavaillon, among others.

From the main railway hubs (Châteaurenard, Cavaillon, Carpentras, Barbentane, Avignon), high-speed trains transport the early produce up the Rhône Valley to Paris and other large cities.

Cereals and Vineyards

The area between Arles and Tarascon, once the centre for growing wheat in Provence, is now producing maize, rape and rice as well. The windmills so dear to Alphonse Daudet have been replaced by modern milling machinery.

Vineyards occupy some 110 000ha/424sq mi and in the plains produce large quantities of table wine *(vin ordinaire)*. On the hillside, where the vineyards are cultivated with care, a delicate wine is produced carrying the general name **Côtes du Rhône** (whose most celebrated vintage is Châteauneuf-du-Pape). It has an estimated 15 000ha/37 050 acres of vineyards that produce high-quality wine.

Lavender and Lavandin

The delicate scent of lavender is characteristic of Provence. This plant is well suited to the climate and calcareous soils of Provence and Haute-Provence (&see *The Green Guide French Alps*). *Lavandin*, a more productive but less fragrant hybrid, is cultivated on the lower slopes (400–700m/1 312–2 297ft) and in the valleys. Today, about 8 400ha/20 748 acres of lavender are cultivated as well as 2 350ha/5 805 acres of *lavandin*. The harvest takes place from July to September according to the region. Though mostly mechanised, the inaccessible or closely planted older fields are still picked by hand. After drying for two to three days, the picked lavender is sent to a distillery. One hundred kilos (220lb) of lavender blossom are needed to produce one litre (0.2gal) of essence (the same amount of *lavandin* flowers yields 10l/2.6gal).

Lavender essence is reserved for the perfume and cosmetic industries whereas the hybrid *lavandin* is for perfumed laundry, soap and cleaning products.

Lavender fields can be spotted on the Vaucluse plateau and in the Drôme and Gard *départements*, north of Nîmes.

Almonds and Olives

Almond trees, which grow all round the shores of the Mediterranean, were first imported into France from Asia in 1548. The development of later-blossoming varieties has led to increased cultivation. The most famous of the local almond confectionery are *calissons* from Aix, lozenge-shaped almond-based sweets coated in white sugar icing.

The silver-green of the olive groves is a common sight in the country round Salon and Nyons.

Sometimes, in the olive plantations, old trees have been cut low to the ground and four suckers can be seen growing in a crown-like shape; these create handsome new trees. The black olives of Nyons, preserved in brine, are a delicacy.

At the Pont du Gard, a magnificent 1 100 year old olive tree, still bearing fruit, stands sentry as you approach the Roman aqueduct.

Truffles

The truffle is an edible, subterranean fungus that develops from the mycelium, a network of filaments invisible to the naked eye. They live symbiotically with the root of the downy oak, known in Provence as the white oak. The truffle is harvested in winter when it is ripe and fragrant.

These small, stunted downy oaks are planted in rows in fields called *truffières*. They are found mainly in south Tricastin, Comtat Venaissin, the Claparèdes plateau and in the Luberon. A superficial breaking-up of the soil and a specified pruning favours the truffle crop, which is harvested from November to April and marketed mostly in Apt, Carpentras, Richerenches, Uzès and Valréas, where several tons of this "black diamond" pass through annually.

Lime Trees and Herbs

Although found in most parts of France, the lime tree *(tilleul)* is cultivated mainly in Provence between Buis-les-Baronnies and Carpentras. At the end of the 19C, the lime tree grew alongside most French roads, whereas today it is planted in orchards and pruned.

The flower is picked in June, depending on the blooming, dried in a shaded, airy dry room, then sold in bags or by the ounce for tea. Mixtures of aromatic plants called *herbes de Provence* have doubled in popularity in recent years. Certain varieties are cultivated traditionally: basil and marjoram are cultivated around St-Rémy-de-Provence, tarragon on the Vaucluse plateau, whereas other varieties such as thyme, rosemary and savory are still gathered from the hillsides where they grow wild, and supply a large proportion of the herbs gathered.

Stock Raising

Sheep raising is an essential resource of all Mediterranean rural economies. Wool, no longer profitable, was abandoned and the sheep are now reared for meat.

Pastis in Provence

Inextricably linked to the game of *boules*, *pastis* is usually drunk around apéritif time, on the outdoor terraces of cafés. It made its first appearance in Marseille in 1922 after aniseed beverages were rehabilitated (they had been banned since 1915 because they were likened to absinth). Proper *pastis* is produced by leaving various aromatic plants (anise, star anise, liquorice, etc.) to macerate in alcohol. By the late 1930s, a host of brands had already made a name for themselves in France: Capon, Pernod, Cap Anis, Pasty-Anis, Bisanis, Stop-Anis, but especially Ricard (locals will usually ask for "*un Ricard*" rather than "*un pastis*"). During World War II, *pastis* was sold in small packets on the black market: mixing the concentrated powder with half a litre of 90° proof alcohol and the same quantity of water would produce a litre of *pastis*. Demand for bottled *pastis* soared once again in the 1960s and there are some chic new brands on the market. You'll find a superb selection at La Maison du Pastis, 108 quai du Port, Marseille (*℘04 91 90 86 77; www.lamaisondupastis.fr*).

The merino variety from Arles is predominant in the Bouches-du-Rhône *département*, however, the area allocated to it diminishes daily. The sheep graze on the meagre *coussouls* from the Plaine de la Crau from 15 October to 15 June. They are then moved up to Alpine pastures. Once a picturesque procession through villages and rugged countryside (known as transhumance), the transfer of the sheep is now done in trucks. In the *garrigues*, flocks of sheep graze on the sparse vegetation. They spend the summer in Larzac, or in the Lozère mountains.

The Camargue is famous for the black bulls and white horses who live in semi-liberty in herds called *manades*.

FISHING

Fishing is a traditional activity in the ports of Languedoc (Le Grau-du-Roi) and Provence (Port-St-Louis, Martigues, Carry-le-Rouet, Marseille, Cassis). But it frequently suffers from the effects of water pollution. Nevertheless, fishermen in these areas annually catch several thousand tonnes of sardines, anchovies, mackerel and eel. The sight of sailor-fishermen unloading their catch and drying their nets still remains one of the ports' most attractive scenes.

In Marseille, the port of Saumaty, located at the foot of the Estaque, can shelter as many as 180 trawlers (1 400m/4 593ft of quays) and offers all the necessary equipment for the preservation of fish.

Small fishing boats still supply the fishmongers of Marseille's Vieux Port. The hustle and bustle and the sing-song cries of the stallholders create a lively, timeless atmosphere that seems to have come straight out of Marcel Pagnol's novels.

INDUSTRIALISATION

In the 1930s, Provence witnessed spectacular industrial development. Around Étang de Berre a vast industrial complex was built: oil refineries; and chemical, aeronautic and metal works. Its centre was the Bassins de Fos complex, inaugurated in 1968. From Marseille to Aix, industrial zones have multiplied and offer a vast range of activities: from soap-making plants to the most modern electronics factories. The hydroelectric installations of the lower valleys of the Rhône and Durance have also contributed to the profound economic upheavals. Hydroelectric production combined with nuclear (*Marcoule*) production has allowed France to strengthen its energy potential. Moreover, the domestication of the two undisciplined rivers has resulted in the possibility of irrigating an immense agricultural area, until then hindered by drought. All these transformations have made Provence one of France's great industrial zones juggling between two types of industry:

♦ **traditional**: minerals (ochre, bauxite, lignite), shipbuilding, foodstuffs, soap-making (Marseille area), building materials, construction and saltworks;

♦ **modern**: petroleum and its derivatives, aeronautics, electronics, nuclear and chemicals.

Light industries have also developed: packaging in Valréas and Tarascon; confectionery in Aix, Apt and Nyons; fruit preserving, and garment and shoe making in Nîmes.

Ochre

The Apt-Roussillon area is one of the main mining and treatment regions in France for ochre (an earthy red or yellow, and often impure, iron ore essentially used as a pigment for paints or as a wash applied for its protective value). The mineral beds can at times be 15m/49ft thick. Ochre in its natural state is a mixture of argillaceous sand and iron oxide. To obtain a commercially pure ochre product, the mineral is first washed and the impurities, which tend to be heavier, settle on the bottom. The lighter weight "flower", which is made of iron oxide and clay, is passed through the filter and into settling tanks. There, after drying, it assumes the look of ochre. It is then cut into blocks. After drying, the ochre is crushed, sifted and at times baked in ovens to darken the pigmentation and obtain a reddish-orange colour. This process is called ochre calcining. The ochre then becomes an unctuous, impalpable powder used commercially. The quality of the ochre from Vaucluse has made France one of its most important producers, with an annual production of about 3 000 metric tons.

Olive Oil

Typically, Provençal oil has always been olive oil. Olives are treated when ripe and picked while still green if used for food preservation. The quality of the oil depends on the quality of the fruit and the treatment (number of pressings). Once picked, the olives are crushed whole with the pit, either by a millstone, hammer mill or roller.

The paste obtained is then distributed on a trolley's nylon discs. The trolley, now loaded, is placed on the sliding piston of a hydraulic press that exerts pressure on the paste, resulting in a mixture of oil and water that is collected in tanks and then pumped into centrifugal machines where the oil and water will be separated. The oil that comes out of the machine is a virgin oil obtained by a first cold-water pressing. The residual pulp *(grignon)* can be pressed again, yielding more oil, though of a lesser grade and taste.

In the past the olive paste was spread by hand onto coconut mats *(scourtins)* which were stacked under the press. For a long time the presses were worked by hand and a horse turned the millstone. The residual pulp was remashed with lukewarm water: a mixture of refined and virgin oil was obtained, classed as second quality and called second pressing. Today, as in the past, the residual pulp treated with chemical solvents in Italy produces oil used for cutting or soap-making. Before this last pressing the olive pit can be separated from the pulp: the pit is ground down into powder and is used by the baker and pastry cook; the pulp is used for compost.

Salt Marshes

People in the Camargue work two large salt marshes: one is south of Aigues-Mortes and spreads over 10 000ha/24 700 acres; the other is south of Salin-de-Giraud and covers over 11 000ha/27 170 acres.

Already improved by the monks in the 13C, the salt marshes increased production in the mid-19C, progressed and then decreased. The present-day global annual production is evaluated at c. 850 000 metric tons.

GOVERNMENT

France is split on an administrative level into 22 metropolitan and four overseas *régions*, which are administered by elected regional councils. These are furthermore divided into 100 *départements* (equivalent to a district or county), in turn administered by general councils. Provence encompasses an area included in three *régions*, consisting of six *départements*: **Gard** in the Languedoc-Roussillon *région* to the west; **Drôme** and **Ardèche** in the Rhône-Alpes *région* to the north; and **Bouches-du-Rhône**, **Var** and **Vaucluse** in the Provence-Alpes-Côte d'Azur *région* to the east.

POPULAR GAMES
BOULES

This popular game is emblematic of Provence: long lazy evenings and animated debates. Contests are played between teams of three *(triplettes)* or four *(quadrettes)*, amid attentive and enthusiastic spectators. The *pointeurs* have to throw their balls, which are weighted with iron, as near as possible to a smaller ball *(cochonnet)*, which has been set at the end of the bowling ground; the *tireurs* have then to dislodge the balls of the opposing team by striking them with their own. The most skilful succeed in doing this and in taking the exact place of their adversary *(faire le carreau)*. Over short distances play is *à la pétanque*, standing within a circle,

Playing the pétanque

Brigitta L. House/MICHELIN

feet together. Over longer distances, above 10m/33ft, the game is called *la longue*; the *tireurs* take a running start and throw their balls after having made three hopping steps from the throwing point.

Among all these shirt-sleeved players, the two Provençal types form a real contrast. One, a native of the mountains, somewhat reserved and distant, shows his pleasure or his disappointment by a smile or frown. The other enacts quite a little drama, which has been happily described:

"Here then is the last ball; it rolls out before the player and you can watch its progress in his face; he broods over it, protects it with his gaze; gives it advice, strives to make it obedient to his voice, hurries or slows its course, encourages it with a gesture or urges it on with a heave of his shoulder, slackens it with his hand; perched on tiptoe, his arm flung out, his face animated by a wealth of varying emotions, he wriggles his body in bizarre undulations; one could almost say that his soul had passed into the ball."

Play is frequently held up by noisy, heated arguments about the distances separating the various balls from the *cochonnet*. Play resumes once measurements have been taken, often with small branches or twigs broken off a nearby tree.

CARD GAMES

The unforgettable scene in the *Bar de la Marine*, where a group of locals take part in a game of *manille*, with the colourful dialogue that typified Marcel Pagnol's work, exemplifies the importance of card games in Provençal society. Provence was the first place in France where playing cards appeared. Minutes drawn up by a Marseille notary, dated 30 August 1381, prohibiting a merchant of the city from playing *nahipi* or *naïbi*, a sort of Happy Families card game, attest to the fact. This card game is nowadays considered the ancestor of modern-day tarot. Following their likely origins in the imperial Chinese court, playing cards reached the Occident during the course of the 13C, via Venetian bankers and merchants, or via the hordes of Tartars from central Asia. Venetian artists, hitherto devoted to religious and secular canvases, succumbed to this trend of painting on card and parchment. Marseille was soon drawn to the charms of this new pastime, as was the Comtat Venaissin, with its close ties with Italy. The 15C gave rise to the game *cinq cents*, also known as the *Marseillais*. The first "professional" card makers appeared around 1631. With the development of new xylographic and typographic processes, replacing wooden printing moulds with copper ones, card production continued to increase dramatically, reaching a rate of 180 000 packs a year by the end of

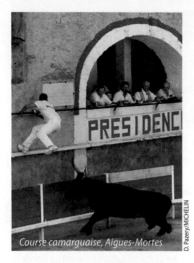
Course camarguaise, Aigues-Mortes
D. Pazery/MICHELIN

the 17C. The 18C was for Marseille the epoch of **tarot**, which originated in Italy. Apart from the set manufactured by Jean Noblet in Paris during the 17C, the oldest tarot cards, said to have been made in Marseille, actually appeared in Avignon in 1713, a city where card makers were exempt from tax.

This privilege was removed in 1754, at which time Marseille established itself as the leading manufacturer. Marseille tarot, the French version of Venetian tarot, from which it copied 78 signs, provided the game with its definitive form, principally under the aegis of the master tarot maker **Nicolas Conver**, who produced a particularly attractive set of cards in 1760. The *Tarot de Marseille*, which was adopted by clairvoyants and soothsayers alike, was also to act as a support for another regional game in the 18C, the **Portrait de Marseille**.

However, the following century the Camoin company, with its exports worldwide, was to distance itself from its competitors by producing over a million sets a year, based on traditional expertise acquired over more than two centuries. The company finally closed its doors in 1974, though its sparkling creations can still be admired in the large collection housed in the Musée du Vieux-Marseille.

FESTIVALS AND COSTUMES
FESTIVALS

The people of Provence have always had a taste for celebration. In the past it was the men who were in charge of the festivities. The fairs, either secular or religious (remnants of Christian celebrations mixed with pagan tendencies), were numerous. There are the feast days that occur throughout the year, and the larger festivals, more or less traditional, attracting thousands of people in a typically colourful Provençal atmosphere.

In April and September, Nîmes and Arles try to outdo each other with their famous *férias*, via the *corrida* (bullfights) or *course camarguaise*, where men called *raseteurs* attempt to grab a rosette *(cocarde)* from between a bull's horns. The latter continues to take place throughout the summer in arenas across the Camargue.

Also in the Camargue, the *Féria du Cheval* in July celebrates the region's four-legged friends – the horse and, of course, the bull.

In canal town Martigues, the Venetian Water Festival includes a nocturnal procession of decorated boats as well as water jousting.

Families will love the Tarasque Festival in Tarascon at the end of June, which celebrates the killing of a mythical medieval monster.

And of course there are the theatre, opera and dance festivals. Be it Avignon, Aix-en-Provence, Orange, Vaison-la-Romaine, Carpentras, Salon-de-Provence or Arles, each of these cities is the venue for an annual artistic festival of top quality (&see PLANNING YOUR TRIP – Calendar of Events).

FARANDOLES

Most of the festivals are a wonderful opportunity to listen to the fife and *tambourin* so delightfully characteristic of the Provence region. The **farandole** is a Mediterranean dance that dates back to the Middle Ages if not to Antiquity, and was danced throughout Arles country. Young men and women, holding either each other's hands or a handkerchief, dance to a six-beat rhythm. The typically Provençal instruments played by the *tambourinaires* are the **galoubet**, a small three-holed flute that produces a piercing sound, and the **tambourin**, a type of drum 75cm/29.5in high and 35cm/13.8in wide, beaten by a *massette* held in the right hand while the other hand holds the *galoubet*. On the drum itself, the head of which is made from calfskin, is stretched the *chanterelle*, a thin strand of hemp or a violin string that produces a rasping sound, poetically called the "song of the cicada".

CHRISTMAS IN PROVENCE

Celebrations surrounding the end of the year begin on 4 December, the feast day of St Barbe, and end at Candlemas on 2 February. The locals start by sowing their "Christmas wheat" *(lou blad de Calendo)* on 4 December. When it starts to sprout, they place it above the fireplace. Three weeks later, people use it as decoration beside the crib or as a centrepiece for the long banquet table. Preparations for the crib take place on the Sunday before Christmas, but it is only at midnight on 25 December that the infant Jesus is laid in the crib. That same night, the whole family ritually performs *Cacho-Fio*, a ceremony during which a Christmas log *(bûche de Noël)* is blessed with a fortified wine and taken round the house three times, before being burned. The family may then be seated to begin their Christmas feast. The table, covered with three overlapping tablecloths, is laid with three chandeliers and three saucers containing the Christmas wheat, as well as 13 loaves of bread. The meal ends with the traditional 13 desserts (*mendiants*: walnuts and hazelnuts, figs, almonds and raisins; fresh fruit; black and white nougat; *pompe à huile*, a flat, brittle loaf made with olive oil). Midnight Mass starts with *lou Pastrage*: the shepherd, the miller and the ancestors enter the church, where the priest lays the infant Jesus in the crib. Then the bells are rung, inviting the procession of shepherds to enter the church: they draw a small cart with a lamb, an offering made to the Infant Jesus. Mass continues with a series of Christmas songs and carols, which retraces the steps of Joseph who was seeking refuge for the night. On 31 December, Provençal people always celebrate the New Year *(an nou)* together as a family. On the first Sunday in January, they pay tribute to the Magi and throughout the month of January, in honour of the Three Wise Men, they eat Twelfth Night cake *(galette des rois)*, a crown-shaped bun decorated with crystallised fruit and containing a lucky charm *(fève)*. These Christmas festivities end on 2 February with Candlemas *(Chandeleur)*, the feast marking the Purification of the Virgin Mary and the presentation of Christ in the Temple 40 days after his birth. Celebrations involve a procession of green church candles. In Marseille, one also eats *navettes*, small boat-shaped biscuits that evoke the arrival of the Saintes Maries in Provence.

PROVENÇAL COSTUMES

It was thanks to the commercial relationship between Marseille and the Mediterranean ports of the Levant that Provence discovered Oriental fabrics. Since the end of the 17C, it has made these its own by adopting printed floral calicos and stitching and quilting techniques. The characteristic patterns of colourful motifs now known as "Provençal prints" are the result of a long evolution of methods and fashions.

Traditional costume in Arles is but one of several different costumes worn all over Provence. It is a reminder of the diversity of the clothing worn by the various social milieux of days gone by: the fisherman's wife of the Vieux Port of Marseille, with the flaps of her coif blowing about in the wind; the flowergirl; the country farmer's wife; the washerwoman; or the peasant woman with her striped underskirts, her huge apron of deep purple canvas and the *capuch* or *capelino*, which envelops her head.

In their traditional festive costume (there is an excellent collection in the Museon Arlaten in Arles), women from Arles wear long colourful skirts and a black under-blouse *(eso)* with tight sleeves; on top a pleated shirt is covered with a shawl either made of white lace or matching the skirt. There are different varieties of headdress, all worn on top of a high bun: *à la cravate* (white percale knotted like rabbits' ears); *à ruban* (with a lace-trimmed velvet ribbon); or *en ailes de papillon* ("butterfly wings" of lace).

The men's costume is less colourful. They wear a white shirt knotted at the collar by a thin tie or ribbon, sometimes covered by a dark-coloured vest upon which hangs a watch chain; canvas trousers are held at the waist by a wide red or black woollen belt. They wear black felt hats with a wide, tilted brim.

FOOD AND WINE
A SUCCULENT CUISINE

Provençal cooking is characterised by garlic and food fried in oil. Garlic was praised by many poets as the "truffle of Provence", the "divine condiment", this "friend of man." Oil (preferably olive oil) replaced butter in all the Provençal dishes.

An old Provençal saying goes, "A fish lives in water and dies in hot oil."

Bouillabaisse

This famous Provençal dish traditionally comprises "the three fishes": the spiny red hog-fish, gurnet and conger eel *(rascasse, grondin, congre)*. Cooks add as many other fish as are available: sea bass *(loup)*, turbot, sole, red mullet *(rouget)*, monkfish *(lotte)* and crustaceans such as crabs, spider crabs *(araignées de mer)*, mussels *(moules)* and sometimes, spiny lobsters *(langoustes)* or crawfish.

These sea delights are cooked together very rapidly in a *bouillon*, emulsified with a small quantity of olive oil and seasoned with salt, pepper, onion, tomato, saffron, garlic, thyme, bay leaf, sage, fennel, orange peel, and maybe a glass of white wine or Cognac – the magic of the results depends on the seasoning.

A *rouille* (pronounced *roo-EE*), or paste, of Spanish peppers, served at the same time, sharpens the sauce and gives it colour.

In a restaurant one is usually presented with a soup plate and toast with which to line it. Some people then spread some of the toast with the *rouille*; others mix it directly into the thickened bouillon soup that arrives in a tureen. To your plateful of toast, *rouille* and soup, you then add bits of the assorted cooked fish and crustaceans. *Bouillabaisse* is a main dish. The fish must be fresh and the dish freshly prepared. It is not a stew: the actual cooking time is only ten minutes.

Aïoli

The other great Provençal speciality is a mayonnaise made with garlic, egg yolks, lemon juice, olive oil and sometimes mustard. It is served with hors-d'œuvres, asparagus and other vegetables, and also as a sauce with *bourride*, the fish soup made from angler fish *(baudroie)*, sea bass *(loup)* and whiting *(merlan)*. It is also the name of a complete dish consisting of boiled vegetables (carrots, potatoes and green beans), boiled fish (cod) and boiled eggs served with the mayonnaise.

Fish and Crustaceans

Local fish dishes include red mullet *(rouget)* cooked whole, sea bass *(loup)* grilled with fennel or vine shoots, and *brandade de morue*, a thick and creamy mash of pounded cod, olive oil and milk, seasoned with crushed garlic.

Fish specialities are associated with individual towns. For Marseille, in addition to *bouillabaisse*, there are clams *(clovisses)*, ascidia or iodine-rich sea-squirts *(violets)*, mussels *(moules)* and sea urchins *(oursins)*, all of which you will find easily in the small restaurants around the Vieux Port. In St-Rémy you will encounter the *catigau*, a dish of grilled or smoked Rhône eel in sauce. In the Camargue, look for *tellines* (edible moluscs) served with a pungent sauce.

Fruit and Vegetables

Raw onion and tomatoes, common favourites among vegetables, are

Three Traditional Recipes

Tapenade

This olive, anchovy and caper-flavoured paste is eaten either as an hors-d'œuvre or as an accompaniment to an apéritif and is spread on slices of bread. In a mortar, place two handfuls of stoned black olives, 2–4 anchovy fillets, 2 soup-spoonfuls of capers, 1 crushed garlic clove, a pinch of dried thyme, and ground black pepper to taste. Crush until you get a rough paste. Add a dessertspoon of mustard, juice from a quarter of a lemon, a dash of brandy (optional), and mix. Lastly, add enough olive oil to give the paste a nice spreading consistency.

Artichauts à la Barigoule

Serves 4. The term *barigoule* is Provençal for mushroom; the name of the dish comes from the manner in which the artichokes are cut, giving them the appearance of mushrooms. Select a dozen small fresh artichokes and remove the largest leaves. Cut off the top two-thirds of the remainder and cook in an open casserole dish over a low heat with some sliced onions and carrots; add some olive oil. After 20–25min, add two glasses of dry white wine, two glasses of stock, two cloves of garlic and a few bacon cubes. Add salt and pepper, then cover once more and simmer for 50min. Serve the artichokes in the sauce.

Daube Provençale

Allow two days for the preparation of this dish. Marinate half a pound of beef cut up into pieces in red wine together with an onion cut in four, a clove of garlic, a bunch of mixed herbs *(bouquet garni)*, salt and pepper. The next day, fry some bacon *(lard)* in hot olive oil, using a casserole dish (preferably made of clay with a shallow lid). Add a chopped onion and two sliced carrots as well as two crushed tomatoes. After browning these, mix in with the meat and continue to fry. Pour in a glass of red wine and bring to a boil. Add two more glasses of water and the garlic, the *bouquet garni* and the peel of an orange. Season with salt and pepper. After the boiling point is reached, turn the heat down and leave to simmer for five hours.

followed closely by *cardoons* (vegetable related to the artichoke, served in white sauce), fennel, peppers, courgettes and aubergines. The art of Provençal cuisine resides in the wide variety of its cooking methods: gratin dishes baked in the oven *(tians)*, soups, salads, stews, fritters, stuffed vegetables, and the like. The most popular fruit is the small green fig or Marseille fig: a juicy, sweet fruit. Peaches, apricots, strawberries, cherries, and grapes are all top quality, not to mention the deliciously fragrant melons from Cavaillon and also watermelons.

Olives

Local olives are both the small, meaty green and black varieties, which are left whole, pitted or stuffed. There is the green olive, picked early then marinated, which comes from Nîmes, and the black olive of Nyons preserved in brine. Nyons and Carpentras are the main olive producing centres.

Cheeses

Provençal artisinal cheeses abound in the weekly markets throughout the region, as well as in speciality shops *(fromagerie)* and covered markets, such as Les Halles in Avignon. Provence is renowned for its sheep- *(brebis)* and goats' milk cheeses, which often come in the form of small, palm-sized packages: firm, semi-soft and soft. These cheeses impart the flavours of the hillside aromatic plants upon which the sheep and goats grazed, enriching their milk. A must-taste salad is *salade de Chèvre Chaud*: the well-dressed greens are topped with toasted slices of baguette covered in melting goat's cheese and herbs.

Specialities

Among the numerous Provençal specialities are the *pieds-et-paquets* (sheep tripe and feet) from Marseille; Arles' sausages *(saucissons)*, often made from bull meat; *gardianne de taureau*, bull stew from the Camargue; Avignon's preserved melons; Aix's *calissons* (almond paste sweets with sugar icing); and *berlingots,* hard candies from Carpentras. In Nîmes try *brandade de morue* (cod fish mash); in Apt, crystallised fruits; Sault's nougat; Nyons' black olives; and Modane's special bread, which is split and stuffed with crystallised fruit.

PROVENÇAL WINES

It was the Greeks who first cultivated vines in Provence on the hills around Massalia (present-day Marseille) and the lower Rhône Valley.

During the Middle Ages, it was the full-bodied red wines of Provence that enjoyed the greatest renown. Only when King René encouraged the production of rosé in the 15C did the red wines' domination of the area loosen. Following the spread of phylloxera, it was not until after 1918 that the vineyards of Provence regained prominence. Over the past 20 years, winemakers have made huge leaps in quality, largely due to strict selection processes and to a complex blending of grapes. Provençal wines are characterised by the blending of several grape varieties in the same wine. This technique was devised in order to anticipate climatic changes (such as drought, which can be aggravated by the *mistral* winds) since these, under certain circumstances, can have an unpredictable effect on the ripening of the grape. In the course of time, Mediterranean French stock has been mixed with Spanish and Italian transplants, with the following drawback: the wines occasionally lack consistency and there are doubts about their ability to age.

The fruity rosé wines of Provence, with their sparkling colour, have become immensely popular (*for more information on the wines of Provence, see the Michelin Green Guide The Wine Regions of France*). Having fully benefited from the introduction of the new vinification process, the wines are now developing greater balance, possess a delightful bouquet and are fresh on the palate, especially when enjoyed young. Compared to rosé wines from other parts of the world, they are dry and vibrant.

The Herbs of Provence

The famous *herbes de Provence* form, along with garlic and olive oil, the basis of the region's cuisine. Coupled with the magic touch of the chef, these fresh ingredients will add their own personality to the frugal, yet fully flavoured and characteristic cooking of Provence.

Among these note: **savory**, often used to flavour goats' or sheep's cheeses; a mix of **thyme** and **bay**, which, combined with tomatoes, aubergines, courgettes, red and green peppers, and onions, is used to make the popular ratatouille (vegetable stew), as well as being an ideal addition to grilled and roast meats; **basil**, which, when crushed with garlic, olive oil, and occasionally bacon and parmesan cheese, is an important ingredient in the preparation of the famous *pistou*; **sage**, its clear, velvety leaves boiled with garlic to make the traditional *aigo-boulido* broth to which nothing more than olive oil and slices of bread are added; **rosemary**, a perfect seasoning for vegetable gratins and baked fish, also used in herbal teas to ease digestion; **wild thyme**, particularly suited to wild rabbit dishes, but which also brings out the best in vegetable soups and tomato-based recipes; **juniper**, an irreplaceable seasoning for pâtés and game; **marjoram**, ideal for stews; **tarragon**, used to spice up white sauces; **fennel**, with its aniseed taste, a superb accompaniment to fish dishes.

The mainly dry whites, with a similarly delicate bouquet, are a perfect accompaniment for fish and seafood dishes.

The contrasting Provençal vineyards have led to a wide variety of rapidly improving reds, ranging from generous and full bodied to supple, delicate wines.

In addition to unique wines, Provence also has its own wine-producing vocabulary: an *avis* is a wine shoot; a *tine* is a vat; and a *crotte* is a cellar.

Southern Côtes du Rhône Wines

They feature many prestigious appellations such as Lirac, Tavel, Châteauneuf-du-Pape, Gigondas, Vacqueyras, Rasteau, Muscat de Beaumes-de-Venise, Côtes du Ventoux and Côtes du Luberon, as well as the regional Côtes du Rhône-Villages.

The right bank of the Rhône offers some fine wines such as **Tavel**, one of the most popular French wines sold abroad. This is a smooth, crystalline rosé, described as "sunlight trapped in a bottle" by the poet Ronsard. North of Tavel, the **Coteaux de Lirac** yield delicate, full-bodied reds and rosés. Listel is a rosé wine *(vin gris du sable)* from the Aigues-Mortes region.

To the west, the balanced **Costières de Nîmes** reds are elegant and powerful although they are not technically part of the Côtes du Rhône appellation.

On the left bank, the warm, structured **Châteauneuf-du-Pape** appellation is one of the most famous names in the Côtes du Rhône area. The reds, characterised by a dark robe (colour) as well as spicy, woody and peppery aromas, are definitely wines for laying down. The whites have a bouquet reminiscent of flowers.

Vacqueyras produces well-constructed reds and elegant whites. The Séguret vineyard yields heady, scented wines; those of **Cairanne**, tannic wines that will improve with age.

Gigondas is a red wine that needs to age in oak casks for a few years; in this respect it can be likened to Châteauneuf-du-Pape.

The **Côtes du Lubéron** reds are light and should be drunk young whereas the whites tend to be fresh and fine. Red wines from the **Côtes du Ventoux** are both structured and tannic, made with grapes that have ripened on the exposed slopes of Mont Ventoux; the lighter varieties should be drunk very young, barely a few months after the harvest *(vins de primeur)*.

Dessert wines are represented by **Rasteau**, with its red or amber robe, and by **Muscat de Beaumes-de-Venise**, renowned for its golden robe and strong bouquet with notes of flower and fruit. They are made by adding alcohol to the the grape juice during the fermentation process, which ensures that the wine is rich in sugar. The Rasteau and Beaumes-de-Venise vineyards are also used to produce red and rosé Côtes du Rhône.

Provence Appellations

In the hills of southern Provence, the wines of **Cassis** have a great reputation, particularly the flower-scented dry whites, though the velvety reds are equally exceptional.

The outskirts of Aix-en-Provence are home to the small **Palette** appellation, a smooth tannic red, often referred to as the "Claret of Provence". Only two landlords share this vineyard, which features the famous Château Simone.

The **Coteaux d'Aix-en-Provence** produce warm reds and dry, lively whites.

The **Baux-de-Provence** appellation is used for red, white and rosé wines that may be drunk young.

The **Côtes de Provence** appellation, on the boundary of this guide around the Massif de la Sainte-Baume, are best represented by its rosés, offering various flavours and textures.

History

Events in *italics* indicate milestones in history.

TIME LINE

PREHISTORY TO THE ROMAN CONQUEST

BC

c. 90 000–40 000 — Neanderthals occupy coastal Provence.

c. 30 000 — Modern early humans (Cro-Magnon) settle in the region, leaving traces, such as the cave paintings in Grotte Cosquer (see CASSIS).

c. 6000 — Neolithic-impressed pottery: the first potters begin turning to agriculture and settle on the sites of Châteauneuf-les-Martigues and Courthézon.

c. 3500 — Chassey culture: the appearance of stock-raising farmers living in villages.

1800–800 — Bronze Age. Ligurian occupation.

8C–4C — Progressive installation of the Celts.

c. 600 — Founding of Massalia (Marseille) by the Phocaeans (see MARSEILLE).

4C — Massalia is at its apex; travels of the Massaliote, Pythéas, into the northern seas.

218 — Hannibal passes through Provence and crosses the Alps.

125–122 — Conquest of southern Gaul by the Romans. Destruction of Entremont and founding of Aix.

102 — Marius defeats the Teutons at Aquae Sextiae (Aix).

58–51 — Conquest of *Gallic Comata* ("long-haired Gaul") by Julius Caesar.

55 — *Caesar lands in Britain.*

27 — Augustus establishes the Narbonensis.

AD

2C — Nîmes at its apex.

284 — Narbonensis is divided into two provinces: Narbonensis on the west bank of the River Rhône, and Viennoise on the east bank.

4C — Arles at its apex; establishment of the dioceses.

416 — Jean Cassien, from the Far East, founds the Abbaye de St-Victor in Marseille.

THE COUNTY OF PROVENCE

471 — Arles taken over by the Visigoths.

476 — *Fall of the Roman Empire.*

536 — Provence ceded to the Franks.

8C–10C — Saracens, Vikings, and Magyars terrorise the land.

843 — By the Treaty of Verdun Provence, Burgundy and Lorraine are restored to Lothair (one of Charlemagne's grandsons).

855 — Provence is made a kingdom by Lothair for his third son, Charles of Provence.

879 — Boso, Charles the Bald's brother-in-law, is King of Burgundy and Provence.

1032 — Provence is annexed by the Holy Roman Empire; the Counts of Provence, however, retain their independence; the towns expand and assert their autonomy.

1066 — *William the Conqueror lands in England.*

1125 — Provence divided up between the Counts of Barcelona and Toulouse.

c. 1135 — First mention of a consulate in Arles.

1215 — *Magna Carta is issued in England.*

1229 — By the Treaty of Paris, Lower-Languedoc returns to France; founding of the royal seneschalship in Beaucaire.

1246 — Charles of Anjou, brother of St Louis (Louis IX), marries Beatrice of Provence, the Count of Barcelona's daughter, and becomes Count of Provence.

1248 — St Louis embarks from Aigues-Mortes on the Seventh Crusade.

1274 — Cession of the Comtat Venaissin to the papacy.

1316–1403 — The popes and schismatic popes at Avignon. Papal Schism (1378–1417).

1337–1453 — *Hundred Years' War.*

1348 — Clement VI buys Avignon from Queen Joan I. Great Plague epidemic.

1409 — University of Aix founded.

1434–80 — Reign of Good King René, Louis XI's uncle (*see AIX-EN-PROVENCE).*

1450 — Jacques Cœur sets up his trading posts in Marseille.

1481 — Charles of Maine, nephew of René of Anjou, bequeaths Provence to Louis XI.

THE ESTATES OF PROVENCE

1486 — The Estates of Provence meet at Aix to ratify the union of Provence to the crown.

1492 — *Christopher Columbus lands in the Americas.*

1501 — Inauguration of the Parliament of Aix as Supreme Court of Justice with limited political authority.

1509–47 — *Henry VIII's reign.*

1524–36 — Provence is invaded by the Imperialists (soldiers of the Holy Roman Empire).

1539 — Edict of Villers-Cotterêts decrees French as the language for all administrative laws in Provence.

1545 — Suppression of Vaudois heretics from Luberon.

1555 — Nostradamus publishes his astrological predictions, *Centuries.*

1558 — The engineer Adam de Craponne builds a canal.

1558–1603 — *Elizabeth I's reign.*

1567 — Michelade tragedy occurs in Nîmes.

1588 — *Defeat of the Spanish Armada.*

1622 — Louis XIII visits Arles, Aix and Marseille.

1660 — Solemn entry of Louis XIV into Marseille.

1685 — Revocation of the Edict of Nantes. Huguenots flee France.

1713 — Under the Treaty of Utrecht the Principality of Orange is transferred from the House of Orange-Nassau to France.

1714–27 — *George I's reign.*

1720 — The Great Plague, which originated in Marseille, decimates Provence.

1763 — Peace of Paris ends French and Indian War (1754–63), marking the end of France's colonial empire in North America.

1771 — Suppression of Aix's Parliament.

FROM THE REVOLUTION TO THE PRESENT

1789 — *The French Revolution;* Storming of the Bastille.

1790 — The constitutional Assembly divides southeast France into three *départements*: Basses-Alpes (capital: Digne), Bouches-du-Rhône (capital: Aix-en-Provence), Var (capital: Toulon).

1791 — Avignon and Comtat Venaissin are annexed to France.

1792 — 500 Marseille volunteers parade in Paris to the song of the Rhine Army, called "La Marseillaise".

1805 — *Battle of Trafalgar.*

1815 — *Battle of Waterloo;* Napoleon's fall.

1837–1901 — *Queen Victoria's reign.*

1854 — Founding of the Provençal literary school: Félibrige.

1859 — Frédéric Mistral publishes the Provençal poem *Mirèio.*

1861–65 — *American Civil War.*

1886 — *Statue of Liberty erected.*

1899–1902 — *Second Boer War.*

1904 — Frédéric Mistral wins the Nobel Prize in Literature.

1933 — Founding of the Compagnie Nationale du Rhône for the harnessing of the river.

1942 — German forces invade Provence.

1944 — 15 August: Allied troops land on the Côte d'Azur.
22–28 August: General de Montsabert and his troops aided by the Resistance movement liberate Marseille from German occupation.

1962 — First hydroelectric power stations of the Durance begin operating.

1965 — Construction of Bassins de Fos complex begins.

1970 — A 6–A 7 motorways link Paris and Marseille.
Creation of the Parc Naturel Régional de Camargue.

1977 — Marseille's Métro system begins service.
Creation of the Parc Naturel Régional du Luberon.

1981 — The TGV, France's high-speed train, links Paris to Marseille.

1991 — Cave paintings and engravings dating from the Upper Paleolithic Era are discovered in the Calanque de Sormiou, south of Marseille; now known as the Grotte Cosquer.

1993 — Olympique de Marseille become the first French football team to win the European Cup.

1994 — A painted cave, known as the Grotte Chauvet, is discovered in the Ardèche gorges.

1999 — Marseille celebrates its 2 600th birthday.

2000 — Avignon is one of nine cities designated a European Capital of Culture.

2001 — The new TGV Méditerranée line south of Valence opens, making Paris a mere 3hr away from Marseille.

2004 — The Millau Viaduct, the world's highest car bridge, opens west of Avignon, facilitating higher speed travel to southern France.

2006 — Aix-en-Provence marks the centenary of the death of artist, and former resident, Paul Cézanne.

2007 — Nicolas Sarkozy is elected President of France and Marseille is one of ten French cities to host Rugby World Cup matches.

2009 — France assumes full membership of NATO.

2013 — Marseilles-Provence designated to become a European Capital of Culture for 2013.

HALLMARKS OF DIVERSITY

Provence is the product of one of the most highly used crossroads of the Mediterranean world, where ancient, medieval, and modern meet. Provence received migrations and invasions from diverse peoples including the Bronze-Age Ligurians, the Iron-Age Celts, the early Greeks, Romans, Visigoths and Arabs. No lesser diversity greets the visitor today, as Provence has become a desirable tourist destination.

PRE-ROMAN SOUTHERN GAUL

Origins: A Melting Pot

During the Bronze Age (1800–800 BC) Ligurians, the probable descendants of the native Neolithic population in northern Italy and southeastern France, inhabited the region. Celts began to infiltrate the area in the 7C, though their mass influx did not occur until about the 5C–4C. In the 7C, the first Greeks were also settling in the area. Phocaeans (Greeks from Phocaea in Asia Minor (Ionia, near Izmir in modern Turkey), founded Massalia (Marseille) around 600 BC in agreement with a Celtic tribe. This period represents a mixing of populations that established ancient Provence's roots in the Celtic-Ligurian civilisation. These diverse populations settled progressively in *oppida*, fortified hill sites. Nages, near Nîmes, St-Blaise overlooking the Golfe de Fos, and Entremont, near Aix, were important settlements and fortified townships.

Greek Presence

Greek settlement and influence is an essential part of the history of Provence's civilisation. The Rhodian Greeks most likely gave their name to the great Provençal river (Rhodanos). However, the Phocaeans were the first to establish a permanent colony: **Massalia**. Massalia rapidly became a powerful commercial city, which founded in turn a number of trading posts: Glanum, Avignon, Cavaillon, and had commercial exchanges with the people of the north (wine and pottery for pewter from Armorica and agricultural products and livestock from Brittany). The colonists brought with them a number of improvements, such as a wine and olive oil industry, the introduction of coinage, and more intricate architecture. But by the 2C, relations between the natives and the Phocaeans from Massalia were deteriorating. The Salian Confederation, which had grouped together the Provençal population, rose against Massaliote imperialism.

Rome and Massalia

During the Second Punic War (218–201 BC), Massalia supported Rome whereas the Salian Franks helped Hannibal cross the region in 218. In 154 Massalia, worried about the threat of attack by the Gauls, obtained the protection of Rome. In 130 BC the powerful Arverni empire threatened southern Gaul's security, Gaul being the key trading centre between Italy and Spain. Rome came to Massalia's aid in 125 and the Roman legions easily conquered the Vocontii and Salian Franks, toppling their capital, Entremont. In 123, date of the founding of Aquae Sextiae (Aix-en-Provence), the Arverni and Allobroges suffered a bloody defeat. The consul Domitius Ahenobarbus relaxed the boundaries of a new province, **Gallia Transalpine**, which became **Narbonensis** (from the name of the first Roman colony of Narbonna) in 118. Massalia remained independent and was recognised as a territory. The Roman domination, which at one time was threatened by the Cimbrian and Teuton invasions in 105 (disaster at Orange) and halted by Marius near Aix in 102, spread irreversibly over the region, not without abuse and pillaging.

ROMAN COLONISATION

Pax Romana

Gaul Transalpine rapidly became integrated in the Roman world and actively supported the Proconsul Caesar during the Gallic Wars (58–51 BC). Marseille, as a result of having supported Pompey against Caesar, was besieged in 49 BC, fell, and lost its independence. The important Roman towns were Narbonne, Nîmes, Arles,

Roman mosaics, Musée de l'Arles et de la Provence antiques, Arles

S. Sauvignier/MICHELIN

and Fréjus. Romanisation accelerated under Augustus, and the Narbonensis was reorganised in 27 BC. Antoninus Pius' (🔾 see NÎMES) reign (2C) marked the apogee of Gallo-Roman civilisation. Agriculture remained Provence's principal activity and trade enriched the towns. Arles profited the most from Marseille's disgrace. Urban affluence was reflected in a way of life entirely focused on comfort, luxury and leisure. Excavations have given us a glimpse of that life.

Arles, the Favoured City

After the troubled times of the 3C, the 4C and 5C brought considerable religious and political transformation. Christianity triumphed over the other religions after the conversion of Constantine. Arles became his favourite town in the west. Marseille remained a commercial centre. Aix became an administrative capital. Nîmes declined, and Glanum was abandoned.

Rural areas suffered from the general impoverishment of the Gallo-Roman world. Large landowners placed heavy demands, and insecurity led to the resettlement of fortified hill sites, such as St-Blaise.

FALL OF THE ROMAN EMPIRE TO PAPAL AVIGNON

Invasion after Invasion

Until AD 471, the date Arles was taken by the Visigoths, Provence had been relatively free from invasions. The Burgundian and Visigoth domination (476 to 508) was followed by the Ostrogoth restoration, a period of some 30 years whereupon the Ostrogoths considered themselves the mandatories of the Far Eastern emperor and revived Roman institutions: Arles thus recovered its praetorian prefects. Religious life continued to progress; several synods were held in Provence towns (Vaison-la-Romaine).

The Bishop of Arles, St Caesarius, had a vast following in Gaul. In 536, Provence was ceded to the Franks and followed the same uncertain destiny as other provinces, tossed from hand to hand

according to the Merovingian dynastic divisions. Decline was rapid.

The first half of the 8C was chaotic and rife with tragedy: Arabs and Franks transformed the region into a battleground. In 855 Provence was made a kingdom, its limits corresponding more or less with the Rhône basin. It soon fell into the hands of the kingdom of Burgundy, whose possessions spread from the Jura to the Mediterranean and were under the protection of the Holy Roman Emperors, who inherited it in 1032. This was a major date in the region's history as it made Provence a part of the Holy Roman Empire, with the area west of the Rhône under the aegis of the counts of Toulouse.

Occitanian Provence

The 10C and 11C marked a major shift in the evolution of Provence's civilisation, which until then was deeply defined by its Greco-Roman past. A new society developed out of the feudal anarchy. Rural life, henceforth, was concentrated in the hillside villages – Luberon, Ste-Baume and the Vaucluse mountains – which depended upon the seigneuries. Many towns sought to recover a degree of autonomy. The Oc language spread. Close links were established between Provence and Languedoc.

The failure of Occitania facilitated Capetian intervention. The Albigensian heresy resulted in the delayed union of the Catalan and Toulousain peoples, who until then had been fighting over Provence against the invaders from the north. The defeat at Muret in 1213 dashed all hope of a united Occitania.

Louis VIII's expedition (siege of Avignon in 1226) and the Treaty of Paris in 1229 brought about the founding of the royal seneschalship in Beaucaire: the west bank of the Rhône was part of France. In the east, the Catalan Count, Raimond Bérenger V, maintained his authority and endowed Provence with administrative organisations. The towns became powerful locally: as early as the 12C they elected their own consuls, whose power increased to the detriment of the traditional lords (bishops, counts and viscounts). In the 13C they sought their independence.

House of Anjou's Provence

The marriage of **Charles of Anjou**, St Louis' brother, to Beatrice of Provence, Raimond Bérenger V's heir, in 1246 linked Provence to the House of Anjou. Charles had large political ambitions: he interfered in Italy and conquered the kingdom of Naples in 1266 before turning towards the Far East.

In Provence, Charles of Anjou's government was very much appreciated. It re-established security. Honest administration managed public affairs, and prosperity returned. Concerning the territories, Comtat Venaissin was ceded to the papacy in 1274 by the King of France and evolved separately.

Charles I's successors, Charles II and Robert I, continued their father's and grandfather's political ideas and political order, and peace reigned during the first half of the 14C. Aix was raised to administrative capital with a seneschal and a court where the officers who presided were in charge of the finances of the county.

The key city was henceforth Avignon, where the Bishop Jacques Duèze, elected pope in 1316 under the name John XXII, established himself. French-born Pope Clement V was already resident in Comtat Venaissin and benefited from the protection of the King of France. Thus John XXII's decision was confirmed by his successor Benedict XII, who began the construction of a new papal palace. The popes' stay in Avignon, which lasted almost a century, brought expansion and extraordinary brilliance to the city.

FROM ANNEXATION TO THE FRENCH CROWN

The End of Provence's Independence

After the second half of the 14C, Provence entered a difficult period. Famine and plague (which struck in 1348), pillaging road bandits, and political uncertainty brought about by the slackness of Queen Joan (granddaughter to King Robert; she was assassinated in 1382),

badly damaged Provence's stability. The population was decimated, the country in ruins. After a violent dispute over succession, Louis II of Anjou (nephew to the King of France, Charles V) aided by his mother, Marie of Blois, and the pope re-established the situation (1387).

Pacification was temporarily slowed by the activities of a turbulent lord, Viscount Raymond de Turenne, who terrorised the country (1389–99), pillaging and kidnapping. His lairs were the fortresses of Les Baux and Roquemartine. Peace was not achieved until the early 15C.

Louis II of Anjou's (d. 1417) youngest son, **King René**, inherited the county at the death of his brother in 1434. He was primarily concerned with the reconquest of the kingdom of Naples but every attempt of his failed, whereupon he turned all his attention to Provence (1447) and came to love it. His reign left happy memories; it coincided with a political and economic restoration that was felt through all of France. King René was a poet and had a cultivated mind fed by his love of the arts. He attracted a number of artists to Aix, who came to take up where the popes' Avignon had left off.

His nephew Charles of Maine briefly succeeded him. In 1481 Provence ceded to Louis XI of France and the region's history was henceforth interlaced with that of the kingdom of France.

Vaudois and Huguenots

The Reformation spread in the south of France as early as 1530, thanks largely to the impetus from merchants and pedlars. Through the Rhône and Durance valleys and Vivarais, Protestantism was stimulated by the brilliance of the Vaudois church located in the Luberon village communities.

The Vaudois heresy went back to the 12C: a certain Peter Waldo or **Valdès**, a rich merchant from Lyon, had founded a sect in 1170 preaching poverty, Evangelism, refusal of the sacraments, and ecclesiastical hierarchy. Excommunicated in 1184, the Vaudois had since been pursued as heretics. In 1530 they were targeted by the Inquisition, and in 1540 the Aix Parliament decided to strike hard by issuing a warrant for the arrest of 19 Vaudois from Mérindol. François I temporised and prescribed a deferment. Instead of calming things down, the religious controversy came to a head. The heretics pillaged Abbaye de Sénanque in 1544. As a riposte, the *Parliament*'s president obtained royal authorisation to enforce the Mérindol warrant and organised a punitive expedition. From 15 to 20 April 1545 blood ran through the Luberon village streets: 3 000 people were massacred, 600 were sent to the galleys, and many villages were razed.

Nevertheless, Protestantism continued to spread, especially west of the Rhône in Vivarais, Cévennes, Nîmes and Uzès. East of the Rhône it was Orange (a Nassau Family principality since 1559) that became a Reformation stronghold. In 1560, numerous churches and abbeys (St-Gilles, Valbonne charterhouse) were pillaged by the Huguenots; violence gave rise to more violence and with it the capture of Orange (1563) by the Catholic partisans. This in turn was answered by the fall of Mornas.

During these tumultuous times Provence and Languedoc-Cévennes split, taking different paths. Provence opted for Catholicism, and the Catholic League recruited fervent partisans in such cities as Aix and Marseille (both of which would have liked to become an independent republic). On the Rhône's opposite shore the situation was different. The people, influenced by the merchants and textile craftsmen who kept the Reformation alive, generally tended to believe in the Protestant movement and Nîmes was its capital. The violent Wars of Religion in southern France brought about a conflict between two peoples of opposing mentalities who were to clash again during the Camisard Insurrection (1702–04).

17C TO THE PRESENT DAY

In the 18C, Provence experienced a golden age for agriculture and commerce. The 19C was a less successful period: industrialisation progressed but rural life suffered from the failure of the silkworm farms and phylloxera, which spread through the vineyards.

In the face of these changes, **Frédéric Mistral** sought to defend the Provençal identity and its traditions. When he died in 1914, Provence was nevertheless wholeheartedly engaged in modernisation.

In the 21C, Provence is now a successful society, relying on heavy industry, agriculture and tourism. The region is renowned for its cultural events, its climate and its produce (wine, honey, rice) as well as for its multiculturalism.

Art and Culture

ARCHITECTURE AND THE VISUAL ARTS
TRADITIONAL RURAL STYLE

The Provençal country house, whether a *mas*, a *bastide* or an *oustau*, features the following characteristics:

- a shallow sloping roof of Roman style; curved terracotta tiles, with a decorative frieze under the eaves, composed of a double or triple row of tiles embedded in the wall and known as a **génoise**;

- stone walls, more or less smoothly rendered (pink or lavender), with no windows on the north side and those on the other three sides just large enough to let in light but keep out the summer heat;

- a north–south orientation, with sometimes a slight turn to the east to avoid the direct blast of the *mistral*; cypresses serve as a windbreak to the north, plane and lotus trees provide shade to the south;

- floors covered with red or brown terracotta tiles *(mallons)*;

Architecture A–Z

Acroterion: ornaments placed at the apex and ends of a pediment of a temple.

Ambulatory: aisle around the east end of a church.

Apse: rounded termination of the central nave opening on to the east end.

Archivolt: arch moulding over an arcade or upper section of a doorway.

Blind arcading: sequences of arches applied to a blank wall for decoration.

Brattice: temporary wooden gallery or parapet for use during a siege.

Caryatid: carved female figure used for support.

Chevet: French term for the east end of a church.

Cippus: small pillar used to mark a burial place.

Claustra: stone railings with vertical bars.

Coffered ceiling: vault or ceiling decorated with sunken panels.

Crocket: carved ornament in the form of a curled leaf or cusp used in Gothic architecture.

Diaphragm arch: transversal arch used to relieve side walls.

Entablature: projecting crown of a façade.

Exedra: niche with a bench around the wall.

Flamboyant: 15C phase of French Gothic architecture; named after the tapering (flame-like) lines of the window tracery.

Fluting: vertical, shallow grooving decorating a column or pilaster.

Foliated scrolls: sculptural or painted ornamentation depicting foliage.

Fresco: mural paintings executed on wet plaster.

Gable: triangular part of an end wall carrying a sloping roof; or steeply pitched ornamental pediments in Gothic architecture.

Génoise: decorative frieze under the eaves, composed of a double or triple row of tiles embedded in the wall.

Historiated: decorated with figures of people or animals.

Hypocaust: an underground furnace for heating.

Jambs: supporting pillars flanking a doorway.

Keystone: middle and topmost stone in an arch or vault.

Lintel: horizontal beam or stone slab surmounting a door or window frame.

Mascaron: medallion carved in the shape of a human head.

Modillion: small console supporting a cornice.

Mullion: vertical post dividing a window.

Narthex: interior vestibule of a church.

Peristyle: columns surrounding or fronting a building.

Pietà: Italian term for the Virgin Mary with the dead Christ on her knees.

Pinnacle: slender upright structure crowning a buttress, gable or tower.

Piscina: washbasin for sacred vessels.

Predella: base of an altarpiece, divided into small panels.

Pulpitum: front section of the stage in an antique theatre.

Retable: ornamental structure set up above and behind an altar.

Rood screen: open screen separating areas reserved for clergy (chancel) and laity (nave).

Rosette: circular window with ornamental tracery radiating from the centre to form a rose-like pattern.

Stucco: decoration of powdered marble, plaster and strong glue.

Transom light: upper section of a door or window.

Triptych: three decorated panels hinged together.

Voussoir: wedge-shaped stone forming part of an arch or vault.

♦ vaulting in dried stone or masonry that completely replaced floorboards.

The **Provençal mas** is a large, low farmhouse rectangular in plan with a sprawling low roof covering the living quarters and annexes. The walls are made of stone taken from the fields or from the Plaine de la Crau, ashlar-stone surrounding the openings. Traditionally, it is divided into two parts by a corridor, for in times past, one side was for the master and the other for the farmer *(bayle)*. This was repeated on the ground floor and on the upper storey.

The kitchen is level with the courtyard, and functions as the centre of the house in spite of its small size. Upstairs are bedrooms with tiled floors, and the attic. The outbuildings and other rooms are used for various purposes according to the importance of the *mas* and the agricultural vocation of the region. The ground floor sometimes has a vaulted cellar facing north. This could be used for stables, shed, storeroom, sheep's pen (at times separated from the *mas*), bread oven and cistern. Above this, the attic space once served as the cocoonery for silkworms, and also as a barn (above the sheep's pen) and dovecote.

The **mas of the Bas Vivarais** are slightly different. They have an attractive pattern of stonework and an additional storey. In a traditional farm, the ground floor, covered by solid vaulting, contains the stables for the smaller animals and the storeroom for wine-making tools. In the cold-room, harvested products as well as hams and sausages are kept. A stone staircase opens on to a **couradou**, a terrace that is generally covered, and leads to the stone or terracotta-tiled kitchen. The cocoonery was often off the *couradou* and until c. 1850 was an essential part of the Vivarais *mas* architectural conception. The sleeping quarters are off the kitchen, and a small wooden staircase leads to the attic. In the wealthier *mas* this may be a spiral staircase in a turret with the bedrooms on the upper floor.

Annexes were often added to the living quarters, such as bread oven, barn, and in the chestnut region, a chestnut dryer, **clède** (or *clédo*).

Nowadays, it is hard to find a *mas* occupied by a traditional farming family. Many of these properties have been bought up for use as holiday homes and have been completely transformed to accommodate modern desires: a jacuzzi where sheep once rested; a TV room where the silkworms once spun; or a microwave where the bread oven stood.

An **oustau** is a typical Provençal farmhouse smaller in size than a *mas* but with the same layout. In the upper Comtat it is called a *grange*. In the past these barn-like buildings were progressively enlarged to house the family, which formed a clan, and the workers. It was small but people compensated for the lack of surface area by adding upper storeys.

A **bastide** is built of fine ashlar-stone and displays regular façades with symmetrical openings. Most often its layout is square in plan with a hipped roof.

Unlike the *mas*, the *bastide* was not necessarily a farmhouse. Thus, its conception was more luxurious, using decorative elements such as wrought iron balconies, exterior staircase and sculpture.

The **gardian's cabin**, the typical Camargue dwelling of bygone days, is a small building (10m x 5m/33ft x 16.5ft) with a rounded apse at one end. The cob walls are low. Only the front façade, with its entrance door, is built in rubble to hold a long ridge beam supported by another piece of wood sloped at a 45° angle, and crossed by a piece of wood to form a cross. Thatched with marsh reeds, *sagnos*, these cabins usually had just two rooms divided by a wall of reeds: the dining room and bedroom.

CELTIC-LIGURIAN

Ligurians and Celts settled in fortified hill sites known as *oppida*, such as Nages, Entremont and Roquepertuse, and created towns organised on a regular plan. Within the fortified walls stood a group of uniform dwellings, a type of hut in unfired stone and brick.

Celtic-Ligurian sculpture honoured, above anything else, the cult of the dead warrior, the town's hero, who they represented in the form of warriors' statues seated cross-legged with people either free-standing or in relief. An important ritual consisted of setting the severed heads of the conquered peoples, or at least the carved version, in the stone lintels. The sculpture exhibited at Roquepertuse perfectly demonstrates this Celtic form of expression.

Analysis of pottery shards confirms that Roquepertuse was densely occupied from the final Neolithic Era (3 000 BC) to around 200 BC, the date of the last destruction of the site. The most prosperous period was between the end of 4 BC to the end of 3 BC, characterised by the widespread use of delicate Mediterranean dishes (cups and pitchers of either painted or unpainted clay, and black glaze from 3C). From being confined to a single sanctuary, as was long believed, Roquepertuse, which is still the subject of detailed research, is in fact a vast complex stretching from the *oppidum* in the north to the sloping village in the south.

Hellenistic influence was also crucial for the region; it directly influenced the native peoples, accelerating the development of their economy and society. Greek construction techniques are evident in the building of St-Blaise and Glanum. Numerous pottery fragments and Greek black figure vases were excavated at Arles, and the stelae found in rue Négrel in Marseille are the oldest examples (second half of the 6C BC) of Greek sculpture in France.

ROMAN CULTURE

Throughout Provence, towns were built on the Roman urban plan. They all boasted remarkable public and private buildings, some of which are still well preserved, giving them a charm all their own. Without dropping Hellenistic influence entirely, the great Provençal towns took Rome as their model.

Towns

Most of the towns were built on either native Hellenistic or Gallic sites. And yet, very often, the desire to settle in a particular spot was that of a colony of veteran legionnaires, as was the case in Nîmes and Orange, who were soon after joined by the civilian population. The urban foundation was laid according to precise rules: having determined the future town centre, two major streets were traced – the *cardo maximus* (north–south orientation) and the *decumanus maximus* (east–west orientation). This created a regular grid pattern in which the grids were squared with sides some hundred square yards wide. This geometric exactitude could appear only on sites where the local topography was suitable, such as in Orange or Arles as opposed to Nîmes and Vaison-la-Romaine.

Where previous edifices had existed, they were razed, as at Glanum, to make room for the new buildings. These towns were not surrounded with walls except at Nîmes, Arles, and Orange, which were granted the honour of surrounding themselves with ramparts (permission obtained from Rome). Defensive walls did not appear until the end of the 3C. Such walls were built with towers and gates corresponding to the main streets.

Streets

The main streets were lined with pavements, at times 50cm/19.7in high and bordered by porticoes that protected the people from sun and rain. The roadway, paved with large flagstones laid diagonally, was crossed at intervals by stepping stones laid at the same level as the pavements but between which horses and chariot wheels could pass and pedestrians could cross over above the dust and mud. Gutters also ran alongside the road and were slightly rounded.

Forum

The forum, a large paved open space surrounded by an arcade, was the centre of public and commercial life in a Roman town. Government offices were located round the forum. These included a temple devoted to the imperial cult, a civil basilica (a type of town hall where judicial and commercial affairs were conducted), the *curia* or headquarters of local government, and at times, a prison.

At Arles the forum had the particularity of being lined with a vast underground gallery, *cryptoporticus*, the origin of which remains a mystery.

Architectural terms

ORANGE – Roman Theatre (early 1C BC)

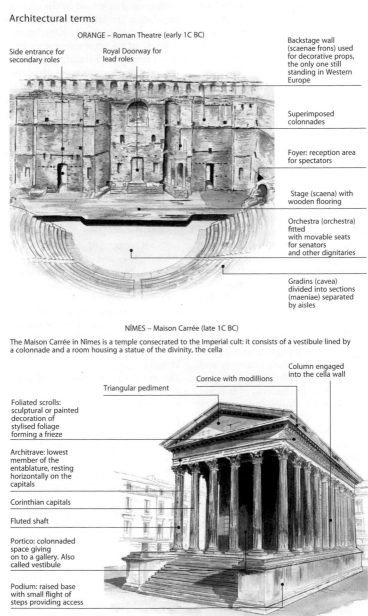

Side entrance for secondary roles

Royal Doorway for lead roles

Backstage wall (scaenae frons) used for decorative props, the only one still standing in Western Europe

Superimposed colonnades

Foyer: reception area for spectators

Stage (scaena) with wooden flooring

Orchestra (orchestra) fitted with movable seats for senators and other dignitaries

Gradins (cavea) divided into sections (maeniae) separated by aisles

NÎMES – Maison Carrée (late 1C BC)

The Maison Carrée in Nîmes is a temple consecrated to the Imperial cult: it consists of a vestibule lined by a colonnade and a room housing a statue of the divinity, the cella

Column engaged into the cella wall

Cornice with modillions

Triangular pediment

Foliated scrolls: sculptural or painted decoration of stylised foliage forming a frieze

Architrave: lowest member of the entablature, resting horizontally on the capitals

Corinthian capitals

Fluted shaft

Portico: colonnaded space giving on to a gallery. Also called vestibule

Podium: raised base with small flight of steps providing access

R. Corbel/MICHELIN

Religious architecture

VAISON-LA-ROMAINE – Plan of the Ancienne Cathédrale
Notre-Dame-de-Nazareth (11C)

This cathedral is a typical example of Provençal church architecture, consisting of a nave without a
transept ending in a semicircular apse.

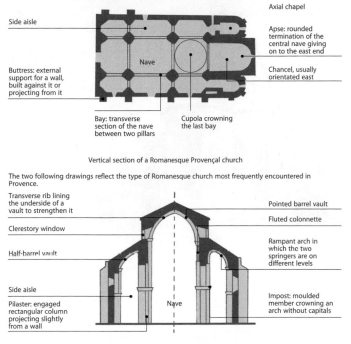

Side aisle

Axial chapel

Apse: rounded
termination of the
central nave giving
on to the east end

Nave

Chancel, usually
orientated east

Buttress: external
support for a wall,
built against it or
projecting from it

Bay: transverse
section of the nave
between two pillars

Cupola crowning
the last bay

Vertical section of a Romanesque Provençal church

The two following drawings reflect the type of Romanesque church most frequently encountered in
Provence.

Transverse rib lining
the underside of a
vault to strengthen it

Pointed barrel vault

Fluted colonnette

Clerestory window

Half-barrel vault

Rampant arch in
which the two
springers are on
different levels

Side aisle

Nave

Impost: moulded
member crowning an
arch without capitals

Pilaster: engaged
rectangular column
projecting slightly
from a wall

Abbaye de SILVACANE – Vaulting in the Chapter-house (13C)

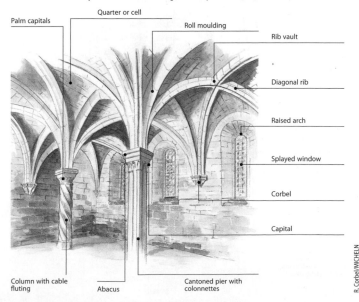

Palm capitals

Quarter or cell

Roll moulding

Rib vault

Diagonal rib

Raised arch

Splayed window

Corbel

Capital

Column with cable
fluting

Abacus

Cantoned pier with
colonnettes

R. Corbel/MICHELIN

Abbaye de MONTMAJOUR – Chapelle Ste-Croix (12C)

The quadrilobed plan of the Chapelle Ste-Croix, based on a Greek cross and representative of 12C Provençal architecture, can be seen in several other buildings of the area.

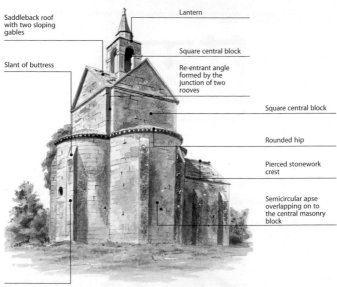

Lantern

Saddleback roof with two sloping gables

Square central block

Re-entrant angle formed by the junction of two rooves

Slant of buttress

Square central block

Rounded hip

Pierced stonework crest

Semicircular apse overlapping on to the central masonry block

Buttress

CARPENTRAS – South Door of the Ancienne Cathédrale St-Siffrein (late 15C)

The South Door, known as the Jewish Door, is Flamboyant or late Gothic: this is evidenced by the window tracery and its sinuous, tapering lines evoking tongues of flame.

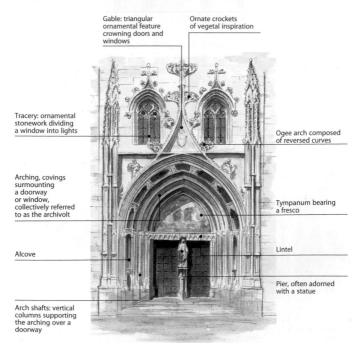

Gable: triangular ornamental feature crowning doors and windows

Ornate crockets of vegetal inspiration

Tracery: ornamental stonework dividing a window into lights

Ogee arch composed of reversed curves

Arching, covings surmounting a doorway or window, collectively referred to as the archivolt

Tympanum bearing a fresco

Alcove

Lintel

Pier, often adorned with a statue

Arch shafts: vertical columns supporting the arching over a doorway

R. Corbel/MICHELIN

Abbaye de ST-MICHEL-DE-FRIGOLET – Retable in the Chapelle
Notre-Dame-du-Bon-Remède (17C)

This 11C chapel is richly decorated with Baroque panelling dating from the 17C. At the far end stands an imposing altarpiece.

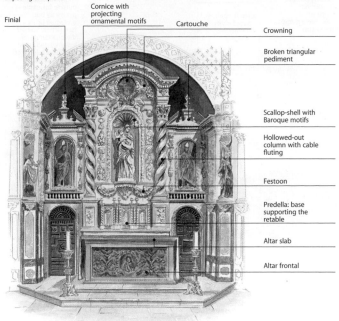

Finial

Cornice with projecting ornamental motifs

Cartouche

Crowning

Broken triangular pediment

Scallop-shell with Baroque motifs

Hollowed-out column with cable fluting

Festoon

Predella: base supporting the retable

Altar slab

Altar frontal

UZÈS – Organ in the Cathédrale St-Théodorit (18C)

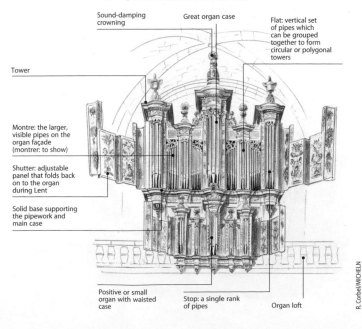

Sound-damping crowning

Great organ case

Flat: vertical set of pipes which can be grouped together to form circular or polygonal towers

Tower

Montre: the larger, visible pipes on the organ façade (montrer: to show)

Shutter: adjustable panel that folds back on to the organ during Lent

Solid base supporting the pipework and main case

Positive or small organ with waisted case

Stop: a single rank of pipes

Organ loft

R. Corbel/MICHELN

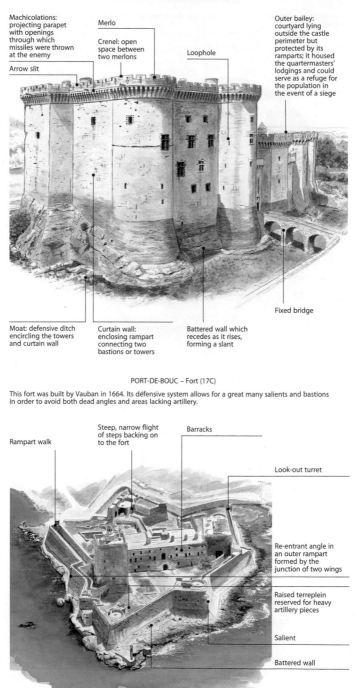

TARASCON – Fortified castle (14-15C)

Machicolations: projecting parapet with openings through which missiles were thrown at the enemy

Merlo

Crenel: open space between two merlons

Loophole

Arrow slit

Outer bailey: courtyard lying outside the castle perimeter but protected by its ramparts; it housed the quartermasters' lodgings and could serve as a refuge for the population in the event of a siege

Fixed bridge

Moat: defensive ditch encircling the towers and curtain wall

Curtain wall: enclosing rampart connecting two bastions or towers

Battered wall which recedes as it rises, forming a slant

PORT-DE-BOUC – Fort (17C)

This fort was built by Vauban in 1664. Its défensive system allows for a great many salients and bastions in order to avoid both dead angles and areas lacking artillery.

Rampart walk

Steep, narrow flight of steps backing on to the fort

Barracks

Look-out turret

Re-entrant angle in an outer rampart formed by the junction of two wings

Raised terreplein reserved for heavy artillery pieces

Salient

Battered wall

R. Corbel/MICHELIN

Civil architecture

AIX-EN-PROVENCE – Pavillon de Vendôme (17-18C)

The main façade features the "great order" advocated by Palladio as early back as the Renaissance, characterised by the display of three superimposed orders: Doric, Ionic and Corinthian.

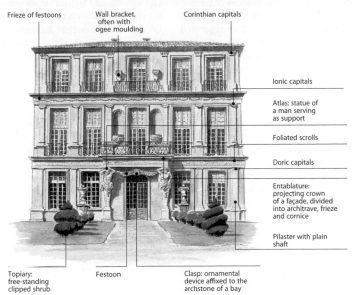

Frieze of festoons

Wall bracket, often with ogee moulding

Corinthian capitals

Ionic capitals

Atlas: statue of a man serving as support

Foliated scrolls

Doric capitals

Entablature: projecting crown of a façade, divided into architrave, frieze and cornice

Pilaster with plain shaft

Topiary: free-standing clipped shrub

Festoon

Clasp: ornamental device affixed to the archstone of a bay

MARSEILLE – Water tower of the Palais Longchamp (19C)

Seeking inspiration from Bernini's work in Rome, the architect Espérandieu built a monumental fountain whose decoration draws heavily upon the aquatic theme.

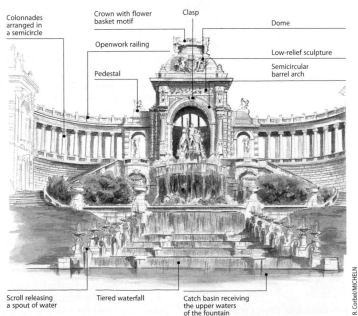

Colonnades arranged in a semicircle

Crown with flower basket motif

Clasp

Dome

Openwork railing

Low-relief sculpture

Pedestal

Semicircular barrel arch

Scroll releasing a spout of water

Tiered waterfall

Catch basin receiving the upper waters of the fountain

R. Corbel/MICHELIN

79

The Art of Building

The art of building was very advanced with the Romans. The rapidity with which their buildings went up was due not so much to the number of people working on a site as to the special training of the workers, their organised working methods, and the use of lifting devices, such as levers, hoisting winches and tackles, that moved heavy materials into place.

Building Materials

For building materials the Romans used the local limestone, which was not hard to dress; stones were easily extracted and shaped into blocks. Romans originally adopted the method of using large blocks of stone without mortar: the stones were held together by their weight, and with dowels or cramps. But builders then revolutionised wall construction by introducing the use of concrete, a manufactured material not unique to any one country. Concrete could be used in the construction of buildings throughout the empire, giving a uniformity and similarity to their edifices.

They also used concrete to fill in cracks or joints, or give to a public building a uniform surface, such as at the Maison Carrée and Amphitheatre in Nîmes, or to wedge the stones together allowing the expansion of a vault.

Orders

The Roman architectural Orders derived from the Greek Orders but with some variation. Roman Doric, still called the

Doric Order, Ionic Order, Corinthian Order

R. Corbel/MICHELIN

Tuscan Order, the simplest and most solid, was found on the monuments' lower storeys. Too severe, it was rarely used by the Romans. The Ionic Order was very elegant but not ornate enough for the Roman architects. It was the Corinthian Order that Romans used frequently because of the richness of its ornamentation. The Composite Order was a combination of the Ionic and Corinthian Orders.

Roofs

Public buildings sometimes had rectangular-shaped roofs held by colonnades inside the rooms. But more often the Romans used rounded vaulting in corridors and galleries where the walls were parallel, groined vaulting in square rooms, and the dome in circular rooms.

Public Buildings

The inhabitants of Roman towns enjoyed bloody combats as much as more peaceful theatrical representations (&see NÎMES).

Due to the influence of Christianity, gladiator fights were forbidden in 404. The games were abandoned at the same time.

Amphitheatres

The amphitheatre (the **arena** was the name of the sand floor) had two tiers of arcades on the outside surmounted by a low storey called the attic. Posts were fixed on the attic to carry a huge adjustable awning, the *velarium*, to shelter the spectators from the sun and rain. The arcades were divided by rectangular pillars decorated with engaged half-columns on the first storey. Inside, enclosing the arena, a wall protected the spectators in the front rows from the wild animals released in the ring. The *cavea* – terraces for the spectators – was divided into *maenia* – tiers of seats generally in groups of four, individually separated by a passage. The seats were strictly allocated, those nearest the arena being for the men with a superior social station. The first *maenia* were reserved for consuls, senators,

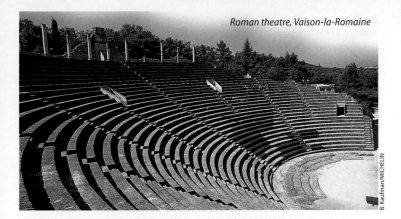

Roman theatre, Vaison-la-Romaine

B. Kaufman/MICHELIN

magistrates and members of local guilds (such as the boatmen of Arles). In another section sat priests, knights and Roman citizens, whereas freemen and slaves sat in the attic. The arcades and three circular gallery-promenades, and the hundreds of staircases and passages, allowed spectators to reach or leave their stepped seats directly. At Nîmes it took less than five minutes for the audience of 20 000 to leave via exits known as *vomitoria*.

Theatres

The Roman theatre, in the form of a half-circle lengthened by a deep stage, was divided into three sections: the *cavea* (auditorium) built in the hollow of a hillside, as in Orange, and crowned by a colonnade; the orchestra, the semicircular section in front of the stage with movable seats reserved for dignitaries; the stage flanked by side rooms, rectangular in shape, which were higher in level than the orchestra. At the back of the stage was a wall (which was as high as the *cavea*) with three doors through which the actors entered.

The stage wall was the finest part of the building. Its decoration included several tiers of columns, niches containing statues (the central niche contained the emperor's statue), marble facing and mosaics. Behind these were the actors' dressing rooms and store rooms. Beyond these again was a portico open to the garden through which the actors entered the theatre. In it, spectators would stroll during the intermissions or take shelter from rain. As in the arenas, a huge adjustable awning, known as the *velum*, could be opened to shelter the spectators from the sun and rain.

Theatrical scenery and machinery were ingenious. Some scenes were fixed; some were superimposed and uncovered by sliding others sideways.

The curtain was only 3m/9.8ft high. It dropped into a slit at the beginning of the play and rose at the end. The basement contained the machinery and communicated with the stage through trapdoors on which the actors could rise from or sink into the ground. Other machines, mounted in the flies, lowered gods or heroes from the heavens, or raised them into the clouds.

The effects men knew how to create were smoke, lightning, thunder, ghosts, and the accompaniment of apotheoses.

All sorts of means were used to obtain perfect acoustics. The mouths of the actors' masks were little megaphones. The large sloping roof over the stage threw the sound downwards, and the upward curve of the seats received it smoothly. The colonnades broke up the echo, and carefully graduated sounding-boards under the seats acted as loudspeakers. One detail shows how far these refinements were carried: the doors on the stage were hollow and made like violins inside. When an actor wished to amplify his voice he would stand against one of these sound-boxes.

Circuses

These were the largest public sites in the Roman world, about four times longer than an amphitheatre, one end of which was oval shaped; they were used for chariot and horse races. The one in Arles was big enough to race about 12 chariots at a time and all that remains of it now is the obelisk that stands in front of St-Trophime church, which was once the finishing line.

Temples

The temple stood on a podium surrounded by columns and consisted of two rooms: the *pronaos* (a vestibule) and the *cella* (a place for the statue of the divinity). The prime example of a temple is the Maison Carrée at Nîmes. In the countryside there were small local temples, *fana* (singular *fanum*).

TRIUMPHAL ARCHES

The arches in Orange, Glanum, Carpentras and Cavaillon resemble the triumphal arches of Rome, raised in honour of victorious generals, but these were built to commemorate the founding of the cities in which they stand and the exploits of the veterans who settled there. They had either one or three openings. The columns decorating the four sides and flanking the central arch were all engaged; later on they became detached. The upper storey was decorated with statues, horse-drawn chariots, and their feats of arms, usually in gilt bronze.

Baths

The Roman baths, which were public and free, were also centres of physical culture, casinos, clubs, recreation centres, libraries, lecture halls and meeting places, which explains the amount of time people spent in them. Decoration in these great buildings was lavish: columns and capitals picked out in bright colours, mosaic ornaments, coloured marble facings, richly coffered ceilings, mural paintings and statues.

Central Heating

The bath's functioning demonstrated the Romans' understanding of the canalisation of water and its subsequent heating. Water was brought from the mountains via aqueducts and placed into cisterns and then distributed by a lead-pipe and cement system of canals; evacuation was conducted through a network of drainpipes.

To heat air and water a number of underground furnaces (hypocausts) like bakers' ovens, in which roaring fires were kept going, were used. The hot gases circulated among the brick pillars supporting the stone floors of rooms and baths, and rose through flues in the walls to escape from chimneys. In this way the rooms were heated from below and from the sides as in modern buildings. The warmest room, facing south or west, had large glazed windows and was used as a solarium. Water at three different temperatures cold, lukewarm and hot circulated automatically by thermo-siphon.

Bather's Route

The bather followed a medically designed route. From the *apodyterium* (changing room), where he would have left his clothes and anointed his body with oil, he entered the *palaestra* (a gymnasium of sorts), where he would warm up performing physical exercises. Then came the *tepidarium* (a lukewarm room), where he thoroughly cleaned himself by scraping his skin with small curved metal spatulas *(strigiles)* that prepared him for the *caldarium* (hot room), where he took a steam bath. He then proceeded into the hot swimming-pool. Having been massaged, he once again returned to the *tepidarium* before continuing on to the *frigidarium* (cold bath) to tone up the skin.

Thoroughly revived the bather dressed and proceeded to take advantage of the baths' other activities, such as lectures, sports, gossip, and the like.

THE ROMAN TOWNHOUSE

Numbers below correspond to the illustration on p83.

Excavations at Vaison-la-Romaine, Glanum or the Fountain quarter in Nîmes have uncovered Roman houses of various types: small bourgeois houses, dwellings (several storeys high) for rent, shops open to the street, and finally, large, luxurious patrician mansions.

Mansions had modest external appearances owing to their bare walls and few windows. But the interiors, adorned with mosaics, statues, paintings and marbles, and sometimes hot baths and a fish pond, reflected the wealth of their owners.

A vestibule and a corridor in the mansion led to the atrium. The **atrium (1)**, which opened onto the street through a vestibule containing the porter's lodge, was a large rectangular court, open in the middle, to the sky *(compluvium)*. A basin called the *impluvium*, under the open section, caught rainwater. Rooms opened off the *atrium*: a reception room **(2)**, a private oratory, a *tablinum* or study, and a library of the head of the family.

The **peristyle (3)** was a court surrounded by a portico (a gallery with a roof supported by columns) in the centre of the part of the house reserved for the family. They reached it from the *atrium* along a corridor called the *fauces*. Here the peristyle was generally made into a garden with basins lined with mosaics, fountains and statues. The living quarters opened all around it: bedrooms, *triclinium* (dining room **4**) and *oecus* (main drawing room).

The annexes included the kitchen with a sink and drain, baths, and a flush lavatory. Other buildings housed slaves' quarters, attics, cellars, stables, etc.

RURAL HOUSING

Experts are just beginning to examine this kind of dwelling. The towns must have been numerous and the settlement of these sites by Romans was done on pre-existing sites. The cadastral plan of Orange seems to show that the Romans tried to organise their territory into square-shaped lots called *centuries*.

R. Corbel/MICHELIN

Roman townhouse

The most common type of house was the villa, 40 of which have been discovered in Provence.

AQUEDUCTS

Grandiose like the Pont du Gard or more modest like Barbegal, aqueducts played an important role in daily life as they carried the water from their source to the town.

ROMAN ROADS

As soon as they settled in Provence, the Romans decided to design and build a reliable network of terrestrial means of communication that would ensure supremacy over the lands they had conquered, while at the same time encouraging the exchange of both goods and ideas. The layout of these roads usually coincided with that undertaken by the Gauls or with the paths *(drailles)* traditionally used by herds of cattle. They were cobbled only at the entrance to cities (country ways were surfaced with small, flat stones arranged tightly together) and dotted with stone or wooden bridges (Pont Julien at Bonnieux, Pont Flavien at St-Chamas), military milestones (1 Roman mile = 1 481m/0.92mi) and relay posts. Three great Roman roads cut across Provence: the Aurelian Way *(Via Aurelia)*, the Domitian Way *(Via Domitia)*, and the *Via Agrippa*. The first connected Rome to the River Rhône, running along the coast through the towns of Antibes *(Antipolis)*, Fréjus *(Forum Jilii)*, Aix-en-Provence *(Aquae Sextiae)*, and Salon-de-Provence *(Salo)* before joining up with the Domitian Way in Tarascon *(Tarusco)*. The *Via Domitia*, which headed towards Spain, helped link northern Italy to southern Gaul. It served the cities of Briançon *(Brigantium)*, Gap *(Vapicum)*, Sisteron *(Segustero)*, Apt *(Aptia Julia)*, Cavaillon *(Cabello)*, Tarascon *(Tarusco)*, Nîmes *(Nemausus)*, Béziers *(Julia Baeterrae)*, Narbonne *(Noarb)*, and Perpignan *(Ruscino)*. Finally, the Via Agrippa was a network built by Marcus Vipsanius Agrippa which started at Arles *(Arelate)* and extended towards Lyon, following the left bank of the Rhône and crossing Avignon *(Avenio)* and Orange *(Arausio)*.

ROMAN INFLUENCE

The brilliant Gallo-Roman civilisation took a long time to disappear after the fall of the Western Empire. The ancient public buildings remained standing and the architects of the Middle Ages took inspiration from them to build churches and monasteries.

A dark age followed (5C–10C) when few buildings were erected, of which only isolated specimens now remain, such as the small baptistries at Aix and Venasque. Early Romanesque art, which developed from Catalonia to northern Italy in the 10C and 11C, did not leave significant examples, either.

The 12C was for Provence one of its most outstanding historic periods during which it underwent a brilliant architectural renaissance. Churches,

remarkable for the bonding of their evenly cut stones with fine mortar work, appeared everywhere. Their style was closely linked to a school which had evolved in the area between the River Rhône, the Drôme, the Alps, and the Mediterranean. This school knew how to capture different influences: from Roman Antiquity came the use of vaults and especially decoration; from Languedoc came the carved portals; from Lombardy came the Lombard arcade or the lions adorning the base of doors; and from Auvergne came the dome on squinches over the nave and in front of the apse.

Below are the essential characteristics of the Romanesque style, the best examples of which were the great sanctuaries in the Rhône Valley: Cathédrale de la Major in Marseille, St-Trophime in Arles, St-Gilles, Cathédrale Notre-Dame-des-Doms in Avignon, Cathédrale Notre-Dame in Orange, and the church in Le Thor.

CHURCHES AND CHAPELS
Plan

Provençal Romanesque churches have descended directly from the Roman basilica and Carolingian church. Their general appearance was of a solid mass. Transepts were rare and shallow. Often there was a single nave with side chapels hollowed out of the thickness of the walls. The east end took the form of an apse with two flanking apsidal chapels,

St-Trophime cloister, Arles

G. Magnin/MICHELIN

where there were side aisles. Only the great pilgrimage churches of St-Gilles (in St-Gilles) and St-Trophime (in Arles) have ambulatories.

Minor buildings (Chapelle Ste-Croix in Montmajour; St-Sépulcre in Peyrolles) present a quadrilobed plan.

Bell Towers

The bell tower is an imposing, most often square, sometimes octagonal structure, that dominated the dome above the transept crossing.

It was sometimes placed above the bay preceding the apse or on the façade. It was decorated with blind arcading known as Lombard arcades or fluted pilasters in the Antique style, or sometimes both.

Side Walls

The walls were usually bare except for the cornice and the plain side doors. Massive buttresses, between which were set the windows of the nave, relieved the austere monotony of the exterior.

West Fronts and Doors

The west front was generally plain, opened by a door surmounted by an *oculus* as the main door was often located on the south side sheltered from the *mistral*. The doors were probably the architectural element most influenced by ancient Greek and Roman art; sometimes they were decorated with a *fronton* directly influenced by the ancient temples, such as the porch at Notre-Dame-des-Doms and the Chapelle St-Gabriel near Tarascon.

During the 12C, façades became more ornate preceded at times by a porch: a large carved tympanum over a horizontal lintel began to be featured. The doorways of St-Gilles and St-Trophime, superbly carved examples, rivalled in quality, size, and beauty the Gothic cathedral masterpieces of northern France.

Interior

Upon entering the Provençal Romanesque church the visitor is struck by the simplicity and austerity of the inside structure, enhanced only by some carved mouldings and cornices, barely visible in the dimly lit interior.

Chancels

This is the part of the church reserved for the clergy. It was usually oven vaulted and linked to the transept crossing with rounded barrel vaulting.

Naves and Vaults

The lofty, moderate though it was, structure of the building's interior was remarkable for the purity of its lines.

The nave was roofed with pointed barrel vaulting in which the downward thrust was more direct than that of the rounded arches, which tended to splay the wall outwards.

The barrel vaulting had already been used in the Roman era, having replaced the easily flammable wooden roofing, used from the 5C to the 11C, which had caused the destruction of many buildings. It was buttressed by pointed arches, also called transverse arches, which came down on thick engaged pilasters in the side walls or down onto slender pillars lining the nave.

The nave was sometimes lined with aisles with quarter-circle or pointed barrel vaulting, which acted as buttresses. Owing to the height of the side aisles there were no tribunes but a decorative band of blind arcading, made of rounded arches, with three arches to each bay, the central arch pierced by a lancet window, which let in very little light. Where the churches had but a single nave the side walls were quite thick in order to compensate for the missing side walls and balance the whole structure.

Transepts and Domes

The construction of the transept was a difficult problem for the architects in the Romanesque period. The groined vaulting made by the crossing of the nave and aisle vaulting had to be of great height in order to support the heavy weight of the central bell tower; the problem was solved by placing a dome on squinches over the crossing in the style of the Auvergne School.

Decoration

Interior decoration was as austere as exterior decoration: decorated capitals usually ornamented with stylised leaves, friezes with interlacing and foliated scrolls, fluting and rope moulding.

The capital with leaves of the Romanesque style was an adaptation of the ancient Corinthian capital: it was formed by a group of leaves arranged according to the style of the Romanesque period (interlacing and stylised decoration). The most picturesque of these capitals were historiated, inspired by religious stories taken from the Old and New Testaments. The cloisters offer the best examples: St-Trophime with its magnificent corner pillars adorned with statues of saints is remarkable. Fine capitals can also be found in the cloisters of Montmajour and St-Paul-de-Mausole (fantastic animals) and the apse of the church at Stes-Maries-de-la-Mer. There are also fragments of carved decoration worth seeing: in Avignon's cathedral there is the bishop's throne; in Apt's cathedral there is the altar.

Abbeys

Provence boasts several fine abbeys. The Benedictine Abbaye de Montmajour near Arles, founded in the 10C, forms a superb architectural ensemble illustrating the evolution of Romanesque forms from the 11C to 13C. It includes two churches (an upper church and crypt or lower church), two chapels, cloisters and its annexes in the characteristic Provençal style: simplicity in the monumental size, the volumes of which were inspired by the Antique style, carved decoration similar to St-Trophime, and perfection in the stone bonding. Cistercian art was represented by three sister abbeys: Sénanque, Silvacane and Le Thoronet (*see the Michelin Green Guide French Riviera for Le Thoronet*).

Sober elegance, austerity and lack of ornamentation were the required rules of the Cistercians, a reformed monastic order founded by St Bernard of Clairvaux. St Bernard had denounced the fanciful nature of Romanesque sculpture, which could distract the monks at prayer. The Cistercians imposed an identical plan everywhere, and they themselves directed the construction.

GOTHIC STYLE

Evolution

Romanesque art survived longer in Provence than it did in the rest of France. In spite of the relatively early appearance of Gothic, limited to two buildings (crypt of St-Gilles, porch of St-Victor in Marseille) and quadripartite vaulting as early as pre-1150, Gothic art was late in taking hold in Provence.

In the early 13C the new vaulting was used to cover buildings only in the Romanesque style. The only buildings entirely in the 13C Gothic style are to be found in Aix: the central nave of Cathédrale St-Sauveur and Église St-Jean-de-Malte, the former priory of the Knights of Malta.

In the mid-14C, there began a new step in Gothic evolution: a school of architecture called the Papal Gothic style began developing in Avignon. The popes attracted to their court artists from different regions of France, Germany, Flanders and Italy.

During the 15C the cardinals embellished Villeneuve-lès-Avignon with palaces *(livrées)*, churches and cloisters; aisles and chapels were added to certain churches. St-Trophime was altered; the Romanesque apse was replaced by an ambulatory and radiating chapels.

The main Gothic churches include: Palais des Papes (Clementine, Grand or Clement VI Chapel), St-Didier, St-Pierre, St-Agricol, Couvent des Célestines, all in Avignon; St-Laurent in Salon-de-Provence; Cathédrale St-Siffrein in Carpentras; the basilica of St-Maximin-la-Ste-Baume; the church in Roquemaure; and especially the charterhouse and church in Villeneuve-lès-Avignon.

Architecture

The Gothic style is marked by the systematic use of quadripartite vaulting and pointed arches. This innovative style, which originated in northern France, revolutionised construction by concentrating the weight of the structure on four pillars directed by stringers and transverse arches. Due to the absence of flying buttresses (characteristic of northern Gothic) the thrust of the vaults was assured by the massive buttresses between which chapels were built.

Inside, the nave was relatively dark, almost as wide as it was high, and ended in a narrower polygonal apse. Its width better accommodated the primary function of the church: Dominican preaching. The wall surfaces required painted decoration.

Église St-Didier in Avignon is considered the best example of southern Gothic in the region, whereas in a building like the basilica in St-Maximin-la-Ste-Baume, southern and northern influences appear. The church of the Couvent des Célestines in Avignon is entirely northern Gothic in style.

Religious edifices were not the only examples of Gothic art in Provence. Civic and military buildings also held an important place. The Palais des Papes in Avignon was one of buildings in the 14C that accommodated the demands of luxury and comfort with those of defence and security.

Decoration

The austere elegance of Provençal Gothic churches is underlined by their lack of decoration.

FINE ARTS

Painting

The Avignon region was for over two centuries (14C–15C) the great centre of Provençal painting. Already in the 13C the frescoes of the Ferrande tower recalled the miniatures painted during St Louis' reign. In the 14C the popes decorating the palace sought out the great Italian masters: **Simone Martini** from Siena and **Matteo Giovanetti** from Viterbo (⟲see the Michelin Green Guide Italy). The charterhouse in Villeneuve-lès-Avignon also contains fine works by Giovanetti. Once the popes had left Avignon, Italian influence diminished, but artistic life underwent

a renaissance in the mid-15C. Good King René was a patron of the arts and attracted master-craftsmen – artists and architects – to his court. Fresco painting lost ground to the Avignon School of panel painting. Artists from the north, Flanders and Burgundy, painted splendid masterpieces such as the Triptych of *The Annunciation* (1443–45) in Aix's Ste-Marie-Madeleine Church and *The Coronation of the Virgin* (1453–54) by Enguerrand Quarton, which is exhibited in the Musée Pierre de Luxembourg in Villeneuve-lès-Avignon.

Nicolas Froment, King René's court painter from Languedoc, painted the famous *Triptych of the Burning Bush* (in Aix's Cathédrale St-Sauveur). Avignon's Petit Palais contains a remarkable collection of lovely 14C and 15C paintings (Avignon and Italian Schools).

Sculpture

In the 14C, sculpture consisted of recumbent figures (John XXII in Avignon's Notre-Dame-des-Doms, Innocent VI in Villeneuve-lès-Avignon's charterhouse, and Cardinal Lagrange in the Petit Palais in Avignon), corbels, keystones and slender capitals. Archaic in style, they tended to draw on the Romanesque tradition.

Renaissance

Although the Rhône Valley was the principal route by which personalities of the Italian Renaissance entered France, Provence remained virtually untouched by the movement.

CLASSICAL PERIOD

The 17C and 18C, by contrast, produced a large number of buildings. They were dignified and austere in design without distinctive regional characteristics. The so-called Jesuit style developed in the Comtat Venaissin churches, bringing with it Italian monumental features such as ornate retables or altarpieces, panelling and baldachins, often obscuring the church's architectural lines. Avignon became the major centre once more, with local artists such as the Mignards and Parrocels producing

Pierre Puget (1620–94)

This highly skilled, multifaceted artist began his career as a young sculptor in Italy, where he trained under Pietro da Cortona. In 1645, Fouquet commissioned him to execute the doorway for the town hall in Toulon – it was to be one of his first great masterpieces. Between 1660 and 1668, the most brilliant period in Puget's career, he was living in Genoa. He was called back to Paris by Colbert, who entrusted him with the decoration of ships' prows belonging to the fleet in Toulon. Wary of the plots and intrigues of Versailles, he chose to live away from the French Court and devoted himself to the ornamentation of several Provençal cities, such as Aix and Marseille. His work is said to be forceful rather than elegant, and his statues, often of monumental proportions, artfully convey power, movement and pathos. His style is strongly reminiscent of Italian Baroque (Bernini, Cortone) and he succeeded in gracing Provence with a personal and highly original touch at a time when the country was largely dominated by Classicism.

His paintings (*Achilles' Education*) and sculptures (*The Faun, The Plague in Milan*), are displayed at the Musée des Beaux-Arts in Marseille, as well as at the Louvre Museum in Paris (the famous *Milon de Crotone* sculpture). His architectural feats include the ovoid dome of the Vieille Charité chapel in Marseille.

religious pictures and **Jacques Bernus** of Mazan carving for churches throughout the region.

In the Gard, there was a great drive to rebuild churches damaged during the Wars of Religion (Église St-Gilles). An entirely novel element was the building of townhouses by the old and new moneyed nobility, the magistracy and others: a few remain in Avignon and Nîmes but the finest line the streets of Aix. These well-proportioned, dignified stone houses are distinguished by doorways coroneted with ironwork balconies often supported by robust caryatids or muscular atlantes. The artists of these works were sculptor-decorators **Jean-Claude Rambot** (1621–94) and **Jean Bernard Toro** (1672–1731), both contemporaries of **Pierre Puget** (see sidebar), the 17C Baroque artist and architect from Marseille.

The 18C saw the continuation of the towns' and cities' embellishment programme, which had begun the previous century: in Nîmes the engineer J-P Mareschal designed the splendid Jardin de la Fontaine.

Among the painters of that period, two stand out: **Carle Van Loo**, who was susceptible to Provençal charm, and **Claude Joseph Vernet**, the painter of seascapes and ports.

19C

The art of architects and civil engineers was mostly practised in the Marseille region where **Henri-Jacques Espérandieu** erected the new Cathédrale La Major and Basilique de Notre-Dame-de-la-Garde, in the fashionable late-19C Romano-Byzantine style, and Palais Longchamp. Roquefavour Aqueduct is a superb civil engineering project that brings to mind the ancient Roman Pont du Gard. The Rove Underground Canal also represents an incredible feat.

Around this time painting benefited from an explosion of talented artists all fascinated by the luminous beauty of the Provençal countryside. The first to study the landscapes of Provence were **J A Constantin** (1756–1844) and **François-Marius Granet** (1775–1849). The Landscape School inspired by **Émile Loubon** (1809–63) also explored the notion of light with painters such as **Paul Guigou** (1834–71), a forerunner of Impressionism, and the Marseille artist **Adolphe Monticelli** (1824–86). This School ceased to exist around 1870 and was replaced by the painters known as "Naturalists": **Achille Emperaire** (1829–98) and **Joseph Ravaisou** (1865–1925) in Aix; **Clément Brun** (1868–1920) and **Paul Sain** (1853–1908) in Avignon;

Joseph Garibaldi (1863–1941), **Jean Baptiste Olive** (1848–1936) and **Alphonse Moutte** (1840–1913; strong realistic scenes of local fishermen) in Marseille. Finally **Félix Ziem**, a resident of Martigues, one of the first to paint in the hills beyond the fishing village of L'Estaque, chose to use colour in its own right and not to create light effects.

Van Gogh

Vincent van Gogh (1853–90), son of a Dutch Calvinist pastor, admirer of Millet and Rubens and influenced by the art of Japanese Ukiyo-e prints, was attracted to Impressionism, and brought his strong personality to his work.

In February 1888, he decided to settle in Arles, seeking a "different light". The two years he spent discovering Provence (Arles, Stes-Maries-de-la-Mer, Les Baux, St-Rémy) correspond to an intense period of creativity: he sought to express with colours and dramatic forms the "terrible human passions" that tormented him and caused him to suffer. He painted intensely the light and forms of Provence: landscapes (*View of Arles with Irises*, *The Alyscamps*, *Starry Night over the Rhone*, *Crau Plain*, *Boats along the Beach*) and portraits (*Portrait of an Old Provençal Peasant*, *L'Arlésienne*, *Madame Ginoux*). His quarrel with **Paul Gauguin**, who had joined him in October 1888, plunged him into despair and madness; he was cared for at St-Paul-de-Mausole near St-Rémy-de-Provence and continued to paint (*Wheatfields*, *Cypresses*, *Starry Night*, *Olive Trees*, *Self-Portrait*). He returned to Paris in May 1890 and committed suicide two months later. He left an enormous legacy of work, of which his Provençal period is perhaps the most intense and fascinating.

Cézanne

Paul Cézanne (1839–1906), unlike Van Gogh, was from Provence. Son of an Aix-en-Provence banker, he left his studies to take up painting. Introduced to the Parisian Impressionists by his friend, the writer Émile Zola, he began as a Romantic studying Delacroix, whose theory of colours he adopted. Having assimilated the Impressionist techniques, he rapidly went beyond them as early as 1879 and began his constructive period; he experimented with large dabs of luminous colour and simple geometric forms. "Everything in nature is modelled after the sphere, the cone and the cylinder", he wrote. He painted still lifes and portraits where colour and form determined the painting's organisation.

After 1890, he hardly ever left his native Provence and devoted all his energy to capturing the Montagne Ste-Victoire on canvas, painting it some 60 times

Gulf of Marseilles seen from l'Estaque (c. 1885) by Paul Cézanne

©Imagestate/Tips Images

without ever being entirely satisfied with his work. His research continued until his death and opened the way to Cubism.

20C

Clearly, for Cézanne, it was impossible for a painting to convey the full brilliance and subtleties of light; only colour could presume to fulfil that role. These views gave rise to a movement that influenced many late 19C and early 20C painters. Provence was now attracting many artists who settled in L'Estaque, following in the footsteps of Cézanne. First **Paul Signac** (1863–1935), who applied his Pointillist technique to Provençal colour (instead of the fine brushwork used in the north of France, here he opted for square, oblong touches, more suitable for catching the vivid sunlight). The Fauves found inspiration in this radiant Provençal setting. Their works played with colours and lines ignoring perspective and chiaroscuro. Matisse, Dufy and Derain all spent time in Provence, together with native artists from the region like **Charles Camoin** (1879–1965), **Auguste Chabaud** (1882–1955), **Alfred Lombard** (1884–1973) and **Louis-Mathieu Verdihan** (1875–1928). Around 1906–08, **L'Estaque** became the privileged meeting place of those artists who were later dubbed the Cubists. **Georges Braque** and **Pablo Picasso** worked together closely in Sorgues; the product of this joint venture was revolutionary, pictorial compositions touching on abstraction.

After World War I, a new generation was experimenting with novel theories, such as Expressionism and Surrealism. **André Masson**, father of spontaneous drawing (a technique that enabled him to break from figurative conventions), settled in the Aix region until his death in 1987 and drew a series entitled *Provençal Landscapes*. **Victor Vasarely** (1906–97) opened a foundation at Gordes to continue his research into optics and kinetics.

Contemporary Times

Today, many of the region's young artists have studied at the École d'Art de Lumigny in Marseille. Two contemporary art museums showcase recent works: the MAC in Marseille and the Carré d'Art in Nîmes.

DECORATIVE ARTS

Provençal Furniture

It was during the 15C that Provençal furniture, until that time considered to be of unsophisticated design, began to follow the lead set by Italy, with the introduction of delicate sculptures, finished off with a Spanish-influenced style of heavily chiselled wrought iron and copper keyholes. The 18C and beginning of the 19C heralded the *grande époque* of Provençal furniture, with the main production centres scattered between the lower valley of the Rhône and the mid-section of the Durance. The period from the Second Empire onwards was characterised among other things by excessive sculptured decoration.

In lower Provence, the Louis XV style reigned absolute from the middle of the 18C onward. Artisans preferred working with walnut, resorting if necessary to the use of box, olive, cherry or pear wood. The pieces of furniture, with their irregular curves, pronounced bends, and curled legs and bases are generally of quite slender proportion, with an abundance of storage units. They include: the **paneiro** or openwork bread bin; **manjadou** or meat safe decorated with ornamental spindles; **estagnié** or pewter cupboard; **verriau**, for glasses; and **saliero** or salt container. The following original items also stand out: the elegant **buffet à glissants**, or sliding sideboard; **radassié**, a large straw-seated sofa adorned with esparto leaves or sprigs of rye, such as those of the *à la capucine* armchairs, distinguishable by their trapezoid seat, setback arm rests, and concave-strutted back. Ornamentation is based on abundant and deep mouldings and sculpted motifs with overriding importance given to vegetation in different forms: acanthus leaves, flower baskets, branches of olive or oak; and the addition of small, curved candle-rings to the angles and to the crest tops. The best-known decorative style is from Arles, a production centre of particular character, where the *paneiro* or bread container, the first mobile cabinets, and *à la capucine* chairs originated.

In upper Provence, sombre lines and decor triumph over furniture of a more rustic style, remaining steadfast throughout the period of influence of the Renaissance and Louis XIII styles. Craftsmen in this part of the region preferred working with mulberry, pine or limewood. Furniture not seen in lower Provence, such as the *vaisselier* or dresser, and the *banc à dossier* or backed bench, are a testimony to the influence of the neighbouring Dauphiné. Simple wall cavities also tend to replace the use of small storage units in evidence in lower Provence.

The Supremacy of Clay

The abundance of excellent quality clay in Provence has given rise to a number of large ceramic centres in the region: the mottle decoration of **Apt** and **Avignon** faience; Allemagne-en-Provence and Moustiers (*see The Green Guide French Alps*); La Tour-d'Aigues; and above all, **Marseille**, where clay has been worked into vessels, both useful and decorative, since ancient times. Under Louis XIV, the wars that emptied the kingdom's coffers resulted in the banning of the use of gold and silver dishes, thus providing an opportunity for the faience industry.

In 1679, the Fabre pottery works at **St-Jean-du-Désert** between Aubagne and Marseille transformed its production to that of faience under the influences of **Joseph Clérissy**, who was from an Aubagne family that had moved to Moustiers. Its blue "Chinese-style" cameos drew inspiration from the first pieces of porcelain imported into France from China. Although St-Jean-du-Désert saw its importance decline after the Great Plague, other earthenware works started to spring up, many of which employed the sharp

fire technique. **Fauchier** created *fleurs jetées*, designs of flowers painted in a seemingly haphazard fashion, and used a distinctive yellow enamel background decoration. The works of **Leroy** are recognisable for their fantastic creatures and human figures set on a background of star-like flowers.

The second half of the 18C represented the zenith of Marseille earthenware, mainly as a result of the activities and talent of **Pierrette Candellot**, a colourful personality originally from Lyon, and the wife of the Marseille pottery manufacturer **Claude Perrin**. Following his death in 1748, his widow, known as **La Veuve Perrin**, guided the family business towards the mild firing technique, consequently obtaining pieces of exceptional quality. She perfected the ornamental Marseille style, introduced fish motifs and sea landscapes, and developed an unusual sea-green background. She also drew inspiration from contemporary trends in jewellery design.

After Veuve Perrin, the last great Marseille earthenware producers were **Joseph-Gaspard Robert** and **Antoine Bonnefoy**, both of whom were able to give to faience an ornamental refinement that until that time had been the prerogative of porcelain. Bonnefoy is famous for his trademark *bouillabaisse* motifs and pastoral scenes reminiscent of the Rococo paintings of François Boucher. Robert created floral motifs set off by black butterflies and a gold border; his dishes bordered in red, white and blue were the last great series to come out of Marseilles. Ultimately, a combination of the competition from porcelain makers, the Revolution, and the blockade by the English naval fleet sounded the death knell for Marseille's faience industry.

The Christmas Crèche

Christmas cribs (*crèche* means crib) have a long tradition in Provence although it was not until the late 18C that they became common and developed a typically local character. A few 18C groups, often highly original and beautifully modelled, may still be seen at a collector's or in a church, but most are now in museums (Musée du Vieil Aix, Musée du Vieux Marseille, Museon Arlaten in Arles, and the Musée National des Arts et Traditions Populaires in Paris).

Church Cribs

Christmas was not an important festival in the early church. Nativity scenes did not form part of the medieval celebrations except for rare low reliefs of the Adoration of the Shepherds or the Kings as in the St-Maximin crypt.

In 1545 the Council of Trent sought to advance the Counter-Reformation through the encouragement of popular piety. The practice of setting up a crib in church arrived in Provence from Italy in the 17C. There is a particularly beautiful crèche from this period in the church of St-Maximin; the carved figures, about 50cm/20in high, are of gilded wood. In the 18C, bejewelled wax figures were introduced with glass eyes and wigs.

Only the head, arms and legs were carved and attached to a richly dressed articulated frame. In the 19C, new materials were introduced, including printed or painted cardboard cut-outs with gaily coloured clothing, figures made from spun glass, cork, clay and even bread dough. By then, all the Provençal churches had adopted the Christmas crib of dressed figures. This kind of Christmas crib can still be seen today.

Live Cribs

At Midnight Mass in many churches – Séguret, Allauch, Isle-sur-la-Sorgue and Marseille – a Nativity play is performed. In Gémenos, children in costume place an infant Jesus in a straw-filled manger. In Les Baux, a little cart, decorated with greenery and bearing a newborn lamb, is drawn into church by a ram and accompanied by shepherds. The procession is headed by angels and fife and tabor players, while the congregation sings old Provençal carols.

Talking Cribs

The 18C passion for marionettes was adapted to produce talking cribs in which mechanical figures enacted the Nativity to a commentary and carols. People came from far and wide to see and hear the talking cribs of Marseille and Aix. Characters were added to the already numerous cast and, as imagination ran wild, historical accuracy and relevance vanished: reindeer, giraffes and hippopotamuses joined the other animals in the stable, and the pope was made to arrive in a carriage to bless the Holy Family. It must have been a sight to see a Napoleon puppet, accompanied by his soldiers and a man-of-war firing salvoes, arriving at the manger! Another new idea came to those presenting a crib close to Marseille station: the Three Kings travelled to the scene in a steam train!

Santon Cribs

The *santon* cribs are the most typical of Provence. They first appeared in 1789 at the time of the Revolution when the churches were closed. **Jean-Louis Lagnel** (1764–1822), a church statue-maker from Marseille, had the idea of making small figures that families could buy at little cost. Labelled *santouns* (little saints) in Provençal, and *santoni* in Italian, abbreviated from *santibelli* (beautiful saints), these figurines had an immediate and wide appeal. They were modelled in clay, fired and naïvely painted in bright colours. Limited at first to biblical personages, they were soon joined by men and women from all walks of life, dressed in local costume: the Holy Family, the Shepherds and their sheep, the Three Kings, the knife grinder, the fife and tabor player, the smith, the blind man and his guide, the fishwife, the wetnurse, the milkmaid, the huntsman, fisherman and even the mayor!

So great was the figurines' success, as virtually every family began to build up a collection, that a Santons Fair *(Foire des Santonniers)* was inaugurated in Marseille, which is still held on the Canebière from the last Sunday in

November to Epiphany. Aubagne was also famous for its *santons*. *Santon* makers established workshops in towns throughout Provence, whereas in the country, men and women made figures in the long winter evenings. The craft reached its peak in the 1820–30s, which is why so many of the characters appear in the dress of that period.

The *santons* of Provence are now known the world over and many families like to add to their collection of characters each year and set up displays during the Christmas holidays.

LITERATURE

Provence is an ancient civilised land, Greco-Latin then Occitanian, which has never stopped influencing poets and writers alike, who expressed themselves in Provençal.

LANGUAGE OF THE TROUBADOURS

The Romance languages evolved out of Vulgar Latin spoken at the end of the Roman Empire. These were Italian, Romanian, Catalan, Spanish, Portuguese, and in France, the Oïl language *(langue d'oïl)* in the north and the Oc language *(langue d'oc)* in the south. *"Oïl"* and *"Oc"* were the words used for "yes" in the north and south, respectively. This distinction, which was formed as early as the Merovingian period, was advanced enough in the 10C and 11C for the two languages to enter into literature separately. Occitan, which appeared in Latin texts for the first time in the 11C, owed its place and influence to the success of 12C courtly literature. The art of the **troubadours**, which developed in the feudal courts of Périgord, Limousin and Gascony, was not confined purely to Provence but encompassed all of Occitania, from Bordeaux to Nice. These troubadours (*trobar* means to find) were inventors of musical airs, both melodies and words in the Oc language, and they created a linguistic community independent of political divisions: Jaufré Rudel from Blaye, Bernard de Ventadour from Limousin, Peire Vidal from Toulouse, and from Provence, Raimbaut of Orange, the Countess of Die, Raimbaut of Vaqueiras and Folquet of Marseille.

Under the Provençal or Limousin name, Occitanian was appreciated by noble foreigners and most of the European courts. The essential inspirational force of the troubadours was love, not passionate love but courtly love, where the patience and discretion of the poet-lover finally won over the lady who accepted the homage of her vassal. Using sound, word pattern, and stanza-structure these poems told of the troubadours' anxieties and hopes.

PROSE AND POETRY

The courtly poem declined in the 13C, its themes having been exhausted. It was replaced by satirical poems known as *sirventès* and prose that told of the lives of the troubadours (the famous *vidas*). This period is marked by the European influence of French, by the setting up of the Inquisition, and by the expansion of the Capetian monarchy.

Occitan, nevertheless, retained its importance. It is said that **Dante** (c. 1265–1321) almost used it to write his *Divina Commedia* and that it was the language spoken at the pontifical court of Avignon. With Latin, Occitan was, in the Middle Ages, the only written administrative language. And yet beginning in the 14C regional differences began appearing in written texts and French was gradually adopted in its place.

Occitanian literature became popular in Italy where it was revived thanks to Dante and returned in force into the Rhône Valley in the form of a sonnet with **Petrarch** (1304–74). Exiled in Avignon, Petrarch fell passionately in love with the lovely Laura de Noves in 1327. His *Il Canzonière* (1348) were a group of sonnets where he expressed his unrequited love for her. The poet, who had retired to Fontaine-de-Vaucluse, also wrote descriptions of Provençal life in his letters; he spoke of shepherds, the Sorgue fishermen, and his climb to Mont Ventoux.

The fatal blow fell upon the Occitan language in 1539, with the adoption of the Edict of Villers-Cotterêts, which decreed that for all administrative purposes the French language, the dialect spoken in the Île de France, and thus Paris, should be used. In spite of that, Occitan survived until the 19C in the theatre, poetry, short stories and legends, chronicles, and didactic and erudite works (dictionaries and anthologies).

One of the regional popular writers of the 16C was **Bellaud de la Bellaudière**. Born in Grasse around 1543, he lived a very active life as a soldier; he was also opposed to the Huguenots. When he was in prison he wrote 160 sonnets, his *Œuvres et Rimes*. His poetry – inspired by Marot, Rabelais and Petrarch – was essentially personal, owing to its familiar realism. His work renewed the Occitan language and he inspired and was joined by Claude Bruey, Raynier from Briançon and François de Bègue.

In the 17C, when the moralist Vauvenargues was born in Aix, and Madame de Sévigné resided at Grignan, **Nicolas Saboly** was composing Provençal **Noëls**: charming, simple works of popular poetry. These happy yet pious canticles, touching and devout, depicted the entire world running in the night towards the newly born baby Jesus. In Saboly's lifetime, church services were still held in Occitan in rural villages as well as in the cities. When French dramatist **Jean Racine** resided in Uzès in 1661 he had a great deal of difficulty making himself understood. Until the Revolution, Occitan was the language spoken daily; only a small elite spoke French, and even then they were bilingual. And yet, the use of Occitan declined steadily, breaking up into different local dialects.

THE FÉLIBRIGE

In the late 18C, Occitan, weakened by the centralised state, was reborn through literature. In 1795, Abbot Favre made history with his *Siège de Caderousse (Caderousse's Seat)*, a satirical poem written in dialect, amusing because of its Rabelais-like truculence. In the 1840s Occitan experienced an explosion: **Joseph Roumanille** (1818–91), a teacher in Avignon and the author of a work *Li Margarideto* (1847), awakened in the young **Frédéric Mistral** (1830–1914) a passion for Provence, its culture, history and Oc language.

As early as 1851, Mistral began writing *Mirèio*. In 1852 the first congress of future *Félibres* was held in Arles. On 21 May 1854, at the castle of Fort-Ségugne, seven young poets writing in Provençal (Roumanille, Mistral, Aubanel, Mathieu, Tavan, Giéra and Brunet) founded the Félibrige. *Félibre* was a word taken from an old song meaning doctor. Félibrige was an association whose goals were to restore the Provençal language and to codify its spelling. It published a periodical *Armana Provençau,* which spread its ideas.

In 1859 Mistral published *Mirèio*, an epic poem of 12 cantos that brought him immense success . Lamartine praised his work and Charles Gounod made it into an opera in 1864. Mistral's literary works included: *Calendau* (1867), *Lis Isclo d'or* (1875), *Nerto* (1884), *La Reino Jano* (1890), *The Song of the Rhône* (1896) and *Lis óulivado* (1912). In 1904 he was awarded the Nobel Prize in Literature.

Mistral was also a fine philologist who patiently collected the scattered elements of the Oc language and recorded their spelling in a monumental dictionary *Lou Trésor du Félibrige*, published in 1878–86. It still serves as a reference book. The Félibrige brought together Occitanian poets and novelists as different as Alphonse Daudet, Paul Arène, Félix Gras, Baptiste Bonnet, Joseph d'Arbaud, Charles Rieu, Dom Xavier de Fourvière, Jean-Henri Fabre, Folco de Baroncelli-Javon and Charles Maurras (political theorist). During the same period, renowned writers of French included: Jean Alcard (a member of the Academy, who wrote *Maurin of the Moors*); Émile Zola, who went to secondary school in Aix and who in his Rougon-Macquart series described the evolution of a family from the south; and

Edmond Rostand, born in Marseille, who wrote the unforgettable *Aiglon*.

THE PRESENT

Although Provence is always present in their works, many of the contemporary writers have gone beyond the regional level and joined the ranks of the top French writers: Jean Giono from Manosque; Marcel Pagnol (*Jean de Florette*, *Manon des Sources*) from Aubagne; René Barjavel from Nyons; acclaimed poet René Char from Isle-sur-la-Sorgue; and Marie Mauron.

Provençal as a spoken language regressed while as a language of culture – successor to the troubadours and Félibres – it progressed. Admittedly the local dialects remain but they are most often ignored by the young and are more prevalent in rural than in urban areas. At the same time, the centralising and unifying role of the state has enhanced the language: the Oc language is recognised in official teaching programmes.

Continuing with the work of the Félibrige society, the goal of the Institut des Études Occitanes (Institute of Occitanian Studies), while still promoting the use of authentic everyday speech, is to seek the unity of a common language, and to restore to Occitania the status it enjoyed in Middle Ages when it extended beyond political limits from the Atlantic to the Mediterranean.

LEGENDS AND TALES

The legends and tales of Provence are a colourful account of its history and geography. These stories depict regional people, customs, institutions, lifestyles, beliefs, monuments and sites. The Greco-Roman heritage shows in Provençal legends where the wondrous accompanies daily life in its humblest activities, where the gods are omnipresent and miracles occur at their behest.

Ancient Myths

For the ancient Greeks, the western Mediterranean was awe-inspiring, yet at the same time, frightening. Each evening the sun set with Apollo's chariot. **Heracles**, Zeus' son, had been to this land and had married Galathea from Gaul. Endowed with incredible strength, he had opened the passages through the Alps. To protect his son's passage through Provence, Zeus showered his enemies with stones and boulders, which became a desert, the Crau. The attraction of this western Mediterranean land inspired the Phocaeans later to found a colony here. The legend of **Protis** and **Gyptis** illustrates this episode. The Marseille navigator, **Pytheas**, is said to have sailed in 4 BC, between the columns of Heracles (Straits of Gibraltar), across the waters to Cornwall and on to Iceland.

Legends of the Saints

Christianity, too, brought its collection of stories. A thousand-year-old tradition ascribes the conversion of Provence in the 1C to the miraculous landing of a boat from Judaea bearing **Lazarus**, **Mary Magdalene**, **Martha** and disciples of Christ. With **St Victor** and **Cassien** they formed a sort of mystic Provençal state and are credited with many wondrous acts. Among the most dramatic is Martha's defeat of the Tarasque monster (&see TARASCON).

Local saints were not in short supply either. Legend has it that **St Mitre**, the beheaded martyr, picked up his head, kissed it, and bore it to the cathedral (&see AIX-EN-PROVENCE). Then there is **St Caesarius**, who captured a puff of sea air in his glove and carried it back to Nyons country. From that moment, a light wind began to blow over the region; the local people took heart and started to cultivate the land. The prosperity of Nyons country dates from this period, and the advantages of the local climate have made it a perfect place for growing olives.

Troubadour Tradition

The legends of Provence were inspired by epic poetry (*chansons de geste*) and courtly prose.

Pierre of Provence, a valiant knight and talented troubadour, lived at his father's

Sorcery

Rare were the villages that did not have at least one *masc* or *masco*.
These people had the power to bewitch humans and animals. If a baby stopped suckling, if horses stopped for no apparent reason, if hunting dogs lost their scent, they had been *emmasqués*. Méthamis, in Vaucluse, is still – even today – a sanctuary of Provençal sorcery. To fight against evil spells a *démascaire* was called in. This person was often a shepherd, because the shepherd was a holder of supernatural powers but was said to be a sworn enemy of sorcerers, someone who held the secrets of nature. The *démascaire* was good and broke the evil spell. He was also a bone-setter and cured sickness with plants.

Other ways of warding off evil spells were possible, such as wearing a piece of clothing inside out or back to front, throwing salt into the hearth, or reciting different invocations while crossing oneself at the same time. To protect houses from the evil eye the custom was to cement a vitrified pebble into the wall. On the sheep-pen door people nailed a magic thistle. Some places are totally magical and mysterious, such as Garagaï at Vauvenargues, a bottomless chasm where strange things happen. Between Arles and Montmajour is the fairies' hole, peopled with supernatural beings.

court in the Château de Cavaillon. Seeing her portrait, the knight fell in love with Princess Maguelone, daughter of the King of Naples, and set out to find her. Received at the Neapolitan court, he was victorious in a series of tournaments where he wore Maguelone's colours. But one day Pierre was kidnapped by Barbary pirates and taken to Tunis where he was imprisoned for seven years. Having served his term, he was finally able to set sail for Provence, but not far from Aigues-Mortes, his boat sank. Mortally wounded, he was brought to the local hospital, headed by Princess Maguelone herself, who had sought through charitable works a way to forget her unhappy love. The lovers met and recognised each other. Pierre was cured.

Not all endings were so happy. One day **Guillem de Cabestaing**, a son of a noble and well-known troubadour, came to sing at the court of the lord of Castel-Roussillon, an ugly, vulgar old man who had a lovely young wife named Sérémonde. Love kindled quickly between these two young people. The lord, having discovered this, killed the handsome Guillem in an ambush, ripped out his heart, and served it to his wife for dinner. Sérémonde responded with: "My lord, you have served me such delicious fare that nothing could ever equal it and

so I swear before Christ, in order to keep the taste fresh for all time, I will never eat again." She then threw herself from the top of a cliff in Roussillon. As her blood spread it coloured the soil, bringing about the origin of ochre.

Child Heroes

A great number of Provençal legends recount the memorable exploits of children and adolescents gifted with a force and extraordinary ingenuity. They generally appeal to Almighty God, the intervention of the saints or magic. This is the case of the shepherd boy **Bénézet**, who built the bridge at Avignon after experiencing a vision in 1177. **Jean de l'Ours**, so-called because he had been brought up with a bear, was another. At the age of 12 he conceived the idea of journeying round France. He forged himself a stout iron staff and, thus armed, killed the horrible dragons that kept a young princess in an enchanted castle. **Guihen l'Orphelin** (the orphan), thanks to his mysterious white hen, which he would stroke while murmuring a special incantation, could become invisible. He was able to free a king and the king's daughter, both whom had been imprisoned by a wicked baron. To thank him the king promised his daughter to Guihen and they lived, of course, happily ever after.

Nature

Renowned for its laid-back Mediterranean lifestyle, Provence's natural treasures range from rocky coastal creeks to the back-country's chalk outcrops, irrigated by the Rhône and her tributaries. This sun-kissed land, where the scent of rosemary and thyme fills the air, provides the ideal refuge for cicadas, who hum among its *garrigues*, olive groves and pine forests.

REGIONS AND LANDSCAPES
TOPOGRAPHY

Formation of the Land

Approximately 600–220 million years ago, during a period called the Primary Era, what is now Provence was covered by a sea that surrounded the continent of Tyrrhenia, contemporary with the Massif Central. Tyrrhenia was formed by crystalline rocks. Vestiges of this land mass included the Maures, Corsica, Sardinia and the Balearic Islands.

During the Secondary Era (220–60 million years ago), erosion gradually levelled Tyrrhenia; the Cretaceous Sea covered practically the whole region. Variations in sea level were caused by materials from the Primary strata carried down by rivers and deposited at the bottom of the sea, forming sedimentary deposits composed either of limestone (e.g. from Orgon) or marl and transformed into regular, parallel layers of rock (strata) in a strip of land lying east to west; this was the Durancen Isthmus.

The Tertiary Era (60–2 million years ago) was marked by important tectonic upheavals that uplifted the sedimentary cover and created the young folded mountains of the Alps and Pyrenees. The strata were uplifted and folded in an east–west direction, giving rise to the Provençal secondary mountains north of Marseille, Toulon and Draguignan (Ste-Baume, Ste-Victoire, Mont Ventoux, Baronnies, Alpilles, Luberon). The sea level rose to the present-day Rhône Valley, and while the Alpilles chain was thrust upwards, the Crau plain sank.

During the Quaternary Era (beginning about 2 million years ago) land mass development continued: Tyrrhenia was submerged beneath the present-day Mediterranean Sea leaving the Maures, Esterel and Canaille mountains. The relief adopted the form it has now, the Rhône corridor emerged, widened and became an important travel route.

The subsiding Crau plain modified the course of the River Durance so that it deviated to join the Rhône. Erosion during glaciation and interglacial periods put the final touches to the landscapes *(calanques)*.

Plains

The plains, such as the Rhône delta, were formed by the constant deposits of alluvial sediments that reclaimed territory from the sea. These plains first spread over the Rhône's east bank, **Comtat Venaissin**, then spread over both banks. On the west side of the river the plains extended to the Lower Languedoc dominated by the *garrigues* near Nîmes. To the east they became the fertile **Petite Crau** and **Grande Crau**.

Romans, medieval monks and small property holders throughout the centuries have improved the land with drainage and irrigation systems.

Two regions, especially, have profited from such systems: Comtat Venaissin and Petite Crau. Market gardens now cover the land creating a fine pattern of tiny plots separated by windbreaks of tall cypress and lower screens of reeds. The **Grande Crau**, separated from Camargue by the Grand Rhône, is an immense desert of pebbles and boulders between which grow tufts of grass known locally as *coussous*. It was used traditionally for the winter pasturing of large flocks of sheep.

The expansion of the industrial zone of Fos and the clearing of the land of stones as well as the irrigation systems have transformed the area; it has lost its pastoral image and with it much of its charm.

Olive groves, almond trees, vineyards and undulating grassland make up the new wealth of these areas.

The **Camargue** is a man-made delta of recent alluvium or silt formed by the Rhône, which holds the sea back by means of dykes. The wetland thus created is one of France's most picturesque regions. The *sansouires*, vast salt marshes, give the area the appearance of an untamed expanse.

Plateaux and Mountains

The Provençal plains are flanked or penetrated by folded mountain chains lying east to west that rise quite abruptly, blocking the horizon. The relief often appears confused, presenting an undisciplined alternation of limestone heights and partitioned-off fertile basins: Apt country, Aigues country (south of Luberon), Aix country (irrigated by the Provence canal) where very varied crops (grain, vineyards, fruit, market gardening) are cultivated. East of the Rhône, from north to south, different landscapes follow one after the other. The western fringe of the **Baronnies** form a complicated structure of hills and slopes of pure beauty wherein reign olive groves and the hybrid *lavandin*. Unique to Provence, the rocky summits of the **Dentelles de Montmirail** display a finely carved-out relief (*dentelle* means lace) of oak and pine forest with vineyards carpeting the slopes. Backed up against the Baronnies is **Mont Ventoux**, an imposing limestone massif that dominates the Comtadin plain at a height of 1 912m/6 275ft.

The **Vaucluse plateau**, also known as the Vaucluse hills, is a vast arid land of karstic relief devoted to raising sheep and to the cultivation of lavender. This limestone countryside is potted with

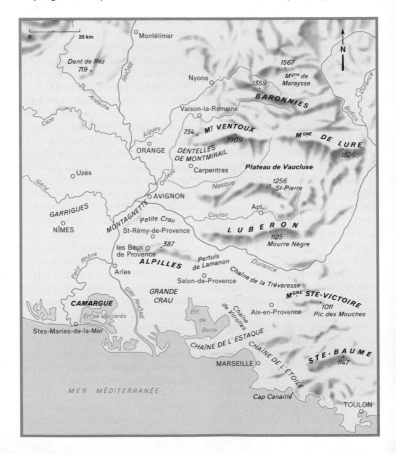

chasms and carved out by gorges. An underground hydrographic network, still largely uncharted, penetrates the limestone and opens out at the Fontaine de Vaucluse.

The **Montagne du Luberon** stretches over some 60km/37mi. Cut in half north to south by the Lourmarin combe, it culminates in the Grand Luberon at Mourre Nègre (alt 1 125m/3 692ft). This region has some rugged but beautiful mountain sites to which villages cling precariously. There is a striking contrast between its wild, forest-clad north face and its more cultivated south face. In the middle of the Rhône plain stand two picturesque ranges: La **Montagnette** and Les **Alpilles**.

East of Aix, **Montagne Ste-Victoire**, a limestone mass pockmarked with caves and chasms, dominates the Aix basin, whereas to the southeast the Trévaresse and Vitrolles ranges bar it from the Étang de Berre. This lagoon is closed to the south by **Chaîne de l'Estaque** and is separated from the St-Mitre hills by the Caronte depression.

The **Chaîne de l'Étoile**, Chaîne St-Cyr, and Massif Marseilleveyre surround Marseille whereas on the horizon looms the long rocky barrier of the **Massif de la Ste-Baume**, which reaches an altitude of 1 147m/3 764ft at the Ste-Baume signal station.

West of the River Rhône, the Cévennes foothills lie north to south receding in the river's direction and the vine-carpeted plain via the *garrigues* of Nîmes. A series of desolate limestone plateaux cut by canyons and gouged out by sometimes huge chasms succeed in tiers; it is an arid, rocky terrain only fit for grazing sheep. In the past, local people earned income by harvesting wild aromatic plants, olives and almonds, and by making goats' cheese *(migou)*. The countryside is criss-crossed by a multitude of dry-stone enclosures, in the middle of which once stood a modest hut *(mazet)* or *capitelle,* similar to the present-day dry-stone huts known as *bories*. There are, however, a few isolated fertile areas: the Uzès basin, the Vistre plain, and the Vaunage (southwest of Nîmes), which are devoted to growing crops, such as orchards and vineyards.

Waterways

On its Provençal passage, the Rhône receives water to the west from the Ardèche and Gard rivers, which come down from the Cévennes, and to the east from the Aigues, Ouvèze and Durance rivers, which come down from the Alps. They all have the same appearance: a trickle of water in an oversized stony bed during periods of drought, a torrent of foaming water during rain storms. The Cévennes receive rainfalls of unusual severity – a single downpour can exceed the annual rainfall of Paris. The rivers expand dramatically. The Ardèche has risen 21m/69ft in one day and its flow has increased from 2.5cu m/88.3cu ft per second to 7 500cu m/264 855cu ft; frequently the water rises 10m/33ft and more. The heavy flow of the Ardèche cuts through the Rhône like a rocket, striking the dykes of the left bank across the way. These 5m/16.5ft high flash-floods are known as "the blows of the Ardèche" *(les coups de l'Ardèche)*.

For the tributaries of the east that come down from the Alps, it is the melting snows that multiply the volume of water. The Durance, for example, expands up to 180 times its usual volume. Fortunately these spates occur in the spring, when the Ardèche and Gard rivers are low. On the other hand, the Durance is almost dry in winter and autumn while the rains from the Cévennes expand the tributaries of the west bank.

Coastline

From the Languedoc coast to the Marseille *calanques*, the form of the coastline changes often. As far as the Golfe de Fos, the shoreline is marked by vast lagoons separated from the sea by narrow sand bars: the mass of alluvial deposits dropped by the Rhône and shaped by the coastal currents has formed offshore bars closing off the lagoons. The encroachment of sand has pushed old ports like Aigues-Mortes inland.

At the Chaîne de l'Estaque, limestone relief reappears and cuts the coastline. From Marseille to La Ciotat the littoral is cut into a great number of coves of which the deepest and most uneven are called **calanques** – they are in fact the submerged extremities of the valleys when the sea level rose after the Quaternary Era's glacial period. Steep cliffs, brown and reddish rocks plunge vertically into the sea from which emerge a number of nearby islands. With small well-sheltered ports and lovely wild creeks, the *calanques* are nirvana for deep-sea divers and climbers.

The Sea

The Mediterranean is the bluest of European seas. This deep cobalt, in painters' parlance, arises from the great limpidity of the water.

The surface water temperature varies by 20°–25°C/68°–77°F in summer, falling to only 12°–13°C/53°–55°F in winter. At a depth of 200 to 4 000m/656 to 13 128ft, the temperature is a constant 13°C/55°F, an important factor in the climate: this great liquid mass cools the area in summer and warms it in winter. As a result of very rapid evaporation, the water is noticeably saltier than that of the Atlantic.

The sea's tide is very slight, averaging 0.25m/9.8in and yet, strong winds can cause variations in height of as much as 1m/3.3ft. This relative stability has singled out the Mediterranean as base level for all the French coast's altitudes.

A calm sea, with short, choppy waves, the Mediterranean can suddenly become violent. When the *mistral* wind rises, often with little or no warning, dangerous storms can surprise unsuspecting yachtsmen.

FLORA

In addition to its beautiful countryside, backdropped by a luminous sky, Provence possesses a unique natural habitat.

Climate and Zones

All vegetation is closely dependent on climatic conditions. In Provence, flowering occurs during the spring, although there is a second blossoming in the autumn that goes on well into winter. The dormant period is during the summer, when the climate's heat only permits plants that are especially adapted to resist drought to grow, such as those with long taproots, glazed leaves that reduce transpiration, bulbs that act as reservoirs of moisture and a protective perfumed vapour. The olive tree and holm oak mark out the distinctly Mediterranean zones, known as *garrigues*. In Haute-Provence the *garrigues* disappear to be replaced by forest cover (downy oak, Scots pine, beech) and moors (broom, lavender, boxwood).

In the Vivarais, chestnut trees add an unusual touch to the landscape.

Olive Trees

The Greeks brought olive trees to Provence 2 500 years ago because they grow equally well in limestone or sandy soils. The olive has been called the immortal tree since, grafted or wild, it will continually renew itself. Those grown from cuttings die relatively young, at 300 years of age. Along the coast the trees reach gigantic dimensions attaining 20m/65.6ft in height, their domes of silver foliage 20m/65.6ft in circumference and trunks 4m/13ft round the base. The olive tree – there are more than 60 varieties – will grow at altitudes

Olive tree

R. Corbel/MICHELIN

Umbrella pine

R. Corbel/MICHELIN

of up to 600m/1 969ft, mainly on valley floors and hillsides, often mingling with almond and fig trees. Its presence marks the limit of the Mediterranean climate. It begins to bear fruit between 6 and 12 years of age and is in full yield at 20–25 years; it is harvested every two years. Locals cultivate early vegetables in the shade of the light-coloured, evergreen foliage of the olive tree.

Oak Trees

There are several varieties of oaks.

The **holm oak** *(Quercus ilex)* has a short thick-set trunk with a wide-spreading thick dome. It grows on arid, calcareous soil at less than 1 000m/3 282ft. It is an evergreen oak, the leaves of which remain a fine dark green. In stunted form it is a characteristic element of the *garrigues* in association with all sorts of shrubs and aromatic plants.

The **kermes**, or scrub oak, is a bushy evergreen shrub rarely exceeding 1m/3.3ft in height. It has a trunk of grey bark with a thick dome of shiny, tough, ragged and prickly leaves. Its name, kermes, comes from the scale-insect that lives on its branches and from which a bright red dye is obtained. The tree can grow on stone-free dry soil but prefers fertile, cool soil.

The **downy oak** or **pubescent oak** *(Quercus pubescens)* is a deciduous tree; the undersides of the leaves are covered with dense short white hairs. It requires more water than the evergreens noted above. The downy oak can be found in the valleys and on the more humid mountain slopes. It is at times found with the maple, service tree and rowan. In its undergrowth grow a variety of shrubs and flowers, most notably the orchid. Truffles develop around the roots of this tree.

Pine Trees

The three types of pine found in the Mediterranean can be easily distinguished by their shape.

The **maritime pine** *(Pinus pinaster)* grows on limestone soil; its foliage is dark blue-green, the bark an orange-red.

The **umbrella** or **stone pine** *(Pinus pinea)* is one of the Mediterranean's most characteristic sights; it owes its name to its easily recognisable shape. It is often found growing alone.

The **Aleppo pine** *(Pinus halepensis)* is a Mediterranean species that grows well in the chalky soil along the coast. Its foliage is light and graceful; its grey bark-covered trunk twists as it grows.

Other Provençal Trees

In towns and villages, the streets and squares are shaded by the smooth-barked **plane trees** or the dark green canopy of the branching **lotus tree** *(micocoulier)*, which yields a fruit mentioned by Homer in the *Odyssey* as inducing a state of dreamy forgetfulness and loss of desire to return home – hence lotus-eaters. Some have identified it as the jujube tree.

The outline of the dark **cypress**, a coniferous evergreen, marks the Mediterranean landscape with its tapered form pointed towards the sky. It is often planted in serried ranks to form a windbreak.

Cypress

R. Corbel/MICHELIN

Almond tree

R. Corbel/MICHELIN

The cypress variety with scattered branches is used for reforestation.

The rosaceous species, the most common **almond tree** prevalent in Provence, bears lovely early spring pink blossoms.

The noble elm tree has practically disappeared from the landscape.

Forest Cover

There are not many forests in Provence and those that exist grow especially in the mountain ranges below 1 600m/5 251ft.

Fine forests of holm or downy oak grow in Grand Luberon, on Montagne Ste-Victoire, and on the Vaucluse plateau.

Petit Luberon is covered with a cedar forest. Beech tree forests grow on the north face of the Massif de la Ste-Baume. A moor of broom spreads along the limestone peaks.

The designation of the word forest beyond these areas indicates copses carpeting vast areas north of the Durance.

Garrigues

The word comes from the Provençal language – *garriga* – and defines an area of second-growth vegetation that appears on calcareous soils in the Mediterranean region following the destruction of the forest. Small *garrigues* can be found in most parts of Provence, but the vast stretch north of Nîmes, carved deeply by the River Gardon, is what most people think of when they hear "*garrigue*". Here the low limestone hills are interspersed with minute parcels of land between the outcrops of white calcareous rock; sometimes the rain has washed the soil down into the valleys leaving vast rocky table lands.

The sparse vegetation is mostly composed of holm oaks, stunted downy oaks, thistles, gorse and cistus, as well as lavender, thyme and rosemary. Short dry grass also provides pasture for flocks of sheep.

In addition to the wild aromatic plants that grow in the *garrigues*, herbs such as basil, marjoram, savory, sage, melissa, mint, laurel and absinth are cultivated commercially.

Environmental Threats

The natural habitat of Provence is under constant attack due to the influx of tourists, and to industrial and urban development.

Forest Fires

The Provençal forest is particularly vulnerable to fires (those of 1979, 1985, and 1986 were catastrophic), the majority of which are due to negligence or arson (most recently in 2005). Over time, these fires gradually disrupt the ecological balance. The oak forests are receding and the soil remains barren for a long period of time. Fire prevention and public awareness (especially that of tourists) will best help combat this devastating problem.

Dial 18 to reach the Fire Department (pompiers).

Pollution

The fast-developing urbanisation and industrialisation programmes in Provence have dealt a heavy blow to the beauty of many natural sites.

The Fos-sur-Mer industrial complex spreads out over the Plaine de la Crau; the area around Étang de Berre, especially its eastern side, has become the bustling suburb (airport, refineries, etc.) of Marseille. In 1957, owing to the high level of polluted water, fishing was strictly forbidden in the lagoon. Discharge of used water from the surrounding towns, St-Martin-de-Crau's rubbish tip and Marseille's main sewer flow into the Calanque Cortiou were all harmful.

Sadly, increased traffic in the region has necessarily resulted in the construction of more and more road networks that are cutting up the countryside and diminishing natural land.

CAVES AND CHASMS

In contrast to the deeply dissected green valleys with their settlements, the Bas Vivarais limestone plateaux roll away to the far horizon, grey and deserted. The calcareous nature of the rock absorbs rain like a sponge and makes the soil very dry.

At the end of the last century, the methodical, scientific exploration of the underground world, with which the name of **Édouard-Alfred Martel** is associated, led to the discovery of a number of caves, which have become a tourist attraction.

In 1935 **Robert de Joly** explored Aven d'Orgnac and encountered its wealth of cave formations. Later on, the discovery of a gaping hole in the chasm led in 1965 to the discovery of a vast network of upper galleries. Our knowledge of the underground system is at present very incomplete and a great many chasms remain unknown to speleologists.

Water Infiltration

Rainwater, charged with carbonic acid, dissolves the carbonate of lime in the region's limestone. Depressions then form that are usually circular in shape and small in size and are known as **cloups** or **sotchs**. This dissolution of the limestone rocks, containing salt or gypsum, produces rich soil particularly suitable for growing crops. When the cloups increase in size they form large, closed depressions known as **dolines**. Where rainwater infiltrates deeply through the fissures in the plateau, the hollowing out and dissolution of the calcareous layer produces wells or natural chasms that are called **avens** or **igues**. Little by little the chasms lengthen and branch off, communicating with each other and widening out into caves.

Underground Rivers

The infiltrating waters finally produce underground galleries and collect to form a more or less swift flowing river. The river widens its course and often changes level, falling in cascades. Where the rivers run slowly they form lakes, above natural dams, known as **gours**, which are raised layer by layer by deposits of carbonate of lime. The dissolution of the limestone also continues above the water level in these subterranean galleries: blocks of stone fall from the roof and domes form, the upper parts pointing towards the surface of the earth. Such is the case with the Upper Chamber at Orgnac, which lies only a few feet beneath the surface of the plateau. When the roof of the dome wears thin it may cave in, revealing the cavity from above and opening the chasm.

Cave Formation

As water circulates below ground it deposits the lime it carries, building up concretions of shapes that seem to defy the laws of gravity and equilibrium.

In some caverns, the seeping waters produce calcite (carbonate of lime) deposits that form pendants, pyramids, and draperies. The best known calcite formations are stalactites, stalagmites, and eccentrics.

Stalactites are formed from the cave roof. Each water droplet seeping through to the ceiling deposits on it some of the calcite with which it is charged, before dripping off. Gradually the concretion builds up layer by layer as the drops are attracted and run down its length, depositing particles before falling.

Stalagmites rise from the floor towards the roof. Drops of water, dripping from the roof in the same place, deposit the calcite particles they carry and build up to form a candle-like shape. This rises towards a stalactite with which it ultimately joins to form a pillar linking the cave floor with the ceiling. Concretions form very slowly indeed; the rate of growth in a temperate climate is about 1cm/0.4in every 100 years.

The **eccentrics** are fine protuberances which seldom exceed 20cm/8in in length. They emerge at any angle, either as slender spikes, or in the shape of small, translucent fans. They are formed by crystallisation and seem to disregard gravity. Aven d'Orgnac, Aven de Marzal and Grotte de la Madeleine contain some remarkable examples.

Arles by the Rhône River bank
©Nicolas Thibaut/Photononstop/Tips Images

AIX AND STE-VICTOIRE

If not the art capital of the world (that title might belong to Rome or Florence), Aix-en-Provence is, at the very least, in the top 10 of art-influencing cities in the world. A must-see for fans of Impressionism, as well as those of 18C architecture, painting and tapestries, this area is a vacation dream-come-true. The area also boasts a long and complex history of religion and politics. Aix is rooted in history. It was founded in 123–122 BC (by Sextius Calvinus), and has not stopped making contributions to world art, religion and education since. It was the capital of Provence during the Middle Ages, and welcomed a golden age of creativity in the 17C, 18C and 19C. Shoppers also flock to Aix, particularly for antiques, pottery and textiles. Provençal fabric dates back to the 17C, when silkworms were bred in the region. Many cotton fabrics are still made using the same techniques that have been used for more than 200 years. Options include fabrics as well as fashions made with the signature regional designs.

Highlights

1 Enchanting clocktower of place de l'Hôtel-de Ville, **Aix-en-Provence** (p114)

2 Possibly the prettiest of all Aix's fountains, **Fontaine des Quatre Dauphins** (p115)

3 Three tiers of intriguing arches, **Aqueduc de Roquefavour** (p117)

4 International Opera and Music Festival (p119)

5 The summit of **Croix de Provence** (p123)

No matter what time of year you plan your trip, you'll be able to find a uniquely-Aix event taking place, making you feel like you chose the perfect time for your trip. In December the Christmas Concert by the Tambourin Academy joins displays of nativity figures, many special mass services and restaurants sporting menus with 13 traditional, symbolic desserts. Spring also brings a lovely mass with Provençal songs at the priory chapel on Ste-Victoire, as well as the festival of the Provence tambourin, and drumming contexts.

For easy trip-planning, the city can be divided into sections, all of which have some must-sees:

The old town (called **Old Aix**) is where the old Roman town once reigned. Stops there include Place de l'Université, home to the Romanesque delights of the St-Sauveur Cathédrale and Cloister, and Cours Mirabeau, the city's main boulevard.

Next up is the tiny **Quartier Mazarin**, built in the 17C and home to some of the city's favourite museums, including the Musée des Tapisseries and the renovated Musée Granet. Don't miss the many decorative fountains around town. In fact, there are so many water features the area is sometimes called "the city of a thousand fountains".

Just 10km/6mi east of Aix is **Ste-Victoire**, both a geographic and artistic landmark for the region. The limestone mountain was the frequent subject of the works of Paul Cézanne; he painted more than 50 images of the peak. Pablo Picasso owned land here and was buried here in 1973.

But the mount isn't just for artistic revelry. Walking and climbing routes available include one that follows 17C pilgrimages, and there are several small villages dotted on the mountain.

Aix-en-Provence★★

Bouches-du-Rhône

This old capital of Provence has kept a great deal of its 17C and 18C character: the sober elegance of its mansions, the graceful charm of its squares, the majesty of its avenues, and the loveliness of its fountains. Aix is also a lively city whose large student population is abundantly evident on the busy café terraces. Around old Aix a new town has developed that is both a spa and an industrial complex – it is the largest centre in France and Europe for processed almonds. Part of the production is used to make the cakes and confectionery of Aix, including the local speciality, sugar-coated *calissons*.

A BIT OF HISTORY
Good King René (1409–80)

Some traces of a prosperous civilisation in Aix under the Roman Emperor Augustus can still be seen in the sophisticated statuary in the Musée Granet. At the end of the 12C, the counts of Provence held a refined and literate court at Aix. The development of the town continued during the 13C, and yet in the 14C its surface area diminished. In 1409 Louis II of Anjou founded the university, but Aix's golden age occurred later, in the second half of the 15C under the reign of Good King René.

A city of 4 000–5 000 people, a bishopric and county seat, Aix exerted a strong influence over the neighbouring countryside, occupied by wealthy townspeople and enhanced by Italian craftsmen. Within the walls lived the burghers, aristocrats and farmers; this category included the shepherds responsible for ensuring a return on livestock investments made by a handful of powerful merchants.

Second son to Louis II and Yolanda of Aragon, René became Duke of Anjou, Count of Provence, and titular King of Sicily and Naples at the death of his older

- ▶ **Population:** 142 534
- ⚲ **Michelin Map:** 340: H-4 or 114 folds 15 and 16 or 528 fold 31 or 524 fold J.
- **Info:** 2 place du Gén.-de-Gaulle, 13100 Aix-en-Provence. ℘04 42 16 11 61. www.aixenprovence tourism.com.
- ◑ **Location** – Take a guided tour of the town (2hr); for information, contact the tourist office (◔*see above*). Buy a 2€ "Pass Card" at the tourist office; use it to receive reduced admissions on guided tours, shows and museums.
- Ⓟ **Parking:** Parking is scarce. Avoid the old town and look for spaces on bd. du Roi-René or on bd. Aristide Briand. Try the covered car parks but these fill up quickly.
- ⊛ **Don't Miss:** The cours Mirabeau and the old town; place Albertas and the Four-Dolphins fountain; the newly renovated Musée Granet; and, of course, Cézanne's sites.
- ◷ **Timing:** Allow half a day for Cézanne's sites and half a day for the old town. Don't miss the markets: you'll come across one every morning.
- ⚇ **Kids:** Visit the dinosaur eggs in the Musée d'Histoire Naturelle, a *calisson* or *santon* maker, and the *santons* fair in December.

brother, Louis III, in 1434. René spoke Latin, Greek, Italian, Hebrew and Catalan. He played and composed music, painted illuminations with meticulous detail, wrote verses, understood mathematics, astrology and geology. In short, René possessed one of the most univer-

King René

sal minds of his time. He was an enlightened patron of the arts, in particular Flemish painters. Dating from his rule are the famous triptychs of the *Annunciation* (said to be by the Master of King René) and the *Burning Bush* painted by Nicolas Froment (of Languedoc origin, he studied in Flanders and Burgundy). By the end of the 15C some 40 artists of quality lived and worked in Aix under contract to René and his nobles. They produced prestigious works of art and contributed to the decoration of mystery plays and popular festivals (such as Corpus Christi, which underwent a brilliant revival).

A man of arts and letters, René did not neglect his obligations as a ruler; he legislated, stimulated commerce and encouraged agriculture. He introduced the Muscat grape into Provence and on occasion cultivated his own vineyards. He was concerned with the health standards of his people and instituted a public service of doctors and surgeons, promulgated a sanitation law and ordained the cleaning up of the different quarters of the city. He was, however, criticised for his heavy taxation as well as his weak currency; the coins he minted, called *parpaillottes*, were of rather base alloy.

At the age of 12, René married Isabelle of Lorraine, who brought him as dowry the Duchy of Lorraine. Their younger daughter, Margaret of Anjou (1430–82), married the English King, Henry VI (1421–71) in 1445. Two years after the death of Isabelle (at 44) to whom he had remained tenderly attached for 33 years, René married Jeanne of Laval, aged 21. This second marriage was as happy as the first. Queen Jeanne, who should not be confused with the 14C Queen Joan I of Sicily, was as popular as her elderly husband among the people of Provence.

Having lost both his son and two grandsons, King René sadly observed his nephew Louis XI annex Anjou to the kingdom of France. Thereafter, instead of dividing his time between Angers and Provence, René never set foot outside the land of sunshine and died in Aix in 1480, aged 71. His nephew Charles of Maine, who had been chosen as his heir, died one year later.

The New Faces of Aix

After the union of Provence to France in 1486, a governor appointed by the king lived in Aix. In 1501 the city became

The Legend of Saint Mitre

Mitre was born in 433 in Thessalonica, Greece, from where he emigrated to Aix to lead a humble life. He preached against the adultery of Arvendus, a local Roman magistrate. According to legend, Arvendus framed Mitre with sabotaging grapes from his vineyard. Through Mitre's prayers, the grapes miraculously sprouted back on the trees. Accused of witchcraft and beheaded, Mitre picked up his head and carried it to the Église Notre-Dame de la Seds *(located at 22 avenue Jean Dalmas)*, where he passed away. In 1383, his relics were transferred to the Cathédrale St-Sauveur. It is said that a liquid seeped out from the right-hand column supporting his white marble tomb, which was used to cure eye sores.

the seat of a newly created parliament, and as a result, in the 17C it experienced another period of growth as one of its social classes became prominent – the men of law. These well-to-do judges and lawyers led stimulating and active lives and consequently proceeded to build magnificent townhouses *(hôtels)* worthy of their name and rank.

At the same time, the urban landscape was transformed: new areas of the city sprang up and developed rapidly (notably the Quartier Mazarin, south of the city); the old ramparts were razed and replaced by an avenue for carriages, which later became cours Mirabeau. In the 18C, the city continued its transformation, with its wide avenues, squares, fountains and new buildings. The old county palace was demolished and a new law court was built in its place.

Into the Modern Age

After the Revolution, Aix suffered a decline as a result of ever-prospering Marseille, although it retained its court and its university.

It was not until the 1970s that it experienced a two fold revival: economic, with the installation of high-tech industries; and cultural, with the growing influence of the university and the creation of the music festival. This growth in economic activity and population was accompanied by a major town-planning project, the extension of cours Sextius and cours Mirabeau, of which the Cité du Livre is the first stage, and which will help to redefine Aix in the 21C.

CÉZANNE
A BIT OF HISTORY

Born in Aix in 1839, **Paul Cézanne** studied at the Collège Bourbon (now Collège Mignet), where he became friends with Émile Zola. He chose "humanities," then enrolled at the Faculty of Law in accordance with his father's wishes, while at the same time painting and writing poetry in the countryside around Jas de Bouffan. This residence in the midst of parkland, acquired by his father in 1859, was a

Cézanne, who loved Aix

In a letter to his son in 1906, Cézanne described his admiration for Aix:
"I go to the country every day, the motifs are beautiful and so my day is spent more pleasantly here than anywhere else".

propitious setting for the development of his artistic work.

Although Cézanne became friendly with Impressionist painters in Paris, he was not successful there. It was on his return to Aix that fame came to him, thanks to the good name he had made for himself among painters such as Monet, Manet, Sisley, and above all, Pissarro.

However, it was not long before Cézanne shook off Impressionist techniques. Using large, luminous patches of colour and juxtaposing them in new ways, he created shapes with exaggerated outlines and relief but simple in form. The countryside around Aix became the dominant subject of his painting. Fleeing Paris in 1870, Cézanne settled at L'Estaque in his mother's house. Finally, in 1904 he achieved recognition in the Paris Autumn Salon.

The **Cézanne Tour** (*see Addresses*) includes a visit to the parts of town habitually frequented by the artist and the areas of the surrounding countryside from which he drew inspiration, in particular **Mont Ste-Victoire**.

Atelier Paul Cézanne (Cézanne's Studio)

9 av. Paul-Cézanne, in the north of Aix along av. Pasteur. Open daily *Jul–Aug 10am–6pm; Apr–Jun and Sept 10am–noon, 2–6pm; Oct–Nov and Mar 10am–noon, 2–5pm; Dec–Feb Mon–Sat 10am–noon, 2–5pm.* Closed 1–3 Jan, *1 May and 25 Dec.* 2€. *Guided tours (30min) daily Apr–Sept 5pm; Oct–Mar 4pm.* 04 42 21 06 53. *www.atelier-cezanne.com.*
When his mother died in 1897, Cézanne had a traditional Provençal-style house built about 500m/547yd from the

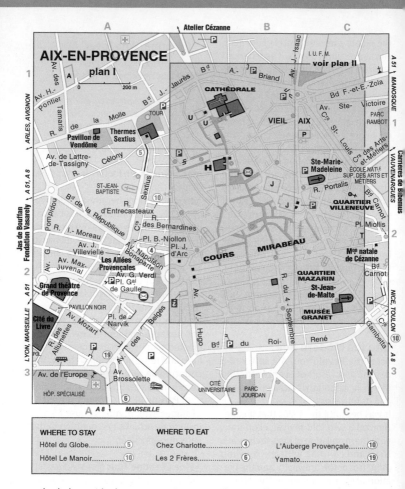

WHERE TO STAY

Hôtel du Globe.................⑤
Hôtel Le Manoir.............⑩

WHERE TO EAT

Chez Charlotte.................④
Les 2 Frères...................⑥

L'Auberge Provençale.........⑩
Yamato..............................⑲

cathedral, outside the ramparts. It was surrounded by a garden with colourful leafy plants growing right up to the windows of the artist's studio.

The studio, called the *Lauves*, where he painted *The Bathers*, among other works, has been left as it was at his death in 1906. A few items of memorabilia are on view.

✎ WALKING TOUR
OLD AIX★★
Allow half a day, including 1hr30min for Quartier Mazarin.

❍ *Start from place du Général-de-Gaulle, more commonly known as the "Rotonde", where there is a monumental fountain.*

The ring of boulevards and squares that encircles the old town marks the line of the ancient ramparts. North of cours Mirabeau, the town's focal point, lies Old Aix, tucked between the cathedral and place d'Albertas. The many pedestrian streets criss-crossing this area make it the perfect setting for an exploratory stroll.

Cours Mirabeau★★
This wide avenue, shaded by fine plane trees, is the hub of Aix, where a verdant tunnel of foliage protects against the hot Provençal sun.

Built in the 17C on the site of the medieval ramparts, the avenue originally had no shops or boutiques, yet, Aix's life now revolves around this very area. Lining the north side of the street are cafés (e.g.

VIEIL AIX
plan II

the **Café des Deux Garçons** at no **53**, once an important meeting place for artists and writers) and shops. A number of bookshops reveal Aix's intellectual and scholarly vocation. On the other side stand the aristocratic façades of the old hotels with their finely carved doorways and wrought-iron balconies supported by caryatids or atlantes from the Puget School.

Hôtel d'Isoard de Vauvenargues

10 cours Mirabeau.

This mansion was built around 1710 with a wrought-iron balcony and fluted lintel. The Marchioness of Entrecasteaux, Angélique de Castellane, was murdered here by her husband, the president of parliament.

Summer evening at Cours Mirabeau

©Romain Cintract/hemis/Photolibrary

Fontaine d'eau thermale

Farther up cours Mirabeau, at its junction with rue Clemenceau, is a natural hot water fountain covered with moss, dating from 1734, whose waters gush out at 34°C/93°F.

Fontaine du Roi René

This fountain marks the end of the avenue. Carved by David d'Angers (19C), the fountain portrays King René holding a bunch of muscat grapes, which he introduced to Provence.

Hôtel du Poët

1 pl. Haut du Cours Mirabeau.
This dates from 1730 and closes off the view down cours Mirabeau to the east. The three-tiered façade is decorated with *mascarons* and some pretty ironwork adorns the first floor balcony.

▷ *Take the street to the right of the Hôtel du Poët.*

Rue de l'Opéra

There are a number of houses of interest on this street. No **18** Hôtel de Lestang-Parade was built around 1650 by Pavillon and Rambot and remodelled in 1830. No **24** Hôtel de Bonnecorse (or Arlatan-Lauris) dates from the 18C. No **26** Hôtel de Grimaldi was constructed in 1680 after drawings by Puget. And no **28** was Cézanne's birthplace.

▷ *Return towards the Théâtre du Jeu de Paume, turning right and then left into rue Émeric David.*

Hôtel de Panisse-Passis

16 r. Émeric David.
Built in 1739, the façade is enhanced by fine wrought-iron and corbelled balconies with fantastically carved heads.

Église Ste-Marie-Madeleine

pl. des Prêcheurs. ◷*Open daily 8.30am–11.30am.* ℰ*04 42 38 02 81.*
The church's west front is modern although the church itself dates to the 17C. At the end of the south aisle, in the fourth chapel, an 18C marble **Virgin**★ by Chastel can be seen. The central panel of the 15C **Triptych of the Annunciation**★ hangs in the north aisle – near the altar to Our Gracious Lady (the other two panels are elsewhere) – and was ordered around 1443–45; it's attributed to Barthélemy d'Eyck, an artist who used *chiaroscuro* effects subtly and inventively.

Fontaine des Prêcheurs

pl. des Prêcheurs.
In this square, you will find Chastel's 18C fountain. Note the atlantes that decorate the doorway of the **Hôtel d'Agut** at no **2** (the former residence of Achille Emperaire, a contemporary of Cézanne), before taking rue Thiers,

Place d'Albertas

©Sean Nel/IStockphoto.com

The Marriage of Mirabeau

Aix played an important role in the life of Honoré Gabriel Riqueti, Count of Mirabeau. He married here in 1772 and was divorced here in 1783. It was here, too, that he was elected to the Estates General in 1789.

The fiery Mirabeau was only 23 when he married Mlle de Marignane. The bride was a rich heiress, and among her suitors featured the best of Provence nobility. Mirabeau, although a count, was ill-favoured. With a big head and a face disfigured by smallpox, he was penniless and moreover had a scandalous reputation. But he was aware of the mysterious attraction he held for women. Cynically, he made a show of his good fortune and left his coach at the door of the Hôtel de Marignane (*see Quartier Mazarin*) before spending the night there. After this scandal, a marriage had to take place. But Mirabeau's father-in-law showed resentment by cutting off the young couple's allowance. Mirabeau displayed no embarrassment at this blow and promptly ran up 200 000 *livres* of debts with Aix merchants. Their complaints were such that a warrant was issued sending him under house arrest to Château d'If and subsequently Fort Joux, where he published his *Essay on Despotism*.

Mirabeau returned to Aix in 1783 to answer a summons for separation instituted by his wife. The eminent orator presented his own defence. His prodigious eloquence secured him victory at a first hearing but he lost on appeal, although it is said that his pleading aroused such enthusiasm and the violence of his language was such that the opposing counsel fainted!

1789 saw the elections to the Estates General. The Count of Mirabeau, who had met with only contempt and rebuff among his peers, decided to represent not nobility but the Third Estate. His election was a triumph and his historic role as an orator began; however, it was also the beginning of Aix's downfall.

where at no **2** you will find the 17C **Hôtel de Roquesante**.
Rue Thiers leads to the top of cours Mirabeau; take the right-hand pavement. At no **55** note the sign of a hat shop founded by Cézanne's father in 1825.

○ *Turn right into rue Fabrot.*

The pedestrian-only rue Fabrot leads to place St-Honoré.

○ *Take rue Espariat.*

Hôtel Boyer d'Éguilles
6 r. Espariat.
This townhouse was built in 1675, most probably by Pierre Puget. Entrance is through a large *porte cochère* that opens into the main courtyard. The **Musée d'Histoire Naturelle** is housed here (*see entry, p116*).

Place d'Albertas★
This square was opened in 1745 and was embellished with a fountain in 1912. It is arranged very much in the style of Parisian squares and has lovely mansions all around it. Concerts are held here every summer.

Hôtel d'Albertas
10 pl. d'Albertas.
Built in 1707, this hôtel includes carvings by the sculptor Toro.

○ *Bear right into rue de l'Aude.*

Hôtel Peyronetti
13 r. de l'Aude.
Italian Renaissance in style, it dates from 1620.

○ *Follow rue du Maréchal-Foch.*

Hôtel d'Arbaud
7 r. Maréchal Foch.
Fine atlantes frame the doorway.

Aix Pass Card

As well as providing a valuable discount to museums and monuments in Aix, the Aix Pass Card also entitles the bearer to discounts to sites in the Aix region and a reduction on Aix network buses. The card can be purchased from tourist offices and participating sites for 2€. A five-day Aix City Pass is also available (≈15€), which includes a free tour of Cézanne's studio and a guided tour of Aix by mini-tram.

Place Richelme

The south façade of the old grain market runs alongside this square, which is broken into sections by two corner statues. *Every morning there is a fresh fruit and vegetable market here.*

Place de l'Hôtel de Ville★

The northwest corner of this attractive square is overlooked by the **clock tower**, which in the 16C used to be the town's belfry. A bell in a wrought-iron cage also dates from the 16C. Each season is represented by a different character. This is also the site of the weekly flower market.

Hôtel de Ville

Built between 1655 and 1670, the town hall was designed by the Parisian architect Pierre Pavillon. Around the splendid paved **courtyard**★, the buildings are divided by pilasters of the Classical order (*see INTRODUCTION – Art*). There is a niche with scrolls on the inside façade.

Ancienne Halle aux Grains

This former grain market was built to the south of the square in the mid-18C. The central part of the building projects forward and is embellished with a pediment carved by Chastel, depicting the Rhône and the Durance. This sculptor spent his life in Aix, a fact evidenced by the many works of art left behind by him. The grain market now houses a post office and administrative centre.

▷ *Go along rue Gaston-de-Saporta.*

In place des Martyrs de la Résistance is the 17C former archbishop's palace, the courtyard of which is used for the music festival, while the buildings house the **Musée des Tapisseries**★ (*see entry, p116*).

Cloître St-Sauveur★

34 pl. des Martyrs de la Résistance. ⊙*Open daily except during religious services May–Oct 9.30am–noon, 2.30–5.30pm.* *Guided tours.* ℘04 42 23 45 65. www.cathedrale-aix.net. These Romanesque cloisters are a delight. The arcades are not buttressed, giving the cloisters a delicate quality. The paired columns and the capitals are adorned with leaves and add elegance to the construction. On a fine corner pillar you will discover a remarkably carved St Peter.

▷ *A door northwest of the cloisters gives access to the adjoining cathedral.*

Cathédrale St-Sauveur★

Rue Gaston-de-Saporta. ⊙*Open daily except during religious services 7.30am–noon, 2–6pm.* ℘04 42 23 45 65. www.cathedrale-aix.net. St-Sauveur is a curious building decorated in all styles from the 5C to the 17C. In the Gothic central nave hang two 15C triptychs. Of the first triptych, depicting the Passion, only the central panel is from the 15C. The second series, the **Triptych of the Burning Bush**★★, is made by Nicolas Froment, court painter to King René. The king and his queen are shown kneeling on either side of the Virgin. The Virgin holding the infant Jesus is in the Burning Bush, similar to that in which God appeared to Moses.

Behind the altar, in the Chapel of St-Mitre, hangs the *Martyrdom of St Mitre*, attributed to the School of Nicolas Froment. The doorway is closed by **panels**★ *(masked by false doors)* in walnut; this sculpture in wood by Jean

Guiramand of Toulon represents the four prophets of Israel and 12 pagan sibyls. The cathedral's west front includes to the right a door in the Romanesque Provençal style, in the middle a Gothic part (early 16C) and to the left a Gothic bell tower (14C–15C).

▶ *Return to cours Mirabeau via place de l'Hôtel de Ville and rue Vauvenargues, rue Méjanes, rue des Bagniers and rue Clemenceau.*

Hôtel d'Arbaud-Jouques
19 cours Mirabeau.
Built in 1700, this building displays a finely decorated stone façade with a carved frieze underlining the first floor.

▶ *Turn left into rue Laroque and then left again into rue Mazarine.*

QUARTIER MAZARIN★
1hr30min
This district of orderly design was built between 1646 and 1651 by the Archbishop Michel Mazarin, brother of the famous cardinal of the same name.

Hôtel de Marignane
12 r. Mazarine.
Late 17C. This hôtel was the scene of Mirabeau's scandalous behaviour towards Mlle. de Marignane.

Fontaine des Quatre-Dauphins★
pl. des Quatre-Dauphins.
At the centre of a small square stands the charming fountain by J.C. Ribaut from 1667.

Église St-Jean-de-Malte
24–26 r. d'Italie. ○*Open daily 10am–noon, 3–7pm.* ☎*04 42 38 25 70. http://moinesdiocesains-aix.cef.fr.*
The church, dating from the late 13C, was the chapel of the Knights of Malta, and was Aix's first Gothic building. Although the façade is austere, the **nave**★ presents the elegant decorative detail of the High Gothic.

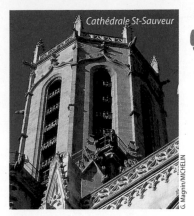
Cathédrale St-Sauveur
G. Magnin/MICHELIN

MUSEUMS
Musée Granet★
pl. St Jean-de-Malte. ○*Open Tue–Sun Jun–Sept 11am–7pm; Oct–May noon–6pm.* ○*Closed 1 Jan, 1 May, 25 Dec.* ▸*Guided tours (1hr30min) 3€.* ◦*4€ (no charge first Sun in month).* ☎*04 42 52 88 32. www.musecgranet-aixen provence.fr.*
On display in this museum is a collection of paintings including the legacies of the Aix painter **François Marius Granet** (1775–1849).
Works from the great European Schools spanning the 16C–19C are exhibited. A gallery devoted entirely to Cézanne presents eight of his paintings. You'll also find works by Klee, Giacometti, Picasso and Mondrian as well as local archaeology finds.

Musée des Tapisseries★
28 pl. des Martyrs de la Résistance. ○*Open Wed–Mon 10am–11.45am, 2–5.45pm.* ○*Closed 1 Jan, 1 May and 25 Dec.* ◦*3€.* ☎*04 42 23 09 91.*
Housed in the former bishop's palace, the Tapestry Museum presents in particular the 19 magnificent tapestries made in Beauvais in the 17C and 18C, including nine famous panels illustrating the life of Don Quixote, after cartoons by Natoire.

Fondation Vasarely★
1 av. Marcel Pagnol, Jas de Bouffan. &○*Open Tue–Sat 10am–1pm, 2–6pm, ticket office closes 30min before*

museum. ∞7€. ℘04 42 20 01 09.
www.fondationvasarely.fr.
This foundation, created by Hungarian artist Victor Vasarely (1906–97), stands on a hill to the west of Aix.
The vast building, consisting of 16 hexagonal structures, has sober façades decorated with circles on alternately black and white squares. Vasarely's research led him to geometric abstractions via lines and graphics. In 1955, the artist evolved into a field where by various optical means he was able to produce visual illusion without the use of movement.

Cité du Livre

8–10 r. des Allumettes. *Méjanes library:* ⊙open Tue, Thu and Fri noon–6pm, Wed and Sat 10am–6pm. ℘04 42 91 98 88. www.citedulivre-aix.com.
The City of Books is a bibliophile's dream. Housed in a modern glass and metal structure, it is home to the prestigious Méjanes library – the 1786 legacy of the Marquis de Méjanes: 80 000 volumes. The project has also opened up new spaces for artistic creation in Aix, most notably a 1 300-seat auditorium, currently the home base of the Ballet Preljocaj *(www.preljocaj.org)*. Numerous events and exhibits are organised in the premises.

♣♣ Musée d'Histoire Naturelle

6 r. Espariat. ⊙Open daily, 10am–noon, 1–5pm. ∞3€ (child no charge). ℘04 42 27 91 27. www.museum-aix-en-provence.org.
This Natural History Museum houses interesting collections of mineralogy and paleontology. The palaeontology section includes general as well as local exhibits, notably a collection of dinosaur eggs from the slopes of Mont Ste-Victoire.

Musée du Vieil Aix

17 r. Gaston-de-Saporta. ⊙Open Tue–Sun Apr–Oct 10am–noon, 2.30–6pm; Nov–Mar 10am–noon, 2–5pm. ⊙Closed public holidays. ∞4€. ℘04 42 21 43 55.
Located in the Hôtel d'Estienne de St-Jean (17C), attributed to Laurent Vallon, the museum presents local memorabilia. On display is a collection of marionettes evoking the talking cribs and the local Corpus Christi procession, porcelain from Moustiers, and *santons*.

🚗 DRIVING TOURS

Montagne Ste-Victoire★★★
Round trip of 74km/46mi, Ⓒ see p122.

Vallée de l'Arc
Round trip of 56km/35mi – about 3hr.

▷ *Leave Aix-en-Provence on N 8 towards Marseille as far as Bouc-Bel-Air.*

Jardins d'Albertas★
At La Croix-d'Or. ♿⊙Open May–Oct; for specific times please call before visit. ∞6€. ℘04 91 59 84 94. www.jardins albertas.com.
These gardens were laid out in 1751 by the Marquis Jean-Baptiste d'Albertas. They blend together different styles including Italian (terraces, antique statues, artifical cave with the Triton fountain); French (flower beds and canals), and Provençal (rows of plane trees).

▷ *At San Baquis, turn right onto D 60A.*

Cabriès
Cabriès is a picturesque hill village with a castle accessed through a clock gateway and a network of narrow streets inside what used to be its fortified town wall.

▶ *Take D 8 back to rejoin D 543 and at Calas, turn left onto 9B, then D 9. Drive alongside the Réaltor Reservoir, a fine 58ha/143-acre stretch of water set amid lush vegetation, and take D 65D to the right, crossing over the Marseille canal. After Mérindolle, turn left.*

Aqueduc de Roquefavour★
This fine aqueduct was constructed to transport the Canal de Marseille across the Arc valley at a point 12km/7.4mi west of Aix-en-Provence. Built from 1842 to 1847 under the direction of Montricher, the aqueduct is made up of three stages – three tiers of arches – supporting the water channel; it is 375m/1 230ft long and 83m/272ft high. Its lower level has 12 arches, the middle level 15 arches, and the top level with its 53 smaller arches carries the canal which transports the waters of the Durance to Marseille.

▶ *Follow D 65 towards Salon-de-Provence and 300m/328yd further on bear right on D 64 uphill.*

Top level of Roquefavour Aqueduct (Sommet)

▶ *After 2km/1mi bear right on a path towards Petit Rigouès and right again to the keeper's house located on the aqueduct's topmost level.*

From the plateau's edge there is a lovely view of the Aix basin, Montagne Ste-Victoire and the Étoile chain. From the car park walk to the top level of the aqueduct where the canal runs.

▶ *Return to D 64 and turn right.*

Ventabren
This tiny village is dominated by Queen Jeanne's castle, now in ruins. Take rue du Cimetière to the foot of the castle ruins to enjoy the splendid **view** of the Berre lagoon, Martigues, the Caronte gap and the Vitrolles chain.

▶ *From D 64A rejoin D 10 on the right, then turn left onto D 543 for the village of Éguilles.*

Éguilles
The village, which has a wonderful view of the Arc valley, is situated on the old Aurelian Way, the present D 17. The town hall, an old castle bought by the Boyer d'Éguilles family in the 17C, has a beautiful façade interspersed with mullioned windows on four levels. From the esplanade, there is a magnificent **view** of the Étoile chain, Les Milles and the Aix plain through which the TGV Med line passes. Stroll through the village to explore the old wash-houses.

▶ *Leave Éguilles to the NE on D 63, and turn right onto D 14. Then take the path to the left up to the plateau d'Entremont.*

Oppidum d'Entremont
🕐*Open Wed–Mon 9am–noon, 2–6pm.* 🕐*Closed 1 Jan, 1 May, 1 and 11 Nov, 25 Dec.* ✆*No charge.* ℘*04 42 99 10 00.* *www.entremont.culture.gouv.fr.*
This capital of the Celtic-Ligurian Saluvii *(les Salyens)* resembled a fortified town by 2C BC, with a surface area of 3.5ha/8.6 acres. It was protected by steep slopes on one side and to the north by ramparts with a sturdy curtain wall reinforced with round towers set at regular intervals. Between two of the towers on the ramparts is a gateway where archaeologists think the Saluvii may have displayed the skulls of their enemies.
Excavations have uncovered many artefacts and works of art, proving that the *oppidum* possessed a high level of civilisation. Entremont artefacts may be seen at the **Musée Granet** (👁 *see entry, p115*).

ADDRESSES

🏠 STAY

Hôtel du Globe – *74 cours Sextius. ℰ04 42 26 03 58. www.hotelduglobe.com. Closed 20 Dec–20 Jan. 46 rooms. ⊡8€.* Rooms are bright, well kept and sound-proofed, and but not luxurious. Good value.

Hôtel Cardinal – *24 r. Cardinale. ℰ04 42 38 32 30. 29 rooms, 6 suites. ⊡8€.* In an 18C building, in the quiet Mazarin quarter, this hotel has old-fashioned elegance and today's comfort. Its location is perfect for exploring the town on foot.

Hôtel St-Christophe – *2 av. Victor-Hugo. ℰ04 42 26 01 24. www.hotel-saintchristophe.com. 60 rooms. ⊡10.80€. Restaurant.* This hotel is right in the centre of the city, near cours Mirabeau, and rooms are decorated in either a 1930s or Provençal style. The lively Brasserie Léopold is decorated in the Art Deco style and offers regional cuisine and typical brasserie dishes. Pavement terrace in fine weather.

Hôtel Le Manoir – *8 r. d'Entrecasteaux. ℰ04 42 26 27 20. www.hotelmanoir.com. Closed 5–25 Jan. 40 rooms. ⊡8€.* A lovely old building, formerly a hat factory. Part of an adjoining 14C cloister has been converted into a summer terrace, creating a unique atmosphere.

Hôtel des Augustins – *3 r. de la Masse. ℰ04 42 27 28 59. www.hotel-augustins.com. 29 rooms. ⊡8€.* Stone vaulting and stained glass are reminders of the origins of this hotel, a stone's throw from cours Mirabeau, which was originally a 15C convent. The rooms, of which two have terraces with rooftop views, are decorated in a modern style.

🍴 EAT

Pizza Capri – *1 r. Fabrot. ℰ04 42 38 55 43. www.pizza-capri.fr.* Very good pizzeria, also serving paninis. Good value for money.

L'Auberge Provençale – *19 cours Mirabeau. ℰ04 42 93 12 51. Closed Mon lunch, Sun.* This is a retreat with a luminous, verdant patio-veranda. All the flavours of Provence and Italy are at your fingertips.

Chez Antoine Côté Cour – *19 cours Mirabeau. ℰ04 42 93 12 51. Closed Mon lunch, Sun.* This is a retreat with a luminous, verdant patio-veranda. All the flavours of Provence and Italy are at your fingertips. Try the *aubergines à la parmesane* and the *calamars farcis*.

Chez Charlotte – *32 r. des Bernardines. ℰ04 42 26 77 56. Closed Aug, Sun–Mon, 24–25, 31 Dec.* Upon entering you are greeted with a nostalgic atmosphere. The main dining room's décor is dedicated to the cinema. Offering traditional and seasonal cuisine, the owner gives special attention to every dish.

La Cigale – *48 r. Espariat. ℰ04 42 26 20 62. Closed 24 Dec–5 Jan and Sun (except summer).* In addition to pizzas, classic dishes are on offer. Graceful décor and a terrace in good weather.

Le Formal – *32 r. Espariat. ℰ04 42 27 08 31. Closed 27 Aug–9 Sept, Sat lunch, Sun–Mon.* A restaurant occupying 15C vaulted cellars adorned with a collection of contemporary paintings. Inventive, well-presented cuisine.

Les 2 Frères – *4 av. Reine-Astrid. ℰ04 42 27 90 32. www.les2freres.com.* As the name suggests, this restaurant is run by two brothers: the older one prepares the delicious, modern cuisine (his labours projected onto a screen in the dining room), while his sibling works front of house. Trendy bistro atmosphere.

Yamato – *21 av. des Belges. ℰ04 42 38 00 20. Closed Mon (except eve in Jul), Tue lunch.* Guests are made to feel very welcome in this small Japanese restaurant. The décor is traditionally Japanese. Veranda, terrace and garden.

Pierre Reboul – *11 Petite-Rue-St-Jean. ℰ04 42 20 58 26. www.restaurant-pierre-reboul.com. Closed 20 Dec–4 Jan, Sun–Mon.* In the heart of the old town, this elegant contemporary restaurant specialises in delicious and innovative cuisine, which focuses on ingredients' quality.

⊖⊜⊜⊜ **Chez Féraud** – *8 r. du Puits-Juif.* 🖀*04 42 63 07 27. Closed Aug, Sun and Mon.* Tucked away in an Old Quarter lane, an appealing place with typical local cuisine (pistou, daube) and grills.

🍷 NIGHTLIFE

Café des Deux Garçons – *53 bis cours Mirabeau.* 🖀*04 42 26 00 51.* Bordered by plane trees, cours Mirabeau's 13 cafés are very popular. The Deux Garçons, known more familiarly as "le 2 G", is the oldest (1792) and most famous of these cafés. Cézanne and Zola used to meet here in the afternoon.

Château de la Pioline – *260 r. Guillaume-du-Vair, Les Milles.* 🖀*04 42 52 27 27. www.chateaudelapioline.fr.* The bar of this hotel-restaurant (16C) is superbly decorated in the style of the Medicis and Louis XVI. Don't miss the large terrace overlooking the 4ha/10-acre French garden.

🛒 SHOPPING

Markets – 👥 **Traditional market** every morning in place Richelme and every Tuesday, Thursday, and Saturday on place des Prêcheurs and place de la Madeleine. **Flower market** every Tuesday, Thursday and Saturday in place de l'Hôtel de Ville, and in place des Prêcheurs on other days.

Antiques – **Antiques market** every Tuesday, Thursday and Saturday in place Verdun. **Antiques fairs** take place in the centre of town every 1st Sun of the month 9am–6pm. Check with the tourist office. **Village des Antiquaires du Quartier de Lignane**, *RN 7, Lignane, 13540 Puyricard.* The place to hunt for antiques.

Crafts – Makers of vases, ceramics, fabrics, baskets and jewellery display their wares on cours Mirabeau at the end of Mar, in mid-May, mid-Jun, mid-October, and mid-Nov.

👥 **Calissons** – Legend has it that these treats were invented to sweeten up Jeanne for her marriage to King René. It seems she felt much happier about her fate after savouring a *calisson* made of almonds, sugar and candied melon. Two exemplary and long-established

places to try these delights include: **Calissons Léonard Parli** – *35 av. Victor Hugo.* 🖀*04 42 26 05 71. www.leonard-parli.com. Closed Sun;* **Confiserie du Roy René** – *13 r. Gaston-de-Saporta.* 🖀*04 42 26 67 86. www.calisson.com.*

Apéritifs – The definitive shop for Provençal liquors and aperitifs is **Liquoisterie de Venelles**, *36 av. de la Grand-Béude, 13770 Venelles.* 🖀*04 42 54 94 65. www.versinthe.net.* Free tours and tastings.

🎎**Santons Fouque** – *65 cours Gambetta.* 🖀*04 42 26 33 38. www.santons-fouque.com.* Visit the atelier where these figurines are made.

Books – **Cité du Livre**, *8–10 r. des Allumettes* is a haven for book lovers. 🖀*04 42 91 98 88. www.citedulivre-aix.com.*

🎭 CALENDAR OF EVENTS

International Opera and Music Festival (www.festival-aix.com) Founded in 1948 by Gabriel Dussurget, this prestigious festival takes place every summer in the courtyard of the archbishop's palace which is converted into a theatre for the event. Concerts and recitals are held in the cathedral, the cloisters of St-Saveur and the Hôtel Maynier d'Oppède. The festival focuses on important operas (in particular those by Mozart) as well as Baroque opera and contemporary music. Among the many illustrious artists who have contributed to the high standards of the festival are conductors Hans Rosbaud and Carlo Maria Giulini and the acclaimed singer Teresa Berganza.

Santons Fair – These figurines can be purchased from *end Nov–Feb along cours Mirabeau.*

Wine Festival – **Festival des Vins et Coteaux d'Aix** – *cours Mirabeau – last Sun in Jul.* An opportunity to sample the rich variety from the vineyards of Aix.

Dance Festival – *end Jul–Aug.* Details are available from the tourist office.

TOURS

Cézanne Tour: early May to early Oct Tue 2–7pm. ⊜28€. 🖀*04 42 16 11 61. www.aixenprovence tourism.com.*

Chaîne de l'Étoile★

Bouches-du-Rhône

This chain of mountains, which belongs to the small Alps of Provence and is a result of the Pyrenean fold, separates the Arc basin to the north from that of the Huveaune to the east. It extends the Chaîne de l'Estaque beyond the shelf of St-Antoine. In spite of the low altitude of its mountain tops, the chain rises spectacularly above the Marseille plain. Its central crest, which spreads out like a fan, ends at 781m/2 563ft at the Tête du Grand Puech.

🚗 DRIVING TOUR

From Gardanne to Aubagne

61km/38mi – about 3hr30min (not including the climb to Étoile peak).

Gardanne

This important industrial town, with its coal mining, bauxite and cement works, was painted by Cézanne. It is a lively place on market days (Wed, Fri and Sun).

👥 Écomusée de la Forêt Méditerranéene

NW of Gardanne on D 7 towards Aix and Valabre. 🕐Open Sun–Fri Jul–second last week in Aug 9am–1pm, 1.30–6pm; Sept–Jun 9am–12.30pm, 1–5.45pm. 🕐Closed public holidays. ⊛5.50€ (child 3.20€). 🞂04 42 65 42 10. www.institut-foret.com.
Dedicated to the ecology of this region, there are interactive displays, footpaths and instructive panels, as well as a botanical trail that helps you explore and learn about the flora and fauna in its natural setting. If you're here around midday, there's a very nice and inexpensive restaurant in the courtyard for lunch.

Michelin Map: 340: H-5.

Info: 31 boulevard Carnot, 13120 Gardanne. 🞂04 42 51 02 73. www.ville-gardanne.fr.

Kids: Ecomusée de la Fôret, Musée du Terroir Marseillais.

▷ *Return to Gardanne and take the D 58 going S, which becomes the D 8. After 7km/4.3mi turn right to Mimet.*

Mimet

This small hilltop village is undergoing considerable expansion. From its terrace there is a fine **view**★ of the Luynes valley, Gardanne and its furnaces.

▷ *Return to the D 8 and bear right. The picturesque D 7 and D 908 skirt the Étoile chain. At Le Logis-Neuf turn left to Allauch.*

Allauch

A large suburb of Marseille, Allauch (pronounced Allau) rises in tiers up the foothills of the Étoile chain. From here you can follow a series of footpaths leading up to the Garlaban hills, much loved by the great Provençal writer Marcel Pagnol.

Esplanade des Moulins

Appropriately named (*moulin* means mill), this esplanade, with its five windmills, one of which has been restored, offers a good **view**★ of Marseille.

▷ *Take the D 44F NW of Allauch.*

After passing Plan-de-Cuques, you will reach Château-Gombert, a neighbourhood of Marseille that has retained the atmosphere of a village.

👥 Musée du Terroir Marseillais
5 pl. des Héros (at Château-Gombert).
🕐*Open Mon–Fri 10am–1pm, 2–5pm, Sat–Sun 2–5pm.* 🚫*Closed public holidays.* 👁4€ *(child 2€).* 📞*04 91 68 14 38. www.musee-provencal.fr.*

The museum is situated in the main square shaded by plane trees. Dedicated to local arts and traditions, it is set out as the interior of an old Provençal dwelling. The kitchen, with its fireplace hood and typical *pile* (sink), is full of ceramics from Marseille, pewter, *terralhas* (culinary pottery), a big clay *tian* (bowl) and mortars for *aïoli* (garlic mayonnaise). There's also a fine display of *santons*.

▶ *Leave Château-Gombert towards Marseille and turn right into Traverse de la Baume-Loubière. Park the car at the Grottes Loubière. A footpath leads to the summit of the Étoile (4hr return on foot).*

Étoile Peak
After a winding trail through a rocky passage you reach the **Grande Étoile** (alt 590m/1 936ft), where a telecommunications tower stands, and then **Étoile peak** (alt 651m/2 136ft). From the shelf separating these last two summits there is a splendid **panorama**★★ over the Gardanne basin to the north and the thresholds that cut the chain's southern slopes.

▶ *Return to Allauch by car by the same way you came. Continue S on the D 4A. At Les Quatres-Saisons bear left and soon after, left again.*

Camoins-les-Bains
This pleasant little spa is surrounded by green countryside. **Marcel Pagnol** (1895–1974), the writer and film director who was born in Aubagne, is buried in **La Treille cemetery** at the town's entrance.

▶ *Return to Camoins-les-Bains and take D 44A to Aubagne.*

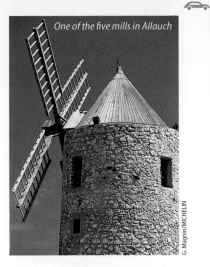
One of the five mills in Allauch

G. Magnin/MICHELIN

ADDRESSES

🛏 STAY

🛏🛏🛏 **Hôtel Les Cigales** – *rte. Enco-de-Botte, 13190 Allauch.* 📞*04 91 68 17 07. www.hotel-lescigales.fr. 7 rooms.* 🍴*7€.* Between Marseille and Allauch, this new establishment, in a tranquil setting, offers cosy, traditional rooms along with a pretty garden and inviting swimming pool.

🍽 EAT

🍽🍽 **La Grignote** – *22 r. Mignet, 13120 Gardanne.* 📞*04 42 58 30 25. Closed Sun and a week in Aug.* A restaurant with good, traditional cuisine.

🛒 SHOPPING
Nougats F et V Brémond – *Parc d'activité de Fontvieille, 13190 Allauch.* 📞*04 42 82 16 16. http://nougat-allauch. com.* The residents of Allauch claim that their town is the birthplace of nougat, which can be sampled at the manufacturers.

La Ste-Victoire★★★

Bouches-du-Rhône

East of Aix-en-Provence lies Montagne Sainte-Victoire, a limestone range which reaches an altitude of 1 011m/3 318ft at its peak, the Pic des Mouches. Oriented west to east, this range forms on its south side a sheer drop down to the Arc basin, whereas on its north side it slopes gently in a series of limestone plateaux towards the Durance plain. A striking contrast exists between the bright red clay of the foot of the mountains and the white limestone of the high mountain ridges, especially between Le Tholonet and Puyloubier. The mountain, immortalised by Paul Cézanne in his paintings, was depicted about 60 times by the artist.

- ♿ **Michelin Map:** 340: I-4
- 🗊 **Info:** 570 av. du Club Hippique, Aix-en-Provence. 𝒫 04 42 64 60 90. wwwgrandsitesainte victoire.com.
- ⊘ **Don't Miss:** The walk up to Croix de Provence.
- 🕓 **Timing:** Access is restricted Jul–Sept (open 6–11am) to prevent fires. In summer, bring a hat and water; in winter, a warm jacket.
- 👪 **Kids:** The Maison de la Ste-Victoire, to find out about the dinosaur eggs found here, now displayed in the Natural History Museum in Aix-en-Provence.

🚗 DRIVING TOUR

Round trip of 74km/46mi – allow 1 day (not including tour of Aix).

▷ *Leave Aix-en-Provence on the D 10 going east; turn right towards the Barrage de Bimont.*

Barrage de Bimont

This vaulted dam across the River Infernet is the principal architectural undertaking on the Canal de Verdon extension. It stands in a beautiful, wooded site at the foot of Montagne Ste-Victoire.

Downstream, superb gorges descend *(1hr there and back on foot)* to the Barrage Zola (a dam built by the engineer François Zola, father of the famous author Émile Zola), the second undertaking in the scheme which supplies water to local towns and villages and irrigation to some 60 local *communes.*

▷ *Return to the D 10 and turn right. Park the car in the small car park to the right of the road at Les Cabassols farm.*

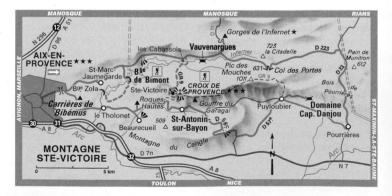

Massif Ste-Victoire

J. Malbure/MICHELIN

Croix de Provence★★★

🚶 *3hr30min round trip on foot.*
Walk along the Venturiers path, a mule track which rises rapidly through a pine-wood before easing off into a winding path (♿easier walking).

The first staging post is at 900m/2 950ft, the Notre-Dame de Ste-Victoire priory, built in 1656 and occupied until 1879. It comprises a chapel and parts of cloisters; a terrace laid in a breach in the wall gives a **view** of the Arc basin and Étoile chain. Bear left of the cloisters to reach the 945m/3 100ft high summit, Croix de Provence, marked by a 17m/55.7ft cross upon an 11m/36ft base. The **panorama**★★★ of Provençal mountains includes: Massif de la Ste-Baume and Chaîne de l'Étoile to the south, then towards the right the Vitrolles, Crau plain, Durance valley, Luberon, Provençal Alps and more to the east the Pic des Mouches. To the east on the crest is **Gouffre du Garagaï**, a chasm 150m/492ft deep, a source of legends.

Vauvenargues

Nestling in the Infernet valley, this village has retained its 17C château, which stands on a rock spur. It belonged to **Picasso**, who lived here and is buried in the park in front of the château.

Beyond Vauvenargues, the road follows steep wooded **gorges**★ of the Infernet, overlooked on the left by the 723m/2 372ft high Citadelle, and reaches the Col des Portes pass. During the descent, the Alpine foothills can be distinguished on the horizon.

At Puits de Rians, take the D 23 to the right, which skirts Montagne Ste-Victoire on its eastern side and crosses the Bois de Pourrières (woods); to your left is the Pain de Munition (alt 612m/2 008ft).

▶ *In Pourrières turn right towards Puyloubier. Take the D 57B; then turn right onto the D 56C.*

Good views of Montagne Ste-Victoire can be enjoyed before the road climbs the slopes of Montagne du Cengle. The D 17, on the left, winds between the imposing mass of Montagne Ste-Victoire and the Cengle plateau.

Saint-Antonin-sur-Bayon

The **⛰️Maison de la Sainte Victoire** (🕐*open Mon and Wed–Fri 10am–6pm, Sat–Sun 10am–7pm;* 🕐*closed 1 Jan, 25 Dec;* 🚫*no charge;* 📞*04 42 66 84 40)* has an exhibition detailing its ecosystem and history (dinosaur eggs). They also organise guided walks.

Before returning to Aix, it is worth making a detour to **Beaurecueil**, which affords the best views of Ste-Victoire, particularly at sunset when the mountain and surrounding countryside are tinted by the sun's rays.

▶ *Return to Aix via the "route Paul Cézanne", which goes through Le Tholonet.*

ADDRESSES

🏠 STAY ‖ EAT

🍽️🍽️ **Au Moulin de Provence** – *33 av. des Maquisards, 13120 Vauvenargues.* 📞*04 42 66 02 22. www.lemoulinde provence.com. 12 rooms.* ⚬*7€. Restaurant*🍽️🍽️. After exploring the village, linger for a moment in this pleasant family-run establishment, offering regional cooking and modest rooms. From the terrace and the pastel-coloured sitting room there are views of the Ste-Victoire mountain.

Just 15km/9mi east of Arles, the limestone hills (rather than true mountains, they are just 387 m at their highest) of the Alpilles change the landscape before your eyes. In relatively small geographic distances you can experience a world's worth of vistas. At one stop you'll see blue hills growing grapes for wine, almonds or olives. At the next some of the country's quaintest villages, followed by open fields and wooden pine or oak forests. Much of the land has been preserved and protected, so you can see the vistas as they were generations ago.

Highlights

1 Breathtaking views at Les Baux Panorama: **Les Alpilles** (p125)

2 Literary inspiration Moulin de Daudet: **Les Alpilles** (p126)

3 Up on a limestone peak: **Abbaye de St-Roman** (p136)

4 Semi-free-ranging wildlife Zoo La Barben: **Salon-en-Provence** (p146)

5 The fragrant Musée des Arômes et du Parfum at **Graveson** (p152)

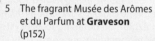

Outdoorsmen and women of all ability levels and interests can find an activity here, from birdwatching to hiking to biking. Among the favorites of birdwatchers is the majestic Bonelli eagle, a small brown eagle with white bellies.

Most trails offer more intense hikes as well as quick walks, thanks to many mountains and valleys, and even some flat stretches for easy biking, so you'll have plenty of options, although summer can be warm, and the flammability of tender underbrush (called "garrigue") makes campfires completely verbotin. Even if you are not an athlete, you'll still want to ride a train through this area, sussing out artistic and literary inspiration, as well as farm-fresh vegetable markets.

Because of their proximity to Arles, and, more so, because of the quality of the light on these hills, the Alpilles appeared in several Vincent Van Gogh paintings.

Starting in the Alpilles, you'll be treated to views of cypress forests, as well as archaeological sites such as of the ruins of the Gallo-Roman Aqueducs de Barbegal. Fontvieille was founded by stone carvers, but in recent memory the focus has been on French 19C author Alphonse Daudet and the collection of his letters about Provence (and the restored windmill to which he referred in his writing). Nearby Tarascon was a favourite of Daudet, but has a claim to fame of its own: its castles. Don't miss the 13C Château du Roi René.

The terrain changes as you approach Barbentane, home to the 17C Château, as well as many plots of land tended for market gardening. Stop in Graveson, where vegetable-growing is still an ancient art. Here farmers still use harnessed horses (oft-decorated with flowers and ribbons) to till the land.

Les Baux-de-Provence gave its name to the mineral bauxite that was found here in the 19C. You can hear that story by visiting the Musée d'Histoire des Baux. Local ruins include the Citadelle and the 16C Hôpital Quinqueran.

Montagnette, a smaller chain of hills, is more fragrant, planted with Provençal herbs, thyme and rosemary. The classic French countryside, dotted with canal views and excellent daily markets, is also home to St-Michel-de-Frigolet Abbey, where Father Gaucher created the legendary Frigolet liqueur. Maillane is a picture-perfect Provençal town: Have the camera ready when you pass these white-tiled roofs.

Les Alpilles★★
Bouches-du-Rhône

The limestone chain of the Alpilles, a geological extension of the Luberon range, rises in the heart of Provence between Avignon and Arles. From afar, these jagged crests rising 300–400m/985–1 313ft appear to be lofty mountains.The arid, white peaks of these summits standing out against the blue sky are reminiscent of some Greek landscapes. At the mouths of the dry valleys that cross the mountain chain, olive and almond trees spread their foliage over the lower slopes. Occasionally a dark line of cypress trees breaks the landscape. In the mountains, the gently sloping lower areas are planted with *Kermes* oaks and pines, but often the rock is bare and peppered with a few scraggy bushes covered by *maquis* or poor pasture suitable only for sheep.

Due to the high risk of fire, access to the forested areas of the Alpilles is forbidden from July to 15 September.

DRIVING TOURS

LES BAUX ALPILLES★★
Round trip starting from St-Rémy-de-Provence. 40km/25mi – allow 4hr.

St-Rémy-de-Provence★
See ST-RÉMY-DE-PROVENCE.

Leave St-Rémy-de-Provence going SW on chemin de la Combette; turn right into Vieux Chemin d'Arles. After 3.8km/2.3mi, turn left at a T-junction onto D 27 (signposted: Les Baux).

Les Baux Panorama (Table d'Orientation)★★★
Just before reaching the top of the hill, on your left, you will see a road tracing the ledge where you can stop and gaze at the magnificent **panorama**★★★ of Les Baux (*see Les BAUX-DE-PROVENCE*).

- **Michelin Map:** 340: D3-E3 or 528 fold 29.
- **Info:** Nature lovers can plan a guided tour of the Caume by contacting the tourist office in St-Rémy-de-Provence, ℰ04 90 92 38 52.
- **Location:** The area is divided between the Alpilles des Baux in the W and the Alpilles d'Eygalières in the E; in the middle is St-Rémy-de-Provence.
- **Don't Miss:** The mill in Fontvieille, made famous by Alphonse Daudet; a tour of the AOC Baux olive oil mills; Christmas markets in Maussane, Mouriès and Eyguières.
- **Timing:** You would ideally spend two or three days exploring the region, particularly at Christmas. If you only have a day, take in two or three villages.
- **Kids:** "La Petite Provence du Paradou", with its *santons* displays; the *santons* museum at Maussane-les-Alpilles and the 'Le Petit Train des Alpilles', which meanders between Arles and Fontvieille.

Return to D 27; bear left on it.

The road winds through Val d'Enfer (*see Les BAUX-DE-PROVENCE*).

Les Baux-de-Provence★★★
See Les BAUX-DE-PROVENCE.

Continue along D 27, then take a right before Maussane-les-Alpilles to connect to Paradou on D 17.

La Petite Provence du Paradou
75 av. de la Vallée des Baux, Le Paradou (towards Fontvieille (D 17)

on the right). ⚐🕐*Open daily Jul–Aug 10am–7pm; Sept–Jun 10am–6.30pm.* ✆*No charge.* ℘*04 90 54 35 75. www.lapetiteprovenceduparadou.com.*
In a decor redolent of rural Provence, *santons* are produced here by *santon*-makers from Aubagne. They are dressed in the local costumes and some are even mobile. They are arranged into evocative scenes of Provence past, with trades (fisherman, miller, shepherd), festivals, daily life (drinking holes, games of cards), and the like.

▷ *Return to the village, taking D 78 to the right through an olive grove.*

Aqueducs de Barbegal
▷ *15min round trip on foot: follow the signposts for aqueduc romain.*

Note the impressive ruins, on the left in particular, of a pair of Gallo-Roman aqueducts. The aqueduct branching off to the west supplied Arles with water from Eygalières some 50km/31mi away. The other one cut through the rock and served a 4C hydraulic flour mill on the slope's south side, the ruins of which provide a rare example of Gallo-Roman mechanical engineering.

▷ *Go right on D 33.*

Fontvieille
🖹*Avenue des Moulins, 13990 Fontvieille.* ℘*04 90 54 67 49. www.fontvieille-provence.com.*
For centuries, the main industry in this small town, where Alphonse Daudet is remembered for his *Lettres de mon Moulin* (1869), has been the quarrying of Arles limestone.

Moulin de Daudet (Daudet's Mill)
Fontvieille. 🕐*Open Feb–Dec daily 9am–7pm.* ✆*2.50€.* ℘*04 90 54 60 78.*
Between Arles and Les Baux-de-Provence, the admirers of Alphonse Daudet's works can make a literary pilgrimage to his mill, the inspiration for his famous *Lettres de mon Moulin (Letters from my Mill)*, a charming and whimsical series of letters and tales from Provence. A lovely avenue of pines leads from Fontvieille to the mill.
Inside the mill, the first floor displays different kinds of millstones. Note at roof level the names of the local winds, positioned according to their source. The small **museum** contains memorabilia of the author.
Alphonse Daudet, the son of a silk manufacturer, was born in Nîmes on 13 May 1840 (d. 1897). An outstanding author of tales of Provençal life and member of the Académie Goncourt, he was also a contemporary of such important 19C literary figures as Zola and Mistral. The **view**★ from the mill is an inspiration, embracing the Alpilles,

Les Alpilles des Baux

D. Pazery/MICHELIN

Beaucaire and Tarascon castles, the vast Rhône valley, and the Abbaye de Montmajour.

▷ *Take D 32 to return to St-Rémy-de-Provence.*

2 EYGALIÈRES ALPILLES★★
Round-trip from St-Rémy-de-Provence. 42km/26mi – allow about 3hr.

St-Rémy-de-Provence★
See ST-RÉMY-DE-PROVENCE.

▷ *Leave St-Rémy-de-Provence on D 5, in the direction of Maussane.*

The road passes the old monastery of St-Paul-de-Mausole and the Roman monuments of Glanum, before continuing deep into the mountains where the landscape is dominated by pine trees.

▷ *After 4km/2.5mi leave the car by the side of D 5 and take the left footpath leading up to the Caume.*

Panorama de la Caume★★
Access is forbidden from 1 July–15 Sep. Alt 387m/1 270ft.
At the top is a television relay mast. Walk to the southern edge of the plateau to enjoy a vast panorama of the surrounding countryside, including the Alpilles in the foreground and the Crau and Camargue plains. From the northern edge, the view encompasses

the Rhône plain, the Guidon du Bouquet with its beak-like outline, Mont Ventoux and the Durance Valley.

▷ *Return to D 5 and turn left.*

The road traverses a pine wood and several small gorges and goes past the Rochers d'Entreconque, former bauxite quarries.

Maussane-les-Alpilles
At the entrance to the town stands the **Musée des Santons Animés** *(rte de Saint Rémy de Provence; open Wed–Mon Apr–Sept 10am–7pm, Oct–Mar 1.30–7pm; 4€ (child 2€); 04 90 54 39 00).* The displays show the evolution of *santon* figurines against a backdrop of Provençal scenery.

▷ *Turn round and by way of D 5, head towards Maussane-les-Alpilles. At the town entrance bear left and immediately left again onto D 78.*

The road runs through olive groves at the foot of the Alpilles before rising gently to a low pass from where there is a view of Les Opiès, a hillock crowned by a tower.

▷ *At Le Destet, turn left onto D 24, which, as it rises, reveals the crest of La Caume. After 7.5km/4.5mi bear right onto D 24B, which leads to Eygalières.*

Eygalières

This small town of narrow winding streets rises in tiers up the hill to an ancient castle keep. Once a Neolithic settlement, it was later occupied by Romans sent to divert the local spring waters to Arles. From the top of the village a view opens out onto La Caume mountains, the Alpilles and then Durance valley.

Le Jardin de l'Alchimiste

Mas de la Brune, Eygalieres. ⏱*Open May daily 10am–6pm; Jun–Oct Mon–Fri 3–6pm, Sat–Sun and public holidays 10am–6pm.* ⌚*7€.* ☎*04 90 90 67 67. www.jardin-alchimiste.com.*

The inspiration for the garden around the 16C Mas de la Brune comes from the alchemist and his quest for the philosopher's stone. The garden contains many Mediterranean plants with medicinal properties.

▷ *Take D 74A, and turn left on D 99 for St-Rémy-de-Provence.*

ADDRESSES

🛏 STAY

🍽🍽 **Hostellerie de la Tour** – *rte d'Arles, 13990 Fontvieille. 9km/5.6mi towards les Baux then take D 78F, then D 17.* ☎*04 90 54 72 21. www.hotel-delatour.com. 10 rooms.* ⌚*9€. Restaurant*🍽🍽*. Closed Nov–mid-Mar.* A truly warm and attentive place awaits you here in this modest inn, which is consistent in its presentation. The rooms are small, pleasantly simple, and quite comfortable. The cuisine is good local fare. There is also a decent swimming pool.

🍽🍽🍽 **Hotel Terriciaë** – *rte de Maussane les Alpilles, 13890 Mouriès. 1.8 km/1.1mi W from Mouriés along D 17.* ☎*04 90 97 06 70. www.mouries-en-provence.com. 29 rooms.* ⌚*12€.* A typical Provençal hotel in the tranquil setting at the foot of the Alpilles makes this hotel an excellent base from which to explore the Bouches-du-Rhône region. Along with an outdoor swimming pool and games room, many of the rooms boast a private balcony.

🍴 EAT

🍽 **La Maison Sucrée** – *r. de la République, 13810 Eygalières.* ☎*04 90 95 94 15.* Delicious crêpes, ice cream and sorbets.

🍽 **La Pitchoune** – *21 pl. de l'Église, 13520 Maussane-les-Alpilles.* ☎*04 90 54 34 84. Closed mid-Nov–mid-Jan, Fri and Mon for lunch.* Situated near the church this pretty 19C house has tastefully decorated rooms and a terrace.

🍽🍽🍽 **Table du Meunier** – *42 c. Hyacinthe Bellon, 13990 Fontvieille.* ☎*04 90 54 61 05. Closed 19–28 Dec, Feb, week of All Saint's Day, Tue (Sept–Jun) and Wed.* The regional cooking in the rustic setting of this old mill attracts customers from far and wide. The terrace harbours a real treasure: a chicken house dating from 1765.

🍽🍽🍽🍽 **Le Bistrot d'Eygalières (Chez Bru)** – *28 r. de la République, 13810 Eygalières.* ☎*04 90 90 60 34. www.chezbru.com. Closed mid-Nov–Apr, Mon, Tue lunch.* An institution. Delicious regional cuisine in attractive surroundings and a good wine list.

🤾 SPORT & LEISURE

🥾 **Hiking** – Take the 15km/9mi footpath along the Alpilles ridge, from Glanum to Eygalières, via Val St-Clerg, following the GR 6 footpath. Other walks of 1–3hr are available.

👪 **Le Petit Train des Alpilles** – *17 bis av. de Hongrie, Arles.* ☎*04 90 18 81 31.* ⌚*9.50€ (child 6€).* A 40min ride between Arles and Fontvieille allows families to discover the plains of Montmajour.

Barbentane
Bouches-du-Rhône

Built against the north slope of the Montagnette, Barbentane overlooks the plain near the confluence of the Rhône and the Durance and is devoted to market gardening. The village has retained part of its 14C fortifications and is worth visiting for its castle.

▶ **Population:** 3 711.
Michelin Map: 340: D-2.
Info: Le Cours, 13570 Barbentane. ℘04 90 90 85 86. www.barbentane.fr.
Location: North of Tarascon (14km/8.7mi) on the D 35.
Timing: Allow a couple of hours to wander around the castle and the streets.

VISIT

Château★★
Guided tours (45min) Easter–Oct Thu–Tue 10am–noon, 2–6pm. ✆7€. ℘04 90 95 51 07.
A Classical 17C façade and terraces with their flower-filled urns overlook formal Italian-style gardens. The interior, enhanced by mementoes belonging to the Marquis of Barbentane, features rich 18C decoration of Italian influence. The vaulting, plasterwork, painted medallions, coloured marble, Louis XV and XVI furnishings, Chinese porcelain and Moustiers faience all add to the charm of this delightful château.

Old Village
All that remains from the fortifications are the two entrance gates, Porte Calendale, which opens onto the Cours, and Porte Séquier above the village.

Maison des Chevaliers (House of the Knights)
2 pl. de l'Pujade. ⊶Closed to the public.
This 12C residence has a lovely Renaissance façade composed of a turret and two basket arches topped by a columned gallery.

Tour Anglica
Overlooking the village, the tower is the keep of the former castle, built in the 14C by the brother of Pope Urban V, Cardinal Anglic de Grimoard. From the terrace there is a good view of Avignon, Châteaurenard and in the distance Mont Ventoux.

A short walk through the pines leads to the well-preserved 18C **Moulin de Bretoul** (Bretoul mill), from where there is a lovely view of the Rhône plain. This is the only remaining example of the many windmills formerly present in the region.

ADDRESSES

✍ STAY

⊜⊜⊜⊜ **Chambre d'hôte Le Mazet de la Dame** – *Draille du Mas de la Dame, 13570 Barbentane. ℘04 90 90 91 73. www.la-dame.com. 2 rooms. ⊊. Weekly rentals possible.* A sweet little *gîte*, with sun-kissed rooms of ochre and soft rose, tile floors: warm, intimate country living. The garden is enchanting, with llamas and horses!

Château de Barbentane
G. Magnin/MICHELIN

Les Baux-de-Provence★★★

Bouches-du-Rhône

Detached from the Alpilles, this bare rock spur – 900m/2 953ft long and 200m/656ft wide – has vertical ravines on either side. A ruined castle and ancient houses make up the spectacular site★★★ of Les Baux, in turn making it one of the most picturesque French villages and a popular tourist destination. The village gave its name to the mineral bauxite, discovered here in 1822.

A BIT OF HISTORY

A warrior line – The Lords of Baux were renowned in the Middle Ages, described by Mistral as "warriors all – vassals never". They were proud to trace their genealogy back to the Magi King, Balthazar, and, so that no one should ignore the fact, boldly placed the star of Bethlehem on their coat of arms.

From the 11C the lords were among the strongest in the south of France, having in their control 79 towns and villages. In 1145–62 they warred against the House of Barcelona, whose rights to Provence they contested. Supported for a while by the German emperor, they finally submitted after having succumbed to a siege at Les Baux itself.

They won titles: members of different branches became variously Princes of Orange, Viscounts of Marseille, Counts of Avellino, and Dukes of Andria (having followed the Capetian Princes of Anjou who were campaigning in southern Italy). One of them married Marie of Anjou, sister of Joan I, Queen of Naples and Countess of Provence. She was destined to tragedy: three times a widow, she died in 1382, smothered by an ambitious cousin.

Turenne, the Brigand – The House of Turenne, from the Limousin, was a great family: two of its members were popes at Avignon, one of whom was Clement VI. Another of its members

▶ **Population:** 381.
♿ **Michelin Map:** 340: D-3.
ℹ **Info:** Maison du Roy, 13520 Les Baux-de-Provence. ✆04 90 54 34 39. www.lesbauxdeprovence.com.
▶ **Location:** Arriving by the D 78 from Fontvieille, you'll notice the perched houses at the entrance of the village.
🅿 **Parking:** Leave your car in one of the car parks – the nearest one to the village costs 5€ for unlimited parking. In summer, unless you get there early, you'll need to park at the side of the road.
👁 **Don't Miss:** The castle and a walk around the old town.
🕐 **Timing:** Allow about 2hr for a visit. Many shops and restaurants are closed November–March.
👥 **Kids:** The Cathédrale d'Images.

was the Viscount Raymond de Turenne, nephew of Gregory XI, who became the guardian of his niece, Alix of Baux, in 1372. His ambitions caused civil war in the region. His pillaging and cruelty terrorised the countryside and he was appropriately named the "Scourge of Provence". His chief delight was to force his unransomed prisoners to jump off the castle walls.

The pope and the Lord of Provence hired mercenaries to get rid of the brigands, but the mercenaries themselves ravaged the enemy territories as well as the territories to be protected; as a result their contract was broken and they were paid to leave the area. Pillaging and fighting broke out again quite soon. The King of France joined Turenne's enemies and in 1399 the "scourge" was surrounded at Les Baux; however, he escaped and fled into France.

The End – Alix was Baux's last princess, and on her death in 1426 the domain, incorporated into Provence, became simply a barony. King René granted it to his second wife Jeanne of Laval. Joined with Provence to the French crown, the Barony revolted against Louis XI in 1483, who subsequently had the fortress dismantled. As of 1528 the Constable Anne de Montmorency, who was titular Lord of Les Baux, undertook a large restoration project on the town, which once again enjoyed a prosperous period. Les Baux then became a centre of Protestantism under the Manville family who administered it for the crown. In 1632, however, Richelieu, tired of this troublesome fief, had the castle and ramparts demolished and the inhabitants were fined 100 000 livres plus the cost of the demolition!

SIGHTS
Hôtel de Manville
Grande Rue.
This 16C mansion, donated to the town by the prince of Manville, boasts a beautiful façade decorated with mullioned windows. It houses the town hall.

Anciens fours banaux
The townspeople came to bake their bread in these ovens.

Rue du Trencat
This street, carved out of the bedrock, leads to the castle.
While descending Grande Rue, note the **Renaissance house** of Jean de Brion, home of the engraver, publisher and printer **Louis Jou** (1881–1968), who devoted his whole life to the art of books.

⬥⬥ WALKING TOUR
THE VILLAGE★★★
1hr.
A walk through the streets of Les Baux is a magical experience, as long as they are not too crowded or full of souvenir sellers.

▷ *Enter through the Porte Mage and turn left towards place Louis-Jou.*

LE PASS "Les Baux jours"
A useful ticket allowing entry to the château, Cathédrale d'Images and the Musée Yves-Brayer. *15€ (child 7.50€). Available from the tourist office.*

Ancien Hôtel de Ville
pl. Louis Jou. ⏱*Open daily 9am–6pm.* *No charge.* ℘*04 90 54 34 39.*
This deconsecrated 16C chapel, formerly the town hall, still has three rooms with pointed vaulting, which house a **Santon Museum**.

▷ *Follow place Louis Jou N. The road forks (before becoming rue de la Caldes); follow it right.*

Porte Eyguières
This used to be the town's only entrance gate.

▷ *Return to the street and continue N to the end of rue de la Caldes. Go towards the right on rue de l'Église.*

Musée Yves-Brayer★
pl. François-de-Hénain. ⏱*Open Apr–Sept daily 10am–12.30pm, 2–6.30pm; Oct–Dec and mid-Feb–Mar Wed–Mon 10am–12.30pm, 2–5.30pm.* *4€ (10.50€ with Cathédrale d'Images).* ℘*04 90 54 36 99. www.yvesbrayer.com.*
The museum houses works by Yves Brayer (1907–90), a figurative painter deeply attached to Les Baux (he is buried in the village cemetery). It is the glowing landscapes of Provence which inspired some of his best paintings, such as *Les Baux* and *Field of Almond Trees.*

▷ *Walk through place François-de-Hénain and you'll reach Église St-Vincent on your left.*

Église St-Vincent★
pl. St-Vincent. ⏱*Open daily 9am–7pm.* *No charge.*
This 12C and 16C church is flanked on its north side by a graceful campanile, the so-called lantern of the dead. Partly car-

ved out of the bedrock, the simple interior is surprisingly light, with stained-glass windows by Max Ingrand.

▷ *A short way further on, you'll come to place St-Vincent.*

Place St-Vincent★
This is a charming, shaded little square. There is a lovely view of the Fontaine Valley and the Val d'Enfer from the terrace.

CHÂTEAU★
45min. Access to the citadel through the Musée d'Histoire des Baux, at the end of rue du Trencat.
🕐*Open daily spring 9am–6.30pm; summer 9am–8.30pm; autumn 9.30am–6pm; winter 9.30am–5pm.* 👓*7.70€.* ✆*04 90 54 55 56. www.chateau-baux-provence.com.*
Since 1991, the citadel has been the subject of an important restoration and development project. The excavation work carried out in 1992 allowed three main periods of occupation of the rocky spur prior to the modern era to be determined: the 2C and 1C BC (second Iron Age), the 5C and 6C (construction of a rampart and scattered dwellings), and the medieval period (construction of a keep).

Musée d'Histoire des Baux
Housed in the old residence of the powerful Tour du Brau family, this History Museum exhibits in a beautiful rib-vaulted room information concerning the most important moments in the history of Les Baux from Antiquity to the present day. Two models of the fortress in the 13C and the 16C illustrate the architectural evolution of the site.

Chapelle St-Blaise
This chapel was the seat of the woollen carders and weavers brotherhood from the 12C. Nowadays it houses a small museum devoted to the olive. Visitors can watch a video entitled "Van Gogh, Gauguin and Cézanne in the Country of the Olive."

Hôpital Quiqueran
This hospital was built in the 16C by Jehanne de Quiqueran, wife of the governor of Les Baux and was in operation until 1787. Nowadays in ruins, there are plans to rebuild it.

Moulin
The old communal mill, the use of which incurred a tax paid to the Lord of Les Baux, stands alongside a paved area used to collect rainwater which then drains into a cistern carved into the rock.

Monument Charloun Riéu
From this monument erected in honour of the poet Charloun Riéu (1846–1924), there is a magnificent view over the plain as far as the Berre lagoon.

Citadelle
Towering over the eastern side of the rocky spur are the citadel ruins. The **Tour Sarrasine** (Saracen Tower) – from the top, a good **view** of the village and castle – and the **Tour des Bannes** remain to the south, dominating a group of 16C houses. A bay of rib vaulting can still be seen in the **Chapelle castrale** (12C–16C), dedicated to St Catherine. The **castle** and the **donjon** (keep) (👣*fairly difficult steps, not recommended for those who suffer from vertigo*) are the remains of a 13C building constructed on the site of the 10C fortress. There is a magnificent **panorama**★★ embracing the Aix countryside, the Luberon, Mont Ventoux and the Cévennes; the tormented shapes of the Val d'Enfer to the north contrast with the gentle countryside of the Vallon de la Fontaine to the west.
Leaning against the northern rampart, the **Tour Paravelle** affords a pretty **view**★ of the village of Les Baux and the Val d'Enfer.

EXCURSIONS
👥 Cathédrale d'Images★
By the D 27, 300m/328yd N of the village in Les Baux stone quarries. 🕐*Open Apr–Sept daily 10am–6pm; late Feb–Mar and Oct–early Jan daily 10am–5pm; 1*

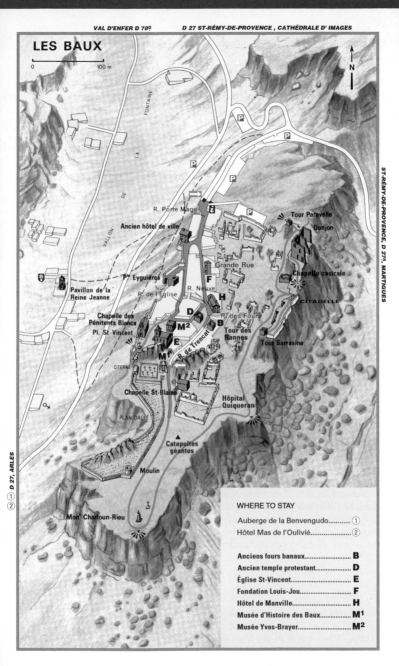

LES BAUX

0   100 m

N

VAL D'ENFER D 78⁰   D 27 ST-RÉMY-DE-PROVENCE, CATHÉDRALE D' IMAGES

ST-RÉMY-DE-PROVENCE, D 27, 27ᴬ, MARTIGUES

D 27, ARLES
① ②

R. Porte Mage

Tour Paravelle
Donjon

Ancien hôtel de ville

Grande Rue

Chapelle castrale

Pᵗᵉ Eyguières

R. Neuve

F

CITADELLE

Pavillon de la
Reine Jeanne

Rᵉ de l'Église

H

Chapelle des
Pénitents Blancs
Pl. St-Vincent

D

Rᵉ des Fours

M²

B

E

Tour des
Bannes

M¹

R. de Trencat

Tour Sarrasine

CITERNE

Chapelle St-Blaise

Hôpital
Quiqueran

PLAN DALÉE

▲ Catapultes
géantes

Moulin

Monᵗ Charloun-Rieu

WHERE TO STAY

Auberge de la Benvengudo............ ①
Hôtel Mas de l'Oulivié.................... ②

Anciens fours banaux............................ **B**
Ancien temple protestant...................... **D**
Église St-Vincent.................................. **E**
Fondation Louis-Jou.............................. **F**
Hôtel de Manville................................. **H**
Musée d'Histoire des Baux.................. **M¹**
Musée Yves-Brayer.............................. **M²**

Jan and 25 Dec 2–5pm. 7.50€ *(child
3.50€); 10.50€/3.50€ with Musée Yves
Brayer (see p131). ☎04 90 54 38 65.
www.cathedrale-images.com.*
Albert Plécy (1914–77) created a place
where he could carry out his research
on the "total image". In the half-light,
the limestone cliffs of the galleries and
pillars act as three-dimensional screens.
The *30min* show changes theme every
year.

Panorama★★★

Continue along D 27 for about 1km/0.6mi and bear right on a steep road (look for parking signs).

This rocky promontory offers the best view of Les Baux and a panorama of Arles and Camargue, Rhône valley, Cévennes mountains, Aix-en-Provence, the Luberon and Mont Ventoux.

Val d'Enfer

Access from the D 27 and D 78G.

A path *(15min)* crosses Hell Valley, a jagged gorge. The caves are still the source of fairytale legends.

Queen Jeanne's Pavillion

Vallon de la Fontaine (on the D 78G). A path leads down to the pavilion from Porte Eyguières. ⊙Free access.

This Renaissance building was built by Jeanne de Les Baux c 1581. Mistral had a copy made for his tomb at Maillane.

ADDRESSES

▧ STAY

◒◉◉◉ **Auberge de la Benvengudo** – *quartier de l'Arcoule (2km/1.2mi southwest of Baux via D 27). ℘04 90 54 32 54. www.benvengudo.com. Closed Nov–Mar. 28 rooms. ⊂15€. Restaurant◒◉◉◉.* Nestled in a cluster of olive groves at the foot of the citadel is this charming Virginia creeper-covered inn. Rooms are plush and open onto a flower-filled garden. The dining room and veranda are decorated in Provençal style. Poolside terrace. Dishes are composed around fresh market produce.

◒◉◉◉ **Fabian des Baux** – *rte Départemental 5 F, 13520 Les Baux-de-Provence. ℘04 90 54 37 87. www.hotelfabiandesbaux.com. 31 rooms. Restaurant ◒◉◉◉. Closed Nov–Jan.* Situated in the village of Baux-de-Provence, this hotel is surrounded by an orchard of olive trees, affording a charming view of the Alpilles mountains. It also has an outdoor pool and a large outdoor patio.

⋎ EAT

◒◉ **Café Cinarca** – *26 r. du Trencat. ℘04 90 54 33 94. Closed 6 Jan–6 Feb, 12 Nov–20 Dec, eves from mid-Sept–Apr and Tue.* If the road to the castle seems never-ending, a pit-stop in this café will refuel you. Well-priced "traditional" food served in a setting crammed with objects and posters. Tables outside under mulberry trees. Also worth a visit for afternoon tea.

◒◉◉◉ **La Riboto de Taven** – *Le Val d'Enfer, 13520 Les Baux-de-Provence. ℘04 90 54 35 23. www.riboto-de-taven.fr. Closed 5 Jan–12 Mar, Wed.* A timbered ceiling and fireplace provide the ambience for this restaurant which serves an ever-changing menu, based on local market produce.

⛒ SHOPPING

WINE AND OIL

Castelas – *rte de St-Rémy, at the foot of Les Baux castle. ℘04 90 54 50 86. www.castelas.com.* Award-winning olive oil and *tapenade*.

Mas de la Dame – *chemin Départemental 5 (on the RD 5). ℘04 90 54 32 24. www.masdeladame.com.* This 16C property, immortalised by Van Gogh in 1889, sells Vallée des Baux wine and olive oil.

EVENTS

Christmas at Les Baux – Midnight mass is held on Christmas Eve in the church of St-Vincent with a nativity scene.

Beaucaire★

Gard

Formerly a stronghold of the Counts of Toulouse, Beaucaire kept watch over Tarascon, across the river, which was part of the Holy Roman Empire. It became famous for its fair, attracting huge crowds for many centuries. The Rhône to Sète canal flows through the town.

BEAUCAIRE FAIR

The fair, launched in 1217 by **Raymond VI of Toulouse**, originally lasted one week. It became a great medieval fair and at its peak in the 18C, it lasted a month every July when as many as 300 000 people gathered to do business, roister and celebrate. So prestigious was the fair that the prices negotiated there served as a reference throughout the kingdom. Streets specialised in single commodities after which many were named: Beaujolais was a wine street; Bijoutiers was a jewellers' row; rue des Marseillais was where oil and soap were sold. On the quayside, traders proffered an array of produce including cocoa, coffee and dates.

The fairground, on the large flat expanse between the castle cliff and the river, was set with stalls offering everything from perfume to pottery. It was also a horse fair. Circus acts with everything from acrobats to elephants amazed onlookers.

This huge success was almost certainly due to the town's position at a crossroads of land and river routes, aided by Louis XI's decree which made it a free port. Today, the Beaucaire Fair is re-created during the "Estivales" Festival, which still attracts a crowd.

❧ WALKING TOUR
OLD BEAUCAIRE★

▷ *Take rue Hôtel de Ville (to the right of cours Gambetta), which leads to place Georges Clemenceau.*

▷ **Population:** 15 099.
🚲 **Michelin Map:** 339: M-6.
🛈 **Info:** 24 Cours Gambetta, 30300 Beaucaire.
  ℘04 66 59 26 57.
  www.ot-beaucaire.fr.
▷ **Location:** 14km/8.7mi N of Arles; 24km/15mi S of Avignon.
🅿 **Parking:** On the banks of the canal.
👫 **Kids:** Les Aigles de Beaucaire, Le Vieux Mas.

Hôtel de Ville
r. de l'Hôtel de Ville.
The town hall is a late-17C mansion by Mansart with a central block flanked by wings outlined by a high, balustraded wall; carved flower garlands surround the windows, and the grand staircase (courtyard) rises behind a double portico of Ionic columns.

▷ *A small arched passageway leads to rue de la République.*

Hôtel des Clausonnettes
21 r. de la République.
Note the Classical façade of this 18C building which backs onto the castle (try to enter the courtyard).

Hôtel de Margaillier
23 r. de la République.
This magnificent 17C dwelling with its carved façade is known as the "house of caryatids" because of the caryatids flanking its porch.

Hôtel de Roys de Lédignan
r. de la République.
Another fine mansion. The street emerges onto **place de la République**, a square with arcades housing numerous craftshops. In the centre of the square is a statue of the *drac*, a local mythological monster who looks rather the worse for wear due to the ravages of time.

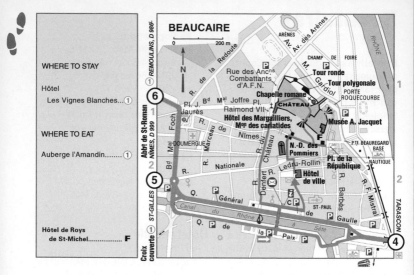

BEAUCAIRE

WHERE TO STAY

Hôtel
  Les Vignes Blanches...①

WHERE TO EAT

Auberge l'Amandin........①

Hôtel de Roys
  de St-Michel.................F

○ *Go back along rue de la République,
then take the street on the right side that
leads up to the castle.*

CHÂTEAU★

Montée du Château. ○*Open daily
Apr–Oct 10am–6pm; Nov–Mar
10am–5.15pm.* ☞*Guided tours 19
Apr–25 Oct Sun 10am; 15 Nov–15 Feb
Sun 2pm (by appointment with the
tourist office).* ○*Closed public holidays.*
⊙*4.40€.* ℘*04 66 59 71 34.*
Built in the 11C on the site of a Roman
camp and remodelled in the 13C, the
castle was dismantled in the 17C on the
orders of Cardinal Richelieu.

Tour polygonale

This unusually shaped tower is also
called the triangular tower.

Curtain wall

A short walk enables the visitor to
admire the sheer curtain wall, the barbican defending a castle entrance, and
the rocky spur of the Tour Polygonale.

≗ Les Aigles de Beaucaire

○*Shows (45min) daily Apr–Jun 2pm,
3pm, 4.30pm; Jul–Aug 3pm, 4pm,
5.30pm; Mar and Sept–Nov 2.30pm,
3.30pm, 4.30pm.* ⊙*10€ (child 7€).*
℘*04 66 59 26 72.*
www.aigles-de-beaucaire.com.

Falconry displays are held within
Beaucaire castle. Kites, eagles and others
glide to evocative music, handled by
falconers clad in medieval costume.

ADDITIONAL SIGHTS
Musée Auguste-Jacquet
(Gardens of Château Beaucaire)

EXCURSIONS
Abbaye de St-Roman★
*Mas des Tourelles 4294, rte de
Bellegarde. 5km/3mi NW by D 999
and the road to the right, then 15min
return on foot.* ○*Open Jul–Aug daily
10am–1pm, 2–7pm; Apr–Jun and Sept
Tue–Sun 10am–1pm, 2–6pm; Oct and
Mar Tue–Sun 2–5pm; Nov–Feb Sun and
public holidays 2–5pm.* ○*Closed 25
Dec.* ⊙*5.50€.* ℘*04 66 59 19 72.
www.abbaye-saint-roman.com.*
This abbey is located on a limestone
peak. It was abandoned in the 16C and
transformed into a fortress. In 1850 the
castle was demolished. A signposted circuit leads to the chapel containing the
tomb of Saint Roman. The **view**★ from
the terrace extends to the Rhône and the
Vallabrègues dam, Avignon, Mont Ventoux, the Luberon, the Alpilles and, in the
foreground, Tarascon and its castle. Note
the graves hollowed out of the rock, the
basin from which rainwater was channel-
led, the monks' cells and a vast hall.

Mas Gallo-Romain des Tourelles

4294 rte de Saint-Gilles. 4km/2.5mi to the west. Leave Beaucaire by the road to Bellegarde. After 4km/2.5mi, turn right for the Mas des Tourelles. ♿🕐*Open Apr–Jun and Sept–Oct daily 2–6pm; Jul–Aug Mon–Sat 10am–noon, 2–7pm; Sun 2–7pm; Nov–23 Dec and Mar Sat 2–6pm.* ✆*4.90€.* ✆*04 66 59 19 72. www.tourelles.com.*

Between the 1C and 3C AD a Gallo-Roman villa covered this area, comprising of a dwelling, a farm and a pottery workshop. Its 17C buildings (sheep barn, present wine cellar, farmhouse), containing archaeological material found in pottery ovens and information on wine production during the Gallo-Roman period, are grouped around a flowered courtyard.

In the Cella Vinaria, a reconstruction of a Roman wine-cellar, a winepress *(calcatarium)*, vat *(lacus)*, press *(torcula)* and large earthenware jars *(dolia)* are worthy of note. Nowadays the *mas* produces ancient wines such as Muslum and Turriculae as well as the AOC Costières de Nîmes wines.

👥 Le Vieux Mas

6.5km/4mi S on D 15 (to Fourques), then a small road to the right towards Mas Taraud, which you follow for about 2km/1mi as far as Mas Végère. ♿🕐*Open Apr–Jun and Sept daily 10am–6pm; Jul–Aug daily 10am–7pm; Oct–Dec and 7 Feb–Mar Wed, Sat–Sun and public holidays 1.30–6pm.* 🕐*Closed 25 Dec.* ✆*6.50€ (child 5€).* ✆*04 66 59 60 13. www.vieux-mas.com.*

Turkeys, geese, ducks and cattle are raised in this traditional *mas* where life seems to have stopped around 1900 with staff dressed in period costume.

ADDRESSES

🏠 STAY

🛏🛏🛏 **Hôtel Les Vignes Blanches** – *67 av. de Farcienne.* ✆*04 66 59 13 12. www.lesvignesblanches.com. 57 rooms.* ⊇*9€. Restaurant*🍽🍽🍽*.Closed 2–29 Jan.* A décor of beautiful colours and an overall fresh, bright feeling. The culinary offering is traditional seasonal cuisine.

🍷 EAT

🍽🍽🍽 **Auberge l'Amandin** – *quartier St-Joseph. 3km/2mi S of the town centre of Beaucaire via D 15 for Fourques then south industrial zone.* ✆*04 66 59 55 07. www.auberge-amandin.com. Closed Sun–Mon for dinner (late Apr–Oct), Sun–Wed for dinner (Nov–early Apr).* Laid out in the stables of an old *mas*, this dining room has a charming Provençal atmosphere. The traditional cuisine is livened up with a wood fire. There are also tables on the terrace facing the garden.

EVENTS

Les Fêtes de la Madeleine – For ten days in July, this summer festival re-creates the glorious past of the Beaucaire Fair. Entertainment includes *abrivados, courses camarguaises* in the amphitheatre (where the "Palme d'Or" trophy is contested), *novilladas* and *corridas* (during the last weekend of the month), fairground rides, dance evenings, fireworks and "casetas" (tents) where Xères wine flows liberally to the sound of flamenco *(www.beaucaire. fr/Estivales).*

Les Beaux Quais – There are markets along the canal banks from Jul–Aug Fri 6pm–midnight.

GUIDED TOURS

Guided tours of the town – *(1hr30min).* Beaucaire offers a variety of tours including that of the château and evening walks. For information and reservations enquire at the tourist office (✆*4.40€; 6.40€ evening; "passport" for all nine tours 22€; www.beaucaire.fr).*

St-Rémy-de-Provence★

Bouches-du-Rhône

Gateway to the Alpilles, St-Rémy symbolises the essence of Provence: boulevards shaded by plane trees, fountains gracing the squares, charming alleyways, and a festive atmosphere, especially on market day and during traditional fairs. Sitting within a region that is a great fruit and market gardening centre, it is a town of gardeners, and has long specialised in the production and trade of flower and vegetable seeds. St-Rémy's main source of income, however, is tourism, encouraged by its thyme- and rosemary-scented streets and the presence of impressive Roman ruins.

A BIT OF HISTORY

The village, founded after the destruction of Glanum, developed under the protection of the Abbaye de St-Rémi of Reims, from which its name is derived. Birthplace of the famous astrologist Michel Nostradamus, St-Rémy has been dazzled by the genius of Van Gogh and the inspiration of the Provençal poets from Roumanille to Marie Mauron (1896–1986).

PLATEAU DES ANTIQUES★★
1km/0.6mi S of St-Rémy – allow 2hr.

◯ *Leave St-Rémy by the D5*

🅿 *Leave your car in the parking area on the right, in front of the triumphal arch.*

The Roman monuments lie on a plateau below the Alpilles' last foothills. In this pleasant spot, from where the view extends over the Comtat plain, Durance valley and Mont Ventoux, stood the prosperous city of Glanum. It was abandoned after Barbarian invasions at the end of the 3C; two magnificent monuments – the mausoleum and commemorative arch – remain.

▶ **Population:** 10 203
◔ **Michelin Map:** 340: D-3 – Local map, *◔see Les ALPILLES.*
🈁 **Info:** Place Jean-Jaurès, 13210 St-Rémy-de-Provence. ℘04 90 92 05 22. www.saintremy-de-provence.com.
🅿 **Parking:** Place de la République or place Jean-Jaurès.
◉ **Don't Miss:** Plateau des Antiques.
◔ **Timing:** Count on spending a day here, especially on market day (Wednesday). It's a good base to explore the surrounding area (Avignon, Arles ...).

Mausoleum★★

This monument is 18m/59ft high and is one of the most outstanding in the Roman world and the best preserved; it lacks but the pinecone finial crowning its dome. For a long time it was believed to have been built as a sepulchre for a noble from Glanum and his spouse. However, the excavations conducted by Henri Rolland have established that it was not a tomb but a cenotaph; that is to say, a monument built in memory of the deceased, around 30 BC.

Low reliefs representing battle and hunting scenes adorn the four walls of the square podium. The first storey, pierced by four arches, bears on the frieze (depicting naval scenes) of the northern architrave an inscription which says "Sextius, Lucius, Marcus, sons of Caius of the Julii family, to their parents". This suggests a posthumous dedication from the three brothers in honour of their father and grandfather.

The second storey is made up of a rotunda with a Corinthian colonnade which encloses the statues of the two figures.

Arc Municipal★

Perhaps contemporary with the mausoleum, that is to say the first years of Augustus' reign, this arch is the oldest Roman arch of the Narbonensis region. It indicated, on the main route to the Alps, the entrance to Glanum. Its perfect proportions (12.5m/41ft long, 5.5m/18ft wide and 8.6m/28ft high) and the exceptional quality of its carved decoration show Greek influence, quite evident at Glanum.

The sole arcade is carved with a lovely festoon of fruit and leaves; inside, it is adorned with a finely carved hexagonal coffered ceiling. On either side of the opening are allegorical symbols of victory and on the sides groups of two prisoners, men and women, down by the victors' booty. The despondency of these figures is well rendered.

Art historians feel that the unique form of this arch, mutilated very soon after construction, has inspired some of the 12C Romanesque doorways such as St-Trophime at Arles.

GLANUM★

rte des Baux-de-Provence. ○*Open Apr–Aug daily 9.30am–6.30pm; Sept Tue–Sun 9.30am–6.30pm; Oct–Mar Tue–Sun 10am–5pm (last admission 45min before closing).* ○*Guided tours (1hr30min).* ○*Closed 1 Jan, 1 May, 1 and 11 Nov, 25 Dec.* ○7€. ○04 90 92 23 79. http://glanum.monuments-nationaux.fr/en.*

The excavations, unearthed since 1921, are located at the main gap of the Alpilles, which dominate them. The site consists of a group of complex structures reflecting several different periods of occupation, grouped by archaeologists into three phases.

A BIT OF HISTORY

The Three Glanum – The origin of the site is a sanctuary venerated by Celtic-Ligurian people known as the Glanics. This native settlement rapidly came into contact with the merchants of Massalia owing to its location close to two important roads. Glanon **(or Glanum I)** developed under Hellenistic influence

as can be seen in the construction, particularly in the technique of bonding (large carved blocks of stone perfectly set without mortar) in the 3C and 2C BC. This Hellenistic community included public buildings (temple, agora, assembly hall, a rampart, which was probably ceremonial and controlled the procession to the sanctuary), houses with peristyles, and a fortified district to the south (sanctuary).

The second phase **(Glanum II)** began with the Roman conquest during the late 2C and with the occupation of the country by Marius' army, which stopped the Teutonic army. The town most probably suffered when the Teutons passed through; the new buildings were then made by the bonding of irregular stones and the majority of the public buildings disappeared.

The last phase **(Glanum III)** follows the conquest of Marseille by Caesar in 49 BC. Romanisation intensified, and under Emperor Augustus the town was rebuilt. In the centre, the old buildings were razed, their debris levelled and filled to make room for a vast horizontal esplanade on which were erected the great public buildings: forum, basilica, temples and baths.

Reception

In the visitors' centre (ticket office), two models of the site, reconstructed frescoes and various fragments of architecture and domestic objects all help to shed further light on the different phases of the site's history.

Gallic Sanctuary

Set up in terraces facing the rising sun, this sanctuary dates from the 6C BC. In this area kneeling warriors were uncovered, as well as stelae with carved skulls identical to those found in the great Salian towns.

Nymphaeum

The source round which Glanum possibly developed is marked by a pool with masonry walls of large, Greek-style stones. In 20 BC Agrippa built a temple next to it, dedicated to

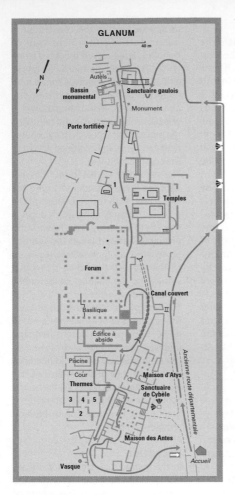

GLANUM

0   40 m

N

Autels
Bassin monumental
Sanctuaire gaulois
Monument
Porte fortifiée
1
Temples
Forum
Canal couvert
Basilique
Édifice à abside
Piscine
Cour
Thermes
3 4 5
2
Maison d'Atys
Sanctuaire de Cybèle
Ancienne route départementale
Maison des Antes
Vasque
Accueil

Temples

Southwest of the forum *(on the left as you go north)* stood twin temples surrounded by a *peribolos* (a court enclosed by a wall), the southern section of which partially covered an assembly hall with its tiered seats. These Roman public buildings, the oldest of their kind in Gaul, date back to 30 BC. Important vestiges of their lavish decoration (blocks of cornice, roof decorations, etc.) as well as exquisite sculpture have been excavated. These vestiges have made it possible, partially, to reconstruct the smaller of the two temples. A monumental fountain **(1)** stood opposite the temples in front of the forum and here a trapezoidal square belonging to a Hellenistic building was laid out, surrounded by magnificent head capital colonnades.

Forum

The forum was built on the ruins of pre-Roman buildings which archaeologists are seeking to identify. It was closed to the north by the basilica (a multi-purpose building mostly for commercial and administrative activities) of which 24 foundation pillars remain and under which Sulla's house was discovered. In the house were uncovered mosaics **(2)**, most likely the oldest ones found in Gaul.

South of the basilica lay the forum square lined on each side by a covered gallery and closed to the south by a great decorated apsidal-ended wall. Discovered underneath the square were a house and a large Hellenistic building.

Covered Canal

This remarkable work, probably a channel which drained the water from the valley and the town, was so constructed

Valetudo, goddess of health (ruins of three fluted columns). A staircase leads to the bottom still fed with water from the spring.

Fortified Gate

This remarkable Hellenistic vestige used, as at St-Blaise, the Massaliote technique of large, well-matched rectangular blocks of stone with merlons and gargoyles. The ramparts, which succeeded at least two protohistoric ramparts, defended the sanctuary and included a postern with a zigzag passageway and a carriage gate.

that the stone covering also served as Glanum's main street pavement.

Baths

These baths date back to the time of Julius Caesar. Their clear plan followed the classical route: a *gymnasium* (**3**), *frigidarium* (**4**), *tepidarium* (**5**), *caldarium*, *palestra*, set up for physical exercise and athletic games, once lined with porticoes, and finally a cold swimming pool, possibly supplied with running water.

Maison d'Atys

This house was originally divided into two parts (peristyled court to the north and pool to the south) joined by a large door. Later a sanctuary to Cybele was set up in the area where the peristyle stood; note the votive altar dedicated to the goddess' ears.

Maison des Antes

Beside Maison d'Atys, this lovely Greek-style house, built according to the 2C BC taste, was laid out around a peristyled central courtyard and cistern. The entrance bay of one of the rooms has preserved its two pilasters *(antes)*.

✎ WALKING TOUR

THE TOWN
Place de la République

Beside the ring road, this square is on the site of the medieval ramparts and is the heart of the town, animated by its café terraces and the bustle on its market days.

Collégiale St-Martin

Bd Marceau. ◷*Open for organ concerts Jul–Sept Sat 5.30pm.* ✆*04 90 92 10 51.*
This collegiate church with its striking façade was rebuilt around 1820 after it had partially caved in. The only remaining 14C feature is the bell tower crowned with a crocketed spire.
The vestiges of the old 14C fortifications line rue Hoche; here can also be seen the **Maison natale de Nostradamus** (Nostradamus' Birthplace) and the 17C **Ancien Hôpital St-Jacques**.

▷ *Take boulevard Victor-Hugo and turn leftt into rue du 8 Mai 1945. In place Jules Pélissier stands the town hall, which was formerly a 17C monastery. Turn right into rue Lafayette, then left into rue Estrine.*

Musée Estrine Centre d'Art Présence Van Gogh

8 r. Estrine. ◷*Open Mar–Apr and Oct–Nov Tue–Sun 10am–12.30pm, 2–6pm; May–Sept Tue and Thu–Sun 10am–12.30pm, 2–7pm, Wed 10am–7pm.* ✎*Guided tours (1hr).* ⊙*3.20€.* ✆*04 90 92 34 72.*
This museum is housed in a handsome private mansion was built in the 18C for Marquis Joseph de Pistoye and was subsequently purchased by Louis Estrine, a master rope maker from Marseille, from whom the house gets its name. Built on three storeys from ashlar masonry, it features a central concave section on its façade into which opens the doorway, surmounted by an elegant wrought iron balcony. Inside, the grand stone staircase leads up to the rooms on the first floor, which are paved with floor tiles and decorated with plasterwork.
The museum has an audiovisual display and thematic exhibitions to illustrate Van Gogh's work and the time he spent at St-Rémy. The upper floors are given over to interesting temporary exhibitions of contemporary art.
On the corner of rue Carnot and rue Nostradamus is the 19C **Fontaine Nostradamus**, decorated with a portrait of the famous medic and astrologer.
A couple of yards further on, place Favier (Le Planet or the former herbal marketplace) is lined with fine 15C and 16C hôtels, the latter of which hosts the Musée des Alpilles: the Hôtel de Sade (15C–16C) and the 16C **Hôtel Mistral de Mondragon**.

▷ *Return to boulevard Marceau, where a detour to the right reveals (at no 11) the former Hôtel de Lubières, also known as the "house of the almond tree".*

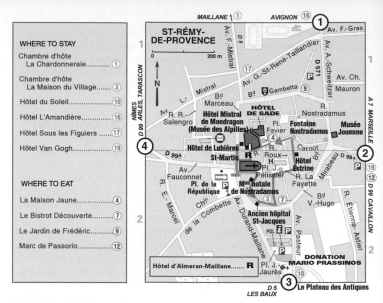

WHERE TO STAY

Chambre d'hôte
La Chardonneraie.......... ①

Chambre d'hôte
La Maison du Village....... ③

Hôtel du Soleil.................. ⑩

Hôtel L'Amandière............. ⑯

Hôtel Sous les Figuiers ...... ⑰

Hôtel Van Gogh................ ⑲

WHERE TO EAT

La Maison Jaune................ ④

Le Bistrot Découverte.......... ⑦

Le Jardin de Frédéric........... ⑨

Marc de Passorio............... ⑫

ADDITIONAL SIGHTS
Musée des Alpilles

pl. Favier. &⊙*Open Tue–Sat and first
Sun of month Nov–Feb 2–5pm; Apr–Jun
and Sept–Oct 10am–noon, 2–6pm;
Jul–Aug 10am–12.30pm, 2–7pm.*
⊙*Closed 1 Jan, 1 May and 25 Dec.*
3€. ℘04 90 92 68 24.

This museum is located in the vast 16C
Mistral de Mondragon mansion built
round a fine courtyard with a round
turreted staircase and overlooked by
loggias. The exhibits relate to popular
arts and traditions including costumes
and old farming techniques. Documents
concerning Nostradamus as well as
minerals from the Alpilles are also
displayed.

Ancien Monastère de
St-Paul-de-Mausole

*av. Van Gogh (off the D 5 in the direction
of Glanum).* &⊙*Open Apr–Sept daily
9.30am–7pm; Oct–Christmas week and
Jan–Mar Tue–Sun 10.15am–4.45pm.*
⊙*Closed 1 Nov and 1 Jan.* *4€.*
℘04 90 92 77 00.

Located near the Roman monuments,
to which its name is linked, this
monastery of Augustinian and later
Franciscan canons was transformed into
a convalescent home in the mid-18C. It
preserves the memory of Vincent Van

Gogh, who asked to be interned here
from 3 May 1889 to 16 May 1890.

He had a workroom on the ground floor
and a bedroom on the first floor. While
here he painted: his life at the hospital,
nature (*Cypress Trees, The Sower*), self-
portraits, and the extraordinary work
The Starry Night.

The small church dates from the end
of the 12C (18C façade) and has a fine
square bell tower with Lombard arcades.
Beside it the **cloisters**★ present a fine
Romanesque décor: the capitals of the
small columns are carved with varied
motifs (foliage, animals, masks).

Mas de la Pyramide

*chemin des Carrières (200m/219yd from
the Monastery of St-Paul-de-Mausole).*
&⊙*Open daily May–Sept 9am–noon,
2–7pm; Oct–Apr 9am–noon, 2–5pm.*
4€. ℘04 90 92 00 81.

This *mas* hewn out of the rock has an
unusual interior layout. It was built in
the old Roman quarries from materials
that were also used for the neighbouring town of Glanum. There is a museum
which displays tools and agricultural
equipment once used by local peasants.
At the centre, the vertical "pyramid" rock
is a reminder of the ground level of the
site before mining began.

ADDRESSES

🛌 STAY

🍽 **Hôtel Van Gogh** – *1 av. J. Moulin.* 🕿*04 90 92 09 05. Closed mid-Mar–Oct. 21 rooms.* ☕*8€.* This simple town centre hotel features rooms decorated with a Provençal note. Those on the first floor have dormer windows. Attractive poolside terrace. Good value.

🍽🍽–🍽🍽 **Hôtel du Soleil** – *35 av. Pasteur.* 🕿*04 90 92 00 63. Closed mid-Nov–mid-Mar. 5 rooms.* Buildingsover a century old (converted metalworks factory) around a vast enclosed courtyard (terrace, garden, swimming pool, fountain). Peaceful, unostentatious rooms.

🍽🍽🍽 **L'Amandière** – *av. Théodore Aubanel. 1km/0.6mi NE.* 🕿*04 90 92 41 00. www.hotel-amandiere.com. 25 rooms.* ☕*7.50€.* A quiet regional building with a pleasant tree-lined flower garden. Peacful, practical rooms with a balcony or terrace. Breakfast is served in the winter garden.

🍽🍽🍽 **Chambre d'hôte La Chardonneraie** – *60 r. Notre Dame, 13910 Maillane, 7km/4.3mi NW.* 🕿*04 90 95 80 12. http://lachardonneraie.com. 4 rooms.* Forming part of an old Provençal *mas*, this charming house is full of allure with its shimmering colours, antique furniture, small garden and swimming pool. At breakfast time the owner will point out the most picturesque footpaths from which to explore the area.

🍽🍽🍽–🍽🍽🍽🍽 **Hôtel Sous Les Figuiers** – *3 av. Taillandier.* 🕿*04 32 60 15 40. www.hotel-charme-provence.com. Closed 10 Jan–13 Mar. 13 rooms.* ☕*12€.* Small hotel full of charm and warmth. The stylish rooms (quilts and antique furniture) boast private terraces shaded by a century-old fig tree. Painting workshop.

🍽🍽🍽🍽 **Chambre d'hôte La Maison du Village** – *10 r. du 8 mai 1945.* 🕿*04 32 60 68 20. www.lamaisonduvillage.com. 5 rooms.* ☕*12€.* This 18C house in the heart of the historic centre is delightfully decorated. Superb rooms and enchanting courtyard-terrace.

🍴 EAT

🍽🍽 **Le Bistrot Dévouverte** – *19 bd Victor Hugo.* 🕿*04 90 92 34 49. Closed last week Aug, Jan–Feb, Sun eve (except Jul–Aug) and Mon.* The characterful bistro and veranda-terrace serve traditional Provençal dishes. Splendid stone vaulted cellar with a fine wine list to be sampled on the spot or taken home.

🍽🍽 **Le Jardin de Frédéric** – *8 bd Gambetta.* 🕿*04 90 92 27 76.* Traditional Provençal dishes in a cosy, smart atmosphere with soft orange and yellow décor. Friendly welcome.

🍽🍽 **Marc de Passorio** – *8 chemin Canto-Cigalo, 1km/0.6mi via 2 (on map). www.restaurant-marcdepassorio.com. Closed 11 Jan–11 Feb, Sun eve and Mon (low season). Reservations recommended.* Elegant atmosphere in the restaurant, which opens onto a flower-decked terrace. Regional dishes, based on the best local produce.

🍽🍽🍽🍽 **La Maison Jaune** – *15 r. Carnot.* 🕿*04 90 92 56 14. www.lamaison jaune.info. Closed Dec–Jan, Tue lunch (Jun–Sept), Sun eve (Oct–Nov and Feb–May), Mon.* This restaurant, with a yellow façade overlooks the old town. A beautiful abode with a large shaded upstairs terrace. Teak furniture and a roof of local tiles. Delicious Provençal cuisine.

🛍 SHOPPING

Le Petit Duc – *7 bd Victor-Hugo.* Using recipes drawn from books of magic spells, the delicacies of Le Petit Duc will surprise you not only for their flavours but also for their names: *oreilles de la bonne déesse* (ears of the good goddess), *pastilles d'amour* (love lozenges) and in particular the town speciality, *pignolat de Nostradamus.*

Santonnier Laurent-Bourges – *on the D5 to Maillane.* From his home in the heart of the countryside, Laurent Bourges has dedicated himself to the profession of *santon* craftsmanship for 44 years. Pay him a visit and he will show you his atelier and, who knows, perhaps divulge some secrets of his ancestral know-how. You might even encounter some celebrities searching for figures to complete their collection.

EVENTS

Festival Organa – Organ festival in the Collégiale St-Martin, Jul–Sept Sat 5.30pm.

Fête de la Transhumance – Whit Sunday from 10.30am: goats, ewes and rams cross the town in celebration of the end of winter as animals move to open pastures. The festivities include a cheese fair, an antique fair and a display of Provençal donkeys.

La Fête du Vin et de l'Artisanat – Around thirty local wine producers bring their best vintages for sale along with arts and craft exhibitors in the town centre on the last weekend of July.

Feria Provençale – Typical *courses camarguaises* in the middle weekend of August, which includes abrivados, and the so-called *carreto ramado*, a ritual procession of a cart drawn by 40 horses.

Noël – At Christmas a *gros souper* (Christmas dinner) market is set up, offering basic ingredients to make a Christmas meal; a pastoral played by the town's inhabitants.

Salon-de-Provence★

Bouches-du-Rhône

The town lies at the heart of France's olive growing country. Today mineral oils hold an important position in the town's commerce. Salon is the seat of the officers' training school for the French Air Force, which was established in 1936. It was also the home of doctor and soothsayer Nostradamus.

A BIT OF HISTORY

Michel de Nostradame (Nostradamus) chose Salon as his home. Born in St-Rémy-de-Provence in 1503, he studied medicine in Montpellier and travelled for 12 years in Europe and the Far East to try to improve the remedies which he kept secret; he also studied esotericism.

The success he achieved with his remedy for the plague epidemics of Aix and Lyon aroused the jealousy of his colleagues. When the epidemics ceased, he retired to Salon (1547) and took up astrology. His book of predictions entitled *Centuries*, written in the form of verse quatrains, was fantastically successful and attracted the attention of Catherine de' Medici. She came to him and had him read Charles IX's horoscope, showering him profusely with gifts. He died in Salon in 1566.

▶ **Population:** 40 147.

Michelin Map: 340: F-4.

Info: 56 cours Gimon, 13664 Salon-de-Provence. 04 90 56 27 60. www.salon-de-provence.org.

Don't Miss: Château de l'Empéri, the house of Nostradamus, a trip to La Barben zoo and castle.

Timing: Allow 2hr or more if you come on market day – Wednesday – on place Morgan.

Kids: La Barben zoo.

WALKING TOUR

TOWN CENTRE
2hr.

Château de l'Empéri
Montée du Puech.

Built on top of Puech rock, this massive castle dominates the old town. Once the residence of the archbishops of Arles, Lords of Salon, the castle was begun in the 10C, rebuilt in the 12C and 13C and remodelled in the 16C; it was transformed into barracks in the 19C but damaged during the 1909 earthquake. A vaulted passage leads to the courtyard decorated with a Renaissance gallery. The 12C Chapelle Ste-Catherine, the main reception room with its finely carved chimney and some 30 rooms, houses the **Empéri Museum**.

Hôtel de Ville

174 pl. de l'Hôtel de Ville.
℘04 90 44 89 00.
This elegant 17C mansion with two corner turrets and a carved balcony nowadays houses the town hall. On place de l'Hôtel de Ville stands the statue of Adam de Craponne (1526–76), a native son of Salon and civil engineer, who made the region fertile through the construction of the irrigation canal bearing his name which carries water from the Durance along the original river course through the Lamanon gap.

Porte Bourg-Neuf

r. du Bourg Neuf.
This gate opposite the town hall is all that is left of the old 13C ramparts.

OLD TOWN

In the centre of the old town the house of Nostradamus is to be seen, before passing through the **porte de l'Horloge** *(rue de l'Horloge)* to reach place Crousillat with its charming 18C fountain, the **Fontaine moussue**.

◗ *Continue along rue des Frères-Kennedy, then turn right into rue de Pontis.*

Collégiale St-Laurent

r. Maréchal Joffre. ℘04 90 56 06 40.
This 14C and 15C church is a good example of southern French Gothic. Inside, admire a monolithic 15C polychrome Descent from the Cross, carved from a single block of stone; the third north chapel contains Nostradamus' tomb.

◗ *Turn back to rue Frères-Kennedy and make for place des Centuries, in front of the castle.*

ADDITIONAL SIGHTS
Musée de l'Empéri★★

Château de l'Empéri, Montée du Puech.
◷*Open Wed–Mon 10am–noon, 2–6pm. Ticket office closes 45min before museum.* ◷*Closed public holidays.*
৶*4.50€. ℘04 90 56 22 36.*
This museum covers the history of the French army from the time of Louis XIV to 1918. The fine rooms enhance the impressive display of 10 000

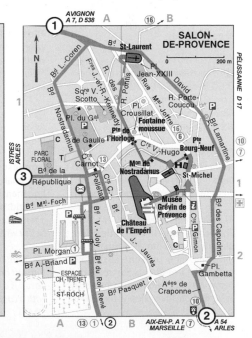

WHERE TO STAY	
Chambre d'hôte Domaine du Bois Vert	(1)
Chambre d'hôte Le Castelas	(7)
Château de la Barben	(10)
Hôtel d'Angleterre	(13)
Hôtel Vendôme	(16)

WHERE TO EAT	
L'Eau à la Bouche	(1)
La Salle à Manger	(6)
La Touloubre	(7)
Le Craponne	(10)
Le Planet	(13)
Le Repaire	(16)

items (uniforms, flags, decorations, cutting and thrusting weapons and firearms, cannons, paintings, drawings, engravings, figures on foot or on horseback) which illustrate the military past with special reference to the Napoleonic years.

Musée Grévin de Provence

pl. des Centuries. ♿🕐*Open Mon–Fri 9am–noon, 2–6pm, Sat–Sun 2–6pm.* 🕐*Closed public holidays.* ⊜*4.50€.* 📞*04 90 56 36 30.*

Some 2 600 years of the history of Provence are retraced here, in the form of 15 waxwork scenes, from the legendary marriage of Gyptis and Protis to the modern day.

Maison de Nostradamus

11 r. Nostradamus. 🕐*Open Mon–Fri 9am–noon, 2–6pm, Sat–Sun 2–6pm.* 🕐*Closed public holidays.* ⊜*4.50€.* 📞*04 90 56 64 31.*

This is the house in which Nostradamus spent the last 19 years of his life. Ten animated tableaux with audiovisual back-up illustrate his life and work.

🚗 DRIVING TOUR

Round-trip of 57km/35.4mi – allow half a day.

▷ *Leave Salon-de-Provence on the D 572 heading E. After Pélissanne a small road on the left leads to La Barben, which occupies a precipitous site in the small Touloubre valley.*

Château de La Barben★

rte du château, La Barben. 👣*Guided tours only (1hr) 4 Apr–11 Nov daily 2–5pm; 30 Jan–29 Mar 2–5pm.* 🕐*Closed 25 Dec and 1 Jan.* ⊜*8€.* 📞*04 90 55 25 41. www.chateaudelabarben.fr.*

The access ramp to the castle offers a plunging view onto the formal French gardens. The present castle was originally a medieval fortress, built before AD 1000, belonging to the Abbaye St-Victor from Marseille and then to King René, who sold it to the powerful Forbin family. This family owned it for some 500 years and remodelled and enlarged it several times, especially in the 14C and 17C, when it was transformed into a stately home. In front of a noble 17C façade is the terrace (Henri IV staircase with double flight of stairs), from where there is a good view of the gardens designed by Le Nôtre and of the Provençal countryside.

Inside, on the second floor, the Empire-style bedroom of Pauline Borghese, Napoleon's sister, and her boudoir ornamented with paper painted by Granet and representing the Four Seasons, are worth noting.

🧍🧍 Zoo de La Barben

13330 La Barben. ♿🕐*Open daily 10am–6pm.* ⊜*13.50€ (child 8€).* 📞*04 90 55 19 12. www.zoolabarben.com.*

This 30ha/12-acre zoo features a number of enclosures in which over 600 animals roam in relative freedom: big cats, monkeys, elephants, giraffes, bison, zebras and birds of prey. There's a little train (⊜*1€*) to get you around.

▷ *Continue left along the D 572.*

The road follows the fertile Touloubre valley; after the viaduct carrying the TGV southeast, there is a lovely view of the Trévaresse range before you. Take a look at the village of **St-Cannat**.

▷ *Leave St-Cannat by the N 7, in the Avignon direction, then turn left onto the D 917.*

Lambesc

This small town possesses a number of fine mansions and fountains from the 17C and 18C. The large 18C church has a remarkable dome. On a 16C gate is a belfry with a clock and Jack.

▷ *Continue along the N 7, in Cazan turn left onto the D 22. 1km/0.6mi SW of Cazan is a road marked Château-Bas, with a car park at the end.*

Château de La Barben

G. Magnin/MICHELIN

Château-Bas

Temple Romain is open Mon–Sat 9.30am–12.30pm, 1.30–6.30pm, Sun and public holidays 10am–12.30pm, 2.30–6.30pm. Closed 1 Jan and 25 Dec. No charge. 04 90 59 13 16. www.chateaubas.com.

The fascinating ruins of a Roman temple and chapel stand in a charming site at the far end of the castle (16C–18C) estate. The **Temple Romain** probably dates from the late 1C BC, a period characterised by many impressive buildings such as the Commemorative Arch at St-Rémy-de-Provence and the Maison Carrée in Nîmes. The remains include part of the foundations, the left side wall, a wall ending in a square pilaster, surmounted by a beautiful Corinthian capital, and a 7m/23ft fluted column still standing intact. Among the surrounding ruins are a second temple and a semicircular precinct (Roman), probably the ruins of a sanctuary.

Continue along the D 22 and turn right onto the D 22C.

Vieux-Vernègues

After passing through Vernègues, the uphill road circles the old village *(the ruins are not open to the public)*, which was destroyed by an earthquake in 1909, and goes on to the small tower from where there is a **panorama**★ *(viewing table)* of a large area of Provence. Follow the winding road to **Alliens**, which has preserved some remains of the city ramparts.

Turn left onto the D 71D and, just after crossing the EDF canal, turn left again onto the D 17D for Lamanon.

Site de Calès

Leave the car in the car park of the fire station and take the path behind the church. www.cales-lamanon.fr. There are two paths; one leads to the caves and castle ruins *(blue signposts – 1hr30min there and back)*, the other to the chapels *(green signposts – 2hr30min there and back)*. The site is closed in July and August.

Nestling on the slopes of the Défens mountain, the Calès site features cliff dwellings overlooked by a medieval castle and chapels.

Caves (Grottes)

Forming a natural amphitheatre, the caves were used as quarries during the Middle Ages, and were inhabited until the late 16C.

Of the 12C fortress there are few vestiges. From the edge of the terrace, by the statue of Our Lady, there are **views** through the forest: north, of the Durance valley and the Luberon; east, of the cliff dwellings; and south, of the Lamanon gap, the Salon plain, Estaque chain, Crau plain and Berre lagoon.

Go back down towards the cirque. The green signposts lead to the **Chapelle St-Denis**, a typical Provençal church, built in the same age as the castle.

Return to Salon via the D 12F and N 538.

ADDRESSES

🏠 STAY

🛏️ **Hôtel d'Angleterre** – *98 cours Carnot.* 📞*04 90 56 01 10. 26 rooms.* ⊑*7€.* This hotel near the museums was once a convent. Simply renovated rooms; some are air-conditioned. Breakfast buffet under a glass cupola.

🛏️ **Gîte Canto Cigalo** – *quartier du Pin, 13430 Eyguières, 9km/5.6mi NW.* 📞*04 90 59 89 85. Closed mid-Nov–mid-Dec. 4-person gîte.* ⊑🍴. Relatively new premises. Rooms are plainly decorated with old-fashioned furniture.

🛏️ **Hôtel Vendôme** – *34 r. du Mar.-Joffre.* 📞*04 90 56 01 96. www. hotelvendome.com. 19 rooms.* ⊑*7€.* A peaceful hotel reputed for its comfort. Some rooms give onto the patio.

🛏️ **Chambre d'hôte Le Castelas** – *Vallon des Euores, 13121 Aurons.* 📞*04 90 55 60 12. www.lecastelas.com. 3 rooms.* ⊑🍴. *Reservations recommended.* Each room is individual. The vast veranda offers a superb view.

🛏️ **Chambre d'hôte Château de la Barben** – *13330 La Barben, 8km/5mi SE.* 📞*04 90 55 25 41. 2 rooms, 2 suites.* 🛏️. *Evening meal for residents.* Beautiful furnishings in these large rooms. Tours of the château available, children's treasure hunts, walks, hunting, fishing...

🛏️ **Chambre d'hôte Domaine du Bois Vert** – *quartier Montauban, 13450 Grans. 7km/4.3mi S of Salon via D 16 and D 19 for Lançon.* 📞*04 90 55 82 98. www.domaineduboisvert.com. 3 rooms. Closed mid-Nov–Feb.* A park of oak and pine trees surrounds this traditional old house. Rooms have old-fashioned, rustic furnishings. Breakfast is served in the large living room or on the terrace facing the garden. Swimming pool.

🛏️ **Chambre d'hôte Le Gallatras** – *rte de Caireval, 13410 Lambesc, 18km/ 11.2mi E.* 📞*04 42 92 75 70. 2 rooms.* ⊑🍴. Magnificent building situated near Lambesc's vineyards. Comfortable rooms.

🍽️ EAT

🍴–🍴 **Le Repaire** – *old village, 13116 Vernègues, 15km/9.3mi NE.* 📞*04 90 59 31 64. Closed Jan, 1 week in Oct.* Just steps from the ruins of the old village, destroyed in an earthquake in 1909. Pleasant setting and pretty terrace in summer. Light fare, good choice of teas and coffees.

🍴 **Le Planet** – *12 pl. Jean-Jaurès, 13450 Grans, 5.5km/3.4mi SW.* 📞*04 90 55 83 66. Closed Feb and Nov holidays, 17 Sept–3 Oct Sun eve Nov–Mar, Mon–Tue.* This old building has preserved its original vaults. The shaded terrace makes a good people-watching spot!

🍴 **La Salle à Manger** – *6 r. du Maréchal Joffre.* 📞*04 90 56 28 01.* Good-quality food served here. Pleasant ambiance and classic décor.

🍴 **La Touloubre** – *29 chemin Salatier, 8km/5mi SE in La Barben.* 📞*04 90 55 16 85. Closed 3 weeks in Feb, Sun eve and Mon.* Plane trees shade the vast terrace of this village inn located along a quiet road. Large country-style dining room. Seven modern rooms available.

🍴–🍴 **Le Craponne** – *146 allées Craponne.* 📞*04 90 53 23 92. Closed 12 Aug–3 Sept, 23 Dec–3 Jan, Wed and Sun lunch, Mon.* The name of this restaurant refers to a benefactor of the region. Dark-wood panelling, yellow walls and rustic furniture. In fine weather, meals served in a small flower-decked courtyard.

🍴🍴 **L'Eau à la Bouche** – *pl. Morgan.* 📞*04 90 56 41 93. Closed Sun eve and Mon.* Joined to a fishmongers, this restaurant brings over fish and seafood from the shop before cooking it so freshness and quality are guaranteed! You will eat either in the simple dining room or on the veranda, which is very pleasant in the summer.

🛒 SHOPPING

Savonnerie Marius Fabre – *148 av. Paul-Bourret.* 📞*04 90 53 82 75. www.marius-fabre.fr. Closed Sat–Sun.* This soap is still made in the original factory, founded in 1900. Visit the museum and shop.

Tarascon★

Bouches-du-Rhône

A tradition dating back some 2 000 years has made Tarascon the city of the Tarasque. In the 19C century Alphonse Daudet brought fame to the town through his character Tartarin. And yet the city has its own claim to fame in the shape of its magnificent castle, with walls which drop straight down to the swift-flowing Rhône river. The city is on the boundary of a rich market gardening region and has become an important fruit and vegetable dispatching centre. Market day is Tuesday, in the town centre.

CHÂTEAU DU ROI RENÉ★★

Bd du Roi René. ⏱*Open 2 Jun–Sept daily 9.30am–6.30pm; Oct–1 Jun Tue–Sun 10.30am–5pm.* 🔊*Guided tours (1hr) available.* ⏱*Closed public holidays.* ∞*6.50€.* 📞*04 90 91 01 93.*

Its location on the banks of the Rhône, its massive appearance which contrasts with its elegant inner architecture, and its exceptional state of preservation, make this building one of the finest medieval castles in France. In the 13C, the castle, opposite the royal city of Beaucaire, defended Provence's western boundary. Captured by Raymond de Turenne in 1399, it was restored soon after to its owners, the Anjou family;

▶ **Population:** 13 376.

🕐 **Michelin Map:** 340: C-3.

🅰 **Info:** Bd de la République, 13150 Tarascon. 📞04 90 91 03 52. www.tarascon.org.

▷ **Location:** Arrive over the bridge from Beaucaire for the best view of the castle. The town is 17km/10.6mi N of Arles and 23 km/14.3mi W of Avignon.

🅿 **Parking:** Free on the ring road and at the foot of the castle.

✪ **Don't Miss:** King René's castle, the old town, the Souleiado textile museum and shop.

🕐 **Timing:** Allow 2hr to visit the castle followed by a walk around the old town.

🔼 **Kids:** Maison de Tartarin and the Tarasque Festival.

Louis II, father of René, decided to have it entirely rebuilt. From 1447 to 1449, **King René** completed the building, which was his favourite residence, contributing all his taste and refinement to the interior decoration.

It is made up of two independent parts: the seigneurial living quarters on the south side flanked by round towers on the town's side and square towers on the

Château du Roi René

G. Magnin/MICHELIN

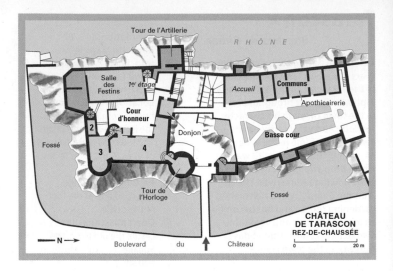

Rhône side, offering a compact mass of walls rising up 48m/157ft; and the inner courtyard on the north side, defended by shorter rectangular towers.

Outer Courtyard (basse cour)

A wide moat spanned by a bridge (once a drawbridge) isolates the group of buildings from the rest of the city. This section includes the recently restored service buildings, including the Hospital of St-Nicolas' **dispensary**: in a finely panelled 18C room there are 200 apothecary jars.

Main Courtyard (cour d'honneur)

Enter the seigneurial living quarters through the keep's zigzag passageway to the main courtyard, around which are the apartments with their lovely, finely carved façades adorned with mullioned windows. A graceful polygonal staircase turret **(1)** serves the different floors; near it a niche shelters the busts of King René and Jeanne of Laval, his second wife. Still on the south side of the main courtyard, climb up some steps to the Flamboyant screen of the chantry **(2)**; opening onto the corner tower is the lower chapel **(3)**, and above it the upper chapel.

To the east and north lie the L-shaped main living quarters which partly overlook the town and include the private apartments, which rise above a lovely gallery **(4)** with pointed barrel vaulting, and communicate with the clock tower.

Seigneurial Living Quarters

The tour of the west wing, which rises above the river, is a visit through the state rooms: the ground floor – banqueting hall (two chimneys); first floor – reception hall (two vast rooms with painted wood ceilings). Then continue to the king's bedroom (in the southwest tower) with a chimney and heating platter; on the second floor are the audience chamber and council room, which were vaulted to support the terraces. In these rooms there are several fine 17C Flemish tapestries. Return to the south wing to see the chaplain's room (sacristy, host oven, corner for the treasury) and the royal chapel, which has kept the king's and queen's oratories and from where they could hear the chantry voices.

Terrace

Access via the artillery tower.

The terrace offers a wide **panorama**★★ of Beaucaire, Tarascon, the Rhône, Vallabrègues undertaking, the Montagnette hills, the Alpilles, Fontvieille, the Abbaye de Montmajour, Arles and St-Gilles plain.

The Tarasque Monster

Tarascon was established on an island in the Rhône as Massalia's trading post. The Romans took it over after the defeat of the Massaliotes. The present castle stands on the site of the Roman camp built by the legionaries. According to a Provençal legend, an amphibious creature periodically climbed out of the Rhône into the town, where it devoured children and cattle and killed anyone attempting to cross the river. To save the town, St Martha came from Les Stes-

Tarasque

G. Magnin/MICHELIN

Maries-de-la-Mer and subdued the beast with the sign of the Cross; the now docile beast was thereupon captured by the townspeople. In celebration of the miracle, Good King René, who often resided in the castle, organised stupendous festivities in 1474. The legend is still recalled in an annual fête.

Go back down by the clock tower; the ground floor houses the galley room, named to commemorate the graffiti and boat drawings made by past prisoners.

🐾 WALKING TOUR

THE TOWN
Even if it is best known for its castle, the town is also worth a visit, for its warm-toned old stone buildings and narrow streets, lined with fine mansions, whose façades have often been carefully restored.

▷ *Enter the town by Porte St-Jean and follow rue Pelletan.*

On the right note the theatre's Baroque façade, with its chubby-cheeked cherubs.

▷ *Continue along rue Proudhon.*

A fine mansion *(no 39)* houses the family business, **Souleïado**, whose shop sells Provençal fabrics printed in warm, bright colours.

WHERE TO STAY

Chambre d'hôte
  Rue du Château............①

Hôtel
  Cadran Solaire...............④

Hôtel du Viaduc...............⑦

Hôtel Les Échevins..........⑩

Hôtel Le Mas
  des Amandiers.............⑬

WHERE TO EAT

Bistrot des Anges.............①

Le Provençal...................④

Cloître des Cordeliers...........**N**
Hôtel de ville.......................**H**

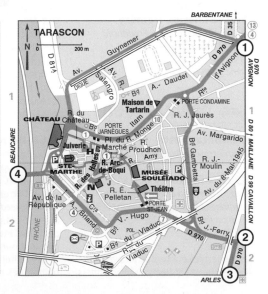

◐ *Continue along this street then, just after the 17C Chapelle de la Persévérance, turn left into rue Arc de Boqui. At the end of this street, turn right towards place du Marché.*

Hôtel de Ville
pl. du Marché. ◐*Open Mon–Thu 8am–noon, 1.30–5pm, Fri 8am–noon, 1.30–4.30pm.* ◐*No charge.* ℘*04 90 91 00 07.*

This 17C building features an elegantly carved façade enhanced by a stone balcony. The first-floor Salle des Consuls, with its panelling and portraits, may be visited.

Rue du Château leads to the picturesque **Juiverie**, the town's former Jewish ghetto.

◐ *Return to place de la Mairie by rue Robert.*

Turn right into rue des Halles, the main street of old Tarascon, where the market was once held. It is lined with picturesque arcaded houses (15C). In rue Ledru-Rollin, on the left, are the 17C galleries of the old cloister, the Cloître des Cordeliers (◐*open Mon–Sat 10am–noon, 2–6.30pm; ℘04 90 91 38 71),* where exhibitions are held.

ADDITIONAL SIGHTS
Musée Charles-Deméry (Souleïado)★ *(39 r.Proudhon).* **Maison de Tartarin** *(55 bis bd Itam; ◐2€ (child 1€), ℘04 90 91 05 08).*

🚗 DRIVING TOUR

La Montagnette
Round-trip of 45km/28mi – allow 4hr.

◐ *Leave Tarascon by the D 80 to the east (in direction of Maillane) and continue along the N 570 via the D 80A, then on the left the D 32.*

Maillane
In the fertile countryside known as the Petite Crau de St-Rémy, Maillane offers the charm typical of a Provençal town with its small squares shaded with plane trees and white tile-roofed houses. Its renown is largely due to the fame of **Frédéric Mistral**, the Provençal poet and one of the founders of the Félibrige movement.

Museon Mistral
11 av. Lamartine. ◐*Open Tue–Sun Apr–Sept 9.30am–11.30am, 2.30–6.30pm; Oct–Mar 10am–11.30am, 2–4.30pm.* ◐*Guided tours only (1hr).* ◐*Closed public holidays.* ◐*4€. ℘04 90 95 84 19.*

This museum is located in the house which Mistral had built and then lived in from 1876 to 1914. Mistral's memory is evoked throughout the various rooms – office, living room, dining room, bedroom – which have been kept as they were at his death.

◐ *Continue to Graveson via the D 5, then left onto the D 28.*

Graveson
Quite charming fortified town whose main street runs alongside a canal. There's a good market here every Friday from May–Oct from 4–8pm. At the end of cours National is the **Musée Auguste-Chabaud**★ (◐*open daily Jun–Sept 10am–noon, 1.30–6.30pm; Oct–May 1.30–6.30pm; ◐closed 1 Jan and 25 Dec; ◐4€; ℘04 90 90 53 02; www.museechabaud.com),* which houses a collection of paintings by this artist, sculptor and poet, who was born in Nîmes and died in Graveson in 1955. He found inspiration in the countryside, rural scenes and festivals of Provence.

Musée des Arômes et du Parfum
Ancien chemin d'Arles. ◐*Open daily Jul–Aug 10am–7pm; Sept–Jun 10am–noon, 2–6pm.* ◐*Closed 1 Jan and 25 Dec.* ◐*5€. ℘04 90 95 81 72. www.museedesaromes.com.*

A few miles to the south on D 80, this perfume museum occupies an old *mas* that once belonged to the monks of St-Michel-de-Frigolet. Traditional techniques related to the making of aromatic scent are presented and explained by a fascinating exhibition: copper stills, collection of old flasks, semicircular racks displaying all types of essences *(orgues de parfumier)* and receptacles for catching the essential oils and floral water after distillation *(essenciers)*.

▶ *Continue to the D 570 and turn right towards Graveson, then left towards Tarascon. Turn left immediately onto the D 81.*

After crossing over the D 970, the road climbs and winds among pines, olive trees and cypresses, in a pleasant setting for a picnic.

▶ *Continue along the D 80 then D 35E.*

Barbentane
♿ *See BARBENTANE.*

▶ *Leave Barbentane to the south, on the D 35.*

Boulbon
An impressive fort dominates the town, which is laid out against the Montagnette hillside.

▶ *Return to Tarascon on the D 35.*

ADDRESSES

🏠 STAY

🛏 **Hôtel de Viaduc** – *9 r. du Viaduc.* ℘*04 90 91 09 99. www.hotelduviaduc.com. 4 rooms.* ☕*5€.* Situated within easy walking distance of the town centre, this hotel is well fitted out. In good weather, breakfast is served on the shaded terrace.

🛏🛏 **Hôtel Le Mas des Amandiers** – *rte d'Avignon, 13690 Graveson, 10km/6mi NE.* ℘*04 90 95 81 76. www.hotel-des-amandiers.com. 3 rooms.* ☕*9€.* Rooms at this hotel, amid almond groves, have rustic furniture; the dining room is decorated with a Provençal note. Outdoor swimming pool. "Botanic" garden.

🛏🛏🛏 **Chambre d'hôte Rue du Château** – *24 r. du Château.* ℘*04 90 91 09 99. www.chambres-hotes.com. 5 rooms. Closed Nov–Jan. Min. stay 2 nights.* Staying in this carefully restored 18C house, situated in a quiet road leading to the château, is like going back in time. Breakfast is served on the flower-decked patio, beneath the dovecote with its red-ochre walls. A dream of a place at a reasonable price.

🛏🛏🛏 **Hôtel Cadran Solaire** – *r. du Cabaret Neuf , 13690 Graveson. 10km/6mi N of Tarascon on N 570.* ℘*04 90 95 71 79. www.hotel-en-provence.com. 12 rooms.*

☕*8€. Closed mid-Nov–mid-Mar.* A sundial adorns the pretty façade of this former coaching inn. Natural beige colours, rush matting on the floor and country furniture in the recently renovated rooms.

🛏🛏🛏 **Hôtel Les Échevins** – *26 bd Itam.* ℘*04 90 91 01 70. www.hotel-echevins.com. 40 rooms.* ☕*10€. Restaurant🍴🍴. Closed Nov–Mar.* Guests will enjoy this 17C dwelling with family atmosphere. Modest but well maintained rooms. Beautiful staircase with wrought-iron railing. Colourful veranda-restaurant and traditional cuisine blown in with the *mistral.*

🍴 EAT

🍴 **Bistrot des Anges** – *pl. du Marché.* ℘*04 90 91 05 11. http://bistrot.des.anges. free.fr.* Amiable restaurant in Provençal style with a summer terrace and light fare on a changing menu. Fresh produce making use of regional ingredients.

🍴🍴 **Le Provençal** – *12 cours Aristide Briand.* ℘*04 90 91 11 41. www.leprovencal-tarascon.com. Closed Sun eve, Mon.* This hotel-restaurant is set in the heart of Tarascon. The restaurant is well recommended locally and the Mediterranean-inspired cuisine uses fresh local produce.

Crusades, collection and countryside collide in Ardèche and Gard, the western most Provençal regions. From here you can immerse yourself in the great outdoors (or underground, if caving is for you), or opt instead to look closely into centuries of religious and political history, dotted with ruins of all shapes and sizes.

Knowing that Aigues-Mortes translates to "dead water", may not make this town sound like your go-to vacation spot. But with its sea marches, salt pans and other topography, this port, rebuilt by Louis IX of France in 13C, is a stop for maritime buffs, history buffs and those who study religious history. In the geography alone, Ardèche is an area with much diversity, as its elevation spans from close to sea level to 1 754m/5 754.6ft at Mont Mézenc. Vallerys, mountains, plateaus and riverside banks all co-exist here, with some sparsely populated regions. The topography makes the area a favorite of canoe and kayak enthusiasts.

Aigues-Mortes was the starting point for both the Seventh and Eighth Crusades, because it gave Louis IX access to the Mediterranean without using a foreign port. Some of this is a little hard to imagine today. In the 14C the sea retreated and the channels dried up. Even without the sea access, you can still explore cafés, shops and the 21C industry for the city: wine-growing. Stop at the place St-Louis and Tour de Constance for a few looks back in time.

Highlights

1 Underground oddities at **Aven de la Forestière** (p164)

2 Contemporary works in a 17C mansion **Musée d'Art Moderne** (p166)

3 Volcanic rock stylings in **Ruoms** (p171)

4 The water works at **Source Perrier** (p180)

5 A wonder of the ancient world **Pont du Gard** (p185)

From the man-made sites at Aigues-Mortes, you should travel to Gorges de l'Ardèche, which are both a natural wonder (the gorges themselves, made by the Ardèche river cutting through limestone), and a manmade wonder (the road that was built to overlook them). The gorges are a nature reserve, with many sites to see, either by car or by train. Try the road between Vallon-Pont-D'Arc to Pont-St-Esprit.

Don't drive by the Belvédère de la Cathédrale, a rock that looks like a cathedral ruin. Opportunities abound for swimming and caving, and even rafting calm enough for kids, for those who want to get out and experience the wilderness.

More wilderness and ancient buildings combine in **Bagnols**, where you can win the trifecta of Roman architecture, art and river rafting. And, what is a trip to France without a visit to the Garrigue and Côtes du Rhône vineyards? Taste Lirac and Tavel wines while here.

The seaside resort of **Le Grau-du-Roi** is dotted with beaches for lapping up the sun. Take a break from the rays at the Seaquarium where you can see sharks and sea lions.

Nîmes is known even to those who haven't visited Provence in the past. Explore this city of the arts, followed by watching bullfighting in the Roman amphitheatre. Stop at the Maison Carrée, one of the best-preserved Roman temples around. There's plenty of shopping in Nîmes, so you can take home the souvenir of your choosing.

Aigues-Mortes★★

Gard

Aigues-Mortes, from *Aquae Mortuae* meaning dead waters, with its large towers and defensive curtain wall, stands in a melancholy landscape of pools, sea marshes and salt pans. This solitary fortified city is a glorious sight, especially during long sunsets on warm, summer evenings.

A BIT OF HISTORY

St Louis' Creation

In the early 13C the King of France, Louis IX (St Louis), possessed no Mediterranean seaport as such. As he was preparing to set out on a crusade to Palestine, Louis IX did not want to embark from a "foreign" seaport like Marseille, for example (foreign, because Marseille was ruled by the Counts of Provence and thus separate from central government). Instead, he sought a site on the coast where he could set up a port of embarkation and a city that would serve to establish and reassert Capetian influence in the region.

In 1240 he obtained, from the monks of the Abbaye de Psalmody, a tract of virgin land frequented only by fishermen. There he rapidly built the Tour de Constance. In order to encourage people to settle on this rather desolate site, the king granted a charter in 1246 that offered many advantages, such as tax exemption and other commercial privileges.

Like the southern bastides (*see The Green Guide Dordogne, Berry-Limousin*), the new town was built on a regular grid plan within a rectangle (550m x 300m/1 805ft x 985ft) cut across by five straight streets that were in turn cut by five cross streets. Clusters of settlements developed in the vicinity of three religious establishments (Notre-Dame-des-Sablons, the Franciscan monastery, and the Psalmody monks' residence), which offered protection from the local winds.

▶ **Population:** 7 115.

Michelin Map: 339: K7 or 528 fold 27.

Info: Place St-Louis, 30220 Aigues-Mortes. ℘04 66 53 73 00. www.ot-aigues mortes.fr.

Location: Take the tourist train (*see Addresses*) or a 2hr guided tour of the town to get an overview of what there is to see and do (*contact the tourist office*). A traditional market can be found on ave. Frédéric-Mistral (*see Addresses*).

P **Parking:** Parking (*fee*) is available in the car park at the foot of the ramparts.

Don't Miss: The panorama from the Tour de Constance.

Timing: See the fortifications first, allowing at least 45min for your visit. Then visit the town site before taking the Excursions.

Kids: A tour of the town in the little tourist train (20min), a walk around the ramparts (45min) or a river-trip by barge.

Setting off for the Crusades

In 1248 a huge armada chartered from Venice and Genoa gathered at Aigues-Mortes, which at that time was linked to the sea by the channel of Grau Louis. An estimated 1 500 ships, carrying 15 000 men plus horses and equipment – the Seventh Crusade – set sail for Cyprus on 28 August.

The Crusaders arrived in Cyprus 23 days later and met with some success before being defeated at al-Mansurah. The king was captured in 1250. In 1270, St Louis embarked with a fleet from Marseille that sailed to Tunis. It was there that he died of the plague, a disease he contracted while attending to his afflicted Crusaders.

The Salted Burgundians

In 1418, during the Hundred Years' War, the Burgundians captured Aigues-Mortes by surprise. The Armagnacs laid siege to the town and were desperate to possess it. In the dead of night, their partisans within the city walls succeeded in killing the garrison guarding one of the gates. They opened the city gates to the besieging army.

The Burgundians were decimated. So numerous were the dead that the corpses awaiting burial were thrown into a tower, named ever since the **Tour des Bourguignons**. To prevent putrefaction, the Armagnacs covered the dead bodies with salt until they could bury them.

Decline

Aigues-Mortes stayed prosperous until the mid-14C, when it had a population of 15 000. However, the sea withdrew and the channels silted. Even the construction of a canal to the coast could not prevent the decline.

The town participated in the Wars of Religion and became a Protestant stronghold. In the 18C the founding of Sète dealt the port a final blow.

The town's activities now include wine growing, which extends over 75% of the municipality, and salt extraction.

VISIT

Allow 1hr

Tall ramparts protect Aigues-Mortes from the salty wind and so it is unscathed by time. The areas surrounding place St Louis and the main streets are teeming with cafés, craft boutiques, souvenir shops and art galleries. In season, the Aigues-Mortes sightseeing train departs every half hour from Porte de la Gardette; you can also enjoy a boat tour on the canal (*see Addresses*).

Église Notre-Dame des Sablons★

Grand'Rue Jean-Jaurès. Open daily 10am–6pm. Guided tour of the chapels including Notre-Dame des Sablons (1hr30min) available from tourist office Mon–Fri. 3.50€. 04 66 53 73 00.

This Gothic church has been frequently modified over the years, even serving as a salt warehouse at one time. Inside, its timber-framed nave adds to the simplicity of the décor: 14C Christ, altar table from the former Abbaye de Psalmody and Chapelle St-Louis. It is lit by contemporary stained-glass windows by local artist Claude Viallat.

Place St-Louis

On this shaded square that marks the heart of the town stands the statue of St Louis (1849) by Pradier. The 17C **Chapelle des Capucins** (open Wed–Sun; 04 66 53 38 60) served as a market before being converted into an exhibition space.

To get to the fortifications, take rue Victor-Hugo to the Organeau gate. From there turn right into boulevard Sud followed by boulevard Ouest, which formerly allowed garrisons to move swiftly. You will then reach the Porte de la Gardette.

FORTIFICATIONS

45min. Access from place Anatole France Open daily Sept–Apr 10am–5.30pm; May–Aug 10am–7pm (last entry 45min before closing). Closed 1 Jan, 1 May, 1 and 11 Nov, 25 Dec. 7€ (child no charge). 04 66 53 61 55. http://aigues-mortes.monuments-nationaux.fr.

Tour de Constance★★

This tower is a circular keep 22m/72ft in diameter and 40m/131ft high (including the turret), with walls 6m/19.6ft thick.

Located northwest of the town, the tower was built between 1240 and 1249. The entrance fort and bridge, which connected the tower to the ramparts, date from the 16C. A defensive system protected the entrance. You can still see the portcullis and the embrasures through which missiles were hurled onto assailants.

The lower room with pointed arches still has its bread oven. The upper floors are approached by a spiral staircase. St Louis' oratory is a minute chapel built into the wall and the upper room, which served as quarters for prisoners. A display case presents various documents covering a period of 500 years and concerning these famous detainees, many of whom were political opponents of the regime: Templars, rebel barons, and Huguenots. Two Protestants held in the tower were **Abraham Mazel**, a Calvinist who escaped down knotted bedclothes with 16 co-religionists in 1705, and **Marie Durand**, whose courage secured her release together with ten of her companions from the cell in which she had been incarcerated for 38 years (1730–68). Note her graffito: *Register* (the verb to resist in Vivarais dialect).

Climb to the summit of the watchtower *(53 steps)* crowned by a wrought-iron cage. In the 13C–16C this protected a lantern that served as a beacon. An immense **panorama**★★ extends over the town and its grid-patterned streets right to left by the Cévennes, the Grande-Motte "pyramids", Montagne de Sète, the Midi salt marshes and the Camargue.

Remparts★★

The ramparts were built after 1272 with stone quarried from Beaucaire and Les Baux. Four sided, and of remarkable unity, the fortifications are a typical example of 13C military architecture. The walls, topped by a watch path, are flanked by towers of different size and importance. The large towers defending the main gates contained two vaulted rooms with terraces.

The ramparts were punctuated by only two gates to the north, whereas, to the south, five gates or posterns offered access to the town from its loading docks. The towers in order of approach are: Tour des Bourguignons; Porte de l'Organeau, an *organeau* being the iron ring to which the ships were moored; Porte des Moulins (Mill Gate), where grain was ground for the garrison; Porte

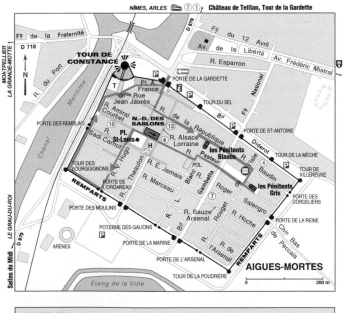

des Galions (Galleons Gate), in front of which moored the galleys; Porte de la Marine (Maritime Gate), a ceremonial entrance; Tour de la Poudrière (the powder magazine); Tour de Villeneuve; Tour de la Mèche (Wick Tower), where a light was kept burning to ignite firearms; and finally, Tour du Sel (Salt Tower).

EXCURSIONS
Tour Carbonnière
◯ *3km/2mi N towards St-Laurent-d'Aigouze.*

A 14C tower, complete with gates, portcullises and battlements, was the advanced barbican of Aigues-Mortes on the old salt road.

ADDRESSES

🛏 STAY

◯◯◯ **Chambre d'hôte Hermitage de Saint-Antoine** – *9 bd Intérieur-Nord, opposite St-Antoine gate. ℰ06 03 04 34 05. www.hermitagesa.com. Closed Jan–Feb. 3 rooms. ⌷.* At the heart of the old town, this small house adheres to traditional Aigues-Mortes architecture. Despite their small size, the three rooms are cosy.

◯◯◯ **St-Louis** – *10 r. Amiral Courbet. ℰ04 66 53 72 68. www.lesaintlouis.fr. Closed Nov–Mar. 22 rooms. ⌷10€. Restaurant◯◯◯.* Inside the city walls, near the Constance Tower, an elegant 18C building with comfortable, colourful rooms. Those on the second floor are more spacious. Enjoy the Provençal-style indoor dining area with fireplace in winter. In summer, there's a pretty, shaded patio.

◯◯◯◯ **Chambre d'hôte Mas de la Montille** – *rte des Stes-Maries-de-la-Mer, 30220 St-Laurent d'Aigouze, 9km/5.6mi N. ℰ04 66 35 59 43. http://masdelamontille. free.fr. 6 rooms. ⌷⌷. Meal◯◯.* Charming, oriental furnishings, the roos are comfortable. Swimming pool, Jacuzzi. Good quality food by reservation.

Château de Teillan
◯ *13km/8mi NE on D 979, then, after St-Laurent d'Aigouze, left on D 288.*

🐾*Guided tours of the interior by appointment only (1hr) mid-Jul–mid-Aug Tue–Sun. ◯3€. ℰ04 66 88 02 38.* Built on a Gallo-Roman site, this former priory of the Abbaye de Psalmody was sold in the 17C and enlarged.
A watchtower (15C) surmounts the main part of the building. There is a fine view from the terrace of the Cévennes, Languedoc plain, Aigues-Mortes and the Camargue. In the park you will find Roman altars and milestones. Note also the remarkable chain water pump in the small vaulted outbuildings.

◯◯◯◯ **Hôtel Canal** – *440 rte de nîmes. ℰ04 66 80 50 04. www.hotel canal.fr. Closed mid-Nov–mid-Dec and 10 Jan–20 Feb. 25 rooms. ⌷11.50€. Restaurant◯◯◯.* At the entrance to the town, opposite the canal, is this contemporary-style hotel. The functional, air-conditioned roooms are well soundproofed. Swimming pool and sundeck.

🍴 EAT

◯◯◯ **Le Café de Bouzigues** – *7 r. Pasteur. ℰ04 66 53 93 95. www.cafe debouzigues.com. Closed first weeks in Dec and Jan.* No, you won't find mussels from Bouzigues here, in spite of the café's name. But you will find a regional menu that changes monthly and a colourful dining room or birdcage-filled courtyard-terrace in which to eat it.

◯◯◯ **La Salicorne** – *9 r. Alsace-Lorraine. ℰ04 66 53 62 67. www.la-salicorne.com. Closed Tue, Mon–Sat lunch, Jan and first fortnight in Feb.* Stonework, exposed beams, a fireplace, wrought iron, a pleasant summer terrace and food with a southern Provence flavour.

◯◯◯◯ **Les Arcades** – *23 bd Gambetta. ℰ04 66 53 81 13. www.les-arcades.fr. Closed Mon and Tue.* Beautiful 16C house in a refined Provençal décor of bare stone. Arcaded tterrrace, regional cuisine, attractive rooms and small pool. Peace and quiet guaranteed.

🛒 SHOPPING

Traditional Market – *av. Frédéric-Mistral. Wed and Sun 8.30am–12.30pm.*

Domaines de Jarras-Listel – *Quai Jarras, rte du Grau du Roi. ℘04 66 51 17 00. www.listel.fr. Tastings and guided tours (1hr) Apr–Oct by appointment. ⌕3€.* The cradle of local *vins des sables*, these vines are grown in the sand. Be sure to sample the *vin gris*, rosé.

La Bandido – *12 r. Pasteur. ℘04 66 53 72 31. Closed Nov–Feb.* Regional clothing and footwear.

EVENTS

Feast of St Louis – *Third weekend in Aug.* Medieval market, processions in historical costumes, tournaments, as well as the embarkation of the king.

Votive Feast – *Second week and third weekend of Oct.* This feast is notable for the typical Camargue races, which are preceded by *abrivados* and followed by lively *bandidos*.

🎣 LEISURE ACTIVITIES

👥 **Tours by Sightseeing Train** – *SEPTAM, Porte de la Gardette. ℘04 66 53 85 20. ⌕4€ (child 2.50€).* Departs every 45min from Porte de la Gardette. From Apr–Sept daily (ride lasts 20min).

👥 **Boat Tours** – **Pescalune Barge**, *46 r. de la Pinède. ℘04 66 53 79 47. www. pescalune-aiguesmortes.com.* Departure from the foot of the Tour de Constance. Trips last 1hr45min and follow the canal of Le Grau-du-Roi and the canal that links the Rhône to Sète. *⌕8€ (child 6€).*

Gorges de l'Ardèche★★★

Ardèche

The Ardèche gorges, overlooked by an audaciously engineered road, rank among the most imposing natural sites in the south of France. The main part of the gorges is now a nature reserve and in 1993 the whole area was listed as a Major Site belonging to France's national heritage.

A TEMPERAMENTAL RIVER

The Ardèche rises in the Mazan massif (alt 1 467m/4 815ft). After a 119km/74mi journey, it flows into the River Rhône, 1km/0.6mi upstream from Pont-St-Esprit. The river slope has a steep gradient, particularly so in the upper valley, but it is in the lower valley that the most surprising examples of erosion can be observed as the river carves a passage through the limestone strata of the plateau, already hollowed out by underground rivers.

The Ardèche's tributaries running down from the mountain accentuate its sporadic yet typically Mediterranean flow: autumn spates give way to a

- 🚲 **Michelin Map:** 331: I7-J8 or 528 folds 1, 2, 14 and 15 or 524 fold 23.
- ℹ **Info:** 1 place de l'Ancienne Gare, 07150 Vallon-Pont-d'Arc. ℘04 75 88 04 01. www.vallon-pont-darc.com.
- ▶ **Location:** The D 290 follows the gorges between Vallon-Pont-d'Arc and St-Martin-d'Ardèche for 38km/23.6mi.
- 👁 **Don't Miss:** Spectacular views of the Haute Corniche and the Pont d'Arc; the caves; descending the gorge by kayak.
- 🕐 **Timing:** Allow a day for the full circuit. Take extra care when driving (there can be traffic jams at the panoramic vistas) and swimming. Be sure to pause and enjoy the vistas along the way.
- 👥 **Kids:** Kayaking down the river in calm water; Prehistoric Zoo at Marzal Chasm; visiting caves.

shallow rivulet in winter, then swell into spring torrents, before subsiding to a comparative trickle during the summer. During the peak flow there is a convergence of flood waters at Vallon-Pont-d'Arc. A wall of water advances down the valley at 15–20kph/9.3–12.4mph! The strength of these flood waters is such that the river pushes the flow of the Rhône eastwards and deposits a pile of rubble in its river bed. In 1890, the overflow of the Ardèche was so strong that it cut through the Rhône and broke the Lauzon breakwater on the opposite bank.

The nature reserve of the Gorges de l'Ardèche (situated between Charmes and Sauze) is a protected area and it is therefore essential to preserve its ecosystem. Note the following:

Do not *light fires, leave litter, pick flowers or branches from trees or stray from designated footpaths. Camping is only allowed on official sites and windsurfing is forbidden.*

🚗 DRIVING TOURS

1 VALLON-PONT-D'ARC TO PONT-ST-ESPRIT

▶ *38km/23.6mi – allow 1 day. Leave Vallon and drive S towards Pont d'Arc.*

A **panoramic road**, the D 290, overlooks (*corniche* style) the gorge, offering views along its way. It follows the left bank of the Ardèche, then after crossing the river at St-Martin-d'Ardèche, returns to Vallon via the *Plateau d'Orgnac*.
The road passes the Château du Vieux Vallon and crosses the River Ibie before rejoining the Ardèche. On the left is the **Grotte des Tunnels**, a cave which once had an underground stream, and then the **Grotte des Huguenots**, which houses an exhibition on speleology and prehistory (*open Jul–Aug daily 10am–7pm; 3.50€ (5.50€ with Grotte des Tunnels); 04 74 96 52 62).*

Pont d'Arc★★
▶ *Park in the car park to the left of the road. To reach the foot of Pont d'Arc, there is a path on the Vallon side 150m/164yd from the viewpoint. The river flows under the natural arch (34m/112ft high, 59m/194ft wide).*

The scenic splendour begins immediately after Pont d'Arc: the river flows in curves punctuated by rapids, all in a 30km/18.6mi gorge enclosed by rock walls 300m/985ft high in some places, coloured in tones of white and grey. The river is jade green.
Beyond Chames, on the floor of the **Tiourre valley**, the road curves to the left creating a rocky **cirque**★ before climbing to the plateau's edge.

Belvédère du Serre de Tourre★★
Poised almost vertically 200m/656ft above the Ardèche, this offers a **view** of the river round the **Pas du Mousse rock** on which stand the ruins of the 16C Château d'Ebbo. Also to be seen are the Falaises de Saleyron (Saleyron cliffs). On the left bank, the tourist road follows the outline of its cliffs and passes through oak forests, first the Bois Bouchas and then the Bois Malbosc.

Belvédères de Gaud★★
The **view** upstream takes in the Gaud meander and the turrets of its 19C castle.

Belvédères d'Autridge★
To reach the two viewpoints take the panoramic curve. The Aiguille de Morsanne (Morsanne needle) soars above the gorges like the prow of a ship. About 500m/0.3mi beyond the coomb, Combe d'Agrimont, new **vistas**★★ open up with the Aiguille de Morsanne in the foreground.

Belvédères de Gournier★★
The viewpoints are situated 200m/656ft above the river. Below, Le Gournier farm lies in ruins in a field bordering the Ardèche, which carves its course through the Rochers de la Toupine (*toupine* means cooking pot).

◯ *Approach the Aven de Marzal by the road running along Gras plateau (D 590, opposite the road to the Belvédère de la Madeleine).*

👤👤 Aven de Marzal (Marzal Chasm)
🕐*Open Mar–Sept daily 11am–7pm; Sept–Nov Sun and Whitsun 11am–5pm.* 💬*Guided tours (1hr).* ◉*8.40€ (child 5.60€).* ✆*04 75 04 12 45.*

Buried under the Gras plateau, this chasm is remarkable for the wealth of limestone formations which range in their oxide colouring from brown ochre to snow white. A metal staircase *(743 steps)* leads to the natural opening in the Gras plateau. The chasm opens into the Salle du Tombeau or Tomb Gallery. Nearby are bones of bear, stag and bison that fell into the cave.

The **Salle du Chien** (Dog Gallery), whose entrance is surmounted by a flow of white draperies, contains a large variety of concretions, eccentrics, brightly coloured organs, disc-like formations, and shapes resembling bunches of grapes. On the way out you'll find the **Musée du Monde Souterrain** (♿ ◉*no charge)*, which recalls the great names and great moments of French speleology: Martel, Robert de Joly, Elisabeth and Norbert Casteret, and Guy de Lavaur.

Kids will love the 👤👤 **Prehistoric Zoo** (♿ *combination ticket with Aven de Marzal* ◉*14.40€ (child 8.90€))*, their very own Jurassic Park.

◯ *Take D 590 back to the gorge as far as Madeleine crossroads.*

La Haute Corniche★★★
This is the most outstanding section of the drive. In close succession, there are unrivalled views of the gorges.

Belvédère de la Madeleine★
There is a fine view of the "Fort" de la Madeleine, which bars the succession of gorges downstream.

👤👤 Grotte de la Madeleine★
🕐*Open daily Apr–Jun and Sept 10am–6pm; Jul–Aug 9am–7pm;* *Oct 10am–5pm; last admission 1hr before closing.* 💬*Guided tours (1hr) available.* ◉*7.50€ (child 4.50€).* ✆*04 75 04 22 20. www.grotte madeleine.com.*

This cave, discovered in 1887, was formed by an underground river which once drained part of Gras plateau. Enter through the Grotte Obscure, then follow a tunnel hewn out of the rock *(steep staircase)* to the Salle du Chaos (Chaos Cave).

Beyond this chamber, divided into two parts by a mass of columns detached from the vault, extends a vast gallery full of richly decorated concretions. The sides of the chamber are covered with small crystallisations resembling coral.

◯ *Approach Aven de Marzal by the road running along Gras plateau (D 590, opposite the road to the Grotte de la Madeleine).*

Belvédère de la Cathédrale★★
15min round-trip on foot.

🚶This affords a breathtaking view of the "Cathedral", a huge rock resembling a building in ruins whose stone spurs proudly overhang the river. Some of the path is quite rough, so be careful.

Grand Belvédère★
View of the end of the gorges and the Ardèche's final bend.

◯ *Follow D 290 downstream from the Grand Belvédère; after 200m/656ft you will see the entrance building to the Grotte de St-Marcel.*

👤👤 Grotte de St-Marcel★
🕐*Open daily 15 Mar–30 Jun and Sept 10am–6pm; Jul–Aug 10am–7pm; Oct–15 Nov 10am–5pm; last admission 1hr before closing.* 💬*Guided tours (1hr).* ◉*7.70€ (child 4.50€).* ✆*04 75 04 38 07. www.grottesaintmarcel.com.*

The opening to this cave, which was discovered in 1835 by a hunter from Aiguèze, is through a natural shelter cut into the side of the rock faces of the Gorges de l'Ardèche. The cave was formed by a subterranean river which has now dried up. It hollowed out a 32km/20mi network of chambers, a section of which is now open to the public.

A tunnel hollowed out of the rock leads through striking passages in which stalactites, stalagmites, draperies and other kinds of formations can be seen: Chamber of the Virgin's Fountain; Painters' Gallery, with different coloured stripes in white (calcite), red (iron oxide) and black (manganese); Chamber of Kings; Cathedral.

A footpath laid out on the site offers a good opportunity of discovering local flora (holm oak, boxwood, cistus) and two megalithic monuments.

▷ *Return to the D 290.*

Belvédère du Colombier★

There's a view down into the bend enclosed by rocky banks. The road follows a loop along a dry valley, skirts the Dona Vierna promontory and makes a wide detour around the Louby valley, the Ardèche's last enclosed bend.

Belvédère du Ranc-Pointu★★

Note the different types of erosion, striation, potholes and caves. Leaving the gorge, the countryside changes completely: the bare defile is replaced by a cultivated valley which opens out as it approaches the Rhône.

On the right stands the village of **Aiguèze**, perched on a rocky outcrop overlooking the Ardèche, the first town since Vallon.

St-Martin-d'Ardeche

This small town is situated at the exit to the gorge and is nowadays on more friendly terms with the river whose floods used to be a bane to

The Discovery

The local word *marzal* identifies a wild grass. The name *marzal* was given in c. 1810 to the forester Dechame, from St-Remèze, after he had fined his wife who had picked some for her rabbits. A little later Marzal was murdered and thrown into a well, the so-called Trou de la Barthe, with his dog. The crime was discovered and the local people began calling the well Marzal. The chasm was actually discovered in 1892 when the speleologist **Édouard-Alfred Martel** (1859–1938) explored it for the first time, but its exact location was lost through incorrect signposting and it was not rediscovered until 1949.

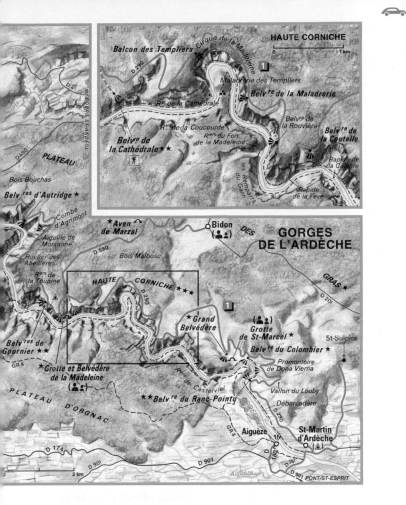

local residents. Surrealist painter Max Ernst stayed here in 1937–40. It is now a holiday centre for bathers, anglers, hikers and canoeists.

▶ *Cross the Ardèche by the suspension bridge (pont suspendu St-Martin), then take D 901 on the right, and turn right again onto D 180.*

Aiguèze
This medieval village with its paved streets is set on top of the last cliffs of the gorges. After passing under an arch cut into the rock, one comes out into a 14C fortress. From the watch-path there is a pretty **view**★ of the end of the canyon, the ruined towers and the

suspension bridge linking Aiguèze to St-Martin-d'Ardèche.

2 ORGNAC PLATEAU
Aven d'Orgnac ★★★
℃*See Aven d'ORGNAC.*

Plateau d'Orgnac
Round-trip of 45km/28mi leaving from the chasm.

▶ *Take D 317 and drive west as far as Barjac.*

Barjac
Barjac is famous for the antiques fairs it organises twice a year (*Easter weekend and the week of the Assumption of the*

Virgin Mary, 15 Aug; *04 66 24 50 09; http://comex.barjac.free.fr)*. The upper part of town is a pleasant place to wander, through streets lined with 18C residences. The elegant **château** has been converted into a cultural centre, with a cinema and multimedia library *(www.tourisme-barjac-st-privat.com)*.

▶ *Turn N onto D 979. At Vagnas, turn right onto D 355. After Labastide on the D 217 turn left.*

Belvédère du Méandre de Gaud★★
This commands an excellent view of the river at the foot of the Gaud cirque.

▶ *Retrace your steps and take D 217 to the left. Soon afterwards, a small road to the right leads to the Forestière chasm.*

▲▲ Aven de la Forestière★
Ⓞ*Open daily Apr–Sept 10am–7pm; last admission 1hr before closing)*. ⌨*5.50€ (child 3.50€)*. *04 75 38 63 08. www.laforestiere.net.*
The dramatically lit chambers are rich in concretions such as the cauliflower-like shapes and macaroni-like strips, which hang from the roof, stalactite curtains, and floors bristling with stalagmites.

THE DESCENT★★★

Vallon-Pont-d'Arc to St-Martin-d'Ardèche: **By Boat**
After a calm stretch, the river bends and enters the gorges. The Charlemagne rapid is passed, dominated on the right by the eponymous rock. The river then passes under the porch of the Pont d'Arc. To the left extends the Estre cirque onto which opens a cave known as the Grotte Chauvet. Shortly after, to the right, are the Grotte d'Ebbo and Pas du Mousse rock, a passage through the cliff to the plateau. The rock on the north bank is the Rocher de l'Aiguille. The Dent Noir rapids are just below the Saleyron cliffs, followed by the Gaud meander and Gaud cirque.

After approximately four hours you should have negotiated the Rochers de la Toupine, which in places is 18m/59ft deep, and be able to see Rocher de la Cathédrale in the distance. Before you actually reach this, you pass one of the openings of the Grotte de la Madeleine, on the left. The river then flows below the Rocher de la Cathédrale and past the Templars peninsula (12C remains), a popular spot with naturists.

The Cirque de la Madeleine is spectacular when seen from water level. Straits, rapids and iridescent reaches follow one another as the river flows between sheer cliff walls. Below the peculiar-looking Coucourde (Provençal for crane) rock and the Castelvieil cliff, the opening of the Grotte de St-Marcel can be seen on the left, and, as you round the bend, the Dona Vierna promontory and the Belvédère du Ranc-Pointu. The cliffs melt away, the valley widens out, allowing a view of Aiguèze's tower on the edge of the rock escarpment to the right.

Vallon-Pont-d'Arc to St-Martin-d'Ardèche: **On Foot**
For a dry walk, leave from Chanes to Gué du Charmassonet (left bank), then cross the river twice, at Charmassonet to Gué de Guitard (right bank) and Gué de Guitard to Sauze (left bank). Otherwise, loops are possible leaving from the plateau.

ADDRESSES

🛏 STAY

Chambre d'hôte La Sérénité – *pl. de la Mairie, 30430 Barjac. ℘04 66 24 54 63. www.la-serenite.fr. Closed Dec–Mar. 3 rooms.* Situated in the heart of the village, this 17C house with blue shutters is covered in Virginia creeper. Painted furniture, knick-knacks, the patina of the walls and hexagonal floor tiles adorn the individually decorated rooms. Delicious breakfast served in front of the fireplace or on the flower-decked terrace in fine weather.

Hôtel Le Clos des Bruyères – *route des Gorges, 07150 Vallon-Pont-d'Arc. ℘04 75 37 18 85. www.closdesbruyeres.fr. Closed Nov–Mar. 32 rooms. ⊆8€. Restaurant ⊜⊜.* The Gorges de l'Ardèche road is magnificent, but its bends are exhausting. Take a break in this local-style house, with arcades opening onto the outdoor swimming pool. Rooms have balconies or overlook the garden. Country cooking in the restaurant with terrace.

🍽 EAT

Le Manoir du Raveyron – *r. Henri Batrbusse, 07150 Salavas. ℘04 75 88 03 59. www.manoir-du-raveyron.com. Closed mid-Oct–mid-Mar.* An enjoyable vaulted dining room where modern dishes are prepared with local market produce.

Le Mas Rêvé – *07150 Labastide-de-Virac. ℘04 75 38 69 13. www.lemasreve.com. Closed Oct–mid-Apr.* A resplendent restaurant and hotel, serving good regional cuisine, in a restored 17C property, with a large inner courtyard and terrace.

DESCENT BY BOAT

Ideal Time– The best time for the descent by boat or canoe/kayak is from Mar–Nov; May, Jun and Sept are ideal as days are longer and it is not too crowded (except at weekends).

Rental – There are about 60 rental firms at Vallon-Pont-d'Arc, Salavas, Ruoms, St-Martin and St-Remèze, offering trips down the gorge independently or with a guide (1–2 days). To fully enjoy the entire trip allow 2 days. Rental rates vary from an average fee of 26€ (1 day) to 36€ (2 days, not including accommodation) per person. A list of rental firms is available from tourist offices *(syndicats d'initiative)* in Ruoms *(26 r. Alphonse-Daudet; ℘04 75 93 91 90; www.ot-pays-ruomsois.com)*, Vallon-Pont-d'Arc *(1 pl. de l'Ancienne Gare; ℘04 75 88 04 01; www.vallon-pont-darc. com) and St-Martin-d'Ardèche (pl. de l'Eglise; ℘04 75 98 70 91; www.ot-stmartin-ardeche.com).* If you are making the trip without a guide, make sure to reserve a pitch at a camp site through a central booking office at the tourist offices listed above.

⚠Caution: Depending on season and water levels, allow 6–9hr for the trip down the gorge (no departures allowed after 6pm). Ask about the trickier passages with rapids; these require expertise in the use of a canoe and are suitable for experts only. It is essential that you know how to swim. Life jackets are compulsory: failure to wear them can result in heavy fines. It is advisable to obtain the map/guide of the area, the *Plan-guide des gorges de l'Ardèche*, published by Association Tourena. The safest way to travel is with one of the trained boatmen of the Ardèche.

Camping – The river flows through a nature reserve. It is possible to picnic anywhere along the river's banks as long as you respect the environment. Camping is only permitted at official sites at Gaud and Gournier *(⊜5.50€ per person or 7€ per tent per night. ℘04 75 88 00 41).*

DESCENT ON FOOT

🚶This requires experience, and hiking equipment is recommended.
If you are walking along the left bank, check the water levels at police stations at the *Service départemental d'alerte des crues (℘04 75 64 54 55)* before you leave. The "des Champs" and the "de Guitard" fords are unavoidable.

Bagnols-sur-Cèze

Gard

The old town of Bagnols is renowned for its charm, its ancient buildings and its Museum of Modern Art. The River Cèze is popular with kayakers.

SIGHT
Musée d'Art Moderne Albert-André★

pl. Mallet, 2nd floor in the town hall.
Open Tue–Sun Sept–Jan and Mar–Jun 10am–noon, 2–6pm; Jul–Aug 10am–noon, 3–7pm. Closed public holidays. No charge. 04 66 50 50 56.
The Modern Art Museum shares the same building as the town hall, a fine 17C mansion. It exhibits contemporary works collected by the painter Albert André, curator 1918–54, and with the private collection of George and Adèle Besson. It is made up of works – oils, watercolours, drawings, sculptures – by Renoir, Valadon, Bonnard, Matisse, Marquet and Van Dongen.

DRIVING TOURS

LE BAS-VIVARAIS
Round trip of 130km/81mi – allow 1 day.

Leave Bagnols-sur-Ceze going W on the D 6, then turn left on the D 166.

Sabran
This old town is perched on a rocky outcrop. From the foot of the giant statue of the Virgin a vast **panorama**★ unfolds over the surrounding countryside.

Return to the D 6, which you will cross and take the D 166.

La Roque-sur-Cèze
The village encircles a Romanesque chapel on a hilltop darkly plumed by cypresses, creating a peaceful **site**★. An arched bridge with pointed cutwaters spans the River Cèze.

- **Population:** 18 545.
- **Michelin Map:** 339: M-4.
- **Info:** Espace St-Gilles, av. Léon-Blum, 30200 Bagnols-sur-Cèze. 04 66 89 54 61. www.tourisme-bagnols surceze.com.
- **Location:** S of the Ardèche gorges (25km/15.5mi) and N of the Pont du Gard (32km/20mi).
- **Timing:** In old Bagnols, you can follow the signposted route (45min) around town.

Follow the path on the left without crossing the bridge.

Cascade du Sautadet★
Caution: *This site is accessible but dangerous. Pay attention to the safety markings.*
This waterfall is unique in the way it cuts into the river bed and for the network of crevasses in which the Cèze runs. From the south there is a lovely view.

Return to the D 166 and continue to the D 980 where you will turn left. After 3km/2mi turn right.

Cornillon
This fortified site offers a walk along its ramparts. From the centre, take in the **panorama**★ of the Cèze valley.

Proceed on the D 298. After St-André-de-Roquepertuis, turn left on the D 167, which runs across an solitary, wild plateau. Take the D 16 in the direction of Rochegude, then take the D 7 to Brouzet-les-Alès.

Guidon du Bouquet★★
The highest point of the Bouquet range is a beak-shaped rock that dominates the horizon between the Gard and Ardèche rivers. From the approach, the ruins of the Château du Bouquet are visible through the clumps of holm oaks. The **panorama**★★ from the summit takes

in the Cévennes *causses* to the west, the crests of the Bas Vivarais range to the north, Mont Ventoux and the Alpilles to the east. From the statue of the Virgin there is a view of the garrigue surrounding Uzès and behind the television mast a view of the Bouquet range itself.

◐ *Returning to Brouzet-les-Alès, take the D 7. Turn right onto the D 37.*

The road rises offering a view of the **ruins**★ (☞ *guided tours available Apr–Oct;* ✆*04 66 24 80 24)* of Château d'Allègre. It continues through the garrigue to the hill village of **Lussan**.

◐ *At Lussan take the D 143, then go left on the D 643 which, lined with clipped boxwood, crosses a garrigue of holm oak to the Gorges de l'Aiguillon, also known as Les Concluses. Leave the car at the end of the road, preferably in the second of the two car parks, in a lay-by halfway down.*

From here there is a **view**★ upstream of the giant holes in the river bed.

Les Conclusès★★
1hr round trip on foot.
The Aiguillon torrent, dry in summer, has hollowed out of the calcareous grey-white rock a rocky defile some 1km/0.6mi long and opened upstream by a natural phenomenon: the **Portail** (Gateway).

◐ *Take the path on the right signposted: Portail.*

As you descend you see the caves on the opposite bank, most notably the Baume de Biou or Bulls' Cave, and come to the promontory and Beauquier pool, fringed by trees at the feet of rock escarpments. Note on the cliff-face three abandoned eagles' eyries. The path ends at the gateway where the rock overhang finally meets above the river's course; the bottom forms a gorge through which the Aiguillon flows when

in flood. Pass under the gateway, then walk through the rocky straits following the river bed for about 200m/219yd (*☞Only accessible in summer*). On the way back, experienced walkers may enjoy climbing back to the car park by way of the riverbed upstream as far as Baume de Biou and from there a rough path *(allow an extra 15min)*.

◐ *Once on the D 143, head for Goudargues.*

Goudargues
The village, ringed by plane trees, is dominated by its church. This former abbey church, partly rebuilt in the 17C and 19C, is interesting for its Romanesque apse, decorated inside by two storeys of arcading.

◐ *Turn right onto the D 298 and return to Bagnols.*

THE GARRIGUE AND CÔTES DU RHÔNE VINEYARDS
Round trip of 50km/31mi – allow 3hr.

◐ *Leave Bagnols-sur-Cèze on the N 86 southwards (direction of Remoulins) to Gaujac, turn right onto the D 310 which passes below the village. Take a dirt road (signposted) uphill (unsuitable for cars).*

Oppidum de St-Vincent-de-Gaujac
☾*Open access.* Perched on a height in the middle of a forest, this site was occupied sporadically between the 5C BC and the 6C AD and then again from the 10C–14C. During the Gallo-Roman era it was a sanctuary with temples and baths. Go through a fortified gate (the vestiges of a curtain wall) to discover the ruins of the medieval fortified stronghold with its cistern and the Gallo-Roman excavations. The latter dates from the Early Empire (1C–3C).
Above the oppidum are the remains of a fanum, a small Roman temple; below are the baths.

▶ *Return to the N 86 and 4km/2.5mi south, after Pouzilhac, turn left onto the D 101.*

St-Victor-la-Coste

On the border of the garrigues and vineyards, this picturesque village huddles at the foot of its castle.

▶ *Continue along the D 101.*

The countryside is covered by the famed Côtes du Rhône vineyards, renowned for their selected grapes.

St-Laurent-des-Arbres

In the past this village belonged to the bishops of Avignon. It has a Romanesque church, a rectangular keep from the Lords of the Sabran's castle, and above the village, a 12C square tower.

▶ *Take the D 26 to Lirac and Tavel.*

These two wine-growing villages have given their names to renowned wines.

▶ *Return to St-Laurent-des-Arbres. At the crossroads with the N 580 turn left. At l'Ardoise, take the D 9 to the left.*

Laudun

This village is dominated by its 14C Gothic church. A long footpath, the GR 42 towards Orsan leads from the church up the Camp de César plateau, from where there is a view of the Rhône. The "Camp de César" (http://vialaudun.free.fr) was occupied from the 5C BC to the 6C AD. A forum and a basilica have been uncovered. Artefacts are exhibited in a gallery on rue de la République (◷open Tue–Fri 8.30am–noon, 1.30–5pm, Sat 9.30am–12.30pm (Jul), Sun 9.30am–12.30pm; ℘04 66 50 55 79).

▶ *Return to Bagnols on the N 580.*

ADDRESSES

🏠 STAY

😊😊😊 **Chambre d'hôte La Tonnelle** – *pl. des Marronniers, La Roque-sur-Cèze, 17km/10.5mi NW. ℘04 66 82 79 37. www.hambre-la-tonnelle.com 6 rooms.* A hotel set beside cypress-crowned rocks.

🍴 EAT

😊😊😊 **Paul Itier** – *rte Nationale 86, Connaux, 13km/8mi S. ℘04 66 82 00 24. Closed Feb school holidays.* A classic rural dining room with a terrace.

Grotte de la Cocalière★

Gard

This cave, northwest of St-Ambroix on the Gard plâteau, contains a network of galleries running 46km/29mi underground.
The site has revealed a prehistoric settlement that was occupied from the Mousterian period (45 000 BC) to the Iron Age (400 BC).

TOUR

◷*Open Jul–Aug 10am–6pm. Mar–Jun and Sept–Oct 10am–noon and 2–5pm.* ●*Guided tours (1hr) available. Temperature: 14°C/57 °F.* ◉*8€.*

◈ **Michelin Map:** 339: J-3.
▶ **Location:** From Les Vans bear left on a road which branches off the D 904 on the left; not far after, the road to the right goes off to Courry.

℘04 66 24 34 74.
www.grotte-cocaliere.com.
At the bottom of the tunnel, a path follows along (about 1 200m/1 312yd) the bottom of a horizontal gallery that adjoins the other galleries. The cave is rich in its variety of concretions, reflected in the pools of water fed by small waterfalls. As you travel

underground you will see discs – huge concretions with a wide diameter that specialists have not yet been able to explain; delicate stalactites that are white (if charged with calcite) or multi-coloured (if charged with metallic oxide); and gours (natural dams). After the speleologists' campsite, walk through the Chaos chamber, where the roof is covered with stalactites and other forms of erosion, to the gallery of frozen falls and eccentrics that overlooks an imposing sparkling waterfall and wells linked to the lower stages where underground rivers flow. Pass through a prehistoric deposit before returning to the entrance area on a small train. Outside, follow the path to discover a dolmen, tumuli, *capitelles*, prehistoric shelters and varied karstic phenomena (caves, sinkholes, and faults).

Le Grau-du-Roi ⚐⚐

Gard

This seaside resort, which grew up around a pretty little port, was part of the town of Aigues-Mortes until 1879. This extends in part from an inland estuary or "grau" formed by a spate in the Rhône during the 16C (in Languedoc, grau designates an open breach in the offshore bar separating the lagoon from the sea). An 18km/11mi stretch of fine sandy beach runs past Le Grau-du-Roi and Port-Camargue, which are both equipped with a variety of sports facilities and attract many holiday-makers in the summer.

THE VILLAGE

The grid-plan of low houses becomes a hive of activity in the summer months, with craft shops and restaurant, but the nerve-centre remains the canal, with its pontoons and old lighthouse, symbol of the town.

ADDRESSES

🛏 STAY & 🍴 EAT

⊜⊜⊜⊜ **La Bastide des Senteurs** – *30500 St-Victor-de-Malcap. 8km/5mi from Grotte de la Cocalière via D 904 and D 51C.* ℘*04 66 60 24 45. www.bastide-senteurs. com. Closed Nov–Mar, lunch in Jul–Aug except Sun and public holidays. 14 rooms.* ⊟*10€. Restaurant*⊜⊜⊜. The young owners have made a charming hotel out of this abandoned country house. You will enjoy the food, the elegance of the décor and the warm welcome. Everything here sings with the flavours and colours of the south! Pretty rooms, swimming pool and a terrace.

▸ **Population:** 7 892
⏱ **Michelin Map:** 339: J-7.
🖽 **Info:** 30 r. Michel Rédarès, 30240 Le Grau-du-Roi. ℘04 66 51 67 70. www.vacances-en-camargue.com.
🕙 **Timing:** Le Grau is the ideal place for a family holiday.
👥 **Kids:** Seaquarium; 18km/11.2mi of beaches!

THE SEASIDE
The Beaches
Between the Passe des Abymes and Les Baronnets stretches 18km/11.2mi of fine sand. A word of advice for bathers: swimming is better from the right bank of the canal (Le Boucanet) than the left.

👥 Seaquarium
Access from boulevard du Front-de-Mer. ♿🕙*Open daily Jul–Aug 9.30am–11.30pm; Apr–Jun and Sept 10am–7.30pm; Oct–Mar 10am–6.30pm.* ⊕*11.30€ (child 8.30€).* ℘*04 66 51 57 57. www.seaquarium.fr.*

Sharks, Mediterranean fish and sea lions will entertain adults and children alike. The small museum is also worth a visit: model boats, fishing nets as well as a history of the resort.

Port-Camargue
Via the D 62B.

Located between the fishing harbour and Point de l'Espiguette, the resort of Port-Camargue was created in 1969. It is the farthermost eastern resort created in the development of the Languedoc-Roussillon coast and has facilities to house 4 500 boats. It's a good departure point for cruising along this coastline.

Phare de l'Espiguette
6km/3.7mi S by a road from the roundabout at the entrance to Port-Camargue. Paying car park in summer.

The road, which passes between beaches and lakes, is a good place to discover a typical Camargue landscape, as well as to observe several species of bird *(observatory next to the Étang des Baronnets, opposite the Maison des vins du Domaine de l'Espiguette)*. The lighthouse which overlooks Point de l'Espiguette stands amid windswept dunes, where tamarisk, thistles, sea rockets and *Cakiles* grow. The immense beaches are a haven for naturists.

ADDRESSES

🛏 STAY

🛌 **Camping Le Boucanet** – *rte de Carnon. 1km/0.6mi NW of Grau-du-Roi.* ☎04 66 51 41 48. www.camping boucanet.fr. Closed 4 Oct–10 Apr. Booking recommended. 458 pitches. For those who like to get their feet wet, some sites are 5m/16ft from the sea! But the swimming pool also has a certain charm. Guaranteed relaxation for adults and children alike; tennis, windsurfing and entertainment for children. Mobile homes and bungalows can be rented.

🛌🛌🛌🛌 **Oustau Camarguen** – *3 rte des Marines, 30240 Port-Camargue. 3k1m/ .8mi S of Grau-du-Roi via D 62B.* ☎04 66 51 51 65. www.oustaucamarguen.com. Closed 12 Nov–19 Mar. 39 rooms. ⚏12€. Restaurant 🍽🍽🍽 (Closed Oct–Apr). This Camargue-style house is situated on the road to the southern beach. The spacious rooms are decorated in local style; some open out onto a small, private garden. There is a terrace for alfresco dining next to the swimming pool. Classic cooking, with grills at lunchtime. Turkish bath and spa.

🍴 EAT

🍽🍽🍽🍽 **Carré des Gourmets** – *pointe de la Presqu'île, Port-Camargue.* ☎04 66 53 36 37. www.spinaker.com. Closed 21–27 Dec, Mon–Tue (Sept–Jun). An enchanting restaurant set in the grounds of the Spinaker Hotel and a terrace overlooking the marina. The menu is creative and contemporary and the hotel rooms are stylised individually with different global décor.

🍽🍽🍽🍽 **L'Amarette** – *8 av. Jean Lasserre, Port-Camargue. 3km/2mi S of Grau-du-Roi via D 62B.* ☎04 66 51 47 63. www.l-amarette.com. Closed Dec–late Jan. This restaurant is situated on the first floor of a 1970s shopping centre. Seafood dishes can be enjoyed on the terrace, which offers good views of the coast.

🛒 SHOPPING

Maison Méditerréenne des Vins et Produits Régionaux – *Domaine-de-l'Espiguette.* ☎04 66 53 07 52. www.maisondesvins-lespiguette.com. This spacious store is packed to the rafters with regional products to buy or taste: wines from Provence and Languedoc-Roussillon, olive oils, rice and salt from the Camargue, cooked dishes, honey and Marseille soap.

🚶 LEISURE ACTIVITY

Horse Riding – *Ranch Lou Seden, 1820 rte de l'Espiguette.* ☎06 27 16 96 27. www.ranch-lou-seden.com. Riding through the dunes for beginners and experts. A 1hr ride will cost 18€.

Labeaume★

Ardèche

When seen from afar, the old village situated on the bank of the gorges of the Beaume merges almost totally into the rock face.

▶ **Population:** 506.
♿ **Michelin Map:** 331: H-7.
🛈 **Info:** 26 rue Alphonse Daudet, 07120 Ruoms. ✆04 75 93 91 90. www.otruoms.com.

VISIT
The Village

Leave the car on the square at the village's entrance and enjoy a stroll along the steep streets, with covered passageways and balconied houses, some of which have been restored. To the left of the church, with its belfry porch (19C) resting on two round columns, take an alleyway to the river bank and a shaded esplanade. For a better view, cross the low-level bridge, and follow the uphill path for a couple of hundred yards.

Gorges de la Beaume★

The walk upstream along the river's north bank, beside the clear waters, across from the eroded limestone cliff, is worthwhile.

EXCURSIONS

11km/7mi – allow 1hr.
▷ *Leave Labeaume on the D 245, then turn left onto the D 4.*

Défilé de Ruoms★

The road goes through rock tunnels and affords plunging views of the river with its green waters. Following the Ruoms defile are the Ligne gorges; there is a good view from the confluence of the Ardèche and Ligne rivers, framed by 100m/328ft high cliffs striped by the rock strata. On the return trip, the silhouette of Rocher de Sampzon appears at the end of the valley.

▷ *Cross the Ardèche towards Ruoms.*

Ruoms

The walled centre of the town lies within a quadrilateral of ramparts flanked by seven round towers. At the heart of the old town is a small Romanesque church with an arcaded belfry faced with motifs worked in volcanic rock. The view is best from Ruelle St-Roch.

▷ *Leave Ruoms on the D 579 towards Vallon, then turn right along the narrow D 161, which winds upwards towards Sampzon after crossing the Ardèche. Park below the old village church.*

Rocher de Sampzon★

45min return journey. First take the tarred path and then the path level with the turning place.
From the summit (television relay mast) there is a panorama including the Vallon basin, the Orgnac plateau and the meanders of the Ardèche.

Défilé de Ruom

J. Damase/MICHELIN

Nîmes★★★

Gard

Situated on the edge of the *garrigue* limestone hills and the Petite Camargue, Nîmes exudes the air of a great city of the arts: proud of its prestigious Gallo-Roman past, yet anxious to open itself up to new ideas. Deeply marked by its Huguenot past, Nîmes is a city of old traditional industries, particularly textiles and the processing of local agricultural products (canning of fruit, wine production). Among the city's gastronomic specialities are *brandade de morue* (◐ *see below*), marinated olives, caladons (almond biscuits) and crispy little Croquant Villaret, a speciality of Nîmes for more than 200 years. The local wine, Costières de Nîmes, has an excellent reputation. Nîmes is also the French centre for tauromachy (bullfighting). The *corridas*, or bullfights, which take place in the Roman amphitheatre, have brought immense popularity and fame to the city.

A BIT OF HISTORY

The Chained Crocodile – Capital of Volcae Arecomici, Nemausus (Nîmes' ancient name originated from a sacred spring around which the town settled) was at the head of a vast territory of 24 settlements between the sea, the Cévennes and from the River Rhône to the Sète mountains, when it accepted Roman domination. The date of Roman colonisation, its founder and the ethnic origin of its colonists are now matters of controversy. Two theories have been put forward: the founder was either Augustus, who settled here in 31 BC with a Roman colony of veterans of the Egyptian campaign (evidence of this settlement is the famous coin stamped with the chained crocodile), or Caesar, with a Latin colony in 44 BC.

Regardless of the issue as to who founded Nîmes, Augustus was the one who heaped privileges on the town

▶ **Population:** 144 092.
◔ **Michelin Map:** 339: L-5.
▫ **Info:** 6 rue Auguste, 30000 Nîmes. ℘04 66 58 38 00. www.ot-nimes.fr.
◉ **Don't Miss:** The Roman arena and Maison Carrée, the Jardin de la Fontaine, the Carré d'Art (and its excellent rooftop restaurant), the Musée du Vieux Nîmes.
◔ **Timing:** If you hate heat, avoid July; if you're against bullfighting, avoid the féria in May, when it will also be difficult to find accommodation.
♟ **Kids:** Roman Amphitheatre; Maison Carrée.

and allowed it to build fortifications 16km/10mi long. The town, situated on the **Domitian Way**, then proceeded to embellish itself with splendid buildings: a forum with the Maison Carrée to the south, an amphitheatre able to hold 24 000 people, a circus, baths and fountains fed by an imposing aqueduct, the Pont du Gard which yielded 20 000cu m/706 314cu ft of water a day. In the 2C the city received privileges from the Emperors Hadrian and Antoninus Pius (whose mother came from Nîmes) and continued to flourish and build (Plotinius' basilica, arrangement of the Fountaine district), reaching its zenith with a population of 20 000 to 25 000 inhabitants.

Religious Struggles – The most significant period of Nîmes history, together with that of the Roman occupation, is the period of bitterly disputed religious differences. In the 5C the Visigoths, who ruled the country (from Toulouse to the River Rhône), clashed with the Catholic population when they tried to impose their beliefs: churches were closed and the Catholics were persecuted well into the 6C.

In the 13C the people of Nîmes sided with the Albigensians. This sect, also known as the Catharist heretics, was in permanent opposition to the Roman church and protested against the corruption of the clergy at that time. Simon de Montfort headed the terrible crusade against these heretics, and the city surrendered in 1213. The war threw the nobility of northern France against that of the south, and ended in the destruction of the Provençal civilisation along with the independence of the princes who ruled over it. In the 14C a wave of intolerance fell upon the Jews; they were expelled and their possessions confiscated. In the 16C Nîmes became a Huguenot city. It was the Geneva of France: three-quarters of its population supported the Reformation.

On 29 September 1567 the Michelade tragedy occurred: 200 Catholics, most of whom were priests, were massacred. There ensued a long dark period of persecution and war in which both sides suffered in turn. The active participation of Nîmes in the War of the Camisards (1700–04) following the Revocation of the Edict of Nantes was followed later the same century by Protestant revenge at the time of the Revolution. The Restoration of the Bourbon monarchy (1814–30) was marked by the White Terror perpetrated by the Catholics.

The Conquest of the West – From the Middle Ages local serge was well known throughout Europe for its hard-wearing quality. Legend has it that Christopher Columbus used it to manufacture the sails of his caravels; this same cloth, which was exported via Genoa, was also used to make sailors' trousers. In 1873, a Bavarian emigrant in the United States called Levi Strauss had the idea of capitalising on its robust qualities to make trousers for gold-diggers and migrants setting out to discover the West. The name "bleu de Gênes" or "blue from Genoa" became "blue jeans" and the brand name "denim" (literally "from Nîmes") still bears testimony today to the contribution made by the city in the conquest of the West.

Férias and bullfighting – The focus of the Whitsun féria (Féria de Pentecôte), created in 1952 in imitation of Spanish bullfighting festivals, is on the amphitheatre (arènes) and the corridas and novilladas (bullfights with young bulls and novice matadors) held inside it. Although the bull reigns supreme, the whole town becomes involved in its traditions: running the bulls along the boulevards, bullfights for eager amateurs in small bullrings nearby, concerts, exhibitions, folklore parades, dances and impromptu events, all of which attract large crowds from far and wide. In the narrow streets local associations open up bodegas (informal bars or restaurants) in which pride of place is given to Spanish food (tapas and paella) and sherries (the dry fino, in particular).

Battered by Storm – Early in the morning of 8 October 1988, a massive thunderstorm, accompanied by torrential rain, struck Nîmes. Although nothing unusual in the region, the rainfall was such that normally dry streams became engorged with water, and even underground water courses forced their way to the surface. Soon the road from Alès turned into a torrent of mud, which invaded the town, carrying everything in its path, throwing trees and cars against walls, and resulting in eight dead and a devastated city.

WALKING TOURS

1 PUBLIC BUILDINGS

This itinerary explores the principal monuments of Roman Nîmes and the "Écusson", the medieval quarter with its winding streets nestling between the tree-lined boulevards. Also worth noting are some of the splendid hôtels particuliers, and elegant townhouses, many undergoing restoration.

Esplanade de Gaulle

This ample square, bordered by the columns of the Palais de Justice and numerous outdoor cafés, looks out onto avenue Feuchères. In the middle

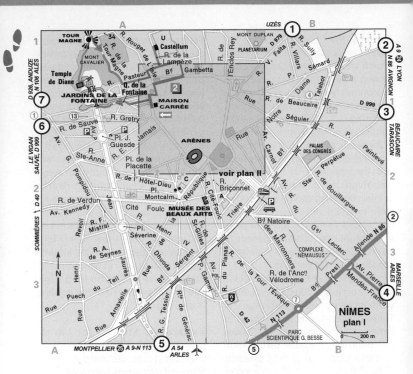

of the square note the Fontaine Pradier, erected in 1848.

🕭 *Go down boulevard de la Libération to reach the amphitheatre.*

👥♿ Amphitheatre (Arènes)★★★

pl. des Arènes. 🕐*Open daily Nov–Feb 9.30am–5pm; Mar and Oct 9am–6pm; Apr–May and Sept 9am–6.30pm; Jun–Aug 9am–7pm; last entry 30min before closing.* 🕐*Closed during performances.* 💶*7.70€ (child 5.90€); "Nîmes Romaine" ticket (Arènes, Maison Carrée, Tour Magne) 💶9.80€ (child 7.50€).* 📞*04 66 21 82 56. www.arenes-nimes.com.*

This beautifully preserved amphitheatre is twin to the one at Arles; most likely from the same period (late 1C–early 2C), with the same layout, similar dimensions and capacity (133m x 101m/436ft x 331ft; seating capacity 24 000). Its differences are slight architectural ones such as the galleries with barrel vaulting of Roman construction which are replaced by

the Greek trabeated form. The Nîmes amphitheatre is ranked ninth out of the twenty most significant amphitheatres discovered in Gaul; however, it is the best preserved of the Roman ones.

From the exterior, the building presents two storeys each of 60 arcades (total height: 21m/68.8ft) crowned with an attic. The building material in hard limestone from Barutel did not require detailed ornamentation: pilasters on the lower register and engaged Doric columns above. Four axial doorways correspond to the four entrances.

The main northern gateway has kept its pediment, adorned with bulls. Inside (climb to the topmost tiers to have a view of the whole), an ingenious system of corridors, stairways, galleries and *vomitaria* (sloping corridors) made it possible for the amphitheatre to be evacuated in a few minutes. Under the arena itself a substructure (68 x 37m/223 x 121ft) made of two vast galleries served as backstage.

Having lost its main purpose when gladiator combats were forbidden in

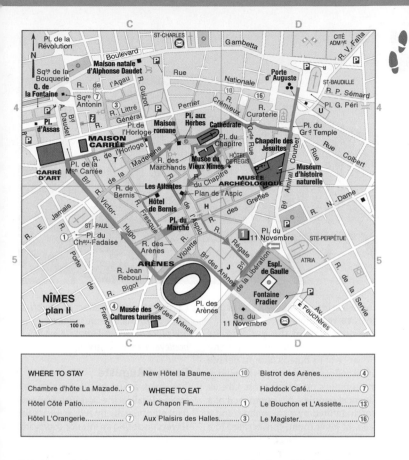

404, the amphitheatre was transformed into a fortress by the Visigoths: arcades were boarded up and towers added, a deep moat was dug around the arena itself and perhaps backed up by a small rampart wall (ruins can be seen in the basement of the Law Courts). In the eastern part of the building, the castle of the Viscounts of Nîmes was later built (two walled arcades lit by small Romanesque windows were preserved). The amphitheatre was, like the one at Arles, overtaken by houses, streets and two chapels; a village was established and numbered 700 inhabitants in the 18C. The demolition of these buildings started in 1809 and restoration soon began. The first *corrida* was performed in 1853.

Two rooms will teach you all about bullfighting and gladiators and there's a good souvenir shop.

◗ *Go up boulevard Victor-Hugo.*

Maison Carrée★★★

pl. Maison Carrée. ◷*Open daily Nov–Feb 10am–1pm, 2–4.30pm; Mar 10am–6pm; Apr–May and Sept 10am–6.30pm; Jun–Aug 10am–7pm; Oct 10am–1pm, 2–6pm; last entry 30min before closing.* ⇔*4.50€ (child 3.70€); 'Nîmes Romaine' ticket (Arènes, Maison Carrée, Tour Magne)* ⇔*9.80€ (child 7.50€).* ℘*04 66 21 82 56. www.arenes-nimes.com.*

This magnificent temple, known as the Square House, is the best preserved of the Roman temples still standing. It was built under Augustus' (late 1C BC) reign and was inspired by the Temple of Apollo in Rome. Consecrated to the Imperial cult and dedicated to Augustus' grandsons, the temple faced the forum

Maison Carrée

Office de Tourisme de Nîmes

and was surrounded by a portico of finely carved columns.

The pure lines of the building, its harmonious proportions and the elegance of its fluted columns denote Greek influence, which is also found in the temple's ornamentation. Like all Classical temples, it is composed of a porch defined by a colonnade, and a *cella*, or inner room, consecrated to a god, which is reached by a stairway of 15 steps. Inside you can watch a 3D film (20min), Heroes of Nîmes, which all the family will enjoy.

◗ *Take the narrow rue de l'Horloge then turn right into place de l'Horloge and then left into rue de la Madeleine.*

Rue de la Madeleine

The main shopping street of Nîmes. At no 13, the Maison Villaret (◗ *see Addresses*) is proud of baking the famous "croquants" biscuits in the same oven for two centuries. No 1, the oldest house in "old Nîmes", displays a finely carved Romanesque façade.

Come out into delightful **place aux Herbes**, a good place for a rest on one of the café terraces, which offer a good view of the west front of the **Cathédrale Notre-Dame-et-St-Castor**, which still has a partly Romanesque frieze depicting scenes of the Old Testament.

◗ *From the narrow street on the left of the cathedral take rue Curaterie and place du Grand-Temple to get to boulevard Amiral-Courbet.*

Porte d'Auguste

This gate, a ruin of the Augustinian fortified wall on the Domitian Way, was flanked originally by two semicircular towers enclosing an interior courtyard, an effective defensive procedure. It still has the two wide passages for chariots and two narrower passages for pedestrians. There is also a bronze copy of the statue of Augustus.

◗ *Go back to boulevard Amiral-Courbet and just after the Archaeological Museum turn right into rue des Greffes and right again into Grand'Rue. Turn left into rue du Chapitre.*

Rue du Chapitre

The Hôtel de Regis (no 14) displays an 18C façade and a lovely 16C paved courtyard.

◗ *Take rue de la Prévôté, which leads into place du Chapitre.*

After the old bishopric, which now houses the Musée du Vieux-Nîmes, return to place aux Herbes before turning left into rue des Marchands.

◐ *Walk under the picturesque covered gallery known as "Passage des marchands". Rue de Bernis will be on your right.*

Rue de Bernis

At the junction with **rue de l'Aspic**, the porch of the **Hôtel Meynier de Sali-nelles** (no **8**) is adorned with three pala-eochristian sarcophagi imbedded in the wall. At no **14**, **Hôtel Fontfroide**, note the superb double spiral grand staircase dating from the 17C. At no **3** rue de Ber-nis, the **Hôtel de Bernis** has a fine 15C façade with mullioned windows.

◐ *Turn left from rue Fresque, an arched passageway leads into place du Marché, where you will find a palm tree, the symbol of Nîmes, while a bronze crocodile is to be found looking in the water of one of the fountains, a sculpture by Martial Raysse.*

② FOUNTAINS

From place de la Maison Carré go up boul-evard Daudet until you reach place d'Assas with its numerous outdoor restaurants. Bear right to get to the aristocratic quai de la Fontaine, bordered by magnificent private residences. Follow the calm, tree-shaded canal with its haughty swans.

Jardin de la Fontaine★★

Entrance through the monumental gate facing rue Jean-Jaurès. ◐*Open daily Jun–Sept 7am–9pm; Oct–May 10am–noon, 2–5pm.* ℘*04 66 58 38 00.*
This garden is the unexpected creation of an 18C army engineer, J.-P. Mareschal, and extends from the famous Nemausus spring up the slopes of Mont Cavalier to the white octagonal form of the Tour Magne.
Since the creation of the garden in the 18C, the spring water has been coll-ected in a mirror-like pool surrounded by balustraded walks, before flowing through pools to the canal.
During Antiquity, this sacred district included the spring, a theatre, temple and baths. Recent excavations have uncovered some of the surrounding area:

to the east on rue Pasteur an opulent 2C mansion; a district for ordinary local people; and at the crossroads of boulevard Jaurès and rue de Sauve, a sumptuous public building (2C), whose function still arouses speculation.
Temple de Diane (◐*open daily Jun–Sept 7am–9pm; Oct–May 10am–noon, 2–5pm;* ◎*no charge*) dates from the first half of the 2C and is known as the Temple of Diana but its true function is unknown. It was most likely part of a vast architectural ensemble, still buried, made up of several different levels (traces of stairs). It was occupied by the Benedictine nuns in the Middle Ages, who converted it into a church, and was destroyed during the Wars of Religion in 1577.

Tour Magne★

Jardin de la Fontaine. ◐*Open daily Nov–Feb 9.30am–1pm, 2–4.30pm; Mar, Sept and Oct 9.30am–1pm, 2–6pm; Apr–May 9.30am–6.30pm; Jun–Aug 9.30am–7pm; last entry 30min before closing.* ◎*2.70€, child 2.30€; 'Nîmes Romaine' ticket (Arènes, Maison Carrée, Tour Magne)* ◎*9.80€ (child 7.50€).* ℘*04 66 21 82 56. www.arenes-nimes.com.*
Located at the top of Mont Cavalier, the city's highest point, the tower is a remarkable vestige of the city defences. It is a three-storey polygonal tower standing 34m/112ft high, but it was weakened by a 16C treasure-seeker who persisted in digging at its base. There is a good **view**★ of Mont Ventoux, the Alpilles, Nîmes, Vistre plain and the *garrigues.*

◐ *Leave the park and go back down to the canal along rue de la Tour-Magne. Turn left into rue Pasteur.*

Castellum

This was the Roman distribution tank to which water, from Uzès, was brought by the Pont du Gard aqueduct, and then distributed in the town. Above it stands Fort Vauban, the citadel built in 1687 to watch over Protestant Nîmes, which today is a university.

▷ *Return along boulevard Gambetta.*

At no 20, the Hôtel Sabrant is the birthplace of Alphonse Daudet.

MUSEUMS
Musée des Beaux-Arts
r. Cité-Foulc. ♿🕐*Open Tue–Sun 10am–6pm (Thu until 8pm Jul–Aug and second Thu of month).* 🕐*Closed 1 Jan, 1 May, 1 Nov, 25 Dec.* ∞*3.79€ (no charge first Sun of month).* ✆*04 66 67 38 21.*

The Fine Arts Museum was remodelled in 1986 by the architect J. M. Wilmotte. On the ground floor there is a large Roman mosaic depicting the marriage of Admetus; it was discovered in Nîmes in the 19C. The museum displays works of art from the French, Italian, Flemish and Dutch Schools (15C–19C) including paintings by Bassano *(Susanna and the Elders)*, Rubens *(Portrait of a Monk)*, Jean-François de Troy *(The Sleeping Reaper)*, Delaroche *(Cromwell and Charles I's Coffin)*, a ceramic figure by Andrea della Robia, a *Madonna and Child* and portraits by Nicolas Largillière and Hyacinthe Rigaud. Local works are represented by the portraits of Xavier Sigalon (1787–1837) from Uzès, a seascape by Joseph Vernet, historical paintings by Natoire, a native of Nîmes, and *Landscape near Nîmes*, by J.-B. Lavastre.

Carré d'Art★
pl. de la Maison Carrée. ♿🕐*Open Tue–Sun 10am–6pm.* ∞*5€ (no charge first Sun of month).* ✆*04 66 76 35 70.*

Designed by the British architect **Norman Foster** to house both the city's Museum of Contemporary Art and its media library, the Carré d'Art stands opposite the Maison Carrée, from which it has copied several of its architectural features. Its collection includes paintings, sculptures and drawings from 1960 onwards, with three main themes: French art from 1960 to the present day, Anglo-Saxon and Germanic artists and Mediterranean identity.

The museum gives precedence to certain key movements in contemporary art such as New Realism, Supports/Surfaces, the BMPT group, Figuration Libre and New Figuration. Some famous names in the museum's collection include César, Jean Tinguely, Sigmar Polke, Christian Boltanski, Gérard Garouste, Martial Raysse, Julian Schnabel, Miquel Barcélo, Annette Messager, the photographer Thomas Struth and local artist Claude Viallat.

There is a good restaurant on the top floor, with sweeping views over the city from the terrace.

Musée du Vieux Nîmes
pl. aux Herbes. 🕐*Open Tue–Sun 10am–6pm.* ∞*No charge.* ✆*04 66 76 73 70.*

This museum is located in the former episcopal palace (17C). It was founded in 1920 by Henri Bauquier, a rival of Frédéric Mistral, and contains numerous local exhibits in a well-restored historical setting. The city of Nîmes reflects characteristics of both Languedoc and Provence, and there are some pieces of furniture typical of both these regions on display here. There's also an interesting display of denim.

Musée Archéologique★
13 bd Amiral-Courbet. 🕐*Open Tue–Sun 10am–6pm.* 🕐*Closed 1 Jan, 1 May, 1 Nov, 25 Dec.* ∞*No charge.* ✆*04 66 76 74 80.*

The Archaeological Museum is located in the former Jesuit College. In the ground-floor gallery, pre-Roman carvings and Roman inscriptions are displayed. Upstairs are Gallo-Roman coins, utensils, headdresses, funerary stelae, oil lamps, glassware and pottery (Archaic Greek, Etruscan and Punic). There is also a collection of cork models of the city's ancient monuments.

Musée d'Histoire Naturelle
13 bd Amiral-Courbet. 🕐*Open Tue–Sun 10am–6pm.* ∞*No charge.* ✆*04 66 76 73 45.*

Located on the first floor of the former Jesuit College. The museum houses a natural history section of stuffed mammals and reptiles from all over the world, and temporary exhibitions.

EXCURSION
Aire de Caissargues

This motorway rest stop is situated between the Nîmes-Centre and Garon interchanges on motorway A 54.

Here, the Neoclassical style colonnade of Nîmes' former theatre has been rebuilt at the end of a tree-lined avenue. The building houses remains, including the "Dame de Caissargues", the skeleton of a 25–30-year-old-woman, dating from 5 000BC, buried in a contracted foetal position and wearing a shell necklace.

🚗 DRIVING TOUR

La Vaunage
Round trip of 44km/27mi – allow about 2hr30min.

▷ *Starting from the Esplanade de Gaulle, take rue de la République, then at the end of rue Jean-Jaurès (roundabout) take rue Arnavielle, opposite, which becomes the D 940, the road to Sommières.*

Caveirac
An imposing 17C horseshoe-shaped château houses the town hall. Two corner towers roofed with glazed tiles, the mullioned windows, gargoyles and a staircase with a wrought-iron balustrade enhance the building. The porch is so big as to straddle the road (D 103).

▷ *Take the D 40 and, after St-Dionisy, turn left into the D 737 for Nages-et-Solorgues. A rocky signposted pathway leads up the hill to the site of the archaeological remains.*

Oppidum de Nages
Nages was one of the five *oppida* of the Iron Age (800–50 BC) that housed the Vaunage population. The living quarters, arranged on the slope's incline and separated by parallel streets, suggest an early Gallic urban plan. The rows of small uniform houses with drystone walls, sometimes quite high, are clearly visible. To begin with,

these dwellings were on a one-room plan with a hearth at its centre; in the 2C BC they were enlarged and subdivided but the comfort remained rudimentary. The settlement was surrounded by fortifications (there were four successive ones) a part of which has been successfully excavated. No public monument has been uncovered except for a *fanum*, a small native temple (70 BC). Roman infiltration did not hinder the *oppidum*'s development which was at its greatest between 70 and 30 BC, the period in which appears the beginning of economic specialisation (presence of a forge).

▷ *On the return trip down, at the village's entrance, take the first street to the left leading to the Roman cistern, which still feeds several of the village's fountains.*

Nages-et-Solorgues
Located on the first floor of the town hall, the **Musée Archéologique** (🕑 *open Mon and Wed 8.30–11.45am, 2–6pm, Tue and Fri 8.30–11.45am, Thu 8.30–11.45am, 5–7pm, ✆04 66 35 05 26*) displays pottery and items excavated from the site of Les Castels. Different aspects of the successive inhabitants' daily life are evoked, such as agriculture, hunting, crafts (metalwork, pottery making, weaving), arms and funerary objects.

▷ *Return to the D 40, turning left onto it.*

Calvisson
This peaceful village lies amid vines in the centre of Vaunage plain and is famed for its Easter procession.

▷ *In the centre of town take the CD 107 for Fontanès; leave the village and bear left on the signposted road indicating Roc de Gachonne.*

From the viewing table located at the top of a tower, there is a view of the red tile-roofed village, Vidourle valley (southwest) and St-Loup peak (east).

Tiled roofs of Calvisson

G, Magnin/MICHELIN

▶ *Return to the D 40, then turn left onto the D 249 and exit at Aubais. The D 142 leads to* **Aigues-Vives**. *After passing under the motorway, it is worth stopping at* **Mus**, *the nearby* **Gallargues** *and* **Vergèze**.

▶ *The D 139 leads to Source Perrier.*

Source Perrier

⚓ Guided tour (1hr) Oct–Mar Mon–Thu 9am–5.30pm (last tour 4pm); Apr–Jun and Sept Mon–Fri 9.30am–7pm (last tour 4.30pm); Jul–Aug Mon–Fri 9.30am–7pm (last tour 5.30pm). ⏰Closed public holidays. ⊛6€. 𝄞04 66 87 61 01. www.perrier.com.

The Source des Bouillens forms an underground lake with a temperature of 15°C/50°F; the natural gas of which is reinserted in the water under pressure. Its beneficial qualities were discovered by Dr Perrier, and marketed by an Englishman, Lord Harmsworth. Annual production now exceeds 800 million bottles. The tour includes various plants for bottling and labelling.

▶ *Return to Nîmes via the D 135 and turn left at Domaine de la Bastide onto the D 613.*

ADDRESSES

🍴 STAY

⊜⊜–⊜⊜⊜ **Hôtel Côté Patio** – 31 r. de Beaucaire. 𝄞04 66 67 60 17. www. hotel-cote-patio.com. 17 rooms. ⊡8€. Charming hotel with a lively feel to it. Very near old Nîmes and the Arènes. Advance reservations around Féria.

⊜⊜⊜ **Hôtel l'Orangerie** – 755 r. de la Tour-de-l'Évêque. 𝄞04 66 84 50 57. www.orangerie.fr. 37 rooms. ⊡9€. Restaurant⊜⊜. A new building with the air of an old *mas*, 1km/0.6mi from the town centre. Spacious and individual bedrooms; some have terraces, some jacuzzis. Provençal theme throughout.

⊜⊜⊜ **Chambre d'hôte La Mazade** – 12 r. de la Mazade, 30730 St-Mamert-du-Gard, 14km/9.3mi W via D 999 and D 1. 𝄞04 66 81 17 56. www.bbfrance. com/couston.html. 4 rooms, 1 gîte. ⊡. Modern equipment combine with antique furniture in the well fitted-out, bright rooms of this B&B in a quiet, rural location.

⊜⊜⊜ **Hôtel Royal** – 3 bd Alphonse Daudet. 𝄞04 66 58 28 27. www.royal hotel-nimes.com. 22 rooms. ⊡9€. Stylish boutique hotel next to the Carré d'Art. Original features and fittings complement minimalist colour and design. Loved by bullfighting superstars, there's an excellent tapas bar, La Bodeguita, downstairs. Can get lively and noisy at weekends.

New Hôtel La Baume – *21 r. Nationale. ℘04 66 76 28 42. www.new-hotel.com. 34 rooms. ☕12€.* This 17C mansion successfully blends contemporary and antique styles. An interior stone staircase leads to the simple bedrooms, a few of which have pretty, French-style painted ceilings.

EAT

Pâtisserie Courtois – *8 pl. du Marché. ℘04 66 67 20 09.* This historic café, with its original 19C interior, serves Nîmes specialities such as ***brandade*** (mashed potato, cod, olive oil, milk) to locals and tourists alike. Excellent cakes and ice-cream, all made on the premises.

Au Chapon Fin – *3 pl. du Château-Fadaise. ℘04 66 67 34 73. Closed Sun lunch.* Friendly bistro-style place at the back of St Paul's church. Market produce is used and there is a good list of regional wines. Terrace in summer.

Bistrot des Arènes – *11 r. Bigot. ℘04 66 21 40 18. Closed Aug, Mon–Wed eves.* Typical Lyonnaise décor at this popular restaurant, serving Lyonnaise and French cuisine.

Aux Plaisirs des Halles – *4 r. Littré. ℘04 66 36 01 02. www.auxplaisirsdeshalles.com. Closed Sun–Mon, public holidays.* A handsome modern dining room (woodwork, designer furniture) and a pleasant flower-decked patio for summer dining. Generous tasty cuisine; fine list of regional wines.

Le Bouchon et L'Assiette – *5 bis r. Sauve. ℘04 6662 02 93. Closed mid-Jul–mid-Aug, 2–17 Jan, Tue–Wed.* This restaurant has a particularly well-designed décor with paintings and antique objects, as well as a very friendly reception. You'll find tasty seasonal cooking here.

Le Magister – *5 r. Nationale. ℘04 66 76 11 00. Closed Sat lunch, Sun.* Art exhibitions adorn the well-worn, wood-panelled walls of this welcoming chalet-type restaurant. Appetising regional fare.

Le Jardin d'Hadrien – *11 r. Enclos Rey. ℘04 66 21 86 65. www.lejardindhadrien.fr. Closed Aug, Sun eve, Mon and Tue lunch.* Away from the crowd, you can eat regional food in the cosy dining room in winter and in summer, enjoy the shady terrace.

NIGHTLIFE

Bar Hemingway – *Hotel Imperator, quai de la Fontaine. ℘04 66 21 90 30. www.hotel-imperator.com.* Opening onto a garden with redwood and cedar trees, a fountain and sculptures, the Hemingway bar of the Hotel Imperator is an oasis of calm and magic. Photographs pay homage to Ernest Hemingway, who wrote ***Death in the Afternoon*** (1962), a magnificent story about bullfighting.

Haddock Café – *13 r. de l'Agau. ℘04 66 67 86 57. Closed Sun.* This place cultivates food (wine by the glass, reasonably priced menu) as much the arts. There is a never-ending series of entertainment including concerts, literary and philosophy evenings and art exhibitions. Behind the zinc bar, owner Philippe presides over what is definitely one of the most dynamic venues of Nîmes' cultural life.

La Grand Bourse – *2 bd des Arènes. ℘04 66 67 68 69. Closed Sun.* With its Napoleon III style coffered ceiling, a terrace facing the amphitheatre and deep comfortable rattan armchairs, this is the most prestigious café in Nîmes. Excellent, professional service attracts customers of all ages and backgrounds.

SHOPPING

BISCUITS

Maison Villaret – *13 r. de la Madeleine. ℘04 66 67 41 79.* Crunchy almond biscuits known as ***croquants*** are sold in the 18C bakery where they were invented.

BRANDADE

Brandade Raymond – *34 r. Nationale. ℘04 66 67 20 47.* The king of ***brandade***! You'll also find other local specialities to take home.

MARKETS

Large market on Mon and organic market Fri mornings on boulevard Jean Jaurès. Flea market Sun mornings in the Costières stadium car park. Evening market Jul–Aug Thu 6–10pm.

PROVENÇAL FABRIC

Les Olivades – *4 pl. de la Maison-Carré. 𝒞04 66 21 01 31. www.lesolivades.fr. Closed Sun–Mon.* The textile industry was born during the reign of Louis XI, when the first workshop was founded. The tradition has continued with Les Olivades. You'll find fabric, linen, home deco and also clothes and bags – all in the patterns of Provence.

WINE

La Vinothèque – *18 r. Jean-Reboul (near arena). 𝒞04 66 67 20 44. Closed Sun–Mon.* Specialist in local wines.

FÉRIAS AND BULLFIGHTING

The best-known Féria, the Whitsun féria, runs Tue–Mon (end May) and includes bars lining the streets, bull runs through the street, bullfights and locals and tourists decked out in Camargue or Flamenco finery; the harvest féria takes place mid-Sept. You'll need to book well in advance for accommodation or stay in another town.

Tickets – *Available from 4 r. de la Violette. 𝒞08 91 70 14 01. www.arenesdenimes. com.* As well as single tickets you can also buy a pass which gives access to the shows and the best seats. Prices vary from 16€ to 91€ for a *corrida* and you should book well in advance.

GUIDED TOURS

Nîmes has been designated as a "Town of Art and History" and the tourist office has a full range of guided tours (2hr), including some in English.

Aven d'Orgnac★★★

Ardèche

The locals paid little attention to the great hole in the ground until 19 August 1935 when Robert de Joly (1887–1968) made an initial exploration. The engineer and speleologist, who explored his native Cévennes, also played an important role in improving the equipment and techniques used in underground exploration. This cave is fascinating because of the natural development of underground streams, fed by infiltration and through fissures in the calcareous rock. The first concretions, which were at times 10m/33ft in diameter, were broken by a major earthquake at the end of the Tertiary Era. These columns, broken or turned upside down, served as a base for more recent stalagmites.

VISIT

Allow 1hr.
🔹Guided tours (1hr) Jul–Aug 10am–5.30pm; Apr–Jun and Sept 10am–noon,

> ⚙ **Michelin Map:** 331: I-8.
> 🗺 **Info:** 1 place de l'Ancienne Gare, 07150 Vallon-Pont-d'Arc. 𝒞04 75 88 04 01. www.vallon-pont-darc.com.
> 🕐 **Timing:** Allow half a day for a visit.

2–5.30pm; Oct–15 Nov 10am–noon, 2.15–4.30pm; Feb–Mar and Christmas school holidays 10.30am–4.45pm. 9.70€ (includes museum Feb–mid-Nov). 𝒞04 75 38 65 10. www.orgnac.com. The constant temperature in the cave is 11°C/52°F, so you are advised to dress warmly. Also bear in mind that you will have to go down 788 steps (lift back up). The **Salle Supérieure** (Upper Chamber), 17–40m/56–131ft high, 250m/820ft long and 125m/410ft wide, contains magnificent stalagmites. The largest are in the middle; a number of growths give them the shape of pine cones. Unable, due to the height of the vault, to join the stalactites to form pillars, the stalagmites have thickened at the base and become quite large; other more recent and thinner stalagmites have piled on top of them like a stack of

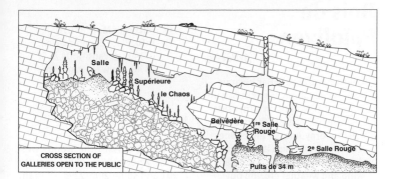

Salle
Supérieure
le Chaos
Belvédère
1re Salle Rouge
2e Salle Rouge
CROSS SECTION OF
GALLERIES OPEN TO THE PUBLIC
Puits de 34 m

plates. Along the walls of the chamber, note the delicate columns which came after the earthquake; some are very tall, either in bayonet shape or standing very straight. Dim light enters through the cave's natural opening.

In **Le Chaos** (Chaos Chamber), encumbered by concretions which have fallen in from the Salle Supérieure, magnificent curtains of varied colours escape from a fissure in the vault. On a level with the viewpoint of the **Première Salle Rouge** (First Red Chamber), the water filtering in, enriched with carbonate of lime through the calcareous layer, has encouraged the formation of a mass of concretions. Nearby is the well, the deepest in the cave at 34m/112ft, which leads into another chamber 180m/591ft deep. The visit finishes with a sound and light show.

Musée Régional de Préhistoire

 Same conditions as the cave.
Rooms arranged around a patio contain the discoveries of excavations carried out in the Ardèche and the north of the Gard regions. Reconstructions (Acheulean hut from Orgnac III, flint knapping workshop, Lion's Head decorated cave) introduce visitors to the way of life of prehistoric humans.

Stalagmites in Aven d'Orgnac

©Guillaume Buffet/Fotolia.com

ADDRESSES

🏠 STAY 🍴 EAT

☞ **Les Stalagmites** – *07150 Orgnac-l'Aven. ℘04 75 38 60 67. www.lesstala gmites.com. 25 rooms. ☐7€. Closed Jan–Feb.* A welcoming and inexpensive family-run boarding house in the village. The traditional food is served in generous portions. In the summer, you can enjoy it in the shade of the trees on the terrace.

Bois de Païolive★

Ardèche

This limestone area of Bas Vivarais stretches over about 16sq km/6sq mi southeast of Les Vans on either side of the River Chassezac. The ground consists of grey Jurassic limestone (Secondary Era), which is both hard and permeable, making it resistant to wind and weather erosion but susceptible to rainwater, full of carbonic acid, which has enlarged the fissures into deep defiles and remoulded the rocks into strange forms. Elsewhere residual rock has turned to clay and encouraged the growth of vegetation (especially the common oak).

A BIT OF HISTORY

Jalès and the Royalists – The basin stretching southeast of Vans, on either side of the village of Jalès, is closely linked to a dramatic period in France's counter-revolutionary history. Between 1790 and 1792, Royalists would congregate at the Château de Jalès. At the time the Civil Constitution of the Clergy was being implemented and this served to accentuate the divide as many bishops ended up supporting the Royalists. On 21 June 1792, the revolutionary cockade was put down at Berrias. Hailed as the leader of the Royalist movement in the area, the Comte de Saillans, whose family originally came from the Dauphiné, plotted an uprising. His plot exposed, soldiers sent to defeat Saillans' men overcame them not far from Courry, south of Vans, on 11 July. Saillans took refuge at the Château de Banne, then decided to flee with a group of his comrades-in-arms.

They were arrested on the road to Villefort and taken to Vans. The crowds, who blamed Saillans for the execution of several Republicans, murdered him and his friends in the street. It is said that a few Royalists succeeded in escaping to the Bois de Païolive, where they died of hunger.

☼ **Michelin Map:** 331: H-7.
🛈 **Info:** Place Léopold Ollier, 07140 Les Vans. ✆04 75 37 24 48. www.les-vans.com.

VISIT

Allow 2hr.
The D 252 crosses the woods west to east. About 300m/328yd from the D 901 and some 20m/22yd off to the right coming from Les Vans stand the rocks known locally as L'Ours (The Bear) and Le Lion (The Lion).

Clairière★

A clearing is accessible to cars near the D 252 in a right-hand bend coming from Les Vans, up an unsurfaced slope. A small picnic area has been set up nearby.

Corniche du Chassezac★★

🚶*30min return journey on foot.*
🅿*Park in the first car park on the left of the road, going towards Mazet-Plage.*
A footpath marked "Corniche" follows the tall cliffs which overlook the deep gorge. After no more than ten minutes' walking you suddenly come upon the grandiose Chassezac gorge winding past below, at the foot of the cave-pitted cliffs. The footpath, a sheer drop of 80m/263ft above the water, leads to the left, opposite a manor house, to a viewpoint located upstream. *Return the way you came.*

Mazet-Plage

15min return on foot. A surfaced path off the D 252 leads 300m/328yd to a campsite along the river bank.
This site is at the end of the Chassezac gorge, which is the only means of access. To reach the higher parts of the gorge, for bathing or climbing places, cross the river going in the direction of Casteljau and park in one of the car parks.
Walk along the Chassezac, going towards the left for about 500m/0.3mi along the shingly beach with its small willows opposite the unusual cave-pitted cliffs.

Banne

6km/3.7mi from the crossroads of the D 901 and D 252. Leave the car in the square; climb up the slope behind the Calvary.

The path leads to a platform overlooking the Jalès depression. From the top, where the ruins of Banne's old citadel lie, there is a vast **panorama**★ extending from the River Gard to the lower Ardèche. Half-buried in the platform's southwest side a long vaulted gallery can be seen, which served as stables to the castle of Banne and which was demolished after the defeat of the counter-Revolutionaries.

Pont du Gard★★★

Gard

This aqueduct, a UNESCO World Heritage Site, served as part of a system which brought spring water from Uzès to Nîmes. The structure was built in 1C, and in spite of its 2 000 years, is in very good condition.

Aqueduct

The Romans attached importance to the quality of the water which they required for settlements. The water was collected preferably on the north slope so as to not heat up in the reservoirs. The water channel was made of stone, either vaulted or tiled and pierced with openings for ventilation and maintenance. Some aqueducts were equipped with settling tanks. The contours of the land were crossed with exceptional engineering – the aqueduct followed its course via bridges, ditches, tunnels and siphons. The aqueduct of Nîmes, some 50km/31mi long, had an average incline of 34cm per km or 1:300, falling before the valley to reduce the height of the bridge. Its daily flow was about 20 000 m3/44 million gallons.

From the 4C the aqueduct ceased to be maintained, so that lime deposits built up, until finally by the 9C the course became blocked and had fallen into disuse. In 1743 a road bridge was added downstream of the aqueduct.

The GR 6 hiking footpath follows the traces of the Nîmes aqueduct in a landscape of scrubland.

- **Michelin Map:** 339: M-5.
- **Info:** Pont-du-Gard site, 30120 Vers-Pont-du-Gard. &08 20 90 33 30. www.pontdugard.fr.
- **Location:** Arrive by the D19 from Uzès or from Remoulins.
- **Parking:** Car parks are located on each side of the River Gardon. Open 6am–1am. 5€ for the day or 13€ for a year.
- **Timing:** You could spend anytrhing from 1hr to a day here, visiting the aqueduct, museum, beach (in summer), walking...
- **Kids:** The 'Ludo'.

Bridge (Pont)★★★

The aqueduct spans the Gardon valley. The golden coloured tone of the old stones complements the countryside.

It is composed of dressed blocks of masonry, some weighing as much as six tonnes, which were held together with iron clamps. The stone was lifted into position by block and tackle with goats as auxiliaries and a winch worked by a human treadmill.

In order to break monotony, the three levels of arches are recessed, the piers in line one above another. Statistical details are: height above the Gardon at low water: 49m/160ft; lowest level: 6 arches, 142m long, piers 6m thick, arches 22m high (466ft, 20ft, 72ft); middle level: 11 arches, 242m long, piers 4m thick, arches 20m high (794ft, 13ft, 66ft); top level with the canal: 35

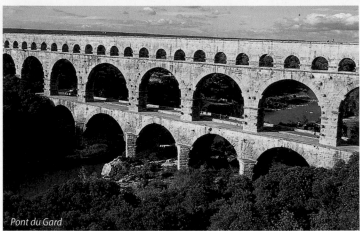

Pont du Gard

B. Kaufmann/MICHELIN

arches, 275m long, piers 3m thick, arches 7m high (903ft, 10ft, 23ft). The bridge was restored under Napoleon III. The architect varied the span of the arches slightly within each range; each arch was constructed independently to give flexibility in the event of subsidence. The stones obtruding from the face were scaffolding supports, and were to facilitate maintenance work and to add interest to the surface, as do the ridges on the piers which held the semicircular wooden frames on which the arches were constructed.

VISIT

Free access to the aqueduct and Mémoires de la Garrigue discovery area. ⏰*Museum, Ludo and cinema are open daily Oct–Apr 9.30am–5.30pm; May–Sept 9.30am–7pm.* ⊘*Ludo and cinema are closed Mon am.* ⊛*7€ (*👪*Ludo child 5€, cinema 4€).*

Left bank

After parking your car you will reach a large embankment with a cafeteria, cinema room, children's activity centre (Ludo), a museum with displays on the region's traditional activities and an area dedicated to presenting the *garrigue*.

Right bank

To the left of the access road, hollowed out of the hill, stands the reception centre which houses a multi-media exhibition/show covering an area of 500m2/598yd2. The show includes films and interactive displays pertaining to the bridge and its construction.

ADDRESSES

🏠 STAY

◔◔◔◔ **Au Temps des Cerises** – *chemin du Garrège, 30210 Vers-Pont-du-Gard, 6km/3.7mi S.* ℘*04 66 03 29 16. www.tempscerises.com. 5 rooms.* Stylish b&b in rural surroundings run by British expats. Delicious breakfast, heated swimming pool, river bathing, *boules* pitch and evening meals available twice a week.

🍽 EAT

◔◔◔◔ **L'Amphitryon** – *pl. du 8-Mai-1945, 30210 Castillon-du-Gard. 6.7km/4mi NE.* ℘*04 66 37 05 04. Closed Tue and Wed (Sept–Jun).* The vaulted dining room with exposed stone walls is in a former converted sheepfold. Eat outside on the pretty terrace in summer. Contemporary-style regional cooking and friendly atmosphere.

🚶 LEISURE ACTIVITY

Kayak Vert – *Berges du Gardon, A9 sortie Remoulins, 30210 Collias.* ℘*04 66 22 80 76. www.canoe-france.com/gardon.* All the family will enjoy a trip by canoe down the Gardon – from a couple of hours (☞20€) to two days (☞44€).

EVENTS

Garrigue en fête – Annual market and picnic weekend. mid-April.

Beach – On the right bank, daily 22 Jun–23 Aug 10am–7pm.

Son et Lumière – Jun–Sept (night).

Heritage Days – Special themed tours throughout the weekend of 19–20 Sept.

Pont-St-Esprit

Gard

The town owes its *raison d'être* and name to the bridge built in 1265–1309 by the Bridge Brotherhood under the protection of the Holy Spirit (St Esprit); it subsequently became an important halting-place on the Rhône. The town's other claim to fame is that the cabinetmaker Michel Bouvier (1792–1874) was born here. He was related to Jackie Kennedy.

▸ **Population:** 9 661.

⛯ **Michelin Map:** 339: M-3 – Local map, ☝️see Gorges de l'ARDÈCHE.

ℹ️ **Info:** 1 avenue Kennedy, Pont-St-Esprit. ☎04 66 39 44 45. www.ot-pont-saint-esprit.fr.

🕐 **Timing:** A pleasant stop near the Gorges de l'Ardèche.

✎ WALKING TOUR

▷ *Take rue St-Jacques, lined with old houses.*

Note in particular the 17C **Hôtel de Roubin** at no 10 and the Maison des Chevaliers (Knights' Mansion) at no 2, a former private residence belonging to the Piolenc, a renowned family of merchants from the Rhône valley, who lived on the premises between the 12C and 1988. This townhouse, enhanced by a pretty gemelled bay window in the Romanesque style, is home to the **Musée d'Art Sacré du Gard** (☝️see opposite).

▷ *Go past the old town hall and walk towards place St-Pierre from rue Haut Mazeau.*

Terrasse

This terrace lies on the east side of place St-Pierre and is bounded to the north by the 15C parish church, to the southwest by the Baroque façade of the Chapelle des Pénitents and to the southeast by the former 17C Église St-Pierre (now deconsecrated) topped by a dome. From the terrace there is a good overall view of the bridge.

A monumental double flight of stairs leads to quai de Luynes. Left, almost at the foot of the bridge, the **Maison du Roi** has fine Renaissance windows.

Pont

The bridge, nearly 1 000m/3 282ft long, is slightly curved upstream against the current; 19 of the 25 arches are original. It used to be defended at either end with bastions and two towers in the middle, now destroyed.

To facilitate navigation – the passage through the bridge had, over the centuries, always been feared by sailors – the bridge's first two arches were replaced by one arch (it was subsequently destroyed during World War II and rebuilt in reinforced concrete).

From the bridge there is a fine view of the Rhône and the town. North of the bridge there is now a vast terrace where the citadel once stood; it was built in 1595 and fortified by Vauban in the 17C. From the centre of the terrace the view extends to the 15C flamboyant doorway of the former Plan collegiate church.

> ▶ *Cross the intersection and then take rue des Minimes and turn left on rue du Couvent; continue along rue Bas-Mazeau, rue Haut-Mazeau and rue St-Jacques to the car.*

MUSEUM
Musée d'Art Sacré du Gard
2 r. St-Jacques. ⏱️Open Mar–Jan Tue–Sun 10am–noon, 2–6pm. Guided tours available. Closed public holidays. 3€. 04 66 39 17 61.
This museum highlights France's religious heritage by presenting and explaining sacred rites and their significance. On the ground floor, a sacristy displaying various sacred articles for celebrating Mass stands alongside a collection of clerical garments (interactive terminal showing a priest donning his robes before celebrating Mass; explanations are then given about the actual proceedings of a religious service). The rooms at garden level encourage visitors to reflect on the meaning of sacred issues, which contribute to reinforcing social cohesion, and on the role of the Bible today in a world characterised by scientific progress.

The collection of religious paintings includes The *Adoration of the Magi* by Nicolas Dipre (c. 1495), while the **Royal Court of Justice**★ on the first floor houses a retable by the Provençal Primitive painter **Raymond Boterie**, illustrating *The Fall of the Angels* (1509–10). Visitors may also admire a former apothecary's surgery and the pharmacy of the St-Esprit Hospital (an outstanding collection of medieval ceramic pieces of Hispano-Moorish inspiration).

St-Gilles★

Gard

Gateway to the Camargue, and of agricultural importance (fruit, Costières wines), St-Gilles' claim to fame is the old abbey, the west front of which considerably influenced Romanesque sculpture in Provence and in the Rhône valley.

A BIT OF HISTORY
St Giles and the Doe – Legend has it that in the 8C St Giles, who lived in Greece, was touched by the grace of God and gave all his money to the poor. He set out from Greece aboard a raft which was borne by the sea to Provence, where he lived alone in a cave for many years. The hermit was befriended by a doe which brought him food, and which he later saved from a huntsman, miraculously snatching the arrow in mid-flight, and so amazing the noble huntsman that he founded an abbey on the site in commemoration of the event. St Giles journeyed to Rome to obtain recognition for the new foundation and was presented by the pope with two doors for the abbey, which he promptly

▶ **Population:** 13 234.
Michelin Map: 339: L-6.
Info: 1 place Frédéric-Mistral, 30800 St-Gilles. 04 66 87 33 75. www.ville-saint-gilles.fr.
Location: 19km/11.8mi S of Nîmes; 11km/7mi W of Arles.
Don't Miss: The abbey, the Peach and Apricot féria in August.

launched on the Tiber and which, after being carried out to sea, landed on the Provençal shore at the same time as the saint on his return.

The Influence of St Giles (11C–12C) – On the site of St Giles' tomb, a sanctuary was raised which became a place of fervent pilgrimage, even more so because of its location on one of the roads to Santiago de Compostela.
In the 12C the monastery reached its peak: the town surrounding it had nine parishes and was prosperous. It owed part of its success to the Crusades: Far

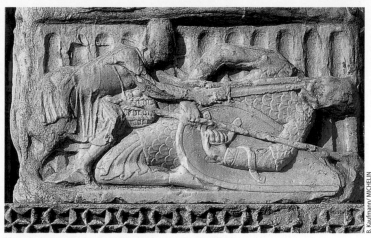

Detail of bas relief on doorway of Abbaye de Saint-Gilles

Eastern goods passed through its port; the crusading pilgrims embarked from here and the people of St-Gilles had trading posts with privileges in the Latin States of Outremer. The St-Gilles Fair held in September became one of the great trading centres between the Mediterranean and northern countries. This prosperity diminished in the 13C owing to the competition of the royal port of Aigues-Mortes.

The Glory and Decline of the Counts of Toulouse – Popes and the Counts of Toulouse protected and enriched the Benedictine monastery. In the 11C Count **Raymond IV** became Lord of St-Gilles, and built up a domain extending from Cahors to the Îles de Lérins, through marriage and inheritance. In 1096 he received Pope Urban II, who consecrated the altar of the new abbey church; the count vowed never to return to his land so as to devote himself to the First Crusade, eventually dying in the Holy Land.

His great-grandson, **Raymond VI**, was ordered by Pope Innocent III to fight against the heretical Albigensians. He received the papal legate, Pierre de Castlenau at St-Gilles, who was assassinated the next day, 15 January 1208. The pope immediately excommunicated Raymond VI. The count submitted and did penance in St-Gilles on 12 June 1209,

being led naked into the church and flagellated in front of Castelnau's tomb. He soon revolted, fighting a losing battle against Simon de Montfort the elder, and later died in 1222. He is represented as one of four figures on the ceiling of the Minnesota Supreme Court in the USA due to his support for city freedoms.

ABBEY

Allow 45min. pl. Jean Jaurès.
Guided tours (1hr) Mon–Sat 10.15am–4.15pm. 4€. Details available from the tourist office.
04 66 87 33 75.

In order to grasp the abbey's importance at the end of the 11C and during the 12C, try to imagine the chancel of the former abbey extending beyond the present chancel and, on the church's south side, the cloisters with their courtyard surrounded by the chapterhouse, refectory, kitchens and basement storeroom, not to mention the other monastic buildings which stretched to the present rue de la République and rue Victor-Hugo.

Secularised and established as a collegiate church in 1538, it suffered irrevocable destruction in 1562 during the Wars of Religion. The Huguenots threw the monks into the crypt's well and set the monastery on fire: the church's vaulting collapsed; in 1622 the great belfry was destroyed. In the 17C the church was shortened by half and its vaulting lowered so that in the future there would be less upkeep. Thus all that is left of a magnificent medieval building are the west face, remains of the chancel and the crypt.

Façade★★

The façade, which dates from the mid-12C, is considered one of the finest examples of Romanesque sculpture in the south of France. The story told is that of Salvation through the different stages in the life of Christ. The sculptors were inspired by the Antique style, notably from the paleo-Christian sarcophagi, as is shown by their use of high relief and the representations of volumes (anatomical proportions) and forms (pleated clothing).

The great frieze reads from left to right and recounts all the events of Holy Week from Palm Sunday to the morning of Paschal Resurrection and the discovery of the empty tomb by the Holy Women.

Ancien Chœur de St-Gilles

This is outside the actual church and corresponds to the part which was devastated in the 17C and razed during the Revolution. The bases of the pillars and the walls indicate precisely the former chancel's layout with its ambulatory and radiating chapels. On either side of the ambulatory, two small bell towers were served by spiral staircases; the one on the left remains: the Vis de St-Gilles.

Vis de St-Gilles★

This spiral staircase served the abbey church's north bell tower. Completed in 1142, it has always been admired by the Brotherhood of Stonemasons who during their habitual tour of France stopped to study it (they left graffiti).

Climb to the top (50 steps) to appreciate the rare quality of the cutting and joining of the stone. The steps rest on the central core and the cylindrical walls. The perfection of the interlocking stone composes a spiral vault of nine voussoirs. The art of the stonemason appears in the double concavity and convexity of each voussoir.

Crypt★

This low church (50m/164ft long, 25m/82ft wide) was the scene of one of the West's most important pilgrimages. It lasted three days and some 50 000 people walked past the venerated tomb of St Giles.

It was once covered with groined vaulting, which remains in several bays to the right of the entrance. Pointed vaulting from the mid-12C is what remains in the crypt; this vaulting is among the oldest known in France. The decoration of certain arches adorned

---

Five Artists to Create a Masterpiece

Art historians identify five stylistic groups with the name of only one master known, that of Brunus.

- Brunus: Matthew, Bartholomew, John the Evangelist, James the Greater, Paul; characteristics: Antique style, heavy, plain.
- Master "of St Thomas": Thomas, James the Less, Peter, low reliefs of the centre door; this sculptor is thought to have worked in the west of France; characteristics: linear quality and typically Romanesque treatment.
- "Soft" Master: apostles, left splay of the centre door, tympanum and lintel of the north door; characteristics: supple drapery modelling the folds around the arms and legs.
- "Hard" Master: apostles, south door; characteristics: long enveloping drapery with voluminous and hard folds sometimes represented in a spiral form, contrasts accentuated by light and shade.
- Master "of St Michael": entablatures on either side of the centre door, St Michael slaying the dragon; characteristic: very expressive style.

with a plain band contrasts with that of the others elegantly ornamented with ribbons and ovolo moulding.

Note the staircase and ramp the monks used to reach the upper church. Sarcophagi, ancient altars and Romanesque capitals are worth admiring, as well as gold, glass, terracotta and fabrics for interiors.

ADDITIONAL SIGHT
Maison Romane
pl. de la Maison Romane.
◷Open Mon–Sat Feb–May and Sept–Dec 9am–noon, 2–5pm; Jun 9am–noon, 2–6pm; Jul–Aug 9am–noon, 3–7pm. ◷Closed public holidays. ◉No charge. ℘04 66 87 40 42.
This Romanesque house is the birthplace of **Gui Faucoi**, elected pope in 1265 under the name of Clement IV. It houses an ethnological room presenting tools and objects relating to the old trades: the shepherd, coopery, life in the fields, the vineyards, olive groves and domestic life. In the "medieval" room, with its magnificent chimney, a small museum contains the ruins of the former abbey church: tympanum, capitals, keystone, 12C low reliefs and sarcophagi.

🚗 DRIVING TOUR

Camargue Gardoise★
73km/45.4mi – allow half a day.
Situated between the Costières and the Petit-Rhône, St-Gilles and Aigues-Mortes, the so-called "Camargue Gardoise" with its marshes and reeds constitutes what is probably the most austere landscape of the Rhône delta. However, its strong links to ancient traditions make it an area that is well worth preserving and exploring.

▷ *Leave St-Gilles via the N 572 for Montpellier.*

The road winds its way through the slopes of the hills crossing the territory of the Nîmes Costières with its numerous vineyards where wine can be bought. To the left there is an area of lakes with the

large lakes of Scamandre and Charnier visible through the reeds.

▷ *Turn left onto the D 179 for Gallician and, from this small wine-producing hamlet, turn right onto the small D 381 road. After the Mas Teissier, turn left and follow the D 401 until you reach the canal that links the Rhône to Sète.*

Pont des Tourradons
From this bridge that stands in isolation among the marshes, there are interesting **views**★ of a typical Petite Camargue landscape: a straight canal, ponds and reeds which seem to merge with the sky in a solitary silence. In the summer herds of black bulls peacefully graze in the pastures of the Cailar. This is surely the definitive scenery of the authentic Camargue.

▷ *Take the D 104 in the opposite direction and turn right onto the D 352 for Vauvert.*

Vauvert
The old centre of this wine-producing village, now a residential suburb of Nîmes, has a covered marketplace which has been converted into an exhibition space (www.vauvert.com).

▷ *Take the N 572 towards Aimargues.*

At the level of the roundabout that leads to the village of Cailar (whose signposts were designed and made by the painter François Boirond), stands the tomb of a famous Camargue bull known as Sanglier (boar).

▷ *Before reaching Aimargues, turn left onto the D 979 for Aigues-Mortes.*

Château de Teillan
ᘛSee AIGUES-MORTES.

Saint-Laurent-d'Aigouze
In the middle of the village square, shaded by large plane trees, stands the arena, next to the church whose sacristy seems to function as a *toril*. It is worth a visit particularly at the end of August

Le Boeuf à la St-Gilloise

Also known as *gardianne des mariniers* (bargeman's bull casserole), this is a local variation on *gardianne de taureau* (bull-meat casserole served with rice).

when the races to celebrate the votive feast take place.

▶ *Continue along the D 146 which goes past the Tour Carbonnière (☞see AIGUES-MORTES). On reaching the D 58 turn left towards Arles.*

In this wine-producing area there are a great number of large *mas*, hidden by the shade of small pine forests.

After 9.5km/6mi turn left onto the small D 179 road for Montcalm St-Gilles.

In the hamlet of **Montcalm** stand the ruins of a large, early 18C house (in very bad repair) where the Marquis de Saint-Veran stayed before his departure for Canada, before dying after the Battle of Quebec. On the right, in a large vineyard, stands a chapel dating from the same period.

ADDRESSES

🛏 STAY

⊜⊜ **Chambre d'hôte Le Mas de Plisset** – *rte de Nîmes.* 🖉*04 66 87 18 91. www.masdeplisset.camargue.fr. 4 rooms. Closed Christmas and New Year.* You know you're in the country when you stay at this farm. Although simple and functional, rooms are comfortable. Swimming pool.

⊜⊜⊜ **Hôtel Héraclée** – *30 quai du Canal.* 🖉*04 66 87 44 10. www.hotel-heraclee.com. 21 rooms.* ⊜8€. Located beside the canal in the centre of the town, this hotel is an ideal base from which to explore the town and the Camargue.

▶ *The very narrow road runs along the Capettes canal all the way to the Mas des Iscles. At the crossing, park in the Centre du Scamandre car park.*

Centre de Découverte du Scamandre

Route des Iscles – Gallician, Vauvert. ⏱*Open Wed–Sat 9.30am–6pm.* ⏱*Closed public holidays.* ⊜*No charge for entry to reserve.* ☞*Guided tours (2hr)* ⊜6€. 🖉*04 66 73 52 05. www.camarguegardoise.com.*

The main purpose of this centre, situated in the Scamandre nature park, is to preserve and manage the marshes as well as raise public awareness of this fragile ecosystem.

Road D 179 on the right leads to Gallician, frequented by many fishermen and situated on the Capettes canal. The canal runs between the Charnier and Scamandre ponds and is a veritable forest of reeds.

▶ *After crossing the canal and Gallician, return to Vauvert via the N 572 on the right.*

☟/ EAT

⊜⊜ **Le Clément IV** – *36 quai du Canal.* 🖉*04 66 87 00 66. Closed Sun and Mon–Thu eve in winter.* Seafood and Camargue specialities served at this rustic restaurant with a lovely view.

🛒 SHOPPING

Maison des Métiers d'Art – *29 Grand Rue.* 🖉*04 66 87 09 05.* Craft workshops: ceramic, glass, pottery and tapestry.

EVENTS

St Gilles – This village is known for its taurine history, especially the Peach and Apricot féria on the third weekend of August (bullfights, Spanish shows).

Uzès★★

Gard

Set in the charming *garrigues* countryside, Uzès is established at the tip of a limestone plateau, overlooking the Alzon valley. The first Duchy of France, the town has preserved its lay-out as a medieval stronghold, embellished in the 17C and 18C as a result of economic prosperity (acquired through the manufacture of linen, serge and silk).

▶ **Population:** 7 935.
Michelin Map: 339: L-4.
Info: Place Albert-1er, 30700 Uzès, ✆04 66 22 68 88. www.uzes-tourisme. com/sitegb.
Don't Miss: The castle, the Saturday-morning market.
Timing: You could easily spend a day here, especially on market days.
Kids: Musée du Bonbon, National Stud, Bouscarasse Water Park, Moulin de Chalier.

A BIT OF HISTORY

The Duchy of Uzès – The old House of Uzès goes back to Charlemagne through its women. After the execution, in 1632, of the Duke of Montmorency in Toulouse, the Duke of Uzès became the most powerful duke and peer of the kingdom.

Poet in Exile – Uzès has its place in the history of French literature, because it was here that **Jean Racine** (1639–99) stayed in 1661 when he was 22 years old. Having been educated under the severe discipline of Port-Royal and the Jansenist College of Harcourt in Paris, Racine sought a change. His family, who watched with horror as their son considered a career in the theatre, sent him to his uncle, vicar-general of Uzès. To entice him away from his worldly associations, his uncle promised him an allowance once he had taken holy orders. Racine spent more than a year here. In his letters, full of humour, he spoke little of theology but much of the countryside, the food, the local dialect (which he could not understand) and his first poems.

The young poet did not pursue the religious vocation so desired by his family, but returned to Paris to become France's greatest Classical dramatist.

WALKING TOUR
OLD TOWN★★
Allow 2hr30min.

▷ *Start at avenue de la Libération and turn right onto boulevard des Alliés.*

On place de l'Église stands the house where **Charles Gide**, the famous economist, was born, uncle of the author **André Gide** (1869–1951), who was awarded the Nobel Prize in Literature in 1947.

▷ *Take rue St-Étienne towards place aux Herbes.*

Rue St-Étienne
Note the imposing Louis XIII-style faceted door at no 1. Farther on to the left in a blind alley is a fine Renaissance façade.

Place aux Herbes★
This picturesque, asymmetrical square is surrounded by covered walkways and has plane trees growing in it. Parts of *Cyrano de Bergerac* (1990) with Gérard Depardieu were shot here. Among the medieval houses, which were converted in the 17C and 18C, notice the **Hôtel de la Rochette**, dating from the 17C and slightly set back and, to the north, a corner house decorated on the side with a turret.

▷ *Near this house turn right into an alleyway, which leads to the unusual and narrow rue Pelisserie. Turn right into rue Entre-les-Tours.*

Tour de l'Horloge
6 r. Entre les Tours.
This clock tower dates from the 12C and is crowned with a wrought-iron bell cage. It was the bishop's tower; it confronted the duke's tower and king's tower at a time when these three powers shared Uzès.

Hôtel Dampmartin
On the corner of rue Jacques-d'Uzès and place Dampmartin.
This mansion displays a Renaissance façade flanked by a round tower; a carved frieze surrounds the first-floor window. Enter into the Renaissance courtyard (staircase).

▷ *Cross place Dampmartin, also surrounded by covered walkways, and take rue de la République.*

Hôtel de Joubert
12 r. de la République.
Fine Henri II-style façade (restored).

▷ *Continue along the street, then turn right into boulevard Gambetta and continue to the Hôtel de Ville.*

Tour Fenestrelle

F. Gégot/MICHELIN

Hôtel de Ville
This dates from the 18C and has a finely laid-out courtyard. From the façade on the side of the château there is a view of the enormous outline of the Ducal Palace and the chapel roof of varnished tiles.

▷ *Turn left along rue Boucairie, formerly a leatherworkers' street.*

At the corner of rue Raffin stands the Hôtel des Monnaies (Old Mint); a sign reminds us that the bishops of Uzès were permitted to strike their own coins during the Middle Ages.

Hôtel du Baron de Castille
The late-18C front of this mansion is preceded by a colonnade.

Ancien Palais Épiscopal
r. de l'Évêché.
This sumptuous episcopal palace was built at the end of the 17C; its right wing houses the public library.

Cathédrale St-Théodorit
r. de l'Évêché.
The 17C cathedral behind a 19C remodelled west front contains a fine Louis XIV-style organa. Note the painted shutters which were closed over the instrument, during Lent.

Tour Fenestrelle★★
This tower which abuts the cathedral's south wall is 12C and is the only relic of the former Romanesque cathedral. This kind of round bell tower is unique in France: it rises 42m/138ft above a square base with six storeys which recede one above the other.

Promenade Jean-Racine
This avenue, which runs into promenade des Marronniers, overlooks the ducal park, the *garrigues*, and the Alzon valley where the River Eure was tapped at its source by the Romans and diverted along the Pont du Gard aqueduct to provide water for Nîmes.

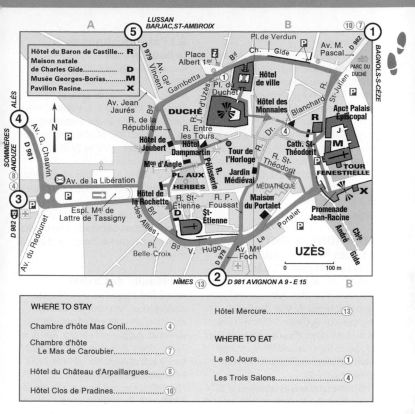

Hôtel du Baron de Castille... **R**
Maison natale
de Charles Gide............... **D**
Musée Georges-Borias....... **M**
Pavillon Racine.................. **X**

WHERE TO STAY

Chambre d'hôte Mas Conil............... ④

Chambre d'hôte
Le Mas de Caroubier.................... ⑦

Hôtel du Château d'Arpaillargues....... ⑧

Hôtel Clos de Pradines.................... ⑩

Hôtel Mercure............................... ⑬

WHERE TO EAT

Le 80 Jours.................................. ①

Les Trois Salons............................ ④

To the left stands the Pavillon Racine, an old tower, once part of the fortifications, restored in the late 18C.

◖ *Return and follow Le Portalet.*

Maison du Portalet
19 Le Portalet.
This is a pretty Renaissance house.

◖ *Return to avenue de la Libération via boulevard Victor-Hugo.*

Duché★
pl. du Duché. ⟿ *Guided tours of apartments and cellars and visit to the tower Jul–Aug 10am–12.30pm, 2–6.30pm; Sept–Jun 10am–noon, 2–6pm (last entry 30min before closing).* ⊙*Closed 25 Dec.* ⊚*15€ (tower only 10€).* ℘*04 66 22 18 96. www.uzes.com.*
From the outside, the ducal palace appears as a feudal *mas* with buildings of various periods exemplifying the rise of the Uzès family.

Courtyard
From left to right are: Tour de la Vicomté (14C tower) with its octagonal turret, commemorating the lords of Uzès' elevation to a viscounty in 1328; Tour Bermonde, a square 11C keep. To the right, at a right angle, lies the Renaissance **façade**★ erected by the first duke in c. 1550 based on plans by Philibert Delorme. At the façade's far end stands a Gothic chapel (restored in the 19C).

Tour Bermonde
This tower is entered up a spiral staircase *(135 steps)*. From the terrace the **panorama**★★ unfolds over the old roofs of Uzès and the *garrigues* landscape; the bell cage of the clock tower can be seen nearby.

Cellars (Caves)
The enormous 11C vaulted cellars house a waxwork reconstruction of the marriage of Jacques de Crussol and Simone d'Uzès in 1486.

195

Apartments

To get into these, go through the doorway in the façade, which opens onto the beautiful Renaissance main staircase, which has coffered, diamond-pointed vaulting. Particularly worth noting in the visit are: the Louis XV great hall, decorated with plasterwork and a Trianon console; the library; the dining room decorated with Renaissance and Louis XIII furniture; and the 15C chapel, which was renovated in the 19C. On the left as you leave notice the 12C **Tour de la Vigie**.

ADDITIONAL SIGHTS
⚐☖ Uzès National Stud (Haras national d'Uzès)

3.5km/2.2mi W. Leave Uzès by the Alès road. After 2km/1.2mi turn left onto the chemin du Mas-des-Tailles (signposted). ♿○*Open 15 Mar–1 Jul Mon–Sat 2–5pm.* ☛*Guided tours (1hr) 15 Jun–15 Sept Tue and Thu 3pm (and 10am Jul–Aug).* ☜*5€ (child 3.50€).* ☎*04 66 22 99 99.*

This horse farm was established in 1974 on a property which included, among other things, a large house dating from the end of the 19C, outbuildings and stables. Modern installations were added to enhance the premises, namely a riding school, racecourses and an obstacle course for the dressage and training of their horses, stallions and Provençal donkeys.

⚐☖ Musée du Bonbon Haribo

Pont-des-Charettes, at the entrance to Uzès on D 981 (Remoulins road). ♿○*Open Jul–Aug daily 10am–7pm; Sept–Dec & late Jan–Jun Tue–Sun 10am–1pm, 2–6pm.* ☜*6€ (child 3€).* ☎*04 66 22 74 39. www.haribo.com.*

Everything you always wanted to know about sweet manufacturing, in particular the various different-shaped "jelly" sweets, so beloved of children (and adults!). Flavour space for smelling and tasting.

⚐☖ Parc Aquatique de la Bouscarasse

Route d'Alès. ○*Open 30 May–30 Aug Mon–Fri 10am–7pm, Sat–Sun and public holidays 10am–8pm; 31 Aug–20 Sept Wed 10am–7pm, Sat–Sun 10am–8pm (dependent on good weather).* ☜*13€ (child 11€); 14.50€/12€ Sun and public holidays.* ☎*04 66 22 50 25. www.bouscarasse.fr.*

With 2 500sq m/2990sq yd of swimming and paddling pools, this place is ideal for families with young children. The large shady park is full of luxuriant plants, with wooden tables for picnics, as well as an open-air theatre and a small snack bar.

⚐☖ Moulin de Chalier

4km/2.5mi. Leave Uzès on D 982, the Anduze road. Turn right just before Arpaillargues onto a road running downhill. ♿○*Open Feb–Dec Tue–Sun 10am–noon, 2–7pm.* ☜*7€ (child 6€), family tickets available.* ☎*04 66 22 58 64. www.jouetmusee.com.*

This 18C stone mill houses the **Musée 1900** with its collection of vehicles, posters and other objects evoking daily life during the Belle Époque. Exhibits include a wide range of vehicles dating from 1870 onwards. The early days of cinema, photography and radio are also represented by magic lanterns (1870), a photo enlarger (1880) and crystal receivers, as well as a section devoted to traditional agricultural activities in the region. The nearby **Musée du Jouet** (Toy Museum), set out in the décor of a recreated railway station, houses a 400m/1 313ft long miniature railway as well as models of the region's sites; the amphitheatre at Nîmes, the Pont du Gard aqueduct and the fortifications at Aigues-Mortes.

St-Quentin-la-Poterie

5km/3mi. Leave Uzès by 1 on the map, the Bagnols-sur-Cèze road. After 2km/1.2mi turn left onto the D 5 and then left again onto the D 23.

The quality of its clay subsoil gave rise to the development of the pottery industry in the village, particularly during the 14C when over 110 000 glazed earthenware tiles were made for the decoration of the Palais des Papes at Avignon. The last brick factory closed its doors in 1954 and the last pipe factory stopped operating in 1974. Ceramists, along with glass artists, have been attracted to the village to continue the tradition. An oil mill in the centre of the village houses the **Maison de la Terre** *(14 r. de la Fontaine)*, which displays a collection of Mediterranean ceramic pieces in the **Musée de la Poterie Méditerranéenne** *(⏱open Feb–May and Oct Wed–Sun 2–6pm; Jun Wed–Sun 10am–1pm, 3–7pm; Jul–Aug daily 10am–1pm, 3–7pm; Sept Wed–Sun 10am–noon, 2–6pm; Nov–Jan by appointment only; ☞3€; ✆04 66 03 65 86; www. musee-poterie-mediterranee.com)*. On the ground floor, the **Galerie Terra Viva** *(⏱open daily 10am–7pm; ☞no charge; ✆04 66 22 48 78; www.galerie-terraviva.com)* displays contemporary ceramic art.

🚗 DRIVING TOUR

51km/32mi – allow about 6hr.

From Uzès to Remoulins

This tour of la Gardonnenque follows the Gardon Valley, passing through a typical landscape of the *garrigue*: rocks uncovered by the action of rain, frost, drought and wind, interspersed with scrub oak, *Cistus*, gorse, asphodel and wild aromatic plants.
Through parched, arid limestone hills, rivers carve picturesque gorges.

▷ *Leave Uzès by the road to the S and turn right onto the D 979, the road to Nîmes, which winds through the countryside offering splendid views of Uzès.*

Pont St-Nicholas

The nine-arched bridge, built in the 13C by the Bridge Brotherhood, spans the River Gardon in a particularly beautiful spot. The D 979 cuts into the overhanging rock as it climbs, affording good views of the Gardon; the right-hand bend at the top (🅿 *car park*) presents a spectacular

view★ along the course of the Gardon gorges.

▷ *Turn left onto the D 135 and, just before Poulx, left again onto the D 127. This is a poorly surfaced road, and passing is sometimes difficult, if not impossible, except in lay-bys hewn out of the rock.*

Site de la Baume★

Park the car after the final bend and take the path (1hr return), which leads to the foot of the gorges.
After passing some ruined buildings, the path reaches a picturesque spot on the banks of the Gardon, which is very popular in summer with bathers. On the opposite bank, the entrance to the cave, the Grotte de la Baume, can be seen in the cliff face.

Poulx

Now a residential suburb of Nîmes, this village still has a pretty little Romanesque church.

▷ *Continue along the D 427, which crosses the garrigue, interspersed with vineyards and orchards. In Carbrières turn left onto the D 3, towards the Gardon valley.*

Collias

A centre for water sports and horse riding, the GR 63 footpath also passes by here, allowing access to the Gardon gorges. The village is also popular among rock climbers, on account of its towering cliffs.

▷ *Follow the D 3, which climbs the Alzon valley, then turn right onto D 981.*

Pont du Gard★★★

⏱see PONT DU GARD.

▷ *Turn left onto the D 228.*

Castillon-du-Gard★

A hilltop village with superbly restored houses built of reddish stone. It can claim the exclusivity of being the only village with a view of the famous bridge.

ADDRESSES

🛏 STAY

🍴🧀🍺 **Château d'hôte Mas de Caroubier** – *684 rte de Vallabrix, 30700 St-Quentin-la-Poterie, 5km/3mi NE.* ☎*04 66 22 12 72. Closed Feb. 4 rooms.* 🛏🍽. This farmhouse, located on a quiet country road offers a friendly welcome and nicely furnished rooms. Pool.

🍴🧀🍺 **Hôtel Mercure** – *rte de Nîmes, via 2 on map.* ☎*04 66 03 32 22. 65 rooms, Restaurant* 🍺🍺 *(eve only).* A group of buildings around a pool and a shaded terrace make up this hotel on the doorstep of Uzès. Bright rooms. An informal guesthouse rather than a chain atmosphere. Provençal-coloured dining room or a pretty terrace in summer.

🍴🧀🍺–🍴🧀🍺 **Château d'hôte Mas Conil** – *chemin de Collorguesm, 30190 Aubussargues, 8km/5mi E.* ☎*04 66 63 97 00. www.masconil.com. Closed 10 days at Christmas. 4 rooms, 1 suite.* 🛏. *Meal*🍴🧀🍺. Not far from the Aubussargues château, this B&B has four well-kept rooms and a family suite. Pool.

🍴🧀🍺🍺 **Hôtel-Château d'Arpaillargues** – *r. du Château, 30700 Arpaillargues, 5.4km/3.3mi W.* ☎*04 66 22 14 48. www.chateaudarpaillargues.com. 29 rooms.* 🍽*14€. Restaurant*🍴🧀🍺🍺. A pretty 18C château with individual rooms overlooking the garden or the village. Friendly atmosphere and good food.

🍴🧀🍺–🍴🧀🍺🍺 **Hôtel Clos de Pradines** – *pl. du Pigeonnier, 30700 St-Quentin-la-Poterie, 5km/3mi NE.* ☎*04 66 57 19 53. www.clos-de-pradines.com. Closed mid–end Nov, 12–end Jan. 18 rooms.* 🍽*12€. Restaurant*🍴🧀🍺 *(closed Tue–Fri lunches Nov–Mar, Sun eve and Mon Sept–Jun).* This hotel offers delightful neo-Provençal-style rooms with, south-facing terraces or balconies. The restaurant serves traditional food.

🍴 EAT

🍴🧀🍺 **Le 80 Jours** – *2 pl. Albert-1er.* ☎*04 66 22 20 78. Closed Wed in winter and Sun.* A modern brasserie with ethnic décor, named after Jules Verne and his writings.

🍴🧀🍺🍺 **Les Trois Salons** – *18 r. du Dr Blanchard.* ☎*04 66 22 57 34. Closed Sun–Mon.* Built in 1699, this house has three dining rooms, hence the name. Modern menu with regional flavours.

🛒 SHOPPING

Annual truffle day *(journée de la truffe)* 3rd Sun in Jan. **Traditional market** Sat am. **Farmers' market** Wed am. *Place aux Herbes.*

Atelier Pichon – *ZA Pont des Charrettes.* ☎*04 66 22 11 86. www.ceramique-pichon.fr.* Manufacture of traditional ceramics, founded in 1802.

La Maison de la Truffe – *27 pl. aux Herbes.* ☎*04 66 63 86 45.* Everything relating to these black diamonds – vinegar, pasta, honey, dog food, liqueurs, oil and even chocolate!

TOURS

Guided Visits – Uzès has been designated a 'Town of Art and History'. Guided tours (2hr) run from Jun–Sept. *Ask at the tourist office.*

EVENTS

Nuits Musicales d'Uzès – Renaissance and Baroque music in picturesque settings during the second half of July *(www.nuitsmusicalesuzes.org).*

Festival Autres Rivages – Hear music from around the world in the Uzès area in July *(www.autres-rivages.com).*

Festival Européen des Arts Céramiques – Takes place in mid-July during even years (next 2010) in St-Quentin. Browse or buy *(www.officeculturel.com).*

Vallon-Pont-d'Arc

Ardèche

An outdoor pursuits resort, Vallon is the recommended starting point for travelling down the Gorges de l'Ardèche by boat. To the southeast, stands the ruins of old Vallon, a feudal village.

SIGHTS

Town Hall Tapestries

1 pl. de la Résistance. ☝ ⊙*Open Mon–Fri 9am–noon, 2–5pm.* ☛*Guided tours available (1hr30min).* ⊜*2.50€.* ☎*04 75 88 02 06.*

The town hall *(mairie)* is located in an old Louis XIII-style mansion, formerly the residence of the counts of Vallon. In the ground floor marriage room hang colourful Aubusson tapestries.

♁♁ "Grotte Chauvet-Pont d'Arc" Exhibition

1 r. du Miarou (behind the town hall). ☝ ⊙*Open Tue–Sun mid-Mar–May and Sept–mid-Nov 10am–noon, 2–5.30pm; Jun–Aug 10am–1pm, 3–7pm; last entry 1hr before closing.* ☛*Guided visits available (1hr30min).* ⊙*Closed public holidays.* ⊜*5€ (child 3€).* ☎*04 75 37 17 68. www.prehistoireardeche.com.*

With a view to preserving the invaluable heritage discovered in the Grotte Chauvet in 1994, a huge exhibition has been organised to enlighten visitors on this major breakthrough dating back to the Upper Palaeolithic Era. A display of photographs, explanatory documents and films explore the various representations of art in the decorated caves of the Ardèche, as well as the daily life of nomadic hunters back in those Prehistoric days (reconstituted scenes).

EXCURSIONS

♁♁ Silkworm Farm (Magnanerie)

3km/2mi towards Ruoms on the D 579. Access along a road branching off to the left coming from Vallon. ⊙*Open Apr–Jun and Sept Tue–Sun 10.30am–*

12.30pm, 2.30–6.30pm; Jul–Aug daily 10.30am–12.30pm, 2.30–6.30pm; Oct–Mar daily 2.30–6.30pm.* ⊜*4€ (child 2.30€).* ☛*Guided tours (45min) Apr–Sept Wed and Sun 10am.* ☎*04 75 88 01 27. www.mamagnanerie.com.*

This is one of the last Vivarois silkworm farms still in operation, with a viewable cocoonery, a vast room containing silkworms on trays made of reeds.

Pont-d'Arc★★

5km/3mi SE via the D 290 (☝see Gorges de l'ARDÈCHE).

Information panel

▶ **Population:** 2 470.

☝ **Michelin Map:** 331: I-7 – Local map, ☝*see Gorges de l'ARDÈCHE.*

🛈 **Info:** 1 place de l'Ancienne-Gare, 07150 Vallon-Pont-d'Arc. ☎04 75 88 04 01. www.vallon-pont-darc.com.

◗ **Location:** On the D 579 between Barjac and Aubenas.

⌖ **Don't Miss:** Le Pont d'Arc (☝*see Gorges de l'ARDÈCHE);* the Grotte Chauvet.

🕐 **Timing:** Allow 2hr to visit Grotte Chauvet and the village; 2hr more to enjoy Pont d'Arc. Be aware that it gets busy in summer.

♁♁ **Kids:** Silkworm farm; and the Grotte Chauvet.

ADDRESSES

🛏 STAY

⊜⊜⊜⊜ **Le Manoir du Raveyron** – *r. Henri-Barbusse.* ☎*04 75 88 03 59. www.manoir-du-raveyron.com. 8 rooms.* 🍽. *Restaurant* ⊜⊜⊜. This 16C buillding, situated in a quiet street, offers cosy and individual rooms. Pleasant flower-filled courtyard. Vaulted dining room where you can enjoy tasty dishes of the day prepared with a regional accent.

Villeneuve-lez-Avignon★

Gard

A tour of Villeneuve-lez-Avignon is the natural complement to a visit to Avignon. This town, the "City of the Cardinals", offers a view – one of the most famous in the Rhône valley – over the "City of the Popes". The best time to contemplate it is at the end of the afternoon, beneath a setting sun, when Avignon appears in all its splendour.

A BIT OF HISTORY

In 1271, after the Albigensian Crusade, the King of France, Philip III the Bold, acquired the county of Toulouse, which extended to the banks of the Rhône. On the opposite shore was Provence and the Holy Roman Empire. The river belonged to the crown, which raised the thorny question of rights: whenever the river flooded parts of Avignon, the French King claimed them as his territory and demanded taxes from the unfortunate citizens.

At the end of the 13C, Philip the Fair founded a new town (in French: *ville neuve*) on the plain, and its population grew rapidly. Grasping the great military importance of the spot, he built a powerful fortification at the entrance to Pont St-Bénézet. The cardinals, arriving at the papal court in the 14C and finding no suitable accommodation in Avignon, began to build magnificent residences (*livrées*) across the river in Villeneuve, until eventually there were 15 of these. The prosperity, which the cardinals' patronage of churches and monastic houses brought to the town, remained long after the papal court had returned to Rome. The kings John the Good and Charles V had built Fort St-André in order to watch over the neighbouring papal kingdom. In the 17C and 18C fine hôtels lined Grande-Rue. In the monasteries, which developed into museums, an active and brilliant lifestyle flourished, until the Revolution swept away the aristocratic and ecclesiastic regimes.

▶ **Population:** 12 741.
Michelin Map: 339: N-5.
Info: 1 place Charles David, Villeneuve-Lez-Avignon. ℘04 90 25 61 33. www.villeneuvelesavignon.com.
Parking: There's a car park at the foot of the fort on avenue Charles de Gaulle.
Don't Miss: The excellent view of Avignon from Philippe-le-Bel tower.
Timing: Allow half a day.

Tour Philippe-le-Bel

av. Gabriel Péri. ◐Open Tue–Sun Apr–Sept 10am–12.30pm, 2–6.30pm; Oct–Nov, Mar 10am–noon, 2–5pm. ◐Closed public holidays. ⊙1.60€. ℘04 32 70 08 57.

Built on a rock near the Rhône, this tower was the key structure in the defence work at the west end of Pont St-Bénézet, on royal land. The first storey was built between 1293–1307. The second floor and watch turret were added in the 14C. The upper terrace *(176 steps)* gives a lovely view of Villeneuve and Avignon, Mont Ventoux, the Montagnette hills and the Alpilles.

Église Notre-Dame

pl. Meissonnier. ◐Open daily Apr–Sept 10am–12.30pm, 2–6.30pm; Oct–Mar 10am–noon, 2–5pm. ◄Guided tours available (30min). ◐Closed public holidays. ⊙No charge. ℘04 90 27 49 28.

This collegiate church dedicated to Our Lady was founded in 1333. The tower which ends the building on the east side was built as a separate belfry, the ground floor of which straddled the public footpath. The monks obtained permission to redirect the path. They blocked off the belfry arcade, converted it into a chancel and linked it to the existing church by adding an extra bay to the nave. Inside, a number of works of art can be found: starting from the back of the church note the tomb of Cardinal Arnaud de Via, rebuilt with its original 14C recumbent figure (second north chapel), a copy of the famous Pietà kept in the Louvre since 1904 (third south chapel), *St Bruno* by Nicolas Mignard and a *Calvary* by Reynaud Levieux.

Rue de la République

The street is lined with a number of livrées (nos **1**, **2**, **3**, **45** and **53**). One of these palaces houses the local **museum** (*see below*), which belonged to Cardinal Pierre de Luxembourg, a cardinal who died having already won saintly repute at the early age of 19 (in 1387). At no 60 a gateway gives access to the Chartreuse du Val de Bénédiction.

Musée Municipal Pierre-de-Luxembourg

2 r. de la République.
&Same as Tour Philippe-le-Bel. ✆3€.
℘04 90 27 49 66.

This museum, in the hotel Pierre-de-Luxembourg, displays magnificent works of art on four floors.

On the ground floor you will find the 14C polychrome ivory **Virgin**★★, carved from an elephant's tusk; it is one of the finest works of its kind. Also worth admiring are: the marble **Virgin**★★ with two faces from the School of Nuremberg (14C); the death mask of Jeanne de Laval, second wife of King René, by Laurana; the chasuble, said to have belonged to Innocent VI; and the 17C veil of the Holy Sacrament, adorned with small pearls. The first floor houses the museum's most beautiful work of art: **Coronation of the Virgin**★★, painted in 1453 by Enguerrand Quarton, from Laon; this artist painted in Aix, then Avignon (from 1447). Fascinated by landscapes and Provençal light, he used bright colours, which emphasised the scene's majesty. The Virgin, with her large cloak, dominates this composition, which

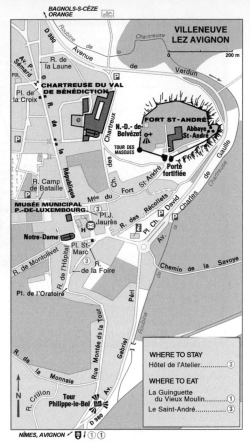

encompasses heaven and earth in the subjects painted.

Note interesting paintings by Nicolas Mignard (*Jesus in the Temple*, 1649) and Philippe de Champaigne (*Visitation*, c. 1644), Reynaud Levieux *(Crucifixion)*, Simon de Châlons and Parrocel *(St Anthony and the Infant Jesus)*.

Chartreuse du Val de Bénédiction★

60 r. de la République. ◯*Open year round (call or see website to confirm hours).* ✆*Guided tours available (1hr15min).* ◯*Closed public holidays.* ✆7€. ℘04 90 15 24 24. *www.chartreuse.org.*

In 1352 the papal conclave met in Avignon and elected the General of the Carthusian Order as Pope, but he refused the throne out of humility. To commemorate this gesture Innocent VI, who became Pope instead, founded

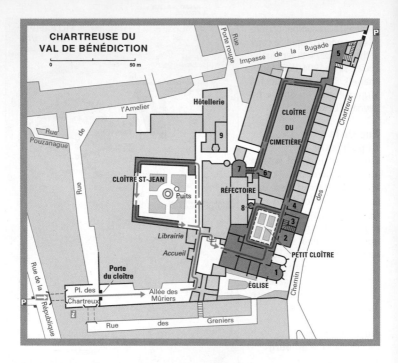

CHARTREUSE DU
VAL DE BÉNÉDICTION

0   50 m

a charter house on his *livrée* in Val de Bénédiction. The house, enlarged by the Pope's nephews after his death, became the most important in France.

The **Carthusian Order** was founded in 1084 by St Bruno. It consisted of Fathers, who used the title Dom, and Brothers, who lived a communal life like monks in other orders. The Fathers, however, lived individually in cells, spending their time in prayer, study and manual work.

Three times a day the monks met in chapel to sing the offices; they took their meals alone except on Sundays, when brief periods of conversation were allowed.

The charter house now houses *colloquia* and seminars and also the Centre National des Écritures du Spectacle (CNES), established to promote the act of writing for public performance (plays, opera and songs). The Rencontres de la Chartreuse, held annualy *(Jul–Sept)*, is linked with the famous annual Avignon theatre festival in July.

Porte du Cloître
The cloister door separates place des Chartreux from allée des Mûriers. The proportions and ornamentation of the 17C door can be admired from inside.

◐ *Pass through the reception area at the end of allée des Mûriers.*

Church
Go through the nave; the apse opens out with a **view**★ on to Fort St-André. The north side apse and nave contain the tomb of Innocent VI **(1)**: the white marble recumbent figure lies on a high plinth of Pernes stone.

Petit Cloître
The east gallery opens into the chapter house **(2)** and the Sacristans' yard **(3)**, with its well and picturesque staircase. The lavabo **(8)** is a circular domed building.

Cloître du Cimetière

The great cloisters, 80m/262ft x 20m/65.6ft, with their warm Provençal colouring, are lined with cells for the Fathers, each cell consisting of a small open court and two rooms, one of which communicates with the cloisters by a hatch. The first cell **(4)** can be visited. The others have been restored and are used as lodgings for writers-in-residence. At the northeast end of the cloisters a passage leads to the bugade **(5)**, the depressed groin-vaulted washroom, which has preserved its well and chimney for drying clothes. Opening off the west gallery is a small chapel of the dead **(6)** off which is another chapel **(7)** which was part of Innocent VI's *livrée*; it is decorated with lovely frescoes attributed to Matteo Giovanetti (14C), one of the decorators of the Palais des Papes. They illustrate scenes from the life of John the Baptist and the life of Christ.

Refectory

The Tinel (18C) is used for concerts. On leaving the cloisters, skirt the crenellated east end of the Tinel; note the bakery **(9)** with its hexagonal tower. On the northeast side, the guest house, remodelled in the 18C, features a lovely façade on its north side.

Cloître St-Jean

The cloisters' galleries have disappeared; however, several of the Fathers' cells remain. In the centre stands the monumental Fontaine St-Jean (18C), which has kept its well and lovely old basin.

Fort et Abbaye St-André★

Montée du Fort St-Andre.
🕐*Open daily Apr–Sept 10am–1pm, 2–6pm; Oct–Mar 10am–1pm, 2–5pm.* ⊚*5€.* 🕿*04 90 25 45 35.*
This fort includes a Benedictine Abbey, the 12C Romanesque Chapelle Notre-Dame-de-Belvézet, and the village of St-André, of which there remain but a few walls. The fort was built in the second half of the 14C by John the Good and Charles V, on an island called Mount Andaon, which became attached to the mainland when the tributary of the Rhône which circled it dried up in the Middle Ages. The magnificent **Porte Fortifiée**★ (fortified gate), flanked by twin towers, is one of the finest examples of medieval fortifications to be seen. Access to the west tower of the fortified gate allows visitors to discover the chamber from which the portcullises were controlled, and an 18C bakery. The terrace *(85 steps)* commands a very beautiful **view**★★ of Mont Ventoux, the Rhône, Avignon and the Palais des Papes, the Comtadin plain, the Luberon, the Alpilles and Tour Philippe-le-Bel.

Abbaye St-André

Gardens: 🕐*open Tue–Sun and public holidays Apr–Sept 10am–12.30pm, 2–6pm; Oct–Mar 10am–noon, 2–5pm.* ⊚*4€.* 🕿*04 90 25 55 95.*
Of the Benedictine abbey founded in the 10C and partly destroyed during the Revolution, there remain the entrance gate, left wing and terraces, held up by massive vaulting. Walk through the **Italian-style gardens**★; the upper terrace offers a lovely **view**★ of Avignon, the Rhône Valley and Mont Ventoux.

ADDRESSES

🏠 STAY

⊜⊜⊜ **Hôtel de L'Atelier** – *5 r. de la Foire.* 🕿*04 90 25 01 84. www.hotel delatelier.com. Closed 3 Nov–17 Dec. 23 rooms.* �}*10.50€.* This charming 16C house features a lovely staircase, antique furniture and exposed beams.

🍴 EAT

⊜⊜ **La Guignette de Vieux Moulin** – *5 r. du Vieux Moulin.* 🕿*04 90 94 50 72. www.guinguettevieuxmoulin.com.* Simple but delicious cuisine. Eat on the patio or in the dining room.

⊜⊜⊜ **Le Saint-André** – *4 bis montée du Fort.* 🕿*04 90 25 63 23. Closed Mon and Tue lunches.* Near the church and the abbey, this restaurant has Provençal décor and tasty food.

ARLES AND THE CAMARGUE

Pack your most comfortable walking shoes when you set out for Arles and the Camargue. These regions of Provence are among the best known, and also the most packed with plenty of must-sees. You can easily wear down shoe soles walking the halls in Arles' many museums and ancient ruins, as well as on trails through the Camargue countryside. If you're a fan of Van Gogh, Arles is the place to visit.

Highlights

No time is a bad time to visit these regions. The Arles city government offers many walking tours in the summer, and these are one of the best ways to make sure you don't miss any of its many highlights. And, where else do you combine artists and bullfighters (particularly around Easter) in the same day? But other seasons are just as attractive with theatre, photography and film festivals, as well as nighttimes cargo boat rides.

Since the Middle Ages, Arles has been a destination for travellers, first as a religious centre. One of the gems in Arles' crown is the number of glorious Gallo-Roman antiquities and items of Romanesque art that are preserved here. Don't miss the ruins of the Roman Theatre or the Amphitheatre, which has also served as a fortress. The Alyscamps cemetery was the starting point for pilgrimages that took medieval believers to Spain. Arles, geographically the largest city in France, is a UNESCO World Heritage Site, thanks to its cultural significance.

But for all those accolades and accomplishments, Arles may be most synonymous with 19C Impressionist Vincent Van Gogh. The home he rented there became a subject in many of his best-known and best-loved paintings, as did the surrounding landscapes (&see The Alpilles for more Van Gogh vistas). Any trip to Arles must include stops at both the Espace Van Gogh, which was once the hospital where he was treated, and Fondation Vincent Van Gogh-Arles, which has a permanent collection of many of his works as well as those of his peers.

Near Arles, but also worlds away, is the Camargue, a nature preserve kept in its pristine state through its designation, both in 1927 and in 1970 as a botanical and zoological nature reserve. The reserve is in an area nestled between two rivers, and is home to flamingos, migratory birds and other wildlife. Abandon your car to explore this area on foot, on two wheels with a bike or in a boat. If you really want to explore like a local, then getting on horseback is preferable: this is the country's cowboy region. Try to ride one of the Camargue horses, smaller, yet often more sure-footed, than others.

Nestled in the Camargue is Parc Ornithologique du Pont-de-Gau, a bird sanctuary that will give you excellent insight to the feathered friends that live in the region. Sightseeing at the Abbaye de Montmajour helps sum up two of the region's golden periods: medieval and 18C. You can see buildings from both time-frames here, a compelling argument for a holiday pilgrimage, if not a religious one.

Arles★★★

Bouches-du-Rhône

Roman capital and a major religious centre in the Middle Ages, Arles preserves glorious Gallo-Roman antiquities and gems of Romanesque art. The development of the Camargue as a protected natural environment has made Arles a rice capital. It is a central market for agricultural produce (raising of Crau sheep) and the largest commune in France, encompassing 77 000ha/300sq mi.

Arles has inspired the praise, in poetry or music, of Mistral, Daudet and Bizet. Its impact in world culture continues to this day: Christian Lacroix, the fashion designer and musical groups such as the Gipsy Kings, being notable Arlésiens.

A BIT OF HISTORY

Arles and Marseille – The excavations undertaken in 1975 under the Jardin d'Hiver have revealed the existence of a Celtic-Ligurian town (known as Theline) colonised by the Greeks from Marseille as early as 6 BC.

The town, which soon took the name of Arelate, met with new prosperity when in 104 BC the Consul Marius built a canal that joined the Rhône to the Fos gulf, greatly facilitating navigation. In 49 BC, when Julius Caesar defeated Marseille, Arles developed economically, becoming a prosperous Roman colony: a crossroads for seven important roads and a major sea and river port.

Roman Arles – A colony of veterans of the Sixth Legion, Arles was granted the privilege of building a fortified wall around the 40ha/99 acres of the official city. A forum, several temples, a basilica, baths and a theatre were built. An aqueduct brought pure water from the Alpilles. The town was spreading at the end of the 1C, with the construction of an amphitheatre. To the south lay the Roquette shipyards. To the east, the Jardin d'Hiver district and the Esplanade were residential, while on the right bank

▶ **Population:** 51 970.
Michelin Map: 340: C-3 or 528 fold 28 or 524 fold 26.
Info: Espl. Charles-de-Gaulle, Bd des Lices, Arles. ℘04 90 18 41 20. www.tourisme.ville-arles.fr.
▶ **Location:** Stroll along Boulevard des Lices, with its huge plane trees and busy café terraces; the atmosphere is especially lively during the market on Saturdays. The Old Town is reached by passing through the Jardin d'Été and following rue Porte de Laure, with its many restaurants. Take a 90min guided tour of the town to get a quick overview (see Addresses).
Don't Miss: The old town with its Roman arena and theatre; the Alyscamps necropolis; the cloisters of St-Trophime and the Musée de l'Arles et de la Provence Antiques.
Timing: Arles' public buildings and museums deserve a minimum of two days. Allow at least 30min for Alyscamps alone. The tour of the Crau Plain requires about 3hr.
Kids: The Roman Amphitheatre; Fête des Gardians; Marais du Vigueirat; the Santonniers' Salon.

of the Rhône, at Trinquetaille, was the large bustling dockland frequented by sailors, boatmen and merchants. A bridge of boats joined the two banks of the river northeast of the town, level with the Bourg-Neuf district.

A Golden Age – In the 5C, Arles was an active industrial centre. Textiles and gold and silver work were manufactured, ships were built, sarcophagi and arms were made, and imperial money was minted. Wheat, pork meat, olive oil, dark and thick wine from the Rhône hills, were all exported. Moreover, stonecarvers, masons and architects from Arles were famous for the quality of their work.

The town possessed five guilds of boatmen. Some sailed the Rhône, the Durance and the many lakes in the region, using rafts carried on inflated goatskins called *utriculaires*. Other Arlésien watermen sailed the Mediterranean.

Prosperity brought political importance: Emperor Constantine established himself and the expansion of Arles reached its apex. The emperor remodelled the northwest district where an imperial palace and the la Trouille baths were built. In AD 395 Arles became the political and administrative capital of the Gauls (made up of Spain, Gaul as such, and Brittany). It was also a great religious centre where 19 synods were held, and its bishops were constantly acquiring importance under the protection of imperial rule.

The Decline– In the 8C, the Franks and Saracens fought over the country, causing a great deal of destruction. In the 9C, Arles was but a shadow of its former self when it became the capital of the Kingdom of Arles, which included Burgundy and part of Provence. It was not until the 12C that the town experienced a political and economic revival and acquired the status of a district governed by elected consuls. Its prestige was considerable as the Germanic Emperor Frederick Barbarossa came to the town in 1178 to be crowned King of Arles in the newly completed Romanesque Cathedral of St-Trophime. In 1239 the burghers of Arles submitted to the Count of Provence.

From that time onwards, the town followed the fortunes of the province: political status was transferred to Aix, and Marseille took its revenge and surpassed Arles in economic prosperity.

As long as the Rhône remained the main commercial route, Arles continued to be relatively prosperous. This was even more the case when the land was upgraded by the Crau irrigation project and the drainage of the marshland. However, the arrival of the railway made river traffic obsolete and dealt a severe blow to trade. Until recently it was the agricultural market centre for the Camargue, Crau and Alpilles.

⚓ WALKING TOUR

PUBLIC BUILDINGS
Roman Theatre (Théâtre Antique)★★
r. de la Calade.
◷Open daily Mar–Apr and Oct 9am–noon, 2–6pm, May–Sept 9am–7pm, Fêtes d'Arles (late Jun–early Jul) 9am–2pm; Nov–Feb 10am–noon, 2–5pm. ◷Closed 1 Jan, 1 May, 1 Nov, 25 Dec and closure at 4pm for concerts (14 Jul–15 Aug). ◎6€ (combined with Arènes). ℘04 90 49 38 20.

Built during Augustus' reign c. 27–25 BC, this theatre was gradually dismantled. As early as the 5C it was used as a quarry for the construction of churches and in the 9C it was transformed into a redoubt before disappearing completely under houses and gardens. It was excavated from 1827 to 1855.

The theatre measured 102m/335ft in diameter and had a seating capacity of 12 000. It was backed up by a 27-arched portico made up of three levels of arcades, of which only one bay remains.

All that is preserved of the stage wall are two columns standing whole amid the ruins, a reminder of the theatre's great past. The stage, curtain slit, orchestra, and part of the tiers are still visible.

Turn right by the amphitheatre to the parvis of the **Collégiale Notre-Dame-de-la-Major** *(pl. de la Major; ◷open on certain religious holidays; ℘04 90 49 38 20)*, an important place for the Confrérie des Gardiens. A terrace allows a fine view of the rooftops of Arles, the Rhône, the Alpilles, and the Abbaye de Montmajour.

Self-Portrait with Bandaged Ear (1889)

©Imagestate/Tips Images

Van Gogh in Arles★★

Vincent van Gogh (1853–90) came to Arles from Paris on 21 February 1888. He first lived at the Hôtel-Restaurant Carrel at 30 rue Cavalerie before renting a small house, or the "Yellow House" as it came to be known, at 2 place Lamartine. This was where he painted The *Sunflowers* among other works to adorn the walls in preparation for the arrival of his contemporary, Paul Gauguin. The Café de la Gare around the corner at 30 place Lamartine became the subject for *The Night Café* (all three sites were destroyed during the Second World War). Vincent adapted quickly to Arles. He dreamed of creating a utopian artists' colony in Arles. His health improved, and he made friends. After much cajoling, Gauguin arrived to stay with him in the Yellow House in October.

Van Gogh's style changed as he moved away from Impressionism. He sought to find "another Japan", as Japanese wood prints fascinated him. The Provençal countryside and its luminosity provided the answer. He painted non-stop: nature, working in the fields, portraits, views of Arles and its surroundings. Among his 200 paintings and 100 drawings were *The Yellow House*, *The Alyscamps*, *L'Arlésienne*, *Crau Plain* and *Langlois Bridge*.

On Christmas Eve 1888, while being plagued by fits of madness and rowing with Gauguin in the street, Vincent's left ear was cut off (whether by him or Gauguin is still in question), wrapped it in a newspaper and asked a local courtesan called Rachel to "keep this object carefully". Vincent was hospitalised. His fortunes went from bad to worse: Gauguin abandoned him and returned to Paris, his friend Roulin, the postman, was sent to Marseille, and in February 1889 a petition circulated in Arles demanding that the *fou roux* ("the redheaded maniac") be confined. He finally decided to leave Arles for the asylum at St-Rémy-de-Provence, arriving on 3 May 1889.

Van Gogh's Bedroom in Arles (1889)

©Peter Barritt/World Illustrated/Photoshot

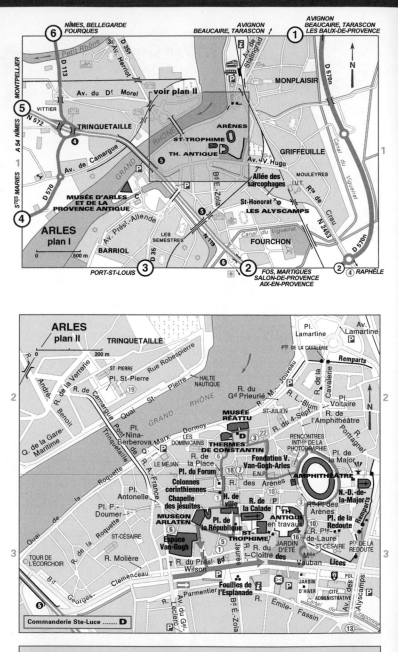

▶ *Bear right to reach the steps that lead to the amphitheatre.*

👥 Amphitheatre (Arènes)★★
Rond point des Arénes.
🕐*Open Mar–Apr and Oct daily 9am– 6pm, May and Sept daily 9am–7pm, Jun–Aug Thu–Tue 9am–7pm, Wed 9am–3pm, Fêtes d'Arles (late Jun–early Jul) 9am–noon; Nov–Feb daily 10am– 5pm.* 🕐*Closed 1 Jan, Easter weekend, 1 May, 6 Jul, Féria du Riz (2nd week Sept), 1 Nov, 25 Dec.* ✆*6€ (child 4.50€) (combined with Théâtre Antique).* 📞*08 91 70 03 70. www.arenes-arles.com.*
This amphitheatre probably dates from the end of the 1C. Transformed into a fortress during the early Middle Ages, it constituted a system of defence. Later on, the arena was transformed into a town of 200 houses and two chapels, built with materials taken from the building itself, which was mutilated but saved from complete destruction. The excavation and restoration began in 1825. Three out of the four medieval watchtowers remain.
The amphitheatre measured 136m x 107m/446ft x 351ft and could seat more than 20 000 spectators. The arena (69m x 40m/226ft x 131ft), as such, was separated from the tiers by a protective wall. The arena was floored and underneath it were machinery, animal cages and the backstage area.

Wander through the upper level of arches in order to understand the building's construction. The spectators would have enjoyed all kinds of games and gladiatorial fighting, which was finally stopped in 404, under the influence of Christianity. Today the amphitheatre hosts bullfighting and cultural events. It was also depicted in the film *Ronin* (1998) with Robert De Niro.
Continue around the amphitheatre to the 18C **Palais de Luppé**, which houses the Vincent Van Gogh Foundation (👁*see Museums*).

▶ *Take rue des Arènes to the right of the palace, then the second street on the right.*

You will pass the former Grand Priory of the Order of the Hospital of St John of Jerusalem (15C), which today houses the Musée Réattu (👁*see Museums*). Take a look opposite at the courtyard of the Commanderie de Sainte-Luce (Social Action Centre).

Palais Constantin – Thermes de la Trouille★
r. du Grand Prieuré. 🕐*Open daily Mar–Apr and Oct 9am–noon, 2–6pm; May–Sept 9am–noon, 2–7pm; Nov–Feb 1–5pm.* 🕐*Closed 1 Jan, 1 May, 1 Nov, 25 Dec.* ✆*3€.* 📞*04 90 49 38 20.*

Amphitheatre with
the medieval watchtower

©wjarek/Fotolia.com

The baths of Arles are the largest (98 x 45m/322 x 148ft) remaining in Provence. They date from Constantine's era (4C). Enter by the *tepidarium*, through to the *caldarium*, which still has its hypocaust.

▷ *Go to rue Maïsto, turn left and left again to reach place and rue de la Sauvage.*

Note the old buildings, including the former palace of the Counts of Arlatan de Beaumont (15C), today the Hotel Arlatan *(no 26; ₢ see Addresses).*

Place du Forum

The actual place du Forum is not on the site of the ancient forum, which lay more to the south. Left of the Hôtel Nord-Pinus, two Corinthian columns surmounted by a fragment of pediment are all that remain of a 2C temple.
A street to the left leads to the Plan de la Cour, a small square lined with historical buildings, including the **Hôtel de Podestats** (12C–15C) and the **Hôtel de Ville**, town hall.
The hall of the Hôtel de Ville gives access to place de la République, in the middle of which stands an obelisk from Arles' Roman circus, moved here in the 17C. The setting is completed with the intricately carved doorway of St-Trophime.

Église St-Trophime★

pl. de la République. ◷*Open Mon–Sat 8.30am–noon, 2–6.30pm, Sun 8.30am–noon.* ⊜*No charge.* ℘*04 90 49 38 00.*
This church, dedicated to St Trophimus, possibly the first bishop of Arles in the early 3C, was destroyed during the Carolingian era (part of the façade built of rubble remains). It was rebuilt at the end of the 11C (transept) and in the first half of the 12C (nave). In c. 1190 the building was enhanced by a magnificent **carved doorway**★★, an example of late Provençal Romanesque style. It displays an ancient Classical arrangement, suggesting the form of a triumphal arch.

Cloître St-Trophime★★

pl. de la République. ◷*Open daily Mar–Apr and Oct 9am–6pm; May–Sept 9am–7pm; Nov–Feb 10am–5pm.* ◷*Closed 1 Jan, 1 May, 1 Nov, 25 Dec.* ⊜*3.50€.* ℘*04 90 49 38 20.*
These cloisters, the most famous in Provence for the elegance of their carved decoration, may have been carved with the help of the craftsmen of **St-Gilles**. The best work is to be found in the north gallery *(on the left upon entering)*, particularly on the magnificent corner pillars decorated with large statues and low relief. The capitals are adorned with scenes from the Resurrection and the origins of Christian Arles, as well as foliage. Note especially, on the northeast pillar, the statue of St Paul, with the deeply incised folds, long under the elbows, the work of a craftsman who was familiar with St Gilles' central doorway.
Of a later period, the east gallery's capitals and pillars recount the major episodes of Christ's life. The south gallery tells of the life of St Trophimus and the west gallery concentrates on typically Provençal subjects such as St Martha and the Tarasque *(₢ see TARASCON).* From the south gallery you can see the cloisters, and above, the former chapter premises, the church nave. Dominating the whole stands the stout plain bell tower. Along the east gallery the refectory and dormitory is the location for the famous annual *santons* fair (Nov–Jan).

▷ *Turn right into rue de la République, then rue du Président Wilson, which leads to the former Hôtel-Dieu.*

Espace Van-Gogh

pl. du Docteur Félix-Rey. ◷*Hall open for temporary exhibitions; free access to courtyard.* ℘*04 90 49 39 39.*
This centre was originally a hospital where Van Gogh was treated in 1889; the courtyard is lined with arcades. Here you will see the recreated garden based both on Van Gogh's painting of this space, *Garden of Arles Hospital*, and from a letter to his sister containing details

of the plants grown herein. There are several shops and cafés here now.

LES ALYSCAMPS★★★

30min.

av. des Alyscamps. ⏲*Open daily Mar–Apr and Oct 9am–noon, 2–6pm; May–Sept 9am–7pm; Nov–Feb 10am–noon, 2–5pm.* ⏲*Closed 1 Jan, 1 May, 1 Nov, 25 Dec.* ✆*3.50€.* ✆*04 90 49 38 20.*

From Roman times to the late Middle Ages, the Alyscamps was one of the most famous necropolises (cemeteries) of the Western world.

In ancient times, when a traveller arrived by the Aurelian Way to the gates of Arles, he made his way to the city's entrance passing along a line of inscribed tombs and mausoleums. And yet the Alyscamps' great expansion occurred during the Christianisation of the necropolis around the tomb of St Genesius, a Roman civil servant, beheaded in 250 for having refused to write down an imperial edict persecuting the Christians. Miracles began to happen on this site and the faithful asked to be buried here. Added to all this was the legend of St Trophimus, who was buried here.

The transfer of St Trophimus' relics to the cathedral in 1152 removed part of the prestige of this cemetery. During the Renaissance, the necropolis was desecrated. City councillors took to offering their guests carved sarcophagi as presents, and monks in charge took funerary stones to build churches and convents and to enclose monastery grounds.

Some sarcophagi are exhibited in the **Musée de l'Arles et de la Provence Antiques** *(see Museums)*, allowing us to get an idea of the splendour of the Alyscamps in its heyday.

▶ *Continue along rue Émile-Fassin to the alley of sarcophagi.*

Allée des Sarcophages

A 12C porch, all that remains of the Abbaye St-Césaire, opens onto the avenue bordered with two rows of

Allée des Sarcophages, Les Alyscamps
©De Agostini/World Illustrated/Photoshot

sarcophagi and also lined with chapels. A number of the sarcophagi are Greek in style with double-pitched roof with four raised corners. The Roman-style ones are identified by their flat top. Some sarcophagi are carved with the three symbols: a plumb line, a mason's level (both signifying the equality of men before death) and a trowel, a type of axe, to protect the sarcophagi from robbers.

MUSEUMS

Musée de l'Arles et de la Provence Antiques★★

Follow bd Georges-Clemenceau to the edge of the Rhône, before passing left under the flyover. ⏲*Open daily Apr–Oct 9am–7pm; Nov–Mar 10am–5pm.* ⏲*Closed 1 Jan, 1 May, 1 Nov, 25 Dec.* ✆*5.50€ (no charge first Sun of month).* ✆*04 90 18 88 88. www.arles-antique.cg13.fr.*

Built on the edge of the Rhône, this triangular construction, designed by Henri Ciriani, houses behind its blue enamel walls a collection of ancient art. A single room groups together large statues. Arranged around the colossal **statue of Augustus** (marble torso, limestone drape), which once decorated the theatre stage wall, are statues of dancers, altars dedicated to the god Apollo, and a cast of the **Venus of Arles**: the copy of a masterpiece of Hellenistic statuary, the original is now displayed in the Louvre. The large **votive shield of Augustus** (26 BC), a marble copy of the

Low-reliefs of a funerary stela, Musée de l'Arles et de la Provence antiques

S. Sauvignier/MICHELIN

golden Roman shield, shows the extent and speed of Romanisation in Arles.

Models illustrate Roman civilisation in imperial times. The museum presents town plans, marked with the important monuments of the Augustan (forum, theatre), Flavian (amphitheatre), Antonine (circus) and Constantine (baths) eras.

Also exhibited is the daily life of the people of Arles, alongside their traditional activities either through objects – tools for weaving dishes – or through sarcophagus reliefs.

The economic role of Arles is evoked through the depiction of its road network and both its land and sea trade (sets of amphorae and marine anchors, lead, tin and copper ingots). One area is given over to religions of the time, where you will find a small faun in bronze (1C BC), and the torso of Sarapis (2C) wrapped in a serpent's coil.

The splendour of the imperial age is exemplified by the **mosaics**, taken from the villas of Trinquetaille (late 2C). A **footbridge** allows visitors to explore these mosaics, which are either geometrical or illustrate a theme such as the Abduction of Europa or the Four Seasons.

Next to the collection of funerary stelae, is the display of **sarcophagi**★★, both pagan and Christian, one of the most important collections after that of Rome. These marble works, carved predominantly in the 4C by craftsmen from Arles and some of which originate from the Alyscamps necropolis, exalted the Christian faith. As well as the sarcophagus known as Phaedra and Hippolytus, note that of the Trinity.

Museon Arlaten★

29–31 r. de la République. ⊙Open daily Oct–Mar 9.30am–noon, 2–4.30pm; Apr–May and Sept 9.30am–noon, 2–5.30pm; Jun–Aug 9.30am–12.30pm, 2–6pm. ⊙Closed 1 Jan, 1 May, 1 Nov and 25 Dec. ⊜1€ (no charge first Sun of month). ℘04 90 93 58 11. www.museonarlaten.fr.

This fascinating Provençal Museum was created by Frédéric Mistral in 1896 and installed, from 1906 to 1909, in the 16C Hôtel de Castellane-Laval, bought by Mistral with the money he was given when awarded the Nobel Prize in Literature in 1904. Worried by the loss of Provençal identity in the face of national centralisation policies, Mistral wanted to preserve the details of Provençal daily life for future generations. At the entrance to the courtyard you will encounter a tiled forum with exedra that led to a small 2C basilica.

The Museon, with its attendants in traditional Arles costume, consists of some 30 rooms devoted to the Arles area and organised by theme (including reconstructions of a baby delivery room and Christmas Eve celebrations). This

Plaine de la Crau★★

The Crau plain, which extends over 50 000ha/193sq mi between the Rhône, the Alpilles, St-Mitre hills and the sea, is a grey-white desert of shingle (round rocks) and gravel that in places reaches a depth of 15m/49ft.

Cultivation

Since the development of a network of irrigation channels, two areas in the north of the Crau are now cultivated. One stretches from Arles to St-Martin-de-Crau, the other lies to the west of Salon. These two areas are gradually merging, so that a drive along the N 113 from Arles to Salon gives little idea of the stony desert that defines the Grande Crau. Windbreaks of poplar and cypress shelter pastures and fields of fruit and vegetables. There are four crops a year of the famous Crau hay (annual crop approximately 100 000 metric tons) – the last of which is grazed in the fields by sheep wintering on the plain.

Sheep farming

The Grande Crau, resembling a huge steppe, is devoted to sheep farming. The traditional breed is the fine-wooled merino, a cross between the Crau country breed and the Spanish merino introduced into France around the early 19C. About 100 000 head graze on *coussouls* (tufts of fine grass growing between the stones) between mid-October and early June.

The departure for summer pastures (transhumance) takes place when the grazing disappears and water becomes scarce. In the past, the procession of sheep, goats, dogs and donkeys, led by the shepherds, would follow established routes to theAlps. It took 12 days on foot to reach the destination, after passing through many villages, whose inhabitants celebrated the passing of the flocks each year. The return journey, which took place as the first snows began, enjoyed the same festive atmosphere.

Nowadays the flock is moved by truck and the area of sheep-grazing land is diminishing.

museum is the most comprehensive of its kind in Provence, with furnishings, costumes, ceramics evoking local customs, crafts and music, items of popular devotion, and documents on the Félibrige as well as the history of Arles and its surroundings.

Musée Réattu★

10 r. du Grand Prieuré.
🕐*Open Tue–Sun 8 Jul–Sept 10am–7pm; Oct–29 Nov 10am–12.30pm, 2–6.30pm; 3 Nov–7 Jul please check website for details.* 🕐*Closed 1 Jan, 1 May, 1 Nov, 25 Dec.* ✆*7€ (no charge first Sun of month).* ℘*04 90 49 37 58. www.museereattu.arles.fr.*
The museum takes its name from the painter Jacques Réattu (1760–1833), who lived here and whose work is exhibited in the museum's galleries. There are also works from the 16C–18C Italian, French, Dutch and Provençal

Schools, as well as a collection of modern and contemporary art. These include paintings by Dufy, Prassinos, Vlaminck, Sarthou and Alechinsky; and sculpture by César, Richier, Bourdelle and Zadkine.

The **Picasso Donation**★ is exhibited in three galleries and displays the variety of techniques mastered by Picasso through 57 of his drawings created in 1971. Other exhibitions include an imposing **collection of photographs**★.

Fondation Vincent van Gogh – Arles

24 bis Rond-Point des Arènes.
🕐*Open Apr–Jun Tue–Sun 10am–6pm; Jul–Sept daily 10am–7pm; Oct–Nov daily 10am–6pm; Dec–Mar Tue–Sun 11am–5pm.* 🕐*Closed 1 Jan and 25 Dec.* ✆*7€.* ℘*04 90 49 94 04. www.fondationvangogh-arles.org.*

The permanent collection includes works of art made in homage to Van Gogh by some of the greatest names in modern culture, such as the painters Francis Bacon, David Hockney, Fernando Botero, Olivier Debré; sculptors Karel Appel and César; photographers Lucien Clergue and Robert Doisneau; writers Viviane Forrester and Michel Tournier; musicians such as Henri Dutilleux; and even fashion designers (Christian Lacroix).

Every year, while the permanent collection is on tour, there is an exhibition on the subject of one of these artists, all of whom have made a donation to the foundation.

Abbaye de Montmajour★
See Abaye de MONTMAJOUR

▷ *2km/1.2mi N of Arles, in the direction of Fontvieille.*

🚗 DRIVING TOUR

Tour of the Crau Plain
93km/58mi – allow 3hr, excluding the Vigueirat.

▷ *Leave Arles on N 453.*

St-Martin-de-Crau
The village houses a museum, **l'Écomusée de la Crau** (*bd de Provence;* ⏱ *open Mon–Sat 9am–noon, 2–6pm;* ⊜ *no charge;* ℘ *04 90 47 02 01; www.ceep. asso.fr*), containing an exhibition on this region, which can be explored through guided tours around the nature reserve at Peau de Meau.

▷ *Take D 24 south as far as the main road (N 568), where you will head in the direction of Martigues.*

La Grande Crau
Green countryside gives way to a progressively more barren landscape, devoid of villages, farms, and agriculture, apart from the very occasional sheepfold and cabin, reflecting the decline of such

pastoral activities as sheep farming. In addition to the encroachment of agriculture from the north, and the installation of several aerodromes, the continued expansion of the Bassins de Fos in the south has changed the appearance of the landscape so dear to Mistral.

▷ *At La Fossette turn right and take N 268 to Port-St-Louis-du-Rhône, then turn right onto D 35, and take D 24 to Mas-Thibert.*

👥 Marais du Vigueirat★
📷 *Guided tousr (1hr) 11am, 2.30pm, 4pm in Mar Wed and Sat–Sun; Apr–Jun Wed–Thu and Sat–Sun; Jul–Aug Tue–Thu and Sun.* ⊜ *5€ (child 2.50€).* ℘ *04 90 98 70 91. www.marais-vigueirat. reserves-naturelles.fr.*
Allow 6hr and take a picnic.

You can visit the marsh alone, on a guided tour along raised footpaths, or in a horse drawn carriage *(2hr;* ⊜ *5€)* taking in local birds and animals such as flamingoes, bulls and horses. Make sure you take mosquito repellent.

The presence of this land, situated between the Arles canal at Bouc (dug in 1827) and the Vigueirat canal (1642), is the work of a Dutch engineer. Thanks to complex drainage and irrigation systems, the level of the water and its salinity are kept under control, thereby maintaining the Camargue's ecosystems.

▷ *Return towards Arles via D 35; take the small signposted street to the right.*

Pont de Langlois
The original bridge, the subject of a famous painting by Van Gogh, was destroyed in 1926. The current bridge, identical to the one in the painting, was rebuilt on the nearby canal that links Arles to Fos.

ADDRESSES

🛏 STAY

⊝🛏 **Hôtel Muette** – *15 r. des Suisses.* ℘*04 90 96 15 39. www.hotel-muette.com. 18 rooms.* ⊑*8€.* Attractive 12C façade overlooking a small square. Soberly Provençal rooms with exposed stone. Breakfast room adorned with bullfighting photos.

⊝🛏 **Hôtel du Musée** – *11 r. du Grand-Prieuré.* ℘*04 90 93 88 88. www.hotel dumusee.com.fr. 28 rooms.* ⊑*7€.* Facing the Musée Réattu, this is hotel was built in the 17C. The rooms are charming, peaceful and cosy, as are the inner courtyards.

⊝🛏–⊝🛏🛏 **Hôtel Acacias** – *2 r. de la Cavalerie.* ℘*04 90 96 37 88. www.hotel-acacias.com. 30 rooms.* ⊑*6€.* Hotel with a cheerful pink façade at the foot of the Porte de la Cavalerie. Colourful and simply furnished rooms. Breakfast room brightened with a mural.

⊝🛏🛏 **Hôtel d'Arlatan** – *26 r. du Sauvage.* ℘*04 90 93 56 66. www.hotel-arlatan.fr. 41 rooms.* ⊑*14€. Closed Jan–Feb.* This graceful 15C residence, with 4C fountations, relives its past through exhibitions of archaeological remains. Décor with personal touches and fine antique furniture.

⊝🛏–⊝🛏🛏 **Hôtel L'Amphithéâtre** – *11 r. Diderot.* ℘*04 90 96 10 30. www. hotelamphitheatre.fr. 28 rooms.* ⊑*7.50–9.50€.* This handsome 17C building is home to snug, revamped rooms. Those in the adjoining townhouse are more spacious and comfortable. Attractive breakfast room.

⊝🛏🛏–⊝🛏🛏🛏 **Hôtel Calendal** – *5 r. Porte-de-Laure.* ℘*04 90 96 11 89. www.lecalendal.com. 35 rooms.* ⊑*12€. Restaurant*⊝🛏🛏*.* This hotel has stylish Provençal interiors, a colourful façade, pretty interior shaded garden and cosy sitting room. Blue and yellow make up the colour scheme. Small tearoom. Provençal salads for summer lunchtimes.

⊝🛏🛏–⊝🛏🛏🛏 **Hôtel Mireille** – *2 pl. St-Pierre (at Trinquetaille).* ℘*04 90 93 70 74. www.hotel-mireille.com. 28 rooms.* ⊑*13€. Restaurant*⊝🛏🛏*.* These two outlying houses stand on the right bank of the River Rhône. Stylish rooms in Provençal style. Small shop selling regional produce. Attentive hospitality. Pleasant poolside terrace lined by mulberry trees. Classic menu in the brightly coloured restaurant.

🍽 EAT

⊝🛏 **Le Criquet** – *21 r. Porte-de-Laure.* ℘*04 90 96 80 51. Closed Wed.* Go for the charming dining room with its beams and exposed stonework rather than the terrace in this little restaurant near the amphitheatre. Once you're comfortably seated, savour the young chef's *bourride* (a kind of fish soup) and other specialities.

⊝🛏 **La Gueule du Loup** – *39 r. des Arènes.* ℘*04 90 96 96 69. Closed mid-Jan –mid-Feb, 1 week in Nov, Mon (except eve) Mar–Oct, Sun.* This restaurant in the historic centre of the town is easy to spot with its foliage-covered façade. A kind welcome and excellent Provençal cuisine.

⊝🛏 **Lou Calèu** – *27 r. Porte-de-Laure, montée Vauban.* ℘*04 90 49 71 77. Closed Sun–Mon.* A real classic: fresh salads, *taureau* stew, lamb with rosemary... All Arle's delights are at your fingertips. An excellent wine list.

⊝🛏🛏 **Ferme Auberge de Barbegal** – *Domaine du Grand Barbegal, 13280 Raphèle-les-Arles, 11.4km/7mi SE.* ℘*04 90 54 63 69. www.barbegal.fr. 5 rooms. Lunch*⊝🛏*. Reservations obligatory.* ⊑*.* The owners of these farm buildings (late 18C) have restored them superbly. Breakast is made with produce grown on the farm. Definitely a place to consider.

⊝🛏🛏 **Le Jardin de Manon** – *14 av. des Alyscamps.* ℘*04 90 93 38 68. Closed 1–27 Nov, 21 Feb–10 Mar, Sun eve Oct–Mar, Tue eve, Wed.* The contemporary srtle dining rooms of this restaurant offer regional, seasonal menus. Pleasant, peaceful and shaded terrace at the back.

🛒 SHOPPING

MARKETS

Traditional market every Wed on boulevard Émile-Combes and every Sat in boulevard des Lices and boulevard Clemenceau. **Antiques** market first Wed of the month in boulevard des Lices. **Christmas** market at the end of November.

CRAFTS

Henri Vezolles Santonnier – *14 rd-pt des Arènes. ℘04 90 93 48 80. Closed Jan.* Exclusive hand-made *santons*, made using two to four different types of clay, are modelled and sold in the shop.

TAUROMACHIE

La Boutique des Passionnés – *14 r. Réattu. ℘04 90 96 59 93. www.passion-toros.com. Closed Sun Jan–Nov, public holidays.* Both a book and music shop, this is a gold mine for *tauromachie* and for music from the south. They organise a cultural festival, *Convivència*, every July.

SWEET TREATS

De Moro – *24 r. du Prés.-Wilson (near the Espace Van Gogh). Closed Sun–Mon, 1 May. ℘04 90 93 14 43.* Specialises in delicious almond biscuits.

TOURS AND DISCOUNTS

Les Alpilles train – *⏱see Les ALPILLES*

Monuments and museums – At the tourist office, you can buy a single pass *(⏺13.50€)* for all sights and museums entitled the *Passeport Avantage*, which is valid for one year. There's also a ticket called *Passeport Arelate (⏺9€, www. festival-arelate.com)*, which allows entry to the sights and to the Musée de l'Arles et de la Provence Antiques.

Tours of the town – (1hr30min) guided tours. Contact the tourist office for information, price and times *(℘04 90 18 41 20; www.tourisme.ville-arles.fr)*. Art lovers can buy a guide *(⏺1€)* that shows you how to get to the Van Gogh sites on foot.

🎭 ENTERTAINMENT

The newspaper *Le César*, available free of charge for tourists at the tourist office and other cultural spots, gives listings of shows in the city.

EVENTS

Fête d'Arles – *early Jun–early Jul (www. fetes-arles.com)*. Over 500 participants take part in a costume festival in the Théâtre Antique.

👥 **Fête des Gardians** – *1 May*. The Gardians attend a mass in Provençal dialect held in Collégiale Notre-Dame-de-la-Major, which includes the blessing of horses. Later, there are typical Camargue games and dancing to the sound of pipes and drums. Every three years (next in 2011), local girls compete for the title "Queen of Arles" *(www. reinedarles.com)*.

Festival Les Suds – *Mid-Jul. ℘08 92 70 08 40. www.suds-arles.com.* World music festival.

Rencontres Internationales de la Photographie – *10 rond-point des Arènes. ℘04 90 96 76 06. www.rencontres-arles.com. Early Jul–mid-Sept.* Throughout this international photography festival there are evenings at the Roman Theatre, exhibitions, courses, talks and activities at various locations across town.

Santonniers' Salon – *Nov–Jan, St Trophime Cloister.* Since 1958, this exhiition has showcased the traditional Provençal models made out of terracotta, attracting thousands of visitors every year.

Tauromachie – The architectural beauty of the amphitheatre acquires even greater appeal when **bullfights** and Camargue games take place: one can almost breathe a sense of antiquity. Bullfights also take place during the férias at Easter *(Easter weekend)*, and during the Rice Festival *(second weekend in Sept)*, which sees the participation of bullfighting's most illustrious figures. With the arrival of spring come the **courses camarguaises**. The most important of these take place during the Fêtes d'Arles with the **Cocarde d'Or** *(early Jul)* and the finals of the **Trophée des As**, which takes place every two years in October, alternating with Nîmes. Booking: **Bureau des Arènes** *(to the right of the main entrance), ℘08 91 70 03 70. www.arenes-arles.com.*

La Camargue★★★

Bouches-du-Rhône

The Camargue, the most original and romantic region in Provence, even France, has been largely preserved in its natural state through its designation in 1927 and 1970 as a botanical and zoological nature reserve. Late spring and early autumn are the best times for a visit: wildlife abounds, the sun shines (but not overpoweringly), and there are the famous pilgrimages to Les Stes-Maries-de-la-Mer. Just make sure you take plenty of mosquito repellent!

Parc Naturel Régional de Camargue

This nature park occupies an area of 85 000ha/328sq mi in the Rhône delta, including the municipalities of Arles and Stes-Maries-de-la-Mer. The main objective of the park, besides its basic policy of protecting nature, is to allow its occupants to live in their natural habitat, while preserving agricultural activity and strictly monitoring both the hydraulic balance of the region and the growing influx of tourists.

GEOGRAPHY
The Rhône Delta

The Camargue is an immense alluvial plain, the product of the interaction of the Rhône, the Mediterranean and the winds. During the end of the Tertiary Era and the beginning of the Quaternary Period while the sea was receding, waterways transported huge quantities of shingle that piled up along the shore creating a shingle bar some dozens of metres wide. On top of this rocky base, marine sediment was deposited after the last glacial period; then, the sea extended to the north shore of the Étang de Vaccarès. However, the landscape changed constantly owing to the conflicting forces of the freshwater Rhône and the sea. The powerful Rhône has shifted its course over the centuries

- **Michelin Map:** 339 and 340: B-4 to D-5.
- **Info:** 5 avenue Van Gogh, Les Saintes-Maries-de-la-Mer. 04 90 97 82 55. www.saintesmaries.com. You should also see the www.camargue.fr.
- **Location:** From Arles, the D570 will take you 27km/16.8mi S to Les Stes-Maries-de-la-Mer whereas the D 36 will take you to Le Sambuc and Salin-de-Giraud. In the middle is the Étang de Vaccarès, which you can explore on foot or by bike.
- **Don't Miss:** The Musée Camarguais to understand the local culture; the Camargue Ornithology Park at Pont de Gau and the village of Les Saintes.
- **Timing:** A few days would be ideal to sample the excellent restaurants, visit a working farm and explore the area on horseback, on foot or by bike.
- **Kids:** Horse riding, an afternoon on the beach, Pont-de-Gau Ornithology Park, Domaine Paul Ricard Méjanes.

– it has occupied the two present arms of its bed only since the 15C – transporting enormous amounts of alluvial deposits: barriers were formed which isolated the marshes; sandbanks created by the coastal currents closed off lagoons. Every year the Grand Rhône, which accounts for 90% of the flow, hollows out 20 million cu m/26.156 million cu yd of gravel, sand and mud from its banks and sweeps them to the sea.

The construction of the **sea wall** and the Rhône dikes in the 19C has partially helped to curb these phenomena. And yet the encroachment of the shoreline – 10–50m/33–164ft a year – continues in several places (l'Espiguette, Sablon Points). Elsewhere, however, owing to continental subsidence, the sea is invading the shore: the **Vieux Rhône and Petit Rhône** promontories have been swept away by southeasterly storms; Phare de Faraman, a lighthouse 700m/0.5mi inland in 1840, was swallowed up by the sea in 1917 so that a new one had to be built; and Stes-Maries-de-la-Mer, once an inland town, is now protected by breakwaters.

Different Faces of the Camargue

Although the Camargue is one vast plain, it is divided into three distinct regions: cultivated, salt marshes, and natural.

The Cultivated Region

North of the delta and along the two arms of its river bed, the Rhône has created banks of fine alluvium (lônes) that make up the best soil. This area, the upper Camargue, is well drained and tillable and started being improved during the Middle Ages. People have battled against water and salt: the level of salt in the soil was increased by intense heat in summer causing evaporation.

Since World War II, great drainage and irrigation projects have been undertaken and have brought satisfactory results. The extent of arable land has considerably increased and large farming units are predominant. Wheat, vineyards, orchards, market gardens, maize, rape, and forage are grown in rotation on this productive soil. But the area is known above all for its **rice** production, even if cultivation has dropped drastically in recent times.

Growing here and there are small clumps of white oak, ash, elm, poplar, robinia and willow trees.

The Salt Marshes

These lie near Salin-de-Giraud (11 000ha/27 181 acres) and Aigues-Mortes (10 000ha/24 710 acres), and appear as a chequerboard of evaporation pans and huge glistening mounds of salt. The production of salt goes back to Antiquity and made, during the Middle Ages, the wealth of the salt abbeys like Ulmet and Psalmody. Industrial salt production started in the 19C.

Between March and September a shallow flow of sea water (not more than a foot deep) is pumped across large "tables" for about 50km/31mi until a saturated solution of sodium chloride has been formed. This is then passed into 9ha/22.2-acre crystallising pans, 12cm/4.7in deep, divided by dikes (cairels). Between late August and early October, when evaporation is complete, the salt crystals are raked to the edge, washed and piled into huge white glistening mounds (camelles), some 21m/69ft high. After further washing, drying and crushing, the salt crystals are ready for use in industry and for animal and human consumption. La Compagnie des Salins du Midi is currently the most powerful company involved in salt harvesting.

The Natural Region

The wild southern delta comprises a sterile plain dotted with lagoons and smaller pools linked to the sea by a number of channels (graus). A desert of sand and marsh with small dunes lining the coast forms a fascinating nature reserve. Roads cross the Camargue, but for a better idea of this nature reserve, walk along the paths laid out by the regional nature park or nature reserve. These flat expanses, cracked by drought and whitened by the efflorescence of salt, are covered with sparse vegetation known as **sansouire**.

Halophilous plants (liking salt), sea lavender and glasswort, green in the spring, grey in the summer, and red in the winter, proliferate and are used to feed the herds of wild bulls. The only shrubs are tamarisks. The reeds serve to make sagno, a screen that protects cultivated land and provides roofing material for the cabins of gardians. The **Îlots des Rièges**, islands that lie at the south end of the Étang de Vaccarès, have a lush vegetation, creating a kaleidoscope of colour in the spring:

Camargue horses

©pigio1958/Fotolia.com

of blue thistles, tamarisks, wild daisies and zinerarias, junipers, yellow irises and narcissi.

Fauna

The fauna is of exceptional variety and quantity. Besides racoons, otters and beavers, which are difficult to find, birds reign supreme in this vast marshy land. There are some 400 different species, 160 of which are migratory.

The bird population changes according to the season due to the migratory birds which come from northern Europe (Finland and Siberia) to spend the winter, such as the teal, or to stop over in spring or autumn, such as the purple heron. Other kinds of birds you might spot are: the cattle egret, which follows the *manades* in order to feed off the insects that the cattle (and bulls) put to flight; the egret; grey heron; black-headed gull; herring gull; cormorant; lark; tit; harrier and finally, the incontestable star of the show, the pink flamingo, instantly recognisable by its pink plumage and long neck. Flamingos live in colonies numbering several thousand and feed on shellfish.

The waters also teem with fish: pike, perch, carp, bream, and especially eel found in the *roubines*, which are fished with long nets *(trabacs)* composed of three pockets sectioned by passages that get narrower. In the past the people lived off their catch. The cistudo, a small aquatic tortoise, and the common snake are also happy in this watery zone.

The **bulls**, black, lithe and agile, with horns aloft, are the stars of the show. They formerly lived wild, but are now kept in **manades**, the local word for herds of livestock. The *manades*, which contribute to the ecological balance of the Camargue, are tending to decline in favour of agriculture and salt production.

The *mas*, the large farm of several hundred acres, is managed by a steward *(bayle-gardian)* and numbers an average of 200 horned cattle plus the horses. In the spring the round-up *(ferrade)* is a colourful event: the young calves (one year old) are separated from the herd for branding by the *gardians*. They are roped, thrown on to their side, and branded on their left thigh with the mark of their owner.

Camargue **horses** are descended from prehistoric animals, the skeletons of which were discovered in a vast horse cemetery at Solutré (north-northwest of Lyon). Small (not more than 14 hands), they possess stamina, sureness of foot, and lively intelligence. The foals are born brown and turn white only in their fourth or fifth year.

Gardians

The *gardian* is the soul of the *manades*, the cowboy of Camargue, in a large felt hat, carrying a long, three-pronged

219

stick, and watching over his herd. Although the hat and stick are kept more and more for traditional fairs, the horse remains the faithful companion of the *gardian* – an excellent horseman. The *gardian*'s saddle, made locally, must offer maximum comfort and security: padding, fenders which fall along the horse's flanks, cage-like stirrups, pommel in front, and cantle behind.

🚗 DRIVING TOUR

Round-trip starting from Arles – 160km/ 99.4mi – allow one day.

▷ *Leave Arles by the southwest (D 570), in the direction of Stes-Maries-de-la-Mer.*

Musée Camarguais★

RD 570, Mas du Pont de Rousty, 13200 Arles. ○*Open Apr–Sept daily 9am– 6pm; Oct–Mar Wed–Mon 10am–5pm.* ○*Closed 1 Jan, 1 May, 25 Dec.* ∞*4.50€.* ℘*04 90 97 10 82. www.parc-camargue.fr.*

This museum has been set up in the old sheep-pen of the *mas* at Pont de Rousty and retraces the history of the Camargue region since the formation of the Rhône delta. The periods studied – including Antiquity, the Middle Ages and the 19C – will familiarise you with the traditional activities linked to the Camargue's natural environment.

A footpath of 3.5km/2.2mi through the estate reveals the crops, pasture and marshlands in between the irrigation canals, all of which form a natural part of the grounds of a Camargue *mas*.

Albaron

Albaron, once a stronghold, as can be seen from its fine 13C–16C tower, is now an important pumping and desalination station.

Château d'Avignon

○*Open Apr–Oct Wed–Mon 9.45am– 5.45pm.* ▪*Guided tours (1hr) 11am, 3pm, 5pm.* ○*Closed 1 May.* ∞*3€.* ℘*04 90 97 58 60. www.cg13.fr.*

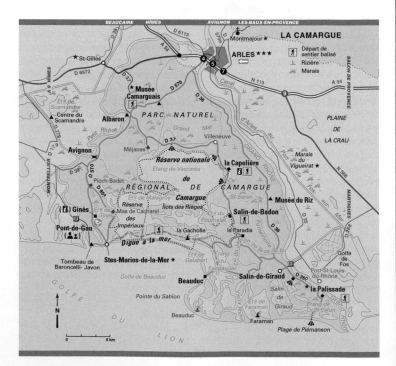

This vast residence with its Classical appearance was modified at the end of the 19C by the industrialist from Marseille, Louis Prat, and is a fine illustration of bourgeois tastes from that period. A tour of the interior reveals beautifully panelled and furnished rooms on the ground floor that are decorated with 18C Aubusson or Gobelins tapestries. A footpath (around 500m/547yd) leads visitors past a variety of trees in the garden.

La Maison du Parc

RD 570, Pont-de-Gau, 13460 Les Stes-Maries-de-la-Mer. ⏱Open Apr–Sept daily 10am–6pm; Oct–Mar Sat–Thu 9.30am–5pm. ⏱Closed 1 Jan, 1 May and 25 Dec. ⊜No charge. ℘04 90 97 86 32. www.parc-camargue.fr.

The Information Centre of the Camargue Regional Park is located on the edge of the Étang de Ginès. Its aim is to make visitors more aware of the fragility of the environment under the park's protection. A permanent exhibition describes the flora and fauna of the Camargue and the working methods and traditions of those who make a living from its natural resources. Large windows overlook the lagoon and marshlands, also giving visitors a good view of many examples of Camargue birdlife as they fly past. Upstairs, there are audiovisual presentations and video films on the subjects of the salt marshes and related activities, pink flamingos and the various projects within the park.

≛≛ Parc Ornithologique du Pont-de-Gau

ﾁ⏱*Open daily Apr–Sept 9am–dusk; Oct–Mar 10am–dusk. ⏱Closed 25 Dec. ⊜7€ (child 4€). ℘04 90 97 82 62. www.parcornithologique.com.*

This bird sanctuary is next to the information centre. By following a trail marked with explanatory panels and observation posts, you can see first hand most of the bird species that live in or pass through the Camargue in their natural habitat: nocturnal and diurnal birds of prey, such as the marsh harrier; waders, such as the avocet or the oyster catcher; grey herons; ducks of all sorts; pink flamingos, and many more.

Les Stes-Maries-de-la-Mer★

ﾁ*See Les STES-MARIES-DE-LA-MER*

▷ *Take the D 38 W and after 1km/ 0.6mi, turn left onto a surfaced road.*

On the left is the tomb of **Folco de Baroncelli-Javon**, the influential writer and Provençal *gardian*, built in 1955 on the site of his property, the Mas du Simbeu, which was destroyed in 1944.

▷ *Return to Les Stes-Maries-de-la-Mer and go north along the D 85A.*

The road crosses Couvin marsh, a saltwater landscape of stunted plants and swamp. Mas de Cacharel, where the film *White Mane* (1953) was made, stands to the right.

▷ *At Pioch-Badet, turn right onto the D 570, towards Arles; at the entrance to Albaron, turn right again, onto the D 37. This winds through rice fields. You can make a 4.5km/3mi detour (bear right) to Méjanes.*

≛≛ Domaine Paul Ricard Méjanes

⏱*Open daily Easter–early Oct without reservation; by reservation the rest of the year. ℘04 90 97 10 10. www.mejanes.camargue.fr.*

The Camargue in microcosm. This estate includes a bullring with regular *courses*; pony trekking, bike hire and horse-drawn carriages; an electric railway runs 3.5km/2mi along Vaccarès lagoon. The centre hosts the spectacular *Festival du Cheval* (Horse Festival) in July. Restaurant Le Mazet (℘04 90 97 10 79; www.mazetduvaccares.camargue.fr) is well worth a visit if you're there at the weekend *(closed Sun eve–Thu)*.

▷ *Continue along the D 37.*

The road crosses an expanse relieved by the occasional clump of trees, reeds and isolated *mas*. On the right there is a small viewpoint that looks out over Vaccarès lagoon towards the Rièges islands.

◉ *In Villeneuve turn right towards Vaccarès lagoon.*

After a little wood the road runs alongside the lagoon, giving a lovely view★ over the Camargue, in all its wild splendour.

La Capelière

◷*Open Apr–Sept daily 9am–1pm, 2–6pm; Oct–Mar Wed–Mon 9am–1pm, 2–5pm.* ◷*Closed 1 Jan and 25 Dec.* ◎*3€.* ℘*04 90 97 00 97.* *www.reserve-camargue.org.*
This is the information centre of the Réserve nationale de Camargue. The reserve covers more than 13 000ha/ 32 123 acres at the heart of the Rhône delta in the area of the Étang de Vaccarès. The centre offers a permanent exhibition, footpaths *(1.5km/09mi)*, and two observatories to help you get better acquainted with the Camargue landscape. To the left, on St-Seren marsh, there is a typical *gardian*'s cabin. The road skirts the Étang du Fournelet.

Salin-de-Badon

◷*Observatories open from sunrise to sunset. Permits can be obtained from La Capelière (Camargue National Reserve information centre).* ◎*3€.* ℘*04 90 97 00 97.*
All year round birds flock to this old salt marsh in their thousands. The Réserve nationale de Camargue has laid out footpaths, put up info panels and built three observatories.

◉ *Retrace your steps to Faraman and carry on to Salin-de-Giraud.*

Salin-de-Giraud

In salt country, this small town on the south bank of the Rhône, with its grid pattern of streets shaded by plane trees, acacias and *catalpas*, is a chemical manufacturing centre. Every district is named after a firm (Péchiney, Solvay).

◉ *Follow the road that skirts the Grand Rhône in the direction marked "Plages d'Arles".*

Viewpoint over the Salt Marsh

The viewpoint beside a salt heap looks out over the Giraud pans and workings.

Domaine de la Palissade★

◷*Open daily 9am–5pm (last admission 45min before closing).* ◷*Closed 1 Jan, 1 May, 11 Nov, 25 Dec.* ◎*3€.* ℘*04 42 86 81 28. www.conservatoire-du-littoral.fr.*
This estate, the property of the Conservatoire du Littoral (Society for the Preservation of Coastlines and River Banks), covers 702ha/1 735 acres and is the only area of the delta not to have been enclosed by dikes. The result is that the scenery here reflects the original character of the lower Camargue: alluvial deposits from the old course of the Rhône; riparial shrubs on the present banks; dunes or hummocks; a type of marsh samphire (*sansouires* in Provençal); fields of sea lavender used for grazing; and beds of reeds and rushes. Three footpaths lead visitors round the estate: one of 1.5km/0.9mi, with info panels and two others, of 3km/2mi and 7.5km/4.7mi, offering less explanations but allowing walkers to penetrate the Camargue.

◉ *Continue towards Plage de Piémanson.*

The road goes along a dike, through a region of lagoons glistening white with salt. Take the chance to have a dip in the Mediterranean at the vast sandy beach of Piémanson (25km/15.5mi).

◉ *Head towards Arles through Salin-de-Giraud.*

Musée du Riz

Rizerie du Petit Manusclat. ♿◷*Open daily 8.30am–noon, 1.30–5.30pm.* ◎*4.50€.* ℘*04 90 97 20 29.*
The Petit Manusclat estate is given over to the cultivation of rice. Its museum describes methods used in the Camar-

gue. Upstairs, there is a pretty *santon* scene displayed in a model of the Roman Theatre at Arles.

> *Take the D 36 and then the D 570, on the right, and head back to Arles.*

🚶 WALK

Along the Sea wall
From the eastern exit to Les Stes-Maries-de-la-Mer, the sea wall is reserved only for those on foot or cross-country bike. The path leads to the **Phare de la Gacgolle** (🕐open Sat–Sun and school holidays 11am–5pm; ⊶no charge; ℘04 90 97 00 97), a lighthouse that houses a long-distance observatory and an exhibition on the coastline. This walk illustrates the Camargue's rich birdlife and landscapes, providing the weather is dry.

From Pertuis to la Comtesse, continue south: the causeway runs between the two lagoons, the **Étang du Fangassier** and the **Étang de Galabert**. Galabert island is the only nesting site in France for pink flamingos. About 8 000 young birds are born here every year. It takes 3–4 years for their plumage to turn from black to pink.

ADDRESSES

🏠 STAY

⊖⊜⊜⊜ **Le Mas du Versadou** – *on the D 179, 30800 St-Gilles-du-Gard.* ℘04 66 87 10 75. www.masduversadou.com. *5 rooms.* This impressive 18C *mas*, set among rice fields, offers antique-filled *gîtes* and rooms whose themes include ancient Rome, Gothic and Mata Hari. After a hard day, bathe in the authentically reconstructed Roman baths or lie by the pool.

🍽 EAT

⊖⊜⊜⊜ **La Chassagnette** – *Domaine de l'Armellière, rte du Sambuc (D 36), 13200 Arles.* ℘04 90 97 26 96. *www.chassagnette.fr. Closed Jan–early Mar, Tue–Wed.* This trendy restaurant serves up local food with a contemporary Japanese twist. When you've finished eating, take a walk around the organic garden or browse the books in the library while enjoying a tea made with herbs you've picked from the herb garden.

🎯 LEISURE ACTIVITIES

Birdwatching – Leave early in the morning, before 10am, or at dusk, Mar–Oct. The best places are the footpaths around La Capelière and the Domaine de la Palissade, the seawall, and the Pont-de-Gau bird park. Just remember to take mosquito repellent and stay quiet!

Courses Camarguaises – These games, where men called *razeteurs* snatch a rosette from between a bull's horns, take place in Easter–September. Ask at the tourist offices in Arles, Les Stes and Aigues-Mortes for details.

Cycling – You can rent bikes from Le Vélociste on pl. Mireille in Les Saintes (℘04 90 97 83 26; www.levelociste.fr) from 7.50€ for two hours. They'll also give advice on self-guided tours.

Horse Riding – Reputable riding centres on the road into Les Saintes include Les Écuries at the Auberge Cavalière Hotel (℘06 09 54 24 40; www.ecuries-cavaliere.camargue.fr) and Ranch La Brouzetière (℘04 90 97 82 40; www.labrouzetiere.camargue.fr). Expect to pay about 35€ for two hours.

Swimming – The best spots are at Les Saintes and Piémanson, south of Salin-de-Giraud.

Walking – The ideal way to see the local flora and fauna is on foot. The best paths are the **GR 653 footpath**; the sea wall; and the footpaths around Domaine de la Palissade, La Capelière and Salin-de-Badon.

Abbaye de Montmajour★

Bouches-du-Rhône

On a hill overlooking the Arles plain lie the ruins of Abbaye de Montmajour, full of history and legends, whose buildings represent two different periods: the medieval and the 18C.

A BIT OF HISTORY

The Struggle against the Marshes – The hill was, for a long time, surrounded by marshes. A Christian cemetery was established here and a group of hermits, who looked after the burial ground, were at the origin of the abbey, founded in the 10C under Benedictine rule. The main occupation of these people was the drainage of the marshland: between the Alpilles and the Rhône.

Decadence – In the 17C the abbey consisted of about 20 monks and "religious" laymen, to whom the king granted a position in the community and more significantly part of the revenues. Their tendency towards frivolity provoked a reaction: the congregation of reformed monks of St-Maur, in charge of restoring discipline, sent new monks to the abbey in 1639; the monks who had been expelled

- **Michelin Map:** 340: C-3.
- **Location:** 2km/1mi from Arles in the direction of Fontvieille. Park in front of the abbey.
- **Timing:** Allow 1–2hr for a visit.

pillaged the abbey. In the 18C part of the buildings collapsed and were replaced by magnificent new constructions. The last abbot, the Cardinal of Rohan, was implicated in the affair of the queen's necklace, with the result that in 1786 Louis XVI proclaimed the suppression of the abbey as retribution.

The Fall and Rise of a National Property – In 1791, Montmajour was sold as a national property. It was bought by a second-hand dealer for 62 000 *livres*, payable over 12 years. To help repay the debt the buildings were dismantled: furniture, panelling, lead, timberwork and marble were loaded on carts and sold. In spite of that, the owner was late in her payments and in 1793 the sale was annulled. The abbey was sold for 23 000 *livres* to an estate agent, who broke up the fine stonework and sold the old buildings to people who converted them into lodgings.

During the last century, the people of Arles and the town itself recovered the buildings little by little. In 1872 the restoration of the medieval buildings was started; the 18C buildings remained in ruins. It provided the film setting for *The Lion in Winter* (1968), starring Peter O'Toole and Katharine Hepburn. The ruins are now a national monument.

VISIT

Open Apr–Jun daily 9.30am–6pm; Jul–Sept daily 10am–6.30pm; Oct–Mar Tue–Sun 10am–5pm (last visit 45min before closing).

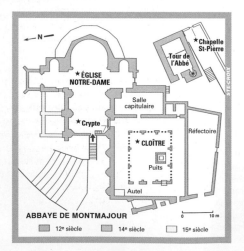

ABBAYE DE MONTMAJOUR

12e siècle   14e siècle   15e siècle

Closed public holidays. ⊚*7€ (no charge first Sun of the month Nov–Mar).* ℘*04 90 54 64 17. www.montmajour. monuments-nationales.fr.*

Église Notre-Dame★

The 12C building in the main part includes an upper church and a crypt or lower church. The upper church was never completed and consists of a chancel, a transept and a nave with two bays. The **crypt**★ was in part built into the sloping rock and in part raised, due to the incline of the land.

Cloisters★

The cloisters were built at the end of the 12C but only the eastern gallery has preserved its Romanesque characteristics. The capitals bear remarkable historiated decoration which has been associated with that of St-Trophime in Arles.

Monastic Buildings

The remaining buildings include the chapter-house with rounded barrel vaulting, the refectory with its interesting pointed barrel vaulting (access from the exterior) and the dormitory, on the first floor above the refectory.

Les Stes-Maries-de-la-Mer★

Bouches-du-Rhône

Between the Mediterranean and the Launes and Impérial lagoons, at the heart of the Camargue, Les Stes-Maries-de-la-Mer can be distinguished by its fortified church. A marina extends to the west.

A BIT OF HISTORY

According to Provençal legend, the boat abandoned to the waves in c. 40 by the Jews of Jerusalem, which, without the aid of sail or oar, landed safely on the shore of Les Stes-Maries, carried Mary, the mother of James, Mary Magdalene, Martha and her brother Lazarus, St Maximinus, Mary Salome, the mother of James Major and John, and Cedonius, the man born blind.

Sara, the two Marys' black servant left behind on the shore, wept aloud until Mary Salome threw her mantle on the water so that Sarah could walk over it to join the others. The legend continues that after erecting a simple oratory to the Virgin on the shore, the disciples separated; Martha went to Tarascon, Mary Magdalene to Ste-Baume. The two Marys and Sara remained in Camargue and were buried in the oratory.

▶ **Population:** 2 341
⚒ **Michelin Map:** 340: B-5 7 – Local map, *see CAMARGUE.*
🛈 **Info:** 5 avenue Van-Gogh, Stes-Maries-de-La-Mer. ℘04 90 97 82 55. www.saintesmaries.com.
🕓 **Timing:** It's particularly busy around 24 May when gypsies come to celebrate their patron saint, Sainte Sara, who is buried in the local church.

SIGHTS
Church★

pl. de l'Église. ℘*04 90 97 88 77.*
From the exterior, the massive crenellated walls of this fortified church are decorated with Lombard arcades at the east end. The keep-like structure of the upper chapel, surrounded at the base by a watchpath and crowned by a crenellated terrace, is dominated by a bell gable (restored in the early 20C). On the south side note the two fine lions devouring their prey which are believed to have supported a porch.

Interior

Enter through the small door on place de l'Église. The Romanesque nave is very dark. South of the nave, protected by a wrought-iron railing, is a well of fresh water for use in time of siege. In the third bay on the north side, above the altar is the Saints Marys' boat which is carried in procession by the gypsies in May and the parishioners in October. South of this altar note the Saints' Pillow, a worn block of marble incorporated in a column and discovered during the excavations of 1448 when the saints' relics were discovered.

Crypt

The altar has been built with part of a sarcophagus; it holds the reliquary containing the presumed relics of St Sara. Right of the altar stands the statue of Sara and ex-votos offered by the gypsies.

Upper Chapel

The chapel is richly panelled in bright green and gold in the Louis XV style. It houses the reliquary shrine of the two Marys. Frédéric Mistral set the final scene of his romance Mirèio in the chapel where his heroine, Mireille, came to pray for help.

Watchpath (Chemin de Ronde)

○ Open Jul–Aug daily 10am–8pm; Mar–Jun and Sept daily 10am–12.30pm, 2–6.30pm; Oct–Nov 10am–noon, 2–5pm; Dec–Feb Wed, Sat and Sun 10am–noon, 2–5pm. ⊚2€. ℘04 90 97 88 77.
53 steps.
Climb to the paved watchpath which encircles the church roof, commanding an unforgettable **view**★ of the sea, the town and the vast Camargue plain.

Musée Baroncelli

r. Victor-Hugo.
○ Open Apr–Sept daily 9am–noon, 2–7pm; Oct Tue–Thu 9am–noon, 2–5pm; Dec–Mar daily 9am–noon, 2–5pm. ⊚2€. ℘04 90 97 87 60.
Located in the former town hall, this museum displays the literature collected by **Marquis Folco de Baroncelli-Javon** (1869–1943), who revived Camargue traditions, on the subject of the agro-pastoral way of life in the Camargue and on the history of the town of Les Stes-Maries. The exhibition comprises also: dioramas illustrating Camargue fauna, including a herons' nesting site; 18C Provençal furniture and display cases devoted to Van Gogh, who painted several works here including *Street in Saintes-Maries* in 1888.

Nineteen Centuries of Pilgrimage

The saints' tomb rapidly became the object of a cult attracting pilgrims from afar, whereas gypsies and other nomads developed a particular veneration for Sarah. By the mid-9C the oratory (believed to date from the 6C) had been replaced by a fortified church which, in 869, was being incorporated into the town ramparts under the personal supervision of the Archbishop of Arles, when suddenly the Saracens made a lightning raid and carried off the archbishop. In the short time it took to collect the ransom of 150 *livres* of silver, 150 mantles, 150 swords and 150 slaves, the prelate died; unperturbed, the Saracens returned with the corpse, set it apart on a throne with a great show of respect as if nothing were wrong, and departed with the ransom before the Arlesians discovered their loss.

In the 11C the monks of Montmajour established a priory and in the 12C rebuilt the church, which was at the same time incorporated into the fortifications. At the end of the 14C the church's fortress-like appearance was reinforced by the addition of machicolations. During the Barbarian invasions the saints' remains were buried under the chancel. In 1448, King René ordered the exhumation of the saints, whose relics were then enshrined with great ceremony and have remained the object of a deep and widespread veneration ever since.

ADDRESSES

🏨 STAY

Méditerranée – *4 r. Frédéric-Mistral.* ℘*04 90 97 82 09. www.mediterraneehotel.com. 14 rooms.* ⊑*6€.* A simple family hotel with plenty of good points: a flower-decked façade, a shady terrace where breakfast is served on fine days, recently decorated rooms, reasonable prices and a good choice of restaurants nearby.

Hôtellerie du Pont Blanc – *chemin du Pont Blanc, 13460 Les Stes-Maries-de-la-Mer.* ℘*04 90 97 89 11. www.pont-blanc.camargue.fr. 15 rooms.* ⊑*6€.* Just off the main road near the village of Les Saintes, this hotel offers an authentic Camargue experience – in one of its Provençal-style rooms or in the traditional *cabane de gardian.* There's a pool to cool off in.

L'Etrier – *chemin bas de Launes.* ℘*04 90 97 81 14. www.letrier.com. 4 rooms. Restaurant* ☺☺☺. Stylish bed and breakfast, built around a *cabane de gardian*, spectacularly located on the Étang de Launes. Ideal for a romantic getaway – just watch out for the mosquitoes!

🍴 EAT

El Campo – *13 r. Victor-Hugo.* ℘*04 90 97 84 11. www.elcampo.camargue.fr. Closed Wed in Jun.* On the main street into the village centre, this is the place to go to eat delicious Camargue food and hear authentic gypsy flamenco.

Hostellerie du Pont de Gau – *rte d'Arles (D 570), 13460 Les Stes-Maries-de-la-Mer.* ℘*04 90 97 81 53. www.pont degau.camargue.fr. Closed 3 Jan–14 Feb.* This is probably the best restaurant in the area for traditional Camargue fare. Situated next to the Ornithology Park, local fish and bull meat dishes are served in the rustic dining room or on the terrace. There are nine rooms if you want to stay over.

Le Mas des Salicornes – *rte d'Arles.* ℘*04 90 97 83 41. www.hotel-salicornes.com. Closed 22–26 Dec, Jan–Feb and lunch.* A small hotel restaurant with a rustic-Provençal setting, offering a constantly changing Camargue style menu.

🛒 SHOPPING

Les Bijoux de Sarah – *12 pl. de l'Église.* ℘*04 90 97 73 73.* Hand-made jewellery. Their speciality is a "gypsy" pendant which is supposed to bring good luck and protect against the evil eye.

Market – Traditional market Monday and Friday in place des Gitans.

EVENTS

Gypsy Pilgrimage – Each May, gypsies from around the world come to celebrate their saint, Sara. After a service in the church on 24 May, her effigy is carried to the sea.

Camargue traditions – The 26 May is Baroncelli-Javon Memorial Day (*see Musée Baroncelli*); it is one of much celebration and local colour. Camargue *gardians*, with the women of Arles in traditional costume, enjoy local dance, *abrivados, courses camarguaises*, etc.

Festival de la Camargue et du Delta du Rhône – One for bird lovers: six days of accompanied walks and exhibitions at the beginning of May.

Feria du Cheval – A celebration of all that is equine, held in mid-July (*www.festivalducheval.camargue.fr*).

🏃 LEISURE ACTIVITY

Port Gardian – *Closed Nov–Feb.* ℘*04 90 97 88 77. www.ffvoile.net.* With its port and large beaches, Stes Maries is a good place to try water sports such as windsurfing, sea kayaking and sailing. A sailing school offers lessons and equipment rental.

In many ways, Avignon is the heartbeat of Provence, the centre of the region's religious, art and cultural history. Immerse yourself in the many traditions of this area by exploring the history-filled city.

Considered the "Windy City" of the south of France, Avignon is easy to get to by train, car or plane. Avignon is nestled on the left bank of the River Rhône, and is filled with Greek, Roman and Gothic architecture while being entertained with a tradition of performing arts dating back to the Middle Ages.

Highlights

1 Roman and Gothic sculpture at Petit Palais: **Avignon** (p236)

2 The artists' art studio and museum Musée Angladon: **Avignon** (p243)

3 Southern Gothic-style Ancienne Cathédrale St-Siffrein: **Carpentras** (p249)

4 The poet's former haunt Musée-Bibliothèque Pétrarque: **Fontaine-de-Vaucluse** (p255)

5 Grotte de Thouzon: **L'Isle-sur-la-Sorgue** (p257)

In the 5C the city suffered the ravages of war, and was damaged in a conflict with the Goths, and again damaged in the 8C. In the 12C Avignon struggled for independence. Between 1307 and 1377, Avignon, not Rome, was the seat of the Papacy, beginning with Pope Clement V at the helm. While this led to conflict within the Catholic Church, it is possibly the one factor that most dramatically shaped and changed Avignon. Even the city's sweets have a papal twist. While in town, try the papaline, a chocolate and liquor confection.

Because of that, the Palais des Papes has to be the first stop on any mention of visiting the area. It is the best place to imagine what it was like to live here as a pope through the ages. Through the years a total of seven popes lived here. The strong fortifications of the palace are still evident, and the palace's mammoth proportions can still be appreciated: it is about the size of four standard French cathedrals.

The popes knew how to find and build an ideal city: Avignon's narrow streets boast pretty plazas, with discoveries at every turn. Most of those are found in Old Avignon, which is dotted with museums, bridges, houses and buildings from Avignon's rich history, from rue des Lice, a street which shows the city's 13C wall, and the place de l'Horloge, home to shops, cafés and paintings of famous actors. Take time for leisurely walking tours through gardens and city streets.

In contrast to the theatrical excitement of Avignon is the bucolic pleasure of the Comtat Venaissin, the surrounding region, and its agricultural centre (and capital) Carpentras. The area has many features that may sound like you are in Paris, including a shopping corridor called rue des Halles and an Arc de Triomphe. But its real attractions are those of an agrarian nature, such as the fantastic Friday farmers' market. Don't miss the 14C synagogue, the oldest in the country. The region was one of the most welcoming to French Jews during the papal period.

Water is the watchword in the valley of Fontaine-de-Vaucluse, with a picturesque spring. Stop by the Ecomusée du Gouffre, which highlights underground limestone structures. Nearby Pernes-les-Fontaines has more than 35 fountains throughout the city, many of which are filled by a nearby spring.

Avignon★★★

Vaucluse

Designated city of art and culture, on the borders of three *départements* (Bouches-du-Rhône, Gard and Vaucluse), Avignon stretches in all its beauty along the banks of the River Rhône. Bell towers emerge from a mass of pink roofs and the city is surrounded by ramparts, dominated by the Rocher des Doms, the majestic cathedral, and the Palais des Papes.
The city is known for its **Festival d'Avignon** founded in 1947 by actor/director **Jean Vilar** (1912–71). Theatrical events, perhaps not so different from the pageants of the Middle Ages, illustrate various art forms (dance, music and cinema) and use the city's enchanting historical monuments as backdrops.

▶ **Population:** 92 454.
🖢 **Michelin Map:** 332: B-10.
🖹 **Info:** 41 cours Jean-Jaurès, 84000 Avignon. ℘04 32 74 32 74. www.ot-avignon.fr.
▶ **Location:** Take the sightseeing train (🖢*see Addresses*) or a guided tour of the city for an overview *(contact the tourist office)*.
🅿 **Parking:** There are paying car parks outside the ramparts – don't drive through the old town.
⊛ **Don't Miss:** Palais des Papes; St-Bénézet bridge; wandering around the narrow streets of the Old Town.
🕐 **Timing:** Allow a couple of days for a visit including half a day for the old town and an hour for the Palais des Papes. Try avoid visiting during the festival in July.
🧑‍🧒 **Kids:** Boat trips on the Rhône; little sightseeing train.

A BIT OF HISTORY

Before the Popes – Only a few ruins remain of the monuments which embellished the flourishing Gallo-Roman settlement of Avenio. Following the barbaric invasions of the 5C, Avignon fell into oblivion through the early Middle Ages. Its rebirth occurred in the 11C and 12C, when Avignon took advantage of the feudal rivalries between the Houses of Toulouse and Barcelona to protect and reinforce its independence: like its Italian counterparts, Avignon formed a small city state. But its commitment in favour of the Albigensians brought about royal reprisals: in 1226, Louis VIII seized the town, ordering its defences razed. Nevertheless, Avignon rose again

Ramparts of Avignon and the Palais des Papes in the background

S. Sauvignier/MICHELIN

quite quickly, and, in spite of losing its independence, regained its former prosperity under the rule of the House of Anjou.

The Popes at Avignon – Avignon's destiny changed in the early 14C with the exile of the pontifical court to France, bringing with it a century of brilliance. The court in Rome had become more or less impossible for the popes, who were incessantly the object of political differences. The Frenchman Raymond Bertrand de Got, elected pope under the name of **Clement V** (1305), decided to establish the court in France, where since 1274 the Holy See possessed the Comtat Venaissin. Clement V solemnly entered Avignon on 9 March 1309, though he did not reside here permanently as he preferred the calm of Groseau Priory, near Malaucène, or Monteux castle, not far from Carpentras. He died in 1314. In 1316, the former Bishop of Avignon, Jacques Duèze, was elected. As **Pope John XXII** he established the papacy here; 1309–77, seven French popes succeeded each other at Avignon, among them **Benedict XII**, who built the papal palace, and **Clement VI**, who purchased Avignon from Queen Joan I of Sicily, Countess of Provence, in 1348.

The Constructive Popes – The city was transformed, and took on the appearance of a vast building site: convents, churches and chapels, not to mention the splendid cardinals' palaces (🕯 see VILLENEUVE-LEZ-AVIGNON), while the pontifical palace was constantly being enlarged and embellished. The university, founded in 1303, numbered thousands of students. The pope wanted to be considered the most powerful ruler in the world. His wealth and munificence shone brilliantly, attracting the notice of the envious, which was why he lived in a fortress and established a line of fortifications to protect the town from mercenary soldiers who pillaged the countryside.

Life in Avignon was pleasant: liberty and prosperity existed and the population jumped from 5 000 to 40 000. A place of asylum for political refugees like Petrarch, the pontifical city also housed a Jewish community. But this tolerance extended, unfortunately, to adventurers, escaped criminals, smugglers, counterfeiters and all kinds of rogues. In these circumstances, the popes thought of returning to Rome; **Urban V** left for the Eternal City in 1367, but hostility in Italy forced him to return to Avignon after three years. **Gregory XI** finally left Avignon in 1376 and died in 1378.

Popes and Schismatic Popes – Hostile to the reforms of the Italian pope **Urban VI**, successor to Gregory XI, the mainly French cardinals of the Sacred College elected another pope, **Clement VII** (1378–94), who returned to Avignon. The Great Schism divided the Christian world; the Avignon pope was recognised mainly in France, Naples and Spain. Popes and schismatic popes mutually excommunicated each other and attempted by any means possible to bring the other down, vying with each other for the papacy's great wealth. **Benedict XIII** (1394–1423) succeeded Clement VII; however, he no longer had the support of the King of France. He fled Avignon in 1403, yet his followers resisted in the palace until 1411. The Great Schism finally ended in 1417 with the election of **Martin V**.

Meanwhile life continued in Avignon as is suggested by the presentation of the *Mystères* (mystery plays enacting an episode of the Scriptures) during Whitsun in 1400, with huge living tableaux and processions that went on for three days and dramatised the Passion of Christ.

Until the Revolution, Avignon was governed by a papal legate and a vice-legate. Intolerance towards the Jews increased: confined to a ghetto, which was locked every night, the Jews had to wear a yellow cap, pay dues, and listen to sermons preached to convert them. Moreover, they were not allowed to mix with Christians, they could only occupy certain positions, and they were under constant surveillance.

Palais des Papes during the Festival d'Avignon

S. Sauvignier/MICHELIN

Avignon was a society of contrast, with a gulf between the wealthy and poor, as evidenced by the confrontation between them from 1652 to 1659. At the Revolution, Avignon was split between the partisans wanting to belong to France and those who wanted the pontifical state maintained. The former won, and on 14 September 1791 the constitutional assembly voted the union of the Comtat Venaissin to France.

PALAIS DES PAPES★★★

Allow 1–2hr.
r. Pente Rapide Charles Ansidei.
🕐*Open daily 1–14 Mar 9am–6.30pm; 15 Mar–Jun and 16 Sept–1 Nov 9am–7pm; Jul and 1–15 Sept 9am–8pm; Aug 9am–9pm; 2 Nov–Feb 9.30am– 5.45pm; last admission 1hr before closing.* ✆*10.50€ (Mar–15 Nov); 8.50€ (16 Nov–Feb); 13€/11€ combined ticket with Pont St-Bénézet.* ✆*04 90 27 50 00. www.palais-des-papes.com.*

The palace is a maze of galleries, chambers, chapels and passages, now empty and deserted. Yet, try to imagine what it was like at the time of the popes.

Picture its luxurious furnishings; sumptuous decoration; discreet comings and goings of prelates and servants; changing of the guards in dress uniform; cardinals, princes and ambassadors arriving and departing; the pilgrims gathered in the courtyard waiting to receive the pope's blessing; or to see him leave on his white mule; the litigants and magistrates creating commotion around the pontifical court.

Construction

This princely residence counts among the largest of its time with an area of 15 000sq m/3.7 acres. It is both a fortress and a palace and is made up of two buildings joined together: the **Palais Vieux** to the north and the **Palais Neuf** to the south; its construction lasted 30 years. The Cistercian Benedict XII brought up in contempt of luxury, had the old episcopal palace razed and entrusted to his compatriot Pierre Poisson the task of building a vast residence that would lend itself to prayer and be well defended. The Palais Vieux thus acquired the appearance of an austere fortress.

Planned around cloisters, its four wings are flanked by towers, the strongest of which, the north tower, Tour de Trouillas, was used as a keep and prison. Clement VI, a great prince of the church, artist and prodigy, ordered the architect Jean de Louvres to carry out the expansion of the palace. The Tour de la Garde-Robe and two new buildings closed off the main courtyard that preceded Benedict XII's palace.

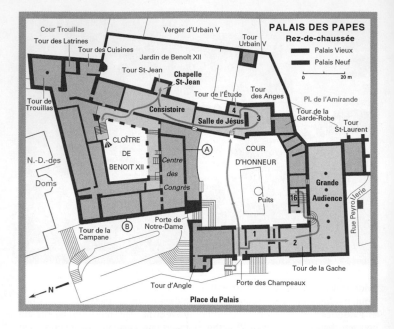

PALAIS DES PAPES
Rez-de-chaussée
■ Palais Vieux
■ Palais Neuf
0   20 m

Cour Trouillas
Tour des Latrines
Tour des Cuisines
Verger d'Urbain V
Tour Urbain V
Jardin de Benoît XII
Tour St-Jean
Chapelle St-Jean
Tour de l'Étude
Tour des Anges
Pl. de l'Amirande
Consistoire
Salle de Jésus
Tour de la Garde-Robe
Tour St-Laurent
Tour de Trouillas
CLOÎTRE DE BENOIT XII
Centre des Congrès
COUR D'HONNEUR
N.-D.-des Doms
Puits
Grande Audience
Rue Peyrollerie
Porte de Notre-Dame
Tour de la Campane
Tour d'Angle
Porte des Champeaux
Tour de la Gache
Place du Palais
N

The exterior was not modified. However, inside, artists sumptuously decorated the rooms, notably the pope's private apartments. The works continued under Clement VI's successors: Innocent VI had Tour St-Laurent built to the south and Tour de la Gache to the west and the decoration completed (fresco on the vault in the Grande Audience); Urban V had the main courtyard laid out with its well and had buildings constructed linking the palace to the gardens, behind the Tour des Anges.

In 1398, and again from 1410–11, the palace was under siege, resulting in the dilapidation of the buildings. Allocated to the legates in 1433, it was restored in 1516 but continued to deteriorate. In a bad state when the Revolution broke out, it was pillaged, with furniture dispersed and statues and sculptures broken. After a particularly bloody episode in 1791, the palace was transformed into a prison and barracks (1810). Occupied by military engineers, it was again mistreated: at least the statutory wash on the walls protected some of the mural paintings.

Unfortunately, in many places, this safeguard came too late: the soldiers had had time to cut the protective coating off the frescoes and sell the pieces to collectors or antique dealers from Avignon.

Exterior

The palace from the outside has the appearance of a citadel built straight out of the rock. Its walls, flanked by ten large square towers, some more than 50m/164ft high, are buttressed by huge depressed arches holding up the machicolations: this is one of the first known examples of such military architecture.

Ground Floor

○ *Go through the Porte des Champeaux and enter the former guard room (reception and ticket office).*

The walls here are decorated with 17C paintings **(1)**.

Petite Audience **(2)**

In the 17C, when this room was in use as an arsenal, the vaulting was decorated with *grisaille* paintings representing military trophies.

▷ Turn round and go back through the Porte des Champeaux.

Main Courtyard (Cour d'Honneur)

Running along the main courtyard to the north is the Conclave Wing **(A)**, which houses the Conference Centre. The Gothic south wing has a number of irregular openings in its façade and the Indulgence window **(15)** on the first floor. It is used during the summer as a backdrop for the theatrical performances of the Avignon Festival.

Treasury

The **Lower Treasure House** (Trésor Bas) is a vaulted room hollowed out beneath the Tour des Anges. Underneath the flagging were the hiding places where bags of silver and gold, silverware and valuable ornaments were kept. The cupboards on the walls contained the accounts ledgers and archives.

The wealth of the popes was considerable. John XXII bequeathed 24 million ducats to his heirs after 19 years as pope. The size of the papal revenue explains why the most important court dignitary was the Chamberlain, that is, the Minister of Finance.

Grande Trésorerie

This small room has an enormous fireplace decorating the north wall. Take the staircase to the **Salle de Jésus**, which used to serve as antechamber to the Consistoire.

Chamberlain's Bedchamber (3)

Situated on the third floor of the Tour des Anges, just below the Papal Bedchamber, this room is magnificently embellished with a 14C painted beam ceiling and with foliated scrollwork covering parts of the walls. Here, too, there are hiding places concealed in the flags on the floor.

Papal Vestiary (4)

This small room in the Tour de l'Étude was converted into a chapel in the 17C by the vice-legates. The original timberwork was reinforced by a stone vault. The walls feature 18C wood panelling.

Consistoire

To debate the great theories of Christianity, the pope and his cardinals met in council in this vast rectangular hall. It was here that the pope announced the name of the newly appointed cardinals and received the sovereigns and their ambassadors in great pomp. It was here also that cases proposed for canonisation were examined. Exhibited in this hall are **frescoes** executed by the great artist **Simone Martini**, which were brought from the porch of Notre-Dame-des-Doms cathedral.

Chapelle St-Jean or Chapelle du Consistoire

This oratory is adorned with lovely frescoes painted from 1346 to 1348 by **Matteo Giovanetti**, Clement VI's official court painter.

On leaving the Consistoire, follow the lower gallery of Benedict XII's cloisters and take the staircase to the banqueting hall. There is a fine view of the **Staff Wing (B)**, where the staff – persons holding various functions – and the main servants lodged. Here you will also discover a fine view of the Tour de la Campane and of Benedict XII's chapel.

First Floor
Grand Tinel or Banqueting Hall

Exhibited in this hall, one of the largest in the palace (48m/158ft long and 10.25m/33ft wide), is a superb series of 18C Gobelins **tapestries**. The immense panelled keel-vaulted roof that takes the form of a ship's hull has been restored. Continue into the **upper kitchen (5)** with its huge chimney in the form of an octagonal pyramid, located on the top floor of the Tour des Cuisines.

This tower was also used as the pantry and provisions storeroom. Next to it, the Tour des Latrines (or Tour de la Glacière – ☛ *not open to the public*) offered common latrines on each floor for the soldiers and staff.

Chapelle du Tinel or Chapelle St-Martial

This oratory is named after the **frescoes** painted in 1344–45 by Matteo Giovanetti of St Martial (apostle from the Limousin, Clement VI's native region). They recount the life of the saint using a harmony of blues, greys and browns.

Chambre de Parement

Next to the pope's bedroom, this antechamber, also known as the Robing Room, was used as a small waiting room by those who had been accorded a private interview with the pope. Two 18C Gobelins tapestries hang on the walls.

Next to the Robing Room on the first floor of the Tour de l'Étude you will find Benedict XII's study **(Studium) (6)** with its magnificent tiles.

Situated along the west wall of the Robing Room was the pope's private dining room **(7)** called the Petit Tinel. Alongside it was the kitchen (or secret kitchen) **(8)**. The rooms in this section of the palace were entirely destroyed in 1810.

Papal Bedchamber (9)

The walls of this room were richly painted against a blue background: birds entwined in vines and squirrels climbing oak trees. Exotic birdcages were painted in the window embrasures.

Chambre du Cerf (10)

This room, known as the Stag Room, was Clement VI's study and is decorated with elegant **frescoes** painted by various Italian artists. The subjects, illustrated against a verdant background, are hunting, fishing, fruit and flower picking, and bathing scenes. The ceiling in larch wood is very ornate. This intimate and cheerful room had two windows. One offered a fine view of Avignon, and the other overlooked the gardens.

To get to the Chapelle Clémentine, cross the **north sacristy (11)** comprising two vaulted bays on diagonal ribs and containing plaster casts of characters who figured significantly in the history of the Avignon Papacy. The bridge was built by Innocent VI to link the pope's private dining room with the chapel and led into the east bay.

Grande Chapelle or Chapelle Clémentine

To the right of the pontifical altar, an opening leads into the **Cardinals' vestry (12)** in Tour St-Laurent, where the pope changed vestments when officiating at High Mass. It contains casts of recumbent figures of the popes:

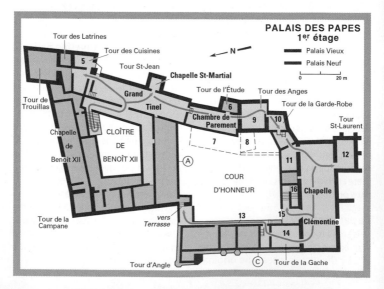

Detail of frescoes depicting the miracle of St Martial, Chapelle St-Martial, Palais des Papes

©Photo Scala, Florence

Clement V, Clement VI, Innocent VI and Urban V.

In this chapel, the Conclave of cardinals came to hear the Mass of the Holy Spirit before returning to the Conclave Wing **(A)** via a narrow passageway called the **Conclave gallery (13)**, which has elegant vaulting.

The **Conclave** was made up of the college of cardinals, who met ten days after the death of the pope, to elect a successor. The first floor of the Palais Vieux was used to receive the cardinals. In order to isolate them from the rest of the world, they blocked up all the doors and windows and did not open them again until they had elected a pope with a two-thirds majority vote. The word *conclave* is derived from Latin, meaning "under lock and key".

Chamberlain's New Bedchamber (14)

This occupies the far south end of the **High Dignitaries' Wing (C)**, which also houses the bedchamber of the Treasury notaries and the Treasurer's apartment.

Terrasse des Grands Dignitaires

Located on the second floor of the High Dignitaries' Wing, this terrace offers an extensive **view**★★ over the upper storeys of the Palais des Papes, the Tour de l'Horloge, the dome of the cathedral, the Petit Palais and, further in the distance, Pont St-Bénézet and the monuments at Villeneuve-lez-Avignon.

Turn back in the other direction to come across the loggia opposite the doorway of the Chapelle Clémentine. From the window of this loggia the pope would bless the gathered faithful in the courtyard below **(15)**.

Ground Floor (Palais Neuf)

Go down the **Grand Escalier (16)**. The right-hand flight of stairs is covered with pointed vaulting, a strong example of the bold architectural design for that time.

Grande Audience

This is a magnificent room with two aisles divided by a line of columns supporting the pointed arches of the vaulting. This is also called the Palais des Grandes Causes (Palace of the Great Causes), as it was here that the 13 ecclesiastical judges formed the Tribunal de la Rota – *rota* (wheel) comes from the circular bench on which they were seated and which is located in the room's last east bay. Around the judges sat the lawyers and the papal court's public servants. The rest of the room was for the public; seating ran along the whole of the room's wall. On the vaulting against a dark blue background sprinkled with stars is a **fresco of the Prophets**, attributed to Matteo Giovanetti in 1352.

◐ *Leave the palace by the Porte des Champeaux.*

⚓ WALKING TOURS

① PLACE DU PALAIS AND THE QUARTIER DE LA BALANCE

Allow 4hr for the round-trip circuit of the place du Palais.

"Promenade des Papes"

This walk gives a striking impression of the height of the building. Follow pretty rue Peyrollerie that leads off from the southwest corner and goes under the enormous buttress supporting the Chapelle Clémentine to emerge on to a square in which there is an attractive 17C townhouse. Go along rue Vice-Légat leading to Urban V's orchard, then go through a covered passageway which opens onto cour Trouillas. The Escaliers Ste-Anne lead up to the Rocher des Doms, giving a different view of the palace.

Rocher des Doms★★

There is a well laid-out garden planted with different species on this bluff. From the terraces you will encounter superb **views**★★ of the Rhône and Pont St-Bénézet, Villeneuve-lez-Avignon with Tour Phillipe-le-Bel and Fort St-André, the Dentelles de Montmirail, Mont Ventoux, Vaucluse plateau, the Luberon hills and the Alpilles.

◐ *Go back down to the garden, in the direction of the Petit Palais.*

Petit Palais

pl. du Palais des Papes.

This was formerly Cardinal Arnaud de Via's residence *(livrée)* before being bought by the pope in 1335 to house the bishopric. The building deteriorated during the different sieges imposed upon the Palais des Papes, and had to be repaired and transformed in the late 15C, especially by Cardinal della Rovere, who subsequently became Pope Julius II. Famous guests resided here: Cesare Borgia in 1498, François I in 1533, and Anne of Austria and the Duke of Orléans in 1660 during Louis XIV's visit to Avignon. Today it houses the paintings of the **Musée du Petit Palais** (⚓ *see Museums*).

Cathédrale Notre-Dame des Doms

pl. du Palais des Papes. ◐*Open daily 8am–6pm.* ⚓*No charge.* ✆*04 90 86 81 01. www.cathedrale-avignon.fr.*

Built in the mid-12C, the cathedral was damaged many times and each time rebuilt and altered.

The porch was added in the late 12C and shelters two tympana (a semicircular one surmounted by a triangular one) once magnificently decorated with frescoes by Simone Martini and now located in the Palais des Papes.

Inside, the single nave with five bays is roofed with pointed-barrel vaulting. The Romanesque **dome**★ that covers the transept crossing is remarkable: to reduce the area, the master craftsman created a series of projections that

Pont St-Bénézet

L. Campion/MICHELIN

supported the dome and its elegant columned lantern.

Hôtel des Monnaies (Mint)

pl. du Palais des Papes.

This 17C townhouse (now the Conservatory of Music Olivier Messiaen) is crowned with a balustrade and has an ornately carved **façade**★ of dragons, eagles, Borghese coat of arms, cherubs and festoons of fruit.

▷ *Take the street to the right of the Hôtel des Monnaies to get to the Quartier de la Balance.*

Gypsies lived in the **Quartier de la Balance** in the 19C. In the 1970s it was renovated. This *quartier* descends as far as the ramparts and the famous bridge of the French children's song, *Sur le pont d'Avignon.*

Rue de la Balance

This is the Balance district's main street. On one side are old restored townhouses with elegant façades, decorated with mullioned windows. By contrast, on the other side you will witness modern, Mediterranean-style buildings with small flower-decked patios and ground level shopping arcades.

Pont St-Bénézet★★

Accessed via ramparts. Rue Ferruce.
&.⊙*Open daily 1–14 Mar 9am–6.30pm; 15 Mar–30 Jun and 16 Sept–1 Nov 9am–7pm; Jul and 1–15 Sept 9am–8pm; Aug 9am–9pm; 2 Nov–Feb 9.30am–5.45pm; last admission 30min before closing.* ⊛*4.50€ (1 Mar–15 Nov); 4€ (16 Nov–Feb); 13€/11€ combined ticket with Palais des Papes.* ℘*04 90 27 51 16. www.palais-des-papes.com.*

In reality Pont St-Bénézet was originally a narrow bridge for people on foot or on horseback. It was never such that one could dance in a ring as in the song lyric, *Sur le pont d'Avignon l'on y danse tout en rond*! Indeed, the people of Avignon did their dancing on the island beneath the arches of the bridge, in other words *sous le pont.*

Spanning two arms of the Rhône to Villeneuve-lez-Avignon at the base of the Tour Phillipe-le-Bel, the bridge was 900m/2 953ft long and composed of 22 arches.

Legend has it that in 1177, a young shepherd boy, Bénézet, was commanded by voices from heaven to build a bridge across the river at a spot indicated by an angel. Everyone thought he was crazy until he proved his divine guidance by miraculously lifting a huge block of stone. Volunteers appeared and formed themselves as the **Bridge Brotherhood** (*Frères Pontifes*), and funds flowed in.

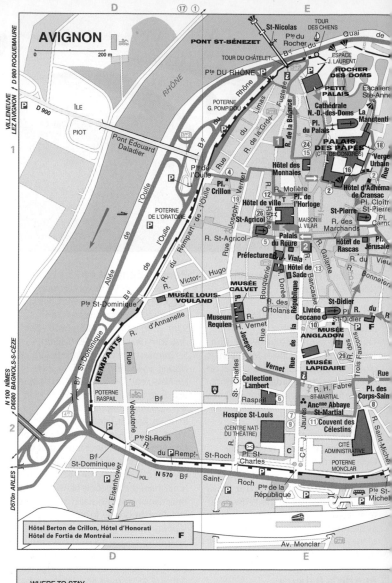

Hôtel Berton de Crillon, Hôtel d'Honorati
Hôtel de Fortia de Montréal .... **F**

WHERE TO STAY

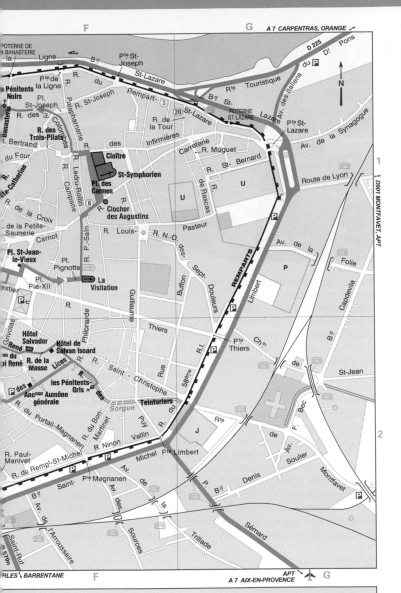

WHERE TO EAT

Place de l'Horloge

G. Magnin/MICHELIN

Within eight years they completed the bridge's construction.

Rebuilt from 1234 to 1237, the bridge was restored in the 15C and then broken by the flooded Rhône in the mid-17C. There is a small display on the history and iconography of this famous bridge to round off your visit.

Remparts★

The actual fortifications (4.3km/2.7mi long) were built in the 14C by the popes. From a military standpoint this is not first-class work: the towers were open to the town, and part of the walls had no machicolations. In fact, the popes had simply wanted to build a preliminary obstacle against attack on the palace. The most interesting part is along rue du Rempart du Rhône to **place Crillon**.

▷ *Return to place de l'Horloge via rue St-Étienne bordered by old townhouses, rue Racine to the right, and rue Molière to the left.*

② OLD AVIGNON
*Start in place de l'Horloge –
allow half a day.*

This route explores the churches, museums and the particularly notable townhouses in the part of Old Avignon to the south and to the east of the Palais des Papes. It also offers you the

opportunity to appreciate the past and present contrasts in this lively city.

Place de l'Horloge
The theatre and town hall overlook this vast square shaded by plane trees and partly occupied by open-air cafés.

In the little streets around place de l'Horloge there are windows painted with effigies of famous actors that call to mind the city's theatrical vocation.

Hôtel de Ville
Built in the 19C, the town hall includes the 14C and 15C **clock tower**.

▷ *Take rue Félicien-David and go around St-Agricol's east end.*

Note the Gallo-Roman rampart ruins.

▷ *Take a left on rue Agricol, then a right on rue Bouquerie.*

Rue Jean-Viala
The street runs between two 18C mansions housing the *Préfecture* (**P**) offices and the general council of the *département* (Conseil Général).

Hôtel de Sade
5 r. Dorée.
Elegant mullioned windows overlook the street. In the courtyard there is a fine pentagonal turreted staircase.

◐ *Head to rue Bouquerie, take a left, then a right on rue Horace-Vernet, which will take you to rue Joseph Vernet.*

Rue Joseph-Vernet

You will see two fine hotels on the right, one of which, the **Hôtel Villeneuve-Martignan** houses the Musée Calvet (◐ *see Museums*).

◐ *Go to the left on rue Joseph-Vernet.*

Rue de la République

This lively and commercial street, which runs into cours Jean-Jaurès (which heads straight into the train station), forms the main axis of the city.

◐ *Go back towards the tourist office.*

From cours Jean-Jaurès turn right (the arcades standing in the neighbouring square are all that remain of the **Abbaye St-Martial**), then left into rue Agricol-Perdiguier to reach the 15C **Couvent des Célestins** (*pl. des Corps-Saints*), built in the northern Gothic style.

◐ *Turn back north onto rue des Lices (on the right).*

Rue des Lices

This street traces the 13C curtain wall. On the left are the 18C buildings of the former almshouse with its façade divided into galleried storeys. It now houses the École des Beaux-Arts (School of Fine Arts).

◐ *At the end of the street bear right on rue des Teinturiers.*

Rue des Teinturiers

The picturesque cobbled street shaded with plane trees follows the course of the River Sorgue, the waters of which were used by the cloth-dyers (after whom the street is named). You can still see several of the large paddle-wheels once used by the printed calico manufacturers to make fine shawls until the end of the 19C. On the right is the Franciscans' bell tower, all that remains of a convent

where Petrarch's unrequited love, Laura, is believed to be buried.

◐ *Turn around and walk back as far as rue de la Masse, on the left.*

Rue de la Masse

At no **36** is the **Hôtel de Salvan Isoard**, a 17C mansion with ornately carved window surrounds; and at no 19 **Hôtel Salvador** is an impressive 18C square mansion.

Rue du Roi-René

At the corner of rue Grivolas stands the **Maison du Roi René**, where the king lived during his visits to Avignon.

Further on, four 17C and 18C townhouses form a remarkable **group**★.

The **Hôtel Berton de Crillon** (no **7**) is emblazoned with portrait medallions, masks, flowers, garlands and adorned with a wrought-iron balcony. In the inner courtyard is a grand staircase with a stone balustrade.

◐ *Take rue des Fourbisseurs until you reach place Carnot. Turn right and head for place Jérusalem*

On the small place Jérusalem is the synagogue, which until the 19C was the heart of the Jewish District, also known as the Carrière.

Paddle wheel on Rue des Teinturiers

S. Sauvignier/MICHELIN

The Penitent Brotherhoods of Avignon

Appearing as early as the 13C, the penitent brotherhoods were at their peak in the 16C and 17C. The brothers were expected to help each other, do public penance, and perform good deeds. The brotherhood they belonged to was identified by the colour of their sackcloth and by the hood that covered their heads during processions. Avignon was a city where many different brotherhoods – grey, white, blue, black, purple and red – coexisted. The White Penitents were the most aristocratic and included among their members Charles IX and Henri III. Each brotherhood had assets and a chapel: a number of these chapels are still standing (the most interesting are those of the Grey Penitents and Black Penitents). During the Revolution they were disbanded and yet several brotherhoods managed to survive.

Place St-Jean-le-Vieux

Set at one corner of the square is a tall, square tower (14C), all that remains of the Commandery of the Knights of St John of Jerusalem destroyed in the 19C.

▷ *From rue St-Jean le Vieux, go to place Pignotte.*

Église de la Visitation

This former convent chapel (17C) has a finely carved façade.

▷ *Take rue P au Saïn to the left, then right on rue Carreterie, which leads to place des Carmes.*

Place des Carmes

On the south side of the square is the Clocher des Augustins, the only remnant of the convent founded here in 1261. The wrought-iron bell tower dates from the 16C.

Église St-Symphorien-les-Carmes

pl. des Carmes. ○*Open daily 8am–noon.* ℘*04 90 27 01 19.*
15C façade – the first north chapel contains three fine 16C statues in painted wood: Christ, Virgin and St John. In the succeeding chapels hang paintings by Pierre Parrocel *(Holy Family)*, Nicolas Mignard *(St Eligius)* and Guillaume Grève *(Adoration of the Magi)*.
A wrought-iron gate to the left of the church marks the entrance to the 14C cloisters.

▷ *Turn left into rue des Infirmières, on the north side of the square, then take the second right onto rue des Trois Colombes.*

Rue Banasterie

This street is named for the basket-makers' guild *(banastiers* in Provençal). At no 13, the 17C **Hôtel de Madon de Châteaublanc** has a façade adorned with garlands of fruit, eagles and masks.

▷ *From place Manguin take the narrow rue de Taulignan to the right.*

Hôtel d'Adhémar de Cransac

11 r. de Taulignan. ✆Guided tours *(1hr) by prior appointment 2–6pm.* ◉*8.50€.* ℘*04 90 86 13 28.*
This small private mansion, dating from the 17C, was redecorated in 18C: its drawing rooms were hung with silk hangings, fireplaces with overmantels and painted decorations. Only two rooms retain their original French-style ceilings. The mansion used to be a part of the St-Martial cardinal's mansion. It was the residence of one Amélie Palun, Countess René d'Adhémar de Cransac (1873–1955), who, along with her poet and Camargue *guardian* friends, dedicated her life to promoting Provençal folklore. There is a collection of items and documents on the subject of Frédéric Mistral, Joseph Roumanille and the Marquis de Baroncelli-Javon.

▷ *Continue straight to place St-Pierre.*

Église St-Pierre
pl. St-Pierre.
🕐*Open Thu 2–5pm, Fri–Sat 2–6.30pm.*
On the church's west façade are two doors adorned with richly decorated Renaissance **panels**★.
Carved in perspective in 1551 by Antoine Valard, the subjects illustrate, on the right, the Virgin and the angel of the Annunciation and on the left St Michael and St Jerome.

▶ *Take rue des Marchands, to the left, off place Carnot, to get back to the place de l'Horloge.*

MUSEUMS
Musée du Petit Palais★★
pl. du Palais des Papes. 🕐*Open Wed–Mon Jun–Sept 10am–6pm; Oct–May 10am–1pm, 2–6pm.* 🕐*Closed 1 Jan, 1 May, 14 July, 1 Nov, 25 Dec.* ✆6€.
✆*04 90 86 44 58. www.petit-palais.org.*
The first two rooms of this museum contain **Romanesque and Gothic sculpture**. Note the carved figure (at the back of the room), which comes from the late-14C monumental **tomb of Cardinal de Lagrange**. The realism of the emaciated corpse, which formed the tomb's base, anticipates the macabre representations of the 15C and 16C.
The **Campana collection**, the major treasure of this museum, brings together a group of Italian paintings from the 13C–16C.
The presentation of the works by the different schools over consecutive periods allow an appreciation of the evolution of the Italian style. Note the strong Byzantine influence that still prevailed in the works of the 13C, the Siennese School, represented by Simone Martini and Taddeo di Bartolo, the international Gothic style (Lorenzo Monaco and Gherardo Starnina), the Florentine School, which concentrated on the form of the drawing in balanced compositions where perspective plays an important role, especially with Bartolomeo della Gatta *(Annunciation)*, and the rediscovery of Antiquity, c. 1500.

> ### Passion in Avignon ...
>
> Get your **"Avignon PASS'ION"** **pass**, valid for two weeks, which offers significant price reductions for visitors to Avignon and Villeneuve-lez-Avignon.

The remaining galleries are devoted to the **painting and sculpture of the Avignon School**. The Avignon School, which can be placed midway between the realism of the Flemish School and the stylisation of the Italian Schools. **Enguerrand Quarton** is represented here by the significant *Requin Altarpiece* (1450–55). On either side of a remarkable *Virgin of Pity* (1457) stand the works of Jean de la Huerta *(St Lazarus and St Martha)* and Antoine le Moiturier *(Angels)*.

Musée Calvet★
65 r. Joseph Vernet. 🕐*Open Wed–Mon 10am–1pm, 2–6pm.* 🕐*Closed 1 Jan, 1 May, 25 Dec.* ✆6€ (7€ with Musée Lapidaire). ✆*04 90 86 33 84. www.musee-calvet.org.*
This celebrated museum is named after its creator, the physician Esprit Calvet. Highlights include a range of sculptures, a collection of silverware and faience and French, Italian and Flemish painting from the 16C to the 19C. Note in particular the *Death of Joseph Bara* by David, *The Four Seasons* by Nicolas Mignard, works by Elizabeth Vigée-Le Brun, and the maritime canvases by the Avignon painter **Claude Joseph Vernet** (1714–89).

Musée Angladon★
5 r. Laboureurs. 🕐*Open Jan Wed–Sun 1–6pm; Feb–Mar Wed–Sun 1–6pm, Tue 2–5pm; Apr–Dec Tue–Sun 1–6pm, public holidays 2–5.30pm.* ✆6€.
✆*04 90 82 29 03. www.angladon.com.*
This lovely 18C mansion was acquired in 1977 by the Avignon painters Jean Angladon-Dubrujeaud (1906–79) and his wife Paulette Martin (1905–88) in order to display their art collections. It contains several paintings by Cézanne,

Sisley, Manet, Derain, Picasso, Modigliani and Foujita. Van Gogh's *Train Carriages* (1888), painted during the artist's stay in Arles, is his only work to be found in Provence today.

On the first floor, you will find a collection of furniture and paintings: a Renaissance dining room, an 18C library with paintings by Joseph Vernet; a Chinese salon, famous for its collection of porcelain (dating from the reign of Emperor Kangxi, 1661–1722) and the studio where the couple's own work is exhibited.

Musée Lapidaire★

65 r. de la République. &. ◯*Open Wed–Mon 10am–6pm.* ◯*Closed 1 Jan, 1 May, 25 Dec.* ◉*2€ (7€ with Musée Calvet).* ℘*04 90 85 75 38. www.musee-lapidaire.org.*

Located in the former chapel of the 17C Jesuit College, this building has a unique nave and is flanked by side galleries where you will find displays of sculpture and stone carvings that together represent the different civilisations that left their mark on the region.

You will encounter the "Tarasque" of Noves, a man-eating monster that is a part of the Celtic bestiary collection. There are a number of statues: Greek, Greco-Roman (a remarkable copy of Praxiteles' *Apollo the Python killer*) and local (Gallic warriors from Vachères). Also, sculpted portraits of emperors (Marcus Aurelius, Tiberius), low reliefs (relief of Cabrières d'Aigues representing a towing scene), sarcophagi and a remarkable series of masks from Vaison.

Musée Louis-Vouland★

17 r. Victor-Hugo. ◯*Open May–Oct Tue–Sat 10am–noon, 2–6pm, Sun 2–6pm; Nov–Apr Tue–Sat 2–6pm.* ◯*Closed 1 Jan, 1 May, 25 Dec.* ◉*4€.* ℘*04 90 86 03 79. www.vouland.com.*

The museum contains a decorative arts collection that concentrates on 18C French **furnishings**: a commode signed by Migeon, an inlaid backgammon table, a money-changer's desk, and an amusing travelling table service stamped with the Countess du Barry's coat of arms.

A fine collection of porcelain and **faience**★ is displayed in two rooms; there are many examples of Moustiers and Marseille wares. Flemish and Gobelins (*Diana the Huntress*, pastoral scenes) **tapestries** hang on the walls. The Far Eastern art collection consists of a number of Chinese vases and plates and ivory polychrome statues. Two galleries are dedicated to the works of Provençal painters.

EXCURSIONS
Villeneuve-lez-Avignon★

▷ *On the Rhône's south (right) bank. Leave Avignon via the bridge pont Édouard Daladier, on the N 100, towards Nîmes.* ℰ*See Villeneuve-lez-Avignon.*

Château de Barbentane★★

9.5km/6mi SW on the N 570, then right on the D 35.
℮*See Château de BARBENTANE.*

Les Alpilles to the Durance

About 2hr. Leave Avignon via the D 571.

Châteaurenard

Of the feudal castle, once belonging to a nobleman named Reynard, only two towers remain on the hill. At its foot, the town has become an important market handling the produce harvested from local market gardens and fruit farms. The two towers house a **Regional History Museum** (◯*open May–Sept Tue–Sat 10am–noon, 2.30–6.30pm, Sun 2.30–6.30pm, Oct–Apr Sat–Thu 3–5pm;* ◉*2€;* ℘*04 90 24 25 50).* From the top of one, the Tour du Griffon, is a fine **panorama**★.

▷ *Head east along the D 28.*

Noves

Noves is an old town with narrow streets, medieval gateways (Porte d'Agel and Porte Aurose) and a 12C church.

▶ *Exit Noves on N 7 for Avignon; after passing the motorway turn right towards Cavaillon. The signpost to the charter house of Bonpas is on the left-hand side of the road.*

Chartreuse de Bonpas

Guided tours (1hr) Mon–Fri 10am–12.30pm, 2–6.30pm, Sat–Sun 10am–7pm. 7€. 04 90 23 67 98. www.louis-bernard.com.

ADDRESSES

STAY

La Ferme – *110 chemin des Bois, Île de la Barthelasse, 5km/3mi N. 04 90 27 15 47. Closed Mon lunch, Wed lunch.* Country-style dining room with beams, fireplace and old stone can be found at this haven of peace. Shaded terrace. 20 guest rooms.

Bagatelle – *25 allées Antoine Pinay, Île de la Barthelasse. 4 90 86 30 39. www.campingbagatelle. com. 10 rooms for 2–4 people at the hotel, 230 placements at the campsite. Prices vary according to accommodation type (camping/half-board/hotel, etc.)* Large campground with a separate hotel. Great setting on a tiny island near Pont St Benezet.

Boquier – *6 r. du Portail Boquier. 04 90 82 94 11. www.hotel-boquier.com. 12 rooms. 8€.* Each room is individually and tastefully decorated, housing between one and four people, depending on the room.

Hôtel Bristol – *44 cours J.-Jaurès. 04 90 16 48 48. www.bristol-hotel-avignon.com. 11 rooms. 11€. Closed 15 Dec–14 Jan.* Situated on the main avenue of the walled city. Spacious and sensibly functional rooms, most overlook the inside courtyards.

Chambre d'hôte Villa Agapè – *13 r. Agricol. 04 90 85 21 92. www.villa-agape.com. 3 rooms. Closed 1–15 May, Jul, Feb.* It's easy to forget the town-centre location of this attractive villa, with its verdant terrace and swimming pool. Occupying two 17C buildings, the hotel has elegant d´´cor and a lovely lounge-library.

Next to a chapel, the Templars built a church and monastery in the 13C. It enjoyed a period of prosperity in the 17C. The charterhouse today houses a wine-growing business: an excellent Côtes-du-Rhône can be sampled. From the terrace there is a clear view of the Alpilles and the River Durance, spanned by a 500m/0.3mi bridge.

▶ *Return to Avignon via N 7.*

Colbert – *7 r. Agricol Perdiguier. 04 90 86 20 20. www.avignon-hotel-colbert.com. Closed Nov–Feb. 15 rooms. 10€.* Simplicity and family home atmosphere in this discreet hotel. Bedrooms are decorated with Provenal colours, antiques and billboards. Don't miss the charming patio and its palm tree.

Hôtel de Blauvac – *11 r. de la Bancasse. 04 90 86 34 11. www.hotel-blauvac.com. 16 rooms. 8€.* The former home of the Marquis de Tonduly, Lord of Blauvac, in the 17C, is one of the best value-for-money hotels in town. Bedrooms and comfortable and full of character.

Mignon – *12 r. Joseph Vernet. 04 90 82 17 30 www.hotel-mignon. com. 16 rooms. 12€.* A small hotel in the heart of Avignon's historic centre, all rooms are soundproofed. Just 5min walk from the palace, 10min walk from the train station.

Banasterie – *11 r. de la Banasterie. 04 32 76 30 78. www. labanasterie.com. 5 rooms.* A Virgin with Child adorns the listed façade of this 16C edifice. A cosy, romantic interior. Rooms are named after chocolate, in tribute to the owner's passion!

Hôtel Cloître St-Louis – *20 r. Portail Boquier. 04 90 27 55 55. www.cloitre-saint-louis.com. 77 rooms. 16€. Restaurant.* Situated in 16C cloisters, part of this hotel was designed by the architect Jean Nouvel. The building uses a variety of materials including glass, steel and stone. Rooms are stylishly minimalist. Pool and solarium on the roof.

⊜⊜⊜⊜ **Hôtel du Palais des Papes** – 1 r. Gérard Philipe. ℘4 90 86 04 13. www. hotel-avignon.com. 27 rooms. Beautiful rooms and beautiful views at this luxurious, reasonably priced hotel in the heart of the historic centre of Avignon.

⊜⊜⊜⊜ **Maison d'hôte Lumani** – 37 r. du Rempart St-Lazare. ℘04 90 82 94 11. http://hoteldanieli-avignon.com. 5 rooms. ⊇12€. Artists are particularly welcome in this fine 19C manor house, which has an attractive courtyard shaded by a couple of hundred-year-old plane treets. Rooms and suites personalised with taste. Warm welcome.

⫣/ EAT

⊜ **Ginette et Marcel** – 25 pl. des Corps Saints. ℘04 90 85 58 70. More a bisto/cafétaria than a restaurant, you can grab a decent sandwich or salad here to take away.

⊜⊜ **Entrée des Artistes** – 1 pl. des Carmes. ℘04 90 82 46 90. Closed 23 Dec–2 Jan, three weeks in Aug, Sat–Sun. The dining room of this restaurant is decorated in the style of a Parisian bistro, with old posters and movie memorabilia. Tables are placed close together and the cooking is traditional. Service is friendly and there is a real scent of the Mediterranean in the air.

⊜⊜ **L'Ami Voyage... en compagnie** – 5 r. Prevot. ℘04 90 82 41 51. French cuisine is served at this cute place set in an old library. An air of elegance reigns here.

⊜⊜ **Le Jardin de la Tour** – 9 r. de la Tour. ℘04 90 85 66 50. www.jardindela tour.fr. Closed Sun–Mon. Situated near the ramparts, this restaurant has a lovely garden. Very agreeable Provençal cuisine.

⊜⊜ **L'Isle Sonnante** – 7 r. Racine. ℘04 90 82 56 01. Closed 3–9 Mar, last week Jun, 26 Oct–19 Nov, lunch in Aug, Sun, Mon. This restaurant near the town hall is proud of its Rabelaisian name. The cosy interior combines rustic style with warm tones. Modern dishes inspired by the region.

⊜⊜ **Piedoie** – 26 r. 3-Faucons. ℘04 90 85 17 32. Closed last week Aug, last week Nov, Feb school holidays, Mon off season, Wed. Beams, parquet flooring and white walls hung with contemporary paintings for the décor and creative cuisine based on market produce. A family atmosphere.

⊜⊜–⊜⊜⊜ **Christian Étienne** – 10 r. Mons. ℘04 90 86 16 50. www.christian-etienne.fr. Historically charged setting in 13C and 14C buildings adjoining the Palais des Papes. Here the chef produces fine cuisine that pays tribute to the Provence of his birth.

⊜⊜⊜ **Le Grand Café** – La Manutention, rue des Escaliers Ste Anne. ℘04 90 86 86 77. www.legrandcafe-avignon.com. Closed Jan, Sun and Mon. Backing onto the buttresses of the Palais des Papes, these old barracks have become an essential part of local life. Locals and tourists all flock here to savour inventive cooking with a Provençal accent. There is also an attractive terrace.

⊜⊜⊜ **Le Moutardier du Pape** – 15 pl. du Palais-des-Papes. ℘04 90 85 34 76. www.restaurant-moutardier.fr. Closed 6–25 Jan, 24 Nov–19 Dec, and Wed from Oct–Mar. This 18C building, listed in France's National Heritage, makes an exceptional setting for a simple, fresh meal. There is a pleasant atmosphere, both in the bistro room, where frescoes depict the story of "The Pope's mustard maker", and on the terrace facing the Palais des Papes.

⊜⊜⊜–⊜⊜⊜⊜ **D'Europe** – 12 pl. Crillon. ℘04 90 14 76 76. www.heurope. com. Closed 22 Feb–9 Mar, 2–31 Aug, 22–30 Nov, 2–9 Jan, Sun–Mon. Elegant 16C mansion with refined décor in the centre of Avignon. Classic dining rooms serve delicious traditional cuisine and there is a pleasant terrace with a fountain. 41 rooms, 3 suites.

⊜⊜⊜–⊜⊜⊜⊜ **L'Essentiel** – 2 r. Petite-Fusterie. ℘04 90 85 87 12. www.restaurantlessentiel.com. Closed Sun. Thie restaurant focuses on the "essential", delighting guests with its generous cuisine, full of sunny French and Italian flavours. Modern décor.

⊜⊜⊜–⊜⊜⊜⊜ **La Mirande** – 4 pl. Amirande. ℘04 90 85 93 93. www.la-mirande.fr. Closed 5 Jan–3 Feb, Tue–Wed. An 18C Provençal décor, antiques, ornaments and a profusion of refined detail set the stunning scene of La Mirande. Inventive menu and appealing terrace-garden. 20 rooms, 1 suite.

🍷 NIGHTLIFE

La Cave Breysse – *41 r. des Teinturiers. ✆04 32 74 25 86. http://cavesbreysse. blogspot.com. Closed Sun.* A very popular wine bar, this is a nice place to enjoy a well-priced glass of wine or an apéritif, and to take in the night, the ambiance and the festivities.

Café In et Off – *pl. du Palais-des-Papes. ✆04 90 85 48 95. Closed mid-Nov–late Feb.* Don't miss the only café that enjoys unbeatable views of the Palais des Papes. The interior is not lacking in appeal but the terrace is definitely the highpoint of this café.

Cloître des Arts – *83 r. Joseph-Vernet. ✆04 90 85 99 04. Open Mon–Sat 7am– 1.30am (during the festival 7am–3am). Closed the first fortnight of Jan.* Sixty varieties of beer from all over the world and a relaxed atmosphere attract beer enthusiasts of all ages, whether among friends or with family.

Woolloomooloo – *16 bis r. des Teinturiers. ✆04 90 85 28 44. www.woolloo.com. Closed 23–25 Dec.* Bearing a long, wild cry for a name, this bar-restaurant nevertheless occupies the very civilised site of a former printing works in the oldest street of the city. The myriad objects brought back by the owner from his worldwide travels adorn this place. Everything from the musical evenings in the bar to the exotic dishes (always using fresh produce from the market) evokes travel. Regular art exhibitions and music.

🎭 SHOWTIME

Le Rouge Gorge – *10 bis r. Peyrolerie. ✆04 90 14 02 54. Closed Sun, Jul–Aug.* The only cabaret in Avignon, the Rouge Gorge, modestly sheltered by the Palais des Papes, unveils the sensual charms of its show every Friday and Saturday, while two Sundays a month there is an operetta lunch. During the week the atmosphere remains lively with numerous themed evenings (Corsican, Latino, Oriental).

🛒 SHOPPING

Markets – **Les Halles Centrales**, *pl. Pie*, traditional covered market Tue–Sun. **Flower market** Sat in *place des Carmes*. **Fair** Sat and Sun, *rempart St-Michel*. **Flea market** Sun in *place des Carmes*.

Honey – **Miellerie des Butineuses**, *189 r. de la Source, St-Saturnin-lès-Avignon. ✆04 90 22 47 52. www.miellerie.fr.* Honey, pollen, and royal jelly, as well as honey-based products.

Chocolate – **Puyricard**, *33 r. Joseph-Vernet. ✆04 90 85 96 33. www.puyricard.fr. Closed 3–17 Aug.* Chocolate lovers go no further: here you'll find some 92 varieties of chocolate in all its possible forms.

Lavender – **Lavande & Co – Pure Lavande** – *61 r. Grande Fusterie. ✆04 90 14 70 05.* A shop full of lavender cosmetics along with demonstrations and information videos.

Home décor – **Terre è Provence** – *26 r. de la République . ✆04 90 86 31 59.* In the same family for several generations, this shop is dedicated to all that is Provence : table settings, textiles with Provençal prints, pottery and porcelain.

🏃 LEISURE ACTIVITIES

👥 Avignon by boat – *CroisiEurope. ✆03 88 76 44 44. www.croisieurope.com.* Audioguide tours from 1hr30 to 4hr of Avignon and along the Rhône.

Coach excursion – **Provence Vision (Cars Lieutaud)** – *36 bd St-Roch. ✆04 90 86 36 75. www.cars-lieutaud.fr. or make reservations at the tourist office.* Offers half- and full-day excursions from Avignon to the Camargue, Pont du Gard, Fontaine-de-Vaucluse, the Alpilles, a lavender tour and a wine tour including Châteauneuf-du-Pape.

👥 Sightseeing train – *Mid-Mar–Jun, Sept–Oct 10am–7pm; Jul–Aug 10am– 8pm. ∞7€ (child 4€). ✆06 11 35 06 66. www.petittrainavignon.com.* Guided visit through Avignon (40min). Departs from place du Palais des Papes.

Trips on the Rhône – "Grands Bateaux de Provence" (*✆04 90 85 62 25. www. avignon-et-provence.com/mireio*) organises several full-day round trip boat outings from Avignon along the Rhône to destinations including Arles, Châteauneuf-du-Pape and the Camargue.

EVENTS

Festival d'Avignon – Every July. It promotes France's cultural life through theatre, dance, lectures, exhibitions and concerts in and around Avignon. *Bureau du Festival d'Avignon, Cloître St-Louis, 20 r. du Portail-Boquier. Information ℘04 90 27 66 50. Reservations ℘04 90 14 14 14. www.festival-avignon.com.* Festival programmes are confirmed in mid-May and from the first two weeks of June

onwards it is also possible to make reservations online *(www.festival-avignon.com)*, at FNAC booking counters and at the main office.

Booking "Festival Off" – The programme for Avignon's Fringe Festival, on at the same time, is available mid-June. *℘04 90 85 13 08. www.avignonleoff.com.*

Hivernales d'Avignon – This contemporary dance festival takes place during two weeks in July. *℘04 90 82 33 12. www.hivernales-avignon.com.*

Animo Nature – *Early Oct at Parc des Expositions d'Avignon. ℘04 90 84 02 04. www.animo-nature.com.* The largest animal show in France.

Carpentras★

Vaucluse

This town continues to thrive as an active agricultural centre. You can witness this first-hand with a visit to the weekly market every Friday morning.

A BIT OF HISTORY

Market centre for a Celtic-Ligurian tribe, then a Gallo-Roman city, and a bishopric, which was temporarily moved to Venasque, Carpentras blossomed when the popes came to Provence. Pope Clement V stayed here frequently from 1309 to 1314, as did the cardinals. Capital of the Comtat Venaissin in 1320, the town profited from papal munificence. It expanded and protected itself, under Innocent VI, with powerful ramparts consisting of 32 towers and 4 gates, demolished in the 19C. With Avignon, Cavaillon and Isle-sur-la-Sorgue, it had a Jewish ghetto up until the Revolution. The most famous local figure was the 18C Bishop Malachie d'Inguimbert, benefactor and founder of the hospital (Hôtel-Dieu), who also founded, in 1745, the famous library named after him, the Bibliothèque Inguimbertine.
Carpentras grew prosperous from the production of madder, a dye-plant introduced in 1768, and the surrounding plain became a fertile garden when a

- ▶ **Population:** 27 451.
- **Michelin Map:** 332: D-9.
- **Info:** 97 place du 25-Août-1944, Carpentras. ℘04 90 63 00 78. www.carpentras-ventoux.com.
- **Location:** The best view of the town is by arriving on the D 950 from Orange (24km/12.4mi to the NW).
- P **Parking:** Free parking on allée des Platanes.

canal, a branch of the Durance, was built in the 19C, enabling the area to be irrigated.

✎ WALKING TOUR
THE OLD TOWN
Allow 3hr. Start south of town in place Aristide Briand.

Hôtel-Dieu
pl. Aristide Briand. ✎ Guided tours of the hospital and pharmacy Apr–Oct. ℘04 90 63 00 78.
This majestic building housing the former hospital dates from the 18C. To the left of the chancel, the Baroque chapel houses the tomb of Monseigneur d'Inguimbert, the hospital's founder. The Hôtel-Dieu was built outside the city wall, to the south, so that the sick

inmates were not subject to the foul air of the city. The tour includes a visit to the **pharmacy**★, largely in its original state, which contains cabinets painted with landscapes and amusing figures, in which there is a large collection of Moustiers faïence (glazed earthenware) jars.

▷ *Cross place du 25-Août-1944 and enter the city along rue de la République, a pedestrian street.*

In place Ste-Marthe note the fine 17C and 18C **Classical façade** to the right along rue Moricelly, to the left the **Chapelle du Collège** *(r. du Collège; ℘04 90 60 22 36)*, built in the Jesuit style. It houses contemporary art exhibits.

▷ *Continue along rue de la République, into place du Général-de-Gaulle.*

Cathédrale St-Siffrein★
r. St-Siffrein. ○*Open daily 7.30am–noon, 2–6.30pm (except for Mass).* ℘*04 90 63 08 33.*
The cathedral was started in 1404, on the orders of Pope Benedict XIII of Avignon, and is a good example of the southern Gothic style. It was finished in the early 16C, and its façade was completed in the 17C with the Classical doorway. Inside, the balcony on the nave's end wall

connects with the bishop's apartments, and from the small room above the first bay he could follow services.

Palais de Justice
pl. du Général-de-Gaulle. ●*Guided tours during school holidays.* ℘*04 90 63 00 78.*
Adjoining the cathedral is the old bishop's palace from the 17C, which now houses the law courts. The halls are decorated with French-style painted ceilings and a frieze of canvases painted in the 17C.

▷ *Take a right and go along the south side of the cathedral.*

Note the cathedral's Gothic south door (late 15C), known as the **Porte Juive**★ or Jewish door, after the Jewish converts who passed through it to be baptised.

▷ *Continue around the cathedral's east end via rue de la Poste to reach place d'Inguimbert.*

Near the east end of the present church are the remains of the original Romanesque cathedral surmounted by an ornate dome (from the railing, look up to see the twisted column topped by a historiated capital).

Medicine cabinets in the Hôtel-Dieu

S. Sauvignier/MICHELIN

Tour de l'Horloge

S. Sauvignier/MICHELIN

Arc de Triomphe

pl. d'Inguimbert.

The Roman municipal arch behind the law courts was probably built in 1C. Its damaged decorations are particularly interesting on the east face, where two prisoners are chained to a tree hung with military trophies.

▷ *Take rue d'Inguimbert to the left, past place du Colonel Mouret, then turn right into rue Raspail.*

This road traces the line of the old city walls.

▷ *After 50m/55yd turn left onto rue des Frères-Laurens.*

After running alongside the chapelle des Visitandines (16C), the street comes to some steps, from the top of which there is a good view of the **Auzon valley** with Dentelles de Montmirail in the distance (&see Dentelles de MONTMIRAIL).

▷ *At the bottom of the steps, take bd. Leclerc to the right.*

Porte d'Orange

pl. Porte d'Orange. ⟐⟐*Guided tours during school holidays.* &*04 90 63 00 78.*

North of the old town centre, this gateway was one of four fortified gateways leading into Carpentras. It is 26m/85ft high, and is all that remains of the fortified wall punctuated by 32 towers built at the end of the 14C.

▷ *Take rue de la Porte d'Orange again and turn left into rue des Halles.*

Rue des Halles

This street is lined with shopping arcades, making it an ideal place for refuge from the heat of summer. Note the **Tour de l'Horloge** (Clock Tower) at the entrance to the street, a remnant of the first town hall (15C).

For a better view of the clock tower, go into the courtyard terrace of the Atelier de Pierre restaurant *(access via rue du Château).* Further on, **passage Boyer** opens off to the right. This glass-covered passage was built in 1848 by a group of unemployed members of the national workshops, *Ateliers Nationaux.*

▷ *At the far end of passage Boyer turn left onto rue d'Inguimbert. This leads into place Maurice Charretier, standing in the place of the old Jewish ghetto. Note the* **façade** *of the synagogue on the right.*

Synagogue★

pl. Maurice Charretier. ⟐*Open Mon–Thu 10am–noon, 3–5pm, Fri 10am–noon, 3–4pm.* ⟐⟐*Guided tours during school holidays.* ⟐*Closed Jewish holidays.* ⟐4€. &*04 90 63 39 97.*

The synagogue, dating from 1367, was rebuilt in the 18C. On the first floor is the panelled sanctuary, simple yet richly decorated. On the ground floor is the oven for baking unleavened bread. In the basement is the pool, dating from the 14C, for women's purification rites.

▷ *Rejoin rue des Halles and walk around the town hall into rue Bidauld.*

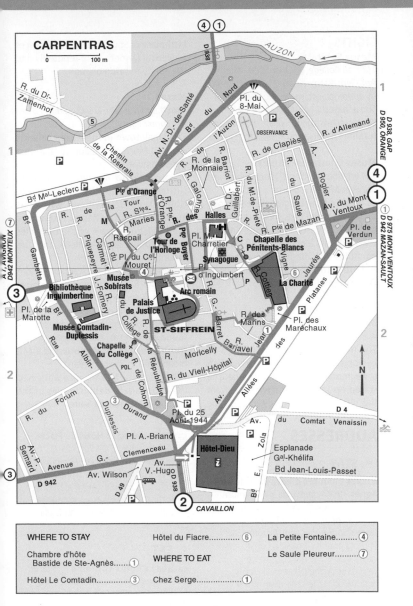

Rue Bidauld leads down to the **Chapelle des Pénitents Blancs**, a 17C chapel with a triangular front door.

▶ *Take rue Cottier.*

La Charité
77 r. Cottier. ☎*04 90 63 46 35.*
Built in 1669 to shelter the poor, the building today houses temporary exhibitions in its cellars.

▶ *Head to place des Maréchaux, turn right, and rejoin rue des Marins.*

This street is lined with fine mansions, such as the Hôtel de Bassompierre with its caryatids.

▶ *Take rue Gaudibert-Barret to the left, an extension of rue Barjavel. Cross avenue Jean Jaurès to rejoin allée des Platanes and return to the Hôtel-Dieu.*

SIGHTS

Musée Sobirats
112 r. du Collège. ⏱Open Wed–Mon Apr–Sept 10am–noon, 2–6pm; Oct–Mar by appointment. ⬤2€ (no charge first Sun of month). 𝒫04 90 63 04 92.
Lovely reconstruction of an 18C mansion: furniture, faïences and tapistries.

Musée Comtadin-Duplessis
234 bd Albin Durand. ⏱Same hours and prices as Musée Sobirats.
One level displays regional mementoes, such as coins and seals, local headdresses and bells for cattle and sheep. Another level exhibits a collection of 16C–20C paintings including those by Parrocel, Rigaud and the Carpentras artists Duplessis and Laurens.

EXCURSIONS

Monteux
4.5km/3mi W via the D 942.
This market-garden centre was visited by Pope Clement V in the early 14C. A tower remains from the castle where he stayed. Also standing are two gates from the 14C ramparts. The town is also the birthplace of St Gentius, patron saint of Provençal farmers, who reputedly had the ability to bring on rain.

Mazan
7km/4.3mi N on the D 942, in the direction of Sault.
This small town in the Auzon valley is close to Mormoiron, Europe's largest gypsum quarry.
Sixty-six Gallo-Roman sarcophagi, surround the **churchyard** of the 12C Notre-Dame-de-Pareloup, which has an underground chapel. From here there is a fine **view**★ of the Dentelles de Montmirail, Mont Ventoux, and Lure mountain.
Near the church, the 17C Chapelle des Pénitents Blancs houses a **museum** *(r. Saint-Nazaire Mazan; ⏱open mid-Jun–mid-Sept Wed–Mon 2–7pm; 𝒫04 90 69 74 27)* exhibiting stone age articles found during the excavations on the south face of Mont Ventoux and a 14C bread oven in the courtyard.
The Château de Mazan, once witnessed the extravagant debaucheries of the notorious Marquis de Sade.

ADDRESSES

🛏 STAY

⬤⬤⬤ **Chambre d'hôte Bastide Ste-Agnès** – *1043 chemin de la Fourtrouse. 3km/2mi NE via D 974 for Bédoin and D 13 for Caromb. 𝒫04 90 60 03 01. www.sainte-agnes.com. 6 rooms. ⬤.*
This old country house is constructed in dry stone. It is hard not to be won over by the ochre bedrooms, antique floor tiles, the charm of the Provençal scented garden and tranquil atmosphere. Pretty swimming pool in what used to be the water cistern.

⬤⬤⬤–⬤⬤⬤⬤ **Hôtel Le Comtadin** – *65 bd Albin-Durand. 𝒫04 90 67 75 00. www.le-comtadin.com. Closed Feb holidays, 20 Dec–7 Jan, Sun Oct–Feb. 19 rooms. ⬤10€. Restaurant⬤⬤.*
This 18C building has been entirely renovated. The majority of the rooms are bright and well fitted out. Breakfast terved on the patio in summer.

⬤⬤⬤–⬤⬤⬤⬤ **Hôtel du Fiacre** – *153 r. de la Vigne. 𝒫04 90 63 03 15. www.hotel-du-fiacre.com. 18 rooms. ⬤10€.* This 18C building in the old town has retained its original bourgeois atmosphere. Rooms are comfortable and charming and there is a pleasant patio-terrace.

🍴 EAT

⬤⬤⬤ **La Petite Fontaine** – *13 pl. du Col.-Mouret. 𝒫04 90 60 77 83. Closed 1 week in Feb, Wed, Sun.* Small dining room decorated with several paintings on the theme of Provence. Food is traditional Provenal cuisine. You can eat lunch on the terrace.

⬤⬤⬤ **Le Saule Pleureur** – *145 chemin de Beauregard, 84179 Monteux, 23km/14.3mi NW. 𝒫04 90 62 01 35. www.le-saule-pleureur.com. Closed 5–12 Jan, 3–17 Mar, 27 Oct–10 Nov, Sat lunch, Sun eve, Mon.* On a busy road, this villa surrounded by a garden has a contemporary dining room and veranda. Creative cuisine.

🍽️🍽️🍽️🍽️ **Château de Mazan** – *pl. Napoléon, Mazan, 21km/13mi N. 𝒞04 90 69 62 61. www.chateaudemazan.com. Closed lunch, 3 Jan–6 Mar, Mon (Nov–Apr), Tue.* Arranged in two charming lounges and a covered terrace, patrons can eat and rest in the house famous for its previous owner, the Marquis de Sade.

🍽️🍽️🍽️🍽️ **Chez Serge** – *90 r. Cottier. 𝒞04 90 63 21 24. www.chez-serge.com. Closed Sun, Mon.* The décor is eclectic and so is the food, varying from delicious traditional Provençal to the new and surprising. The shaded terrace fills up shortly after noon.

🛒 SHOPPING

Market – *r. de Carpentras. Fri 8am–12.30pm.* The Carpentras market has produce of such fine quality that it was elected "marché exceptionnel" in 1996. There is a very colourful atmosphere, conducive to finding good bargains.

Truffle Market – *pl. Artistide Briand. Fri 8am–noon. Closed late Nov–Feb.* The region around Carpentras supplies over half of France's truffles and this is one of the region's most important markets.

Chocolaterie Clavel – *30 r. Porte-d'Orange. 𝒞04 90 67 31 30.* A major **Truffle Market** – *place Artistide Briand* personality in Carpentras, René Clavel never ceases in his search for perfection in the creation of new chocolates, the most celebrated of which are the *rocailles de Provence*. Other specialities worth trying are the lavender truffles and amusing figures made of marzipan.

Confiserie Bono – *280 allée Jean-Jaurès. 𝒞04 90 63 04 99. www.confiseriebono.fr. Closed Sun.* Established in 1925, Bono is a master of the Provençal confectioners' tradition. Using ancient techniques, they make handmade candied fruits, a wide range of jams and conserves, including lemon.

Berlingots

S. Sauvignier/MICHELIN

Nougats Silvain – *rte de Venasque, 84210 St-Didier. 𝒞04 90 66 09 57. www.nougats-silvain-freres.fr. Closed Jan, Mon (Feb–Apr).* The Silvain brothers invite you to share their passion, with a show and tasting. They call themselves "nougat farmers" because they grow their own almonds and collect their own honey.

Confiserie du Mont-Ventoux – *1184 av. Dwight Eisenhower. 𝒞04 90 63 05 25. www.berlingots.net. Closed Sun–Mon.* You will find the famous *berlingot* everywhere in town, but in this shop a rainbow of flavours awaits you. Stop by in the morning to watch these treats being made.

EVENTS

Estivales – *64 r. Vigne. 𝒞04 90 60 46 00.* This festival of music, dance, theatre and fine arts takes place during the second half of Jul.

Truffle and Wine Festival – Come tempt yourself with everything relating to truffles, fine food and wine. Tastings, cooking demonstrations and more on the first Sun in Feb.

TOURS

Guides conduct 90min tours Apr–Sept daily 10.30am, 3.30pm, 5pm. Enquire at the tourist office, which also provides a map for a self-guided tour.

Fontaine-de-Vaucluse

Vaucluse

Vallis Clausa (the "enclosed valley"), from which this *département* gets its name, is best known for its fountain, the famous resurgent spring that rises in a picturesque site dear to Petrarch and is the source of the River Sorgue. It is in winter or spring, during the floods, that the stream is at its most dramatic, when the water level rises 150cu m/39 625 gal per second. By dramatic contrast, in the summer or autumn, the flow is reduced to a mere 4.5cu m/1 188.7 gal per second.

A BIT OF HISTORY
Petrarch

On 6 April 1327 in an Avignon church, this great poet and humanist – a familiar member of the pontifical court in Avignon – met the lovely **Laura de Noves**, with whom he fell passionately in love. However, this love remained platonic: Laura was married and virtuous, but she inspired many of the poet's works throughout his life. Ten years after his first meeting with her, Petrarch, who was only 33 years old, retired to Vaucluse. He remained here for 16 years seeking peace in the tranquil Sorgue valley. During his stay Laura died of the plague in Avignon in 1348.

▶ **Population:** 671.
♿ **Michelin Map:** 332: D-10.
🛈 **Info:** Chemin de la Fontaine, Fontaine-de-Vaucluse. ☎04 90 20 32 22. www.oti-delasorgue.fr.

The poet died 26 years later in Arquà Petrarca near Padua. He never forgot her during those long years.

Fontaine-de-Vaucluse★★

30min return on foot. From place de la Colonne, where a commemorative column of the fifth centenary (1304–1804) of Petrarch's birth stands, take chemin de la Fontaine, which climbs gently, following the River Sorgue.

The Fontaine-de-Vaucluse is one of the most powerful resurgent springs in the world. It is the outlet of an important underwater river fed by rainwater draining through the Vaucluse plateau pitted with numerous chasms *(avens)*, through which the speleologists have searched for the underground Sorgue. The exploration of the fountain's chasm began as early as the 19C and continues to this day. The last record was 315m/1 034ft deep and was achieved in August 1985 with the help of a small remote-controlled submarine equipped with cameras.

The cave from which the River Sorgue emerges is at the foot of a rocky cirque

Fontaine-de-Vaucluse

S. Sauvignier/MICHELIN

formed by high cliffs. In front of it stands a pile of rocks through which the waters filter. During heavy flooding the water reaches the level of the fig trees growing in the rock above the cave mouth, before racing away over the rocks in a vivid green fury of tumbling foaming water.

SIGHTS

Musée-Bibliothèque Pétrarque

Rive Gauche de la Sorgue. ○*Open Wed–Mon Apr–May, 1–15 Oct 10am–noon, 2–6pm; Jun–Sept 10am–12.30pm, 1.30–6pm; 16–31 Oct and All Saints' Day 10am–noon, 2–5pm.* ○*Guided tours year round by appointment.* ○*Closed 1 May, 25 Dec.* ⊕*3.50€.* ℘*04 90 20 37 20. www.vaucluse.fr/569-le-musee-petrarque.htm.*

This library-museum is located at the heart of the village in a house said to be built on the site of the house where Petrarch once lived. Upstairs, there is an exhibition of drawings and prints (16C–19C) relating to the poet and his life, as well as a collection of old editions of his writings. On the ground floor there is a rotating display of works by artists linked with the site of the Fontaine-de-Vaucluse and of writings by René Char illustrated by Zao Wou Ki, Braque and Vieira da Silva.

Écomusée du Gouffre

Chemin du Gouffre. ♿○*Guided tours (45min) Feb–mid-Nov 9.30am–12.30pm, 2–6.30pm; last visit 1hr before closing.* ⊕*5.50€.* ℘*04 90 20 34 13.*

The underground museum presents the **Casteret collection**★ of limestone concretions (calcite, gypsum, aragonite) assembled over 30 years of underground exploration by the speleologist. Different sites have been reconstructed: stalactite and stalagmite caves, chasm and rubble, rivers, waterfalls, natural dams and caves with human imprints.

Musée d'Histoire (1939–45)

chemin du Gouffre. ♿○*Open Wed–Mon Apr–May and 1–15 Oct 10am–noon, 2–6pm; Jun–Sept 10am–6pm; 16–31 Oct and All Saints' Day 10am–noon, 2–5pm; Nov–Dec Sat–Sun 10am–noon, 2–5pm (Mar 6pm).* ○*Closed 1 May, 25 Dec.* ⊕*3.50€.* ℘*04 90 20 24 00. www.vaucluse.fr/549-musee-d-histoire-1939-45.htm.*

This history museum, sited in a plain and functional building, offers a historical, literary and artistic view of the years 1939–45 within a modern framework. The first section of the museum describes daily life in occupied France; the second, the activity of the Resistance in the Vaucluse *département*, through the testimonies of those involved in or observing events during the "dark years". An audiovisual support helps to situate local history within the national context.

EXCURSION

Saumane-de-Vaucluse

4km/2.5mi NW. Leave Fontaine-de-Vaucluse on the D 25, then turn right onto the D 57.

The road follows the hillside across the limestone slopes of the Vaucluse mountains, before arriving at this village perched above the Sorgue valley. Here stands the 15C castle belonging to the family of the **Marquis de Sade**. From the square, which contains a 16C stone cross, there is a **view** across the Sorgue valley, the Luberon and the Alpilles.

Cabrières-d'Avignon

5km/3mi S on the D 100A.
℗*Leave the car in the car park by the town hall.*

The Château des Adhémar (○*closed to the public*) was built in the 11C and partially rebuilt in the 17C in a Renaissance style. It was the backdrop to the tragic events of 20 and 21 April 1545, when Vaudois Lutheran "heretics", who had taken refuge there under the leadership of local Eustache Marron, were massacred by Meynier d'Oppède's Roman Catholic forces.

Walk around the château (*go along rue du Vieux-Four then go left up chemin Eustache-Marron at the edge of open countryside*) to see the ramparts linking the five towers, vestiges of the original fortifications.

L'Isle-sur-la-Sorgue

Vaucluse

L'Isle-sur-la-Sorgue is set at the foot of the Plateau de Vaucluse. The branches of the River Sorgue and the avenues lined with plane trees add coolness to this charming site, which is particularly popular among antique dealers. It is also well known for its Sunday morning market. For a long time the town was a very active industrial centre: weaving, dyeing, tanning and paper, grain and oil mills flourished; some ten wheels set the beat of this bustling town.

SIGHTS
Roues à Eau
Near place Gambetta, at the corner of the Caisse d'Épargne's garden, is a wheel, similar to those which worked the silk factories and oil mills. Seven other old waterwheels still exist: one in place Émile-Char, two others in boulevard Victor-Hugo, three in rue Jean-Théophile and one on quai des Lices.

Hôpital
pl. des Frères Brun. ◷*Some areas are viewable. Ask at reception.* ⊗*No charge.* ℘*04 90 21 34 00.*

▶ **Population:** 18 015.
⌖ **Michelin Map:** 332: D-10.
▤ **Info:** place de la Liberté, L'Isle-sur-la-Sorgue. ℘04 90 38 04 78. www.oti-delasorgue.fr.
🅿 **Parking:** Paying car parks along the river.
☺ **Don't Miss:** Antique shops, Sunday morning market.

Admire in the hall the gilded wooden Virgin, the grand staircase embellished by an 18C wrought-iron banister, a chapel with 18C woodwork, and pharmacy with Moustiers faience pottery jars. An additional attraction is the peaceful garden, decorated with an 18C fountain.

EXCURSIONS
Le Thor
5km/3mi W along the N 100 for Avignon.
Once the capital of the white dessert grape, Chasselas, Le Thor has diversified its agricultural activities to include market gardening and tree and shrub growing.
The bridge over the Sorgue, the church and its precinct create a picturesque scene. Remaining from the Middle Ages are the ruins of the ramparts and the belfry.

L'Isle-sur-la-Sorgue

©Cynoclub/Dreamstime.com

Grotte de Thouzon

3km/2mi N of Thor on the D 16.
🕏Guided tours (45min) Jul–Aug daily
10am–6pm; Apr–Jun, Sept–Oct daily
10am–noon, 2–6pm; Mar Sun 2–6pm;
last visit 30min before closing.
∞6.90€. ℘04 90 33 93 65.
www.grottes-thouzon.com.

The cave opens at the foot of the hill crowned by the ruins of Thouzon castle and a monastery. It was discovered in 1902 by chance after a blast on the site of a former quarry.

The visitor walks 230m/755ft along the bed of the old underground river, which carved this gallery, to a not very deep chasm. On the cave roof, which rises to 22m/72ft, are delicate stalactites of rare quality. In addition the cave presents oddly shaped, beautifully coloured concretions.

ADDRESSES

🏠 STAY

😊😊😊 **Chambre d'hôte Le Mas de la Coudoulière** – *1854 rte de Carpentras. 2km/1.2mi north of Isle-sur-la-Sorgue via D 938 for Carpentras. ℘04 90 38 16 35. 6 rooms.* This hotel is situated in what was originally a 17C monastery that used to grow hemp and madder. Rooms have been decorated in the spirit of bygone times. The evening meal is served in the vaulted dining room or under the hundred-year-old chestnut tree in the summertime. Self-contained accommodation is also available.

🍴 EAT

😊😊 **Le Carré d'Herbes** – *13 av. des Quatre Otages. ℘04 90 38 23 97. Closed Jan, Tue–Wed, Thu lunch.* This small restaurant is located in a courtyard surrounded by antique shops. It is unusually decorated with red walls, an oxidised metal ceiling, wooden seats and a terrace in the aviary. Provençal specialities on the menu.

😊😊😊 **L'Oustau de l'Isle** – *147 chemin du Bosquet. ℘04 90 20 81 36. www.restaurant-oustau.com. Closed 3 weeks in Nov, 3 weeks in Jan, Tue–Wed in winter (lunch in summer).* A stone's throw from the old town, this restaurant reflects the colours and flavours of Provence: painted furniture, brightly coloured tablecloths and southern-influenced dishes.

🍷 NIGHTLIFE

Au Rendez-vous des Marchands – *91 av. de la Libération. ℘04 90 20 84 60. www.antikfrance.com.* Is this an antique shop in a café or a café in an antique shop? It is hard to say where one ends and the other begins; what is certain is that this place is full of originality and charm. Terrace bordering the Sorgue.

Café de France – *14 pl. de la Liberté. ℘04 90 38 01 45.* This delightful café is a member of The Association of Historic Cafés of Europe. Take your pick from a choice of salads, sandwiches and other dishes you can enjoy on the terrace. The cerebral might enjoy „Philosophy Night" on the first Sun of each month.

🛒 SHOPPING

Le Village des Antiquaires de la Gare – *2 bis av. de l'Égalité. ℘04 90 38 04 57. Closed Tue–Fri.* This is one of the biggest antique centres in town: 80 dealers grouped together in an old weaving factory.

Bidal Alain – *2420 rte du Thor. ℘04 90 20 72 83. www.sculptures-bidal.com.* A haven for everything limestone from fountains to fireplaces.

Antique fairs – There is an antiques fair on Easter weekend and mid-Aug.

Les Délices du Luberon – *1 av. du Partage-des-Eaux. ℘04 90 20 77 37. www.delices-du-luberon.fr. Open daily.* This family-run business sells mouthwatering local produce including *tapenade*, aubergine caviar, sun-dried tomatoes, olive oil, honey, jam, etc.

Pernes-les-Fontaines★

Vaucluse

Located on the border of the Vaucluse plateau, Pernes-les-Fontaines was the capital of Comtat Venaissin (968–1320) before Carpentras. The town gets its name from the 40 or so fountains, in which it takes great pride. These decorate the numerous squares in its urban districts. Most of them were built in the middle of the 18C, following the discovery of a large spring near Chapelle St-Roch. The older fountains have since been restored. Like most of the towns on the Vaucluse plateau, Pernes-les-Fontaines has canning factories. Fruit – cherries, strawberries, melons, grapes – is especially abundant in the region.

▶ **Population:** 10 410.
Ⓖ **Michelin Map:** 332: D-10.
ⓘ **Info:** place Gabriel Moutte, Pernes-les-Fontaines. ☎04 90 61 31 04. www.ville-pernes-les-fontaines.fr.
Ⓟ **Parking:** Best to park in the car park near the tourist office.
Ⓓ **Don't Miss:** The fountains – there are 40 of them!

One of many fountains in town

S. Sauvignier/MICHELIN

WALKING TOUR

Allow 1hr for those wishing to explore the winding streets of the old town.

▷ *Start at the church of Notre-Dame de Nazareth.*

Notre-Dame de Nazareth

pl. Église Notre-Dame.
The oldest parts of the church date from the late 11C. Opposite, the willow-shaded River Nesque is spanned by an old bridge, which leads to the Porte Notre-Dame.

Porte Notre-Dame★

On one of the bridge's piles is the small 16C chapel of Notre-Dame-des-Grâces with its elegant cast-iron bell tower. On the left is the 17C covered market.

Fontaine du Cormoran

Quai de Verdun. This, the most interesting of the fountains in Pernes, owes its name to the cormorant with outspread wings which is perched on top of it. The base is decorated with low reliefs and masks.

▷ *Turn right onto rue Victor-Hugo, which runs parallel to the Nesque river. Take rue de Brancas and immediately turn right.*

Tour de l'Horloge

Montée du Donjon. Ⓞ*Open daily 10am–5pm (except in bad weather).* ☜*2€.* ☎*04 90 61 31 04.*
This keep was part of the fortified wall which protected the castle of the Counts of Toulouse. From the top of the clock tower there is a panorama to the west over the Comtat plain and the countryside around Avignon; in the background, to the north and east, the Dentelles de Montmirail and Mont Ventoux.

**PERNES
LES-FONTAINES**

WHERE TO STAY

Chambre d'hôte
Mas Pichony............①

WHERE TO EAT

Dame l'Oie........................①

Hôtel de Vichet ....**G**
Fontaine du Cormoran ...**E**
Hôtel de ville.................**H**

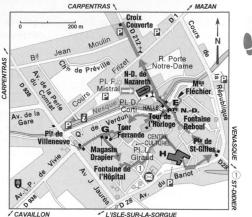

▷ *Continue down rue Victor-Hugo
where you will pass in front of the Clos
de Verdun, a miniscule park which
stands on the site of an old olive-press.*

Tour Ferrande

*r. Victor-Hugo. ⸙⸙Guided tours
(45min) Jul–Aug Mon–Fri 10am; rest of
the year by appointment with the tourist
office. ⸨2€. ☏04 90 61 31 04.*
This 13C tower overlooks a small square
which contains the Gigot fountain. Go
up a staircase to the third floor, which is
decorated with 13C frescoes depicting
the Virgin and Child, St Christopher and
Charles of Anjou.

▷ *Go to the end of rue Gambetta.*

Porte de Villeneuve

This 16C gate is flanked by two round,
machicolated towers.

▷ *Turn back and take rue de
la République on the right.*

On the corner of rue Gambetta and
rue de la République, the magasin
Drapier houses the Musée du Costume
Comtadin. Opposite, notice the 16C
Hôtel de Vichet with its wrought-iron
balcony.

▷ *Turn left onto rue Barreau.*

Fontaine de l'Hôpital

r. Barreau.

13C frescoes, Tour Ferrande

S. Sauvignier/MICHELIN

This fountain dates from 1760 and draws its name from its position opposite the Hôtel des Ducs de Berton, which was once a hospital.

▷ *Take the narrow rue de Brancas on your right.*

Hôtel de Ville
pl. Aristide Briand.
This 17C mansion once belonged to the Dukes of Brancas. The courtyard is further enhanced by a striking fountain and its vast portico (1750).

▷ *Turn left into rue du Bariot, which leads to Porte de St-Gilles.*

Porte de St-Gilles
This square tower was part of the 14C fortifications.

▷ *Cross the tower and continue towards rue Raspail.*

At no 214, set back on the right, lies the Hôtel de Jocas with its beautiful Louis XV doorway. Note the 17C Fontaine Reboul, also known as the "Grand' Font" (Big Fount), with its fish-scale ornamentation.

ADDRESSES

🛏 STAY

🍽🍽🍽 **Chambre d'hôte Mas Pichony**– *1454 rte de St-Didier.* ✆*04 90 61 56 11. www.maspichony.com. Closed Nov–Mar. 5 rooms.* 🚗🍴. From this 17C Provençal farmhouse you get a great view of Mont Ventoux: the house, which is surrounded by vineyards, is picture-postcard Provence. Rooms are alluring. Swimming pool.

🍴 EAT

🍽🍽 **Dame l'Oie – Le Troubadour** – *56 r. Troubadour-Durand.* ✆*04 90 61 62 43. Closed 15–end Feb, Tue in low season, Mon.* Built around a stone fountain surmounted by a fine goose, the yellow and white Provençal décor serves as a showcase for a delightful collection of white ceramic geese. Classic cuisine with a speciality known as *caprice de dame l'oie* and local wines.

Venasque★
Vaucluse

Built on a foothill of the Vaucluse plateau, Venasque dominates the Carpentras plain. The rich calcareous soil, benefiting from irrigation, nourishes vegetables and fruit that are distributed nationwide. The Ouvèze, Sorgue and Durance rivers have created vast, fertile alluvial plains that have brought prosperity to market towns such as Orange, Avignon, Cavaillon and Carpentras; some of these same towns have become very large dispatching centres.

A BIT OF HISTORY
The village was, before Carpentras, the Comtat's bishopric and gave its name to the Comtat Venaissin. Located between

▸ **Population:** 1 131.
⏿ **Michelin Map:** 332: D-10.
🛈 **Info:** Grand'Rue, Venasque. ✆04 90 66 11 66. www. tourisme-venasque.com.
⊛ **Don't Miss:** The Baptistry.
⏱ **Timing:** Allow 2hr.

the Rhône and Durance rivers and Mont Ventoux, the territory was under the Counts of Toulouse's rule; and like all the county's other possessions it was affected by the Albigensian heresy and united under the crown in 1271. It was ceded three years later to Pope Gregory X by Philip III, the Bold, and remained under papal authority until 1791 when it once again became part of France. This enclave had its own administration; its law courts were

Merovingian Baptistry

B. Kaufmann/MICHELIN

located at Carpentras, capital of the Comtat, having superseded Pernes-les-Fontaines in 1320. Made up of the rich Vaucluse Plain, Comtat Venaissin occupies the largest and most southerly basin of the Rhône Valley.

THE VILLAGE

Stroll through the peaceful streets of the village, among the artists' workshops (painters, potters and ceramicists) and the tastefully restored houses, often decorated with pergolas.

During the walk, admire **place des Comtes-de-Toulouse**, a reminder of the village's history. From **esplanade de la Planette** and **Tours Sarrasines**, remains of medieval fortifications, there are fine views to be had of Mont Ventoux and the Dentelles de Montmirail.

Baptistry★

Entrance right of the presbytery.

🕐*Open 5 Jan–5 Apr, 12 Oct–13 Dec 9.15am–noon, 1–5pm; 6 Apr–11 Oct 9am–noon, 1–6.30pm.* ⚙*3€; 2€ on 14 Jul, Fête Votive (in mid-Aug).* 🕿*04 90 66 62 01.*

The Baptistry, most likely from the 6C or the Merovingian period and remodelled in the 11C, is one of France's oldest religious buildings. The Greek cross plan, with groined vaulting over the centre square, has unequal arms ending in apsidal chapels, each oven-vaulted with blind arcading on slender marble columns with Antique or, in the case of the east apsidal chapel, Merovingian capitals. The hollow in the floor was for the font.

Église Notre-Dame

pl. de l'Eglise.

The church, which is connected to the Baptistry by a long corridor, contains a 17C carved altarpiece and a 15C Avignon School **Crucifixion★**.

EXCURSION

10km/6mi E on the D 4 towards Apt.

The **Route des Gorges** goes up the gorges through the **Forêt de Venasque**. After climbing 400m/1 312ft the road reaches Col de Murs pass (alt 627m/2 057ft). Beyond the pass there are views of the Apt basin and Roussillon.

ADDRESSES

🏠 STAY ⅋ EAT

⊜⊜ **Hotel Les Remparts** – *r. Haute.* 🕿*04 90 66 02 79. www.hotellesremparts. com. 8 rooms. Restaurant*⊜⊜⊜. *Closed 15 Nov–15 Mar.* A hotel and restaurant built on the old fortifications of this hill-top village, whose streets are pleasant to explore. Eat in one of the smart, colourful dining rooms, decorated with old cinema posters.

THE LUBERON

In some ways the Luberon is a microcosm of Provence itself, with artist-luring landscapes, a sunny Mediterranean climate, verdant farmland, and a rich, long history. In the 11C monks were drawn to the area and built their monasteries. As recently as the 1970s, people gravitated towards Luberon because of areas with communal ideals.

Tourists gravitate here for other reasons, primarily to see the quaint villages that are the highlight of the area. These centuries-old hamlets include Apt, Bonnieux, Gordes, Ménerbes, Roussillon and other well-known destinations. Most of these villages are more than 1 000 years old and have the architecture and history to keep the curious occupied as they explore the winding streets and steep staircases. Most villages have hardy perches, lookouts that allowed dwellers to protect and defend themselves during centuries of conflict. Visitors also value the pristine condition of Le Luberon, which offers many opportunities for hiking and biking.

Highlights

1 The mouthwatering Musée de la Boulangerie: **Bonnieux** (p267)

2 Baroque Provençal architecture at Synagogue et Musée Juif Comtadin: **Cavaillon** (p270)

3 Cemetery of the (literary) stars Lourmarin: **Le Luberon** (p279)

4 Former home of Marquis de Sade in **Lacoste** (p280)

5 Everything there is to know about wicker Musée de la Vannerie: **La Tour d'Aigues** (p293)

Picturesque Apt dates back to the 3C. Today it is known for crystallised fruit and preserves, lavender essence and truffles, all delectable delights you may find at the excellent Saturday market. While in Apt, stop at the Cathédrale Ste-Anne, the first sanctuary in France dedicated to Ste-Anne.

Bonnieux is a good home base for exploring the Luberon area, and makes it easy to reach other villages by car.

If you are in the Luberon for the produce, you must stop in Cavaillon, where melons and other fruits are harvested. Use caution when driving on the scenic Combe de Vidauque. But its hairpin turns are worth navigating thanks to the remarkable views afforded from the route. The Maison du Parc is particularly appealing for those who want to cycle through the area.

Gordes is oft cited as the region's prettiest village. Visit the Village des Bories to learn about the rural life that has thrived here over the ages. Abbaye de Sénanque can be seen from Gordes. Monks lived here in austerity and silence and you'll see that in the plain and un-ornamented buildings that make up the abbey.

Ménerbes was the setting for British author Peter Mayle's *A Year in Provence* books, but artist Pablo Picasso stayed here and sang the area's praises long before Mayle. Where else besides wine country could you go to the Musée du Tire-Bouchon, a museum devoted to the genius that is the corkscrew?

Le Luberon is a range of mountains (Petit Luberon and Grand Luberon) with both evergreens and deciduous plants and trees, and, of course, those legendary herbs of Provence growing in its soil. Be sure to see the bories, which are dry stone huts built into the limestone that keep a constant indoor temperature no matter what is happening outside. They were inhabited from the Iron Age to the 18C.

Roussillon is home to ochre rock quarries. The rock is used to create pigment used to paint everything from homes to pottery.

Ansouis

Vaucluse

Located between the River Durance and the Grand Luberon foothills, the town was built on the southern slope of a rocky spur crowned by a castle.

VISIT

Château★

pl. du Château. 🕭 *Guided tours (1hr) Apr–Dec Wed–Mon 2.30pm, 4pm.* ⊜*7€.* ℘*04 90 09 82 70. www.chateau-ansouis.com.*

At the beginning of the 12C the Barons of Ansouis built a medieval castle on the foundations of an old fortress. The castle has now been in the Sabran family for centuries. Stone steps and a ramp lead to a spacious chestnut walk, dominated by a monumental and harmonious façade in gold-coloured stone. The main door, lavishly decorated with pyramidal bosses and over which hangs the Sabran crest, is worthy of particular note. The coffer-vaulted grand staircase, dating from the Henri IV period, leads to the guardroom embellished with 17C–19C arms and armour.

The terrace boasts a beautiful view of the Durance gap and the Trévaresse range while the gardens are a delightful surprise.

Musée Extraordinaire

r. du Vieux Moulin. 🕐*Open daily Apr–Sept 2–7pm; Oct–Mar 2–6pm.* ⊜*3.50€.* ℘*04 90 09 82 64.*

The 15C vaulted cellars of this ancient building house a small museum devoted to underwater life. Works displayed are by painter, ceramicist and stained-glass artist **G Mazoyer**.

EXCURSIONS

Le Luberon★★★
🕭*See Le LUBERON*

Château Turcan: Musée de la Vigne et du Vin

Leave Ansouis heading towards La Tour-d'Aigues, then turn immediately right onto D 56 towards Pertuis. After

▶ **Population:** 1 105.
🕭 **Michelin Map:** 332: F-11 or 114 fold 2 or 528 fold 31; 🕭 *see Le LUBERON.*
🖽 **Info:** Place du Château, Ansouis. ℘04 90 09 86 98. www.tourisme-ansouis.com.
▣ **Location:** Between Loumarin (8km/5mi W) and La Tour-d'Aigues (8km/5mi E).
🅿 **Parking:** Car park at the entrance of the village.
🕐 **Timing:** Allow 1hr to visit the castle, before wandering around the village. Allow half a day if you want to visit the nearby museums.

2km/1.2mi, turn left (signposted) onto a gravelled track lined with cypress trees. 🕭🕐*Open Sept–Jun Mon–Tue and Thu–Sat 9.30am–noon, 2.30–6pm, Wed and Sun by appointment only; Jul–Aug Mon–Sat 9.30am–1pm, 2.30–7pm, Sun by appointment only.* 🕐*Closed 1 Jan, 1 May, 1 and 11 Nov, 25 Dec.* ⊜*3€.* ℘*04 90 09 83 33. www.chateau-turcan.com.* Established in the 1860s by Louis Turcan, a self-professed "pharmacist winegrower", this vineyard incorporates 25ha/62 acres of the Luberon landscape. The museum encompasses the history of wine and the tools that cultivate vines.

Château d'Ansouis

G. Magnin/MICHELIN

Apt

Vaucluse

The Roman colony of Julia Apt was a prosperous ancient city and a bishopric in the 3C. Today, Apt, a small bustling town in the Calavon Valley known for its crystallised fruit and preserves, lavender essence and truffles, is also the main centre for ochre mining in France. Apt is a good excursion centre for trips to the Luberon. A colourful, animated market is held here on Saturday mornings, where you can find a rich variety of Provençal produce, including organic *(bio)* delights. Apt is also the scene of a traditional pilgrimage that takes place on the last Sunday in July.

WALKING TOUR

Allow 1hr and at least 2hr on market days.

▷ *From place de la Bouquerie take rue de la République until you reach place du Septier, which is adorned with beautiful private residences. Go to place Carnot and turn right onto rue Ste-Anne.*

Cathédrale Ste-Anne

104 r. Cassin. Open Mon–Fri 9am–noon, 2.30–6pm, Sun 2.30–6pm (except during religious services). 04 90 04 85 44. www.apt-cathedrale.com.
This cathedral is the first sanctuary dedicated to Ste Anne in France. It holds the saint's reliquaries brought back from the Orient in the 3C, which, according to legend, were miraculously found by Charlemagne during a trip in 776.

Chapelle Ste-Anne

The first chapel off the north aisle was built in 1660, when Anne of Austria came on pilgrimage. The furnishings include a large reliquary bust of Ste Anne; a marble group of Ste Anne and the Virgin by the Italian Benzoni; and the family tomb of the Dukes of Sabran.

▶ **Population:** 11 229.
⊙ **Michelin Map:** 332: F-10 or 114 fold 2 or 528 fold 31.
ℹ **Info:** 20 avenue Philippe de Girard, Apt. 04 90 74 03 18. www.luberon-apt.fr.
▷ **Location:** Arriving from the west (Gordes is 25km/15.5mi E via D 2 and D 4, Cavaillon at 34km/21mi E via N 100), you must go through suburbs before arriving in the centre of town: place de la Bouquerie.
🅿 **Parking:** Paid parking on the quays, free on the banks. Free shuttle bus on Saturday mornings (market day) every 30min from 9am, leaving from Viton car park and train station.
⊙ **Don't Miss:** Saturday's market, Luberon National Park Centre, the Ochre Tour.
🕐 **Timing:** Allow 1–2hr to walk around town or half a day for the ochre tour.
👥 **Kids:** Unique landscapes of Colorado de Rustrel.

Treasury (Trésor)

In the sacristy of Ste Anne's chapel are displayed 11C and 12C liturgical manuscripts, shrines decorated with 12C and 13C Limoges enamels, 14C Florentine gilded-wood caskets, Ste Anne's shroud, and an 11C caliph's coat brought back from the First Crusade (1096–99).

Crypt

Composed of two floors: the upper crypt is in the Romanesque style and contains an altar supported by a Romanesque capital and 13C sarcophagi; the lower crypt is Pre-Romanesque. At the back of the two crypts stand two tombstones.

▷ *Continue along rue des Marchands, which passes through the bell gate, to place du Postel.*

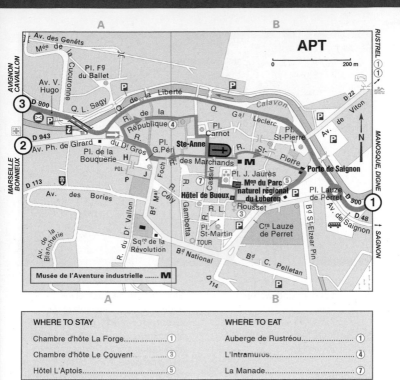

APT

Musée de l'Aventure industrielle .... M

WHERE TO STAY	
Chambre d'hôte La Forge	①
Chambre d'hôte Le Couvent	③
Hôtel L'Aptois	⑤

WHERE TO EAT	
Auberge de Rustréou	①
L'Intramuros	④
La Manade	⑦

Porte de Saignon

Rue St-Pierre leads to this medieval gate, part of the town's remaining fortifications.

▶ *Go along cours Lauze-de-Perret to rue Louis-Rousset, which leads back into the old city.*

Note the 16C **Hôtel de Buoux** on the corner of rue Paul-Achard. The **Maison du Parc du Luberon** (◔ *see opposite*) is housed in a former private hotel at 60 place Jean Jaurès.

▶ *Turn right into rue Casin, which leads back to rue des Marchands; turn left and continue to place Gabriel-Péri.*

Note the lovely Classical façade of the *sous-prefecture*, flanked by two fountains with dolphins.

▶ *Return to place de la Bouquerie via rue du Dr-Gros.*

MUSEUMS
Maison du Parc naturel régional du Luberon

60 pl. Jean Jaurès. ◔*Open Mon–Fri 8.30am–noon, 1.30–6pm.* ◌*No charge.* ☎*04 90 04 42 00. www.parcduluberon.fr.*

Visitors to the centre learn about the natural environment and rural life in the Luberon Natural Park through exhibitions, documents, local products and walking tours.

🚗 DRIVING TOUR

OCHRE TOUR★★
49km/30.5mi – allow about 3hr30min.

▶ *Leave Apt on N 100 in the direction of Cavaillon. Turn right on D 149 in the direction of Bonnieux.*

Pont Julien

This 3C BC arched bridge was on the ancient Domitian Way linking Italy to Spain. It was mounted on two piers

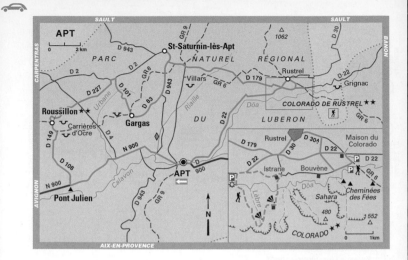

pierced to allow flood-waters to pass through them.

○ *Take D 108, then D 149 in the direction of Roussillon.*

Roussillon★★
♿ *See ROUSSILLON*

○ *Leave Roussillon on D 227.*

Watch for fine views, to the right, of the ochre cliffs and the Luberon range, and to the left, of the Vaucluse plateau.

○ *Bear right on D 2 and right again on D 101.*

In a field to the right you can see the settling tanks used for the processing of ochre.

○ *On entering Gargas bear left on D 83 and left again on D 943.*

St-Saturnin-lès-Apt
This village is overlooked by old castle ruins and a Romanesque chapel. ♿Take the alley left of the village church and climb to the chapel for a view of the Apt countryside and Luberon range.

○ *Follow D 179 and then D 30 to Rustrel.*

👥 Colorado de Rustrel★★
Guides and maps available at the Maison du Colorado, ℘04 90 04 96 07 and at Rustrel's town hall, ℘04 90 04 98 49. Leave your car in one of the paying car parks, either by the banks of the Dôa, or on D 22. Footpaths are well marked; walking time for each loop is indicated by a signpost at the start of the trail. www.colorado-provencal.com.
🚶This gigantic colorado with its ochre-coloured landscape of cliff faces, clay-capped earth pillars with jagged crowns (Cheminées de Fées – fairies' chimneys), the spot known locally as "the Sahara", the Cirque de Barries, waterfalls, and the "river of sand" can be explored on different walks.

🚶 The 2hr loop *(recommended for experienced hikers)* begins at the Colorado campsite, on D22. Follow the yellow blaze marks. Leave the Rustrel iron foundry to the right. The slope down into the valley of the Lèbre contains vermilion rocks. Climb back up the valley to the foot of the old phosphate quarries known as "Terres Vertes" (green earth). Later, be sure to stop in the village of Rustrel for a well-deserved refreshment.

○ *Return to Apt on D 22.*

ADDRESSES

🛏 STAY

Hôtel L'Aptois – *289 cours Lauze Perret.* ☏*04 90 74 02 02. www.aptois.fr. Closed 25 Dec–1 Jan. 29 rooms. ⊑8€.* Deep in the forest, the owners of this 19C building offer a warm welcome.

Chambre d'hôte Le Couvent – *36 r. Louis-Rousset.* ☏*04 90 04 55 36. www.loucouvent.com. Closed 11–23 Feb. 5 rooms. ⊑.* Inside the walls of this 17C convent, you will forget you are in the centre of Apt. Stylish rooms overlook the garden.

Chambre d'hôte La Forge – *Notre-Dame-des-Anges, 84400 Rustrel, 10km/6mi NE.* ☏*04 90 04 92 22. www.laforge.com.fr. 5 rooms. ⊑.* Huge 19C house deep in the Luberon with swimming pool and sundeck. Rooms are of a good size. Bike rental for excursions son the Luberon.

🍴 EAT

Auberge de Rustréou – *3 pl. de la Fête, 84400 Rustrel.* ☏*04 90 04 90 90.* For a long time this inn has had a very good reputation, which it retains. Enjoy dining in a tranquil space decorated in warm tones, situated in a serene village at the gateway to the *colorado provençal.*

L'Intramuros – *120 r. de la République.* ☏*04 90 06 18 87. www. loucouvent.com. Closed Sun–Mon, Nov–20 Dec.* In the town centre, this place serves true Provençal cuisine based on local market produce. Charming interior. Take away or eat in.

La Manade – *36 r. Jules Ferry.* ☏*04 90 04 79 06. Closed Tue eve, Wed and Sat.* This restaurant has been taken over by a dynamic and welcoming young team who offer seasonal, regional dishes in the rustic dining room or on the terrace.

🛒 SHOPPING

Markets – There is a traditional market every Saturday morning; and a farmer's market every Tuesday (cours Lauze de Perret).

Boulangerie Au Pierrot d'Antan – *quartier Brieugne, 84400 Rustrel.* ☏*04 90 04 95 45. Closed Mon.* This small bakery is so good it is well worth the extra mile.

Confiserie Aptunion – *N 100 Salignan.* ☏*04 90 76 31 07. Closed Sun (Jan–Oct).* In the heart of the Luberon, this superb factory shop offers a range of crystallised fruits.

Bonnieux★

Vaucluse

This perched village, situated on a Luberon promontory, is an ideal base to explore the area.

UPPER BONNIEUX

Start from pl. de la Liberté by the steep vaulted passageway, rue de la Mairie, to reach the terrace situated below the old church. By car take the road to Cadenet and a steep surfaced path on the left.

Terrasse

From the terrace there is a lovely **view**★ of the Calavon Valley; to the left, of the hilltop village of Lacoste; and further to

▸ **Population:** 1 441.
Ⓒ **Michelin Map:** 332: E-11.
🅱 **Info:** 7 place Carnot, Bonnieux. ☏04 90 75 91 90. www.tourisme-en-luberon.com.
🅿 **Parking:** Available at the bottom of the village.

the right, of the edge of the Vaucluse plateau to which cling the hilltop villages of Gordes and Roussillon. In the background, Mont Ventoux stands out.

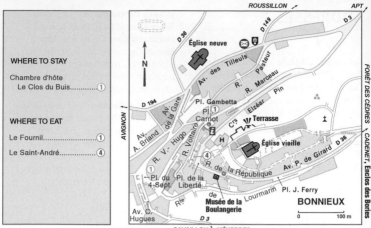

Musée de la Boulangerie

12 r. de la République.

🕐*Open Wed–Mon Jul–Aug 10am–1pm, 2–6pm; Apr–Jun and Sept–Oct 10am–12.30pm, 2.30–6pm.* 🚫*Closed 1 May, 25 Dec.* ⊜3.50€. 📞*04 90 75 88 34.*

The museum illustrates the work of a baker, with utensils, and literature on the bakery trade.

EXCURSION
Cedar forest

5km/3mi along the Loumarin road. Allow 2hr.

Imported from the Moroccan Atlas, these cedars were planted in upper Bonnieux in 1862. There is now a footpath with eight stopping points giving information on plants of the Luberon area.

ADDRESSES

🏠 STAY

⊜⊜⊜⊜ **Chambre d'hôte Le Clos du Buis** – *r. Victor-Hugo.* 📞*04 90 75 88 48. www.leclosdubuis.com. 8 rooms. Closed mid-Jan–mid-Feb, mid-Nov–mid-Dec.* Situated near the church, this old house used to be a grocery and bakery and there is still a bread oven in the sitting room. The attractive bedrooms are bright and airy and have terracotta flooring. Behind the house there is a pleasant garden and swimming pool.

Bonnieux – a typical hillside village

G. Magnin/MICHELIN

EAT

🍽 **Café Restaurant Le Saint-André** – 1 pl. de la Liberté. ℰ04 90 75 80 92. Closed out of season. Good for a pit-stop or lunch on the terrace, which offers a good view of the Calavon Valley.

🍽 **La Flambée** – rue Victor Hugo. ℰ04 90 75 82 20. Closed Mon (Oct), Sat–Sun (Nov–Dec). Grilled foods and wood fire pizzas among other specialties (daube provençale, pain de chèvre, truffes, gibier) in a friendly, unpretentious family-run restaurant. The decor is rustic and the terrace overlooks the Calavon Valley.

🍽 **Le Fournil** – 5 pl. Carnot. ℰ04 90 75 83 62. Closed Dec–Jan, Mon, Tue. The cave-like dining room of this house, which is built on the rock, assures a pleasant coolness during your meal. For sun worshippers, there is a terrace in the square in the summer. Regional dishes on the menu.

CRAFTS

Atelier Marie-Christine Denniel – route de la Gare. ℰ 04 90 75 91 43. www.christine-denniel.com. Hand-painted ceramics in ancient and contemporary designs.

Cavaillon

Vaucluse

The name Cavaillon, to the French, conjures up fragrant melons and the early vegetables of spring. The melons are sweet and rose pink inside and their harvest begins in May. They are grown, along with other produce, in the extensive market gardens that surround the town and make it France's largest designated "national market", with an annual turnover of nearly 800 000 metric tons.

▸ **Population:** 25 819.
📍 **Michelin Map:** 332: D-10.
🛈 **Info:** Place François-Tourel, Cavaillon. ℰ04 90 71 32 01. www.cavaillonluberon.com.

🚶 WALKING TOUR
LOWER CAVAILLON

▸ *From place Tourel walk towards the adjacent place du Clos, which used to be the site of a melon market.*

Arc Romain
pl. du Clos.
On the square lie the ruins of a small, delicately carved Roman arch dating from the 1C BC which stood near the cathedral at the intersection of the main streets of the Roman town and was re-erected here in 1880.

▸ *Take cours Sadi Carnot and turn right into rue Diderot.*

Cathédrale St-Véran
pl. Joseph d'Arbaud. ⏱Open Apr–Sept Mon 2–4pm, Tue–Sat 10am–noon, 3–6pm; Oct–Mar Mon 2–4pm, Tue–Sat 10am–noon. ℰ04 90 76 00 34.
The cathedral is dedicated to the patron saint of shepherds, who was Bishop of Cavaillon in the 6C. The original Romanesque structure was enlarged by side chapels, from the 14C to the 18C. The façade was almost entirely rebuilt in the 18C and the east end holds a fine pentagonal apse.

▸ *Take Grand-Rue, which crosses the old part of Cavaillon.*

Pass the façade of the Grand Couvent before going through the Porte d'Avignon, part of the town's remaining fortifications.

▸ *Turn right along cours Gambetta to reach the square of the same name, then turn right again into the pedestrian-only shopping street, rue de la République.*

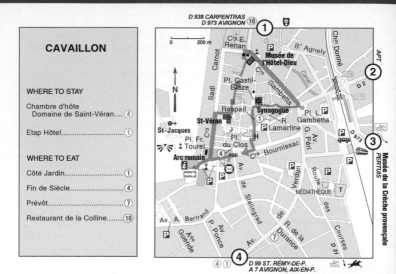

This area was known as the *carrière*, formerly the Jewish ghetto. On the right is rue Hébraïque, which leads to the **synagogue**.

Synagogue et Musée Juif Comtadin

r. Hébraïque. Open May–Sept Wed–Mon 9.30am–12.30pm, 2.30–6.30pm; Oct Wed–Mon 9am–noon, 2–5pm; Nov–Apr Mon and Wed–Sat 9am–noon, 2–5pm. 3€ (ticket includes admission to Hôtel-Dieu). 04 90 76 00 34. www.cavaillon.org.

The original synagogue was built on this site in the 14C, making it the oldest in France. Rebuilt in 1772–74, this synagogue, together with that of Carpentras, is one of the last examples of Baroque Provençal architecture. The interior is ornamented with delightful wood panelling painted grey and decorated with blue and yellow touches. A superb wrought-iron balustrade encircles the gallery. The museum contains a miscellaneous collection of objects and documents: manuscripts, prayer books and sacred articles. In the basement are the baths reserved for the women's purification rites.

The Melon Festival

This festival takes place the weekend before 14 July. There are exhibitions, tastings, processions of flowered carts, reconstructions of an old market and fireworks all centred around the theme of the melon, the symbol of Cavaillon. This is a welcoming town so contingents from other cities are invited to join the festivities, including candied-fruit makers from Apt and vintners from Beaumes-de-Venise. *Délice de Melon* is the name of an aperitif made from

the pulp of melon steeped in alcohol with the addition of sugar, served with crushed ice.*www.melondecavaillon.com.*

▶ *Return to place Tourel by rue Raspail and, on the right, cours Bournissac.*

COLLINE ST-JACQUES
The hill can be reached on foot taking a signposted footpath which starts at the Roman arch (allow 45min).

▶ *It is accessible also by car (5.5km/3.4mi) by way of the D 938 towards Carpentras; then to a road to the left uphill, just beyond a crossroads.*

From the viewing table the **view**★ embraces the Cavaillon plain, Mont Ventoux, the Coulon Valley, the Vaucluse plateau, the Luberon (quite near), the Durance Valley, and the Alpilles. Continue to the **Chapelle St-Jacques** *(colline St-Jacques;* ◷*open daily 10am–6pm),* a 12C chapel, which stands in an attractive garden among cypresses, pines and almond trees.

🚗 DRIVING TOUR

Orgon
▶ *Leave Cavaillon via the D 99 in the direction of St-Rémy and Tarascon. After the Durance river and the motorway, take the D 26 on the left.*

The city, crossed by N 7, lies in the Durance plain. It overlooks the ridge which separates the Alpilles to the west and the Montagne du Luberon to the east. It is home to an interesting **church** (Église) from the 14C. The choir and nave are slightly out of alignment.
Crowning the hill overlooking the town to the south *(road subject to restrictions),* the **Chapelle Notre-Dame-de-Beauregard**'s terrace (✆*04 90 73 34 81)* presents a fine view of the Durance Valley and the Luberon mountains.

St-Andiol
▶ *10km/6mi west, leave Cavaillon on the D99 towards St-Rémy, then turn right in Plan-d'Orgon onto the N 7 towards Avignon.*

Napoleon's Woes

Fleeing Avignon in April 1814, **Napoleon Bonaparte**, on his way to exile on the island of Elba, stopped at an inn in Orgon. A hostile crowd, alerted by the Royalist drummers, gathered. The excited mob wanted to lynch him but he was saved by the mayor of Orgon and fled. He was able to reach the Auberge de La Calade near Aix.

This large farming town was founded by pioneering monks from Montmajour and was the childhood town of French Resistance hero Jean Moulin (1899–1943).

Les Taillades
▶ *5km/3mi E via the D 143. At the roundabout, follow signposts to "Vieux Village".* 🅿*Park the car on the square in the front of the town hall.*

At the far end of the Petit Luberon range, this little village comes as a surprise with its houses perched on what look like enormous stone stalagmites, creating a striking yet serene **site**★. Quarrymen literally hacked away at the foundations of their homes to obtain molasses, a highly prized sandstone.
Follow the road to the church that climbs in a spiral and go past the tower. To your left you will see a strange statue, the "Morvellous", supposedly of St Veranus. A former graveyard opposite the church of St-Luce overlooks the village: ancient dwellings, troglodyte constructions and, wherever you look, vertical partitions carved into rock.

▶ *Retrace your steps and turn right after Auberge des Carrières into rue des Carrières.*

A vaulted archway leads into this quarry hollowed out of the village itself. Its sheer rock walls form a roughly circular space, the **théâtre des carrières** *(place de la mairie; www.lestaillades.fr).* This forms a striking setting for open air concerts every summer.

▶ *Continue on the D 143 to the Cavaillon crossroads.*

The road comes to **moulin St-Pierre**, a watermill on the canal de Carpentras that still features its great paddle-wheel. It was used for grinding madder before becoming a flour mill, a role it played until 1870.

Combe de Vidauque

▶ *5km/3mi southeast. Leave Cavaillon on the D 973 and fork left towards Vidauque.*

The road is very steep and takes a hair-pin course (⟳*one-way traffic, speed limit of 30kph/18mph*), skirting the wild Vidauque combe and offering magnificent plunging **views**★★ of the surrounding countryside: the tip of the Vaucluse plateau and Cavalon Valley (north), the Alpilles and Durance Valley (south and west), and below, the Cavaillon plain.

▶ *Take the Trou-du-Rat road down to D 973 into which you turn right towards Cheval-Blanc to return to Cavaillon.*

ADDRESSES

🛏 STAY

⊜⊜ **Etap Hôtel** – *175 av. du Pont. ℘08 92 68 07 91. 47 rooms. Closed Jan.* 🛏. Easy to find off the motorway, this economy-chain hotel. Comfortable, no-frills, functional rooms. Good value.

⊜⊜⊜ **Chambre d'hôte Domaine de St-Véran** – *13660 Orgon. ℘04 90 73 32 86. 4 rooms. Closed Jan.* 🛏. Beautiful house set in huge gardens, shaded by pines and cypress trees. Tastefully decorated by the owner, the rooms are stylish, the lounge is cosy and there's a pool.

🍴 EAT

⊜⊜ **Fin de Siècle** – *46 pl. du Clos (1st floor) ℘04 90 71 12 27. http://findesiecle. facite.com. Closed 16 Aug–4 Sept.* The décor inside this restaurant is inspired by the Empire, with images of Napoleon III. Quite kitsch. Traditional cuisine and friendly service. Patio-terrace.

⊜⊜⊜ **Côté Jardin** – *49 rue Lamartine. ℘04 90 71 33 58. www.cotejardinpro-vence.com. Closed Sun, Mon eve, Tue eve (in winter).* Slightly out of the town centre, the discovery of this ochre-painted restaurant with its wall friezes will come as a pleasant surprise. In the summertime tables are laid out around a small fountain in a pretty courtyard situated in the garden. Mediterranean cuisine.

⊜⊜⊜ **Prévôt** – *353 av. Verdun. ℘04 90 71 32 43. www.restaurant-prevot.com. Closed part of Aug or Sept (check), 2–7 Jan, 25 Feb–5 Mar, Sun–Mon (except public holidays).* The décor celebrates the melon in all forms: pictures, knick-knacks, chandeliers, crockery and so on. Formal dining atmosphere. An entire menu is dedicated to the melon family!

⊜⊜⊜ **Restaurant de la Colline** – *chemin des Chênes Verts, Ermitage St-Jacques, 4km/2.5mi dir. Avignon-Carpentras. ℘04 90 71 44 99. www.restaurant-la-colline.abcsalles.com Closed Jann, Mar and Mon eve Nov–May.* Peaceful, bright environment combined with local wines and a varied menu of good-quality dishes.

🛒 SHOPPING

Patissier-chocolatier Étoile du Délice – *57 pl. Castil-Blaze. ℘04 90 78 07 51. www.etoile-delice.fr.* Melons of course, this time enrobed in chocolate and baptized *melonettes*. The melon sorbet (seasonal) is smells wonderful (*call ahead to order*).

Market – Traditional market every Monday morning.

Gordes★★

Vaucluse

The houses of Gordes rise in picturesque tiers above the Imergue Valley on the edge of the Vaucluse plateau, facing the Luberon. The site was already occupied by humans as far back as the Neolithic era. The first inhabitants, the Vordeuses, a tribe of Celtic-Ligurian descent, named the city Vorda. Over the centuries this appellation underwent a number of phonetic changes to finally become Gordes. The site★ can best be seen from a rock platform (no barrier) about 1km/0.6mi from the village on the Cavaillon road, the D 15.

VISIT
The Village★

It is pleasant to walk through this charming town along the *calades* – small paved, sometimes stepped alleyways lined with gutters defined by two rows of stone – with vaulted passageways, arcades of old, tall houses and rampart ruins. The shops, craftshops and lively market add to the atmosphere.

Château

pl. du Château. ○*Open daily 10am–noon, 2–6pm.* ○*Closed 1 Jan and 25 Dec.* ⊚*4€.* ℘*04 90 72 02 75.*
The Renaissance château stands on the village's highest point. It was rebuilt by Bertrand de Simiane on the site of a 12C fortress. The north face, flanked by round machicolated towers, is austere, the south monumental, relieved by mullioned windows and small turrets. In the courtyard note the fine Renaissance

- **Population:** 2 126.
- **Michelin Map:** 332: E-10.
- **Info:** Place du Château, Gordes. ℘04 90 72 02 75. www.gordes-village.com.
- **Parking:** From April–November you'll have to park in one of the paying car parks (⊚5€).
- **Timing:** Spring and autumn are the best times to visit.
- **Kids:** Village des Bories.

door (the soft limestone has been worn away by erosion). Inside, in the great hall (first floor) two flanking doorways show off a splendid **chimney-piece★** (1541) with ornate pediments and pilasters, shells and flowers.
In July and August, plays and concerts are held in the courtyard of the castle.

🚗 DRIVING TOUR

Les Bories to Sanctuaire de Répit

Round trip of 12km/7.4mi – allow 2hr.

▷ *Leave Gordes on the D 15 towards Cavaillon; just beyond the fork with the D 2 turn right onto a tarred road which leads to a car park in the village.*

Abbaye de Senánque★★
See Abbaye de SENÁNQUE

Village des Bories★★
○*Open daily 9am–dusk.* ○*Closed 1 Jan and 25 Dec.* ⊚*5.50€ (child 3€).* ℘*04 90 72 03 48.*
This village is now a Museum of Rural Life with 20 restored *bories* (see Le LUBERON) between 200 and 500 years old, grouped around a communal bread oven. The larger *bories* served as dwellings the others were either sheepfolds or various outbuildings. They were inhabited until the early 19C but their origin and use remains something of a mystery: were they permanent or

Village des Bories
S. Sauvignier/MICHELIN

seasonal dwellings, or, were they used as refuges during troubled times?

▶ *Return to the D 2 and bear right; turn left on the D 103 towards Beaumettes and left again onto the D 148 towards St-Pantaléon; continue along this road about 100m/109yd to the place called Moulin des Bouillons.*

Moulin des Bouillons

&🕐*Open Apr–Oct Wed–Mon 10am–noon, 2–6pm.* ☜*5€.* 𝄞*04 90 72 22 11.*
This bastide (16C–18C) has been transformed into a museum dedicated to the history of olive oil, and contains an **olive press**★ made from a whole oak tree trunk weighing seven tonnes. It is Gallo-Roman in appearance, and it is the oldest preserved press of its kind. The history of lighting and olive oil through the ages is also explained.

ADDRESSES

🏨 STAY

☞☞🛏 **Chambre d'hôte la Badelle** – *7km/4.3mi S of Gordes via D 104 for Goult.* 𝄞*04 90 72 33 19. www.la-badelle.com. 5 rooms.* The outbuildings of this ancestral farm have been converted into bedrooms. They are pleasantly simple with antique furniture and terracotta floor tiles. There is a kitchen available for guests' use in the summertime.

☞☞🛏🛏 **Chambre d'hôte Le Mas de la Beaume** – *84220 Gordes.* 𝄞*04 90 72 02 96. www.labeaume.com. 5 rooms.* Peace, a view of the village and the song of cicadas will all seduce most city dwellers! This Provençal *mas* has a garden with olive and almond trees, lavender and nice spacious rooms full of local colours. Swimming pool and Jacuzzi.

▶ *Continue along the D 148 in the direction of St-Pantaléon.*

St-Pantaléon

The Romanesque church of this village is built out of the rock, the central nave of which part dates back to the 5C. Surrounding the church is a rock necropolis, or cemetery, most of the tombs of which are child-size, and was most likely a sanctuary of grace. Children who died before they were baptised were brought here by their parents; according to legend, they revived for the duration of a Mass during which they were baptised, they then died again and were buried here.

▶ *Leave St-Pantaléon from the north and join the D 104A, then the D 2 which returns to Gordes.*

🍴 EAT

☞☞ **La Farigoule** – *Les Imberts (D 2, between Gordes and Cabrières-d'Avignon), 84220 Gordes. 4km/2.5mi from Gordes.* 𝄞*04 90 76 92 76. Closed Wed eve, Thu.* A beautiful covered terrace, this restaurant offers Provençal dishes that are really bursting with flavour, and at good prices.

🍸 NIGHTLIFE

Le Renaissance – *pl. du Château.* 𝄞*04 90 72 02 02. Closed mid-Nov–mid-Feb.* This bar-restaurant-hotel has the benefit of a sunny terrace overlooking the streets of the historic centre and the castle in the square. It featured in Ridley Scott's film *A Good Year* starring Russell Crowe – as did most of Gordes!

CRAFTS

Easter market – During Easter weekend, the town turns into a big street market featuring arts and crafts.

Annie Sotinel – *Les Porquiers, rte de Goult.* 𝄞*04 90 72 05 71. www.latoisondart.net. Open daily 3–8pm. Closed mid-Jan–mid-Feb.* Textile designer who works with silk, alpaca, mohair and cashmere.

Le Luberon★★★
Vaucluse, Alpes-de-Haute Provence

Midway between the Alps and the Mediterranean lies the mountainous Luberon range. This region is full of charm: striking solitary woods and rocky countryside plus picturesque hilltop villages and dry stone huts.

- **Michelin Map:** 332: E-11 to G 11.
- **Info:** La Maison du Parc, 60 place Jean Jaurès, Apt. ℰ 04 90 04 42 00. www.parcduluberon.fr.
- **Don't Miss:** The Petit Luberon with its pretty perched villages such as Bonnieux and Ménerbes.
- **Timing:** Allow half a day for the Petit Luberon circuit and a day for the Grand Luberon.

GEOLOGICAL NOTES

Natural Habitat – The Montagne du Luberon is a gigantic anticlinal fold of calcareous rock of the Tertiary Era running east to west. The range is divided from north to south by the Lourmarin coomb into two unequal parts: to the west the Petit Luberon forms a plateau carved by gorges and ravines where the altitude rarely exceeds 700m/2 297ft; whereas to the east, the massive summits of the Grand Luberon rise up to 1 125m/3 692ft at Mourre Nègre.

The contrast between the north and south slopes is no less great. The northern face, steep and ravined, is cooler, more humid and wears a fine forest of downy oaks. The southern face, turned towards Aix, is more Mediterranean in its vegetation (oak groves, rosemary-filled *garrigues*), and with its sunny slopes, crops and cypresses, announces the delightful countryside along the River Durance.

The diversity of the vegetation is a delight to nature lovers: oak forests, Atlas cedar (planted in 1862) on the heights of the Petit Luberon, beech, Scots pine, moors of broom and boxwood, *garrigues*, an extraordinary variety of aromatic plants (herbs of Provence) clinging here and there to the rocky slopes. The *mistral* contributes, provoking unusual local changes: holm oaks are blown onto the northern exposed slopes and downy oaks onto the southern exposed slopes. In winter the contrast between the evergreens and deciduous trees is striking. The fauna is equally rich: snakes (seven different varieties), lizards, warblers, blue rock thrushes, owls and eagles.

Hilltop Villages – The Luberon has been inhabited by humans since prehistoric times. Villages appeared during the Middle Ages, clinging to the rock face near a waterhole. The tall houses with their imposing walls huddled close

Parc Naturel Régional du Luberon

Founded in 1977, the park incorporates 60 communes covering 185 145ha/457 503 acres including the *départements* of Vaucluse and Alpes-de-Haute-Provence (that is, from Manosque to Cavaillon and the Coulon – or Calavon – Valley to the Durance). Its goal is to preserve the natural balance of the region with the aim of improving the living conditions of villagers, the promotion of agricultural activity through irrigation, mechanisation and the reorganisation of the holdings. The main developments in the tourist industry are the opening of tourist information offices and museums at Apt, Buoux and La Tour-d'Aigues, and the creation of nature trails (through the cedar forest at Bonnieux, the ochre cliffs of Roussillon, the Viens *bories* and the cultivation terraces at Goult, as well as thematic tourist routes such as the "Route de Vaudois". It also produces attractive publications.

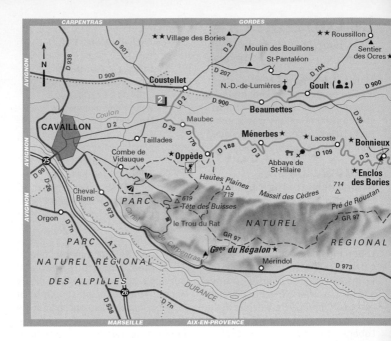

together at the foot of a castle or church; most of them had rooms cut out of the rock. Men left their homes to work in the surrounding countryside and when necessary they lived in dry stone huts called *bories*. Their livelihood was obtained mostly from sheep, olives, grain and vineyards as well as lavender and silkworms. Each parcel of cultivated land was carefully cleared of stones – the stones were grouped into piles called *clapiers* – and bordered by low walls which served to protect the land from soil erosion. The flocks were also contained within a close of dry stone. Traces of these arrangements are still visible in the rural landscape. This traditional economy was swept away by the agricultural improvements of the 19C and 20C: villages lost their inhabitants and fell into ruins. Nowadays, the trend is reversing itself: village populations are increasing at an almost constant rate, and the villages themselves have been well restored.

Bories – On the slopes of the Luberon and the Vaucluse plateau stand these curious dry stone huts, one or two floors high, called *bories*. They are either alone or in groups forming a very picturesque unit; there are about 3 000 of them. They were sometimes just tool sheds or sheep pens but many were inhabited over the different periods from the Iron Age until the 18C.

Bories

G. Magnin/MICHELIN

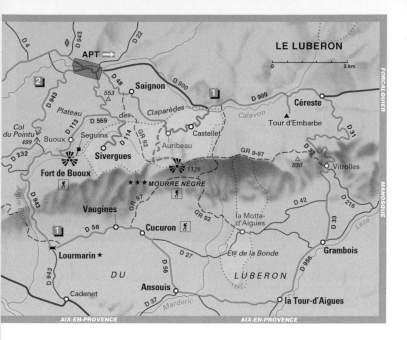

The *bories* were built with thin slabs of limestone. These stones called *lauzes* are on average 10cm/3.9in thick. Specialised *masons* knew how to select the *lauzes* and assemble them without either mortar or water. As the walls were raised, each stone course was carefully made to underhang the preceding one, so that at a height of 3 to 4m/10 to 13ft, the diameter diminished to the point of being reduced to a small opening which could be closed by placing one slab on it. To avoid the infiltration of water, the different layers of stone were slightly inclined towards the exterior.

The *bories* came in several forms. The simplest are round, ovoid or square, consisting of one room and one opening to the east or southeast. The interior was limited to hollow niches used for storage. The temperature of the *borie* remained constant whatever the season. Larger dwellings exist, especially at Gordes. They are rectangular, with a few narrow openings and their organisation was similar to that of a traditional farm: disposed around a courtyard encircled by a high wall were the living quarters, bread oven and outbuildings.

ACTIVITIES IN THE PARK
🚶 Walking/Hiking

The French National Rambling Federation issues two guides called *GR 9 Tour du Luberon* and *G20 Ballades dans le Parc Naturel Régional du Luberon*. The Maison du Parc will give you information about **guided walks** (*no charge*) as well as bed and breakfast accommodation. There is also a guidebook for footpaths in the region.

🚲 Cycling

The Maison du Parc has created a route especially for cyclists, stretching from Cavaillon to **Forcalquier**★ (around 100km/62mi): signposts have been set up at all main crossroads (white heading from Cavaillon towards Forcalquier, ochre in the opposite direction); additional road signs with further information are to be found in 25 nearby villages. The Vélo-Loisirs en Luberon association has indicated accommodation where cyclists are welcomed.

Château de Lourmarin

G. Magnin/MICHELIN

DRIVING TOURS

1 GRAND LUBERON★★
Round trip from Apt – 119km/74mi –
allow half a day (not including climb to
Mourre Nègre).

▷ *Leave Apt on the D 48 going*
southeast on avenue de Saignon.

As the road climbs, the hilltop site of
Saignon, the Apt basin, the Vaucluse
plateau and Mont Ventoux all come
into view.

Saignon
The village, close to a tall rock, contains
a Romanesque church.

▷ *Continue along the D 48.*

The road skirts Claparèdes plateau with
its scattered *bories*.

▷ *Leave the car at Auribeau; exit from*
town northwards and bear left on the
unsurfaced road towards Mourre Nègre.
The **GR 92** *leads to the summit.*

Mourre Nègre★★★
Half a day return journey on foot.
Mourre Nègre at 1 125m/3 692ft is
the highest point of the Montagne
du Luberon. The **panorama**★★★
embraces four points of the compass:

the Montagne de Lure and Digne pre-
Alps (northeast), the Durance Valley
with Montagne Ste-Victoire in the
background (southeast), Étang de Berre
and the Alpilles (southwest), Apt basin,
Vaucluse plateau and Mont Ventoux
(northwest).

▷ *Return to the D 48 and continue*
through Auribeau.

Castellet
The tiny terraced hamlet is now a
lavender distillery centre. The road
crosses a *garrigue* landscape before
reaching the Calavon Valley.

▷ *Turn right on the N 100. After*
crossing the River Calavon follow a
small road on the right for 2km/1.2mi.

Céreste
This old Roman village was on the
Domitian Way, which linked Italy to the
Rhône delta in Roman times.
The village still has some of its
fortifications and constitutes a lovely
architectural unit. The surrounding earth
is rich in remarkable fossils (fish, plants)
which have formed in the calcareous
strata.

▷ *Leave Céreste in the direction of*
Forcalquier and turn left into avenue
du Pont-Romain.

The so-called Roman bridge, which is in fact medieval, can be seen on the right, spanning the River Encrème. The *Nid d'Amour* or Love Nest (below the village near to the Encrème) is a curious fountain-tank beneath a stone vault, fed by two streams gushing from the rock and extended by a pool corbelled into the rock.

▷ *From Céreste take the D 31 to the left.*

The road winds up the north slope of the Grand Luberon offering lovely views over the Calavon Valley to the Vaucluse plateau. The road then descends the southern slope passing through Vitrolles down onto the plain via the D 42; just before St-Martin-de-la-Brasque, continue along the D 27, which skirts the Étang de la Bonde.

Cucuron
Opposite the church, on the first floor of the 17C Hôtel de Bouliers, is a small museum: the **Musée Archéologique Marc Deydier** (r. de l'Église; ⊙ open *Wed–Mon 10.30am–noon, 2–5pm*; ❀no charge; ℘04 90 77 20 82), which is dedicated to prehistory, the Gallo-Roman period and later local traditions. From the terrace below the keep, there is a fine view over the Cucuron basin to Montagne Ste-Victoire on the horizon.

▷ *Leave Cucuron on the D 56 going southeast.*

Ansouis
📍*See ANSOUIS.*

▷ *Leave Ansouis on the D 135 and turn right onto the D 45 and then immediately left onto the D 27.*

Lourmarin★
This village at the foot of the Montagne du Luberon is dominated by its château built high on a rock bluff. The British writer **Peter Mayle** resides in the area. **Albert Camus** (1913–60), author of *L'Étranger* (The Stranger) and *La Peste* (The Plague), is buried in the cemetery, together with the author **Henri Bosco** (1888–1976).

Château de Loumarin★
⊙*Open Jun–Aug daily 10am–6pm; May and Sept daily 10–11.30am, 2.30–5.30pm; Mar–Apr and Oct daily 10.30–11.30am, 2.30–4.30pm; Feb and Nov–Dec daily 10.30–11.30am, 2.30–4pm; Jan Sat–Sun (please call).* ❀*5.50€.* ℘*04 90 68 15 23.* www.chateau-de-lourmarin.com.
The château is partly 15C and partly Renaissance. The Renaissance wing has remarkable stylistic unity and contains large chimney-pieces ornamented with caryatids or Corinthian columns.
The grand staircase ends dramatically with a slender pillar supporting a stone cupola. The château offers a lovely view of the Durance Valley and the olive grove lying within the grounds.

▷ *The D 943 travels northwest up the Lourmarin coomb.*

The River Aigue Brun has cut narrow gorges through the rock. The road goes through a children's holiday camp (16C–18C château) before crossing a bridge and reaching a group of houses.

▷ *Just before these houses turn right onto the narrow path (car park).*

Fort de Buoux
2hr return journey on foot plus 45min visit. Go through the gate and follow the path beneath a vertical rock wall to the porter's lodge. ⊙*Open daily dawn–dusk.* ❀*3€.* ℘*04 90 74 25 75.*
The rock spur on which the fort stands is a natural defence which has, in succession, been occupied by Ligurians, Romans, Catholics and Protestants. Louis XIV ordered its demolition in 1660; there nevertheless remain three defensive walls, a Romanesque chapel, houses, silos hewn out of the rock, a keep, a Ligurian sacrificial altar and a concealed staircase.
From the rock spur, where a medieval keep once stood, there is a fine view of the Upper Aigue Brun Valley.

▷ *Return to the holiday camp and turn right onto the D 113.*

Beyond Buoux village the road returns to Apt along a picturesque route.

2 PETIT LUBERON★
Round trip from Apt – 101km/63mi – about 6hr.

▷ *Leave Apt by the D 943 and turn right immediately onto the D 3, which winds through vineyards.*

Bonnieux★
♿*See BONNIEUX*

▷ *Leave Bonnieux south on the D 3 then bear left on the D 109.*

The road winds along the slope of the Petit Luberon; pause and look back for a pretty view of Bonnieux.

Lacoste
This hill-top village has an elegant 17C belfry and is dominated by the ruins (which now host events; *www. pierrecardin.com*) of a 42-room château, which belonged to the Sade family. The **Marquis de Sade** (1740–1814), author of erotic works, was the Lord of Lacoste for 30 years. He was extremely fond of the stage and gave orders to build an extravagant theatre that could accommodate over 100 people. Condemned several times, he escaped and hid here; but in 1778 he was caught and imprisoned.

▷ *Continue to Ménerbes via the D 109; note the quarries which extract a well-known freestone in the area near Lacoste.*

Abbaye de St-Hilaire
Located on a pretty site facing the Luberon, this former monastery (now private property) was occupied by the Carmelites in the 13C–18C.

Ménerbes★
♿*See MÉNERBES*

▷ *Go south along the D 3 and then take the D 188.*

Oppède-le-Vieux★
Leave the car in the car park just after the village, to explore it on foot.
The terraced **site**★ of the village on its picturesque rocky spur, once partially abandoned, has come to life again through its careful restoration by numerous artists and writers. An old gateway in the walls leads from the old village square to the upper village, crowned by its 13C collegiate church and ruined castle (founded by the Counts of Toulouse and rebuilt in the 15C and 16C). The fine **view**★ from the church terrace is of the Coulon Valley and Vaucluse plateau, Ménerbes and, from the rear of the castle, of the ravined north face of the Luberon.

▷ *Cross the Maubec wine region (D 176, D 29). Turn left instead of right onto the D 2 and, on leaving Robion, bear left on the D 31 to the intersection with the Vidauque road, which you take to the left.*

This very steep winding road (one-way road; speed limit 30kph/18mph), skirts the wild Vidauque coomb and offers magnificent plunging **views**★★ of the surrounding countryside: tip of Vaucluse plateau and Coulon Valley (north), Alpilles and Durance Valley (south and west), and below, Cavaillon plain with its market-gardens .

▷ *The road branches off to the right on the so-called Trou-du-Rat road leading to the D 973, which you take to the right in the direction of Cavaillon. Here, turn right to rejoin the D 2.*

Coustellet
The **Musée de la Lavande** (*rte de Gordes;* ♿🕐☕*open daily Feb–Mar and Nov–Dec 9am–12.15pm, 2–6pm, Apr and Oct 9am–1pm, 2–6pm, May–Sept 9am–7pm,* ☞*6€,* ☎*04 90 76 91 23,*

www.museedelalavande.com) has a collection of old copper stills. Products on sale are made from lavender grown at the Château du Bois in the commune of Lagarde d'Apt.

▷ *3km/2mi after Coustellet bear right on D 207 towards Moulin des Bouillons.*

Musée du Moulin des Bouillons
🕭 *See GORDES*

St-Pantaléon
🕭 *See GORDES*

▷ *The N 100 returns to Apt, climbing the Coulon Valley. On the left is ochre country.*

ADDRESSES

🛏 STAY

🍴🍴 **Hostellerie L'Aiguebelle** – *pl. de la République, Céreste.* ☎*04 92 79 00 91. www.hotel-luberon-aiguebelle.com. 17 rooms. ⊑7€. Restaurant🍴🍴. Closed 14 Nov–13 Feb.* Before or after visiting the medieval ruins, take a break in this unpretentious hotel in the heart of the village. Rooms are simple and bright. Simple local cooking which is both tasty and very reasonably priced.

🍴🍴🍴 **Chambre d'hôte La Maison des Sources** – *chemin des Fraisses, 84360 Lauris. 4.5km/3mi SW of Lourmarin.* ☎*04 90 08 22 19. www.maison-des-sources.com. 4 rooms.* Standing against a cliff which shows traces of a cave dwellers' settlement, this renovated farmhouse has limewashed rooms. One room has four four-poster beds! Downstairs two vaulted rooms serve as a drawing room and dining room.

🍴🍴🍴 **Hôtel L'Oustau dï Vins** – *La Font du Pin, 84460 Cheval-Blanc, 7km/4.3mi W of Mérindol.* ☎*04 90 72 90 90. 6 rooms.* Situated in 20ha/49 acres of woodland at the foot of the Luberon mountain, this well-restored old farm has pretty, ochre-coloured Provençal-style rooms, all with a personalised decor. Attractive stove and wrought-iron furniture in the breakfast room. The wine-producing owner will help you discover the wines of the region. Swimming pool.

🍴🍴🍴 **Maison Gouin** – *44 rte d'Apt, Coustellet. 7km/4.3mi NW of Ménerbes.* ☎*04 90 76 90 18. Closed three weeks in Nov, Sun, Wed.* Run by the same family since 1928, this butcher's shop extends into a dining room and a terrace.

Cooking based on fresh market produce, with wines that you select yourself from the cellar. An unusual place.

🍴🍴🍴 **La Table des Mamées** – *1 r. du Mûrier, 84360 Lauris, 4.5km/2.8mi SW of Lourmarin.* ☎*04 90 08 34 66. www.latabledesmamees.com. Closed 20 Nov–3 Dec, Sun eve, Mon.* In this village restaurant, grandmother's recipes can be enjoyed by guests eating in the 14C and 15C vaulted dining rooms. Musical evenings at weekends.

🍽 EAT

🍴🍴🍴🍴 **L'Auberge de Cheval Blanc** – *481 la Canebière, 84460 Cheval-Blanc, 5km/3mi SE of Cavaillon.* ☎*04 32 50 18 55. www.auberge-de-chevalblanc.com. Closed Sat lunch, Sun eve (Oct–Jun), Mon (Oct–Jun).* This unassuming roadside inn is a pleasant place to stop and eat. The sunny-coloured dining room is completely new. The cooking is classic, with Provençal flavours.

🛒 SHOPPING

La Ferme de Gerbaud – *Campagne Gerbaud, 84160 Lourmarin.* ☎*04 90 68 11 83. Guided tours Apr–Oct. 5€.* A bumpy track leads to this estate, dedicated to growing plants and herbs for perfume and medicinal purposes. The guided visit will show you how to grow plants as well as their properties and uses. The shop sells herbs, honey, essential oils …

MARKETS

Curcuron – Tuesday mornings.
Lacoste – Tuesday mornings.
Lourmarin – Friday mornings.
Oppède-le-Vieux – Sat mornings

Ménerbes★

Vaucluse

This old village occupies a picturesque site on a promontory of the Luberon's north face. In 1573 the Calvinists captured the stronghold by a ruse, and it took five years and a large ransom to dislodge them.

▶ **Population:** 1 157.
🖿 **Michelin Map:** 332: E-11.
🗊 **Info:** ⏱*See BONNIEUX.*
🅿 **Parking:** Leave your car in the car park at the entrance to the village.
🕒 **Timing:** Best to come out of season

VISIT

Place de l'Horloge

The square is overlooked by the town hall's bell tower with its simple wrought-iron bell cage. In one corner of the square stands a Renaissance mansion with a round-arched doorway. Look out for the **Maison de la Truffe et du Vin** (House of Truffles and Wine; ℰ*04 90 72 38 37; www.vin-truffe-luberon.com*) in the square.

17C first French corkscrew, Musée du Tire-Bouchon

Musée du Tire-Bouchon/Domaine de La Citadelle

Église Saint-Luc

🕒*Open for concerts.* ℰ*04 90 72 68 53. www.musicalesluberon.com.*
The church stands at the end of the village and dates back to the 14C when it was a priory dependent on St-Agricol of Avignon. Behind the east end there is a fine **view**★ of Coulon Valley, the villages of Gordes and Roussillon (with its ochre cliffs), Mont Ventoux, the Vaucluse plateau and the Luberon.

An Artist's Village

Ever since **Peter Mayle** published *A Year in Provence*, Ménerbes has become famous the world over: it has even been known for coachloads of Japanese and American tourists who turn up to visit this small village. But before the English writer, other artists had already discovered this charming spot in the Luberon: Picasso stayed here in 1946 and the place has often been frequented by celebrities including Albert Camus and the painter Nicolas de Staël, who in 1953 bought the small castle west of the town (once a medieval fortress) and had it converted into a private residence.

Citadelle

This 13C fortress (rebuilt in the 16C and 19C) has preserved part of its defence system with its corner towers and machicolations. Owing to its strategic position it played an important part during the Wars of Religion.

Musée du Tire-Bouchon

On the D 3 towards Cavaillon. 🕒*Open Apr–Oct daily 10am–noon, 2–7pm; Nov–Mar Mon–Fri 9am–noon, 2–6pm, Sat 9am–noon.* 🕒*Closed public holidays.* ⊛*4€.* ℰ*04 90 72 41 58. www.domaine-citadelle.com.*
Nestling in the wine-producing estate of La Citadelle, this museum displays 1 000 corkscrews from the 17C to today, carved in different materials (horn, ivory, gold and silver) and presenting a variety of shapes (the letter T, animals, an effigy of Senator Volstead, who promoted the laws on Prohibition in the United States in the 1920–1930s). The different methods used to uncork wine are well illustrated through a remarkable display of models including the very first French corkscrew (17C). Visitors may also be taken on a tour of the wine cellars, complete with a tasting of Côtes-de-Luberon wine.

ADDRESSES

ℙ/ EAT

◎🍽🍽🍽 **Auberge de la Bartavelle** –
r. du Cheval-Blanc, 84220 Goult. 6km/
3.7mi NE of Ménerbes via D 218 and D 145.
📞04 90 72 33 72. Closed Tue–Wed. The
owner has renovated this old Provençal
house himself. The vaulted dining
room has restored antique furniture
and in summer extends onto a street-
side terrace (closed to traffic). Regional
cooking using fresh produce.

Roussillon★★

Vaucluse

The village stands on an unusual site
on the highest of the hills between
Coulon Valley and Vaucluse plateau.
These striking hills, composed
of ochre rock of many different
shades featured in the local houses,
enhance the village and the
surrounding countryside.

OCHRE LAND

A visit to Roussillon, as well as giving you
an opportunity to explore the beautiful
village, also gives a good overview of
all stages of ochre production, from
the quarries where it is extracted, to
the processing factory, to colouring the
walls of the village.

ᒋᒐ Sentier des Ocres★

*Departure in front of the cemetery
opposite place du Pasquier. Circuits of
either 30min or 1hr available.* 🕐*Open
daily Jul–Aug 9am–7.30pm; Sept–Jun
please phone tourist office for details.*
🕐*Closed during rainfall.* ◎*2.50€ (child
no charge).*
This signposted footpath, dotted with
information panels, provides an
introduction to the ochre hill's flora
(holm oaks, juniper) and its landscape
of ancient quarries: note the **aiguilles
des fées**, which dominate the famous
chaussée des géants★★, imposing
jagged cliffs.

ᒋᒐ Conservatoire des Ocres et Pigments Appliqués★

*On the road to Apt (D 104), about
1 km/0.6mi from place du Pasquier.*
♿🕐*Open 8 Feb–Jun and Sept–15 Nov
daily 9am–1pm, 2–6pm; Jul–Aug daily*

> ▸ **Population:** 1 265.
> 🖉 **Michelin Map:** 332: E-10 –
> local map 🖉 see APT:
> Ochre Tour
> 🚩 **Info:** Place de la Poste.
> 📞04 90 05 60 25. www.
> roussillon-provence.com.
> ▶ **Location:** Coming from
> Apt (12km/7.4mi SE) or
> Gordes (10km/6mi W), you
> will arrive in the car park in
> place du Pasquier. Parking
> is scarce in summer.
> 🕐 **Timing:** The village
> looks its best at sunset.
> ᒋᒐ **Kids:** The Sentier des
> Ocres, the Conservatoire
> des Ocres.

*9am–7pm; 15 Nov–7 Feb Wed–Sun
9am–1pm, 2–6pm.* 🕐*Closed 1 Jan,
25 Dec.* 💬*Guided tours (50min)
available.* ◎*6€ (child 4€).*
📞04 90 05 66 69. www.okhra.com.

J.P. Brazs/MICHELIN

Range of natural ochre colours

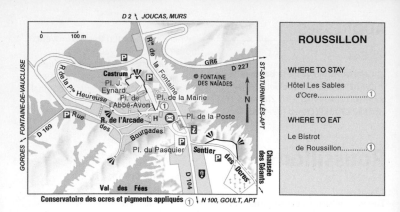

This workshop, closed in 1963, used to transform ochre extracted from the quarries. Ochre in its natural state is a mixture of argillaceous sand and iron oxide. To obtain a pure ochre product, the mineral is washed and the heavier sandy impurities settle to the bottom. The lighter-weight mixture of iron oxide and clay is passed through a filter and into settling tanks where the clay gradually accumulates in layers. The water is evacuated and the ochre is left to dry all summer; it is then cut into blocks. To finish the drying process and to darken the pigmentation, the ochre is baked in ovens (to obtain a red colour, yellow ochre is baked at 450°C/842°F). Finally it is crushed, sifted and put in sacks or barrels.

The Village★

With its narrow little streets, splendidly colourful ochre-clad houses, and arcades full of artwork and pottery, Roussillon is a continual enchantment, particularly with the warm light of sunset.

Start from the tourist office *(place de la Poste)* and turn left into rue des Bourgades and follow rue de l'Arcade, a partially covered stepped street. Pass under the belfry to get to the castrum.

Castrum

Viewing-table. From this platform the view extends northwards to Vaucluse plateau and the white crest of Mont Ventoux, southwards to the Coulon Valley and Grand Luberon.

Go via place Pignotte to reach the far end of the watchpath, from where there is a lovely view of the **Aiguilles du Val des Fées**, vertical clefts in an ochre cliff-face.

▶ *Rue des Bourgades leads back to the start of the walk.*

ADDRESSES

🏠 STAY

⊜⊜⊜ **Les Sables d'Ocre** – *quartier Les Sablières, 4km/2.5mi S towards Goult then take D 149.* ☎04 90 05 55 55. www.roussillon-hotel.com. 22 rooms. ⊜10€. Restaurant⊜⊜⊜. Situated in the heart of a 1ha/2.5-acre park area, this hotel offers comfortable, air-conditioned guest rooms with terraces overlooking the garden or the swimming pool.

🍽 EAT

⊜⊜ **Le Bistrot de Roussillon** – *pl. de la Mairie.* ☎04 90 05 74 45. Closed Mon–Tue. The terrace looks out over the roofs of the village and the Val des Fées. This creates an ideal setting in which to savour Provençal cuisine prepared by the owner, not forgetting the local wines. The dining room is ochre coloured and there are also tables outside in the lively square.

Abbaye de
Sénanque★★
Vaucluse

Nestling in the hollow of a small canyon of the Senancole, which opens onto the Vaucluse plateau, the harmonious ensemble of buildings of the Abbaye de Sénanque (lovely view coming from Gordes on D 177) stands in a desolate site. On arrival, as one takes in the abbey church's east end, set in a sea of lavender, one feels perfectly in tune with the tranquil atmosphere which this seat of Cistercian monasticism exudes.

A BIT OF HISTORY

Foundation and Development – The foundation, in 1148, of Sénanque by a group of monks who had come from Abbaye de Mazan (Haut-Vivarais) fits into the great Cistercian expansion of the 12C. This monastic movement, directed and inspired by St Bernard of Clairvaux, preached an ascetic ideal and prescribed the strict application of Benedictine rule involving isolation and poverty in its monasteries.

The way of life of the Cistercians was thus demanding: divine service, prayer and pious reading alternated with manual labour to fill long days where rest did not exceed seven hours; meals were taken in silence and the monks slept in a dormitory without any comfort. Cistercian austerity influenced the architectural and artistic conceptions of the Order. St Bernard decreed that buildings be plain and stripped of all ornamentation that could divert the attention of those who prayed: no coloured stained-glass windows, statues, paintings or carved tympana. This characteristic can be found in the other two Cistercian abbeys of Provence: Abbaye du Thoronet (&see The Green Guide FRENCH RIVIERA) and Abbaye de Silvacane (&see Abbaye de SILVACANE). They are collectively known as "les Trois Soeurs Provençales" (the Three Sisters of Provence).

ⓖ **Michelin Map:** 332: E-10.
ⓘ **Info:** Abbaye Notre-Dame de Sénanque, Gordes. ℘04 90 72 05 72. www.senanque.fr.
ⓞ **Timing:** Allow 1hr. To respect the silence of the six monks who live here, the only visit is via a guided tour (in French).

Sénanque prospered rapidly to the point that, as early as 1152, the community had enough members to found another abbey in Vivarais. It profited from numerous gifts, starting with the land of the Simiane family and later the land of the Lords of Venasque. The monastery set up outlying farms *(granges)* worked by laybrothers recruited from the peasant population.

Sénanque's peak occurred in the early 13C, but prosperity led to corruption: the order accumulated wealth incompatible with its vow of poverty.

Decadence and Renaissance – In the 14C Sénanque entered a decadent period. Recruitment and fervour diminished while lack of discipline increased. And yet, thanks to the energetic rule of an abbot during the end of the 15C, the situation improved and until the mid-16C the monastery once more strove to respect the ideals of its founders. Unfortunately, in 1544, Sénanque fell victim to the Vaudois Revolt: monks were hanged by the heretics and several buildings were razed. This was the final blow; the abbey was never able to recover. At the end of the 17C, in spite of the efforts of the abbots, the community numbered only two monks. Nevertheless, the south wing of the monastery was rebuilt at the beginning of the 18C.

Sold as state property in 1791, Sénanque miraculously fell into the hands of an intelligent owner who not only preserved it from destruction but also consolidated it. Bought by an ecclesiastic in 1854, it was returned, soon after, to its monastic vocation; new buildings were added flanking the older ones and 72 monks were installed. The anticlerical beliefs of the Third Republic brought about their eviction twice. In 1927 a dozen monks returned and remained for some 40-odd years, then moved for a period to the Lérins Islands (St-Honorat) and finally returned to resume monastic life in the abbey in October 1989.

TOUR

Guided tours (1hr) Jul–Aug Mon–Sat 9.50am–4.30pm, Sun 2.30–4.30pm; Jun and Sept Mon–Sat 10.10am–4.30pm, Sun 2.30–4.30pm; Apr–May Mon–Sat 10.10am–4.30pm; Feb–Mar and Oct–14 Nov Mon–Sat 10.30am–4.35pm, Sun 2.30–4.35pm; 15 Nov–4 Jan and 19–31 Jan daily 2.50 and 4.20pm. ⏱Closed on religious holidays. ✆7€.

This is a fine example of Cistercian architecture. The early monastery is complete with the exception of the laybrothers' wing, which was rebuilt in the 18C. The medieval parts are built in local ashlar stone. The abbey church has kept its original roof of limestone slabs (lauzes) surmounted by a square bell tower; contrary to custom it was built facing north rather than east, as the builders had to compensate for the rigours of the local terrain.

▷ *The tour starts on the first floor of the dormitory, northwest of the cloisters.*

Dormitory (Dortoir)

This vast pointed barrel-vaulted room with transverse arches, lit by a 12-lobed oculus and narrow windows, is paved in brick. This is where the monks slept fully dressed on a simple straw pallet. They were roused in the middle of the night for the first service (nocturns), which took place at 2am, soon followed by matins at dawn. The dormitory now houses an exhibition on the abbey's construction.

Abbey Church (Église)★

Begun in 1160 with the sanctuary and transept, the church was completed in the early 13C with the nave. The purity of line and great and austere beauty, emphasised by the absence of all decoration, create a place of worship and meditation.

Stand at the back of the nave to admire the harmony of the proportions and masses. The transept crossing is crowned by a large dome on elaborate squinches (small arches, curved stone slab, fluted pilasters which recall the style of churches from Velay and Vivarais). The sanctuary ends with a semicircular apse pierced by three windows, symbolising the Trinity, and flanked by four apsidal chapels. Nave, transept and aisles are covered with flat stones resting on the vault itself.

Abbaye de Sénanque

B. Kaufmann/MICHELIN

Cloisters (Cloître)★

Late 12C. The cloisters' galleries are covered with rounded barrel vaulting with transverse arches held up by carved brackets. Decoration appears on the capitals (leaf-work, flowers, rope and palm-leaf moulding and interlacing) and yet it remains discreet.

The cloisters open onto the different rooms of the conventual buildings, each of which has its specific function.

Conventual Buildings (Bâtiments conventuels)★

Chapter house (salle capitulaire)

The room is roofed with six-pointed vaults held up at the centre on two pillars. Under the abbot's leadership the monastic community met here to read and comment on the Scriptures, receive the novices' vows, to keep vigil over the dead and to make important decisions.

Warming room (Chauffoir)

Access via a narrow passage. One of the two original chimneys remains in a corner. The heat was essential to the transcribers, who were bent over their manuscripts all day.

Refectory (Réfectoire)

Parallel to the west gallery of the cloisters. It was extensively damaged in the 16C and has recently been restored to its original appearance.

Laybrothers' wing (Bâtiment des convers)

South of the cloisters, this building which was remodelled in the 18C housed the laybrothers, who lived separately from the monks, meeting them only during certain services or when working in the fields.

ADDRESSES

🛏 STAY

⊖⊖🛏 **Chambre d'hôte Les Hauts de Véroncle** – 84220 Murs, 8km/5mi NE. 🞉04 90 72 60 91. http://hauts.de.veroncle. free.fr. Closed Nov–Mar. 3 rooms.
Apart from the song of the cicadas nothing disturbs the peace of this *mas*, situated in the middle of scrubland. Rooms are simple and whitewashed. A self-catering cottage is also available. Dine under the arbour in the summertime. If you want to go for a walk, ask about the so-called *chemin des sept moulins* (seven mills path).

Abbaye de Silvacane★★

Bouches-du-Rhône

Set in a pastoral landscape on the Durance's south bank, the Abbaye de Silvacane, with its pink-tiled roofs and small mutilated square bell tower, offers a perfect example of plain Cistercian beauty. It is the ideal setting for musical events *(see sidebar)*.

Michelin Map: 340: G-3.

Info: Abbaye de Silvacane, La Roque-d'Anthéron. ℘04 42 50 41 69. www.ville-la-roque-d-antheron.fr.

Timing: Allow 1hr.

A BIT OF HISTORY

From its Founding to the Present – In the 11C the monks from St-Victor of Marseille established themselves on this insalubrious land surrounded by "a forest of reeds" *(Sylva cana)*, from which the monastery derives its name.

The monastery became affiliated with Cîteaux and in 1144 received a donation from two benefactors: Guillaume de la Roque and Raymond de Baux, allowing a group of Cistercians from the Abbaye de Morimond to settle here.

Protected by Provence's great lords, the abbey prospered; it accomplished large land improvement projects in the region and in turn founded Abbaye de Valsainte near Apt. In 1289 a violent confrontation occurred between it and the powerful Abbaye de Montmajour of the Benedictine Order; monks pursued each other and some were even taken as hostages. The conflict ended in a trial and Silvacane was returned to its rightful owners, the Cistercians.

But even more serious were the pillaging of the abbey in 1358 by the Lord of Aubignan and the severe frosts of 1364, which destroyed the olive and wine crops. This set off a period of decline, which ended in 1443 with the annexation of the abbey to the chapter of St-Sauveur Cathedral in Aix.

It became the village of Roque-d'Anthéron's parish church in the early 16C, and suffered during the Wars of Religion. When the Revolution broke out the buildings were already abandoned; the abbey was sold as state property and converted into a farm.

In 1949 the buildings were bought by the state and are gradually being restored: on the foundations discovered in 1989, to the west, the monastic buildings, the fortified wall in coated quarry-stone, and the monks' guest house have all now been restored.

Abbaye de Silvacane

S. Sauvignier/MICHELIN

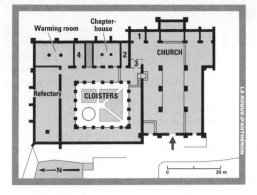

TOUR

🕐 *Open 28 May–30 Sept daily 10am–6pm; 1 Oct–27 May Wed–Mon 10am–1pm, 2–5pm (last entry 1hr before closing).* 🔊 *Guided tours (1hr) Sept–Jun Sun 2.30pm; Jul–Aug daily 10.30am and 4pm.* 🕐 *Closed 1 Jan, 1 May, 25 Dec.* ⚭ *6.50€.*

Church (Église)

The church, built on a slope between 1175 and 1230, features different levels, which are noticeable when one views the west façade with its several openings: a central door, two side doors topped with small off-centred windows, three windows and an oculus adorned with mouldings on the upper floor.

The three-bayed nave ends in a flat east end. Each arm of the transept has two chapels. Note how the architect had to take into account the very steep slope of the land by placing the south aisle, nave, the north aisle and the cloisters at different levels.

In the north chapel of the north arm of the transept **(1)** are the fragments of the tomb of Bertrand de Baux (c. 1137–1181), grandson of the founder, who began the church's construction.

Cloisters

Located at a lower level (1.6m/4.5ft) than the church, the cloisters date from the second half of the 13C, although the gallery vaulting is still Romanesque. Powerful rounded arches open on to the yard; they were originally adorned with paired bays.

Conventual Buildings

Except for the refectory these were all built from 1210 to 1230.

The **sacristy (2)** is a long narrow room next to the **library (3)** located under the north arm of the transept. The **chapter house** recalls the one at Sénanque: six-pointed vaults falling on two central pillars. After the **parlour (4)**, which was used as a passage to the exterior, comes the **warming house**; also with pointed vaulting, it has kept its chimney. Above is the **dormitory**. The large and magnificent **refectory** was rebuilt from 1420 to 1425.

The capitals are more decorated than in the other rooms; the room is well lit by high windows and a large rose window; the pulpit remains.

The laybrothers' wing has completely disappeared. Excavations have uncovered the ruins of the gatehouse and the abbey's precinct wall.

Music in the Monastery

Buildings which once echoed the chanting of monks now echo classical music as the abbey hosts the **Festival International de Quatuors à Cordes du Luberon** (*http://pagesperso-orange.fr/festival-luberon-quatuors*) and the **Silvacane Festival of Vocal Music**, among others.

La Tour-d'Aigues

Vaucluse

Nestling at the foot of the Luberon mountains, the region around Aigues is a delightful countryside made up of fertile, sun-drenched vineyards, cherry orchards and market gardens, in stark contrast to the wild barrenness of the neighbouring hills. Founded in the 10C or 11C, the town owes its name to a tower which was a precursor of the keep of the present castle. In high season the Festival du Sud Luberon is held here.

SIGHTS

Château

🕐 *Open Nov–Mar Sun–Tue 2–5pm, Wed–Sat 10am–noon, 2–5pm; Apr–Jun and mid-Aug–Oct Sun–Tue 2.30–6pm, Wed–Sat 10am–1pm, 2.30–6pm; Jul–mid-Aug daily 10am–1pm, 2.30–6pm.*
🕐 *Closed 1 Jan, 24, 25, 31 Dec.*
⊚4.50€. 𝒫04 90 07 50 33.
www.chateaulatourdaigues.com.
The château was rebuilt in 1555–75 in the Renaissance style by an Italian architect (Ercole Nigra) on a vast terrace overlooking the Lèze; Catherine de' Medici stayed here in 1579. Burned in

▶ **Population:** 3 912.
♿ **Michelin Map:** 332: G-11.
🛈 **Info:** Le Château, La Tour-d'Aigues. 𝒫04 90 07 50 29. www.souriredu luberon.com.

1782 and again in 1792 when it was ruined, it is now being progressively restored by the Vaucluse *département*. The monumental entrance gate takes the form of a richly decorated triumphal arch: Corinthian columns and pilasters, a frieze of the attributes of war and an entablature surmounted by a triangular pediment. In the centre of the bailey is the keep restored to its 16C Italian plan; in a corner the chapel.

Inside, the network of underground cellars now house exhibition, projection and conference rooms as well as collections from the two museums below.

Musée des Faïences

During the course of the restoration work carried out on the château's cellars a large quantity of glazed earthenware was discovered. The finest pieces from these finds have been brought together in this museum which offers the visitor a comprehensive illustration

Entrance gate of Château de la Tour-d'Aigues

G. Magnin/MICHELIN

of the work produced in Jérôme Bruny's Tour-d'Aigues factory between 1750 and 1785.

Musée de l'Habitat Rural du Pays d'Aigues

This museum contains a modern display drawing heavily on audiovisual methods: a history of Provençal man's evolution from his origins to the present.

Slides, illuminated maps, miscellaneous objects (early casts, tools, reconstruction of a silkworm farm) and models depict the development of local rural life.

DRIVING TOUR

112km/69.5mi – allow 1 day.

At the foot of the Luberon mountains flows the Durance, the great fluctuating river which follows a course parallel to the Mediterranean before joining the Rhône at Avignon. This was not always the case, however: at the end of the last Ice Age, the swollen waters burst through the Lamanon gap on a more direct route to the sea, depositing a huge mass of rock and stone over the wide expanse of what is now the Plaine de la Crau.

The Durance's flow is irregular, with violent rainstorms provoking devastating flood-waters, though the river is gradually being harnessed to serve the local economy. The Serre-Ponçon reservoir helps to control its course as well as maintaining irrigation of the plains of the Basse-Durance during dry periods.

It is rare for any one region to be as well served by canals as Provence is between the Durance and the sea. Each was constructed for one of three purposes: irrigation (such as the 16C Canal de Craponne, one of the oldest in Provence), the provision of town and factory water and the production of electricity.

The river's waters have regained their purity, as shown by the numerous fish, cormorants, herons and beavers which make it their home.

Chapelle du St-Sépulcre, Peyrolles-en-Provence

G. Magnin/MICHELIN

▷ *Leave Tour-d'Aigues by the D 135 eastwards and proceed towards Mirabeau.*

On the left after the village, the N 96 goes through the **Défilé de Mirabeau** where the river bends sharply to the west and emerges from Haute-Provence into the Vaucluse through this dramatic narrow channel cut out by the action of the water.

▷ *After crossing the Durance by the* **Pont Mirabeau,** *and the motorway, turn right onto the N 96 near the Centrale de Jouques power station and follow the green waters of the EDF canal, which begins at the Cadarache dam and runs parallel to the Durance until Mallemort.*

Peyrolles-en-Provence

Little remains of the town's medieval fortifications except for a belfry crowned by a wrought-iron bell cage and a round tower (in ruins) near the church.

Château de Peyrolles-en-Provence

Hôtel de Ville. ⊙*Open Mon–Fri 8am–noon, 2–5pm.* ℘*04 42 57 89 82. www.peyrolles-en-provence.fr.*
Once a residence of King René and today the local town hall, this castle was converted into a mansion in the late 17C.

The interior features a grand sweeping staircase and 18C gypsum furnishings. From the east terrace, decorated with a fountain portraying a gladiator, there is a pretty view of the Durance Valley.

Meyrargues

The town is dominated by its château (now a hotel) rebuilt in the 17C. A pleasant walk leads to the remains of a Roman aqueduct (below the castle) which brought water to Aix-en-Provence and continues to the wild Étroit gorges.

◯ *On leaving the town, turn right onto the D 561 in direction of Roque-d'Anthéron, then left onto the D 15 towards Puy-Ste-Réparade.*

Rognes

Rognes is located on the north face of the Chaîne de la Trévaresse. It is famous on two accounts: for the well-known Rognes stone much used for construction locally, and for its truffles (market in December).

The **church** *(23 place de l'Eglise; ℘04 42 50 25 63; www.lestroispierres.org)* built in the early 17C is decorated with a remarkable group of **ten altarpieces**★ (17C–18C).

◯ *Take the picturesque D 66 to return to the D 561, and turn left.*

Centrale de St-Estève-Janson (power station)

This is where the Canal de Marseille begins. Dug in the 19C, it supplied the city with drinking water for many years.

Bassin de St-Christophe

A vast reservoir in a setting of rocks and pine trees, at the foot of the chaîne des Côtes.

◯ *The road crosses and then follows the EDF canal.*

Abbaye de Silvacane★★

℮ *see Abbaye de SILVACANE.*

La Roque-d'Anthéron

At the centre of the town stands the 17C **Château de Florans** *(place Louis Auguste Forbin; now a private clinic)* flanked by round towers. This acts as a backdrop to the prestigious International Piano Festival *(www.festival-piano.com)*.

◯ *Continue along the D 561 to the D 23C on the right. Beyond the town of Mallemort turn onto the D 32 to cross the river; turn left onto the D 973. Continue for 2km/1.2mi and just before a bridge, bear right onto a small road which skirts a quarry.*

Gorges du Régalon★

*1hr15min there and back on foot.
A short distance further on, bear right,
ignoring the uphill road on the left.
Leave the car in the parking area;
take the path opposite which skirts the
stream; cross the olive grove on your left
and go through a narrow gap to enter
the gorges.
(a) It will be cold (an advantage
on hot days); (b) the rocks are often
slippery, so go suitably clad; (c) on rainy
days the stream becomes a rushing
torrent and the expedition should
not be ventured.*

The route follows the bed of the stream,
runs beneath a rock between the sides
of the gorges and over a sometimes
slippery section before coming to a cave.
The tunnel bends sharply into a passage
100m/328ft long and 30m/98ft high but
only 80cm/30in wide in places. The cave
and passage are the most remarkable
parts of the gorges.

▶ *At the end retrace your steps. After
returning to the car, take the D 973 on
the left.*

Lauris

A picturesque village with streets
lined with 16C–18C houses. From the
promenade de la Roque, the visitor can
explore the terraced gardens of the
castle, which dominate the Durance
Valley.

Cadenet

This town was an important centre for
basket making, thanks to the proximity
of the Durance; from the beginning of
the 19C until the mid-20C, its willow
beds were harvested for the production
of wicker. The industry reached its
zenith between the 1920s and 1930s
after which, as a result of competition
from rattan imported from the Far East,
production diversified into providing
household items and various decorative
objects. You can find out all about it at
the **Musée de la Vannerie** *(av. Philippe
de Girard; open Thu–Sat and Mon
10am–noon, 2.30–6.30pm, Sun and Wed*

Le Tambour d'Arcole

In the main square there is a statue
of André Estienne, the famous
drummer boy, born in Cadenet in
1777. He served in Napoleon's northern Italy campaign of 1796 and, in
the midst of the battle against the
Austrians and Italians for the Arcole
Bridge, he swam the river and beat
such a tattoo that the Austrians
mistook it for artillery fire; as they
retreated the French advanced to
capture the bridge and win the
battle.

---

*2.30–6.30pm; 3.50€; 04 90 68 24
44),* which is situated on the site of the
former La Glaneuse workshop.

Pertuis

Capital of Aigues country and birthplace
of Mirabeau's father, the town retains a
14C battlemented tower (St-Jacques),
13C clock tower, a castle ruin and the
Église St-Nicolas. This church, rebuilt in
the 16C, contains a 16C triptych and two
17C marble statues given to the monks
of the town by Cardinal Barberini.

▶ *Return to La Tour d'Aigues by
the D 956.*

ADDRESSES

🛏 STAY

Logis le Mas de Jossyl – *av.
du Parc, La Roque d'Antheron. 04 42
50 71 00. www.masdejossyl.fr. 28 rooms.
12€. Restaurant.* A pleasant
hotel with an olive garden and an
outside swimming pool.

🍽 EAT

Auberge de la Tour – *rue
Antoine de Tres. 04 90 07 34 64. Closed
early Nov, early Jan, Sat lunch, Sun eve,
Mon.* The relaxed atmosphere gives this
village-centre restaurant the feel of a
bistro. Carefully prepared dishes with a
Provençal flavour.

The second city to be established in France, the major port city of Marseille is 26 centuries in the making. Founded by the Phoenicians around 600 BC, and taken over by the Greeks in 540 BC, Marseille was isolated from both the region and the nation until the 19C. The city boasts years of tradition and history, as visible from 16C fortifications and modern-day monuments.

Highlights

1 Protected natural land of **Parc du Mugel** (p306)

2 Inspiration for the Cubists **L'Estaque** (p308)

3 The breathtaking gilded sculpture at **Basilique de Notre-Dame-dela-Garde** (p307)

4 A peak into the shipwrecks and maritime of years gone by **Musée des Docks Romains** (p326)

5 Architectural genius Le Corbusier's **Cité Radieuse** (p315)

While it does not have the flash of its nearby Riviera cities, like Nice, nor the bucolic charm of small villages in Provence, its streets are worth strolling, with parks, small neighborhoods, museums and, of course, maritime sights. And, the residents of Marseille do know how to have a good time. From a traditional Carnival to kite-flying, a garlic fair, and even waterjousting, there's always something going on in this port city. Thanks to the Euroméditerranée project, which began in 1996, Marseille continues to evolve, as more creative businesses, industry and educational facilities are welcomed to town.

Access to fresh seafood makes gastronomy one of the city's best activities. Creative chefs have opened high-end restaurants throughout the city, leaning on the city's cornucopia on local ingredients. Leave room in your schedule (and your appetite) to taste as many as possible. You won't want to miss the moules marinière, the local preparation of mussels, the navette, orange-blossom pastry in the shape of a boat, or the local Cassis white wine. You may have had bouillabaisse and aioli elsewhere, but it is worth it to savor the Marseille variety. Top of your restaurant "must-eat" list should be the local institutions Dégustation Toinou and Chez Fonfon. Fresh seafood is not the only bonus of being a port city. Being on the water helped Marseille build industry in oil pressing, soap making and flour milling. Stock up on some fragrant soaps as a souvenir.

You'll hear locals speaking in their local dialect, as you explore Marseille's streets and ports. Start at the Vieux Port, which is easy to find because all streets in town lead here. After you see (and smell) the fish market, check out the Baroque façade of the Hôtel de Ville and the wrought-iron balcony of the 18C Pavillon Daviel. You can take a quick ferry ride from one side of the Vieux Port to the other to get a better vantage point.

Marseille's independent traditions continued into the 20C when architect Le Corbusier built his first housing complex here. The modern design reflected new principals of community design.

Nearby Aubagne is home to clay quarries and a long tradition of local pottery. The Ateliers Thérèse-Neveu shows a retrospective of this art form.

The area surrounding Marseille is well-loved for its calanques, a name which comes from the Provençal for "steep slope" And that's what you'll see on these limestone cliffs, with breathtaking turquoise water views. One of the best-known is En-Vau, which has a stony beach. If you want to see the sights from water level, there are several companies that offer boat tours. Small fishing villages are nestled in between the calanques near Chaîne de l'Estaque. Much of this area is protected land, leaving it pristine for viewing.

Aubagne

Bouches-du-Rhône

In the Huveaune valley, Aubagne lies in a verdant basin, dominated to the northwest by the Chaîne de l'Étoile. Its location is favourable to industrial expansion and local food production (important agricultural market centre). The once-fortified town has preserved some of its old ramparts and a 12C church remodelled in the 17C. The beloved Marcel Pagnol (1895–1974), author, playwright and film-maker, was born here and lived at 16 cours Barthélémy.

A BIT OF HISTORY

Aubagne's pottery tradition, which developed as a result of its clay quarries, dates back to Antiquity. This tradition became established during the Gallo-Roman period with the manufacture of *amphorae* and ceramics and turned to tile production in the Middle Ages.

In the 19C, the production of *santons* was started, carried on today in a score of cottage industries dotted throughout the old town. The ceramic coating of ships such as the *Normandie*, the *France* or the *De Grasse* originates from Aubagne's workshops.

WALKING TOUR

The historic centre lies within the ancient fortified ramparts of which a few vestiges remain, namely the 14C Gachiou doorway, one of the seven original gates that gave access to the medieval city. The small, narrow streets reveal a number of architectural curiosities – the quaint triangular belfry of the late 17C Chapelle de l'Observance *(place de l'Observance)*, the Tour de l'Horloge and its superb wrought-iron bell tower, the fine, white Baroque front of the Chapelle des Pénitents Blancs and the more Classical façade (1551) of the Chapelle des Pénitents Noirs (chemin de St-Michel).

▶ **Population:** 44 682.

Michelin Map: 340: I-6 or 114 folds 29 and 30.

Info: 8 cours Barthélémy, Aubagne. ℘04 42 03 49 98. www.oti-paysdau bagne.com.

Location: The town is 15min by TER train from Marseille.

Timing: Allow half a day to visit Pagnol sites and *santons* makers.

Ateliers Thérèse-Neveu

8 montée de la Cour de Clastre. &. ◷ *Open Tue–Sun 10am–noon, 2–6pm.* ◷ *Closed 1 May.* ◌ *No charge.* ℘04 42 03 43 10.

This huge exhibition hall occupies the former workshop of Thérèse Neveu, who was a famous *santon* maker from Aubagne. It is devoted to the art of clay and other related industries. It features a standing retrospective on the history of ceramics in the town and hosts temporary exhibitions on a variety of themes associated with *santons* and pottery.

Le Petit Monde de Marcel Pagnol

esplanade de Gaulle. ◷ *Open daily 9am–12.30pm, 2.30–6pm.* ◌ *No charge.* ℘04 42 03 49 98. *www.marcel-pagnol.com.*

This display consists of a crib with *santons* illustrating the popular characters that feature in Pagnol's films and literary works.

EXCURSIONS
Musée de la Légion Étrangère★

Access via D 2 towards Marseille, turn right on D 44A. ◷ *Open Tue–Wed and Fri–Sun 10am–noon, 3–6pm.* ◷ *Closed 9, 10, 11 July.* ◌ *No charge.* ℘04 42 18 12 41. www.legion-etrangere.fr.

On the ground floor, the great hall opens onto the Salle d'Honneur, which exhibits memorabilia belonging to the Legion's great leaders. On the first floor are exhibited numerous historical documents, photographs, arms and uniforms, including the wooden hand of Captain Jean Danjou, who led the Legion in their heroic last stand during the Battle of Camarón (1863). Camerone Day is still celebrated by Legionnaires on 30 April.

ADDRESSES

♀/ EAT

☻ **Café des Arts** – *10 r. du Jeune Anacharsis.* ✆*04 42 03 12 36.* One of the nicest eating places near cours Foch. Young and animated clientele. Dishes of the day, much appreciated by locals, are served on the terrace or in the dining room.

☻ **La Cardeline** – *4 r. Torte.* ✆*04 42 84 02 99. Closed Sun eve and Mon.* This restaurant, situated in an alley in the old town, has everything you could want inluding great regional cooking.

☒ SHOPPING

Markets – Traditional market Tue, Thu, Sat and Sun along *cours Voltaire*.
Antique market on the last Sun of the month at the Tourtelle.

Poterie Ravel – *av. des Goumes.* ✆*04 42 82 42 00. www.poterie-ravel.com. Closed Sun–Mon.* Terracotta objects and pottery pieces for the garden and home are found in this place, which has been running since 1837. Contemporary, historical and classical styles available. Worth a visit for the displays alone.

Étang de Berre★

Bouches-du-Rhône

The Étang de Berre (Berre Lagoon), 15 530ha/60sq mi in extent and nowhere more than 9m/29.5ft deep, has been France's principal petroleum port for about the last 80 years. The Canal de Caronte, dredged out where there was once a lagoon of the same name, provides a passage to the Mediterranean, as does the underground Rove section of the Marseille-Rhône canal. The lagoon is fed fresh water by the Arc and Touloubre rivers and the EDF canal (Électricité de France) and is ringed by limestone hills: the Lançon chain to the north, the Vitrolles to the east, the Estaque to the south, and the St-Mitre to the west.

A BIT OF HISTORY

The region was largely uninhabited when, in 1920, under the San Remo Agreement, France obtained the right to purchase the major part of Iraq's

- ⚅ **Michelin Map:** 340: F5.
- ▤ **Info:** 30 allée Jean-Jaurès, Istres. ✆04 42 81 76 00. www.istres.fr.
- ◗ **Location:** The south and southwest of the Étang are industrialised whereas the north is wilder.
- ⊛ **Don't Miss:** Miramas-le-Vieux, old Istres and St-Chamas.
- ◷ **Timing:** Allow a day for exploring the lagoon.
- ♟ **Kids:** Les Jardins d'Alizée farm.

annual crude oil production. The lagoon was transformed into the ideal port for shallow-draught oil tankers, at the same time harbours also began to be developed on the Golfe de Fos: the French BP company set up at Lavéra in 1922–24, Shell-Berre at the Pointe de Berre in 1928 and the Compagnie Française de Raffinage at La Mède in 1934. Esso has had installations in Fos since 1965.

At the turn of the 19C, the peaceful lagoons and deserted Crau plain were an ideal testing ground for pioneer aviators. The very first military aerodrome was established in Istres before World War I and still operates today. Since then it has expanded considerably and now occupies 2 031ha/5 017 acres.

Until 1940, Berre was the most important hydroplane base of the National Marines. When a civil airport was required for Marseille, the Marseille-Provence airport was sited at the east end of the Étang de Berre at Marignane.

The growth in demand for oil, apparent even in 1938, brought about the transformation of Lavéra soon after the war, to enable 90 000t tankers to dock and pump their cargoes directly into onshore installations. In the 1960s a new port was constructed at Martigues. The lagoon complex is also the terminal of the South European Oil Pipeline. This line, inaugurated in 1962, supplies a dozen European refineries.

However, the petrol crisis of 1973 led to a slight reduction in the capacity of the refineries, which were obliged to adapt to the fall in demand. The petrochemicals industry has continued to develop in more recent years, contributing to a transformation of the landscape.

The modern installations are but the latest of human constructions in the area; buildings still above ground and excavations reveal the presence of earlier inhabitants at St-Blaise, Pont Flavian, built by the Romans, the medieval hamlet of Miramas-le-Vieux and the 17C walls of Port-de-Bouc.

🚗 DRIVING TOUR

113km/70mi round-trip– allow 1 day.

▷ *Start from Martigues.*

Martigues
ⓒ *See MARTIGUES.*

▷ *Leave Martigues by the D 5.*

St-Mitre-les-Remparts
The old town, encircled by 15C ramparts, stands just off the road. A network of small streets and alleys leads to the church where there is a view of the Étang d'Engrenier.

▷ *Leave St-Mitre-les-Remparts by the D 51.*

There is a good view on the right of the Étang de Berre; the road skirts the Étang de Citis before passing the foot of the hill on which stands Chapelle St-Blaise, the east end of which is just visible among the pine trees.

St-Blaise Archaeological Site
ⓒ *See ST-BLAISE*

Istres
Despite the town's rapid development, the old village of Istres still retains its Provençal appearance. The **Musée Archéologique d'Istres** *(4 pl. du Puits Neuf;* 🕐 *open Mon–Sat 9am–noon, 2–6pm;* 🕐 *closed 1 Jan, 1 May, 25 Dec;* ⊘*no charge;* ℘*04 42 11 27 72)* presents local history: palaeontology, zoology, prehistory, underwater archaeology, and the economic life of Istres, Fos and Miramas.

▷ *Circle the Étang de l'Olivier by way of the D 53 and then turn left onto the D 16, which returns to the Étang de Berre.*

Miramas-le-Vieux
The small town on a flat ledge of rock has preserved its medieval ramparts and the ruins of its 13C castle.

▷ *Return to the D 10 and take the D 16 across the way and then the D 70D. At Le Pont-de-Rhaud bear right onto the D 70A.*

Cornillon-Confoux
At the centre of the hill village stands a small Romanesque church with a bell gable and modern stained-glass windows by Frédérique Duran. There are good local **views**★ from the walk

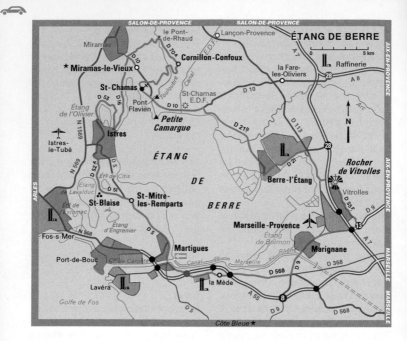

which starts at the church and circles the village.

▷ *Take the D 70 and a tourist road on the right to St-Chamas.*

St-Chamas
The town is dominated by a small, triple-arched aqueduct. The church is 17C with a Baroque west front.

Pont Flavien
This bridge, to the south of St-Chamas, crosses the Touloubre in a single span.

▷ *Continue along the D 10, which passes the St-Chamas Power Station (Centrale de St-Chamas), the EDF canal's final project. Turn left onto the D 21 and left again after 1.7km/1mi onto an unsurfaced road. Park the car.*

Lançon Viewing Table★★
(Table d'orientation de Lançon)
15min return on foot.
Steps (48) lead to the top of a rock from where there is a view over the lagoon to the surrounding hills.

▷ *Turn round and once on the D 21 continue to Berre-L'Étang.*

Berre-l'Étang
The town lives off fishing and its chemical factories.

▷ *Continue first along the D 21, then the N 113 on the right. Finally, turn left for Vitrolles.*

Rocher de Vitrolles
Leave your car at the main entrance of the cemetery, then go up the 75 steps.
The town of Vitrolles, now hidden by an ample industrial and residential area, is famous for the unusual ruiniform rock that dominates it. At the top of the rock, on the southernmost tip, there is a Saracen tower (11C), and on the opposite side a chapel dedicated to Notre-Dame-de-Vie, the aviators' guardian.
The immense **panorama**★ embraces the lagoons of Berre, the oil installations of Lavéra, the port of Fos-sur-Mer and the refinery of La Mède. Just outside the village, ⚲⚲**Les Jardins d'Alizée** farm *(zone agricole de valbacol; ◔open daily 9am–7pm with booking; ∞4€ per child for a half day visit; ℘04 ⓦ ℙ JU*

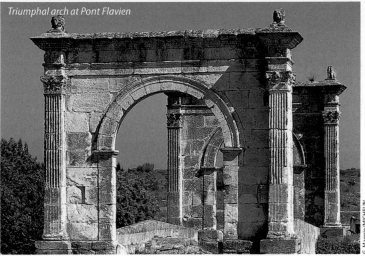
Triumphal arch at Pont Flavien

G. Magnin/MICHELIN

46; www.jardal.com) offers children the opportunity to discover the local fauna of the area through activities, workshops and a miniature golf course.

▶ *Leave Vitrolles by the D 55F. At the N 113 crossroads, cross onto the D 9, which runs alongside the Marseille-Provence airport.*

Marignane
In the 17C, Marignane acceded to the status of marquisate. The castle, the **Château des Covet**, remains from this period and currently houses the town hall. Originally built in the 13C by Guillaume des Baux, the château was taken over in the 17C by the Covets, a wealthy family of tradesmen. It is to them that the château owes its fine Classical façade. The small **Musée d'Arts et Traditions Populaires** evokes the traditions, history and activities of the area *(r. de Covet; ⏱ open Wed 2–5pm, Sat 9am–noon; ⊘ no charge; ℘ 04 42 88 95 36).*

▶ *Follow the N 568 back to Martigues, which crosses the Marseille-Rhône canal.*

Massif des Calanques★★
Bouches-du-Rhône

The Massif des Calanques, with Mont Puget (565m/1 854ft) its highest peak, stretches almost 20km/12.4mi between Marseille and Cassis. With its solid limestone, dazzling whiteness, and weather-worn pinnacles, it has long attracted nature lovers for its wild beauty. However, its unique character and exceptional charm stem above all from its deep and narrow

- 🐾 **Michelin Map:** 340: H-6 to I6.
- ℹ **Info:** 🐾 see *MARSEILLE* and *CASSIS*
- 🌄 **Don't Miss:** Lunch in the sun in the fishing village of Goudes.

indentations, the famous *calanques*, which have been chiselled out along its coastline, creating a majestic union of sea, sky and rocks.

🐾 *Some paths dangerous for children.*

BACKGROUND
What is a Calanque?

The word *calanque* (from the Provençal *cala* meaning steep slope) describes a narrow and steep-sided coastal valley that has been bored into the solid rock by a river, whose course was usually guided by a fault, during the periods of the sea's retreat, and which has subsequently been submerged by the waves during cycles of flooding. Such fluctuations in sea level result from the alternation of glaciation and deglaciation on the earth's surface over the course of the past two million years. The most recent rise in the water level, an average of 100m/330ft, occurred 10 000 years ago, flooding caves inhabited by prehistoric man. The *calanques*, none of which are longer than 1.5km/0.9mi, extend towards the open sea via large underwater valleys, and though they can be compared to the *abers* of Brittany, should not be confused with fjords, which are shaped by glaciers.

A fragile, remarkable site

The absence of any form of surface water and the area's dryness can be explained by the permeability of the limestone, the proliferation of faults, and low levels of rainfall. The temperature regulation of the sea, the sun's glare on the high, bare rocks and the area's sheltered position away from the *mistral* all combine to create an exceptionally hot microclimate on the southern slopes of this massif, conditions that occasionally result in winter temperatures 10°C higher than those on its northern side. Some typically tropical and extremely rare species of vegetation have been able to survive the periods of climatic cooling that occurred during the Quaternary period, creating today a botanical reserve of valuable scientific interest. This in a paradoxical context in which vegetation continues to suffer, the main culprits of which are the area's dryness, the felling of trees for the local lime kilns, excessive grazing and the repeated forest fires that decimate the range.

From the time of the first fire ordered by Julius Caesar in 49 BC to the catastrophic blaze on 21 August 1990 and further fires in July 2009, the forests of the Massif des Calanques have suffered indescribable damage over the centuries. Increasing protective measures have been introduced in recent years: since 1975 the area has benefited from the protection granted natural monuments and sites. Following the 1990 disaster, measures restricting public access during the summer months were stepped up.

Flora and Fauna

In this semi-arid environment, the best adapted flora include copses or thickets of green oaks, viburnum, wild olive trees, myrtle and mastic. In addition to woods of Aleppo pine, stony scrub oak, rosemary, and heather-carpeted *garrigue* also predominate.

Ground where vegetation damage is widespread is also home to areas of brachiopods. Samphire and sea lavender also grow along the coast, replaced higher up the slopes by a thin cushion of plants including the rare Marseille Astragalus or "mother-in-law's cushion" with its fearsome thorns.

Europe's largest lizard and longest snake can also be found in the *calanques*: the ocellar lizard can grow to 60cm/1.96ft and the Montpellier grass snake can reach 2m/over 6.5ft in length.

Birds nest mainly on the coastal cliffs and outlying islands.

The most common, the herring gull or *gabian*, which feasts on the rubbish left behind by careless visitors, is increasing rapidly in number. The most rare, Bonelli's eagle (about 15 pairs), is a beautiful diurnal bird of prey with white, grey and dark brown plumage.

EXCURSIONS
Goudes

◯ *Leave Marseille by the promendade de la Plage.*

An old fishing village, nestled amid grandiose rocky scenery. There is no beach, but there are a number of small local restaurants frequented by the local Marseillais.

A Peaceful Retreat

Faithful to a tradition that dates back to the 16C, no effort is spared on the part of the town dweller to purchase his *cabanon*, which was, until recently, a modest building: a fisherman's hut, a cabin in the hills, or a small village house where Sundays and summer holidays were spent. Although nowadays the hut is more likely to be a comfortable (and expensive) villa, and the stay lengthened to weekends and school holidays, a typical day in the *cabanon* is not so far removed from the picture painted in the operettas of Vincent Scotto. The morning is reserved for fishing or a trip to market. Afternoons, the household gathers in the shade of the terrace to sip an iced *pastis*, before a hearty lunch accompanied by *aïoli*. Cicadas chirp you to sleep during the siesta hour. Evenings are whiled away at the *pétanque* court, and the after-dinner hours devoted to *belote* card games, a last chance for amicable dispute before turning in for a sound sleep, with all the cares in the world having been left in the noise and pollution of the city.

> ◐ *Continue as far as Callelongue where the tarmac road ends.*

Callelongue

This tiny cove has several *cabanons* or cabins and provides shelter for a small flotilla of boats.
🚶*(45min). From there you can get to the calanque of Marseilleveyre and its little pebble beach.*

Sormiou★

🚶*(45min) Leave Marseille on either ave de Hambourg or chemin de Sormiou. Park in the car park at the entrance to the tarmac road blocked off to vehicles. Walk down to the calanque.*
Considered by the local Marseillais population to be the best of all the calanques, there are numerous *cabanons*, a small port, a beach, and several fish restaurants.
Sormiou is separated from Morgiou by the **Cap Morgiou**, a viewpoint affording magnificent views of both *calanques* and the eastern side of the massif.

Morgiou★★

🚶*(2hr) From Marseille take the same route initially as for Sormiou; turn left and follow the "calanque Morgiou" signs (you will pass the famous prison, Les Baumettes). Park near the "sens interdit" (no entry) sign; continue on foot along the paved road.*
A wild setting with tiny creeks for swimming, crystal-clear water, *cabanons* clustered at the far end of the valley,

Calanque d'En-Vau

©Edite Artmann/Dreamstime.com

restaurant, small port. Not to be missed!

Sugiton★★

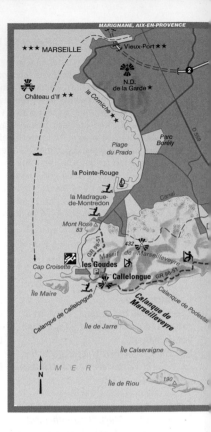 (1hr30min) From Marseille take bd Michelet as far as Luminy; park in the car park near the École d'Art et d'Architecture and continue on foot along the forest track.

A small *calanque* with turquoise water, it is well sheltered by its surrounding high cliffs. It is popular with naturists.

En-Vau★★

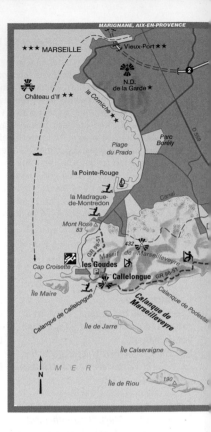 (2hr 30min) Access via Col de la Gardiole (Route Gaston-Rebuffat beginning opposite the Carpiagne military camp); leave your car in the Gardiole car park. 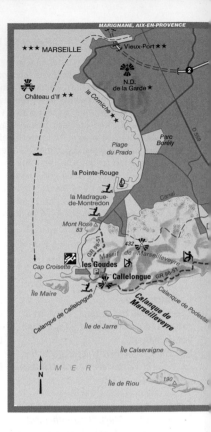 (2hr) Or, from Cassis, walk past Port-Miou and Port-Pin calanques.

The best known of all the *calanques* with its white cliffs, emerald water, and stony beach. It is encircled by a forest of rock pinnacles overlooked by the "Doigt de Dieu" (Finger of God).

Port-Pin★

 Access via Col de la Gardiole (same directions as En-Vau – 3hr) or Cassis (skirting Port-Miou calanque – 1hr30min).

A spacious *calanque* with a sandy beach surrounded by pine trees.

ADDRESSES

♈ EAT

⊜⊜⊜⊜ **Le Lunch** – 13009 Calanque de Sormiou. &04 91 25 05 37. Closed mid-Oct–mid-Mar. Reservations required. If you want to have lunch at the water's edge in a wild setting, then this is the place to come. Seafood is very much the order of the day here and is "just-caught" fresh. Access to the **calanque** is strictly controlled and only those who have reserved at the restaurant may bring their cars.

BOAT TRIPS

From Marseille – ICARD Maritime, quai des Belges. &04 91 33 03 29. www.visite-des-calanques.com. Trips in catamarans to Cassis along the coast. ⊜10–25€.

From Cassis – Les Bateliers de Cassis. &04 42 01 03 31. www.calanques-cassis. com. Departure from the port of Cassis (45 min) visiting Port-Miou, Port-Pin and En-Vau, without landing. ⊜13€. Evening trips available in summer.

From La Ciotat – Les Amis des Calanques, quai Ganteaume. &06 09 35 25 68. www. visite-calanques.fr. Trips in catamarans with glass bottoms. ⊜16–25€.

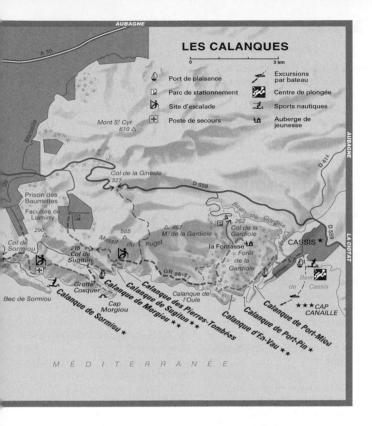

LES CALANQUES

0   3 km

Symbol	Meaning	Symbol	Meaning
⚓ Port de plaisance		Excursions par bateau
P Parc de stationnement		Centre de plongée
Site d'escalade		Sports nautiques
Poste de secours		Auberge de jeunesse

THE CALANQUES

Access – ⊘No access either on foot or
by car to the *calanques* between 1 July
and the second Sunday in September,
or on days when the *mistral* is blowing
fiercely. Even when access to the
calanques is permitted, restrictions may
apply in bad weather conditions, particularly on weekends. Spring is probably
the best time to visit.

Boat trips – An excursion by boat
is a practical way of discovering the
calanques in summer when access to
them by land is strictly controlled. But
be aware that the sea can be rough.

Walking – There are no direct approach
roads by car to the *calanques* with the
exception of the less attractive coves
of Goudes, Callelongue and Port-Miou.
The only way to reach the others is on

foot. Footpaths are often steep and
rocky: it is advisable to get yourself the

IGN map *Les Calanques de Marseille à
Cassis (www.ign.fr)*. It is strictly forbidden
to pick any form of vegetation, stray
from marked paths, smoke or light a fire
at any time of the year. Make sure you
are equipped with walking boots and
detailed maps; carry water with you as
there is none available on the paths;
take necessary precautions against the
harmful effects of the sun.

Experienced hikers will be tempted
to walk the GR 98-51 footpath from
Callelongue to Cassis (see local map), an
incomparable 28km/17.4mi hike (allow
11–12hr) along towering cliffs, with
spectacular views of the most secret
calanques.

Cassis ⚓

Bouches-du-Rhône

Cassis, a bustling fishing port, lies in an attractive **setting**★ at the end of a bay between the Puget heights and Cap Canaille. It is a popular summer resort with three beaches. Boat trips to the *calanques* are a popular excursion (🕑 see p303).

🚗 DRIVING TOUR

Corniche des Crêtes★★

▷ *From Cassis to La Ciotat 19km/12mi – allow 45min.*

The stretch of coast road between Cassis and La Ciotat skirts the crests of the Canaille, a limestone range that rises from the sea in white cliffs, some of the tallest in France – 362m/1 188ft at Cap Canaille, and 399m/1 310ft at the Grande Tête.

▷ *Leave Cassis in an easterly direction, on the road to Toulon (D 559), and during the ascent take a signposted road to the right. At Pas de la Colle, turn left.*

▶ **Population:** 7 788.
🖢 **Michelin Map:** 340: I6.
🅱 **Info:** Quai des Moulins, Cassis. ℰ 08 92 25 98 92. www.cassis.fr.
◗ **Location:** 25km/15.5mi E of Marseille.
🅿 **Parking:** Your best bet is to get the bus from Marseille (40min).
🔊 **Don't Miss:** The *calanques*, Cap Canaille.

Mont de la Saoupe

The **panorama**★★ from the television mast at the top includes Cassis, the Île de Riou and Chaîne St-Cyr to the west, the Chaîne de l'Étoile and Massif de la Ste-Baume to the north, La Ciotat and Cap de Sicié to the southeast.

▷ *Return to Pas de la Colle and continue uphill.*

Note the views of Cassis and La Ciotat.

Cap Canaille★★★

From the guard rail on the cape there is an outstanding **view**★★★ of the cliff face, Massif de Puget and the *calanques* and Massif de Marseilleveyre.

Port of Cassis

G. Magnin/MICHELIN

The Grotte Cosquer

This underwater cave, located near the Cap Morgiou headland, was discovered in 1985 by the Cassis diver Henri Cosquer. Scientists quickly proved the authenticity of the cave art, which includes seals, penguins, fish and even human handprints. A neutronic activation dating method, able to analyse minuscule quantities of organic matter, has dated the handprints to 27 000 BC and the animal drawings to approximately 17 000 BC, one or two millennia prior to those found at Lascaux, which are similar in both style and technique. The cave is closed to the public.

▷ *Beyond Grande Tête, turn right towards the coastguard station.*

From the **Coastguard station (semaphore)** the **view**★★★ embraces La Ciotat, Cap Sicié and Cap Canaille (telescope).

▷ *Return to the crest road; bear right for La Ciotat.*

The descent into town passes quarries, pinewoods, and the "pont naturel", a natural limestone arch.

ADDRESSES

🛏 STAY

◒🛏🛏 **Hôtel Le Clos des Aromes** – *10 r. Abbé Paul Mouton. ☎04 42 01 71 84. www.le-clos-des-aromes.com. 14 rooms. Restaurant◒🛏🛏. Closed 4 Jan–end Feb, Tue and Wed lunch, Mon.* Located in the centre of the village, this old building has all the charm of a mansion. Enjoy the Provençal cooking, served on a flower-decked terrace in the summertime. Its rather small bedrooms are colourful and cosy. Mediterranean atmosphere.

🍴 EAT

◒🛏🛏 **La Vieille Auberge** – *14 quai Jean-Jacques-Barthélemy. ☎04 42 01 73 54. Closed Wed and Sun eves (Oct–Apr). Reservations recommended.* Passed from father to son, the cuisine of this lovely inn is traditional and Provençal. At the water's edge; terrace in summer.

◒🛏🛏🛏 **La Presqu'île** – *2km/1mi SW of Cassis on the Port-Miou road. ☎04 42 01 03 77. www.restaurant-la-presquile.fr. Closed 11 Nov–28 Feb, Sun eve (Sept–May), Mon.* Perched on the Calanques road, just opposite Cap Canaille, admire the stunning sight of the steep cliffs plunging down to the turquoise-blue waters. If the chill of the evening makes you shiver, take shelter in the dining room decorated with Provençal colours.

TOURS

Little train tour aboard Le Petit Train de Cassis *Mar Sat–Sun 2.15pm–5.15pm (also 11.15am Sun); Apr and Oct–15 Nov on the hour daily 2.15pm–5.15pm; May Sept daily 2.15pm–6.15pm (also 11.15am Sun and daily Jul–Aug). ✺6€ (child 3€). ☎04 42 01 09 98. www.cpts.fr.* A little train takes passengers on a 40min commentated tour from the tourist office along the port to the *calanque* of Port-Miou and back.

🍷 BARS

Bar de la Marine – *5 quai des Baux. ☎04 42 01 76 09. Closed 4 Jan–1 Feb.* A simple, friendly place, this bar takes pride in attracting artists and actors passing through this popular summer resort. For those who wish to remain incognito behind a pair of Ray-Bans, it is worth ordering a *pastis* on the terrace while silently admiring the view. At 10pm the K6 disco, also owned by the Bar de la Marine, opens.

EVENTS

The Cassis Wine Festival and the Feast of St-Éloi *(first Sun in September)* offers a good opportunity to sample some excellent wines, in particular white wine, of a region that is divided among 12 wine producers.

La Ciotat♨♨

Bouches-du-Rhône

La Ciotat, where the houses rise in tiers above the bay of the same name, has been a port since ancient times. Roman occupation, Barbarian invasion and devastation were followed by a revival in the Middle Ages, and from the 16C the provision of a merchant fleet in the eastern Mediterranean. The city continues to fulfil its maritime vocation, particularly by running large shipbuilding yards specialising in oil and methane tankers. However, the worldwide crisis in the shipbuilding industry has scored a direct hit here, and the city is having to adapt to different technologies and to seek new areas of commercial activity, such as tourism. Its beach and fishing port, its cliffs, *calanques* and sea bed attract numerous visitors all year round.

SIGHTS
Clos des Plages

The district has been developed as a resort just north of the new harbour (*Nouveau Port*, with 850 berths), with hotels and seaside villas lining the beach, making it ideal for family outings. Marking one of the squares open to the sea is a monument to the Lumière brothers, who brought fame

> ▶ **Population:** 32 126.
> ⚫ **Michelin Map:** 340: I-6.
> 🔲 **Info:** Boulevard Anatole-France, La Ciotat. ℘04 42 08 61 32. www.tourisme-laciotat.com.
> ◗ **Location:** Leave the Marseille–Toulon motorway at exit 9 and then follow the D 559 and av. Émile-Bodin, which brings you into town.
> ◔ **Timing:** This is a pleasant resort for a family holiday outside July and August, when the beaches become packed.
> 👪 **Kids:** OK Corral.

to the town with the first showing of a motion picture in 1895.

Vieux Port

This old harbour has all the charm of a small fishing port, with its quaysides overlooked by warm façades and lively restaurants.

Parc du Mugel

Access by quai de Roumanie.
◔*Open daily Apr–Sept 8am–8pm; Oct–Mar 9am–6pm.* ∞*No charge.* ℘*06 23 79 55 92.*
Located at the tip of Cap de l'Aigle, this natural protected area favours abundant

Vieux Port

©Christian Musat/IStockphoto.com.

and varied vegetation (cork trees, mimosa and arbutus). At the top (steep path), some 155m/509ft, there is a lovely view of La Ciotat and its surroundings.

The Ciotat Calanques

1.5km/0.9mi. Leave La Ciotat along quai de Roumanie, avenue des Calanques and turn left into avenue du Mugel.
These rocky inlets known as *calanques* can also be visited on board a catamaran-type boat with a glass bottom, affording underwater views.

Calanque du Mugel

The inlet is dominated by the rock of Cap de l'Aigle. There is a good view of Île Verte from here.

▶ *Take avenue des Calanques and bear left into avenue de Figuerolles.*

Calanque de Figuerolles★

15min return on foot.
A short green valley leads to the small clear-water inlet. This curious site is characterised by strangely eroded rocks, including the "Capucin", an isolated crag projecting forwards on the right, and cliffs featuring cavities with sharp edges and a smooth, polished interior.

Île Verte★

30min return by boat from the Vieux Port. Departures on the hour Apr–Jun and Sept Mon–Fri 10am–noon, 2–5pm, Sat–Sun 10am–6pm; Jul–Aug 9am–7pm; Oct please call.
Return fare 9€. *06 16 40 83 50.*
www.laciotat-ileverte.com.
The rock at Cap de l'Aigle, so clearly a bird of prey (*aigle* means eagle) when

seen from the small fort on Île Verte, is what gave the point its name. Lie on the beach, swim and picnic.

ADDITIONAL SIGHTS
Musée Ciotaden

1 quai Ganteaume. Open Wed–Mon Jul–Aug 4–7pm; Sept–Jun 3–6pm. Closed public holidays.
3.20€. *04 42 71 40 99.*
www.museeciotaden.org.
Inside the former town hall are mementoes and documents about this seafaring town and its past, including a room dedicated to the Lumière brothers.

Chapelle Notre-Dame-de-la-Garde

Follow chemin de la Garde for 2.5km/1.5mi by car, until you reach a brilliant white housing estate, then 15min on foot. Open Mon–Fri 1.30–5.30pm, Sat 3.30–6pm.
04 42 71 43 82.
At the chapel, bear right onto a path which leads to a terrace (*85 steps cut out of the rock*). The **view**★★ embraces the full extent of La Ciotat bay.

EXCURSION
👤👤 OK Corral

19km/12mi NW on the D 3 then take the N 8 to the left. Open 8 Mar–4 Nov (please check website for specific times). 18€ (child 15.80€). *04 42 73 80 05.*
www.okcorral.fr.
Downhill from the N 8, in the centre of a pine forest clearing, lies this Wild West-themed amusement park. A chair lift and a small train provide a comfortable tour of the park.

ADDRESSES

🍽 STAY

Hôtel R.I.F. – *Calanque de Figuerolles.* *04 42 08 41 71. www.figuerolles.com.* 9 rooms. 7€. Restaurant. *Closed Nov.* A few steps lead down to this house tucked away in an isolated *calanque* where a terrace affords an excellent view. Provençal-coloured

rooms are in bungalows in the pretty garden. The beach is a stone's throw away and canoes are available to hire. Best to reserve in advance.

Hôtel Rose Thé – *4 bd beau Rivage. *04 42 83 09 23. www.hotel-la-ciotat.com.* 19 rooms. 7€. In a building dating from the thirties, this hotel is located on the sea front, with Art Deco stylings and a restaurant with an open terrace. The hotel is located 100m/ 328 ft from the beach in a 3ha/7 acre forest with good amenities and a swimming pool.

¶/ EAT

⊜⊜⊜ **Auberge Le Revestel** – *quartier Liouquet.* ✆*04 42 83 11 06. www.revestel.com. Closed a fortnight in Dec, early Jan–mid-Feb, Sun eve, Wed.* A cosy and bright restaurant on the coastal road of La Ciotat. The dining room offers clear views of the sea and the cuisine offered is regional and contemporary.

🏃 LEISURE ACTIVITIES

Boat Trip to the Calanques
Ⓒ*See the CALANQUES*

Markets – The **traditional** market is held every Tuesday in place Évariste-Gras and on Sundays at the Vieux Port. In July and August there is a **craft** market every evening from 8pm–1am at the Vieux Port.

Parc Régional Marin de la Baie de la Ciotat – Information at the town hall. Famous for the rich diversity of its seabed life, La Ciotat bay is now a protected regional park, thanks to strict measures enforced for its preservation, whereby fishing, deep-sea diving and mooring are strictly regulated. The **Centre Permanent d'Initiatives pour l'Environnement de la Côte Provençale** (✆*04 42 08 07 67; www. atelierbleu.fr)* offers diving lessons and underwater tours.

In the Lumière brothers' footsteps – *Ask at the tourist office.* Tour themed around these film-maker brothers.

Chaîne de l'Estaque★

Bouches-du-Rhône

The Chaîne de l'Estaque, which divides the Étang de Berre from the Mediterranean, is an unusual limestone formation, arid in appearance and almost uninhabited except for a few small fishing villages sheltered by deep inlets *(calanques)* in the steep coastline. The area is much appreciated by the locals from Marseille and is known as the "Côte Bleue", due to the intense cobalt or sapphire blue of its sparkling waters.
The Parc Marin de la Côte Bleue, a natural marine reserve, extends along the coast between the ports of Niolon and Carro, at the foot of the Massif de la Nerthe.
Note that fishing, scuba diving and mooring are prohibited.

Ⓒ **Michelin Map:** 340: F-5 to G-5.
🈸 **Info:** Espace Fernandel, Avenue Aristide Briand, Carry-le-Rouet. ✆04 42 13 20 36. www.carry-lerouet.com.
🈁 **Don't Miss:** A fun way to explore the coastline and its beaches is by train. Ⓒ*See Addresses.*
🕐 **Timing:** You could spend a week here at one of the hotels or campsites or you could spend a day visiting the villages by car, bus or train.

🚗 DRIVING TOUR

Marseille to Port-de-Bouc 74km/46mi – about 4hr.

▶ *From Marseille take the motorway on the coast and exit at St-Henri-L'Estaque.*

GETTING THERE

BY CAR: A transverse road cuts across the mountain chain, running along the hinterland (except between Carry and Sausset-les-Pins). Most of the harbours can only be reached down a dead-end road. In the summer, especially during weekends, access to the *calanques* of Niolon and Redonne is sometimes prohibited to reduce the risk of fire in an area with a particularly fragile ecosystem.

BY TRAIN: Between Marseille and Martigues there is a train which makes several stops at the beaches of the Côte Bleue. The train is fun to ride, as it chugs along through tunnels and past gorgeous views of the sea, blowing its whistle to warn daydreamers who enjoy rambling along the tracks!

L'Estaque

A number of avant-garde painters made the village famous between 1870 and World War I. It was partly here that the foundations of modern art were laid – especially Cubism from 1908–10 – by Cézanne, Renoir, Braque and Dufy. Inhabitants from Marseille are now attracted here by the fish shops, the restaurants, as well as the odd stall that continues to make *chichi frégi* – delicious doughnuts. You can enjoy a panoramic view from the place de l'Église in the old town. From here take in the ports and islands, and the picturesque rooftops of the old village, to see what attracted the artists.

> *Turn right onto the N 568 going west towards the Rove. Before the railway bridge, turn right along the Carrière Chagnaud road. Pass under the railway before turning down the slope to the entrance.*

Canal Souterrain du Rove

The tunnel was cut in the 1920s beneath the Chaîne de l'Estaque to link the Marseille docks and the Étang de Berre, and was used regularly by 1 200 metric ton barges until it was obstructed by a rockfall in 1963. It is more than 7km/4.3mi long and dead straight – one can still see daylight at the far end. Height, width and water depth respectively are 15.4, 22 and 4.5m (50, 72 and 15ft).

> *After passing the village of Rove, which is famous for its fromage frais made from goats' milk, turn left onto the D 5 and left again onto the D 48. On*

Calanque de Niolon

G. Magnin/MICHELIN

Oursinades

The glorious days that usually characterise the winter months are the setting for the "Oursinades", a sea urchin festival which takes place in January in Sausset and February in Carry. The streets around the port are literally invaded with long tables where people sit down to tuck into sea urchins and other seafood accompanied by white wine. A lively time is guaranteed!

approaching Niolon, the winding road descends steeply towards the port.

Niolon★

The lovely little village retains a traditional atmosphere where it clings to the hillside above a *calanque* of the same name. It is a good spot for deep-sea diving (*see Addresses: Centre UPCA de Niolon).

▶ *Return to the D 5, which will be on your left. An arid landscape leads to Ensuès. On entering the village turn left and take the D 48D.*

La Madrague-de-Gignac

The village, set in a lovely site, lines a *calanque*, which faces Marseille across the water. A narrow road (alternate traffic circulation) leads from the port to the Anse de la Redonne.

▶ *Returning to Ensuès make a left turn onto the D 5, which goes down the Vallon de l'Aigle, bordered by pines and holm oaks.*

Carry-le-Rouet⌂

This one-time fishing village is now a seaside resort. Summer residences can be seen in the woods that line the bay. There are plenty of seafood restaurants on the port where you can eat sea urchins, among other specialities.

Sausset-les-Pins⌂

This fishing village and seaside resort has a fine promenade from where one can look across the sea to Marseille.

▶ *D 49 leaves the coast and winds its way up the massif. Drive toward La Couronne by way of the D 49B. Turn right before the church and head for Cap Couronne.*

Cap Couronne

From the lighthouse on the point there is a view right round to Marseille, with the Chaîne de l'Estaque in the foreground, the Chaîne de l'Étoile and the Marseilleveyre. The huge beach of La Couronne is very popular and is a favourite spot among Marseille's young set.

Carro

The attractive small fishing village and resort lies well protected at the back of a rock-strewn bay. There is a fish market held every morning at the port.

▶ *Leave Carro via the D 49 and continue to Les Ventrons.*

The road climbs through an arid landscape of dark pines against white limestone and, at 120m/394ft, looks back *(observation tower)* over the industrial harbour complex of Lavéra, Port-de-Bouc and Fos.

▶ *At Les Ventrons turn right onto the D 5 for Martigues.*

Martigues
See MARTIGUES

▶ *Turn left onto the N 568.*

Port-de-Bouc

The port is protected by a fort erected by Vauban in 1664 on the southern bank of the passage. The 12C tower, part of these fortifications, is now a lighthouse.

ADDRESSES

🛏 STAY

◔◔**Auberge du Mérou** – *Calanque de Niolon, 13740 Niolon, 5km/3mi from Rove, on the road to Niolon.* ℘*04 91 46 98 69. www.aubergedumerou.fr. 5 rooms.* ⌴*9€. Restaurant*◔◔◔. *Closed Sun and Mon evenings during low season.* Decorated as cabins in a boat, the rooms look out over the port of Niolon. The restaurant is known for its seafood.

🍴 EAT

◔◔◔◔**Les Girelles** – *r. Frédéric Mistral, Sausset-les-Pins.* ℘*04 42 45 26 16. www.restaurant-les-girelles.com. Closed 2–24 Jan, Sun evening low season, Mon and Tue lunch (Jun–Aug), Wed except eves in season.* The terrace bordering the beach is very popular with locals. Inside, there is a pretty model ship and plenty of picture windows that make the most of the view. Appetising and well-presented cooking.

🎣 LEISURE ACTIVITIES

Markets – Sausset-les-Pins has a **traditional** market on Thursday morning at the quai du Port, and Sun morning along av. Armand-Audibert. **Fish** market daily from 9am at quai du Port.

Centre UPCA de Niolon – *18 chemin de la Batterie, Le Rove, Niolon.* ℘*04 91 46 90 16. http://niolon.ucpa.com. Closed mid-Nov–end Feb.* This is one of Europe's largest diving centres, catering for all levels from beginners to instructors.

Fos-sur-Mer★

Bouches-du-Rhône

Perched on a rocky outcrop, Fos evokes the typical idea of a Provençal village. It is named after the Fosses Mariennes, a canal dug at the mouth of the Rhône by Marius' legions in 102 BC (*fosse*: canal). The development of the new complex, the largest in southern Europe and which complements the port of Marseille, was begun in 1965 on the Golfe de Fos. The advantages of the site, some 10 000ha/24 700 acres, are a deep-water channel, a low tidal range, and the stony surface of the Plaine de la Crau that makes an ideal foundation for an industrial estate.

VISIT
The Village★

The village retains the ruins of its 14C castle, which once belonged to the Viscounts of Marseille, as well as the église St-Saveur *(quartier de l'Hauture)*, with its Romanesque nave. The chief attraction, however, lies in the views from the terrace and rampart garden.

▶ **Population:** 15 734
◔ **Michelin Map:** 340: E-5.
🏠 **Info:** Place de l'Hôtel de Ville, Fos-sur-Mer. ℘04 42 47 71 96. www.fos-sur-mer.fr.

The Port
The combined Marseille-Fos complex is the largest port in France and third in Europe.

EXCURSIONS
Port-St-Louis-du-Rhône
15km/9.3mi SW.
A town and port have developed around the St-Louis tower, built to defend the mouth of the Grand Rhône in the 18C. The dock, was constructed in 1863 and is now part of the Marseille complex. Its lock and the large Fos-Rhône canal make it the key point for river and maritime-river traffic between Europe and the Mediterranean.

Port-de-Bouc
See Chaîne de l'ESTAQUE

Marseille★★★

Bouches-du-Rhône

Twenty-six centuries of history have contributed to making Marseille the oldest of the great French cities. The city has always been fiercely independent, resulting in its isolation from the national community until the 19C. Even today, although proud of being France's second city, it has retained its own distinct character: a combination of authenticity and hardworn clichés. The distinctive local dialect, the cries of the fishmongers on the Vieux Port or of the *boules* players, all combine to create the soul of Marseille. And yet it does not survive on its reputation alone, it is a city which has progressed with the times: developing ambitious projects including "Euromediterranée", which includes the redevelopment of the Joliette docks and trams in the city centre. Marseille is standing as a candidate for the European Capital of Culture 2013.

A BIT OF HISTORY

The Founding of Massalia – Around 600 BC galleys manned by Phocaeans (Greeks from Asia Minor) landed on the coast in Lacydon creek, which is now the Vieux Port. The Greeks, who were expert traders, quickly made the city prosperous. After their defeat by the Persians in 540 BC, the city became home to several different colonies of people. They set up busy trading posts at Arles, Nice, Antibes, Agde, Le Brusc, the Hyères islands, and inland at Glanum, Cavaillon and Avignon. With the Celtic-Ligurians, intense trade concentrated on arms, bronze objects, oil, wine, salt, most likely slaves and ceramics.

Masters of the sea between the straits of Messina and the Iberian coast, and dominant in the Rhone valley, the Massalians controlled trade in amber and raw metals in particular: silver and pewter from Spain or Brittany, copper

▶ **Population:** 839 043.

🕭 **Michelin Map:** 340: H-6.

🖸 **Info:** 4 La Canebière, Marseille. ℰ04 91 13 89 00. www.marseille-tourisme.com.

▷ **Location:** For an overview, take Le Grand Tour or the tourist train (ⓒ*see Addresses*). All streets lead to the **Vieux Port** where people congregate. Visit the fish market that takes place every morning on **quai des Belges**. For a **breathtaking view** of Marseille, head up to **Notre-Dame de la Garde church**: on the left rise Pomègues and Ratonneau islands, Château d'If and in the distance the Massif de Marseilleveyre; opposite is the port overlooked by Fort St-Jean (14C–17C) with Parc du Pharo in the foreground. The city's main **shopping** street is rue St-Ferréol.

🅿 **Parking:** Like in any big city, finding a parking space is usually a problem. There are several underground car parks but consider taking the convenient metro system (ⓒ*see Addresses*).

🕲 **Don't Miss:** The Vieux Port, the old Panier district, the Corniche and a boat trip over to Château d'If – for a fantastic view of Marseille from the sea.

🕙 **Timing:** Start at the Vieux Port. From here you can get the metro, a bus (no 83 for the Corniche) or a ferry to your chosen destination.

👪 **Kids:** Natural History Museum; an Olympique de Marseille soccer match; Château d'If; the Prado beaches.

from Etruria. After a period of eclipse, the city regained its splendour in the 4C. The coastal region was developed and planted with fruit and olive trees and vines. Greek sailors pushed further south as far as Senegal and to the north explored the Baltic coast as far as Iceland. Massalia was administered as a republic and widely recognised as a cultural centre.

The excavations around the Vieux Port and the Bourse commercial district have enabled historians to establish the layout of the town: it covered 50ha/124 acres and was built facing the sea on the hills of St-Laurent, Moulins and Carmes. It was surrounded by ramparts and featured two temples (one celebrating Artemis and the other Apollo), as well as several other monuments.

Rome Comes to Massalia's Aid – The Romans, taking advantage of the occasion to acquire more influence, entered Provence in 125 BC, rescuing Massalia for the Salian Franks and beginning their conquest. For three years battles raged as the Salian Frankish tribe harassed the land but Roman tenacity triumphed. Transalpine Gaul was founded with Aix and Narbonne as colonies. Massalia remained an independent republic allied to Rome; it kept a strip of territory along the coast.

Roman Marseille – At the moment when the rivalry between Caesar and Pompey was at its height, Marseille was forced to decide for one or the other of the two Roman generals. It backed Pompey, making the wrong choice. Besieged for six months, the town at last fell in 49 BC; Caesar stripped it of its fleet, its treasures and its trade. Arles, Narbonne and Fréjus were enriched with its spoils. Nevertheless, Marseille remained a free city and maintained a brilliant university, the last refuge of Greek teaching in the West.

After the invasions, Marseille remained an active port which continued to trade with the Far East; it was the object of violent rivalry between the barbarian leaders. In 543 the plague arrived in Gaul for the first time and the town's decline began in the 7C. Pillaging by the Saracens, the Greeks and Charles Martel pushed the town back behind the fortifications of the bishopric on St-Laurent hill.

Maritime Development – As early as the 11C the old Phocaean city mobilised all its shipping resources and put its shipyards to work. In 1214 Marseille became an independent republic, but only for a short time, as in 1252 it submitted to the rule of Charles of Anjou. During this prosperous period (12C–14C), during the Crusades, Marseille competed with Genoa for the rich supply trade in war material and food to the Crusaders.

Not only did the city reap great profit from this, but it was granted ownership of a section of Jerusalem with its own church.

Fort St-Jean and Cathédrale de la Major (left)

G. Magnin/MICHELIN

Marseille, now rich again, sought new outlets. Its sailors began to trade along the Catalan coast and often sailed as far as the Levant, Egypt and North Africa. In the early 15C prosperity was undermined by crises which came to a head in 1423 when the fleet from Aragon pillaged the city. Under the influence of two clever merchants, the Forbin brothers, trade started up again. Jacques Cœur installed the main office of his bank here.

The Great Plague – In the early 18C Marseille's population was about 90 000. It had profited from an edict of franchise since 1669 and from a monopoly of trade with the Levant. It subsequently became a huge warehouse of imported products (textiles, food products, drugs); and was preparing to launch into trade with the West Indies and the New World, when in May 1720 it fell victim to a dreadful curse. A ship coming from Syria, the *Grand St-Antoine*, was stricken with several cases of the plague. When it arrived in Marseille, it was put under quarantine at the Île de Jarre. Despite the precautions taken, the epidemic struck the town in circumstances which are still unclear. The *Parliament* at Aix forbade all communication between Marseille and the rest of Provence under penalty of death. Despite this and the construction of a "Plague wall" 28km/17.4mi long, ordered by the papal vice-legate, the plague spread to Aix, Apt, Arles and Toulon. In two years 100 000 people died, 50 000 of whom were from Marseille.

Commercial Activity – In only a couple of years the city had re-established its demographic and economic energy. By 1765 the city had returned to the 1720 demographic level with c. 90 000 inhabitants. Trade flourished with Latin America and the West Indies; Marseille began importing sugar, coffee and cacao. Industrialisation began and fortunes made with soap- and glass-making,

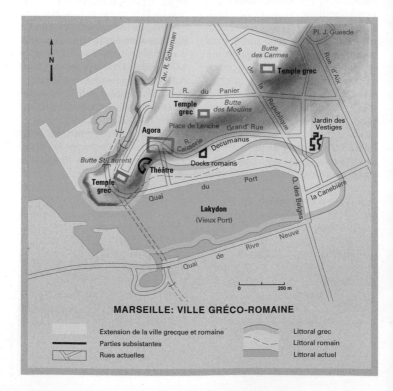

MARSEILLE: VILLE GRÉCO-ROMAINE

Extension de la ville grecque et romaine
Parties subsistantes
Rues actuelles

Littoral grec
Littoral romain
Littoral actuel

sugar refining, glazed earthenware (faïence) and textiles.

The city welcomed the Revolution with enthusiasm. In 1792, volunteers from the city popularised the "*Marseillaise*", composed by Rouget de Lisle (⊚ *see sidebar p320*). Marseille was the first city to demand the abolition of the monarchy. The tyranny of the Convention, however, became unbearable for Marseille and it rebelled.

Under the Empire, Marseille became Royalist, the city's trade having been hard hit by the continental blockade. Under the Second Empire, Marseille became Republican; urban projects were undertaken (the opening of the present rue de la République, construction of Palais Longchamp, Notre-Dame de la Garde basilica, the Cathedral, Pharo Palace and park). The conquest of Algeria put an end to the Barbary pirates and the opening of the Suez Canal in 1869 both contributed to the stimulation of economic activity.

The Present and Future – The German-Italian bombing of 1940 and that of the Allies in 1943–44 to prepare for their landing in Provence caused widespread damage and fatalities. In January 1943, under the pretext of public health, the Nazis evacuated 40 000 inhabitants from the old district in order to raze the streets between rue Caisserie and the Vieux Port.

After the Liberation Marseille threw all its energy into reconstruction programmes. The most striking project of this period was the **Cité Radieuse**, built between 1947–1952 on boulevard Michelet. Nicknamed the *Maison de Fada* or crazy house, this complex by **Le Corbusier** has a bold and innovative design. It is now much studied by architects worldwide and is open to the public.

Today, hit by economic recession, Marseille is seeking a new role, symbolised by the building of the futuristic local government office, designed by Will Alsop. A 25-year "Euro-Mediterranean" development project aims to remodel the city between the Belle de Mai, St-Charles train station and La Joliette, with the creation of cultural, economic and maritime centres.

☙ WALKING TOURS

① OLD MARSEILLE
VIEUX PORT★★
Begin at the Vieux Port, to which all streets lead.

The Phocaeans landed in this creek in 600 BC. It was here that, until the 19C, all Marseille's maritime life was concentrated. The quays were constructed under Louis XII and Louis XIII. In the 19C, the depth of two fathoms was found to be insufficient for steamships of large tonnage and new docks were built.

Hôtel de Ville
pl. Villeneuve de Bargemon.

A town hall has existed on this site since the 13C. The present building and its façade, an example of Provençal Baroque architecture, date from the middle of the 17C. The king's coat of arms above the main entrance is a copy of a work by **Pierre Puget** exhibited in the Musée des Beaux-Arts (⊚ *see Museums*).

Passing to the left of the building, notice the 16C **Maison Diamantée** (*r. de la Prison*), so called because of the faceted stones of its façade. Today it houses the Musée du Vieux Marseille (⊚ *see Museums*).

▷ *Take a few steps into Grand Rue; no 27 bis is the Hôtel de Cabre.*

Hôtel de Cabre
27 bis Grand Rue.

Built in 1535 and spared when much of the district was destroyed in 1943, this is one of the oldest houses in the city. Its Gothic, composite style is typical of civil Marseille architecture.

▷ *Return to place Daviel.*

Pavillon Daviel and Hôtel-Dieu
pl. Daviel.

The former Law Courts building, the Pavillon Daviel (mid-18C), has a beautiful

Vieux Port and Basilique de Notre-Dame-de-la-Garde

G. Magnin/MICHELIN

wrought-iron balcony decorated in the style typical of Marseille known as *à la marguerite or* daisy style, and a harmonious façade of pilasters.

The imposing **Hôtel-Dieu** which dominates the port is typical of hospital architecture of the second half of the 18C; note the arrangement of space and the superimposing of its arcaded galleries.

◐ *From here go towards the Quartier du Panier.*

Quartier du Panier★

Built on the Moulins hill on the site of ancient Massalia, the Panier district is all that remains of old Marseille since the Liberation. In the past its inhabitants, the majority of whom were of modest means and lived mainly from the sea, made the most of their tiny plots of land by constructing tall buildings. Just at the time when it was gradually becoming something of a ghetto, Le Panier reaped the benefits of a large renovation and development programme to turn the restored Vieille Charité into a **museum** (◐ *see opposite*). The area, with its narrow streets dissected here and there by flights of steps and where the tall façades are gradually regaining their former colours, is best explored on foot, preferably between shopping and lunchtime, at the end of the

morning: the **Montée des Accoules**, symbol of the area, but also **rue du Panier**, rue Fontaine-de-Caylus, rue Porte-Baussenque, rue du Petit-Puits, rue Ste-Françoise, rue du Poirier, and rue des Moulins which leads to place des Moulins. This charming and highly picturesque quarter of Marseille can be seen as a melting pot where Naples, Catalonia and the Mediterranean coast mingle with the French West Indies, Vietnam or the Comoro Islands to produce scenes which delight the senses: washing hangs from windows, the air is full of the scents of basil and *ratatouille* and bursts of Marseille French, and its inimitable turns of phrase, can be heard everywhere.

Centre de la Vieille Charité★★
2 r. de la Charité.

This well-restored former hospice is a fine architectural unit built from 1671 to 1749 based on the plans of Pierre and Jean Puget. The buildings, created originally to shelter the deprived, stand around the central **chapel**★, a fine Baroque building with an ovoid dome by Pierre Puget. The façades looking onto the courtyard present three storeys of arcaded galleries in elegant pink and yellow-tinted Couronne stone.

Nowadays the building houses the **Musée d'Archéologie Méditerrané-enne**, the museum of African, Oceanic and native American art (MAAOA), a poetry centre and a variety of exhibitions (&see Museums).

○ *Go round the left side of the Vieille Charité, turn left and left again into rue de l'Évêché, then turn right to reach the Major.*

Cathédrale de la Major
pl. de la Major. ○*Open Tue–Sun 9am–noon, 2.30–5.30pm.* ℘*04 91 90 53 57.*
A huge and sumptuous construction started in 1852 in Roman-Byzantine style. It was originally built at the instigation of the future Napoleon III, who wished to conciliate both the Church and the people of Marseille.

Ancienne Cathédrale de la Major★
pl. de la Major. ○━*Closed to the public.*
The "Old Major", in stout contrast, is a fine example of mid-11C Romanesque, truncated in the 19C to make space for the building of the new cathedral. Only the chancel, transept and one bay of the nave and side aisles remain.

○ *Go past the esplanade de la Tourelle and make for the small church of St-Laurent.*

Belvédère St-Laurent
Parvis de Saint-Laurent.
Located on the parvis of St-Laurent church, the old fishermen's parish of the St-Jean district, it offers a fine **view**★ of the Vieux Port, the entrance to the Canebière, the Étoile chain, Notre-Dame de la Garde basilica and the **Forts St-Jean and St-Nicolas**, built by Louis XIV in an attempt to control the town; the Fort St-Nicolas was stormed on 30 April 1790 and members of the Royal Family were imprisoned in Fort St-Jean, which now hosts **Musée des Civilisations de l'Europe et de la Méditerranée** (&see Musems).

Place de Lenche
This lively square with façades embellished with wrought-iron balconies is located on the presumed site of the agora of the Greek town; there is an interesting view of Notre-Dame de la Garde and the Théâtre de la Criée.

○ *Go to the landing stage of the legendary Ferry-Boat, which takes you to quai de Rive Neuve.*

② RIVE NEUVE
Quai de Rive-Neuve
It was only relatively recently that the shallows that inconvenienced this part of the port were dredged and the quayside

Centre de la Vieille Charité

B. Kaufmann/MICHELIN

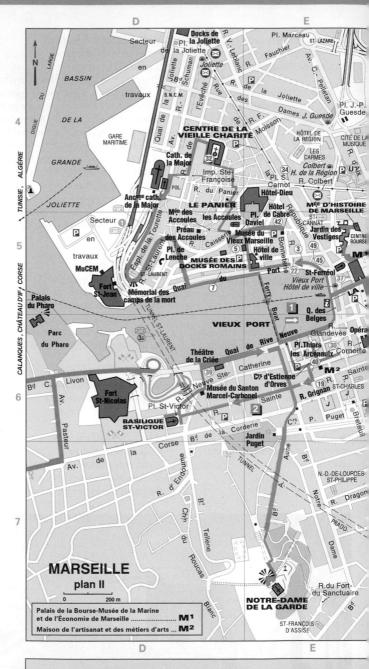

MARSEILLE
plan II

0 — 200 m

Palais de la Bourse-Musée de la Marine
et de l'Économie de Marseille .... **M¹**

Maison de l'artisanat et des métiers d'arts ... **M²**

WHERE TO STAY		WHERE TO EAT	
Hôtel Azur..............................⑯	Hôtel Relax..............................㉚	Axis................................①	
Hôtel Edmond Rostand........⑲	Hôtel Vertigo..................㉜	Bateau-Restaurant	
Hôtel Hermès......................㉒	New Hôtel Vieux Port......㊲	Le Marseillois...............③	
Hôtel Le Ryad......................㉗	Radisson SAS Hotel........㊳	Café des Épices............⑤	

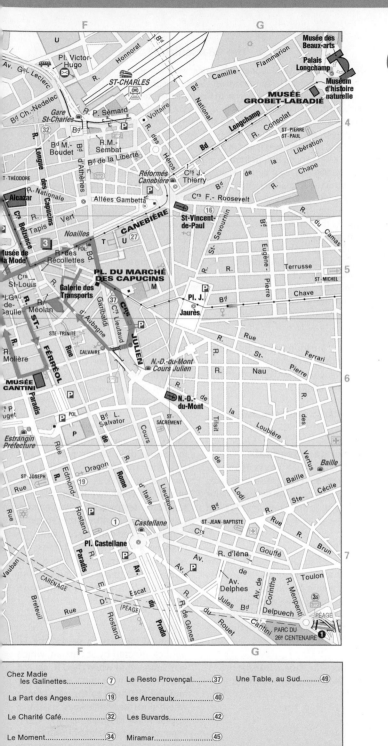

The "Marseillaise"

On 20 April 1792, Revolutionary France declared war against Austria. In Strasbourg, General Kellerman asked Claude Joseph Rouget de Lisle, a talented captain and composer-songwriter in his spare time, to write "a new piece to celebrate the departure of the volunteers"; the Chant de guerre pour l'armée du Rhin (War Song for the Rhine Army) was written on the night of 25 April. Soon adopted by a batallion from Rhône-et-Loire and carried south by commercial travellers, the Chant was heard in Montpellier on 17 June.

On 20 June, a young patriot from Montpellier on assignment in Marseille, François Mireur, sang it during a banquet offered by the Marseille Jacobin club, located at rue Thubaneau. Enthusiasm was such that the text of the song was distributed to 500 national guards from Marseille, who had been called to arms for the defence of Paris. Re-named *Chant de Guerre aux Armées des Frontières* (War Song for the Border Armies), the anthem was sung at each of the 28 stages of the journey towards the capital, with increasing success and virtuosity.

On 30 July, the impassioned verses sung by these warm southern voices, ringing out across the St-Antoine district, was referred to by the electrified crowd as the Chant des Marseillais (Song of the Marseillais). A few days later, the new anthem, on the storming of the Tuileries, was given its definitive name. The *Marseillaise* became the national anthem on 14 July 1795 and once again, after a long period of eclipse, on 14 February 1879.

improved. Surrounded by beautiful buildings in Neoclassical style, the quai de Rive-Neuve is nowadays livelier than its opposite bank.

▷ *Enter the shipyard district via place aux Herbes.*

Quartier des Arcenaulx

In the Italian-style **cours Honoré-d'Estienne-d'Orves** are several cafés and restaurants, as well as the remains of the Arsenal's buildings, at no **23** and no **25**.

Place Thiars

This pleasant square, dating from the end of the 18C, is full of restaurants and bars where *bagna freda* (anchovy paste and small raw vegetables) is often served with your apéritif; it is situated on the former naval construction site of the shipyard.

▷ *To reach the basilica take rue Marcel-Paul (steps) and rue Sainte on the right.*

Basilique St-Victor★

3 r. de l'Abbaye. ◯*Open daily 9am–7pm.* ✎*2€ (crypt).* 𝄞*04 96 11 22 60. www.saintvictor.net.*
This church is the last relic of the famous abbey known as the "key to Marseille harbour" founded in the early 5C by St John Cassian, a monk from the Far East, in honour of St Victor, patron saint of sailors and millers, who suffered martyrdom in the 3C by being slowly ground between two millstones. The sanctuary, destroyed in a Saracen raid, was rebuilt in c. 1040 and subsequently remodelled and strongly fortified.
From the outside it is truly a fortress. The porch, which opens into the Tour d'Isarn, is roofed with heavy pointed vaulting (1140) which is among the oldest in Provence.

Crypt★★

The most interesting part is the 5C basilica, erected by St Cassian, which was submerged when the 11C church was built. Near it are the cave of St Victor and the entrance to the catacombs where, since the Middle Ages, St Lazarus and St Mary Magdalene have been venerated. In the neighbouring crypts a remarkable series of ancient pagan and Christian sarcophagi can be seen. In the central chapel, near the so-called St-Cassian sarcophagus, is a shrine (3C) discovered in 1965, which contained the remains of town martyrs on the tomb of which the abbey was built.

◗ *Go down rue Neuve Ste-Catherine and the steps which lead to quai de Rive-Neuve.*

The **Théâtre National de Marseille-La Criée** *(30 quai de Rive-Neuve; ℘04 91 54 70 54; www.theatre-lacriee.com)*, whose reputation has been made by the Marcel Maréchal company, is located in the former fish auction house *(criée)*, which was moved near to the Estaque in 1975.

◗ *Take the car or the no 60 bus from cours Jean Ballard to go up to the basilica. To reach it on foot take boulevard Aune (at the very end of cours Pierre Puget) and walk through the pretty park.*

Basilique de Notre-Dame de la Garde

Leave the car on "Plateau de la Croix" (car parks). ◷*Open daily 7.25am–7.15pm.* ☛*Guided tours available.* ℘*04 91 13 40 80. www.notredamedelagarde.com.*
The basilica was built by Espérandieu in the mid-19C in the then fashionable Romano-Byzantine style. It stands on a limestone outcrop (alt 162m/532ft) on the site of a 13C chapel also dedicated to Our Lady. Surmounting the belfry (60m/197ft high) is a huge gilded statue of the Virgin. The interior is faced with multicoloured marble, mosaics and mural paintings by the Düsseldorf School. Numerous ex-votos cover the walls, whereas in the crypt is the lovely Mater Dolorosa in marble carved by Carpeaux.
A magnificent **panorama**★★★ can be enjoyed from the parvis of the basilica.

③ THE CANEBIÈRE
Built as Marseille expanded in the 17C, this avenue, the most famous in the city, derives its name from a hemp rope factory (hemp: *canèbe* in Provençal) which once existed here.

◗ *Start on the left-hand pavement of the Vieux Port.*

To the right of rue St-Ferréol a covered passageway and escalator lead to the Centre Bourse shopping centre which houses the **Musée d'Histoire de Marseille**★ *(�Ġsee Museums).* From here make for the Jardin des Vestiges which was brought to light during works for the layout of the quarter.

Jardin des Vestiges
Rue Henri Barbusse.
The fortifications of the Greek town, the horn shape of the ancient port surrounded by its 1C quays, and an entranceway into the town dating from the 4C make up this archaeological garden. During the Phocaean period, this site was located beside a swamp which slowly dried up in the 3C and 2C BC. In the second half of the 2C BC a new wall was built, from which interesting ruins remain: square towers, bastions and stepped curtain walls. Note the construction of the stone blocks hewn out of pink limestone from the cape of Couronne. A road dating from the Roman period enters the town through

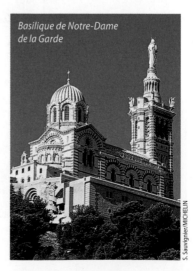

Basilique de Notre-Dame de la Garde

S. Sauvignier/MICHELIN

WHERE TO STAY

Chambre d'hôte
Villa Marie-Jeanne.................⑦

Chambre d'hôte
Villa Monticelli....................⑩

Hôtel Benidorm.......................⑲

Hôtel Le Corbusier...................㉕

Hôtel Le Richelieu...................㉘

Hôtel Les Cigales....................㉚

WHERE TO EAT

Chez Fonfon............................①

Cyprien..................................⑩

L'Épuisette............................⑬

Le Salon Provençal.................㊳

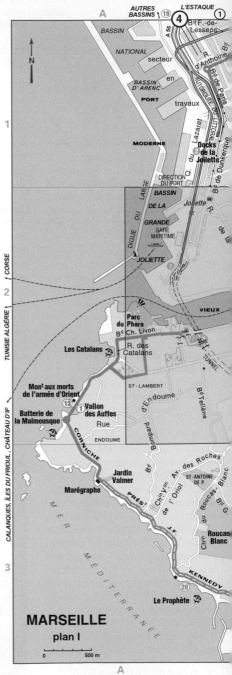

MARSEILLE
plan I

0   500 m

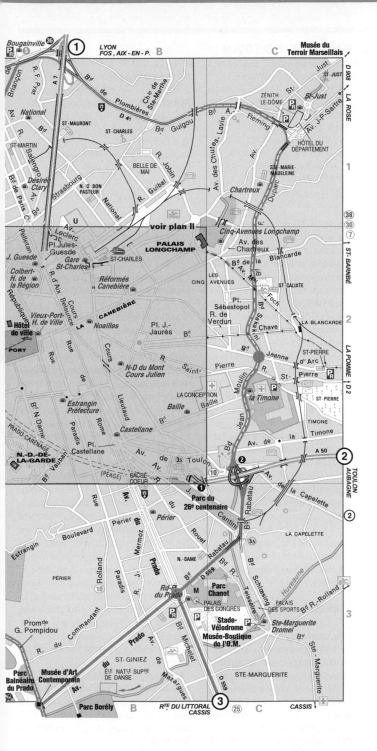

voir plan II

GETTING AROUND TOWN

METRO: This is the most convenient mode of transport; the two lines operate from 5am to 9pm (to 12.30am on Fri, Sat and Sun). From 9pm to 1am during the week, the metro is substituted by the "fluobus". Tickets are sold in the form of magnetic cards and are valid for a single trip (*ticket solo: 1.50€*), 1 day (*carte journée: 5€*) or for several journeys (*carte liberté: 6.30€ for 5 journeys, 12.60€ for 10*). Free network maps are given out at ticket offices. *04 91 91 92 10. www.rtm.fr.*

FERRY BOAT: Trips from one side of the Vieux Port to the other (saving you about 800 paces!): place aux Huiles to the town hall. *Journeys daily 9am–7pm. No charge. http://ferryboat-marseille.com.*

---

an older gate (2C BC), one of the flanking towers of which is still identifiable. Going back along the Canebière, several buildings are remarkable for the quality of their architecture, recalling the past glory of the street, especially on the right-hand side: the mid-18C rocaille facades of buildings between rue St-Ferréol and cours St-Louis; the Baroque-style building (1671–72) on the corner of cours St-Louis (nos **13**), which was to have formed one side of the Place Royale designed by Pierre Puget, but never finished; and two typical Second Empire buildings, no **53** (now a department store) and no **62** (Hôtel Noailles).

At no **58** cours Belsunce is the glass canopy of the famous **Alcazar** theatre which, after lying abandoned for decades, has now become the city's main library, the **Bibliothèque Municipale à Vocation Générale** (**BMVR**; *www.bmvr. marseille.fr*).

▷ *Go down to the shopping area which extends south of the Canebière. Turn right into boulevard Garibaldi and then immediately left.*

Cours Julien

Until 1972 this was the Marseille wholesale market for market garden produce. It has now been renovated and here you will find specialist restaurants and antique or clothing shops. The roads leading off to the east of the cours, such as rue de Bussy-l'Indien, rue Pastoret, rue Crudère, rue Vian, are slightly on the "fringe", their façades covered with artists' graffiti (note the front of La Maison Hantée, rue Vian) and the clubs and cafés which come to life as night falls.

▷ *Take the footbridge spanning cours Lieutard to reach rue d'Aubagne.*

Rue d'Aubagne, which also has its share of unusual establishments (e.g. the grocery shop at no **34**), leads to the "belly of Marseille", still lively, even if of less economic importance. Rue du Musée and rue Rodolph-Pollack specialise in exotic and African hairdressers; **place du marché des Capucins**, opposite Noailles metro station, is a hub for the local stall-holders or *partisanes*. The air rings with their loud cries, urging passers-by to purchase their lemons and beans. In the narrow **rue Longue-des-Capucins** the atmosphere of which is part souk, part flea market, the air is full of different scents: spices mingled with coffee, pitted or marinated olives, anchovies, herbs and dried fruit.

Rue des Halles-Charles-Delacroix (a former fish market, now demolished), lined with grocery stores and shops selling exotic wares, leads to rue Vacon, where Provençal fabrics are displayed, as well as to "Saint-Fé", the rue St-Ferréol, which is the main pedestrian-only shopping street of the city (*see Addresses*).

The **Musée Cantini** (*see Musems,*) is housed in the 17C Hôtel de la Compagnie du Cap Nègre, which was donated to the city. Return to the Canebière and take rue Paradis, a busy shopping street, on the right.

LA CORNICHE★★
You can drive down the Corniche but it is almost impossible to find a parking place.

Parc du Pharo
bd Charles Livon.
This park is situated on a promontory above the entrance to the Vieux Port. Enjoy the **view** from the terrace near the Pharo palace *(http://palaisdupharo. marseille.fr)*, built for Napoleon III. There is an underground auditorium in the park.

Corniche Président-J.-F.-Kennedy★★
This Corniche runs for nearly 5km/3mi – almost entirely along the sea-front. It is dominated by elegant villas built at the end of the 19C.
Level with the **Monument aux morts de l'armée d'Orient** *(60 Corniche Kennedy)*, attractive views open out towards the coast and the islands. A viaduct crosses the picturesque Auffes valley.

Vallon des Auffes
Access through boulevard des Dardanelles, just before the viaduct.
This tiny fishing port, crowded with traditional boats and ringed with *cabanons*, inspired Vincent Scotto. For a pleasant and timeless evening, choose an outdoor restaurant along the port, where you can appreciate the changing light of the setting sun.

Promenade de la Plage
This is the extension of the Corniche to the south, running alongside the **plages Gaston-Defferre**, a leisure area bordered by gardens with children's playgrounds which contains pleasure pools and artificial beaches. On the other side of the road there are several restaurants.
The Pointe Rouge, on the opposite side of the Prado roundabout, with its replica of Michelangelo's *David*, is an important sailing centre.

Château et Parc Borély
134 av. Clot-Bey. *Open Mon–Fri 10am–6pm.* *04 91 25 26 34.*
Built between 1767 and 1778 by the Borély, a family of wealthy merchants, the château will house the town's Museum of Decorative Arts once restoration work is complete.
The **park**, with its network of paths, extends to the east with beautiful **botanical gardens** *(av. du Prado; open daily 9.30am–noon, 1–6pm; 3€; 04 91 55 25 06)* is the venue every year for the extremely popular Provençal and Marseille *boules* competition, so typical of Marseille life.
You can continue to the little Montredon beach, where, in "La Campagne Pastré", an attractive 19C bastide, the superb **Musée de la Faïence** *(see Musems)* is housed, and as far as the Calanques des Goudes and Callelongue.

THE PORT
The old port had become inadequate, with ships crowded four or five rows deep, so in 1844 a law authorised the construction of a dock at La Joliette; later the docks of Lazaret and Arenc were built and the port area was enlarged through the addition of further docks to the north.
The city has retained some traditional Marseille activities, based on maritime trade industries: oil pressing, soap-making, flour milling, semolina production and metalworking.

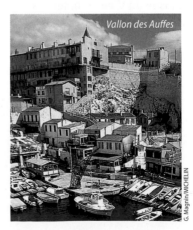
Vallon des Auffes

G. Magnin/MICHELIN

The two World Wars, the fact that larger ships could no longer use the Suez canal and decolonisation dealt Marseille a heavy blow. Reconversion and modernisation, mainly in the oil and chemical sectors, have brought about a shift in the main industrial activities to the area around the Étang de Berre and the Golfe de Fos. The new installations, administered by the Port Autonome de Marseille, have made this one of Europe's leading ports.

La Joliette Docks

Access: Metro Joliette. Entrance at place de la Joliette, through the administrative buildings.

Situated between the new port of La Joliette and the railway line, these warehouses were built from 1858 to 1863 and based on an English design. Almost 400m/1 312ft long, they are the embodiment of Marseille's economic peak as the Gateway to the Orient.

The use of stone, brick and cast iron in the construction, which nowadays is a specific feature of this type of architecture, was intended to prevent the risk of fire. Other installations connected to the activities of the docks, which were renovated in 1991, now hold plays and exhibitions, enabling the visitor to admire the remarkable vaulted cellars.

MUSEUMS

OLD MARSEILLE
Musée du Vieux Marseille★

Maison Diamantée, r. de la Prison.
Closed for renovation for the forseeable future. 04 91 55 28 68.

A selection of the collection is visible at the **Musée d'Histoire de Marseille** *(Square Belsunce – Centre Bourse; open Mon–Sat 12–7pm; closed public holidays; 04 91 90 42 22)* while restoration work is being finished. The ground floor contains 18C Provençal furniture and domestic objects. The staircase with its coffered ceiling goes up to the first floor where a number of 18C cribs in spun glass or resin-and-breadcrumbs and a large collection of *santons* (1830–early 1900s) are

exhibited. Another room is devoted to Marseille's old district, with a relief model of the town in 1848, while another room contains miscellaneous items concerning the great plague of 1720. On the second floor, displays of costumes, engravings and paintings illustrate 19C Marseille life.

Musée des Docks Romains★

pl. Vivaux. Open Tue–Sun Jun–Sept 11am–6pm; Oct–May 10am–5pm. Closed public holidays. 2€ (guided tours 2.50€). 04 91 91 24 62.

During reconstruction work in 1947 the remains of some commercial Roman warehouses used for storing *dolia* (large earthenware jars) were uncovered, dating from the 1C to the 3C. The museum contains objects found on the site, which date from the Greek period to the Middle Ages. A model reconstruction illustrates the site and its surroundings. The warehouse complex consisted of a ground floor level opening out onto the quay and a first floor level, which was probably connected by a gateway to the main street of the city, which is now rue Caisserie. The ground floor housed the *dolia* for grain, wine and oil. The history of trade in Marseille is retraced in the museum with the help of ceramic- and metalware and amphorae, retrieved from shipwrecks, and coins and measures. A potter's kiln demonstrates how amphorae were made.

Centre de la Vieille Charité★★

2 r. de la Charité. Open Tue–Sun Jun–Sept 11am–6pm; Oct–May 10am–5pm. Closed public holidays. Musée d'Archéologie méditerranéenne 2€; Musée des Arts Africains, Océaniens et Amérindiens 2€; temporary exhibitions 4€. 04 91 14 58 59.

The rich and varied collection of this museum, bringing together some 900 artefacts from the Near East, Greece, Etruria and Rome, constitutes one of the few provincial museums able to offer an almost complete picture of ancient Mediterranean civilisations.

The Alcazar Music Hall

Long since closed down, the renowned Alcazar music hall is still cherished by the people of Marseille and has become something of a legend.

The Alcazar first opened its doors in 1857 on the present cours Belsunce and for over a century was the home of variety shows. Here, against a backdrop of Moorish-inspired décor, mime artists, pastoral players, "Marseille review" entertainers, music-hall celebrities, fortune tellers, bawdy comedians, local eccentrics and, in later years, rock stars, all performed. The operettas of Vincent Scotto and Sarvil, performed by well-known French singers, developed their own style here, while at the same time the spirit of the Alcazar carried more than a hint of Marcel Pagnol.

The music hall reached its zenith between 1920 and 1950, with such artists as Mayol, Mistinguett, Rina Ketty and Maurice Chevalier, a regular performer here since his very first appearance at the age of 16. Raimu, Fernandel, Tino Rossi and Yves Montand all made their débuts at the Alcazar, the last in a Western-style repertoire which dubbed him the "young swing star of 1941".

Performing at this mythical venue was indeed a test: the audience here, as in the nearby Opéra, were merciless and would not tolerate a single note out of key or any vocal weakness, seizing the first opportunity to heckle, shout jibes or burst into raucous laughter. The performers nonetheless appreciated the skill and generosity of the theatre: stars tried out their shows at the Alcazar before heading up to Paris. The Alcazar closed down in 1964: one of the last celebrities to triumph there was the French pop singer Johnny Halliday.

Musée d'Archéologie Méditerranéenne★

First floor, north wing.

Egypt: Spanning the beginning of the Old Kingdom (2 700 BC) to the Coptic period (3C and 4C AD), this collection of approximately 1 600 pieces provides a complete overview of art, funerary rites, religion and daily life in Pharaonic Egypt.

Near East: Assyrian pieces from the palace of Sargon II at Dur-Sharukin (present-day Khorsabad) and the Assurbanipal Palace at Nineveh.

Cyprus: With as many as 185 artefacts, the collection of Cypriot antiquities is the largest to be found in any French provincial museum. It includes pieces of pottery with a shiny red surface bearing incised or light relief decoration dating from the Early Cypriot Bronze Age, Mycenaen-type funerary objects crafted in the Late Cypriot Bronze Age and turned ceramic pieces decorated with concentric circles from the Cypriot Geometric period.

Greece, Magna Grecia: Statues of marble Cycladic idols precede an exhibit dating from the Minoan civilisation; ceramics decorated with geometrical motif friezes are characteristic of the 9C and 8C BC. Corinthian works influenced by Eastern art (aryballos and alabaster: perfume vases ornamented with animal or floral motifs), black-figure ceramics, red-figure ceramics and sculptures of a naked young man *(couros)* or a clothed young woman *(koré)*.

Etruria, Rome: Ceramics in *bucchero nero*, where the carefully smoothed black paste rivals the shine of the silver pieces; funerary painting from Chiusi and Tarquinia, Vulci in stone sculpture, Cerveteri and Veii (sculpture of *koré*).

Roquepertuse and the Celtic-Ligurians – Roquepertuse is situated in the commune of Velaux (north of Vitrolles) where various excavation projects have unearthed a remarkable archaeological collection. This includes painted, sculpted and engraved fragments, statues of warriors sitting cross-legged, huge birds and the bicephalous **Hermes**★, a magnificent sculpture of two heads attached by a mortice and tenon joint. The "broken heads" portico consists of three monolithic pillars, the upper part of which is hollowed out with cephaliform cavities which were intended to hold skulls.

Musée des Arts Africains, Océaniens et Amérindiens (MAAOA)★★

Second floor, north and east wings.

After the Musée de l'Homme in Paris, this museum has the richest collection of artefacts from Africa, Oceania and the Americas of any museum in France. The works are exhibited on one side against a black background, illuminated by indirect lighting, while the opposite exhibit provides the corresponding explanatory text.

Salle Pierre-Guerre

In this room are objects donated by Pierre Guerre, as well as other masks, sculptures, reliquaries and other daily objects mainly from West Africa.

Salle Antonin-Artaud

The objects in this room recall the civilisations of Oceania and the Americas: ceremonial paddles, a headdress mask from Wayana (Brazil), shrunken human heads (*tsantsas* of the Jivaros Indians, Ecuador) and other cult objects. The Gastaut collection brings together a unique set of sculpted, engraved and shaped human skulls, illustrating the ancient civilisations of Oceania and Amazonia. Finally, the François Reichenbach Collection consists of popular objets d'arts from Mexico.

Musée des Civilisations de l'Europe et de la Méditerranée (MuCEM)

Fort Saint-Jean, Quai du Port. ◷*Open Tue–Sun Jun–Sept 11am–6pm; Oct–May 10am–5pm.* ⦸*Closed public holidays.* ⊜*2€.* ℘*04 96 11 63 22. www.mucem.eu.*

This museum is dedicated to European cultures, which also houses the collections of the former Museum of Arts and Popular Traditions in the Bois de Boulogne. It is an ongoing project.

AROUND THE CANEBIÈRE
Musée d'Histoire de Marseille★

Square Belsunce, Centre Bourse. ♿◷*Open Mon–Sat noon–7pm.* ⦸*Closed public holidays.* ⊜*2€.* ℘*04 91 90 42 22.*

The museum is located at the end of the Jardin des Vestiges. It traces the history of Marseille in its Provençal context from prehistoric to Gallo-Roman times through archaeological finds, documents and models. The model of Greek Marseille in the 3C and 2C BC shows the horn shape of the ancient port, complete with slipways.

A Roman merchant vessel dating from the 3C, preserved through freeze-drying, shows the wide range of wood used in naval construction of the time: the keel is made of cypress, the stem of umbrella pine, the keys and plugs of olive or ilex, and the planking and interior covering of larch and Aleppo pine.

Musée de la Marine et de l'Économie de Marseille

Palais de la Bourse, 9 la Canebière. ◷*Open Tue–Sun Jun–Sept 11am–6pm; Oct–May 10am–5pm.* ⦸*Closed public holidays.* ⊜*2€.* ℘*04 91 39 33 33.*

This maritime and commercial museum displays several models of sailboats and steamships; paintings, watercolours, engravings and plans illustrate marine history and the history of the port of Marseille, from the 17C to the present.

Musée de la Mode

11 La Canebière. ♿◷*Open Tue–Sun Jun–Sept 11am–6pm; Oct–May 10am–5pm.* ⦸*Closed public holidays.* ⊜*2€; temporary exhibitions* ⊜*4€.* ℘*04 96 17 06 00. www.espacemodemediterranee.com.*

This museum has temporary exhibitions on costume and fashion themes.

Musée Cantini★

19 r. Grignan. ◷*Open Tue–Sun Jun–Sept 11am–6pm; Oct–May 10am–5pm.* ⦸*Closed public holidays.* ⊜*2€.* ℘*04 91 54 77 75.*

This museum specialises in 20C art after World War II until 1960, with particular attention to Fauvist, early Cubist, Expressionist and Abstract art, including works by Matisse, André Derain (*Pine Forest, Cassis*), Raoul Dufy *(Factory in the Estaque)*, Alberto Magnelli (*Stones no 2*, 1932), Dubuffet *(Striking Woman)*, Kandinsky, Chagall, Jean Hélion and Picasso. The presence of a number of Surrealist artists in Marseille during the last war is represented with paintings by André Masson (*Antille*, 1943), Max Ernst (*Monument to the Birds*, 1927), Wilfredo Lam, Victor Brauner, Jacques Hérold, Joan Miró and rare drawings by the Marseille artist Antonin Artaud.

The port of Marseille, a local subject of inspiration along with l'Estaque, is represented on canvases by Marquet, Signac and the Marseille specialist in this subject, Louis Mathieu Verdilhan (1875–1928). Finally, the collection features a few works by 20C artists who defy classification: Baltus *(The Bather)*, Giacometti *(Portrait of Diego)* and Francis Bacon *(Self-Portrait)*.

LONGCHAMP DISTRICT
Musée Grobet-Labadié★★

140 bd Longchamp. ⊙*Open Tue–Sun Jun–Sept 11am–6pm; Oct–May 10am–5pm.* ⊙*Closed public holidays.* ∞*2€.* ℘*04 91 62 21 82.*

The bourgeois interior of this town house has been preserved, with its fine Flemish and French (16C–18C) tapestries, furniture, 18C Marseille and Moustiers faïence ware, religious gold and silver plate, wrought-iron work and old musical instruments. Fine paintings hang on the walls: Flemish, German and Italian Primitives, French School covering the 17C–19C. The museum is enriched by a collection of drawings by European schools from the 15C to the 19C.

Palais Longchamp★
bd Philipon.

This imposing building was constructed by the Nîmes architect Henri Espérandieu from 1862 to 1869. In its centre stands a neatly concealed water tower embellished by fountains; it is linked by colonnades to the Musée des Beaux-Arts *(on the left)* and the Musée d'Histoire Naturelle *(on the right).*

Musée des Beaux-Arts★
Palais Longchamp. ⊶*Closed for restoration until 2011.*

∴ Musée d'Histoire Naturelle★
Right wing, Palais Longchamp. ⊙*Open Tue–Sun 10am–5pm.* ⊙*Closed public holidays.* ∞*4€ (child 2€).* ℘*04 91 14 59 50. www.museum-marseille.org.*

Rich zoological, geological and prehistoric collections are exhibited. Four hundred million years of history of the Provence-French Riviera region are retraced, and a safari museum illustrates the diversity of the animal kingdom throughout the world. A gallery is devoted to Provençal flora and fauna. The various **aquariums** present a standing exhibition on white waters in Provence under the title "Eaux vives, du Verdon aux Calanques".

La Canebière

The fame of this street spread worldwide, thanks to sailors of all nationalities who visited the great Mediterranean port. The operettas of Vincent Scotto and popular songs from the inter-war years also contributed to making this avenue the symbol of the bustling city. The street's real period of glory lasted for three-quarters of a century, until the Occupation, when it was the crossroads for the whole public transport system and where all the city's fashionable cafés, cinemas and department stores were gathered. Today it has lost its prestige; despite a "Plan Canebière" aimed at rehabilitating the area by implanting administrative offices, it is still a far cry from its former glory, especially after nightfall. An indication of its renewal is the recent reopening of the Nouvelles Variétés, one of the great café/concert venues of the 1930s, now transformed into an art house cinema.

SOUTHERN DISTRICTS

From the promenade de la Plage, once level with the Escale Borély, turn into avenue de Bonneveine and continue to the intersection with avenue d'Haifa, where a large metal thumb sculpted by César can be seen.

Musée d'Art contemporain

69 av. d'Haifa (not on map). &♿○*Open Tue–Sun Jun–Sept 11am–6pm; Oct–May 10am–5pm.* ○*Closed public holidays.* ⊛*2€.* *04 91 25 01 07.*
This museum has been constructed via the juxtaposition of identical modules. The permanent collection, which concentrates on French artists and gives pride of place to artists either born or living in Marseille, brings together the different trends in contemporary art from the 1960s to the present day: structured movements, such as New Realism, the Support-Surface or Arte Povera group, but also eclectic work from the 1980s and maverick art which resists all attempts at classification. This rewarding collection includes work by César, Richard Baquié, Jean-Luc Parent, Daniel Burren, the complex creative approach of Martial Raysse, Jean-Pierre Raynaud, Tinguely, Yves Klein, contributions by Robert Combas and Jean-Michel Basquiat as well as exhibits of the sometimes underrated art of our culture: cartoons and graffiti.

Musée de la Faïence★

157 av. de Montredon (not on map). &♿○*Open Tue–Sun Jun–Sept 11am–6pm; Oct–May 10am–5pm.* ○*Closed public holidays.* ⊛*2€.* *04 91 72 43 47.*
Walk past the Parc Borély and proceed towards Pointe Rouge. The museum is situated at the far end of the Parc de Montredon. Set up in the Château Pastré, a fine 19C mansion built at the foot of the Marseilleveyre massif, this museum is devoted to the art of ceramics, from the early Neolithic Era up to the present day. A great many of the collections feature exhibits from Provence, and particularly Marseille, where the manufacturing of faience pottery was considerable in the late 17C and 18C.

EXCURSIONS

Îles du Frioul

Sea crossing: leaves from Quai des Belges, Vieux Port. ⊛*10€ return to If or Frioul and* ⊛*15€ to both. For times, contact Frioul If Express* *04 91 46 54 65. http://frioul.cityway.fr.*

👥 Château d'If★★

Accessible by boat from Embarcadère Frioul If Express, 1 quai de la Fraternité. ○*Open 4 Apr–14 Sept daily 9.30am–6pm; 15 Sept–5 Oct Tue–Sun 9.30am–6pm; 6 Oct–Mar Tue–Sun 9am–5.30pm; 1–3 Apr daily 9am–5.30pm.* ○*Closed 1 Jan, 25 Dec.* ⊛*5€ (child no charge).* *04 91 59 02 30. http://if.monuments-nationaux.fr.*
Alexandre Dumas (1802–70), the popular 19C French author of *The Three Musketeers*, gave this castle literary fame by imprisoning three of his heroes here: the Man in the Iron Mask, the Count of Monte Cristo and Abbé Faria. Built rapidly from 1524 to 1528, Château d'If was an outpost destined to protect the port of Marseille. In the late 16C the castle was encircled by a bastioned curtain wall. After falling into disuse, it became a state prison where Huguenots and various political prisoners were held; their cells can be visited.
The **panorama**★★★ from the old chapel terrace is remarkable, taking in the harbour, the city and the Ratonneau and **Pomègues** islands, linked by the new port of Frioul.

Massif des Calanques★★

See Massif Les CALANQUES

Chaîne de l'Estaque★

See Chaîne de l'ESTAQUE

ADDRESSES

🛏 STAY

⊝⊜ **Hôtel Benidorm** – *734 chemin du Littoral (Estaque), 12km/7.4mi NW. Bus 35, 36.* ☏*04 91 46 12 91. 26 rooms.* ⊑*6€.* The only hotel in Estaque, the building is white and rooms are simple and practical. Reasonable prices.

⊝⊜ **Hôtel Relax** – *4 r. Corneille.* ⊚*Vieux Port.* ☏*04 91 33 15 87. www.hotelrelax.fr. 21 rooms.* ⊑*7€.* Situated near Marseille's shopping area and a 2min walk from Vieux Port, the location is ideal. Rooms are neatly laid out with homely furnishings.

⊝⊜ **Hotel Le Richelieu** – *52 Corniche Kennedy. Bus 83.* ☏*04 91 31 01 92. www. lerichelieu-marseille.com. 21 rooms.* ⊑*8€.* Charming hotel near the Catalans beach. Seven types of rooms and prices with or without views (and bathrooms!). No 5 has a view to die for.

⊝⊜–⊝⊜⊜ **Hôtel Azur** – *24 cour Franklin Roosevelt.* ⊚*Réformés.* ☏*04 91 42 74 38. www.azur-hotel.fr. 18 rooms.* ⊑*8€. Restaurant*⊝⊜. Very near tje Canabière, this hotel has is in typical Provençal style. Rooms are spread across four floors; some give onto the garden, where you can take breakfast. Friendly staff.

⊝⊜–⊝⊜⊜ **Hôtel Edmond Rostand** – *31 r. du Dragon.* ⊚*Castellane.* ☏*04 91 37 74 95. www.hoteledmondrostand.com. 15 rooms.* ⊑*8.50€.* Clean, simple contemporary rooms with comfortable beds. Very reasonable price.

⊝⊜–⊝⊜⊜ **Hôtel Vertigo** – *42 r. des Petites Maries.* ⊚*Vieux Port.* ☏*04 91 91 07 11. www.hotelvertigo.fr. 2 renovated hostels, cabins and a private house.* ⊑. Situated in the historic Belsunce neighbourhood, this place offers varying accommodation types from hostel-style sharing to twin or double rooms. Very nicely renovated.

⊝⊜⊜ **Chambre d'hôte Villa Marie-Jeanne** – *4 r. Chicot.* ⊚*Cinq Avenue Long Champs.* ☏*04 91 85 51 31. 3 rooms.* ⊑*12.50€.* A 19C building in a residential quarter of the city. Traditional, elegant Provençal touch, old-fashioned furniture with modern amenities.

⊝⊜⊜ **Hôtel Le Corbusier** – *280 bd Michelet. Bus 21, 22.* ☏*04 91 16 78 00. www.hotellecorbusier.com. 21 rooms.* ⊑*9€. Restaurant*⊝⊜. *Closed 1 week in Jan.* This unique hotel is located on three floors of Le Corbusier's Cité Radieuse, a short bus ride from the centre of town. Rooms all have original minimalist features and accessories and there's a 360-degree view from the roof. Great location for football fans as it's a 10min walk from the Stade Vélodrome.

⊝⊜⊜–⊝⊜⊜⊜ **Chambre d'hote Villa Monticelli** – *96 r. du Cdt-Rolland.* ⊚*Rond-Point du Prado.* ☏*04 91 22 15 20. www.villamonticelli.com. 5 rooms.* ⊠. ⊑. This Art Deco building near the centre has as an unusual, colourful interior. Modest, comfortable rooms.

⊝⊜⊜–⊝⊜⊜⊜ **Hôtel les Cigales** – *rte Enco-de-Botte, 13190 Allauch, 15km/9.3mi NE.* ☏*04 91 68 17 07. www.hotel-lescigales.fr. Reservations advised. 6 rooms, 1 suite.* ⊑*7€. Restaurant*⊝⊜. A recent building between Marseille and Allauch, rooms are tranquil and families welcome. Garden with pool.

⊝⊜⊜⊜ **Hôtel Hermès** – *25 r. Bonneterie.* ⊚*Vieux Port.* ☏*04 96 11 63 63. www.hotelmarseille.com/hermes/ hermes_us/hotel.html. 28 rooms.* ⊑*8€.* Unpretentious, centrally located hotel with small well-kept rooms; those on the fifth floor have a terrace overlooking the quayside. Panoramic rooftop sundeck.

⊝⊜⊜⊜ **Hôtel Le Ryad** – *16 r. Sénac de Meilhan.* ⊚*Vieux Port.* ☏*04 91 47 74 54. www.leryad.fr. 9 rooms.* ⊑. The Moroccan-inspired beautiful, stylish rooms are very inviting. Visit the colourful tea room in the afternoon or the hotel's little restaurant.

⊝⊜⊜⊜ **New Hôtel Vieux Port** – *3 bis r. Reine-Elisabeth.* ⊚*Vieux Port.* ☏*04 91 90 76 24. www.new-hotel.com/vieuxport. 42 rooms.* ⊑*14€.* Well located in the centre of Marseille by the Vieux Port, this hotel's rooms are pretty and decorated in exotic themes: Pondichery, Rising sun, Arabian Nights, Vera Cruz or Tropical Africa. An invitation to relax and unwind!

⊜⊜⊜⊜ **Radisson SAS Hotel** – *38 quai de Rive Neuve. ⋒Vieux Port. ℘04 88 92 19 50. www.radissonblu.com. 189 rooms. ⌷12€. Restaurant⊜⊜⊜.* Right by Vieux Port, this plush establishment, between Fort St-Nicolas and Théâtre de la Criée, is furnished beautifully. Immaculate, bright rooms. Enjoy the hotel's bar, café or restaurant.

⊌ EAT

⊜ **Le Salon Provençal** – *pl. Benjamin Chappe, 13190 Allauch, 15km/9mi NE. ℘04 91 68 39 92. Closed Thu.* An adorable small place in old Allauch. Amiable tea parlour, terrace and three small rooms where you can eat in peace.

⊜⊜ **Axis** – *8 r. Ste-Victoire. ⋒Castellane. ℘04 91 57 14 70. www.axis-restaurant.com. Closed 3–31 Aug, 24–30 Dec, Sat lunch, Sun, Mon eve.* The seasonal, contemporary-style cuisine makes this establishment worth a detour. Modern décor, with views of the chefs in action. Charming welcome.

⊜⊜ **Le Café des Épices** – *4 r. Lacydon. ⋒Vieux Port. ℘04 91 91 22 69. Reservations advised.* This tiny resturant seats just 20, but the esplanade terrace and its olive grove in the background are delightful.

⊜⊜ **Le Charité Café** – *2 r. de la Charité. ⋒Colbert. ℘04 91 91 08 41.* Very pleasant brasserie. Salads, sandwiches, desserts and drinks, etc. to eat in or take away.

⊜⊜ **Charles Livon** – *89 bd Ch. Livon. ℘04 91 52 22 41. Closed Aug, Sat lunch, Sun, Mon lunch.* Opposite the Palais du Pharo, this restaurant has a minimalist décor adorned with orchids. Reinterpreted regional cuisine; fine selection of Provence and Rhône wines.

⊜⊜ **Chez Madie Les Galinettes** – *138 quai du Port. ⋒Vieux Port. ℘04 91 90 40 87. Closed Sat lunch in Jul, Sun.* Near the museums of Old Marseille, this Povençal restaurant with terrace gives onto the old port. A fair selection of hot and cold dishes.

⊜⊜ **Cyprien** – *56 av. de Toulon. ⋒La Timone. ℘04 91 25 50 00. Closed 31 Jul–2 Sept, 24 Dec–2 Jan, Mon eve, Sat lunch, Sun, public holidays.* This restaurant near the place Castellane offers classic, tasty cuisine and a décor to match. Interior adorned with floral touches and paintings.

⊜⊜ **Miramar** – *12 quai du Port. ⋒Vieux Port. ℘04 91 91 10 40. www.bouillabaisse.com.* This restaurant, serving bouillabaisse and other fish specialities on the Vieux Port, has a very 1960s stylewith varnished wood and red chairs.

⊜⊜ **La Part des Anges** – *33 r. Sainte. ⋒Vieux Port. ℘04 91 33 55 70. www.lapart desanges.com.* This wine bar is fairly lively in the evening. Taste wine by the glass or bottle or take away. Cold cuts, cheese, etc. to accompany the wine. Rustic décor.

⊜⊜ **Le Resto Provençal** – *64 cours Julien. ⋒Cours-Julien. ℘04 91 48 85 12. Closed Sun, Mon, Wed eve (except Mon and Wed in Aug), every afternoon in Aug.* A cosy place with Provençal specialities including sea bream soup and fig tart.

⊜⊜ **Une Table, au Sud** – *2 quai du Port (1st floor). ⋒Vieux Port. ℘04 91 90 63 53. Closed 1–28 Aug, 3–11 Jan, Sun–Mon.* This colourful restaurant delights both the eye and the taste buds, thanks to its inventive cuisine with delicious southern accents, as well as views of the forts and hilltop basilica.

⊜⊜ **La Virgule** – *27 r. de la Loge. ⋒Vieux Port. ℘04 91 90 91 11. Closed Sun–Mon.* Culinary surprises await you at this restaurant with black, white and steel décor.

⊜⊜⊜ **Les Arcenaulx** – *25 cours d'Estienne-d'Orves. ⋒Vieux Port. ℘04 91 59 80 30. www.jeanne-laffitte.com. Closed Aug, Sun.* Dine surrounded by books which cover the walls of this restaurant: it's combined with a bookshop and publishers, located in the orignal warehouses of the 17C Arsenal des Galères. Large terrace and sun-kissed cooking.

⊜⊜⊜ **Bateau-Restaurant Le Marseillois** – *quai du Port-Marine, just by the Town Hall. ⋒Vieux Port. ℘04 91 90 72 52. www.lemarseillois.com. Closed Sun–Mon, Feb.* A 19C building opposite the *mairie*. Provençal cuisine, particularly seafood.

⊜⊜⊜ **Les Buvards** – *34 Grand'Rue.*

Vieux Port. 04 91 90 69 98. Friendly bistro with tasty, affordable cuisine and a decent wine list. Great place to meet in the evenings.

Chez Fonfon – *140 Vallon-des-Auffes. Bus 83.* 04 91 52 14 38. *www.chez-fonfon.com. Closed 30 Dec–15 Jan, Mon lunch, Sun.* The dining room of this renowned restaurant dominates the Vallon des Auffes harbour. Every morning fresh fish and seafood are brought in by "pointus", the local fishing boats.

l'Épuisette – *quartier du Vallon des Auffes.* 04 91 52 17 82. *Closed 5 Aug–5 Sept, Sun–Mon.* Set near the rocks in the picturesque Auffes valley, this restaurant takes you on a pleasant culinary voyage in a light, warm and refined atmosphere. Attentive staff.

Le Moment – *5 pl. Sadi Carnot. Colbert.* 04 91 52 47 49. *www.le moment-marseille.com.* Run by chef Christian Ernst, this new trendy restaurant near the old port offers two a contemporary dining room, sitting rooms upstairs, workshops, wine library and takeaway dishes. Fantastic cuisine in refined surroundings.

NIGHTLIFE

Bar de la Marine – *15 quai Rive-Neuve. Vieux Port.* 04 91 54 95 42. The setting for Marcel Pagnol's *Marius et Fanny* trilogy, you're more likely to find the beautiful people having a drink here these days. A great spot for pre- or post-dinner drinks – if you can get a seat.

Café Parisien – *1 pl. Sadi-Carnot. Colbert.* 04 91 90 05 77. *www.cafe-parisien.fr. Closed Sun.* At weekends this attractive baroque-style café hosts musical events based on the themes presented in the monthly art exhibitions.

TOURS

Guided Tours – *By reservation at the tourist office. 6.50€.* Guided tours (2hr) take place on various themes, in several languages, most days.

Le Grand Tour (bus) – *Leaves from quai du Port daily, on the hour from 10am. 18€ (20€ 2 days).* 04 91 91 05 82.

www.marseillelegrandtour.com. Hop on-hop off bus tour (1hr 30min circuit) with audio commentary in several languages that takes you around all the major sights.

Tourist train – *Leaves from quai du Port. 7€ (child 4€).* 04 91 25 24 69. *www.petit-train-marseille.com.* There are two itineraries: to Notre-Dame de la Garde going past the Basilica of St-Victor (year-round) and Le Panier, the old town (Apr–Oct).

EVENTS

Programmes are listed in local newspapers (*La Provence, www. laprovence.com; La Marseillaise, www. journal-lamarseillaise.com*) and the tourist office also distributes a small monthly magazine, *In Situ*.

Festival de Marseille – *Jun–Jul.* 04 91 99 02 50. *www.festivaldemarseille.com.* Theatre, music and dance festival takes place in atmospheric venues in the city.

Fiesta des Suds – *www.dock-des-suds. org.* In late October, this world music festival brings 50 000 spectators to Marseille and vibrates with the music and traditions of the Mediterranean.

Folklore – International Folklore Festival at Château-Gombert takes place in early July *(www.roudelet-felibren.com).*

Pétanque World Championships – Preliminary games in Parc Borély, finals at the Vieux Port. A very popular event frequented by celebrities who, after a few throws, let the champions take over. First week in July *(http://mediterranee. france3.fr/mondial-petanque).*

Santons Fair – Extensive selection of the finest *santons* in Provence displayed in the centre of town end-Nov–end-Dec.

SHOPPING

BOOKS
Librairie-galerie-restaurant des Arcenaulx– *25 cours d'Estienne d'Orves. Vieux-Port.* 04 91 59 80 40. *www. les-arcenaulx.com.* Home of publisher Jeanne Laffitte. Specialises in books on Marseille, Provence and food; old and rare books. Quality gifts and restaurant.

CLOTHES

The main shopping street is rue St-Ferréol, which has many individual and chain boutiques plus Galeries Lafayette. Adventurous dressers might like to visit Marseille's well-known designer, **Madame Zaza** *(73 cours Julien; ⊕Notre Dame du Mont; ℘04 91 48 05 57; www.madamezazaofmarseille.com)* for colourful, daring outfits.

MARKETS

Fish market every morning on *quai des Belges*. Food markets are open Mon–Sat mornings in *cours Pierre Puget, place Jean-Jaurès* (la Plaine), *place du Marché-des-Capucins* and *avenue du Prado. Boulevard La Canebière* has a flower market every Tuesday and Saturday morning; this market is also set up on *avenue du Prado* every Friday morning.

Every second Saturday of the month *cours Julien* has a book market and second-hand books and records can be bought daily outside the Palais des Arts. Finally, there is a fleamarket on Sunday mornings in *avenue du Cap-Pinède*.

OLIVE OIL

Lei Moulins – *4–6 bd Tellène. ⊕Estrangin Préfecture. ℘04 91 59 49 78. www.leimoulins.com. Closed Sun, Mon.* Cave-like shop in the St-Victor quarter. You'll find an interesting selection of olive oil from the Med and also a selection of jams made on the premises.

SANTONS

Santons Marcel Carbonel – *47–49 r. Neuve-Ste-Catherine. ⊕Vieux Port. ℘04 91 13 61 36. www.santonsmarcelcarbonel.com. Closed Sun. Guided visits Tue and Thu on request.* Visit the workshop where the famous *santons*

Savon de Marseille

S. Sauvignier/MICHELIN

are made. Take a browse through the little museum before hitting the shop.

SOAP

La Compagnie de Provence – *18 r. Francis Davso. ⊕Vieux Port. ℘04 91 33 04 17. www.lcdpmarseille.com. Closed Sun.* Marseille soap and natural products make this shop smell wonderful.

Savonnerie de la Licorne – *34 cours Julien. ⊕Notre Dame du Mont. ℘04 96 12 00 91. www.savon-de-marseille-licorne.com. Mon–Fri 8am–5pm, Sat 10am–6pm.* The only artisan-made soap in the centre of town. Perfumes include rose, violet and pastis. Visits of the workshop on request.

Four des Navettes

G. Magnin/MICHELIN

SWEET TREATS

Four des Navettes – *136 r. Sainte. ⊕Estrangin Préfecture. ℘04 91 33 32 12. www.fourdesnavettes.com.* It is impossible to celebrate Candlemas without a *navette*, which are believed to protect houses from sickness and catastrophe. These biscuits, flavoured with orange blossom, are bought from the city's oldest bakery; their recipe has been jealousy guarded for two centuries. There is also lavender-flavoured chocolate, replete with the scent of Provence.

🏃 LEISURE ACTIVITY

👥 **Football** – People here are obsessed with football and their local team, Olympique de Marseille, known as l'OM *(www.om.net)*. Try and get a ticket for a match at the Stade Vélodrome, if not, watch it on TV at the Brasserie de l'OM on quai des Belges at the Vieux Port. Souvenir shirts are available at the Stade, bd Michelet or on La Canebière.

Martigues
Bouches-du-Rhône

Martigues took its name in 1581 after the union of the three villages of Jonquières (now the shopping centre), Ile (the old town with its canals) and Ferrières (tourist office and Musée Ziem). Set on the banks of the Étang de Berre and linked to the sea by the Canal de Caronte, Martigues, once a small fishing village, has been transformed and enlarged as a result of the expansion of the oil industry and its subsidiaries around Lavéra-Étang de Berre. In the past, painters (Corot, Ziem) and writers (Charles Maurras) alike were captivated by the luminosity and charm of this typical Provençal port; thus Martigues acquired great renown in literary and artistic circles.

- ▶ **Population:** 46 318.
- ◔ **Michelin Map:** 340: F-5 – local map, ◔see *Étang de BERRE*.
- ▮ **Information:** Rond-Point de l'Hôtel de Ville, Martigues. ℘04 42 42 31 10. www.martigues-tourisme.com.
- ☺ **Don't Miss:** Provençal water jousting on the canals (June–August); St Peter's Day Festival (end June); Venetian Festival (start of July).

VISIT
Miroir aux Oiseaux★
Pont St-Sébastien on Île Brescon affords a view of the brightly coloured pleasure craft along Canal St-Sébastien. Popular with painters, this spot is known as the Birds' Looking Glass.

Musée Ziem
bd du 14 Juillet, Quartier Ferrières.
◔*Open Wed–Sun 2.30–6.30pm.*
◉*No charge.* ℘*04 42 41 39 60.*
www.ateliermuseal.net.
Grouped around the works of Félix Ziem (1821–1911), painter of landscapes and oriental scenes, are works by Provençal artists from the 19C and 20C. Also exhibited in the museum are collections of local ethnology and archaeology and an exhibition of contemporary art.

EXCURSIONS
Étang de Berre★
Round trip of 113km/70mi by the D 5.
Allow one day
(◔see Étang de BERRE).

Fos-sur-Mer★
9km/5.6mi by the N 568. Allow 2hr
(◔see FOS-SUR-MER).

ADDRESSES

☞ STAY
⊜⊜ **Le Cigalon** – *37 bd du 14-Juillet.*
℘*04 42 80 49 16. www.lecigalon.fr.*
21 rooms. ⊐*7€.* Located a few minutes from the centre of the "Venice" of Provence, this family-run hotel has a colourful, eye-catching façade. The rooms are simple but beautifully kept and air-conditioned; the food is Mediterranean and served in a typically Provençal décor.

⑊ EAT
⊜⊜⊜ **Le Moulin de Paradis** – *av. Georges Braque.* ℘*04 42 42 36 36.*
www.hotelsaintroch.com. Closed 25 Dec–1 Jan. A restaurant serving Provençal cuisine with a terrace with a view of the 16C tower.

⊜⊜⊜⊜ **Le Garage** – *20 av. Frédéric Mistral.* ℘*04 42 44 09 51.*
www.restaurantmartigues.com.
Closed Sat lunch, Sun eve, Mon. Centrally located with fashionable décor and a modern menu.

St-Blaise

Bouches-du-Rhône

With the sea, the River Rhône, the Étang de Berre as well as other small lagoons and the vast Crau plain not far away, the oppidum of St-Blaise (in the commune of St-Mitre-les-Remparts) is a historic site, the wealth of which depended, during the Hellenic occupation, on the working and trading of salt. After being abandoned for some 400 years, it was reoccupied between the 4C and the 14C.

◔ **Michelin Map:** 340: E-5.
▷ **Location:** Coming from Martigues on the D 5, you arrive at the roundabout of St-Mitre. Go left on the D 51 towards St-Blaise along the Étang de Citis. After 2km/1mi, you'll see the car park. Climb a path on the left to the medieval wall surrounding the excavations.
◔ **Timing:** Allow 1hr.

VISIT

◔*Open Wed–Sat May–Sept 9am–12.30pm, 2–5.30pm; Oct–Apr 9am–12.30pm, 2–4.30pm.* ◔*Closed public holidays.* ✆*No charge.* ℘*04 42 49 18 93.*

The settlement of St-Blaise (its ancient name could be Heraclea or Mastramellè) takes the form of a fortified spur, the natural defences of which, huge vertical cliffs, are reinforced by ramparts from the Hellenic period; these were built on the most accessible side, which overlooks Lavalduc valley.

Etruscan St-Blaise

The oldest traces of human existence date back to early 5000 BC. The group of small lagoons, which link the east arm of the River Rhône to Berre lagoon, most probably contributed to the discovery of the site by Etruscan sailors in the 7C BC. They established a trading post and began a successful trade: exchanging salt collected here for wine from Etruria. The settling of the Phocaeans at Marseille in c. 600 BC brought about serious competition between St-Blaise and Marseille; nevertheless, the discovery of Etruscan, Corinthian and Ionian pottery has proved that the settlement progressed.

In the second half of the 7C, the settlement formed a proto-urban town surrounded by a wall. As in Entremont, a lower and an upper town were established. The dwellings were built

of stone on a square plan; one in the lower town still has its walls at a height of 0.9m/35.4in.

A long period of transition (475–200 BC) then took place, after a fire, marked by the departure of the Etruscans from the trading post, and Marseille took over. It has been suggested that there was a possible period of withdrawal judging from the absence of human dwellings.

Hellenistic Ramparts★

From the late 3C to the mid-1C BC the settlement reached its apex: commerce picked up under the influence of Marseille, which held St-Blaise without, however, making it a colony.

Large projects for levelling of the terrain preceded the establishment of an urban plan and a strong fortified wall. The very high **Hellenistic ramparts**★ were raised under the direction of Greek craftsmen between 175 and 140 BC; they are more than 1km/0.6mi long and cut by towers and bastions, equipped with three posterns and a gateway and crowned at the top with merlons. The wall was equipped with a system of water evacuation via channels. It had hardly been finished when the settlement underwent a violent siege (dozens of cannonballs have been discovered) which historians are still trying to date. According to a recent theory, having escaped the control of Marseille a short time after the ramparts were completed, St-Blaise may have been taken over by the Romans during their conquest from

125 to 123 BC. After this event, St-Blaise went through a period of total decline; after its brief reoccupation in the mid-1C BC the site was totally abandoned for four centuries.

Palaeochristian and Medieval St-Blaise

With the rise of insecurity at the end of the Roman empire, the Hellenistic fortifications were reused: in the 5C the wall was surmounted by an ornamentation of irregular blocks of stone. Two churches were built: St-Vincent (the apse of which is near the ancient main gate) and St-Pierre (destroyed in the 9C). A necropolis (tombs carved into the rock) extended to the south. The living quarters of this settlement were unfortunately difficult to identify among the other ruins.

In 874, Ugium (the name of the settlement at that time) was destroyed by the Saracens. It recovered slowly, St-Pierre was rebuilt in the 10C, then burned down, then reconstructed again in the 11C (substructures have been found near the chapel of St-Blaise). In 1231, at the plateau's northernmost point a new wall was built to protect the town of Castelveyre (its new name) with its new church Notre-Dame-et-St-Blaise around which the dwellings nestled.

In 1390 Raymond de Turenne's band of brigands pillaged the town. The site was never to be resettled; the last inhabitants settled at St-Mitre. At the end of the spur, a fine view of the Étang de Lavalduc and the Bassins de Fos opens out (&see FOS-SUR-MER).

St-Maximin-la-Ste-Baume★★

Var

St-Maximin lies at the centre of a small basin, once the bottom of a lake, not far from the source of the Argens in a region of flat depressions; the village is flanked to the north by wooded hills and vineyards and to the south by the mountainous foundations of the Massif de la Ste-Baume. The village takes its name from St Maximinus who, according to legend, converted its inhabitants to Christianity and is buried here, on the spot of what subsequently became a Dominican monastery and basilica.

A BIT OF HISTORY

During the Revolution the Dominicans were expelled, but by good fortune the basilica and monastery housed Lucien Bonaparte, Napoleon's youngest brother, then officer in charge of military stores. He turned the cathedral into a food depot and saved the organ from harm by having the Marseillaise played

▶ **Population:** 14 183.
 Michelin Map: 340: K-5.
▪ **Info:** Place de-l'Hôtel-de-Ville, St-Maximin-La-Ste-Baume. &04 94 59 84 59. www.la-provence-verte.net.
P **Parking:** Car park near place du Marché.
 Don't Miss: Basilica.
 Timing: Allow half a day.

regularly upon it. The young officer, with an intelligence second only to Napoleon's, became a well-known figure in the town, as he developed into a rousing speaker and was elected president of the local Jacobin club.

BASILICA★★

6 pl. Jean Salusse. *Open daily 9am–6.30pm.* *No charge.*
&04 94 78 00 19. *Allow 45min.*
The Ste-Marie-Madeleine Basilica is constructed on the foundations of a 6C Merovingian church, where in 1279 the tombs of Mary Magdalene and St Maximinus were discovered. The

Detail of the sarcophagus of St Cedonius

D. Pazery/MICHELIN

sarcophagus contained the relics of the saints which were hidden in 716 from the Saracens. The spot was indicated by the saint herself in a dream. In 1295 Pope Bonifacio VIII acknowledged the relics and on the site of the crypt Charles of Anjou had a basilica and monastery built. He installed the Dominican friars who were in charge of guarding the relics and supervised what soon became a major pilgrimage.

Exterior

Devoid of transepts and ambulatory, the basilica has a squat appearance reinforced by the absence of a belfry, its incomplete west front, and the massive buttresses reaching the nave walls. It is the most important example of the Gothic style in Provence, combining the influences of the north, such as Bourges, with local architectural traditions.

Interior

The building comprises a nave, chancel and two aisles of remarkable height. The two-storey, 29m/95ft high nave has pointed vaulting; its keystones bear the arms of the Counts of Provence and Kings of France; the very large chancel is closed off by a pentagonal apse. The aisles, which were only 18m/59ft high to allow for a clerestory, end with quadrangular apsidal chapels. The side chapels were raised less than the aisles so as to allow the light to filter through.

1) The organ, which has a double case and still has the pipes saved by Lucien Bonaparte, was made by the lay Dominican Isnard of Tarascon and ranks with the one in Poitiers' cathedral as one of the finest 18C instruments in France.

2) Fine gilded wood statue of John the Baptist.

3) 15C altarpiece of the Four Saints: Lawrence, Anthony, Sebastian and Thomas Aquinas.

4) Rosary altar with 18C gilded wood statue of the Virgin; 16C altar front carved with four low reliefs of Mary Magdalene.

5) 17C wooden choir screen with wrought-iron inlets emblazoned with the arms of France.

6) Choir stall panelling enclosing 94 stalls, decorated with 22 17C medallions of saints of the Dominican Order, carved by Vincent Funel.

7) 17C stucco decoration by J Lombard before which stand, to the right, a terracotta of Mary Magdalene's communion, to the left, a marble of the saint's ecstasy and, at the centre, the altar surmounted by a glory.

8) Pulpit carved in 1756 by the Dominican Louis Gaudet, with representations on the sounding board, of immense size, of the ecstasy of Mary Magdalene, and

on the staircase, panels of her life. The rail is cut from a single piece of wood and is a masterpiece in itself.

9) 15C Provençal School predella (lower part of the altarpiece) illustrating the beheading of John the Baptist, St Martha taming the Tarasque and Christ appearing to Mary Magdalene.

10) 16C painted wood **retable**★ by Ronzen of the Crucifixion, surrounded by 18 medallions.

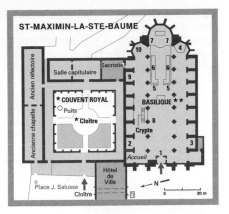

Crypt

The crypt was the funeral vault of a late 4C–early 5C Roman villa. It contains four 4C sarcophagi: St Mary Magdalene, St Marcella and St Susan, St Maximinus and St Cedonius.

At the back there is a 19C reliquary containing a cranium venerated as that of Mary Magdalene. Four stone tablets depict figures of the Virgin, Abraham and Daniel (c. 500).

Royal Monastery★

pl. Jean Salusse. ⏰*Open daily 9–11.30am, 2–6pm.* ⛔*Closed 31 Dec.* 🎟*No charge.* 📞*04 94 86 55 66. www.hotelfp-saintmaximin.com.*

Now the Hotel Le Couvant Royal (⛬⛬⛬⛬), the royal monastery began in the 13C at the same time as the basilica, and was completed in the 15C. The elegant **cloisters**★ (now used for events) include 32 bays. Its garden contains an abundance of foliage: boxwood, yew, lime and cedars. It hosts St-Maximinus Musical Evenings in summer.

The convent buildings include a chapel with vaulting in the form of a depressed arch, the refectory of five bays and the **chapter house** (housing the hotel's restaurant) with its pointed vault above slender columns ending in foliated capitals and held by low corbels. The building also houses the town hall.

Hôtel de Ville, Saint-Maximin-la-Sainte-Baume

©Daniël Leppens/Dreamstime.com

Dentelles de Montmirail is one of Provence's small mountain ranges, but there is nothing small about the opportunities for adventure you can have here. "Dentelle" translates to "lace". The mountains got this moniker because of the way they look against the horizon. That profile also has the effect of making the mountains look higher than they actually are.

Highlights

1. Unsurfaced roads and great views of Col de Cayron: **Montmirail** (p342)

2. Geologic finds from the world around at the Sault Museum: **Sault** (p344)

3. Valson's excavated ruins at Musée Archéologique Théo-Desplan: **Vaison-La-Romaine** (p348)

4. A 1C theatre hewn out of rock, Théâtre Romain: **Vaison-La-Romaine** (p349)

5. Winter sports paradise of Mont Serein: **Mont Ventoux** (p354)

Road sign to the summit of Mont Ventoux

© Craig Miller/IStockphoto.com

On a slope of the mountain lies Source Vauclusienne du Groseau, a natural spring where the Romans built an aquaduct. Oft-snow-capped Mont Serein is home to winter resorts: stay in a chalet here and have quick access to the chair lifts.

The Dentelles are reachable mainly by car, but once there, they are good choices for horse riding and hiking, too. After these outdoor activities, stop at some of the wineries to try the local red Grenache wine. Don't miss the local honey or nougat either. Other fruits found in this region are grapes for sweet Muscat wines.

Sault is a good starting point for excursions to the pretty vantage point of Mont Ventoux. Built in a semicircle, Sault stands above the Gorges de la Nesque, offering spectacular views. Before you launch your trip from here, be sure to see the jagged Cire rock from Sault's viewpoint.

You'll build up your calf muscles walking the steep streets of Séguret. But the walk is worth it, because you can take in views of quaint homes and churches once you get to the top.

Mont Ventoux, nicknamed the Giant of Provence, is the highest peak of the Dentelles. Its name comes from the word vent, which translates as "windy", and the top of the peak lives up to its name. While the roads can be closed occasionally due to these winds, for the most part, the Dentelles offer year-round walking and climbing. There are 650 different climbing routes, many of which are steep, with rocky ridges, made for experienced climbers. The mountains are forested with pines and oak trees, particularly picturesque in spring, and greener than other Provençal forests.

For those whose outdoor adventure quotiant is a little lower, the small town of Vaison-la-Romaine, on the River Ouvèze, offers as much to see as many bigger cities. People flock here to see the Roman Ruins, which offer a glimpse into 1C life, with additional excavations ongoing. One fascinating site in town is Colonnaded Street, a gravel street that was never fully excavated. The Provençal town is stocked with shops selling local delicacies, including honey and lavender.

Dentelles de Montmirail★

Vaucluse

The pine and oak-clad heights, sometimes blanketed with vines, are the foothills of Mont Ventoux and owe their name (*dentelle* means lace) to the outline of the peaks. The geological cause of these sharp peaks lies in the upper strata of Jurassic limestone having been forced upright by the folding of the earth's crust and then eroded by wind and weather into needle-thin spikes and ridges. Although not very high in altitude (St-Amand: 734m/2 409ft), the Dentelles have a more alpine appearance than their taller neighbour (Mont Ventoux: 1 909m/6 265ft). The hills, broom-covered in May and June, attract painters and naturalists as well as walkers of all abilities.

🚗 DRIVING TOUR

From Vaison-la-Romaine
60km/37mi round trip – about half a day.

▷ *Leave Vaison-la-Romaine on the D 977, the road towards Avignon. Turn left after 5.5km/3.4mi onto the D 88.*

- ♿ **Michelin Map:** 332: D-8 to D-9.
- 🛈 **Info:** Place du Marché, Beaumes-de-Venise. ℘04 90 62 94 39. www.ot-beaumesdevenise.com.
- ⊘ **Don't Miss:** The village of Séguret, wine-tasting in Gigondas and Beaumes-de-Venise.

The road climbs into the mountains, disclosing views of the Ouvèze valley to the west.

Séguret★

This picturesque village, built against the side of a steep hill, is well worth a visit. At the village entrance, walk through the covered passage into the main street and continue past the 15C Mascarons fountain and the 14C belfry to the 12C St-Denis church.
From the square *(viewing-table)* the view embraces the Dentelles, the Comtat Venaissin and, to the far north, the line of the Massif Central. A ruined castle and a network of steep streets lined with old houses all add character.

▷ *On leaving Séguret turn left onto the D 23 for Sablet and then take the D 7 and the D 79 for Gigondas.*

Vineyard at the foot of the Dentelles de Montmirail

B. Kaufmann/MICHELIN

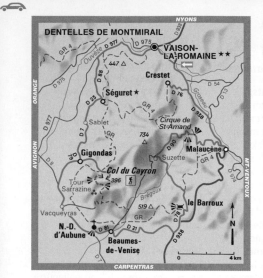

DENTELLES DE MONTMIRAIL

high, offer all the complexity of features relished by rock climbers. Park the car and bear right (*1hr return journey on foot*) on the unsurfaced road which winds through the Dentelles. There are splendid **views**★ of the Rhône plain backed by the Cévennes, Vaucluse plateau and Mont Ventoux. The road passes below a ruined Saracen tower (Tour Sarrazine).

▶ *Return to the car and take the D 7, then turn left towards Vacqueyras. Continue left along the D 81, which winds through vineyards and olive groves.*

Gigondas

The village has given its name to the local red Grenache wine, one of the grands crus of the Côtes-du-Rhône appellation. There are many opportunities to sample and buy direct from the producers.

▶ *By way of Les Florets, where there is an alpine club hut, drive to the Col de Cayron.*

Col de Cayron

Alt 396m/1 300ft. This pass is at the centre of the Dentelles' principal peaks which, with faces rearing nearly 100m/328ft

Beaumes-de-Venise

A terraced village, on the southernmost foothills of the Dentelles, which produces a delicious fortified sweet white wine from the Muscat grape.

▶ *Leave Beaumes-de-Venise eastwards on the D 21, bear left on the D 938 and left again on the D 78.*

Le Barroux

🅿 *Car park at entrance to the village.*
The picturesque village, with sloping streets, is dominated by the lofty sil-

Vineyards of Gigondas

©Sunset/Tips Images

houette of its **castle** (🕐 *open Jul–Sept daily 10am–7pm; Apr–May Sat–Sun 10am–7pm; Jun 2.30–7pm; Oct 2–6pm; ⬛3.50€; ☎04 90 62 35 21; www.chateau-du-barroux.com).* This huge quadrilateral construction, flanked by round towers, originally (12C) guarded the Comtat Venaisson plain. Remodelled in the Renaissance, burnt down during the Second World War, then restored once more, the castle was, until the 18C, the seat of several lordships, including that of Rovigliasc (note the coats of arms above the square tower doorway). After visiting the chapel, the lower rooms and the guard room, walk through the different floors, where contemporary exhibitions are on display in several of the rooms. There is a fine view from the gardens.

▷ *Leave Le Barroux N towards Suzette and meet up with the D 90.*

After Suzette the road enters the vertically walled Cirque de St-Amand. The road rises to a small pass which affords a good **view**★ on one side of the Dentelles and on the other of Mont Ventoux, Ouvèze valley and the Baronnies.

Malaucène

This typical Provençal town is surrounded by an avenue shaded by huge plane trees. The 14C fortified church was once a part of the ramparts.

Go through Porte Soubeyran, the gate beside the church, into the old village of fountains and oratories, with a belfry crowned by a wrought-iron bell cage at its centre. Take the path to the left of the church to the Calvary for a view of Mont Ventoux.

▷ *The D 938 NW climbs the fertile Groseau valley. Turn left onto the D 76.*

Crestet

Park in the castle car park. The village has a 14C church standing in a square lined by an arcade which is decorated at the centre with a fountain. Narrow streets between Renaissance houses climb the hill crowned by a 12C **castle**, from where there is a view of the village, the Ouvèze, Mont Ventoux and the Baronnies.

▷ *Return to the D 938 and turn left for Vaison-la-Romaine.*

ADDRESSES

🛏 STAY

◛◛ **Chambre d'hôte La Farigoule** – *Le Plan-de-Dieu, 84150 Violès, 10km/ 6mi W of Gigondas. ☎04 90 70 91 78. www.la-farigoule.com. 5 rooms. Closed Nov–Easter.* This 18C wine-producing estate has maintained all its authenticity. The hosts, formerly booksellers, have given each room the name of a Provençal poet whose books are also provided. Breakfast is served in a vaulted room.

🍴 EAT

◛◛ **La Bastide Bleue** – *rte de Sablet, 84110 Séguret. ☎04 90 46 83 43. http://pagesperso-orange.fr/labastide bleue. Closed Tue (Oct–Mar), Wed (Sept–Jun).* Situated in the stables of an old coaching inn, this restaurant serves authentic country cooking. In the summer the shady courtyard serves as a terrace. There is also a swimming pool surrounded by a garden, and a few rooms full of character.

🛒 SHOPPING

Caveau de Gigondas – *pl. du Portail, 84190 Gigondas. ☎04 90 65 82 29. www.chateauneuf.dk/gigondas/en/ caveauen.htm.* This shop, run by an association of 50 wine producers, allows visitors to taste a variety of wines without being obliged to make a purchase.

EVENTS

Les Prémices de la Vigne – Celebrations in all the wine-producing villages the Saturday after Ascension Day.

Sault

Vaucluse

The town is built in a semicircle, 765m/2 510ft up on a rock promontory at the west end of the Vaucluse plateau above the Gorges de la Nesque. Its position makes it an ideal centre for excursions to Mont Ventoux. Sault is at the centre of an important lavender-growing region and is known for its nougat and honey.

> **Population:** 1 285.
>
> **Michelin Map:** 332: F-9.
>
> **Info:** Avenue de la Promenade, Sault. ℘04 90 64 01 21. www.sault enprovence.com.

SIGHTS
Terrace

At the north end of the town, offering a lovely view of the Vaucluse plateau, the entrance to the Nesque gorges and Mont Ventoux.

Museum

r. du Musée. ○*Open Jul–Aug Mon–Sat 3–6pm.* ∞*No charge.* ℘*04 90 64 02 30.* Located on the first floor of the library, the museum contains prehistoric and Gallo-Roman remains, coins, arms, geological finds and a collection of old documents, as well as a mummy and other Egyptian artefacts.

DRIVING TOURS

MONT VENTOUX★★★
Allow 2hr – ascent via the eastern face.

▷ *Leave Sault on the D 164. For description and local map* ⌖*see Mont VENTOUX.*

PLATEAU D'ALBION
Round trip of 30km/18.6mi – 1hr30min.

▷ *Leave Sault on the D 30 towards St-Christol.*

The Albion plateau, with its fissured calcareous landscape, has all the physical characteristics of a limestone *causse*. Over 200 underground caves or *avens* have been discovered here, many with narrow openings which are

difficult to spot. The most beautiful viewed from above is the "Crirvi" cave near St-Christol; the deepest in the region include the Aven Jean-Nouveau with its 168m/551ft vertical shaft at its entrance, and the 600m/1 969ft deep Aven Autran, also near St-Christol, with abundant flowing water at its base. The distinctive feature of these caves is their ability to absorb rainwater down into the branches of an underground system buried deep in the calcareous rock: the main branch of this vast system emerges in the famous Fontaine-de-Vaucluse.

▷ *Turn back on the D 30 towards Sault then, after 4km/2.5mi, turn right onto the D 95.*

St-Trinit

A 12C church is all that remains of an old medieval priory which was accountable to the Abbaye St-André at Villeneuve-lez-Avignon.

▷ *Continue to Aurel on the D 950 towards Sault, then take the D 1, which branches off to the right, and finally the D 95.*

Aurel

From the D 950 the village, overlooking the Sault plain and its fields of lavender, appears suddenly below, along with its old fortifications and robust church with its light-coloured stone.

GORGES DE LA NESQUE★★
75km/46.6mi – allow about 3hr.

▷ *Leave Sault to the SE along the D 942, a scenic road that runs along the Nesque river.*

The River Nesque rises on the east face of Mont Ventoux and after some 70km/43mi flows into a tributary of the Sorgue, west of Pernes-les-Fontaines. In its upper reaches, the most attractive part of its course, the river has cut a spectacular gorge through the calcareous rock of the Vaucluse plateau.

Monieux

This picturesque old village perched above the Nesque is overlooked by a high 12C tower connected to the village by what remains of a defensive wall. Some of the village's medieval houses have retained their old doors.

Viewpoint (Belvédère)★★
Alt 734m/2 409ft.

The viewpoint *(left of the road)*, signalled by a stela bearing verses from Mistral's *Calendau*, overlooks the gorges and the jagged **Cire rock** (872m/2 862ft high). The descent begins with a passage through three tunnels, between which the road affords beautiful views of the site. At this point the Nesque runs in a cleft buried so deep in lush vegetation that only the murmuring of the fast-flowing crystal-clear waters over its pebble-strewn bed can be heard.

The D 942 moves slightly away from the gorge to cross the Coste Chaude coomb. At the exit to the fourth tunnel there is a good **view** back along the gorge to the Rocher du Cire. The road runs below the ruined hamlet of Fayol, buried beneath luxuriant Provençal vegetation. The landscape then changes suddenly as the river emerges into the Comtat Venaissin plain, and the horizon expands to include Mont Ventoux to the east and Carpentras and its countryside straight ahead.

The beautiful Hermitage coomb leads to the village of **Villes-sur-Auzon**, an important agricultural centre which lies on the wooded slopes of Mont Ventoux. It is centred on a large square overlooked by old houses and is ringed by a street of plane trees and splashing fountains.

▷ *Take the D 1 towards la Gabelle.*

As the road crosses the plateau, Mont Ventoux, the Dentelles de Montmirail and the Carpentras basin fill the horizon. At the entrance to La Gabelle the view extends to the opposite slope, with the Nesque gorges in the foreground and the Luberon mountains in the background.

▷ *From La Gabelle continue north, cross the D 1 and head towards Flassan.*

The road descends into a cool valley studded with pines and spruce.

Flassan

The minute village has ochre-walled houses and a typically picturesque Provençal square.

▷ *The D 217 and D 1 on the left lead back to Sault.*

ADDRESSES

🏠 STAY 🍴 EAT

⊝⊝⊜ **Ferme Les Bayles** – *84390 St-Trinit, 9km/5.6mi E of Sault via D 950 and a secondary road. ☎04 90 75 00 91. http://lesbayles.free.fr. 5 rooms.* This old sheepfold makes an ideal setting for a return to nature. Chicken, guinea-fowl, duck and rabbit are all on the menu at this farm-inn. Five simple rooms and a cottage are available for hikers, cyclists and riders. Riding centre and swimming pool.

⊝⊝⊜ **Le Provençal** – *r. Porte-des-Aires. ☎04 90 64 09 09. www.hotel-relais.fr. Closed mid-Nov–Dec, Tue (Oct–Apr).* Don't be fooled by the simple façade: this restaurant is well known by inhabitants of the region for its unpretentious, friendly atmosphere. Dishes prepared by a young chef and imbued with all the colour of the region, to be enjoyed in the dining room or on the shaded terrace.

Vaison-la-Romaine★★

Vaucluse

Built along the banks of the River Ouvèze, in the middle of a corrie of wooded hills, Vaison-la-Romaine, a small Provençal town full of charm, will enchant those who love old historical places. Rarely does a town offer such a complete and picturesque ensemble: vast fields of ancient ruins, Romanesque cathedral and cloisters, and the old town dominated by its castle. As well as becoming a busy tourist hub during the music festivals, Vaison thrives as an agricultural centre where wine, fruit and mountain produce (honey, lavender, truffles) are the source of prosperous trading.

A BIT OF HISTORY

The City of the Vocontii – Southern capital of the Vocontii, a Celtic tribe, Vaison (Vasio Vocontiorum) became part of Roman Provence, which was conquered at the end of the 2C BC and covered all southeastern Gaul. Very early on it received the status of federated city (and not colony) which allowed it a great deal of autonomy. Allied with Caesar during the Gallic Wars (58–51 BC), the Vocontii lived side by side with the Romans; and among them illustrious men appeared: the historian Trogus-Pompeius and Nero's tutor Burrhus.

Cited as one of the Narbonensis' most prosperous cities under Roman rule, Vaison covered some 70ha/173 acres and had a population of approximately 10 000. Unlike the colonial examples of Arles, Nîmes and Orange, the city did not expand with a Romanised urban plan, as was customary, because a pre-existing rural plan prevented the surveyors from tracing a regular grid plan and placing living quarters and public buildings in their rightful place.

sThe result was a very loose urban layout. Immense dwellings were built right in the centre of the city, replacing the earlier buildings.

▶ **Population:** 6 313.

Michelin Map: 332: D-8. Local maps, *see DENTELLES DE MONTMIRAIL* and *Mont VENTOUX*.

Info: Place du Chanoine Sautel, Vaison-la-Romaine. ℘04 90 36 02 11. www.vaison-la-romaine.com.

Parking: Arriving from Orange (28km/17.4mi SW) or Carpentras (27km/16.8mi S), use the car park in place Burrus.

Don't Miss: The Roman ruins, the old town, the cloister.

Timing: Allow 2hr to visit the Roman ruins and more if you want to explore the old town; there's a market here on Sundays in summer.

It was not until the last third of 1C AD, under the Flavians, that it was decided to create straight streets: properties had to be remodelled accordingly, the façades of houses were realigned and their axes modified, while porticoes and colonnades were erected. The archaeologists have established that the luxurious domi were much larger than those in Pompeii. They were built over a period of 250 years, and yet Vaison was not restricted to just this kind of dwelling; excavations have unearthed small palaces, modest dwellings, huts and tiny shops. The large public buildings, except for the theatre and baths, have not been traced.

Over the Centuries – Partially destroyed in the late 3C, Vaison rose again during the 4C with a reduced urban plan. The seat of a bishopric, it ranked highly in the 5C and 6C in spite of Barbarian occupation, and two synods took place here in 442 and 529.

The following centuries were marked by a sharp decline and by the desertion of the lower town, to the profit of the old

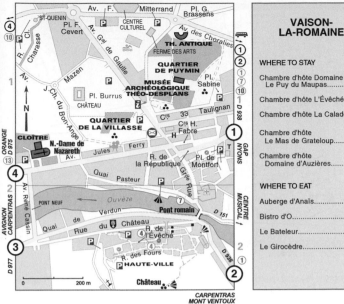

VAISON-LA-ROMAINE

WHERE TO STAY

Chambre d'hôte Domaine
Le Puy du Maupas.............①

Chambre d'hôte L'Évêché......④

Chambre d'hôte La Calade.....⑦

Chambre d'hôte
Le Mas de Grateloup..........⑩

Chambre d'hôte
Domaine d'Auzières............⑬

WHERE TO EAT

Auberge d'Anaïs..................①

Bistro d'O.........................④

Le Bateleur.......................⑦

Le Girocèdre.....................⑩

town on the river's south bank where the Count of Toulouse built a castle. The medieval upper town was abandoned in the 18C and 19C and the modern town fortified the Gallo-Roman city.

WALKING TOUR
ROMAN RUINS★★
Allow 2hr. Quartier de Puymin:
⊙ open daily Nov–Feb 10am–noon, 2–5pm; Mar and Oct 10am–12.30pm, 2–5.30pm; Apr and May 9.30am–6pm; Jun–Sept 9.30am–6.30pm; La Villasse:
⊙ open Tue afternoon–Mon Nov–Feb 10am–noon, 2–5pm; Mar and Oct 10am–12.30pm, 2–5.30pm; Apr and May 10am–noon, 2.30–6pm; Jun–Sept 10am–noon, 2.30–6.30pm. ⊛8€ (including Musée archéologique). ℘04 90 36 50 48.

The ancient ruins are spread over 15ha/37 acres. The centre of the Gallo-Roman city (forum and precincts) is covered by the modern town, and so only the peripheral quarters, rich with information on life at Vaison and its inhabitants in the 1C AD, have been uncovered.
At present the excavations are progressing towards the cathedral in the La Villasse quarter and around

Puymin hill, where a shopping district and a sumptuous *domus*, the **Peacock villa** with its mosaics, were recently unearthed. On the northern boundary of the ancient town, the excavated baths (some 20 rooms) have revealed that they were used until the late 3C and then destroyed.

QUARTIER DE PUYMIN
Maison à l'Apollon Lauré
This *domus*, a large urban dwelling belonging to a wealthy Vaison family (partly buried under the modern road network), features a very elaborate interior which favoured a sumptuous and comfortable lifestyle. As one enters, via the Roman street, a vestibule then a corridor lead to the *atrium* **(1)** around which the various rooms have been laid out, including the *tablinum* (study and library reserved for the head of the family). The atrium had in its centre, under the open section, a square basin *(impluvium)* which caught the rainwater.
Note the room **(2)** where Apollo's head (in the museum) was found, the main reception hall or *oecus* **(3)**, the peristyle and its basin. The annexes include the kitchen **(4)** with its twin hearths, and the

347

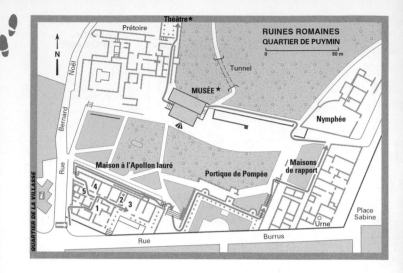

private bath **(5)** with its three rooms: *caldarium*, *tepidarium*, *frigidarium*.

Portique de Pompée

This elegant public promenade, a sort of public garden, 64m x 52m/210ft x 171ft, consisted of four galleries with niches *(exedra)*, covered originally with a lean-to roof, surrounding a garden and pool, in the centre of which stood a square aedicule. The well-excavated north gallery presents three *exedra* into which were placed the casts of the statues of Sabina, Diadumenos (Roman copy of the statue by Polyclitus which is exhibited at the British Museum) and Hadrian. The west gallery is also almost entirely excavated, while the other two galleries are buried under the modern buildings.

Rented Houses

This residential complex consists of a block of dwellings (to rent) several storeys high, for citizens of modest means. Note the large urn *(dolium)* for provisions.

Nymphaeum

This features various buildings of a cistern set around a spring, which was collected into an elongated basin, called a *nymphaeum*.

Further on to the east the shopping district and Peacock villa were excavated *(closed to the public)*.

Musée Archéologique Théo-Desplans★

&. ⊙*Open daily Nov–Feb 10am–noon, 2–5pm; Mar and Oct 10am–12.30pm, 2–5.30pm; Apr–May 9.30am–6pm; Jun–Sept 9.30am–6.30pm.* ⊛*8€ (including Roman Ruins).* ℘*04 90 36 50 05.*

This fascinating archaeological museum displays the finds excavated at Vaison. Different aspects of Gallo-Roman civilisation are presented thematically: religion, living quarters, pottery, glassware, arms, tools, ornaments, toiletries and imperial coins. The statues are remarkable. They are all in white marble; in chronological order: Claudius (dating from 43) wearing a heavy oak crown; Domitian in armour; naked Hadrian (dating from 121) in a majestic pose in the Hellenistic manner; Sabina, his wife, represented more conventionally as a great lady in state dress. Two other pieces are worthy of interest: the 2C marble head of Apollo crowned with laurel leaves, and a 3C silver bust of a patrician and mosaics from the Peacock Villa.

▷ *Go to the theatre by following the west slope of the Puymin.*

Théâtre Romain★

The theatre was built in the 1C, repaired in the 3C and dismantled in the 5C. Its dimensions (95m/312ft diameter, 29m/95ft high) reveal that it was slightly smaller than the one in Orange (103m/338ft, 36m/118ft); it had a seating capacity of 6 000 people (Orange held 9 000 to 10 000 spectators).

Also like the theatre in Orange, it was built against the hillside; its tiers were rebuilt by Jules Formigé (1879–1960; Inspector-General of Historical Monuments). The entire stage was hewn out of the rock and the pits containing the machinery and curtain have been well preserved. Discovered amid the ruins were the fine statues exhibited in the museum. Another feature, unique among the Roman theatres in Provence, is the existence of part of a top gallery portico.

QUARTIER DE LA VILLASSE
Main Street and Baths

On entering the site of the excavations, walk on the paved main street, under which runs a drain going down towards the Ouvèze and the modern buildings. On the west side of the street is a parallel passageway lined with colonnades reserved for pedestrians only; shops, located in the main houses' outbuildings, lined it. On the east side of the street lie the baths, which are surrounded by deep drains. The great room has a pilastered arcade.

Maison au Buste d'Argent (House of the Patrician of the Silver Bust)

Across from the baths in the shopping street is the entrance **(1)** to the vast domus, in which was discovered the silver bust (ⓒ *see museum p344*) of its opulent owner. Sprawled over about 5 000m2/53 820sq ft, the *domus* is complete: paved vestibule, *atrium* **(2)**, *tablinum* **(3)**, a first peristyle with garden and pool and then a second larger peristyle also enhanced with garden and pool. On the south side of the house stands another where mosaics **(4)** were found as well as frescoes around an *atrium*. North of the second (larger) peristyle is the private bath **(5)**, which is preceded by a courtyard. Nearby, to the east, lies a large hanging garden which enhanced the wealthy property.

Maison au Dauphin (Dolphin House)

In its early stages, c. 40 BC, this house occupied the northeastern section of a large enclosure in a non-urban setting. The central part of this vast house, which covers 2 700sq m/29 066sq ft, is laid out around a peristyle **(7)** decorated by a pool in dressed stone. To the north, covering 50sq m/538sq ft, there are the private baths **(8)** with the *triclinium*, a large dining room used for banquets, along the west edge. The *atrium* **(6)** led

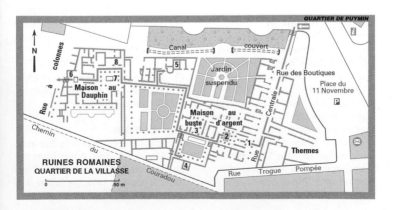

QUARTIER DE PUYMIN

Canal · couvert

colonnes

8

6 · 7 · 5

Maison au Dauphin

Rue · à

Chemin

du

Jardin suspendu

Maison au buste d'argent
3 · 2 · 1

Rue des Boutiques

Place du 11 Novembre

Rue · Centrale

Thermes

4

RUINES ROMAINES
QUARTIER DE LA VILLASSE

Couradou

Rue Trogue Pompée

0 · 50 m

N

Maison au Buste d'Argent

S. Sauvignier/MICHELIN

into the colonnaded street; this was one of the entrances to the house.

To the south stands another peristyle, a pleasant garden complemented by a large pool, with three *exedra* and faced with white marble, as well as fountains and formal gardens.

Colonnaded Street

Not completely excavated, this street borders the Maison au Dauphin along 43m/141ft. It was not a paved street; its surface, like many other street surfaces, was made of gravel.

ADDITIONAL SIGHTS

The exceptional archaeological site for which Vaison is justly famous should not cause the visitor to neglect the medieval town, starting with the cathedral, which is reached from Quartier de la Villasse by following avenue Jules-Ferry.

Ancienne Cathédrale Notre-Dame-de-Nazareth

Avenue Jules-Ferry. ○*Open daily Mar–May and Oct 10am–noon, 2–5.30pm; Jun–Sept 9.30am–noon, 2–5.30pm; Nov–Feb 10am–noon, 2–4pm.* ℘*04 90 36 02 11.*

This beautiful Provençal Romanesque-style building still has its 11C chevet, made from a solid rectangular block of masonry, its apsidal chapels and its walls, reinforced in the 12C at the same time that the nave was covered in by a barrel vault. The discovery of Gallo-Roman architectural fragments leads

experts to believe that the cathedral was built on the ruins of a civic building with a basilical ground plan.

Outside, the chevet is decorated with cornices and foliated friezes imitating Antique decoration. Inside, the nave includes two bays with pointed barrel vaulting and one bay topped by an octagonal dome on squinches decorated with the symbols of the Evangelists. It is lit through windows cut at the base of the vaulting.

Cloître★

○*Open daily 9 Feb–8 Mar 3–5pm; Apr–Jun 3–6pm; Jul–Sept 10am–12.30pm, 2–6.30pm; Oct 10am–noon, 2–5pm (last entry 15min before closing).* ➤*Guided tours available (1hr30min).* ∞*1.50€.* ℘*04 90 36 02 11.*

The cloisters are adjacent to the cathedral and were originally built in the 12C and 13C; the southeast gallery is a 19C reconstruction. The capitals in the east arcade are the most elaborately decorated: acanthus leaves, interlaced designs or figures.

▷ *Return to the avenue and turn right along quai Pasteur, which runs along the right bank of the Ouvèze.*

Pont Romain

The Roman bridge has only one arch, 17.20m/56.5ft wide. Apart from the parapet, rebuilt after the dramatic flood on 22 September 1992, the bridge is as it was 2 000 years ago.

HAUTE VILLE★ (UPPER TOWN)

▶ *Start from place du Poids and go through the 14C fortified gateway, dominated by the belfry tower and its 18C wrought-iron bell cage.*

The 14C fortifications which surround the city's steeply sloping streets were built in part using stones from the ruins of the Roman town. Take the time to amble through the picturesque maze of alleyways (rue de l'Église, rue de l'Évêché, rue des Fours) and squares (place du Vieux Marché) decorated with lovely fountains. The successful restoration of the warm-coloured stone houses roofed with old Roman tiles evokes a typical Provençal village of yesteryear.

The church dates from the 15C and there is a fine view of Mont Ventoux from the parvis. A steep path leads to the castle, built by the Counts of Toulouse at the end of the 12C on a rock overlooking the upper town.

EXCURSIONS

There are two signposted footpaths with loop around the surrounding countryside, one of 18km/11.2mi and one of 37km/23mi. Maps are available at the tourist office.

Rasteau

10km/6mi W on the D 975.

The vineyards of Rasteau produce wines under the two official appellations of Côtes-du-Rhône and Rasteau (dessert wines known as *vins doux naturels*). The **Musée du Vigneron** *(route de Roaix; ⏱ open Thu–Mon Jun and Apr–Sept 2–6pm; Jul–Aug 10am–6pm, guided tours available (30min); 2€ (guided tours 5€); ℘04 90 83 71 79; www.beaurenard.fr)* with a display of winegrowing equipment used long ago and a large collection of vintage Châteauneuf-du-Pape will certainly be of interest to amateur oenologists.

Brantes

28km/17.4mi E by the D 938, then left onto the D 54 until Entrechaux. There take the D 13 towards Mollans and finally turn right onto the D 40.

This fortified village presents an impressive **site**★ at the foot of Mont Ventoux, on the northern face of the Toulourenc valley. It contains a Chapelle des Pénitents Blancs, now used for exhibitions, the remains of a Renaissance manor house (lovely sculpted doorway) and a richly decorated church.

ADDRESSES

🛏 STAY

Chambre d'hôte Domaine le Puy de Maupas – *rte de Nyons, 84110 Puyméras. 7km/4.3mi NE. ℘04 90 46 47 43. www.puy-du-maupas.com. Closed Nov–mid-Mar. 5 rooms.* 🛏. A house set among vines, next to the cellar of this wine-producing property. Breakfast is served facing Mont Ventoux. Evening meals offer the opportunity to taste the house wines. Swimming pool.

Chambre d'hôte La Calade – *r. Calade, 84110 St-Romain-en-Viennois. 4km/2.5mi NE. ℘04 90 46 51 79. www.la-calade-vaison.com. Closed Oct. 4 rooms.* 🛏. A former barn built against the village walls welcomes its guests in a lovely courtyard, where breakfast is served on fine days. Its slightly monastic rooms will appeal to those who like the ascetic style. The terrace, at the top of the tower, offers a splendid view.

Chambre d'hôte Domaine des Auzières – *84110 Roaix, 9km/5.6mi W. ℘04 90 46 15 54. www.auzieres.fr. 5 rooms.* 🛏. It's hard to find somewhere more isolated! Huge house surrounded by lavender with beautiful, spacious rooms. Breakfast in the dining room or on the terrace. Swimming pool.

Chambre d'hôte L'Évêché – *r. de l'Évêché. ℘04 90 36 13 46. www.eveche-vaison.com. Closed 15 Nov–15 Dec. 5 rooms.* 🛏. This pleasant 16C house in the upper part of town was once part of the bishop's palace. Carefully decorated rooms, prettily furnished, arranged on several levels. Lovely views.

Chambre d'hôte Mas de Grateloup – *rte de Villedieu, 84110 Buisson, 7km/4.3mi NE. ℘04 90 28 17 95. www.masgrateloup.com. 5 rooms, 3 suites. ⌂. Meal⊜⊜.* Converted 18C farm in pure Provençal style set in 6ha/15 acres of woodland. Very pleasant all round.

▼/ EAT

⊜⊜ **Auberge d'Anaïs** – *rte de St Marcellin les Vaison, 84340 Entrechaux, 5km/3mi SE. ℘04 90 36 20 06. www.aubergeanais.com. Closed 15 Nov–1 Mar, Mon Mar–Nov.* Surrounded by vines and olive trees, this inn is a popular meeting place for locals. Relaxed dining room, tasty cooking and lively atmosphere.

⊜⊜ **Le Girocèdre** – *Le Village, 84110 Puyméras, 6km/3.7mi NE. ℘04 90 46 50 67. www.legirocedre.fr. Closed Mon.* At the top of the village is this building perched on an outcrop of rock, whose caves, originally carved out to raise silkworms, today serve as wine cellars. Under the cedars, olive, fig and tamarisk trees, the terrace is delightful in summer. Two small cottages.

⊜⊜⊜ **Le Bateleur** – *1 pl. Théodore-Aubanel. ℘04 90 36 28 04. www.le-bateleur.com. Closed Mon (Sept–Jun), Sun (Jul–Aug).* This pleasant establishment in old Vaison offers simple, up-to-date dishes. Some tables overlook the Ouvèze.

⊜⊜⊜ **Le Bistrot du'O** – *r. du Château. ℘04 90 41 72 90. Closed mid-Nov–mid-Dec, Mon lunch, Sun.* An elegant bistro, popular with the locals. Décor has vaulting, stone and a mix of old and contemporary furniture. Menu changes daily. Carefully chosen wine list.

⇥ SHOPPING

Markets – *pl. François Cevert* (Tue and Sun am); *pl. Montfort* (3rd Sun in month); *pl. de la Poste* (Thu eve Jun–Aug).

Cave de Rasteau – *rte. des Princes d'Orange, 84110 Rasteau. ℘04 90 10 90 14. www.rasteau.com.* Selling and tasting of Côtes du Rhône wines.

Moulin à huile Chauvet – *Porte Major, 26170 Mollans-sur-Ouvèze. ℘04 75 28 90 12. Closed Mon–Fri (Apr–Jun).* Selling and tasting of olive oil.

Mont Ventoux★★★

Vaucluse

Mont Ventoux is the most dominant feature of Provence's Rhône Valley. The climb to Mont Ventoux is one of the loveliest excursions of Provence; the panorama from the peak is immense. With a height of only 1 909m/6 265ft, Mont Ventoux cannot rival the Alps or Pyrénées for altitude; and yet its location in front of the Alps, far from any rival peak, its bold outline above Carpentras plain and the Vaucluse plateau, all combine to give it an astonishing majesty. It has become one of the most infamous stages in the *Tour de France* history.

- ♿ **Michelin Map:** 332: E-8.
- 🛈 **Info:** Espace Marie-Louis-Gravier, Bédoin. ℘04 90 65 63 95. www.bedoin.org.
- ▶ **Location:** There are two ways to access the summit: from the north on the D 974 and from the south. Or you can go on foot …
- ◷ **Timing:** Allow half a day to do the circuit described.

VEGETATION

The lower slopes are covered with the trees and plants typical of Provence, while at the summit polar species such as Spitzbergen saxifrage and Icelandic poppy flourish. The flowers are at their best in early July. The forests which once covered the mountainside were felled from the 16C on, to supply the naval shipyards in Toulon; replanting has

Summit of Mount Ventoux

Fr. Isler/MICHELIN

been going on since 1860. Aleppo pine, holm and downy oaks, cedar, beech, pitch pine, fir and larch form a forest cover which at about 1 600m/5 251ft is replaced by a vast field of white shingle. During the autumn a climb to the top through the multicoloured landscape is enchanting.

WEATHER

There is nearly always a wind on Mont Ventoux, as its name suggests (*vent* means wind), particularly when the *mistral* is blowing. The temperature at the top is on average 11°C/20°F lower than at the foot; rainfall is twice as heavy and filters through the fissured limestone of the Vaucluse plateau.

In winter the temperature may drop at the observatory to -27°C/-17°F), the mountain is usually snow-capped above 1 300m/4 267ft to 1 400m/4 595ft from December to April, and the slopes at Mont Serein on the north side and Chalet-Reynard on the south provide good skiing.

🚗 DRIVING TOUR

ASCENT★★

Ascent of the north face. Allow 1 day.
🅐**Caution:** *Roads may be blocked Nov–May; call in advance ☎08 36 68 02 84; www.meteo.fr. Round trip of 63km/39mi starting from Vaison-la-Romaine (👣 see map overleaf).*

The itinerary uses the D 974, a road made in 1933 for tourists ascending Mont Ventoux by the north side. Although the incline is similar to the one on the south side, it is less trying during the hot summer months because of the breeze. During a storm, the road can be obstructed by fallen earth for the last 3km/2mi but does not stop traffic. These conditions simply require more attention on the part of the driver.

▷ *Leave Vaison-la-Romaine by the D 938, to the southeast. After 3.5km/2.2mi turn left onto the D 54.*

Entrechaux

The village, overlooked by the ruins of a castle with its 220m/722ft defensive keep, was formerly a possession of the Bishops of Vaison.

▷ *Return to the Malaucène road via the D 13.*

Malaucène

👣*See DENTELLES-DE-MONTMIRAIL.*

▷ *Leave Malaucène east on the D 974.*

Source Vauclusienne du Groseau

This spring forms a pool of clear water as it emerges from several fissures at the foot of a steep slope (over 100m/328ft), beneath trees to the left of the road. The Romans built an aqueduct to carry the water to Vaison-la-Romaine.

The road continues up the northern slope revealing a good view of the Vaucluse plateau, climbing up the steepest and most ravined face of the mountain; it crosses pastures and pinewoods near the Mont Serein refuge.

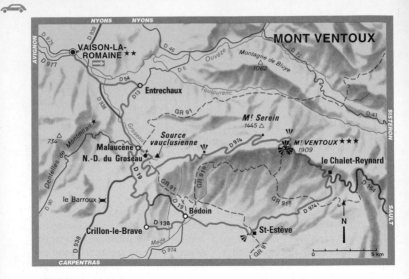

The viewpoint beyond the Ramayettes hut offers a fine **view**★ of the Ouvèze and Groseau valleys, the Massif des Baronnies and Plate summit.

Mont Serein

Winter sports resort: chalets are charmingly set in the snow fields; and it is well equipped with ski-lifts (www.stationdumontserein.com).

The panorama becomes wider and includes the Dentelles de Montmirail and the heights along the Rhône's west bank. Two more long hairpin bends lead to the top.

Mont Ventoux Summit★★★

The summit, which rises to an altitude of 1 909m/6 265ft, is spiked with scientific equipment: an air force radar station and a television mast. In summer the summit may be shrouded in cloud or midday mist; it is advisable to set out early or remain at the top until sunset. In winter the atmosphere tends to be clearer but the last stage of the ascent should be made on skis.

The view from the car park extends over the Alps, particularly the Vercors range (viewing table). The platform on the south side offers a **panorama**★★★ (viewing table): it swings from the Pelvoux massif to the Cévennes by way of the Luberon, Ste-Victoire, Estaque hills, Marseille, the Étang de Berre, the Alpilles and the Rhône valley.

On very clear days the Canigou is visible way over to the southwest in the Pyrenees. At night the Provençal plain is a wonderful sight as it is transformed into a dark carpet studded with clusters of glittering lights. The sight extends to the Étang de Berre and coast where the lighthouses regularly probe the darkness.

The corniche road, which winds down the south face through a vast tract of shining white shingle to woods, is the oldest road built (c. 1885) to serve the observatory. In 22km/13.7mi of hairpin bends to Bédoin (alt 310m/1 017ft), it descends 1 600m/5 251ft.

Le Chalet-Reynard

Excellent local slopes have made Le Chalet-Reynard a popular resort for skiers from Avignon, Carpentras and other nearby towns.

The road goes through the forest; pine trees, beeches, oaks and cedars give way to vines, peach and cherry orchards and a few small olive groves. The view extends across the Comtadin plain; beyond Vaucluse plateau appears the Luberon.

▶ *Leave the D 164 on the left to return to Sault (see SAULT) by the Nesque Valley.*

St-Estève

From the famous sharp bend, now straightened, which featured in the Ventoux car racing competition to the summit, there is a good **view**★ on the right of the Dentelles de Montmirail, the Comtat plain, and left onto Vaucluse plateau.

Bédoin

This village, which is perched on a hill, has picturesque small streets, leading to the classical Jesuit-style church, which contains several elegant altars.

▶ *Take the D 138.*

Crillon-le-Brave

Nestling on an overhang facing the Mont Ventoux, Crillon-le-Brave is a quaint perched village with vestiges of its former fortifications.

▶ *North of the village, take the untarred road leading up to the Belvédère du Paty.*

Belvédère du Paty★

From this viewpoint, there is a panoramic **view**★ down onto the picturesque terraced village of Crillon-le-Brave and the ochre clay quarries; to the right emerge the Alpilles, and opposite them the Comtat Venaissin, bounded by the Vaucluse plateau, and to the left is Mont Ventoux.

▶ *Take the D 19 and D 938 to return to Vaison-la-Romaine.*

ADDRESSES

🛏 STAY

🍽 **Hôtel Garance** – *Ste-Colombe. 4km/2.5mi E of Bédoin.* ☎04 90 12 81 00. www.lagarance.fr. *14 rooms.* ⚏7.50€. *Closed Nov–Mar.* A restored old farm in a hamlet surrounded by vines and orchards, overlooked by Mont Ventoux. The rooms have contemporary furniture, Provençal colours and old floors. Those at the back are preferable, with a view of the "giant of Provence". Swimming pool.

🍽🍽🍽 **Hotel de Crillon-le-Brave** – *pl. de l'Église, 84410 Crillon-le-Brave.* ☎04 90 65 61 61. www.crillonlebrave. com. *Closed Jan–early Mar. 32 rooms. Restaurant*🍽🍽🍽. This 17C building situated opposite Mont Ventoux is reminiscent of Cézanne's paintings. Provençal rooms, lovely vaulted dining room in the former stables, gorgeous shaded terrace and elegant Italian garden. Local food and wines.

🍴 EAT

🍽🍽 **Le Vieux Four** – *r. du Vieux-Four, Crillon-le-Brave.* ☎04 90 12 81 39. *Closed 15 Nov–1 Mar, Mon, lunch Tue–Fri.* This female chef has set up her restaurant in the old village bakery. You can eat in the bakehouse, with its old oven still in place, or on the terrace on the ramparts, with a view of Mont Ventoux.

🍽🍽🍽 **Le Mas des Vignes** – *rte du Mont Ventoux, 84410 Bédoin. 6km/3.7mi E of Bédoin.* ☎04 90 65 63 91. *Closed Nov–Apr, Jul–Aug lunch except Sun and public holidays, Tue lunch, Mon.* From this pretty *mas* overlooking the valley, the view extends as far as the Dentelles de Montmirail and the Comtat plain. Enjoy the simple cooking in the dining room or on the terrace.

🏃 LEISURE ACTIVITIES

Cycling – A guide detailing 18 circuits (10–49km/6–30.4mi) for all levels is available from local tourist offices.

Horse-riding centre Le Ménèque – *583 rte du Ménèque. 9km/5.6mi E of Bédoin.* ☎04 90 65 66 39. *Closed Thu afternoon.* Horse-riding excursions and lessons.

Night climbs – The tourist offices of Bédoin and Malaucène organise night climbs on Fridays in Jul and Aug to see sunrise from the summit.

Bordered by the Rhône and Durance rivers, Vaucluse is a lush growing area, with natural highlights ranging from cliffs to colored ochre. Like much of the rest of Provence, Vaucluse is also home to many significant architectural and historical sites, dating from the Romans through the 20C. The area has been used for decades as a place that politicians, clergy and other kinds of public figures could sneak away and recharge. They can sit and look at some of the country's most beautiful villages while eating local truffles and sipping local wine without interruption.

Highlights

1. The basics of olive oil production at Moulin Ramade: **Nyons** (p361)
2. Old Fortress: **Bollène** (p357)
3. Arc de Triomphe: **Orange** (p365)
4. Grotte de Rochecourbière: **Grignan** (p360)
5. Tasty treats at the truffle markets in **Richerenches** (p371)

Like many towns in the region, the hill town of Bollène was owned by the Avignon popes. Stop there to see the fortress and ruins of a church that played a role in the 16C War of Religion as well as other architectural sites. Also, because of the hills, you can see views of Cévennes and la Vallée du Rhône, not to mention the Côtes du Rhône wine trail.

Speaking of wine, Vaucluse is home to Châteauneuf-du-Pape, the area now known for its Rhône Valley wines. The popes promoted the area as a winemaking area, but the wines have become more respected in recent years, aided by newer strict regulations for the wine-growing region. Today the area grows 13 varieties of grapes, but the majority are Grenache, Mourvedre and Syrah. Work your way through your favourites in tasting rooms; there are 300 wineries here, so you'll be sure to find one that works with your route and schedule.

In addition to wine, you can visit the fortress and castle of Château des Papes, from which the area takes its name. From here you'll also see terrific views of the valley of the Rhône.

On to Grignan, the history of which is well documented in letters of Mme de Sévigné to her daughter. Thanks to that correspondence you can imagine how the hills smelled and looked in the 17C, and compare it to the sights and fragrance of today. These hills are still alive with lavender, sunflowers and truffles.

Mild weather is good for travellers and olive growing alike in Nyons on the River Eygues. If travelling between November and February, you're in for some agritourism: the olive oil mills are active and you can see the process of pressing. There's also a Musée de l'Olivie, where you can learn the history of and more about the processing of the delectable treat. The Old Nyons district is chock-full of 13C buildings.

At one point in history or another, Orange has been under rule by Romans, Dutch and the French since 35 BC, but it is the Roman monuments here that are the most noteworthy. In fact, many historians consider these among the most impressive in Europe. Orange is also a great town in which to listen to music, including an annual international opera festival.

Visual art, with many ongoing exhibitions, is one of the strengths of Valréas. The city, on the left bank of the Coronne River, is also known for its agriculture and light industry.

Bollène

Vaucluse

This hill town, 23km/14.3mi north of Orange, has been an agricultural marketing centre since the days of the Avignon popes, when it was one of their richest possessions. A few houses and fine doorways remain as mementoes of the past in what is now a typical Provençal town, with wide shaded boulevards marking the line of the ancient ramparts and a web of narrow streets at the centre.

VISIT

Collégiale St-Martin

Montée de la Paroisse. ℘04 90 30 11 38. The former parish church (12C–16C) is now used for exhibitions. Its robust bell tower stands atop the hill overlooking the town's rooftops from the east.
Go through the lovely Renaissance doorway to admire the size of the nave covered with a vast timberwork saddleback roof.

Belvédère Pasteur

From this small public garden, set around the former Romanesque **Chapelle des Trois-Croix** *(which hosts the musée Pasteur, with art exhibtions)*, there is a pleasant view of the town and its surrounding countryside.

EXCURSION

Mornas

11km/7mi S via the D 26, which cuts through Mondragon and is dominated by the castle ruins. Then take the N 7.
The village of Mornas clings to the foot of a sheer cliff (137m/450ft) on which lie the ruins of a **fortress**.

🚶 Fortress

🔦*Guided tours (1hr15min) Apr–Jun Mon–Fri 11am–noon, 2–5pm; Sept–mid-Oct Sat–Sun 11am–noon, 2–5pm.* ⌾5€ *(child 5€). Themed visits Jul–Aug daily*

▶ **Population:** 13 835.
🜨 **Michelin Map:** 14 130.
🜨 **Info:** Place Reynaud de la Gardette, Bollène. ℘04 90 40 51 45. www.bollenetourisme.com.
🚶 **Kids:** Themed tour of Mornas fortress.

11am–5pm; Mar–Jun Sat–Sun and public holidays 11am–5pm; Sept–mid-Oct Sat–Sun 11am–5pm. ⌾8€ *(child 6€).* ℘04 90 37 01 26. www.forteresse-de-mornas.com.
The fortress features a vast curtain wall, 2km/1.2mi long, flanked by either semicircular or square towers. At the top are ruins of the keep and chapel. The castle was also the scene of a terrible episode during the Wars of Religion: it fell into the hands of the sinister Baron des Adrets, who forced all the Catholic inhabitants to jump off the top of the cliff! Kids will love the themed visits, led by guides in medieval costume.

Suze-la Rousse

7km/4.3mi E via the D 994.
Suze was the epicentre of Tricastin during the Middle Ages. The hill is dominated by a 14C **castle** *(⌾open Apr–Jun and Sept–*

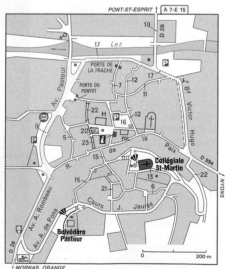

357

Oct daily 9.30am–11.30am, 2–5.30pm; Jul–Aug daily 9.30am–11.30am, 2–6pm; Nov–Mar Wed–Mon 9.30am–11.30am, 2–5.30pm; ○*closed 1 Jan, 25 Dec;* ⊛*3.50€;* ℘*04 75 04 81 44)* which is reached via a drive through a plantation of truffle oaks (some 30ha/74 acres). It was remodelled during the Renaissance.

The castle houses the **University of Wine** (℘*04 75 97 21 30; www.universite-du-vin.com)*, which has a tasting room and offers courses in oenology.

ADDRESSES

♀/ EAT

⊖⊜⊜⊜ **Campagne, Vignes et Gourmandises** – *Ste-Cécile-Les-Vignes. 11km/7mi E along D 8.* ℘*04 90 63 40 11. www.restaurant-cvg.com. Closed Christmas–mid-Jan, Sun for dinner, Mon.* Located in a tranquil area, this restaurant serves modern Provençal cuisine.

🛒 SHOPPING

Markets – Every Mon and Sat morning in the centre of Bollène from place des Récollets to boulevard Gambetta.

Châteauneuf-du-Pape

Vaucluse

The town has given its name to the most prestigious of all the Rhône wines. The original vineyard was planted in the 14C on land belonging to the Avignon popes, who summered here, and the wine was consumed locally until the mid-18C when its renown began to spread. For a long time it was sent in barrels to Burgundy for improvement. In c. 1880 phylloxera ravaged the vineyard, resulting in its ruin. It was subsequently replanted. In 1923 the wine-growers' association laid down strict rules defining the area, the management of the vineyards, harvest dates, the selection of grapes (13 approved varieties), vinification, and vintage labelling. Today, 300 vineyards grow 3 300ha/8 154 acres of vines.

VISIT
Château des Papes
The ruined fortress commands a splendid **view**★★: the valley of the Rhône, Roquemaure and the ruins of Château de l'Hers, Avignon with Notre-Dame-des-Doms and the Palais des Papes clearly outlined against the

▶ **Population:** 2 107.
⚬ **Michelin Map:** 332: B-9.
🚩 **Info:** Place du Portail.
℘04 90 83 71 08.
www.paysprovence.fr.

more distant Alpilles, the Luberon and the Vaucluse plateau, the Dentelles de Montmirail and, further off, Mont Ventoux, the Baronnies, and Lance mountain.

Emblem of the Holy See on a bottle of Chateauneuf-du-Pape

Musée des Outils de Vigneron

Cave Brotte, Le Clos. ⏱*Open daily Apr–Oct 9am–1pm, 2–7pm; Nov–Mar 9am–noon, 2–6pm.* ⏱*Closed 1 Jan, 1 Nov, 25 Dec.* ✆*No charge.* ☎*04 90 83 70 07. www.brotte.com.*

This museum, owned by the Brotte family of wine-makers, is devoted to the world of wine and the tools used to produce it. The tour is conducted in the order that wine is produced: from work in the vineyard (plough, hoes, pruning clippers), its treatment (copper sulphate spraying-machines), harvesting (baskets, wine press), work in the cellar (funnel, 16C press, huge 14C barrel) and related subjects such as cooperage, graf-ting, weights and measures, phylloxera, bottling and corking.

ADDRESSES

🏨 STAY   🍴 EAT

🍷🍷🍷🍷**Château des Fines Roches** – *rte. de Sorgues.* ☎*04 90 83 70 23. www. chateaufinesroches.com. 8 rooms.* ☕*16€. Restaurant* 🍷🍷🍷🍷*. Closed 2–27 Nov, Sun afternoon–Tue afternoon (28 Nov–Apr).* This château was once home to the Marquis de Baroncelli of Camargue. It has fabulous views over the vineyards. Gourmet regional cuisine and stylish, spacious rooms. A real treat.

Grignan★

Drôme

Located on an isolated rocky hillock, the imposing château belonging to Adhémar de Monteil overlooks the old town of Tricastin and owes its fame to the delightful letters written in the late 17C by Mme de Sévigné to her daughter, Mme de Grignan.

▶ **Population:** 1 464.
🚲 **Michelin Map:** 332: C-7.
🅿 **Info:** Place du Jeu-de-Ballon, Grignan. ☎04 75 46 56 75. www.tourisme-paysde grignan.com.

Madame de Sévigné and Grignan

When Mme de Sévigné's daughter married the Count of Grignan, Lieutenant-General of Provence, in 1669, the girl's mother commented: "the prettiest girl in France is marrying not the most handsome of young men (the count was very ugly!) but one of the most honest in the kingdom".

From that time on, she entered into a correspondence with her daughter which lasted 20 years, wherein she recounts, with a keen eye and nice turn of phrase, life at the court of Louis XIV, Paris society, visits to the country and day-to-day domestic matters.

Mme de Sévigné spent several long stays at the château. She enjoyed her visits and described the château as "very fine and magnificent", adding characteristically "one eats well and there are masses of visitors". She gives a mouthwatering description of how the partridges were fed on thyme, marjoram and other herbs to give them flavour, how the quail had fat and tender legs, the doves were succulent and the melons, figs and muscat grapes perfect. Although she admired the view from the terrace, she preferred the cool fragrance of the nearby grotto to write in; her only complaint was the *mistral*, which she viewed as a personal enemy, describing it as "that bitter, freezing and cutting wind".

Mme de Sévigné died at the château in 1696 aged 69 from over-fatigue after nursing her sick daughter. She was buried in the château's chapel, but during the Revolution her head was dispatched to Paris for examination by avid phrenologists. It has since disappeared.

Château de Grignan

B. Kaufmann/MICHELIN

VISIT
Château★★

chemin du Ronde. ◷*Open Apr–Jun
and Sept–Oct daily 9.30am–11.30am,
2–5.30pm; Jul–Aug daily 9.30am–
11.30am, 2–6pm; Nov–Mar Wed–
Mon 9.30am–11.30am, 2–5.30pm.*
◷*Closed 1 Jan, 25 Dec.* ⌖*5.50€.*
℘*04 75 91 83 55.*

The castle was remodelled in the 16C
by Louis Adhémar, Governor of the
Galleys of Provence, and by François de
Castellane-Adhémar, Mme de Sévigné's
son-in-law.

The Renaissance south façade (restored
in 1913) overlooks the garden in the
lower courtyard. The Well Court opens
onto a terrace enclosed by a Gothic
gallery on the left and by Renaissance
wings on the right and at the far end.

The great staircase, the drawing-rooms,
the audience chamber, the Count of
Grignan's apartments, Mme de Sévigné's
bedroom and dressing room, the chapel,
the Gothic staircase and the panelled
Adhémar gallery are also open.

Louis XIII and Louis XV period **furnishings**★ are worthy of note as are the
walls, which are hung with Aubusson
tapestries (17C mythological scenes).

Église St-Sauveur

R. St-Sauveur. ◷*Open daily Apr–Oct
10am–7pm; Nov–Mar 10am–6pm.
http://collegiale.grignan.free.fr.*
Inside this 16C church you'll find, to the
left of the altar, the marble headstone
for Mme de Sévigné.

Grotte de Rochecourbière

*Take the D 541 S out of Grignan.
After about 1km/0.6mi, park and walk
back to the stone steps on the right.*
This grotto was one of Mme de Sévigné's
favourite places, where she loved to sit
and write.

EXCURSION
Taulignan

7km/4.3mi NW on the D 14 and D 24.
Separating Dauphiné and Provence, this
agricultural town remains ensconced
within its medieval fortifications. It
has 11 towers (nine round and two
square) arranged in a circle, joined by
a curtain wall (machicolations remain
in several places), into which dwellings
are integrated.

Admire the ancient façades with their
ogee-arched doorways and mullioned
windows (rue des Fontaines) and
go through (to the northeast) Porte
d'Anguille, a fortified gate flanked by
two towers.

ADDRESSES

ⓎＥAT

🍽️🍽️🍽️ **Le Relais de Grignan** – *route de Montélimar. 1km/0.6mi west of Grignan on D 541. ℰ04 75 46 57 22 . Closed a week in Jan, Sun and Wed eves, Mon.*
A large house built alongside an olive grove with an attractive terrace under the trees.

🛒 SHOPPING

Ayme Truffes – *Domaine de Bramarel, Grignan. ℰ04 75 46 52 20. www.ayme-truffe.com.* Making four kinds of truffle since 1850: Black Truffle, Brumale Truffle, Summer Truffle, Bourgogne Truffle.

Nyons

Drôme

Situated on the River Eygues, where it emerges from a gorge into the Tricastin plain, within a protective ring of mountains, Nyons basks in a pleasant climate in which exotic flora flourishes; the mild winters attract many visitors. The olive groves surrounding Nyons (olives and oil are marketed by the town) give it a very Provençal look.

- ▶ **Population:** 7 065.
- 🚗 **Michelin Map:** 332: D-7.
- 🛈 **Info:** Place de la Libération, Nyons. ℰ04 75 26 10 35. www.paysdenyons.com.
- 👁 **Don't Miss:** Learning about – and tasting – olive oil.
- 🕐 **Timing:** Come for the market on Thursday mornings; from mid-May–mid-September, there's also one on Sunday mornings.

OLIVE OIL MILLS

There are six mills in the Nyons area; each operates from November–February.

Moulin Ramade

7 Impasse du Moulin (access to the west via 3 on the map). 🕐*Open Mon–Sat 8.30am–noon, 2–6.30pm; Off-season Mon–Sat 9am–noon, 2–5.30pm.* 🕐*Closed public holidays.* 👣*No charge.* ℰ*04 75 26 08 18. www.moulinramade.com.*
The first gallery houses millstones and presses used in the production of olive oil. The second gallery is specialised in refining and stocking the produce.

Vieux Moulins

4 promenade de la Digue. 🎧*Guided tours (30min) Sept–Jun, Christmas Tue–Sat 11am, 3pm; Jul–Aug Mon–Sat 11.30am, 3pm, 4pm.* 👣*4€.* ℰ*04 75 26 11 00. http://vieuxmoulins.free.fr.*
Old 18C and 19C oil mills can be seen, in which the oil is produced using traditional methods. You may also visit an old soap factory.

Vignolis: Coopérative du Nyonsais

pl. Olivier de Serres. 👣🕐*Open daily 9am–12.30pm, 2–7pm; off-season 9am–12.15pm, 2–6.30pm.* 🕐*Closed 1 Jan, 1 May, 25 Dec.* 👣*4€; 2€ for tour* ℰ*04 75 26 95 01. www.vignolis.fr.*
In this wine and oil cooperative, two adjoining rooms are devoted to the production of virgin olive oil (70% of

Olive products from Nyon

B. Kaufmann/MICHELIN

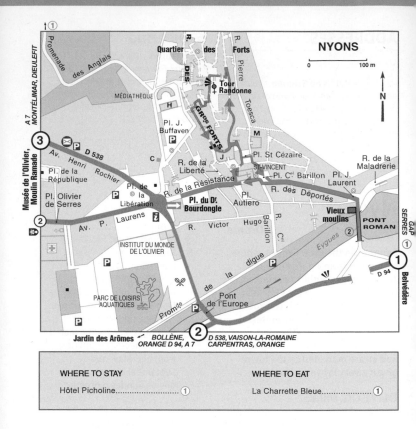

WHERE TO STAY	WHERE TO EAT
Hôtel Picholine.............................①	La Charrette Bleue.....................①

production), obtained by only one mechanical pressing without further treatment.

The remaining olives, the tanche variety, or Nyons black olives, are subsequently processed for canning. The cooperative also houses the **Musée de l'Olivier**.

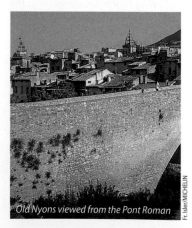

Old Nyons viewed from the Pont Roman

Fr. Isler/MICHELIN

Musée de l'Olivier

&⊙*Open same hours as Coopérative.*
Guided tours (45min) available.
2€. *04 75 26 95 09.*

This Olive Museum includes a wide variety of utensils, presses, tools and so on used in the production of olives and olive oil; there is also a group of items, such as lamps, showing how oil can be used.

ADDITIONAL SIGHTS
Old Nyons★

This old district is built on a hill overlooking the town. Start from the arcaded place du Dr Bourdongle.

Take rue de la Résistance and rue de la Mairie to rue des Petits Forts, a narrow alley lined with low-roofed houses (early 14C). In the square at the end of it a 13C tower, Tour Randonne, houses the tiny chapel of Notre-Dame-de-Bon-Secours. Bear left on rue de la Chapelle, to reach **rue des Grands-Forts★**, a long covered gallery where the thick walls have been pierced with windows to allow the light to filter through. Go under the tall vaulted gateway, the ruins of a feudal castle, and bear left into rue Maupas, a stepped street which leads back to rue de la Mairie. Proceed via place St Cézaire and place Barillon to reach the banks of the River Eygues.

Pont Roman (Vieux Pont)★
This 13C–14C humpbacked bridge spans the Eygues with a single 40m/131ft arch, one of the boldest in the Midi.

EXCURSIONS
Viewpoint (Belvédère)
▷ *Cross the Eygues over the Nouveau Pont, bear left on the D 94, leaving the Pont Roman on the left; pass under the tunnel and turn right.*

From the rocky spike (bench) the view embraces old Nyons overlooked by Angèle mountain (alt 1 606m/5 271ft), and the deep, narrow Eygues Valley to the right contrasting with the wide basin, to the left, where the new town has spread.

Promenade de Vaulx
Round trip of 8km/5mi.

▷ *Leave Nyons by the promenade des Anglais (northwest of town plan) and after 300m/328yd turn right.*

The narrow, winding but nicely laid out road runs along the hillside through olive groves. It offers good views of Nyons, Eygues valley and the Baronnies massif.

▷ *On the descent to the D 538, leave the road on the right to Venterol and return to Nyons via the D 538.*

ADDRESSES

⌂ STAY

⊜⊜⊟ **Hôtel Picholine** – *promenade Perrière. 1km/0.6mi N via promenade des Anglais. ℘04 75 26 06 21. www.picholine 26.com. Closed three weeks in Feb and a fortnight in Nov. ⌐9.50€. Restaurant ⊜⊜⊟. Closed Mon (Nov–Mar), Tue.* Situated on a private road, this large building makes for a pleasant stopover in the hills of Nyons. The idle will definitely enjoy the garden, the swimming pool shaded by the light foliage of olive trees and the attractive terrace.

⌁ EAT

⊜⊜ **La Charrette Bleue** – *7km/4.3mi NE via D 94 (rte du Gap). ℘04 75 27 72 33. www.lacharrettebleue.net. Closed Sun eve (Oct–Mar), Tue lunch (Nov–Mar) and eve (Sept–Jun), Wed.* Yes, there is a blue cart perched on the roof of this pretty *mas* adorned with Roman tiles. If the sun is too bright on the terrace, try the cool dining room with its exposed beams and old flagstones. Country cooking prepared by the book.

⌂ SHOPPING
Moulin Autrand-Dozol – *4 promenade. de la Digue, Le Pont Roman. ℘04 75 26 02 52. www.moulin-dozol.com. Closed three weeks in Oct.* 18C mill selling AOC olive oil, tapenade, honey, soaps and all kinds of regional products.

Distillerie Bleu Provence
58 promenade de la Digue. ℘04 75 26 10 42. www.distillerie-bleu-provence.com. Closed Tue in Jan. This essential oils distillery invites you on guided visits (45min) with 'smellings'. Shop.

EVENTS
Les Olivades – Olive Festival the weekend before 14 July.

Alicoque – Celebration of the new olive harvest, first weekend of Feb.

Fête de l'Olive Piquée – market of olive products, Saturday before Christmas.

Le marché aux olives – olive market on Saturday morning (Nov–Jan), in Mirabel aux Baronnies.

Orange★★

Vaucluse

Gateway to the Midi, at the crossroads of two motorways, Orange is famous for its prestigious Roman public buildings including the triumphal arch and the Roman Theatre. These monuments serve as the stage for the international music festival, the Chorégies, which features top international opera singers. An important market centre for fruit, Orange also has industrial (canning, chemicals) and military (air base, Foreign Legion) activities. In 1981, the triumphal arch, Roman theatre and its surroundings were inscribed as a UNESCO World Heritage Site for the remarkable manner that they have stood the test of time.

▶ **Population:** 29 859.
🚲 **Michelin Map:** 332: B-9.
🈁 **Info:** 5 Cours Aristide-Briand, Orange.
  🖉04 90 34 70 88.
  www.otorange.fr.
👁 **Don't Miss:** The Roman antiquities, of course!
🕐 **Timing:** Allow 2hr for sightseeing. There's an all-day market here from mid-June–mid-September.
👥 **Kids:** Camp Feodal.

A BIT OF HISTORY

Roman Orange – Established in 35 BC, the Roman colony of Orange welcomed the veterans of the Second Legion. The town had a well-ordered urban plan, enhanced by public buildings and surrounded by fortifications which protected some 70ha/173 acres. It was at the head of a vast territory, which the Roman land surveyors laid out with precision. Lots were attributed with priority to the veterans, the next lots were rented out to the highest bidders and the remaining lots belonged to the collective. In this way the Roman state encouraged colonisation and the development of land at the natives' expense. Until 412, when the town was ransacked by the Visigoths, Orange prospered.

Dutch Orange – In the second half of the 12C, the town became the seat of a small principality in Comtat Venaissin; its prince, Raimbaut d'Orange, was a famous troubadour who sang of his love for the Comtesse de Die. Through marriage and inheritance Orange ended up belonging to a branch of the Baux family, heir also to the German principality of Nassau. In the 16C the then prince of Orange and Nassau, William the Silent, transformed his fief into the United Provinces with himself as first *stadthouder*. At the same time, the town became Protestant and fell victim to the ravages of the Wars of Religion, but it succeeded in preserving its autonomy.

Orange is justly proud of the fact that the preferred title of the glorious royal dynasty of Holland is Prince or Princess of Orange; and its name has been given to a state, cities and rivers in South Africa and the USA. While governing the Low Countries and even England, the House of Orange-Nassau did not forget its tiny enclave in France.

In 1622 Maurice of Nassau surrounded the town with strong ramparts and built a large castle. Unfortunately, for economic reasons as well as through lack of time, he took the stones necessary for his fortifications from the Roman ruins which had not been destroyed by the Barbarian invasions. This time nothing was left standing except the theatre, part of the ramparts and the triumphal arch, which had been transformed into a fortress.

French Orange – During the war against Holland, Louis XIV coveted the Principality of Orange. It was the Count of Grignan, Lieutenant-General to the King in Provence and Mme de Sévigné's son-in-law, who captured the town. The ramparts were razed and the castle demolished. In 1713 the Treaty of Utrecht ceded Orange to France.

ROMAN MONUMENTS
Allow 2hr.

Arc de Triomphe★★
At the entry to the town on the N 7.
P *Free parking at the crossroads.*

The arch stands on the north side of the city on the old Via Agrippa, which linked Lyon to Arles. It ranks third among the Roman constructions of this type owing to its dimensions: 22m/72ft high, 21m/69ft wide and 8m/26ft deep and is one of the best preserved, particularly the north face.

Built c. 20 BC and dedicated later to Tiberius, the arch commemorated the campaigns of the Second Legion. It has three openings flanked by columns and displays two unusual architectural features: a pediment above the central opening and two attic storeys. It was surmounted at the time of its construction by a bronze *quadriga* (a chariot drawn by four horses harnessed abreast) flanked by two trophies.

Its exuberant decoration is linked to Roman Classicism and the plastic beauty of the Hellenistic style. Admire the scenes of battles and arms captured, which recall the conquering of Gaul, and naval symbols evoking Augustus' victory over the fleet of Antony and Cleopatra.

Roman Theatre
(Théâtre Antique)★★★
r. Madeleine Roch. ○*Open daily Nov–Feb 9.30am–4.30pm; Mar and Oct 9.30am–5.30pm; Apr–May and Sept 9am–6pm; Jun–Aug 9am–7pm.* ⊜*7.90€ (combined ticket with Musée d'Orange).* ℘*04 90 51 17 60. www.theatre-antique.com.*

Built during Augustus' reign, the theatre is rightly the pride of the city, as it is the only Roman theatre which has managed to conserve its stage wall almost intact. This impressive stage wall (103m/338ft long and 36m/118ft high), which Louis XIV had qualified as the finest wall of the kingdom, is the theatre's external façade. Its upper storey was made up of two rows of corbels pierced with holes to hold up the poles for the *velum*, which shaded the spectators from the sun. Below, 19 blind arcades corresponded with rooms inside, corridors and staircases.

The semicircle, the *cavea*, held up to 8 000 to 9 000 spectators seated according to their social station. It was divided into three sections of 37 tiers of seats and separated by walls. Below, the orchestra was in the shape of a half circle; along it were three low tiers of seats where movable seats were set up for the high-ranking citizens.

Arc de Triomphe

B. Kaufmann/MICHELIN

Théâtre Antique

Grégoire Saint Martin © Office de Tourisme Orange

On either side of the stage, large rooms, one on top of the other (entrance is now from the lower room, west side), were for receiving the public, and housed the backstage.

The stage, fitted with wooden flooring, under which the machinery was kept, measured 61m/200ft long and 9m/29.5ft wide of performing area; it was raised above the orchestra by about 1.1m/3.6ft. It was held up by a low wall, *pulpitum*. Behind was the curtain slot (the curtain was dropped during the performances). The stage wall was as high as the topmost tier, and displayed a richly ornate decoration of marble facing, stucco, mosaics, several tiers of columns and niches for statues, including the imperial one of Augustus (3.5m/11.5ft) which was brought back to its original location in 1951.

The stage wall had three doors, each of which had a particular function. The royal door in the centre was used by the principal actors for their entrances, whereas the two side doors were for secondary actors. From the top row one can hear someone speaking in the semicircle. The actors' masks amplified their voices, and the large sloping roof which protected the stage was also useful acoustically.

OLD ORANGE

> *Starting from the theatre, follow rue Caristie until it joins rue de la République, the city's main street.*

Vieil Orange

The streets of the old town centre are very animated and pleasant to stroll along. Note the statue of the troubadour-prince Raimbaut d'Orange while crossing place de la République and heading towards the cathedral, the **ancienne Cathédrale Notre-Dame de Nazareth** *(r. de Renoyer;* ⓒ *open daily 8.30am–5pm)*, by turning right into rue Fuseerie then, after place du Cloître, left into rue de Renoyer.

There are plenty of lively cafés and restaurants with pavement terraces in place Georges-Clemenceau, where you can admire the **Hôtel de Ville** with its 17C belfry. From place de la République, rue Stassart leads to a little square shaded with plane trees, **place aux Herbes**, which you cross to return to the theatre via rue du Mazeau.

COLLINE ST-EUTROPE
St Eutrope Hill

> *Drive up montée des Princes d'Orange-Nassau. Leave the car in the car park in front of the public gardens.*

The main avenue crosses the moat of the former castle of the Princes of Orange; the excavations (left of square Reine-

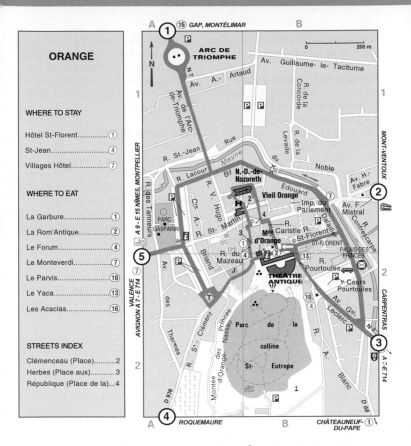

Juliana) have uncovered important ruins. At the far north end of the park, near a statue to the Virgin, there is a viewing table offering a beautiful **view**★ of the Roman Theatre in the foreground, the city of Orange with its tiled roofs, and the Rhône plain enclosed by mountains.

ADDITIONAL SIGHTS
Musée d'Orange

r. Madeleine Roch. ◔Same as Roman Theatre. ☞4.50€; 7.90€ (combined ticket with Roman Theatre). ✆04 90 51 17 60. www.theatre-antique.com.

This museum, which occupies a former palace built in the 17C by a Dutch nobleman, displays in the courtyard and ground floor lapidary vestiges from the Roman monuments (no longer standing) and the castle of the Princes of Orange. One gallery contains fragments (meticulously reconstructed) of the renowned Roman **land survey** of

Orange (◔see above), unique in France. On these marble tablets, the historians have identified the well-planned grid pattern, the administrative subdivisions and topographical references (roads, mountains, rivers, swamps) and finally written information on the judicial and fiscal status of the land.

The museum's other rooms are devoted to the history of Orange, local traditions, painting, and a collection of printed fabrics from 18C Orange.

EXCURSIONS
Caderousse

6km/3.7mi to the W, by the D 17.

This village is located on the banks of the Rhône and has often been subject to flooding. On the town hall's façade left of the door, four plaques indicate the level reached by the rise of the flood-waters. Since 1856 a dike with surrounding ramparts has protected the village from the flood-waters.

Harmas Jean-Henri-Fabre

Rte d'Orange, Sérignan du Comtat. 8km/5mi by the N 7 and D 976 to Sérignan. Near the entrance to the village. ◷*Open Apr–Jun and Sept–Oct Thu–Fri, Mon–Tue 10am–12.30pm, 2.30–6pm, Sun 2.30–6pm; Jul–Aug Thu–Fri and Mon–Tue 10am–12.30pm, 3.30–7pm, Sun 3.30–7pm.* ⊜*5€.* ℘*04 90 30 57 62. www.museum-paca.org/ harmas-infos.htm.*

This is the house of Jean-Henri Fabre (1823–1915), the famed entomologist.

ADDRESSES

🏨 STAY

⊜⊜ **Hôtel St-Florent** – *4 r. du Mazeau.* ℘*04 90 34 18 53. www.hotelsaint florent.com. 17 rooms.* ⊒*7€. Closed Feb.* Situated just a stone's throw from the Roman Theatre, this original little hotel is bound to surprise you. All the paintings are by the owner and each room is decorated individually with furniture chosen to fit its particular style. A delight.

⊜⊜ **Villages Hôtel** – *23 chemin de Queyredel, ZAC de la Brunette.* ℘*08 92 70 75 59. www.villages-hotel.com. 70 rooms.* ⊒*from 5€.* Part of an economy chain of hotels, this hotel is near the town centre and is fairly priced. Functional, comfortable rooms.

⊜⊜–⊜⊜⊜ **Hôtel St-Jean** – *1 cours Pourtoules.* ℘*04 90 51 15 16. 22 rooms.* ⊒*7€. Closed 20–27 Dec.* Former post house backing onto St-Europe Hill, and neighbour to the old theatre. Original lounge hewn ino the rock and bedrooms of varying sizes, all furnished differently.

🍽 EAT

⊜⊜ **Les Acacias** – *pl. de la Mairie, 84100 Uchaux, 9km/5.6mi N, dir. Bollène.* ℘*04 90 40 60 59. Closed Tue eve, Sat lunch.* Traditional dishes are served at this nicely decorated place. Pizzas and grilled food on the menu. Popular at lunchtime.

The visit includes the scientist's office, where display cases contain his collections of flora and fauna, and a gallery in which his watercolours are hung. A tour of the botanical garden ends the visit.

🎭👥 Camp Féodal

500m/547yd from the toll booth of A 7–A 9, then exit 21 for central Orange. 🔄*Guided tours (1hr45min).* ⊜*6€ (child 4€).* ℘*06 43 85 36 18. http://camp-feodal.skyrock.com.* A re-created medieval war camp with jousting and workshops to entertain all the family.

⊜⊜ **La Garbure** – *3 r. Joseph-Ducos, 84230 Châteauneuf-du-Pape.* ℘*04 90 83 75 08. www.la-garbure.com. Closed Jan, 15–30 Nov, Sat–Mon lunch in season, Sun– Mon out of season.* The dining room is decorated with lively colours. The regional menus concocted by the owner are sure to please you. Eight guest rooms.

⊜⊜ **Le Monteverdi** – *443 bd E. Daladier.* ℘*04 90 29 53 77.* Cosy yet trendy décor (earthy tones, communal tables, lounge area); tasty cuisine matching the ambience.

⊜⊜ **Le Parvis** – *55 cours Pourtoules.* ℘*04 90 34 82 00. Closed 9 Nov–1 Dec, 11 Jan–2 Feb, Sun–Mon.* Polished parquet flooring and contemporary paintings create an elegant atmosphere in this restaurant. Contemporary cuisine with a Provençal note.

⊜⊜ **La Rom'Antique**– *5 pl. Silvain.* ℘*04 90 51 67 06. Closed 3 weeks in Jan, 2 weeks in Oct, Sat lunch, Sun eve, Mon.* Not the most beautifully decorated place, but excellent quality food and tempting desserts.

⊜⊜ **Le Yaca** – *24 pl. Silvain.* ℘*04 90 34 70 03. Closed Tue for dinner, Wed.* The owner really goes out of her way to please clients.Everything is home made, fresh and not at all expensive in this small restaurant located a few steps away from Roman Theatre. There is a small, vaulted, Provençal style dining room with flowers on the tables. Terrace in the summer.

⊜⊜–⊜⊜⊜ **Le Forum** – *3 r. de Mazeau.* ℘*04 90 34 01 09. Closed 25 Aug– 10 Sept, 23 Feb–10 Mar, Sat lunch, Sun eve, Mon.* Small restaurant hidden in a tiny, narrow street, a stone's throw from the ancient theatre. Elegant Provençal-style décor. Traditional cuisine prepared with fresh produce.

⊜⊜⊜ **Alons'O Bistro** – *58 cours Aristide-Briand.* ℘*04 90 29 69 27. Closed Sat lunch, Thu.* A plain entrance belies a delightful Provençal décor. A menu based on fresh, local produce, regularly updated throughout the seasons.

⤳ SHOPPING

Chocolaterie Bernard Castelain – *rte d'Avignon, Châteauneuf du Pape.* ℘*04 90 83 54 71. www.chocolat-castelain.com. Closed Sun.* Try the house speciality *'le palet des Papes'* before checking out the little museum.

EVENTS

Chorégies – *pl. Silvain.* ℘*04 90 34 24 24. www.choregies.com.* Opera festival in the Roman theatre, mid-Jul–early Aug.

Orange se Met au Jazz – *every year in late June.* Annual jazz festival.

Valréas

Vaucluse

Lying in the fertile Coronne valley, Valréas is an important centre for agriculture and light industry (printers, factories making metal furniture, cardboard or plastic articles).

A BIT OF HISTORY

The Avignon papacy wanted to possess Valréas, a neighbour to the Comtat Venaissin. In 1317, Pope John XXII bought the town from the Dauphin Jean II, but a strip of land still separated the two pontifical states. Worried about the expansion of the papal lands in this region, King Charles VII forbade further sales of land to the popes, thus creating this papal enclave. In 1791, after a referendum, France annexed the territory. Valréas is a now a canton of Vaucluse *département* entirely surrounded by the Drôme *département*.

Le Petit St-Jean – This is a charming tradition which has survived 500 years. Every year, on the night of 23 June, a small boy (3–5 years old) is crowned Le Petit St-Jean (Little St John). Symbolising St Martin, the city's patron saint, Le Petit St-Jean parades through torch-lit streets on a litter, blessing people along the way.

▶ **Population:** 9 732.
 Michelin Map: 332: C-7.
 Info: Av. Maréchal Leclerc, Valréas. ℘04 90 35 04 71. www.ot-valreas.fr.
 Location: Although in the heart of the Drôme, Valréas (10km/6mi E of Grignan on the D 941) is attached to the Vaucluse.
 Timing: From November to March, the truffle market takes place here on Wednesdays and in Richerenches on Saturdays.

A procession of 300 costumed figures follows him in a colourful and animated atmosphere. For one year Valréas is placed under his protection.

THE TOWN

The town lies within plane tree-shaded boulevards planted on the site of former ramparts of which only the **Tour du Tivoli** *(cours Tivoli)* remains. In the old town are several fine houses: at no 36 Grande-Rue is the **Hôtel d'Aultane**, its door topped by a coat of arms; on the corner of rue de l'Échelle is **Hôtel d'Inguimbert** adorned with modillions and mullioned windows; on place Gutenberg stands **Château Delphinal** with machicolations.

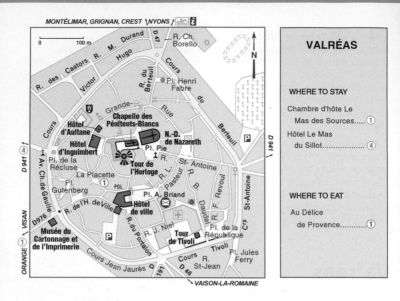

Hôtel de Ville

8 pl. Aristide Briand. ⓃOpen Mon–Thu
*8.30am–noon, 1.30–4pm, Fri 8.30am–
1pm.* ⓃClosed public holidays.
ⓃNo charge. ✆04 90 35 00 45.
This former 18C mansion belonged to
the Marquis de Simiane, who married the
granddaughter of Mme de Sévigné. The
oldest part of the mansion dates back
to the 15C; a majestic façade overlooks
place Aristide Briand. The library, on the
first floor, with its 17C wood panelling
from the former hospital, contains papal
bulls and manuscripts.

Église Notre-Dame de Nazareth

pl. Pie. ⓃOpen daily 9am–noon,
2–6pm.
The most interesting part of this Provençal Romanesque church is its south
door of four recessed orders resting on
small columns.

Chapelle des Pénitents Blancs

pl. Pie. ⓃGuided tours available.
please phone tourist office for details.
A lovely wrought-iron gate announces
the way to the 17C chapel. The chancel
is adorned with carved stalls and a lovely
flowered coffered ceiling.

Musée du Cartonnage et de l'Imprimerie

3 av. Maréchal Foch. ⓃOpen Apr–Oct
*Wed–Sat and Mon 10am–noon, 3–6pm,
Sun 3–6pm; Nov–Mar Wed–Sat and
Mon 10am–noon, 2–5pm, Sun 2–5pm.*
ⓃClosed public holidays. Ⓝ3.50€.
✆04 90 35 58 75. www.vaucluse.fr.
Valréas, an important centre of
cardboard production, offers tourists
an opportunity to follow the different
processes involved in the manufacture
of cardboard since the 19C.

🚗 DRIVING TOUR

Round trip of 40km/25mi – allow 2hr.

▷ *Leave Valréas W on the D 941.*

Grignan★
Ⓝ*See GRIGNAN*

▷ *Take the D 541 and turn left
onto the D 71.*

Chamaret

A clock tower, converted from a fine
belfry, relic of the massive castle
perched high on a rock, dominates the
landscape with an all-encompassing
view of Tricastin.

▶ *Continue along the D 71.*

The road is bordered by fields of lavender separated by truffle oaks and cypresses.

Montségur-sur-Lauzon

In front of the town hall, take the street on the left, turn right and then take the uphill path to the hillock on which lies the old village.
A network of streets allows the visitor to discover the old town and leads to the castle's old Romanesque chapel.

▶ *Take the D 71B going E.*

There are good views of Montagne de la Lance and the Nyons countryside.

Richerenches

Founded as a command post by the Templars in the 12C, the town is now an important truffle market. It still retains its fortified wall flanked by four round corner towers. Left of the church lie important temple ruins.

Truffle markets

Richerenches is known as the truffle capital. It has received the title of *site remarqable du goût*, an award given to places that promote the culinary excellence of their local specialities. Every year in January, a special Mass is held for members of the Confrèrie du diamant noir ("Brotherhood of the black diamond"), and the congregation is invited to put truffles in the collection box. You can buy yours at the market: in Richerenches on Saturday and Valréas on Wednesday *(Nov–Mar)*.

▶ *The D 20, SE, crosses Visan and continues on to Notre-Dame-des-Vignes.*

Chapelle Notre-Dame-des-Vignes

chemin de Notre-Dame-des-Vignes, Visan. ◷*Open Jun–Oct Tue and Thu–Sat 10am–11.30am, 3–6pm, Wed and Sun 3–6pm.* ☏*04 90 41 90 50.*
The nave of this 13C chapel is decorated with 15C panelling; in the chancel is a 13C polychrome wood statue of the Virgin, the object of a popular annual pilgrimage on 8 September.

▶ *Go past Visan and take the D 976 to return to Valréas.*

ADDRESSES

🛏 STAY

⊜⊜⊜ **Chambre d'hôte Le Mas des Sources** – *chemin Notre-Dame-des-Vignes, rte de Vaison-la-Romaine, 84820 Visan.* ☏*04 90 41 95 90. www.mas-des-sources.com. 3 rooms.* ☲. *Evening meal* ⊜⊜⊜. *Closed Nov holidays.*
Situated among the vines, this restored farm proposes cosy, antique-filled rooms (including one family room). Special theme weekends around wine, olive oil and, of course, truffles.

⊜⊜⊜ **Hôtel le Mas du Sillot** – *Les Plans, 84600 Grillon, 8km/5mi W.* ☏*04 90 28 44 00. 18 rooms.* ☲5€. *Evening meal*⊜.
Set in the heart of 600hà/1.48 acres of orchards on the edge of the Enclave des Papes, this old farm building is lovely. Rooms are a bit small, but well fitted out nonetheless. Prices very reasonable for the area.

🍴 EAT

⊜⊜⊜ **Au Délice de Provence** – *6 La Placette.* ☏*04 90 28 16 91. www.resto.fr/audelicedeprovence. Closed a fortnight in Jul.* A pleasant little place to stop and cheer yourself up with classic cooking, in the town centre. A good choice of menus at very reasonable prices.

EVENT

Corso de la Lavande – *first week of Aug, Valréas.* A celebration of lavender including a float parade, concerts and a wine festival.

INDEX

INDEX

INDEX

INDEX

MAPS AND PLANS

MAP LEGEND

	Sight	Seaside resort	Winter sports resort	Spa
Highly recommended ★★★	🏛🏛🏛	✵✵✵	‡‡‡
Recommended ★★	🏛🏛	✵✵	‡‡
Interesting ★	🏛	✵	‡

Additional symbols

🛈	Tourist information
═══ ═══	Motorway or other primary route
❶ ❶	Junction: complete, limited
⊨═══ ═══	Pedestrian street
⊨====⊨	Unsuitable for traffic, street subject to restrictions
▭▭▭ ----	Steps – Footpath
🚆 🚉	Train station – Auto-train station
🚌 S.N.C.F.	Coach (bus) station
──•──	Tram
🅐	Metro, underground
P R	Park-and-Ride
♿	Access for the disabled
✉	Post office
☎	Telephone
✉	Covered market
•✕•	Barracks
△	Drawbridge
∪	Quarry
✕	Mine
B F	Car ferry (river or lake)
🚢	Ferry service: cars and passengers
🚤	Foot passengers only
③	Access route number common to Michelin maps and town plans
Bert (R.)...	Main shopping street
AZ B	Map co-ordinates

Sports and recreation

🏇	Racecourse
⛸	Skating rink
🏊 🏊	Outdoor, indoor swimming pool
🎬	Multiplex Cinema
⛵	Marina, sailing centre
⛺	Trail refuge hut
□–■–■–□	Cable cars, gondolas
□+++++□	Funicular, rack railway
🚂	Tourist train
◆	Recreation area, park
🎭	Theme, amusement park
⊽	Wildlife park, zoo
✺	Gardens, park, arboretum
⊛	Bird sanctuary, aviary
🚶	Walking tour, footpath
🍎	Of special interest to children

Selected monuments and sights

◉ ➡	Tour - Departure point
🏠 ⸸	Catholic church
🏠 ⸸	Protestant church, other temple
▨ ▨ 🕌	Synagogue - Mosque
▬▬	Building
■	Statue, small building
⸸	Calvary, wayside cross
◎	Fountain
●━■	Rampart - Tower - Gate
⊶	Château, castle, historic house
∴	Ruins
◡	Dam
✿	Factory, power plant
☆	Fort
∩	Cave
▣	Troglodyte dwelling
⊓	Prehistoric site
▼	Viewing table
Ⓦ	Viewpoint
▲	Other place of interest

Abbreviations

A	Agricultural office (Chambre d'agriculture)
C	Chamber of Commerce (Chambre de commerce)
H	Town hall (Hôtel de ville)
J	Law courts (Palais de justice)
M	Museum (Musée)
P	Local authority offices (Préfecture, sous-préfecture)
POL.	Police station (Police)
▣	Police station (Gendarmerie)
T	Theatre (Théâtre)
U	University (Université)

COMPANION PUBLICATIONS

MICHELIN MAPS

Motorists who plan ahead will always have the appropriate maps at hand. Michelin products are complementary: for each of the sites listed in *The Green Guide*, map references are indicated which help you find your location on our range of maps.

To travel the roads in this region, you may use any of the following:
- the regional maps at a scale of 1:250 000 - 300 000 **no 527**, which cover the main roads and secondary roads, and include useful indications for finding tourist attractions. These are good maps to choose for travelling in a wide area. In a quick glance, you can locate and identify the main sights to see. In addition to identifying the nature of the road ways, the maps show castles, churches and other religious edifices, scenic view points, megalithic monuments, swimming beaches on lakes and rivers, swimming pools, golf courses, race tracks, air fields, and more.

And remember to travel with the latest edition of the **map of France no 721**, which gives an overall view of the region of Provence, and the main access roads which connect it to the rest of France. The entire country is mapped at a 1:1 000 000 scale and clearly shows the main road network.

Michelin is pleased to offer a route-planning service on the Internet: **www.ViaMichelin.com**. Choose the shortest route, a route without tolls, or the Michelin recommended route to your destination; you can also access information about hotels and restaurants from *The Red Guide*, and tourists sites from *The Green Guide*.

Bon voyage!

Michelin Apa Publications Ltd

A joint venture between Michelin and Langenscheidt

58 Borough High Street, London SE1 1XF, United Kingdom

No part of this publication may be reproduced in any form
without the prior permission of the publisher.

© 2010 Michelin Apa Publications Ltd
ISBN 978-1-906261-89-4
Printed: November 2009
Printed and bound in Germany

Although the information in this guide was believed by the authors and publisher to be accurate
and current at the time of publication, they cannot accept responsibility for any inconvenience,
loss, or injury sustained by any person relying on information or advice contained in this guide.
Things change over time and travellers should take steps to verify and confirm information,
especially time-sensitive information related to prices, hours of operation, and availability.